▶ **Consumer Reports Travel Letter** A monthly newsletter designed to help you track down the best travel values. Presents strategies for finding the best airfares, hotel rates, and rental-car rates. Offers warnings about frauds and scams; ways to avoid hassles; and other timely guidance for travelers.

▶ **Consumer Reports on Health** A monthly source of frank, objective, reliable reporting on nutrition and fitness; preventive measures and new treatments; medical breakthroughs and medical hype; and health frauds and other critical issues.

▶ **Consumer Reports New Car Price Service and Used Car Price Service** The best ways to feel assured of getting a good deal—if you're thinking of buying a car. See the ads at the back of the book for details.

▶ **Consumer Reports Facts by Fax** A 24-hour toll-free hotline that puts recent Consumer Reports articles in your hands in minutes. For details, see the ad at the back of the book.

About Consumers Union

- We are not influenced by any company or manufacturer.

- We are a nonprofit organization established in 1936.

- We receive no products or revenue from any manufacturers.

- We anonymously buy all the products we test at retail just like you.

- We prohibit the commercial use of our material and of our name—CONSUMER REPORTS.

1995 BUYING GUIDE

The December 15, 1994, issue
of CONSUMER REPORTS
Volume 59, No. 13

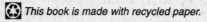 *This book is made with recycled paper.*

CONSUMER REPORTS (ISSN 0010-7174) is published 13 times a year by Consumers Union of U.S., Inc., 101 Truman Avenue, Yonkers, N.Y. 10703-1057. Second-class postage paid at Yonkers, N.Y., and at additional mailing offices. Canadian postage paid at Mississauga, Ontario, Canada. Canadian publications registration no. 9277. Title CONSUMER REPORTS registered in U.S. Patent Office. Contents of this issue copyright © 1994 by Consumers Union of U.S., Inc. All rights reserved under International and Pan-American copyright conventions. Reproduction in whole or in part is forbidden without prior written permission (and is never permitted for commercial purposes). CU is a member of the International Organization of Consumers Unions. Mailing lists: CU occasionally exchanges its subscriber lists with those of selected publications and nonprofit organizations. If you wish your name deleted from such exchanges, send your address label with a request for deletion to CONSUMER REPORTS, P.O. Box 53029, Boulder, Colo. 80322-3029. Postmaster: Send address changes to the same address.

A note to readers

Here it is: The 1995 Buying Guide, Consumers Union's perennial, handy compendium of useful information to help you get through another year in a challenging marketplace.

We introduced the first Buying Guide in 1937. It had 238 pages and was labeled: "Confidential to Members of Consumers Union of U.S." It was sized to fit compactly into a pocket or handbag. The intention was to gather, in one place, the best advice we could provide consumers in that era of tough times and little information.

Each year, we still aim to gather, in one place, the best advice we can provide consumers. Now, the Buying Guide is 400 pages packed with information presented concisely and, we hope, in a way that's easy to use. Since we're in a race with an ever-changing marketplace, the Buying Guide issue can only be a year-end "final." Still, within those constraints, our ongoing improvements now provide you with a volume that contains:

■ Our latest buying advice on the major products.

■ Our latest brand-name Ratings, as published in recent issues of CONSUMER REPORTS, with specially updated prices and models.

■ Repair histories to help you gauge reliability.

■ Product recalls to help you avoid unsafe products.

■ A directory of the last time we published articles on various subjects, products, and otherwise.

For many of our subscribers, this small book serves as a kind of big stick. Subscribers have told me that when they walk into a store with this book, they create a better balance between buyer and seller. They've got facts to penetrate any blather and hype and comparative data to help make the selection process less mysterious and more sensible.

And, equally important, the information in this volume comes from an organization that is beholden to no one but consumers, takes no outside advertising in its publications, and refuses all free samples and contributions from commercial interests. We buy our products in the marketplace, just as you do, test them impartially, and tell you plainly what we found.

With these thoughts, I wish you a year of sensible and satisfying shopping.

Rhoda H. Karpatkin

Rhoda H. Karpatkin
President

Contents

RELIABILITY

AUDIO/VIDEO

PHOTOGRAPHY

APPLIANCES

HOME

YARD & GARDEN

RECREATION & HEALTH

AUTOS

RECALLS

INDEXES

About the Buying Guide

Each year, the Consumer Reports Buying Guide collects and updates buying advice on all major consumer products. Available on newsstands and in bookstores or as the 13th issue of CONSUMER REPORTS magazine, it combines in one handy volume product-buying wisdom distilled from years of product testing along with the latest brand-name Ratings.

The reports in the Buying Guide provide the basic buying information you need—the pros and cons of the choices you'll have to make, what you can expect to pay, and an explanation of features available, both worthwhile and worthless.

The thumb index gives you fast access to the contents: information on autos, audio and video gear, appliances, health and exercise items, yard and garden equipment, products for the home office, home-care appliances, and photography equipment.

For easy reference to past issues of CONSUMER REPORTS, you'll find an eight-year index of the last full report at the back of this book. The date of recent reports is also given at the top of each Ratings table. Back issues of CONSUMER REPORTS are available in most libraries. Some reports are also available by fax: See page 390.

The Buying Guide guides you to brands that have shown themselves to be reliable—information available only from CONSUMER REPORTS. For the brand Repair Histories of products such as refrigerators, washing machines, dishwashers, air-conditioners, lawn mowers, and TV sets, see page 15. For model-by-model reliability information on cars, see the Frequency-of-Repair charts that start on page 324.

The Buying Guide also collects a years' worth of product recalls, based on notices issued by governmental agencies, as published in the monthly issues of CONSUMER REPORTS from November 1993 through October 1994. See page 367.

Using the Ratings

Once you've narrowed your choices, the Ratings in the Buying Guide can help point you to specific brands and models.

Because of the time required for testing and reporting, some models listed in the Ratings may no longer be available. Just before the Buying Guide goes to press, however, we verify model availability and prices for most products with manufacturers. Products that have been discontinued are marked Ⓓ in the Ratings. Such products may still be available in some stores. For some products, we've identified a "successor model" to the model that was tested. A successor, according to the manufacturer, is similar in performance to the item tested, but it may have different features. Such products are marked Ⓢ in the Ratings.

The general price ranges we give in the reports are based on real prices you'd pay in the stores. In most cases, however, the prices in the Ratings are manufacturers' approximate or suggested retail prices—prices that are often much higher than real store prices. Discounts may be substantial, particularly for electronics and photography equipment.

Our ratings are based on laboratory tests, panel tests, reader surveys, and expert judgments of products bought at retail, usually without regard to price. If a product is judged high in quality and appreciably superior to other products tested, we give it a check rating (✔). If a product offers both high quality and relatively low price, we deem it **A Best Buy**. A product's Rating applies only to the model listed, not to other models sold under the same brand name, unless so noted.

About Consumer Reports & Consumers Union

CONSUMER REPORTS magazine is published monthly by Consumers Union, a nonprofit independent testing organization serving only consumers. We are a comprehensive source for unbiased information about products and services, personal finance, and health. Since 1936, our mission has been to test products, inform the public, and protect consumers.

We buy all the products we test on the open market. Our shoppers buy in stores; we receive no special treatment or discounts.

We test products under controlled laboratory conditions. Most of our testing is done in 42 state-of-the-art labs at our National Research and Testing Center in Yonkers, N.Y.

We survey our millions of readers to bring you exclusive information on the reliability of autos and major products. Survey data also help us rate insurance and other services.

We report on current issues of widespread concern, bringing you information on health, money, and your well-being as consumers.

We accept no ads from outside companies, unlike other magazines. Our income is derived from the sale of CONSUMER REPORTS and other services and from nonrestrictive, noncommercial contributions, grants, and fees. The ads in CONSUMER REPORTS and the Buying Guide are for our other services, all of which share the same aims. We don't permit use of our reports or Ratings for any commercial purpose. If that happens, we take whatever steps are open to us. Reproduction of CONSUMER REPORTS in whole or in part is forbidden without prior written permission (and never for commercial purposes).

Subscriptions. CONSUMER REPORTS: U.S. rates: $24 for 1 year, $39 for 2 years, $54 for 3 years, $69 for 4 years, $84 for 5 years. Other countries: add $6 per year. (The Canadian rate is $35 if paying in Canadian dollars; Goods & Services Tax included GST #127047702.) For subscription service or to change an address, write to Subscription Director, CONSUMER REPORTS, P.O. Box 53029, Boulder, Colo. 80322-3029. Please attach or copy your address from the back cover of a monthly issue.

Contributions. Contributions to Consumers Union are tax-deductible. Contributors of $1000 or more (limit: $5000) can become Lifetime Members, receiving a lifetime subscription to CONSUMER REPORTS. For information, write to CU, Dept. MEM, 101 Truman Ave., Yonkers, N.Y. 10703-1057.

Readers' letters. They should be sent to CONSUMER REPORTS, P. O. Box 2015, Yonkers, N.Y. 10703-9015. We regret we are unable to respond to individual letters.

Back issues. Back issues of CONSUMER REPORTS up to 12 months old are available from Back Issue Dept., CONSUMER REPORTS, P.O. Box 53016, Boulder, Colo. 80322-3016: Single copies: $4; the Buying Guide: $10.

Bulk reprints. Selected health and personal-finance reports are available (10 copies min.). Write to CU, Reprints Dept., 101 Truman Ave., Yonkers, N. Y. 10703-1057.

Other Consumers Union services

New Car Price Service. To help you negotiate a deal on a new car, a printout compares sticker price to dealer's cost. See page 400 for details. **Used Car Price Service.** Before you buy, sell, or trade in a used car, find out the current market value in your area. See page 399. **Consumer Reports Books.** More than 100 helpful books in print; see back cover for some of our titles. **Facts By Fax.** Specially edited reports from CONSUMER REPORTS are available by fax or mail. See page 390 for more information. **Consumer Reports Travel Letter.** Monthly newsletter with travel advice. $39 a year. Write CU, Dept. GH, 101 Truman Ave., Yonkers, N.Y. 10703-1057. **Consumer Reports on Health.** Monthly newsletter with information on health issues. $24 a year. Write CU, Dept. GH, 101 Truman Ave., Yonkers, N.Y. 10703-1057. **Zillions.** Bimonthly magazine for kids 8 years and up. $16 a year (6 issues), $26 for 2 years. Write CU, Dept. GH, 101 Truman Ave., Yonkers, N.Y. 10703-1057.

RELIABILITY

Getting things fixed

To better your chances of trouble-free service, it makes sense to purchase brands with a good track record. You'll find some of the latest brand Repair Histories for many big-ticket items such as a TV set, washer, or air-conditioner beginning on page 15. While the data are historical, they've been quite consistent over the years.

Even the best products, though, can experience problems. When trouble arises, you have three basic options: throw it out, try fixing it yourself, or get it fixed.

Option 1: Don't fix it

The same designs and manufacturing methods that have given us better, cheaper, and more durable goods have made it difficult or impossible to repair some of them. These days, manufacturers prefer plastic for many uses because it can be fabricated in a single molding operation. Working with metal requires more steps on the assembly line, and adds to the cost of the product. When metal is required, manufacturers cut costs by crimping parts together instead of welding or bolting them. The result: $9 mixers, $15 coffee-makers, and other low-priced wares.

Trouble is, products with a crimped, welded, or permanently sealed, molded housing are practically impossible to service. When such products break, you have little choice but to throw them out.

Even if a product is repairable, the cost of repairs is so high that fixing the product may not make sense. Repairers charge $30 to $38 an hour on average. Replacement parts can be quite expensive, particularly if the product has been designed in pre-assembled units or modules. When you replace a module, you have to buy necessary parts along with the unnecessary.

HOW LONG THINGS LAST

A product's useful life depends not only on its actual durability but also on such intangibles as your own desire for some attribute or convenience available only on a new model. These estimates are from manufacturers and trade associations.

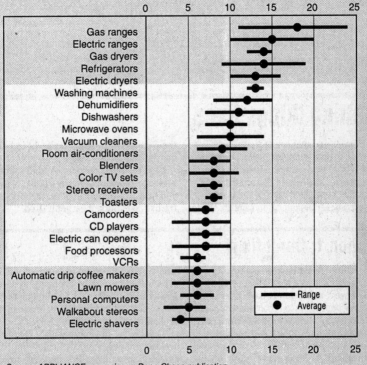

Age at which products are replaced (years)

Source: APPLIANCE magazine, a Dana Chase publication.

Nowhere are changes more evident than among electronic products. Solid-state components have revolutionized just about every device we plug in or pop batteries into. They've led to products that are smaller, lighter, smarter, and because they run cooler, more reliable. But such products are harder to service than old tube-based products. Diagnosing trouble requires more expertise, because obvious signs of failure are rare. Servicers are reluctant to repair parts individually. When an integrated circuit is faulty, they replace the entire circuit board. As a result, electronic failures are often costlier to fix than mechanical ones. Readers responding to a 1992 survey said they didn't fix three-quarters of inexpensive products such as blenders, blow dryers, boom boxes, and telephones. One in three larger, more expensive items—washing machines, TV sets, vacuum cleaners—also went unfixed.

Environmental issues. Getting something fixed is often better for the environment than just throwing it away and getting a new one. There's less waste, less use of resources and associated pollution. But if a new product is much more efficient than the old one, such as a refrigerator, it may be better to replace the old one than to keep it.

The issue of disposal is complicated if the products contain environmentally harmful substances: chlorofluorocarbons from refrigerators; heavy metals like lead in circuit boards and cathode-ray tubes; cadmium in rechargeable batteries; mercury in old fluorescent lights, thermostats, and silent wall switches. If a landfill isn't properly maintained, these chemicals can leach and contaminate ground water supplies. If trash is incinerated, mercury can escape into the air and heavy metals contaminate the ash. Clearly, it's time for manufacturers to cut back, where possible, on the harmful ingredients that go into durable goods, and for government and industry to increase recycling of the useful ingredients. Eventually, the U.S. may need to address the disposal of durable goods on a national level, as Germany has. There, recently enacted regulations require manufacturers to take back used refrigerators, TV sets, computers, and other appliances to reclaim useful material.

In the meantime, America's consumers don't have many good choices for disposing durable goods. One option is to extend the life of an old but functioning appliance by selling or giving it away. Sometimes a shelter, school, or other nonprofit group can use an appliance. Some utility companies take old refrigerators at no charge. You may find groups that accept used goods through your town's or state's environmental agency or under "Recycling" in the Yellow Pages.

Option 2: Fix it yourself

Doing a repair yourself saves money and often leads to more satisfaction with the job, our readers told us. People are most likely to fix products with mechanical innards: clothes dryers, lawn mowers, vacuum cleaners, ranges, washing machines, and such. Many electronics manufacturers specifically advise against do-it-yourself repairs because of the product's complexity and potential shock hazard.

How-to advice. Major appliance manufacturers offer the amateur the most help. General Electric, Whirlpool, Sears, and Frigidaire, for instance, provide technical assistance through a toll-free telephone number. GE and Whirlpool also publish manuals for amateurs. Other companies sell technical service manuals for their products, but they're not an easy read. Many books—from Consumer Reports

Books, Time-Life Books, Readers Digest Books, and other publishers—offer general fix-it-yourself advice.

Getting parts. Even the least handy person can "fix" a mixer with banged-up beaters, say, if they can find the replacement parts, which isn't always easy. Here are tips when scouting for parts:

■ Make sure the model number is correct. Check the appliance itself; don't rely on information in the manual or on the packaging.

■ Contact the manufacturer directly. It's usually faster and easier than trying to locate a source yourself. Phoning is speedier and more effective than writing, especially if there is a problem. Some companies will sell you the part directly; others will refer you to a parts distributor. Most companies have a toll-free telephone number.

■ Try local stores for common parts. Mass merchandisers like K Mart often carry replacement parts like carafes for coffee makers. Electronics specialty stores like Radio Shack are a good source for cordless-phone batteries. Parts stores or appliance dealers might also have parts on hand, but you may have to hunt through the Yellow Pages to find such stores.

■ With inexpensive small appliances, a single part can cost almost as much as a new appliance. We paid $13 for a Black & Decker coffee carafe; the complete appliance sells for $15 at discount.

Option 3: Have it fixed

Repairs rank high on the list of transactions that make people anxious, with good reason: Nearly one-quarter of readers in our survey were dissatisfied to some degree with work done for them on major appliances and other big items. Problems cropped up 42 percent of the time on average. Repairs done on small appliances were even less satisfactory. Readers complained most about work done on expensive electronic products—computers, camcorders, VCRs, TV sets—complex products likely to be repaired in the shop. Mechanical goods—major appliances, lawn mowers, vacuum cleaners—had the fewest problems.

It's possible, however, that at least some "satisfied" customers were unknowingly satisfied with repairs that were unnecessary. It happened to us when our engineers "broke" vacuum cleaners, VCRs, and washing machines and sought repairs in three major cities. Charges for the same simple repair varied by as much as 350 percent.

Unfortunately, the consumer's weapons against potential unscrupulousness are puny, a fact that itself causes much of the anxiety in seeking a repair. But there are ways to minimize the risk.

Types of service. There are three basic types: factory service, in which the company has its own service center or service fleet; authorized service, privately run businesses accredited by companies to fix their brands (the store that sells the product sometimes acts as an authorized repairer); and independents, who set their own policy.

Manufacturers typically require factory or authorized service for warranty work. The owner's manual usually provides instructions for obtaining repairs and a toll-free number to call for the name of the nearest factory-authorized service center.

Manufacturers train factory and authorized technicians on the latest equipment. Companies presumably ensure a certain level of quality in their factory service. They can also hold authorized repairers to standards of performance by threatening to revoke their contractual agreement with the repairer if there are too many complaints. Factory service, which is primarily available for large appliances, holds one advantage over authorized service: Authorized repairers sometimes earn a commission for parts. That can lead to unnecessary replacement of parts.

Independents can be a good choice for work on products whose warranty has expired. But check the repairer's reputation with friends and neighbors.

Repairs at home. For emergency repairs such as loss of refrigeration, companies try to respond within 24 hours. The response time for other repairs is one to three days. Companies may charge extra for Saturday or evening service.

Prior to scheduling an appointment, ask if there's a "trip" charge. The fee, typically $30 to $45, is applied to work that's done out of warranty. It includes travel to and from your home and a minimum labor charge. Expect to pay it even if you don't go ahead with the work.

Find out whether you'll pay flat or hourly rates. If the charge is by the hour, how is it billed? By the quarter hour is common. If you're having a large TV set fixed, ask whether there is a separate transportation fee if the set must be hauled to the shop.

Arrange to be home on the day of the service call. That way, there will be less temptation for a repairer to do other than what is really needed.

Finally, ask about the repair warranty. And request to keep any replaced parts. By doing so, you'll know that a part you are billed for was actually replaced—and the repairer will know that a check on cheating is at least possible.

Repairs in the shop. If repairs are going to be made in-store, first get an estimate. Ask whether the service includes a standard cleaning or whether it costs extra. Ask how long the repair should take. One of our readers' biggest complaints about repairs was that they took more than two

HOW MUCH TO FIX?

Average paid by readers.

Most

Camcorders	$100
25-27" TV sets	100
19-20" TV sets	80
VCRs	80
13-14" TV sets	78

Least

Stereo receivers	$50
Lawn mowers	50
Mid-sized microwave ovens	40
Vacuum cleaners	40

Source: 1992 Annual Questionaire

weeks. Also, find out the typical waiting time for parts. If the parts are on back order from the factory, be prepared to wait several weeks or more.

Tell the repairer you want all replaced parts returned to you. Be sure to get a signed claim check that shows the date your product went to the shop and describes the item by brand, model, and serial number.

If there's still a problem. First, try to resolve the problem with the repairer. If you're still unhappy, write the manufacturer's main customer relations office. Include in your correspondence the model and serial number, proof of purchase, and a copy of the written diagnosis.

If you are still unhappy, complain to the Better Business Bureau in your area and notify any local or state consumer agencies.

If you have trouble with the repair of a major appliance and can't resolve it, you can bring the problem to the attention of MACAP—the Major Appliance Consumer Action Panel—an independent complaint-mediation group. To find out if MACAP can help, write to them at 20 North Wacker Drive, Chicago, Ill. 60606.

Extended warranties

With an extended warranty or service contract, you're betting that the appliance will break down after the manufacturer's warranty expires—but before the extended warranty does—and that the cost of repairs will exceed the cost of the contract. It's possible, but it's a long shot. Not only are products today more reliable, but they are often constructed in such a way that makes any defect likely to appear early on, within the first 90 days or so, when the manufacturer's own warranty is likely to be in effect. That's particularly true of solid-state electronic circuitry.

Retailers push extended warranties aggressively for one simple reason: Stores can make more money selling extended warranties, priced from $50 to $500, than they can from the sale of merchandise. According to the National Association of Retail Dealers of America, a trade group, extended warranties carry average gross-profit margins of more than 77 percent. (Other estimates are lower, only 40 to 65 percent.)

Extended warranties are a good deal for retailers because they're such a bad deal for consumers. It's estimated that fewer than 20 percent of products covered by such agreements are ever brought in for repair, either because they don't break during the warranty period or because their owners prefer to replace them when they do.

Service contracts pose another sort of risk. Over the past several years, a number of warranty companies have gone bankrupt, leaving customers with worthless pieces of paper. Some states have introduced protective legislation. The proposals range from the toothless—merely requiring warranty firms to register with the state—to measures requiring a warranty contract be backed by an insurance company.

If the idea of extra protection is appealing but you'd rather not pay for it, consider using your credit card. Items bought with American Express cards and some standard Visa and MasterCards (and all their "gold" cards) automatically double the manufacturer's warranty for a maximum period of up to one year.

To qualify, you simply present the original store receipt and a copy of the manufacturer's warranty at the time you file a claim. In addition to their warranties, some MasterCards and all American Express cards toss in 90 days' worth of purchase insurance to replace or repair merchandise that is stolen or damaged. (Visa provides extra purchase insurance, too, but it excludes goods that are lost and certain types of damage.

Credit card purchases are further protected under the terms of the Fair Credit and Billing Act. It lets you "charge back" the purchase of an unsatisfactory product or service before you've paid the bill. You can request that the card issuer withhold payment to the retailer. The protection applies to items priced at more than $50 and purchased in your home state or within 100 miles of your mailing address. You must have shown a good-faith attempt to settle the problem with the store before asking to halt payment.

Our advice—as it has been for years—is to avoid extended warranties. It doesn't make a lot of sense to insure against small risks that you can cover out of your own pocket, if need be. You'd be better off taking the money an extended warranty would cost and set it aside as a repair fund. And if you feel you need some protection, buy with your credit card.

Repair Histories

Every year, CONSUMER REPORTS asks its subscribers to share their experiences with various products by answering questions on the Annual Questionnaire. One benefit is the automobile Frequency-of-Repair charts, beginning on page 324. Another result is what you'll find in this chapter—repair histories for various brands of major appliances, electronic items, and other products.

The graphs that follow represent the percentage of products in each brand that have ever been repaired, as reported to us by subscribers in the survey. It's important to keep two things in mind: Repair histories apply only to brands, not to specific models of these products. And the histories, being histories, can only suggest future trends—not predict them exactly. A company can at any time change its products' design or quality control so substantially as to affect their reliability. But our findings over the years have been consistent enough for us to

be confident that these repair histories can greatly improve your chances of getting a more trouble-free product.

Note, too, that the repair histories of different products are not directly comparable. Data for each graph have been adjusted differently—to compensate for differing age distributions, for instance—and the experiences summed up by different graphs may cover different years of purchase. The text associated with each graph explains exactly what type of product is covered and whether any special assumptions were made in the graph's preparation.

Use the following graphs in conjunction with the product reports elsewhere in the Buying Guide. Some of these brand Repair Histories have already appeared in the 1994 monthly issues of CONSUMER REPORTS; some appear here for the first time; others will be updated in the 1995 issues of CONSUMER REPORTS.

VCRs

Based on nearly 230,000 responses to our 1993 Annual Questionnaire. Readers were asked about any repairs to VCRs bought between 1988 and 1993. Data have been standardized to eliminate differences among brands due solely to age and how much the VCRs were used. Differences of less than 3 points aren't meaningful.

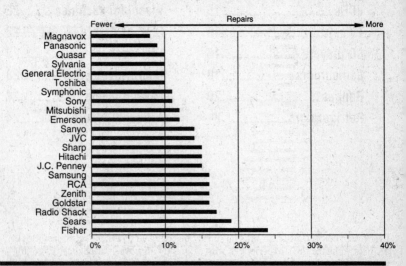

Television sets: 13-inch and 14-inch

Based on more than 42,000 responses to our 1993 Annual Questionnaire. Readers were asked about any repairs to a 13-inch color TV set with remote control bought new between 1988 and 1993. Data have been standardized to eliminate differences among brands due solely to age. Differences of less than 3 points aren't meaningful.

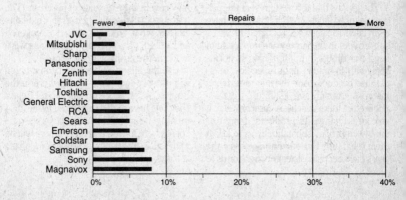

Television sets: 19-inch and 20-inch

Based on more than 97,000 responses to our 1993 Annual Questionnaire. Readers were asked about any repairs to a 19-inch or 20-inch color TV set with remote control bought new between 1988 and 1993. Data have been standardized to eliminate differences among brands due solely to age. Differences of less than 3 points aren't meaningful.

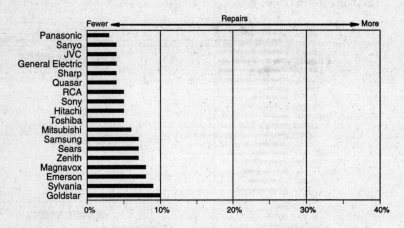

Television sets: 25-inch and 27-inch stereo sets

Based on more than 96,000 responses to our 1993 Annual Questionnaire. Readers were asked about any repairs to a 25-inch to 27-inch color TV set with remote control bought new between 1988 and 1993. Data have been standardized to eliminate differences among brands due solely to age. Differences of less than 3 points aren't meaningful.

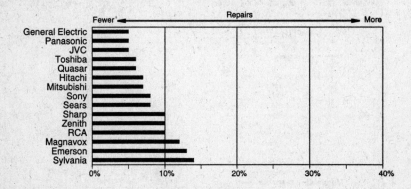

Compact-disc players

Based on more than 108,000 responses to our 1993 Annual Questionnaire. Readers were asked about any repairs to a single-play or changer tabletop model bought new between 1990 and 1993. Data have been standardized to eliminate differences among brands due solely to age and how much the CD players were used. Differences of less than 4 points aren't meaningful.

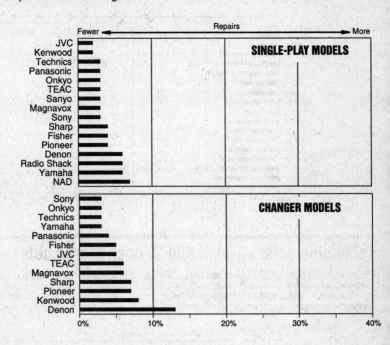

Fewer ← Repairs → More

SINGLE-PLAY MODELS

- JVC
- Kenwood
- Technics
- Panasonic
- Onkyo
- TEAC
- Sanyo
- Magnavox
- Sony
- Sharp
- Fisher
- Pioneer
- Denon
- Radio Shack
- Yamaha
- NAD

CHANGER MODELS

- Sony
- Onkyo
- Technics
- Yamaha
- Panasonic
- Fisher
- JVC
- TEAC
- Magnavox
- Sharp
- Pioneer
- Kenwood
- Denon

0%   10%   20%   30%   40%

VHS camcorders

Based on more than 27,000 responses to our 1993 Annual Questionnaire. Readers were asked about any repairs to a VHS camcorder bought new between 1988 and 1993. Data have been standardized to eliminate differences among brands due solely to age and how much the camcorder was used. Differences of less then 4 points aren't meaningful. VHS repair rates cannot be compared directly with those of compact camcorders because the VHS models tended to be older and used more than the compacts.

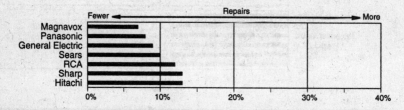

Compact camcorders

Based on more than 35,000 responses to our 1993 Annual Questionnaire. Readers were asked about any repairs to a compact (8mm or VHS-C) camcorder bought new between 1988 and 1993. Data have been standardized to eliminate differences among brands due solely to age and how much the camcorder was used. Differences of less than 4 points aren't meaningful. Repair rates of compacts cannot be compared directly with those of full-sized VHS models.

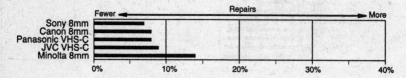

Gas ranges

Based on nearly 17,000 responses to our 1993 Annual Questionnaire. Readers were asked about any repairs to a freestanding, single-oven, self-cleaning gas range bought new between 1987 and 1993. Data have been standardized to eliminate differences among brands due to age. Differences of less than 4 points aren't meaningful.

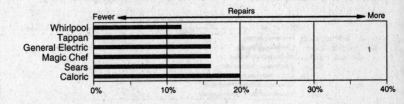

Electric ranges

Based on more than 27,000 responses to our 1993 Annual Questionnaire. Readers were asked about any repairs to a freestanding, single-oven, self-cleaning electric range bought new between 1988 and 1993. Data have been standardized to eliminate differences among brands due to age. Differences of less than 4 points aren't meaningful.

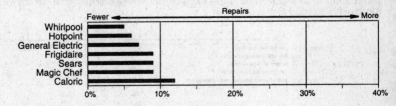

Side-by-side refrigerators

Based on more than 38,000 responses to our 1993 Annual Questionnaire. Readers were asked about any repairs to side-by-side, two-door, no-frost refrigerators bought new between 1986 and 1993. Data have been standardized to eliminate differences among brands due solely to age. Differences of less than 4 points aren't meaningful.

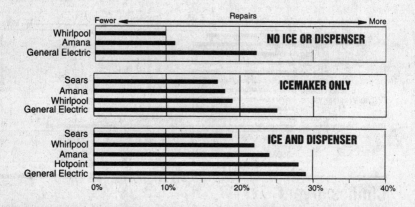

Top-freezer refrigerators

Based on more 83,000 responses to our 1993 Annual Questionnaire. Readers were asked about any repairs to top-freezer, two-door, no-frost refrigerators bought new between 1986 and 1993. Data have been standardized to eliminate differences among brands due solely to age. Differences of less than 4 points aren't meaningful.

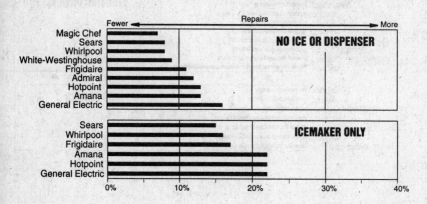

Washing machines

Based on more than 177,000 responses to our 1993 Annual Questionnaire. Readers were asked about any repairs to a full-sized washer bought new between 1986 and 1993. Data have been standardized to eliminate differences among brands due solely to age. Differences of less than 4 points aren't meaningful.

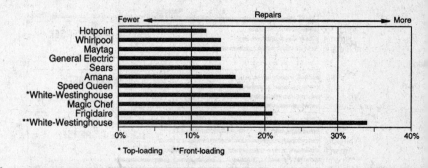

Clothes dryers

Based on more than 139,000 responses to our 1993 Annual Questionnaire. Readers were asked about any repairs to a full-sized electric or gas clothes dryer bought new between 1987 and 1993. Data have been standardized to eliminate differences among brands due solely to age. Differences of less than 4 points aren't meaningful.

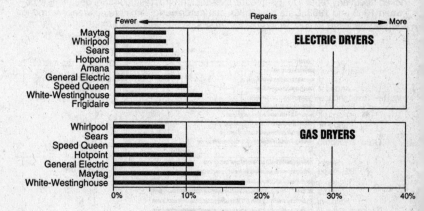

Dishwashers

Based on more than 149,000 responses to our 1993 Annual Questionnaire. Readers were asked about any repairs to installed dishwashers bought new between 1987 and 1993. Data have been standardized to eliminate differences among brands due solely to age and degree of use. Differences of less than 4 points aren't meaningful.

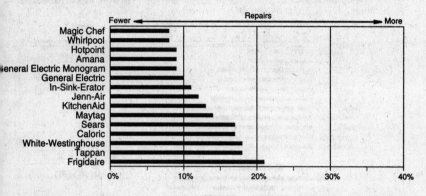

Microwave ovens

Based on more than 98,000 responses to our 1993 Annual Questionnaire. Readers were asked about any repairs to medium and large-sized microwave ovens with electronic touch controls bought new between 1988 and 1993. Data have been standardized to eliminate differences among brands due solely to age. Differences of less than 3 points aren't meaningful.

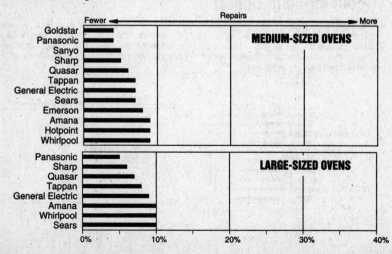

Walk-behind lawn mowers

Based on more than 64,000 responses to our 1993 Annual Questionnaire. Readers were asked about any repairs to any push or self-propelled gasoline mower with an engine between 3.5 and 5.0 horsepower and a cutting swath of 20 to 22 inches that was bought new between 1988 and 1993. Data have been standardized to eliminate differences among brands due solely to age and how much the lawn mowers were used. Differences of less than 4 points aren't meaningful.

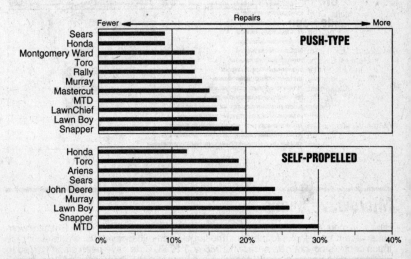

Room air-conditioners

Based on more than 15,000 responses to our 1993 Annual Questionnaire. Readers were asked about any repairs to a window-mounted room air-conditioner with cooling capacity under 10,000 BTU/hour that was bought new between 1988 and 1993. Data have been standardized to eliminate differences among brands due solely to age. Differences of less than 3 points aren't meaningful.

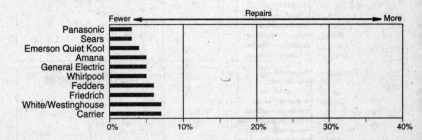

AUDIO & VIDEO GEAR

Two trends continue to drive home-entertainment products: digital technology and home theater. Digital technology is being used in more and more components, from new digital audio recording media to fancy features on receivers and TV sets. Home theater is also having far-reaching effects:

■ Most big-screen TV sets are stereo and can be connected to a separate sound system. More and more sets come with audio amplifiers capable of directly driving external loudspeakers. Many big-screen TV sets can switch among several video sources. Sets with a 27-inch screen are among the premier sellers, and large-screen sets are the fastest-growing part of the market. True high-definition television

remains years away, but manufacturers are starting to introduce wide-screen sets with screens shaped like a theater's.

■ Most stereo receivers these days are "audio/video" receivers, capable of serving as the switching center for a home-theater system. Many mid-priced models come with special sound-effects features like Dolby Pro Logic. Pro Logic decodes and plays a special sound track through multiple speakers to add sounds such as ricochets or the swoosh of airplanes.

■ Speakers, once sold only in pairs, are available singly and in threes, the better to simulate a theater sound system.

■ Hi-fi sound has become a common feature in VCRs, the machines that started home theater.

■ Laser-disc players, once considered something of a technological dodo, have taken on new life, primarily because they deliver superb picture and sound quality.

■ Remote controls, formerly a mere accessory, are now a product in their own right, often capable of day-to-day operation of the whole show.

At its fanciest, a home theater can cost more than a car. But setting up a home theater can be inexpensive and simple: upgrade your VCR to a hi-fi model (for as little as $275), hook up the TV set to a pair of external speakers ($100 or so), or add a patch cord to connect the TV set to the stereo (about $5). Even if you build a system from scratch, you can do it for well under $2000 and still get good performance. Here's what to consider:

Decide which component is the heart of the system. Until recently, you had no choice. It had to be the stereo receiver, whether or not you watched TV and listened to music in the same room. That has changed now that many big-screen TV sets can drive external speakers directly and switch among several video sources. For a TV-based system, plan on spending at least $500 for a 27-inch set with decent speakers and audio and switching features.

If you already have a TV set with an audio output, you can set up a receiver-based system for much less. Because receivers typically have more powerful amplifiers and greater switching capabilities than even the best-equipped TV set, using a receiver as the heart of the setup lets you build a more powerful and versatile system. A receiver costs as little as $150. For an A/V model that decodes Dolby Pro Logic sound, you'll pay at least $280.

Choose the sound-effects package. You typically make this choice in buying a receiver, although some TV sets now come with sound-effects circuitry built in.

The most basic sound setup is two-channel stereo using a pair of speakers. All the configurations of surround sound require additional speakers.

■ Dolby Surround, the at-home version of the Dolby Stereo used in movie theaters, deciphers the channels on the Dolby-encoded sound track of movie videos and a growing number of TV programs. It supplies a pair of ambience speakers with a signal providing the sound effects and echoes that make the action seem to envelop you. With the falling price of Pro Logic (see below), plain Dolby Surround seems headed for the exits.

■ Dolby Pro Logic, representing a significant improvement over Dolby Surround, and, at only a slightly higher price, is fast displacing Dolby Surround. Pro Logic enhances the separation between the front and rear channels and separates some sound, such as dialogue, for a fifth center-channel speaker, which is positioned above or below the TV set so that the sound seems to come directly from the screen.

To drive the center channel, Pro Logic requires an additional amplifier. Most Pro Logic receivers have the amplifier built in; some low-end models come with the Pro Logic circuitry, but not the amp.

■ Dolby 3 stereo, found on many Pro Logic receivers, lets you experience some of the surround-sound effect with only three speakers. Sounds that would normally emanate from the rear speakers are rerouted to the front speakers, but at a slightly lower volume than the sound for the front channels.

■ The ambience modes, found on most surround-sound receivers, are usually created with digital signal-processing, which adds echo to the sound signal on the way to the rear speakers. By selecting "stadium," "concert hall," or "night club" settings, you can simulate environments with various acoustic characteristics.

Plan on spending at least $250 for a receiver that decodes Dolby Pro Logic, plus an additional $100 or so for the center-channel speaker.

Set up the loudspeakers. Some TV sets have built-in "psychoacoustic" effects, which enable speakers located only a couple of feet apart to simulate the spaciousness of full-blown stereo. Convincing as these effects may be, they can't compare with the sound produced by a set of good loudspeakers placed for maximum stereo effect. Expect to pay about $200 to $400 for a main pair. The pair of rear, adjunct speakers in a Dolby setup can be cheaper, since ambience sounds don't tax a speaker's capabilities.

In a two-speaker setup, the speakers go on either side of the TV set. Rear speakers should point away from the listener, since you want ambience sounds to seem as if they're coming from all around you. The fifth speaker in a Dolby Pro Logic setup goes near the TV screen for dialogue and other sounds that make the most sense coming from the picture.

Check the speaker and receiver specifications before you buy to be sure that components are compatible. Many high-quality speakers, particularly those of American origin, have an impedance rating of 4 ohms. (Impedance measures resistance to electric current.) But many receivers, particularly Japanese products, are designed to work with speakers rated at 6 ohms or more. Using the wrong speakers can overheat and damage receiver circuits, especially during steady play at high volumes.

Multiple pairs of speakers complicate the picture. Two sets of speakers connected in parallel, as some receivers require, are a more difficult load than the same two sets of speakers connected in series, as other receivers require.

Choose the playback devices. At a minimum, a home theater setup needs a hi-fi VCR. Hi-fi models are fairly inexpensive, available at discount for less than $300. Laser-disc players are generally more expensive: $400 and up.

Consider the remote control. "Universal" remote controls, which operate more than one type of component, regardless of brand, often come with high-end TV sets and VCRs. Such remotes can be bought separately, too, for $15 and up. Don't count on tossing out the remotes you've collected—you'll still need them to perform specialized functions. For more information on remote controls, see the report on page 38.

Select the rest of the gear. To round out the list of home-entertainment possibilities, there are camcorders, analog or digital recording decks, headphones, and CD players.

Several new technologies have come on the home entertainment scene during the past couple of years. For instance, noise cancellation, a new technology that reduces noise from ambient sound, has begun to appear in some stereo headphones. Digital audio, represented by Philips's Digital Compact Cassette and Sony's Mini-disc, combines CD-quality sound with the ability to record as well as play. Interactive home multimedia devices, such as those marketed by Philips and Panasonic, give the family TV set computerlike capabilities. Digital audio and interactive multimedia are still expensive, with uncertain futures. Wait until the dust settles before investing in either one of them.

Make connections. Connectors range from phono plugs to multipronged S-connectors; wires range from thin speaker wire to coaxial cable. Avoid thin speaker wire; ordinary lamp cord (16 gauge or lower) is better and cheaper for hooking up speakers. Be sure to trim the ends of the wires carefully to keep the two wires from shorting together. Keep audio cables away from power cords to avoid excess hum.

Cable systems and home theater

While consumers await the completion of the fabled information superhighway, some of the boulevards and streets already in place—the cable systems that serve many U.S. homes—can stand repairing.

Cable reception can founder in three places: The signals transmitted by the cable company can be inferior; the distribution system—the cable and all the associated equipment—can degrade the signals; or the cable-converter box itself can introduce problems.

Cable boxes. Today's cable-ready sets are designed to tune channels as if they were present directly at the set's input. Many cable subscribers must use cable boxes to get premium channels like HBO; in some systems, subscribers must use them to receive all channels. These boxes—set-top converters and descramblers—act as electronic go-betweens, one more link for signals to negotiate before they're fed to your TV set. Unfortunately, the boxes are sometimes a weak link.

Cable boxes often render a TV set's remote control useless for changing channels. You may need the cable company's remote—at perhaps a dollar or two in monthly charges—to change channels. One remedy: universal remote controls, which work most brands of cable boxes along with the TV set.

Hooking up a VCR to a TV set with a cable box can be cumbersome and add a layer of complexity to VCR programming. To address the problem, new versions of the *VCR Plus* programming system found on many models have been redesigned to control a cable box.

Further, the cable box can make it difficult or impossible to view two channels simultaneously on a set with the picture-in-picture (PIP) feature. At worst, you may need *two* boxes in order to display PIP.

Cable sound. When cable systems were first being wired, no one foresaw the sweeping changes in store for TV. Less-than-superb audio might have gone unnoticed before the days of hi-fi TV. Now, poor sound just gets reproduced more faithfully.

Even though you may watch programs that are broadcast in stereo and your TV set or VCR indicates it's receiving in stereo, your cable company may not properly process the signal. If your "stereo" sound is practically mono, the problem is likely to be most noticeable with Dolby Surround and other ambience effects, which require clear stereo separation.

More annoying, noise can be introduced into the system—and the better your system, the worse it sounds. Buzz can come from the extra information that many cable systems use in scrambling the signal. Your only recourse is to complain to the cable company and hope that it will soon upgrade its equipment or switch scrambling methods. Hum can result from electrical power leaking into the audio signal. That problem, which can be caused by voltage differences in electrical grounds, may be more easily solved by the cable company.

Some cable systems simulcast the audio track of their pay channels on a separate frequency in the FM band, with potentially far better sound quality; some systems also include the basic channels or at least the music channels, like MTV. Many A/V receivers are set up to receive such simulcasts. (The simulcasts are assigned broadcast frequencies where there are no local radio stations on the dial.) There may be an extra installation or monthly charge to hook up your stereo receiver to the cable.

For those dissatisfied with the quality of cable service, hope is on the way, in the form of satellite transmissions. Heavily promoted by RCA, the new system will use an 18-inch receiver dish to capture signals and route them to the TV, with supposedly

higher picture and sound quality. After the initial cost, expected to be $700 to $900, the monthly charge should be competitive with cable ($20 to $30).

Buying the gear

Our basic shopping advice is easily summed up: Shop around, and don't buy more than you need.

Home electronics equipment is often sharply discounted from the list price. The extent of discounting depends, in part, on where you buy. Audio/video salons tend to charge list or close to it; discount houses and mail-order sources usually provide better deals, but you have to know exactly what you want.

What do you get by buying a brand's more expensive models? Often, small but tangible improvements in performance, convenience, or versatility.

Sometimes, however, you pay extra for a name and a look. Mass-market brands, such as *RCA* and *Panasonic* in video and *Sony*, *Pioneer*, *Technics*, and *JVC* in audio, are widely available in stores and by mail, usually at substantial discount. Prestige brands, such as *Proton* and *ProScan* video products, are sold primarily through specialty audio and video dealers, with little discounting. Some companies—Sony, RCA, and Panasonic among them—manufacture separate lines of merchandise in order to reach both markets.

Our tests have shown no substantive performance advantage for the prestige brands. Indeed, prestige audio brands tend to give you fewer features for the money than mass-market brands. (That allows the control panels of many prestige products to be a model of simplicity.)

Aficionados of hi-fi equipment have always put together a system one piece at a time, shopping carefully for just the right

speakers or the cassette deck nonpareil. That strategy still makes sense, according to our test results. A single company rarely excels at making every component.

Keep in mind, however, that the differences in performance we find between the best and the rest are often fairly small. Even "rack systems," the everything-provided audio systems that are snubbed by audiophiles, can produce good sound.

The increasing interconnectedness of audio and video gear, however, provides good reasons to choose many or all components from the same manufacturer. Remote controls, for instance, may enjoy expanded capability if the components are of the same brand. And special taping conveniences built into modern cassette tape decks work only with a same-brand compact-disc player.

Check our brand Repair Histories, where available; they start on page 15. Repairs of electronic equipment can be costly, averaging around $50 to $65 for audio components and around $80 to $100 for video components, according to a recent survey of our readers.

Don't buy an extended warranty—it's a bad investment. If solid-state electronic circuitry fails, it usually fails early, within 90 days or so, when the manufacturer's own warranty is apt to be in effect. Belts and other parts that wear out with heavy use usually aren't covered, nor is accidental breakage. Stores make much of their profit from these contracts, so prepare yourself for a hard sell. See page 14 for the report on extended warranties.

TV sets

▶ Ratings on page 52. ▶ Repair records on page 16.

As with much home electronics gear, you can get more TV for your money than in the past. Manufacturers continue to wring better performance from the existing broadcast system while moving fancier features down the price curve. The 27-inch set—once considered large, now routine—has been a beneficiary of these trends.

Better pictures. One milestone in tube design was the Trinitron approach pioneered by Sony more than 20 years ago. A recent innovation, the Invar tube (named for the nickel-iron alloy that guides the electron beam to the screen's phosphors), makes it possible to produce exceptionally bright pictures without sacrificing clarity. Now, comb-filter circuitry, which is built into most large sets, improves picture clarity by minimizing shimmery false colors and increasing resolution.

The latest picture improvements include darkening the front of the picture tube to enhance contrast in bright settings.

Despite those improvements, picture quality is still limited by the broadcast and cable format that allows, at most, 330 lines of horizontal resolution. Most sets we've tested come close enough to that limit—at 320 lines or so—for most TV-watching. (Sets without a comb filter are apt to resolve just 270 lines.) S-VHS videotapes and laser-disc players can produce 400 to 425 lines, if the TV set can render them.

The next major improvement in picture quality won't come until HDTV (high-definition television) becomes widely available, probably several years from now. If prototype HDTV sets we've seen at industry trade shows are any indication, HDTV will be well worth the wait. When it first arrives, though, it's likely to be expensive—

$1000 to $2000 more than conventional large-screen sets. HDTV's arrival shouldn't affect owners of existing TV sets. Government plans are for conventional TV broadcasting to continue alongside HDTV for years to come.

Meanwhile, manufacturers have begun selling forerunners of tomorrow's HDTV sets, recognizable by their wide screens and high price tags. While these models can offer better picture quality than traditional sets—achieved through a technology known as IDTV (improved-definition television)—they should not be confused with high-definition sets.

Better sound. TV sound has also improved over the past decade. As stereo telecasts and hi-fi sound tracks on videotapes have become the norm, the ability to decode multichannel TV stereo (MTS) has also become commonplace. More and more sets feature sound enhancements, like Dolby Pro Logic, with the amplifiers built in to power extra speakers.

Good sound starts with good fidelity—the ability to reproduce wide tonal range. Sound from the best TV sets compares favorably with that of a decent compact component system.

But good tone quality alone cannot provide the sound effects that some movies beg for. Internal speakers that are too close together or too small cannot reproduce stereo in all its glory.

The "side firing" speakers on some TV sets offer a better illusion of stereo, as long as the set is not enclosed in cabinetry. Some sets offer electronically enhanced stereo, or "psychoacoustically" altered sound, as an alternative to hooking up external speakers. In those sets, electronics manipulate the audio cues reaching listeners' ears to create the illusion of a wider sound stage, which also can sometimes make dialogue sound unnatural. It's most effective in movies with exotic sound effects. The SRS (sound retrieval system) is a particularly effective two-speaker system.

Closed captioning. By law, all new TV sets with a 13-inch screen or larger must be able to display captions—strips or full screens of text—encoded into broadcast, cable signals, and some rental tapes. The most obvious beneficiaries of this are hearing-impaired viewers. Such captions also show promise as teaching tools for preschoolers learning to read and as a way to watch TV in bed without disturbing others. Sets with this ability are already showing up in restaurants, allowing diners to follow sports events without the sound on.

The choices

In the world of television, screen size defines the subtype.

Mini. Color TV sets with screens of three inches or so are still in the fancy-gadget stage of evolution. The picture comes from a liquid-crystal display (LCD) rather than a regular TV set's cathode-ray tube. To look its best, the picture has to be viewed nearly head on. Some LCD sets display fairly good pictures, but not as good as tube sets. Bright outdoor lighting makes the picture all but vanish, and even in shaded areas the picture is only marginally acceptable. Color mini sets are priced as high as a full-sized TV set: $100 to $600.

13-inch sets. Sets this size are regarded as "second" sets, so makers tend to make them plain. As a rule, expect monophonic sound, sparse features, a remote control, and a price tag of $200 to $300.

20-inch sets. With corners squared off, most brands' 19-inch sets grew to 20 inches on the diagonal. Once the standard living-room set, TV sets of this size are in-

creasingly regarded as a second set. Don't expect high-end picture refinements such as a comb filter or high-performance picture tube except in the pricier models. You can expect an acceptable-to-very good picture, stereo capability, and extra inputs to accept programming from a VCR and a laser-disc player. Sets this size offer lots of features and typically sell for $200 to $500.

Large-screen TV sets. Sets 25 inches and larger are the fastest-growing sizes. Three brands account for nearly half of U.S. sales of large-screen TV sets: *RCA, Magnavox,* and *Zenith.* Sets with a 25- or 26-inch screen tend to be the economy models; those with 27-inch screens offer more features. Sets in the 25- to 27-inch range are priced from about $300 to more than $1500. High-end models have fancy sound systems and complex but versatile remotes.

Sets with screens 31 inches and larger usually have enhanced sound systems and various high-end features, such as the ability to recall customized picture and sound settings or picture-in-picture. Prices range from less than $1000 to more than $2500. The largest TV sets in this size weigh hundreds of pounds each—too wide and too high for conventional component shelving.

Rear-projection sets. These offer still more picture area—40 to 70 diagonal inches—but less clarity than a conventional tube. You'll need a viewing distance of at least 10 feet for a 50-inch set, more for larger ones. (The rule of thumb: The closest viewing distance is four times the screen height.) Brightness and, to a lesser extent, color vary as you move left or right, up or down. Big-screen sets come with plenty of features, such as ambient sound and custom audio and video settings. Expect to pay from $1500 to more than $5500.

Features and conveniences

Comb filter. This circuitry improves picture quality by increasing resolution and cleaning up image outlines. A must for the best picture.

Remote control. Just about all TV sets come with an infrared remote control. The simplest such device may only switch the set on and off, change channels, and adjust volume. More versatile units can mute sound, shut the set off with a timer, block a channel from view, and control a VCR. On some sets, nearly all controls have been moved to the remote, a mixed blessing unless the remote is well designed. See the report on remote controls, page 38.

Electronic channel scan. Direct tuning, which lets you hop from one station to another, is standard. "Auto program" automatically tunes the TV only to channels that are active in your area. Most sets let you delete little-watched channels from the up/down channel scan.

Cable ready. These sets can receive cable TV signals (except for scrambled premium movie channels) without using the cable company's decoder box. This feature is now commonplace. High-end models offer two cable (antenna) inputs, for basic and for scrambled channels.

MTS stereo. MTS (multichannel TV stereo) means the TV set has a built-in stereo decoder and amplifier to reproduce stereo broadcasts. Some low-priced sets from RCA and General Electric create a pseudostereo sound instead of the standard MTS variety.

Inputs/outputs. Audio and video jacks come mainly with sets 20 inches and larger.

Many of the largest sets have more than a dozen. For hooking up a hi-fi VCR, laserdisc player, camcorder, or sound system, the set needs at least one video input, one stereo audio input and output.

Other features. These include an alarm timer to turn the set on or off; block-out to eliminate certain channels; channel labeling; a timer to help skip commercials; and adjustments that smooth images and perform subtle color corrections.

Reliability

Years of reader surveys have yielded this generalization: larger sets have been more likely to need repair than 13- or 20-inch sets. According to our surveys, no single brand has been the most reliable across all set sizes. Among 25- to 27-inch sets, some of the more reliable brands have been *Panasonic, JVC, GE, Toshiba*, and *Quasar*. See the Repair Histories, pages 16 and 17.

Buying advice

With good picture quality the norm these days, the choice of a TV set is likely to hinge on several other factors—features, reliability, price, or perhaps the design of the remote control. If possible, try out the remote functions before buying.

Don't put too much stock in comparisons of the picture you see on sets displayed in a store. You can't be sure that those TV sets are getting a uniform picture signal or that they have been uniformly adjusted.

VCRs

▶ Ratings on page 68. ▶ Repair records on page 16.

In their second decade on the market, VCRs have become nearly as popular as televisions. Picture quality is about as good as it's going to get, at least until a future development such as HDTV or digital video comes along. For now, expect a flood of features, many of which are secondary to what most people need: good picture and, for home theater, hi-fi sound.

These days, nearly all VCRs use the VHS format or its high-end variant, S-VHS. Out of more than 40 brands, three—*RCA, Magnavox,* and *Panasonic*—account for about one-third of all VHS VCRs sold in the U.S. Other big brands include *JVC, Sharp, General Electric, Sony,* and *Zenith.*

The Beta format has all but vanished; only Sony, its inventor, still sells Beta equipment, primarily to the TV industry, to Betaphiles, and to consumers outside the U.S. Newer formats such as 8mm and its cousin, Hi8, have come along to accommodate a new breed of small-sized camcorders, and a small number of VCRs are sold in those formats. Like Beta-format machines, machines with those formats do not accept VHS cassettes.

Although the VCR market has settled down in recent years, big changes loom on the horizon. Consumer electronics companies are now at work on standards for digital VCRs, offering improved picture and sound quality, that could reach the market within several years. Technological improvements also raise the possibility of recordable video discs in the not-too-distant future.

The choices

VCRs cost anywhere from less than $200 to more than $2000. Certain key features mark off rough price levels.

The basic VCR. While some very low-priced models are just playback machines (VCPs—videocassette players), the basic VCR has been the two-head player with monophonic sound, priced at less than $200. Two play/record heads are all you need for everyday recording and playback.

An extra pair of heads offers some advantages: cleaner freeze-frames in the longer-play EP speed and sometimes a slightly better picture during regular playback. Four-head models outsell two-head

models and may soon be regarded as basic. Four-head models start at about $200.

Hi-fi models. Hi-fi stereo is resoundingly better than the older, "linear" stereo technology, which lays sound tracks along the edges of the tape. Hi-fi VCRs record the audio tracks as diagonal stripes across the tape's width under the video track. The result is near-CD sound quality, with excellent reproduction across a wide range of audio frequencies, and virtually no flutter or noise. Hi-fi VCRs use two extra heads on the drum and are sometimes referred to as "six head" machines. The typical price range is $250 to $600.

Super VHS. You'll pay a premium of about $200 for this technical refinement of VHS. S-VHS gives a sharper picture than normal VHS. S-VHS also stands up better if you're making multiple tape-to-tape copies. To take full advantage of the S-VHS format, you need a high-resolution source of pictures (S-VHS or Hi-8 camcorder) and a high-resolution TV set—preferably a model equipped with an S-video jack.

S-VHS is partially compatible with regular VHS—an S-VHS machine can tape and play in VHS mode, but an S-VHS tape can't be played in a regular VHS machine (although some conventional VHS machines offer "Quasi-S-VHS" playback). To record in S-VHS, you need special, more expensive, S-VHS tapes; the player automatically senses the tape type and adjusts the tape mode accordingly.

S-VHS models generally are priced $550 to $2000 or more.

Features and conveniences

Year by year, fancy features migrate down from higher- to lower-priced models.

Remote control. Even low-end models usually come with a remote. See the report on page 38.

HQ. HQ (high quality) refers to small technical refinements that reduce some of the video noise and other picture defects that a VCR can introduce into a recording. Virtually every VHS VCR has the HQ designation.

Digital tracking. Now found on nearly all VCRs, this eliminates the need to adjust the tracking control for each tape viewed, useful when playing tapes recorded on other units.

Easy programming. On-screen programming is almost universal. The VCR shows a menu on the TV screen that prompts you through the process of choosing times and dates for the programs you want to record, up to several days or weeks in advance. Some VCRs simplify setting the clock by automatically switching to and from daylight saving time on the appropriate dates.

Even though on-screen programming is a great improvement over previous methods, it's still too complicated for many people. *VCR Plus* simplifies it even further. *VCR Plus* is sold as a separate product for $60, or as a built-in feature that adds $20 to $80 to the list price of a VCR. It enters the time and channel information automatically when you tap in the special three- to seven-digit program code that appears in the TV listings of many newspapers and magazines. Newer versions of *VCR Plus* have the ability to record multiple channels from a cable box, a feature older versions lacked.

Matsushita incorporates its own simplified programming controls on the remotes of most *Panasonic* and *Quasar* models. On *Panasonics*, it's called Program Director; on *Quasars*, it's called E-Z Dial Programming. You enter each piece of information—date, start time, stop time, and channel—by turning a dial. Then you send the information to the VCR with the Transmit button.

The newest wrinkle in programming is the voice-activated remote. It lets you call out the channel and time to record. In our last test, we found it unwieldy to use.

Programming is likely to become even simpler when the next generation of smart "set-top boxes" comes along, to help people cope with the increasing complexity of TV technology.

Camcorder jack. All VCRs let you plug in a camcorder of any format. More and more models have the jacks on the front of the VCR, where they are easy to reach.

Picture tricks. They include such features as multiple-speed slow-motion and fast-motion, frame advance, and freeze frame. Most of these extras are more gimmick than useful additions.

Taping features. One-touch recording (OTR) simplifies taping. A tape-time-remaining indicator can save running out of tape five minutes before the end of the movie. Index search lets you mark the tape and then move rapidly to the next mark. Real-time search or Go-to lets you enter a location on the tape and then speeds through the tape. A Skip button advances the tape in 30-second increments.

Tape-editing functions. Of interest mainly to those who make home videos, these features include: flying erase heads, for glitch-free assemble edits; an Edit switch that boosts the signal when copying a tape to improve the quality of second-generation signals; a Synchro-edit jack to coordinate a compatible camcorder or a second VCR used as a source; advanced editing features such as insert editing; a Jog-shuttle control, which helps locate a tape segment by running the tape backward or forward at continuously variable speeds; audio and video dubbing abilities; and a character generator for adding written titles or captions.

The tests

CU's engineers check the performance of each model at both SP (standard play) and EP (extended play) speeds. We make tapes on each VCR, then play them back on laboratory monitors. A panel of staffers judges them for such factors as blurriness, graininess, streaking, and the presence of unnatural-looking edges to images.

In the laboratory, CU engineers measure the same tuner factor we check in TV sets—selectivity for blocking out adjacent signals. Our audio tests measure the same factors we check on tape decks—flutter, signal-to-noise ratio, and frequency response. And of course, we evaluate convenience and features.

Reliability

VCRs are finicky machines. According to our 1993 Annual Questionnaire, 13 percent of the machines bought from 1988 to 1993 have needed repair at least once. *Magnavox, Panasonic, Quasar, Sylvania, General Electric,* and *Toshiba* have been among the least troublesome brands. *Fisher* VCRs have needed repairs more often than any other brand. See the brand Repair Histories on pages 16 and 17.

Buying advice

There's no clear correlation between purchase price and picture quality. As a general rule, more money buys more features and convenience.

A two-head VCR or a basic four-head model is all you need if you're primarily interested in taping TV programs for viewing later. If you want to take advantage of movies with a stereo sound track or hook the VCR into your stereo system as part of a home theater, concentrate on a hi-fi VHS model. A hi-fi VCR produces superb sound, but only when it's piped through good loudspeakers.

If you're interested in editing video tapes, check that the VCR and camcorder have compatible synchronization provisions. Unfortunately, there's still no standardization of synchro-editing features.

HOW TO BUY VIDEOTAPE

In the real world of imperfect TV reception and VCR performance, differences between brands of videotape are likely to be all but unnoticeable. For many uses, the strategy of buying the cheapest tape may be perfectly fine.

Differences are likely to show up most when the signal quality is high-quality, as from a camcorder. In addition, manufacturers recommend that high-grade tapes be used for videos you expect to keep for many years (although we know no evidence showing the quality of standard-grade tapes diminishes faster than that of high-grade ones). Peace of mind alone may justify spending the extra dollar or so to buy a high-grade videotape for taping important events. Our top-rated VHS tape, *TDK Hi-Fi Extra High Grade,* costs $4.

Time-shifting vacationers may want to consider T160 and longer videotapes. These superlong tapes we tested aren't noticeably lower in quality than the standard-length cassettes. Some extra-length tapes, including the top-rated *TDK HS T160,* $4, offer good value.

We recommend stocking up on video tape whenever it's on sale. Prices range from about $1 to $12. You can also save by buying in quantity—four packs, five packs, and so on.

To protect videotapes you care about: ■ In the event of catastrophe, make a duplicate copy and store it away from the original. ■ Enclose videotapes in plastic boxes to seal them from smoke, dust, and dirt. ■ Store tapes in moderate temperature and humidity. Never leave tapes in direct sunlight or leave them in a hot vehicle. ■ Seldom-played tapes should be "exercised"—taken out for a spin every year or two at least.

Camcorders

▶ **Repair records on page 19.**

The great battle of video formats has left camcorder users with two major tape formats: 8mm and VHS-C and their higher-resolution cousins, Hi8 and S-VHS-C.

Panasonic, the VHS-C market leader, plays up the format's compatibility with VHS VCRs, even though hooking up an 8mm camcorder to a TV set is very easy. The main advantage of 8mm is its longer playing time—two hours, versus 40 minutes for VHS-C at standard speed—plus the fact that flutter-free sound is standard on 8mm. Both formats have held their own in fierce competition; both are likely to stick around for the foreseeable future.

One new design replaces the viewfinder with a color LCD screen at the rear of the camcorder. That novel design, heavily promoted by Sharp, fared no better than many other models in our tests and had some major shortcomings.

There are some 30 brands of camcorders on the market. A handful of brands—*Sony, Panasonic, Canon, Sharp, JVC,* and *RCA*—account for most of the sales.

Most camcorders get their power from a rechargeable nickel-cadmium (nicad) battery that gives about an hour of taping on a full charge. Many models also offer batteries of smaller capacity (to save weight) or larger capacity (for longer shooting). Consider buying a spare (about $60).

Unless fully discharged before recharging, nicad batteries temporarily lose some of their capacity. To get around that, many models have a charger than discharges the battery before recharging.

The choices

8mm. Small, light, easy to tote, 8mm is the best-selling format. Its higher-resolution, "high band" version is Hi8. Cassettes hold up to two hours of footage; 2½-hour cassettes exist but are not readily available. Sound quality is the equal of hi-fi models in the other formats. Cassettes cost about $5; Hi8 tapes cost more. For playback, you connect a cable from the camcorder to your TV or VCR. You can also connect the camcorder to your VCR to make copies or edit VHS tapes; 8mm VCRs are also available. Prices of 8mm camcorders range from about $450 to $1500 or more. Expect to pay a few hundred dollars extra for Hi8.

VHS-C. JVC introduced this compact version of VHS. The high-band version is S-VHS-C. Cassettes are playable in a VHS VCR with a battery-powered adapter (supplied with the camcorder or available in camcorder stores) that will work with any VHS VCR. Cassettes, at about $6 apiece, hold just 40 minutes at fast speed, 120 minutes at slow speed. Prices for VHS-C start at about $500, S-VHS-C at about $1200.

Full-sized VHS. This was the old standard, now fading. Though these models are heavy and bulky, some people prefer them for their stability. The high-band version is S-VHS. Standard VHS cassettes are widely available; T-120 (two-hour) tapes cost about $3 each. A full-sized VHS camcorder can double as a VCR to play rented movies. This is the bargain format now, with prices ranging from $500 to $1100 on many models.

Features and conveniences

Standard features include date/time labeling, fade, headphone jack (to monitor the audio portion), microphone jack (for recording music), and jacks for playback or recording to another camcorder or VCR. You can also expect a motorized zoom lens whose "macro" range lets you make close-ups of subjects within an inch of the lens; automatic exposure and sound-level controls; a flying erase head that helps deliver clean scene changes even if you re-record something; and auto-focus, which keeps the image sharp as the subject or the camera moves.

Also standard is automatic white balance. This circuitry keeps colors normal under different lighting conditions.

Other features available on some camcorders include:

Color viewfinder. Found on a growing number of models, this lets you view scenes in color, but the picture is not always as crisp or bright as that provided by a black-and-white viewfinder.

Image stabilization. Also increasingly common, this tries to iron the jitters out of hand-held shots—particularly useful with small, light units. This feature's effectiveness varies considerably from brand to brand. A video tripod is still the best tool for steady shots (see the report on tripods on page 80).

Digital gain-up. Helps create passable pictures in dim light. It works by slowing the shutter speed. The downside: Moving subjects or fast panning leaves a blur.

Sound. The 8mm format has audio capabilities inherently superior to VHS but not hi-fi VHS and VHS-C models. The built-in mike in most camcorders is better suited for capturing speech than music.

Remote control. More and more commonplace, especially on 8mm models, a remote makes it easy to use the camcorder for playback and editing. It also works as an alternative to a self-timer.

Reset-to-auto switch. A single switch on some models restores all settings to their normal automatic mode so that you don't have to check each control.

Manual exposure control, found on a few models. Automatic exposure generally works well but doesn't offer the flexibility of a manual override, which is helpful in some lighting situations.

Special picture effects. Some models in the middle-to-top brand lines include crude animation and time lapse effects. Freeze-frame and other digital special effects also show up on some of those models.

Title generator. Some models permit superimposing printed titles and captions created with a built-in character generator. Others let you photograph and superimpose titles from artwork or signs. Most let you select a color for the title.

Wide-screen pictures. This feature lets you record images in a format similar to that of letterboxed movies. It's not especially useful, unless you have one of the pricey new TV sets whose picture tube has a 16:9 aspect ratio.

Reliability

Most people don't use their camcorders a lot—readers who own a camcorder bought since 1988 report taping an average of just six hours per year. Even so, nearly 1 in 10 camcorders needed repair. Among compact models, *Minolta* 8mm required the most repairs. *Sony* 8mm, *Canon* 8mm, *Panasonic* VHS-C, and *JVC* VHS-C have been among the more reliable compacts. Among the most reliable VHS brands: *Magnavox, Panasonic, General Electric,* and *Sears.* See the brand Repair Histories on page 19.

Buying advice

Picture quality overall is quite good. It's not likely to improve much more until high-definition television or digital video reach the market. High-band models generally provide a noticeably sharper picture than regular models. VHS and VHS-C are slightly more convenient for playback of tapes, but that's about their only advantage. 8mm has longer recording times and better sound. Compared with VHS, 8mm and VHS-C cameras are much easier to lug around and their pictures are comparable.

With any type, you'll need a tripod for professional results. For fast panning, a tripod-mounted compact is more manageable than a VHS model because the compact's viewfinder is at the rear rather than forward on the side as it is with a VHS. See page 80 for the report on tripods.

Remote controls

The remote control is now a standard accessory for virtually every type of home-entertainment gear. It has also become a product in its own right.

Dedicated remote. It operates only the component it comes with, typically the cheapest TV sets, VCRs, and receivers.

Unified remotes. This type also comes packaged with a component, but offers more flexibility—it operates at least one other product of the same brand, often in a limited way.

Universal remotes. This type is often included with high-end TV sets, VCRs, and receivers, or sold as a stand-alone product, priced from $20 to $225. It operates gear from a variety of makers. Many work video gear only; some work everything.

The appeal of universal remotes goes beyond that of simplifying the home-entertainment experience. If you want to replace a lost remote, a universal remote control can sell for less than a replacement from the manufacturer. Similarly, if a remote is broken, you can often buy a new universal model for less than it would take to repair the old device.

Universal remotes can be "code entry" models, "learning" models, or a combination. Code-entry remotes, programmed with the codes for major-brand components, are easy to use: Just tell the remote which brand and model to emulate by entering the codes listed for your components. But code-entry remotes often don't support the advanced commands needed for programming a VCR or work with components more than a few years old.

Learning remotes mimic virtually any command found on other remotes, but are more complicated to set up. To program one, you align the remote with the remote whose commands you want it to learn, then execute those commands. A low-battery indicator is especially useful for a learning remote, which can be quite cumbersome to reprogram if the battery dies.

Buying advice

The simplicity of most code-entry universal remotes limits them to only basic functions, which may be just fine for everyday use. Remotes of the learning variety are more difficult to use and tricky to program, but they control more functions. Hybrid models combine the best of both types: easy setup and powerful functions. Simplified models are probably best as second remotes, useful when all you need is to change channels or volume.

Well-designed models let you operate components with a minimum of button-pressing or on-screen menu navigation. They feel balanced and comfortable to hold and are easy to use with one hand. Buttons are organized and differentiated by size, shape, or color. Often-used buttons should stand out. Especially handy are four-way rocker switches or north/south buttons that control volume and channels.

Receivers

▶ Ratings on page 62.

If any component exemplifies the growing importance of video and home theater, it is the receiver. Two of every three units sold are designed to shuttle video as well as audio signals between the other components. Nearly as many offer some type of surround sound, an important feature for home theater.

But the basic function of the receiver, however, remains the amplification of sound from audio components and the built-in radio tuner. Our tests have shown that, regardless of price, the amp almost always performs very well. Where models differ is in amplifier power output, FM radio performance, and the presence of such conveniences as input jacks for plugging in ancillary equipment.

Receivers are sold under more than 30 brand names. Five—*Pioneer, Sony, Kenwood, JVC,* and *Technics*—account for more than 60 percent of the market, however.

The choices

The premium charged for video-switching capability depends on the brand. Companies such as Pioneer, Sony, and JVC have switched virtually their entire lines over to audio/video receivers. Other companies retain audio-only receivers at the low end of their price lines. Some prestige brands offer nothing but audio receivers, but even those are starting to recognize video functions as more than a frill.

Prices range from $150 to more than $1900. By spending more, you don't necessarily get better sound. You get:

Power. Low-end receivers may produce only 35 to 45 watts per channel of amplifier power, while high-end models crank out 100 watts or more and come with extra amplifiers to drive the additional speakers that are essential to home theater.

More isn't necessarily better. How much you need depends on your speakers, the size of the room, and the type of music you play. In most applications, 50 watts per channel is ample. Receivers in the 100-watt range are necessary only if you're driving multiple pairs of speakers at loud volumes in large spaces or are using speakers that are particularly inefficient. (Low-efficiency speakers need more power than a high-efficiency model to produce the same volume level.) The box on page 41 can help you calculate your power requirements.

Sound. Two-channel stereo is the most basic sound effect, suited primarily to listening to music. For watching movies or videos, Dolby Surround or Dolby Pro Logic provides greater realism through special circuitry that deciphers the sound effects encoded on many movie videos. Dolby Surround uses a second pair of speakers to carry the sound effects and echoes that make the action seem to surround you. Dolby Pro Logic adds a fifth speaker to carry "center" sound from the direction of the TV screen. Look for a model that includes an amplifier for the fifth channel. As prices for the superior Dolby Pro Logic drop to nearly the level of plain Dolby Surround, the latter seems to be fading from the market.

Dolby 3 Stereo, a feature on many Pro Logic receivers, lets you experience all five channels in the surround mode with only three speakers. Sounds that would normally emanate from the rear speakers are rerouted to the front three speakers and dispersed at slightly lower volume than the sounds for the main channels. The feature works, but has a more dramatic effect if rear speakers are used. Another sound effect common on middle-of-the-line receivers is ambience mode, which simulates the acoustics of a stadium or concert hall.

Dolby Pro Logic models start at $250. See the discussion about choosing a sound-effects package on page 26.

Lucasfilm THX is the latest in sound-system technology. It comes closer to movie theater realism but costs $1600 or more.

Audio/video switching. Any receiver can handle sound from a stereo TV set or a VCR if you connect the video source's audio outputs to auxiliary inputs on the back of the receiver. An A/V receiver does more; it is essentially a control center for selecting the component you want to hear; either a video source (a TV set, VCR, or laser-disc player) or an audio source (a CD, cassette tape, or radio).

Elaborate controls. Mass-market receivers tend to be encrusted with knobs, dials, levers, and lights. More controls do more, but they make the product more complicated. Prestige brands, on the other hand, make a virtue of simplicity—no flashy display, perhaps no remote, limited switching and dubbing capability—even on high-priced models. Ultimately, the solution to the growing complexity of controls on full-featured receivers may be similar to what works with the VCR—a TV-based on-screen menu system. Several versions are already out.

Features and conveniences

Some features—a pulsing bar graph of the sound "profile," say—may do more for a receiver's image and marketability than for its use. Here are the major features:

Graphic equalizer. This fancy tone control for contouring the sound shows up even on low-priced models. Equalizers with fewer than seven "bands," as they are

called, don't accomplish much more than regular bass and treble controls. Most high-end models now offer an equalizer as part of digital signal processing.

Digital electronic tuning. It's the standard method of radio tuning. Digital tuning captures a station at its precise frequency, thus minimizing noise and distortion. Tuning is generally accomplished with an up/down Seek button that searches for the next listenable station along the dial. Handiest are tuners that step in increments of 200-kilohertz, the distance between FM channels in the U.S. Some models let you directly enter a station's frequency on a numeric keypad, the method we prefer. When you tune past either end of the band, wraparound tuning jumps automatically to the opposite end.

Remote control. Most receivers now have one, usually adorned with rows and rows of undifferentiated tiny buttons, the way video remote controls used to be.

Switched outlet. It lets you plug other components into the receiver so that you can shut off the whole system when you turn off the receiver.

Tone-control bypass is useful for temporarily defeating tone settings so you can listen to a recording in its pristine form.

Loudness switch. It boosts the bass when the volume is down, compensating for the human ear's insensitivity to bass at low volume. A variable control allows the most flexibility.

Mute switch. It turns sound off without changing the volume-control setting.

Multi source. Handles two sound sources at once—useful, for example, for sending a movie soundtrack to the home-theater speakers and music from a CD to the home office.

The tests

Our evaluation is based primarily on a standard battery of laboratory tests, chiefly of the FM tuner. A first-rate tuner reproduces sound free of background noise and distortion. If sensitive enough to pull in weak signals, a receiver should resist interference from electrical sources, aircraft, and other radio signals.

We consider a model's convenience, especially of the control layout, and the usefulness of features.

Reliability

Receivers are stable components that typically last for years and years.

Buying advice

If you want to power a modest system purely for music listening or are content with stereo-only sound from your TV or VCR, a low-end receiver, rated at 50 watts per channel, should be quite satisfactory.

Such a receiver costs $150 or so.

Although some low-priced receivers can handle a TV/VCR/stereo setup without a problem, you'll probably have to buy a model higher in the line if you want the receiver to be the heart of a home-theater system. Models in the $300-to-$450 range typically come with Dolby Pro Logic and enough jacks to accommodate a complicated system and enough power to run more than one set of loudspeakers. If you have a full-sized center speaker, look for a receiver with 50 to 60 watts in the center channel. Some models with this capability are priced no higher than weaker models.

Before buying any receiver, make sure it matches your other components and meets their power requirements. See "How Much Power Do You Need?," below.

HOW MUCH POWER DO YOU NEED?

Even inexpensive receivers have plenty of power. But if you want an idea of how much power a system actually needs, here's how to figure it:

Determine the "liveness" of your listening room. A space with hard floors, scatter rugs, and plain wood furniture will be acoustically live; one with thick wall-to-wall carpet, heavy curtains, and upholstered furniture, relatively dead. Locate the room size (in cubic feet) and type (live or dead) at right and note the multiplier. That figure, multiplied by a speaker's minimum power requirement as noted by the speaker manufacturer, gives the watts per channel needed.

Let's say you have a 4000-cubic-foot room with average acoustics and speakers that require 12 watts of power. The multiplier from the chart, 1.5, times the watts needed, 12, equals 18. At minimum,

you need an amplifier with 18 watts of power per channel to drive the speakers at moderately high volume. To be safe and to do justice to CDs or bass-heavy music, double or triple the figure.

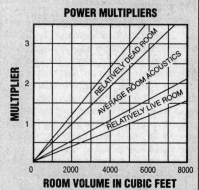

POWER MULTIPLIERS

RELATIVELY DEAD ROOM
AVERAGE ROOM ACOUSTICS
RELATIVELY LIVE ROOM

MULTIPLIER

ROOM VOLUME IN CUBIC FEET

Loudspeakers

▶ Ratings start on page 55.

Loudspeakers are the last place to economize in setting up a music system, but that doesn't mean you have to spend a fortune to get good sound. In our tests, we found some very good inexpensive speakers, suitable as main speakers in a basic system or as front speakers in a home theater setup.

Speakers tend to differ most in their ability to handle bass, which is critical for enjoying jazz, pop, or movie music. Besides that, differences elsewhere in the audio spectrum give each speaker its own distinctive sound, which you may or may not like. Also, what you hear depends a great deal on the size and furnishings of the room, the speakers' placement, and the type of music.

The four and a half million speakers sold each year comprise more than 300 speaker brands, many of them from small, specialty companies, which are often American. The leading manufacturers are Bose and Radio Shack, which account for more than one-quarter of all sales.

The choices

Classic loudspeaker configuration has not changed much in 30 years: The rigid box containing a large bass speaker (the woofer) and a much smaller treble speaker (the tweeter). There may also be a third speaker (the mid-range) that handles middle tones between the highs and lows. Most speakers direct all the sound out the front. Some are designed to radiate some sound upward or to the rear, bouncing sound waves off a nearby wall.

As a practical matter, a speaker needs a big woofer to make big, loud bass. Speaker manufacturers have long tried to design around that fact, with some success.

Certain miniature speakers, for instance, are able to deliver more bass than their size would seem to indicate, though at the expense of volume.

Prices for speakers run from $50 or so a pair to more than $10,000. What more money primarily buys, at every size level, is a deeper reach into the bass.

Here are the main choices:

Small speakers. Miniature speakers are smaller than a shoebox; they typically cost $100 and up per pair. Most are seriously deficient in reproducing bass.

"Powered" speakers are miniatures that have their own built-in amplifier. Typically powered by batteries, such speakers are what makes walkabout tape players or portable CD players small, easy-to-carry sound systems. Powered speakers are increasingly being sold to help turn home computers into "multimedia centers." Powered speakers are priced from $30 to $300.

One variant of the self-powered speaker is the wireless speaker, which comes with a separate transmitter. A pair of wireless speakers can sit up to 15 feet away from the transmitter and are handy in a space where you can't easily run wires.

Bookshelf speakers can fit on a bookshelf sideways. They're appropriate for undemanding listening in a medium-sized room or as the second pair of speakers in a surround-sound system. Bookshelf speakers typically are priced $200 to $550 per pair.

Ambience speakers are another type of small speaker, typically priced less than $150 per pair. They are intended for use as the adjunct, rear speakers in a Dolby Surround system. Many are magnetically shielded and are sold singly, to serve as the center-channel speaker in a Dolby Pro Logic setup. These speakers don't need much bass capacity, since the bass in a Dolby system is carried by the main speakers.

Main speakers. Medium-sized models can fill a medium-sized room with loud sound and a large room with fairly loud sound. In speakers this size, the woofer can push the large volumes of air needed to reproduce a full, rich, loud bass sound. Figure on spending at least $300 for a decent pair.

Large speakers include audiophile equipment, such as electrostatic speakers, in which tall, thin plastic diaphragms replace speaker cones. Such equipment is necessary to fill a very large room; in a smaller setting it's overkill. Speakers this big can cost $700—or thousands.

Some speakers save space by fitting into interior walls, a design that is becoming more and more popular.

Three-piece systems. Another popular type of speaker, the three-piece "subwoofer/satellite" system, separates the tweeter and mid-range speakers from the bass subwoofer. The tweeter and the mid-range speakers, which supply much of the stereo effect, are small and fit unobtrusively among furnishings, while the large bass section can be concealed behind a sofa or in a corner behind the TV set. In our tests, three-piece systems have rendered sound less accurately than conventional speakers. Figure on spending anywhere from $350 to $800.

The tests

To measure speaker performance, we set up laboratory instruments to take measurements in an echo-free chamber and in a 14x23-foot carpeted, furnished room not unlike an ordinary living room.

For most speakers, we measure accuracy from a frequency of about 30 hertz in the bass to about 16,000 Hz in the treble and rate them on a 100-point scale. We don't rate ambience speakers below 100 Hz.

Tweaking a receiver's tone controls can improve a speaker's accuracy—dramatically, in some cases—and also help compensate for a room's acoustical drawbacks. We've learned that most listeners will find it difficult to pick the more accurate of two models if the spread in our scores is eight points or less.

We also measure the minimum power the receiver must supply to a speaker to produce fairly loud sound in a medium-sized room.

Reliability

Loudspeakers are very stable components and likely to be problem-free.

Buying advice

Before you buy speakers, be sure that you can return or exchange them if you dislike the sound they generate in your home. Try to audition them in a good listening room at the store. Compare only two pairs of speakers at a time; stay with the pair you prefer and judge it against the next pair. Take a recording whose music you know well—one that gives both bass sounds and treble a good workout.

Speakers, especially low-priced ones, tend to differ most in the low frequencies. The difference is most noticeable in the bass extension—a speaker's ability to reproduce the very lowest audible tones. Bass-handling, particularly at high volumes, is another aspect of low-frequency performance. That is important if you favor the driving bass sounds typical of fusion jazz, say, or contemporary dance music.

Once you have particular speakers in mind, be sure that your receiver will be able to supply enough power to drive them, and that speaker impedance is not too low for the receiver's amplifier to handle (see "Set Up the Loudspeakers" on page 27 and "How Much Power Do You Need?" on page 41).

Compact-disc players

▶ **Ratings on page 59.** ▶ **Repair records on page 18.**

Virtually every CD player we've tested through the years is capable of reproducing superb hi-fi sound. All the traditional indicators of quality sound—wide dynamic range, accurate (flat) frequency response, and freedom from noise and distortion—can be taken for granted. The minor differences we've noted in sound-reproduction capabilities are not apparent except to a laboratory instrument or a trained listener. Performance differences have been confined to how well the players overcome adverse conditions such as being bumped or playing a damaged disc. Recent models have gotten better at compensating for such problems.

Such perfection has helped the CD player conquer the world of sound. The technology of recording information for playback with lasers has also crept into the world of video. Laser-disc players typically also play CDs as well as the LP-sized laser discs. On the horizon are machines that play video compact discs. Kodak's system for putting still photos on CDs—"Photo CD"—isn't wildly popular, but is gaining ground. And CD players are increasingly packaged with computers as "CD-ROM" drives—to work as multimedia systems.

The world of home audio compact-disc players is dominated by Sony, which makes more than one of every four players sold in the U.S. Other major brands include *Pioneer* (the leader in laser-disc players), *Technics*, and *JVC*.

The choices

Table-model components. These are available as single-disc models and multiple-disc changers. Prices start around $100 for a low-end single-disc player and around $175 for a multiple-disc changer.

One changer design uses a "magazine," a slide-in box the size of a small, fat paperback book. Magazines typically hold six discs, but some models take more—up to 100 in a CD "jukebox."

The alternative changer design is a carousel, holding five or six discs. Carousels are somewhat easier to load than magazines but not as convenient for storing a whole collection of CDs. Most use a slide-out drawer, a few load from the top. Top-loading models cannot be sandwiched into a stack of other stereo components.

Portable players. Some are scarcely bigger than the disc itself; others are part of an overgrown boom box. Portable models sell from about $100 for a small, simple unit, to more than $250 for a fancy system. Basic models may have only rudimentary controls. More elaborate versions come with such features as a rechargeable battery pack, a built-in radio tuner, a cassette deck, or a panoply of controls similar to what you find on a table model. Many boom-box systems have detachable speakers with a bass-boost feature. Portables can easily be hooked into a sound system or plugged into a car stereo through either a CD input jack or an adapter that fits into the cassette slot.

Features and conveniences

The CD world is rife with jargon referring to technical specifications, particularly those connected with the conversion of digital information to analog sound waves: "oversampling," "MASH technology," "dual digital/analog converters," "bit stream" technology, triple laser beams, and so forth. None of that stuff is apt to make a difference you can consistently hear, our tests have shown.

The extras on a CD player don't always go hand-in-hand with price. Less expensive models may be just as generously endowed with features as more expensive ones. Features are most limited on portables.

Standard on just about all home component models are a remote control and features that let you play, pause, stop, select a track, and program selected tracks to play in the order you choose. (Changers let you skip from one disc to another.)

Also typical is a display that indicates which track is being played and the elapsed playing time. Other common options, even on basic models:

Shuffle play. This mixes the playing order into a random sequence. Look for non repeat shuffle.

Numeric keypad. It lets you program by punching in track numbers directly rather than fussing with Up/down buttons. It's common on remotes, less so on consoles.

Calendar display. This starts by showing the number of each track on the disc; as the disc plays, the track numbers disappear one by one. Such a display is especially handy for making tapes, since it reminds you which tracks you have already programmed.

On/off pause. It's handier than having to hit Play to resume playing.

Headphone jack. This is useful for listening without disturbing others.

Fade control. This makes the music fade out slowly, then stop.

Music sampling. This lets you play a few seconds from each track to help you choose which to listen to or tape.

Programming aids. Programming a CD player means telling the unit to play tracks in a particular order. Some players even remember your programs. This feature, called Favorite-track selection or Custom file, works by having the player read and remember programs you've encoded on the discs. Some models have a Delete-track function that will remember to skip over unwanted tracks.

Taping aids. Various features to make taping easy work best with a same-brand tape deck. Auto-edit lets you punch in the recording time of one side of a tape for the CD player to suggest a track order that fits. With a player that features synchronized recording, you don't have to be present during the taping. You connect a cable from the player to a same-brand deck with Auto-reverse. When the deck is ready to record on the second side of the tape, it sends a signal to the CD player, and the taping resumes. Models with Music-peak finder can search for the loudest passage on a disc, letting you set the recorder to the proper sound level. Running total adds up track time as you program the disc so that you can tell how many tracks will fit on a given tape. Digital output jacks let you connect a CD player directly to a digital tape or minidisc recorder.

Special effects. Digital signal processing is a technique that simulates the acoustics of a concert hall or stadium.

The tests

Besides making the usual sound checks, we see how well the players can cope with adversity: bumps in playback and purposely damaged discs. We also measure how fast the players can jump from track to track.

Reliability

The repair rate for most brands of compact-disc players bought from 1990 to 1993 has been about 5 percent, according to our readers' experiences. Magazine changers have been more likely to need repair than either single-play or carousel models. Among the single-disc players, *JVC* and *Kenwood* were among the more reliable

COMPACT DISCS: MUSIC AND BEYOND

Compact discs have moved beyond the record store. They've taken oven the encyclopedia business and are beginning to replace computer diskettes. The rise of CDs reflects the move to convert electronic information to digital encoding, a trend called convergence.

Converting information to digital storage has many advantages: Noise and interference can be virtually eliminated; duplicates are perfect copies of the original; large amounts of information can be stored in a very small space at shrinking prices; and computers can manipulate digital information in ways that are difficult or impossible by any other means.

A dozen or so CD formats and seven types of player now exist. Among them:

■ CD audio. This is the oldest and most prevalent format—the invention that all but killed the LP record. CD players and all of the newer players can play music from CDs.

■ CD-ROM (read-only memory). This format is designed to let you retrieve data from the CD to use on a computer. Thousands of titles are available, including encyclopedias, games, and children's books.

■ CD-I. Interactive discs that run on Philips and Magnavox CD-I players.

■ CD-I video. A CD-I disc with a full-motion movie. Requires a special adapter to run on a CD-I player.

■ Sega CD. Holds game software for Sega game systems.

■ Photo CD. Stores about 100 high-quality photos from slides or prints that can "play" on most CD-ROM players.

■ 3DO. A promising new game format with improved graphics and sound. So far, few titles are available.

■ CD+G. Contains still images to accompany music; not widely used.

■ CD+MIDI. Plays on a specially equipped player and keyboard synthesizer; not widely used.

■ CD-V. Holds up to 20 minutes of sound and 5 minutes of video for music videos; not widely used.

brands. *Denon* had the worst record of the changers; *Sony, Onkyo, Technics, Yamaha* among those with the best. We don't yet have data on the reliability of portables. For more information, see the brand Repair Histories on page 18.

Buying advice

Good audio performance from a compact-disc player is a given. Virtually every CD player we've tested can reproduce superb hi-fi sound. Product differences boil down to how well the players handle physical abuse and what features they offer. If you need to save money in your system, do it here. By spending less, you give up niceties, not performance.

Changer models are priced a little higher than single-play units but offer the convenience of hours of uninterrupted play. We prefer the carousel design; it's easier to load and unload than the magazine type.

If uninterrupted playing isn't crucial, consider a single-play model. You're likely to get more features for the money than you would with a changer.

Cassette decks

▶ Ratings on page 66.

The conventional cassette deck is still the medium of choice for recording and playing music at home. Despite the analog deck's inherent limitations—slow access to individual tracks and a limited ability to capture the whole audible spectrum—today's best decks can satisfy all but the most critical ear. And the decks do it at a far lower price than the new, rival digital technologies:

■ The digital compact cassette deck (DCC), a component that first reached stores in 1992, offers better compatibility than other new media. DCC decks can play conventional cassettes and also record and play digitally. When recording on digital tape, DCC relies on a data-compression process that leaves out those parts of a musical program that other sounds mask. In essence, it records only what you hear, and ignores inaudible sonic information. In our tests of DCC, digital recordings sounded close to compact discs and better than any conventional tape deck. DCC decks have copy-protection circuitry that creates perfect copies of CDs, but prevents digital copying of those copies. Decks sell for about $750 to $1000.

■ The Minidisc, or MD, developed by Sony, is the first consumer-priced compact-disc medium that can both record and play. MD uses data-compression technology similar to that used on digital compact cassettes. It is a 2½-inch disc that can play up to 74 minutes. Sound is near CD quality. Players provide nearly instant access to tracks, random play, and other features found on CD players. The Minidisc also incorporates copy protection circuitry. Portable and compact-sized recorders sell for about $700.

■ Digital audio tape (DAT) cassettes,

which also offer compact-disc quality sound, have had a toehold in the U.S. for several years. But, since the tiny DAT cassettes aren't compatible with conventional decks, a DAT owner is faced with the prospect of building a new tape library from scratch. Like DCC and MD, DAT decks incorporate copy-protection circuits. Component-sized decks sell for about $600 to $800; portables, for about $600.

■ Recordable compact disc (CD-R) can produce discs playable on any standard CD player. Decks currently cost about $5000, but are expected to drop in price in a few years.

Promising as these new technologies seem, they won't send cassette tape the way of the LP record overnight. If you already have an extensive collection of tapes, it makes sense to stay with a conventional tape deck. If you choose the right deck, you won't sacrifice much in the way of performance. Some of the decks we've recently tested can deliver sound approaching the quality of digital tape or CDs.

The choices

Full-sized component tape decks are the most popular size. Despite the more than 30 brands available, more than half of all U.S. sales go to *Sony, Pioneer, JVC*, and *Technics* models. Component decks start at $80 or so to well over $1000. To get a deck that performs well, expect to pay anywhere from $200 to $500. Spend less, and you'll probably sacrifice performance. Spend more, and you'll get more features, though they may not improve the deck's performance significantly.

Portable decks include boom boxes and—typically for playback only—walkabouts. You can hook up most walkabouts to a stereo system. Their basic playing performance can be quite acceptable, although the small controls may not be very convenient. Boom boxes sell for about $40 and up; walkabouts, $20.

Among component decks, there are two main types: Single-deck and dual-deck machines. Tape changers that hold five or six cassettes are a novelty.

Single-deck machines. They're generally regarded as serious machines, geared to the audio-buff market. We've found that the tape drive in a single-tape deck is often a cut above the drives in a comparably priced dual-deck machine.

Dual-deck machines. Also called "dubbing" decks, they lend themselves to copying tapes and playing cassettes in sequence. For those conveniences, you usually have to give up a little in audio performance. We've found that these decks tend to suffer slightly more from flutter and are slightly less accurate than single-deck units.

Features and conveniences

Here are the features you're most likely to encounter:

Adjustable bias control. Modern tape coatings can potentially deliver a wider dynamic range than standard ferric oxide (Type I) tape. By increasing the "bias" (an ultrasonic signal the deck uses to reduce distortion), many decks can handle high-energy ferric (Type II) and metal (Type IV) tape. A deck with automatic Tape-type switches is able to sense the type of tape loaded and switch bias accordingly. To fine-tune the bias setting, some decks have a manual control you set by ear. Some decks boast an Auto-bias feature that fine-tunes the bias, which eliminates a lot of fiddling.

Noise-suppression circuits. Numerous techniques have been employed to mute tape hiss, including reformulating the tape itself. Most decks lean heavily on electrical signal-processing to reduce noise. To utilize the circuits, a tape must be recorded and played back with the same circuitry. Standard are Dolby B and Dolby C; virtually all prerecorded cassettes use Dolby B. Better still, and available on all but low-priced models, is Dolby S, which records at near-digital quality. Another system, dbx, has all but disappeared.

Two-button recording. A single Record button makes it too easy to start recording accidentally.

Auto-return or Memory rewind. Both let you cancel a recording and get the tape back to the starting point. Auto-return is easier to use.

Auto-reverse. This reverses the tape automatically when it reaches the end so you can hear both sides without having to flip the tape. Many dual-deck models can play or record both sides of two tapes in sequence, a feature called Relay play or Relay record.

Quick reverse. Similar to Auto-reverse, but faster.

Music search. This feature locates a particular selection by looking for the silences between selections.

Tape scan. You can locate a desired selection on a tape by moving from song to song, playing the first few seconds of each.

Record mute. This feature inserts a silence between selections when you record continuously, say from a CD or an LP. The silences act as signposts for the Music search and Scan features.

Tape counter. Look for one that shows elapsed time in minutes and seconds. Even better is a counter that shows how much time is left on the tape.

Recording-level meters. These days, meters are lighted bar graphs rather than swinging needles. If you do a lot of recording, look for a deck with 12 or so segments on its recording-level meter. Numerous segments make it easy to establish the peak level of the music you are recording and to set the appropriate level. A large knob makes it easier to adjust the level.

Three heads. A deck with three heads doesn't necessarily produce better recordings than one with two heads, but it is more convenient to use for recording. The third head makes it possible to monitor a recording as you make it. On machines with bias adjustment, the third head also makes it easier to fine-tune the bias setting.

Dubbing. Dual decks dub, or copy, tapes at the press of a button. Many decks have an Edit dub feature that stops recording while you change tapes or fiddle with the playback deck. A High-speed dubbing feature cuts recording time in half, but also degrades the music somewhat.

CD synchro helps coordinate recording from a CD. It requires using the same-brand CD player and deck. Pushing a Synchro button cues up the deck and starts recording the instant the music begins.

The tests

We check decks for speed accuracy and flutter, which can make music sound wavery or watery. We measure frequency response—how smoothly a deck responds to sounds. We also measure dynamic range—the span between the loudest and the softest sound a unit accurately records.

Buying advice

Mass market brands like *Sony* and *Technics* represent excellent value; a high-priced audiophile brand won't necessarily perform any better.

If you intend to make a lot of tapes, look for a tape deck that comes with three heads, adjustable bias control, Dolby B and

HOW TO BUY CASSETTE TAPE

Except for packaging, audio cassettes haven't changed significantly in years. That's good, because they're one of the best bargains in the electronic world—inexpensive, yet high performing.

Tapes differ in playing time—C-60, C-90, and so forth. A C-90 tape plays 45 minutes per side. Tapes longer than C-90 haven't performed well in our tests.

Tapes also differ in the type of coating applied to them and the strength of the signal—known as the bias—needed for a tape deck to control distortion. Here are the types:

Type I ("normal"). This is the oldest type sold, the lowest quality and, at $1 to $2.50 per tape, the lowest priced. Its ferric-oxide coating is easily overwhelmed by louder sounds and, when sounds are soft, it produces a background hiss. Type I tape is best suited for speech, nondemanding music, or recordings that will be played under less than ideal con-

ditions, such as in a boom box.

Type II ("high bias"). This type, which uses a high-energy ferrite coating, minimizes tape hiss and handles high frequencies better than Type I. Use this type to record FM broadcasts, to make tapes for the car from CDs, or to make tapes for a walkabout. Expect to pay $2 to $4 per cassette.

Type IV ("metal"). This is the highest grade of tape. Not all decks can take advantage of its capabilities when recording, but all should be able to play back tapes already recorded. Type IV is best for the most demanding applications, such as a live concert or music from a compact disc for listening at home. Prices range from about $3 to as much as $14 per tape.

Don't assume that the highest-priced brand is the best—in our tests, it wasn't. We found that heat-resistant cassettes performed as claimed. They're typically priced about $12.

C, and noise-suppression circuitry.

If you'll be taping CDs, look for Auto-edit or Synchro-edit features. You may want to pay a premium for Dolby S circuitry.

Copying tapes? Look for a dual-deck unit. For those who are primarily interested in playing tapes, a single-deck unit will suf-fice. For playing long periods of uninter-rupted music, choose a dual deck equipped with such features as Auto-reverse and Music search.

If you'll be making live recordings, look for a deck with a microphone jack or a pair of jacks if you want to record in stereo.

Rack stereo systems

In years past, a good hi-fi system consisted of a set of components—receiver, loud-speakers, turntable—carefully selected to match the others' specifications. For those who couldn't afford to buy all the separate pieces at once or didn't want the hassle of picking and choosing them, manufactur-ers offered all-in-one stereo systems that in-cluded everything in a single box. Such systems were generally low cost and low-fi, with small, cheap speakers incapable of emitting decent sound.

Today, many prepackaged or "rack" sys-tems (notably those with good speakers) are worthy of respect. They comprise a floor-standing rack to house the compo-nents and a pair of floor-standing speak-ers—all the elements of a serviceable stereo setup sold as a unit. When small, such systems may be designated as "mini-," "midi-," or "micro-" component systems.

Their turnaround is due in large part to CD players, even the cheapest of which can produce superb sound. Unlike the com-pact stereos of years past, some rack sys-tems we've tested lately perform every bit as well as a good set of separate, low-priced "mix-and-match" audio components.

Prices of rack systems—anywhere from $500 to about $1200—compare favorably with those of a separate-component system but are more expensive than a smaller com-pact system. Ten brands account for about three-quarters of all sales of full-sized rack systems. The major brands are *Sony*, *Soundesign*, and *Pioneer*.

Features and conveniences

More money buys more features, but not necessarily better overall performance as our tests showed. Here's what to expect from the individual components:

Receiver. Most have the essentials: A capable, digital AM/FM tuner with station presets; at least 80 watts of power per stereo channel (enough to rattle your win-dows); and an accurate amplifier. More fea-ture-laden models include the ability to switch video signals from a VCR, TV set, or laser-disc player; outputs for a second set of speakers; and Dolby Pro Logic circuitry for five-speaker home-theater effects.

Speakers. These aren't likely to win any awards. The cabinets, designed to match the height of the rack itself, tend to be made of cheap, lightweight materials. The speakers themselves are far from the best designs. The best in the Ratings, found on *Sony* systems, compared favorably with low- to mid-priced speakers we've tested in the past. Most of the rest can be made to sound decent with some tweaking of the re-ceiver's tone controls. Several delivered pretty good bass, at the expense of accura-cy. Systems with Dolby Pro Logic in our tests included the requisite five speakers.

Compact-disc player. A single-play unit or a five- or six-disc changer are standard on most systems. (For fans of vinyl, *Optimus* systems still offer a turntable.) Quality is comparable to a low-end component, with all the basic controls and a complement of useful features. A few models produced slightly more noise and were a bit less capable playing damaged discs than the separate players we've tested.

Cassette deck. A good-quality, dual-well deck is standard. But a number of manufacturers cut corners: some decks may lack Dolby noise-reduction circuitry, recording-level controls, a tape counter, or the ability to record on the highest-quality, Type IV ("metal") tape.

Overall design. Cost-cutting also shows here. Cabinets, made of plastic-covered particle board typically take an hour to assemble. Designs vary considerably from brand to brand. One may allow shelf space for an extra component, while another lacks enough electrical sockets for even those components that come with the system. Controls—knobs, switches, and remotes—offer more style than convenience.

Buying advice

Many rack systems are a good value, compared with low-priced separate components. Features on individual components vary considerably from system to system. So, if Dolby Pro Logic, say, or the ability to make high-quality tape recordings is important to you, examine a system's components to make sure the appropriate features are included. Be particularly cautious about extremely low-priced "bargain" systems. One we bought for less than $300 gave the impression of having more components than it had and produced muddy, distorted sound at one-third the loudness of a decent rack system.

Walkabout stereos

The walkabout can hold a tape player, an AM/FM radio, or both. Sony invented the walkabout and remains the major brand.

The choices

Radio/tape players. These average $50 or so, but can run more than $100.

Tape players. Cassette-only models cost about $25. They're typically smaller and lighter than units with radio tuners.

Radios. Radio-only models are even cheaper (less than $20) and lighter.

Digital sound/minidiscs. Play-and-record mini-discs share many of the advantages of CDs. DCC plays regular and digital tapes. Priced from $500 to $900.

Features and conveniences

The typical radio/tape player has the basics you need to play a cassette or tune a station. Features beyond that include Auto-reverse; digital tuning; bass booster (such as "Megabass"), which puts more oomph in the low range; water resistance, which offers some protection from rain and sweat; and recording, so you can tape lectures or interviews (look for a unit with a built-in mike). Recording models may also have a tape counter, pause, or a switch for tape type. Tested models with Dolby B had much less tape hiss than those without it.

Buying advice

Most walkabouts produce surprisingly good sound, roughly equivalent to what you'd hear with a low-priced home audio system. When you pay more than $75, you get such conveniences as digital tuning with station-presetting capability, Dolby noise suppression, and a bass booster.

RATINGS LCD TV SETS

▶ **See report, page 30.** Last time rated in Consumer Reports: December 1993.

Brand-name recommendations: LCDs with an active-matrix display performed much better than those with a passive one. The active-matrix *Sony FDL-380* sells for much less than comparable models and includes a built-in radio with good sound.

For the typical LCD set, expect: ■ Below average or poor tone quality. ■ Fair picture quality at best, compared with that of conventional sets, even indoors with strong signals. ■ Poor performance outdoors. ■ Full portability on battery current (but can run on household current). ■ Screen 4 in. or smaller, suitable for narrow-angle viewing from about 2 ft. away. ■ VHF and UHF channels. ■ Earphone and video jacks. ■ Only basic features, no frills. ■ Dark gray case.

Notes on the table: Price is the mfr.'s suggested retail. **Weight**, including batteries, is to the nearest ¼ pound. **Battery** columns show how long a set produced a usable picture with fresh alkaline batteries. **Tuning type** is **search** (you press Up and Down buttons to get to the next active channel) or **programmable** (you program the set to scan 12 or more channels in any order). Ⓓ indicates model discontinued or replacement not similar.

RATINGS OVERVIEW

Listed in order of picture quality

Better ◀———▶ Worse
⊖ ⊖ ○ ⊖ ●

Brand and model	Price	Weight	Picture quality	Sensitivity	Tuning	Batteries
ACTIVE MATRIX						
Casio TV-7700B	$450	1¾ lb.	⊖	○	Search	4½ hr.
Sharp 4M-T30U	699	1¾	⊖	○	Program	2¼
Sony FDL-380	399	2½	⊖	○	Search	5
Sony FDL-K400	699	1¾	⊖	◒	Program	①
PASSIVE MATRIX						
Casio TV-7500	350	1	◒	○	Search	3½
Memorex 16-163 Ⓓ	200	¾	◒	◒	Search	2
Citizen T740-1A Ⓓ	399	1½	●	●	Program	2¼

① *Offers optional rechargeable battery pack.*

RATINGS DETAILS Models listed alphabetically

Casio TV-7500	Picture control(s) inconvenient or hard to use. No Color-intensity control.
Casio TV-770B	Picture control(s) inconvenient or hard to use.
Citizen T740-1A Ⓓ	Picture control(s) inconvenient or hard to use. Wired remote control.
Memorex 16-163 Ⓓ	Picture control(s) inconvenient or hard to use. No Color-intensity control.
Sharp 4M-T3OU	Widest viewing angle among tested LCD sets. Has Screen dimmer.
Sony FDL-380	Built-in radio. Adjustable-angle stand doubles as carrying handle. No Color-intensity control. Above average tone quality.
Sony FDL-K400	Battery pack for portable use not supplied. Wireless remote control. Has Screen dimmer to prolong battery life.

RATINGS SMALL TV SETS

▶ **See report, page 30.** Last time rated in Consumer Reports: December 1993.

Brand-name recommendations: Among the larger sets, the eight-inch *Sony* produced the best picture, but at $379, it's also the most expensive. The nine-inch *RCA*, whose picture quality was nearly as good, costs less and includes a built-in FM radio which has fair sound. (Both have successor models that should perform similarly.) Among five-inch sets, choose between the *Magnavox* and the *GE*, which has been discontinued but may still be available.

For the typical small set, expect: ■ Good picture quality, with 8- to 10-inch sets; fair quality with 5-inch sets. ■ For 8- to 10-inch sets: Average or better color fidelity; wireless remote control; most other standard TV-set features. ■ Operation on household current or using a car adapter. ■ Broad-angle viewing. ■ VHF, UHF, and cable channels. ■ Earphone jack and audio/video input jack. ■ Average or better color fidelity.

Notes on the table: Price is the mfr.'s suggested retail. Ⓢ indicates tested model has been replaced by successor model; according to the mfr., the performance of new model should be similar to the tested model but features may vary. Not tested. Ⓓ indicates model discontinued or replacement not similar.

RATINGS OVERVIEW Within types, listed in order of overall picture quality

Better ◀━━━▶ Worse
⊖ ⊖ ○ ⊙ ●

Brand and model	Price	Overall score	Picture quality			Selectivity
			CLARITY	CONTRAST	OVERALL PICTURE	

8- TO 10-INCH

Brand and model	Price	Overall score	CLARITY	CONTRAST	OVERALL PICTURE	Selectivity
Sony KV-8AD12 Ⓢ	$379	▬▬▬▬	⊖	○	⊖	○
RCA EO 9535KW Ⓢ	329	▬▬▬	○	○	○	⊖

Ratings continued ▶

Ratings continued

Brand and model	Price	Overall score	Picture quality			Selectivity
			CLARITY	CONTRAST	OVERALL PICTURE	
8- TO 10-INCH *continued*						
Emerson TCO916	$329		⊖	○	○	●
Panasonic CT-10R10 Ⓢ	320		○	⊖	○	●
Magnavox RDO946	300		○	⊖	⊖	●
5-INCH						
GE 7-7660 Ⓓ	269		⊖	⊖	⊖	⊖
Magnavox RDO510	300		⊖	⊖	⊖	⊖
Emerson TCO561	299		●	⊖	●	●

RATINGS DETAILS   Models listed alphabetically

Emerson TCO561	Manual tuning; 12 channels. Built-in radio. Angle stand collapses easily. Below average in color fidelity. Much worse than average VHF and UHF sensitivity.
Emerson TCO916	Direct tuning; 113 channels. Sleep timer with auto shutoff. No earphone jack. Better than average VHF sensitivity.
GE 7-7660 Ⓓ	Search tuning; 12 channels. Built-in radio. No earphone jack. Bracket for cabinet mounting.
Magnavox RD0510	Search tuning; 12 channels.
Magnavox RD0946	Direct tuning; 99 channels. Sleep timer with auto shutoff.
Panasonic CT-10R10 Ⓢ CT-10R11, $320	Direct tuning; 99 channels. Sleep timer with auto shutoff. Bracket for cabinet mounting. Skip timer lets you view other channels during commercials, then return.
RCA EO 9535KW Ⓢ E09303KW, $329	Direct tuning; 125 channels. Built-in radio. Sleep timer with auto shutoff. Bracket for cabinet mounting. Display shows time. Better than average VHF and UHF sensitivity.
Sony KV-8AD12 Ⓢ KV9PT40, $379	Direct tuning; 125 channels. Sleep timer with auto shutoff. Bracket for cabinet mounting.

RATINGS 3-PIECE LOUDSPEAKERS

▶ **See report, page 42.** Last time rated in Consumer Reports: March 1993.

Brand-name recommendations: Give first consideration to the top five systems. They are comparable but don't reproduce sound identically.

For the typical 3-piece loudspeaker, expect: ■ A pair of satellite speakers for the midrange and treble and a bass module. ■ Satellites that can be wall-mounted or placed on a bookshelf and a bass module that can be hidden behind drapes or under a table. ■ Satellites available separately. ■ Spring-loaded connectors that take stripped wire or single or double "banana" plugs.

Notes on the table: Price on top is the mfr.'s suggested retail for the satellites: underneath, for the bass module or system. Satellite prices are per pair. Models with identical scores are bracketed and listed in order of tone-corrected accuracy. **Accuracy** shows how accurately speaker reproduced sound. **Impedance** indicates speaker's compatability with a receiver; our measurements, then mfr.'s. **Minimum power** is our estimate of the lowest receiver power needed to play music that has a full frequency range loudly in a medium-sized room. Ⓢ indicates tested model has been replaced by successor model; according to the mfr., performance of new model should be similar to tested model but features may vary. Not tested. Ⓓ indicates model discontinued or replacement not similar.

Listed in order of performance, based on accuracy and bass capability

Better ◀━━━━▶ Worse
⊜ ⊖ ○ ⊝ ●

Brand and model	Price	Overall score					Accuracy corrected/raw	Bass	Impedance	Min. power
		P	F	G	VG	E				
Yamaha NS-A325/ YST-SW100LP Satellite: 8x5x4 in. Bass module: 23x8x16 in. Ⓢ YST-SW120, $499	$170 pr. 449 pr.						92/90	⊜	7/6	13
Bose Acoustimass 5 Series II Satellite: 7x3x5 in. Bass module: 14x8x19 in.	799						91/89	○	5/6	15
NHT Zero/SW-1V Satellite: 9x6x6 in. Bass module: 20x8x13 in. Ⓢ Super Zero SW-1P, $650	200 pr. 300						89/87	⊜	6/8	30
Boston Acoustics SubSatSix Series II Satellite: 8x5x5 in. Bass module: 14x8x17 in.	500 pr.						90/83	⊜	3/8	38
Design Acoustics PS55/PS-SW Ⓓ Satellite: 6x7x10 in. Bass module: 22x11x17 in.	220 pr. 350						87/82	⊜	6/6	12

Ⓓ *Bass module can be used as low stand.*

Ratings continued ▶

Ratings continued

Brand and model	Price	Overall score (P F G VG E)	Accuracy corrected/raw	Bass	Impedance	Min. power
Celestion 5/CS135 Satellite: 14x8x10 in. Bass module: 21x8x14 in.	$249	▬▬▬	90/78	⊖	4/8	18
Bose Acoustimass 3 Series II Satellite: 4x5x5 in. Bass module: 8x8x15 in. Ⓢ Series III, $469	469	▬▬▬	89/85	◒	4/5	18
Advent Mini-Advent A1063 Satellite: 11x7x5 in. Bass module: 13x9x16 in. Ⓢ Mini-Advent II, $179 pr.	289 pr.	▬▬▬	86/86	○	4/6	18
Cambridge Ensemble II Satellite: 8x6x5 in. Bass module: 14x8x17 in.	837	▬▬▬	87/80	⊖	4/—	36
Cambridge Ensemble 'Vinyl Clad' Ⓓ Satellite: 8x6x5 in. Bass module: 12x21x5 in.	499 pr.	▬▬▬	84/82	○	4/—	36
JBL Pro III Plus Satellite: 10x6x6 in. Bass module: 16x14x14 in.	659	▬▬▬	87/74	○	4/4	18
Celestion 1/CS135 Satellite: 11x6x9 in. Bass module: 8x21x14 in.	399	▬▬▬	85/73	⊖	4/8	29
Polk RM3000 Ⓓ Satellite: 7x4x5 in. Bass module: 13x20x13 in.	800 pr.	▬▬▬	85/77	◒	5/8	23
AR Athena System Ⓓ Satellite: 8x5x5 in. Bass module: 8x17x16 in.	599 pr.	▬▬▬	84/76	○	4/6	23
Phase Tech PC 40/50 Mark II Satellite: 10x7x6 in. Bass module: 14x14x15 in. Ⓢ 50 Mark III, $350	380 pr.	▬▬▬	83/72	⊖	4/6	29
Realistic Minimum 7W/ Subwoofer Ⓓ Satellite: 8x5x5 in. Bass module: 13x16x18 in.	120 150	▬▬▬	83/71	⊖	5/8	18
Infinity Micro II Satellite: 8x7x7 in. Bass module: 16x10x15 in.	779	▬▬▬	82/73	○	4/7	29
Pioneer S-3D-K/SW-55 Ⓓ Satellite: 11x7x5 in. Bass module: 22x8x17 in.	550 pr.	▬▬▬	82/73	◒	6/8	17

Brand and model	Price	Overall score					Accuracy corrected/raw	Bass	Impedance	Min. power
		P	F	G	VG	E				
ADS SubSat 3 Satellite: 9x6x6 in. Bass module: 19x9x8 in.	$799						81/70	⊖	3/8	48
Altec Lansing System 3 Satellite: 9x4x4 in. Bass module: 10x20x12 in.	600						79/70	⊖	6/4	15

RATINGS LOW-PRICED LOUDSPEAKERS

▶ **See report, page 42.** Last time rated in Consumer Reports: March 1994.

Brand-name recommendations: The 15 speakers at the top of the Ratings performed to such a similar overall standard that you can safely choose among them based on size and price.

For the typical loudspeaker in this class, expect: ■ Pairs. ■ Tendency to reproduce low frequencies less accurately than expensive models. ■ Mfr.'s impedance rating of 6 or 8 ohms. ■ Rectangular shape varying widely in size.

Notes on the table: Price is the mfr.'s suggested retail per pair. **Accuracy** shows how well the speaker reproduced sound with and without corrections. **Best sound.** The adjustments, measured in decibels, to the bass and treble controls to achieve optimum sound. **Bass** reflects the ability to loudly and clearly reproduce the lowest-frequency tones. **Impedance** indicates the speaker's compatibility with a receiver; measured in ohms. The first figure is the mfr.'s rating, the second our measurement. * indicates mfr. rating not available. **Minimum power** is our estimate of the lowest receiver power needed to play music loudly that has a full frequency range in a medium-sized room; measured in watts. Ⓓ indicates model discontinued or replacement not similar.

		E	VG	G	F	P
		⊜	⊖	○	◑	●

Listed in order of accuracy

Brand and model	Price	Overall score					Accuracy	Best sound	Bass handling	Imped-ance	Min. power
		P	F	G	VG	E		BASS/TREBLE			
Bose 301 Series III 10½x17x9¼ in.	$369						91/89	0/+2	⊜	8/7	19
Boston Acoustics HD9 21x11¼x8¼ in.	340						91/89	+1/+2	⊜	8/5	13
DCM CX-17 17x9x10 in.	370						94/90	+1/+3	○	8/6	18

Ratings continued ▶

Ratings continued

Brand and model	Price	Overall score (P F G VG E)	Accuracy (Bass/Treble)	Best sound (Bass/Treble)	Bass handling	Imped-ance	Min. power
JBL J2080 D 22½x11x10 in	$260		91/89	+2/+2	⊖	8/7	13
Pioneer CS-G303 26½x15x12½ in.	310		88/87	0/+1	⊜	6/9	7
Celestion 5 MKII 13¾x8x10 in.	399		91/89	0/+1	○	8/6	18
Paradigm 3se-MkII 20½x10x11½ in.	419		89/85	+1/+3	⊜	8/5	25
Acoustic Research M3 D 21¼x9¼x15 in.	245		94/86	+3/+5	◒	*/5	15
Cerwin-Vega L-7-B 14x9x9 in.	340		90/84	+3/+4	⊖	8/8	11
Design Acoustics PS-8c D 13½x9¾x11¼ in.	280		93/83	+2/+5	⊖	8/6	20
Infinity RS 325 17x9x10¾ in.	319		89/89	0/+1	○	6/4	17
Sony SS-U610 29½x15¾x10½ in.	280		90/80	-2/+5	⊜	8/10	11
Yamaha NS-A820A D 22x10½x10¾ in.	360		90/89	0/+1	○	6/5	19
Allison AL 110 16x9½x9½ in.	266		88/88	0/0	○	6/4	33
Pinnacle AC 800 18¾x10½x11 in.	299		90/84	+1/+4	○	8/4	19
Polk Audio S6 21¼x10¼x7¾ in.	400		91/85	+2/+4	○	8/4	16
Optimus (Radio Shack) STS 1000 22¾x14¾x12½ in.	260		85/84	+1/+2	⊖	8/8	12
B & W DM600 14x8x9½ in.	350		89/86	+1/+3	◒	4/4	45
B.I.C. Venturi V620 D 22¾x9x11 in.	300		89/86	+1/+3	◒	8/7	22
Cambridge Soundworks Model Six 18¼x11¼x7½ in.	240		85/85	0/0	⊖	8/7	10
Advent Prodigy Tower II 28¾x10x8½ in.	300		85/83	+1/+2	○	8/5	25
Altec Lansing 96 32x8¾x10 in.	400		87/80	+1/+5	⊖	8/4	27
Technics SB-CX300 18½x10½ x10 in.	198		88/87	0/+5	⊖	6/4	42

RATINGS CD PLAYERS

▶ **See report, page 44.** Last time rated in Consumer Reports: March 1994.

Brand-name recommendations: The low-priced models we tested sound just as flawless as expensive models. Among carousel changers, the *Sony CDP-C435*, $240 (and its successor, *C445*, $330), delivers fine performance, a full array of features, and a good brand-reliability record. Among magazine changers, look to the *Pioneer PD-M702*, $245 (and its successor, *PD-703*, $315). If you want to spend less and don't mind changing discs, choose the *Technics SL-PG440*, the top-rated single-player.

For players in this class, expect: ■ Excellent sound quality. ■ Remote control. ■ Headphone jack. ■ Play, Pause, Stop, Track-select, Program functions, Repeat-track, Calendar display, Music-sampling. ■ Audible fast-scanning. ■ Shuffle mode for random play. ■ On changer, a carousel that holds 5 discs, or a magazine that holds 6 plus a 7th in a single-play drawer. ■ On carousel models, ability to change up to 4 discs while a disc plays. ■ 3- to 6-sec. interval before a disc starts playing and between tracks; 10- to 15-sec. time to change discs.

Notes on the table: Price is the mfr.'s suggested retail. **Overall score** is based primarily on sound quality (excellent for all models) and performance. **Performance: Error correction** shows how well a player compensates for dirty or scratched discs. **Bump resistance** is how well the player handles the thumping of heavy footsteps or, for portables, being carried around. **Taping ease** includes features for taping from a disc. ⑤ indicates tested model has been replaced by successor model; according to the mfr., the performance of new model should be similar to the tested model but features may vary. Not tested. ⑩ indicates model discontinued or replacement not similar.

RATINGS OVERVIEW
Within type, listed in order of performance

E VG G F P
◓ ◒ ○ ◐ ●

Brand and model	Price	Overall score	Performance		
			ERROR CORRECTION	BUMP RESISTANCE	TAPING EASE
CAROUSEL CHANGERS					
Sony CDP-C435 ⑤	$240	▬▬▬▬	◓	○	◓
Denon DCM-340	300	▬▬▬	◓	○	◐
Philips CDC935 ⑤	245	▬▬▬	◓	◓	○
Yamaha CDC-635 ⑤	290	▬▬▬	◓	◓	◐
Magnavox CDC794 ⑤	200	▬▬▬	◓	◓	◓
Technics SL-PD947 ⑤	240	▬▬▬	◓	○	○
Teac PD-D880	190	▬▬▬	◓	◓	◐
Goldstar FH-R20R ⑩	170	▬▬▬	◓	◓	◐
Sherwood CDC-5030R	275	▬▬▬	○	○	◐

Ratings continued ▶

Ratings continued

Brand and model	Price	Overall score	Performance		
			ERROR CORRECTION	BUMP RESISTANCE	TAPING EASE

CAROUSEL CHANGERS *continued*

Brand and model	Price	Overall score	ERROR CORRECTION	BUMP RESISTANCE	TAPING EASE
Onkyo DX-C110 Ⓢ	$265	▬▬▬▬	⊖	⊖	⊖
Optimus CD-7500	230	▬▬▬	⊖	⊖	○
Fisher DAC-503	250	▬▬▬	○	⊖	⊖
JVC XL-F211TN Ⓢ	250	▬▬▬	○	○	⊖
Kenwood DP-R5750 Ⓢ	230	▬▬▬	⊖	⊖	⊖

MAGAZINE CHANGERS

Brand and model	Price	Overall score	ERROR CORRECTION	BUMP RESISTANCE	TAPING EASE
Pioneer PD-M702 Ⓢ	245	▬▬▬▬	⊖	⊖	○
JVC XL-M409TN Ⓓ	280	▬▬▬	⊖	⊖	⊖
Kenwood DP-M6650 Ⓢ	245	▬▬▬	○	○	○

SINGLE PLAY

Brand and model	Price	Overall score	ERROR CORRECTION	BUMP RESISTANCE	TAPING EASE
Technics SL-PG440	160	▬▬▬▬	⊖	⊖	⊖
JVC XL-V261TN	220	▬▬▬	⊖	⊖	⊖
Onkyo DX-710	220	▬▬▬	⊖	○	○
Pioneer PD-202 Ⓢ	145	▬▬▬	⊖	⊖	⊖
Kenwood DP-2050 Ⓓ	200	▬▬▬	⊖	○	⊖
Sony CDP-311 Ⓢ	189	▬▬▬	⊖	⊖	○
Teac PD-555 Ⓓ	90	▬▬▬	⊖	⊖	⊖

PORTABLES

Brand and model	Price	Overall score	ERROR CORRECTION	BUMP RESISTANCE	TAPING EASE
Panasonic SL-S550 Ⓢ	219	▬▬▬	⊖	⊖	⊖
Sony DISCMAN D-113CR Ⓢ	179	▬▬▬	⊖	⊖	⊖
JVC XL-P80 Ⓢ	200	▬▬▬	○	⊖	⊖
Sony DISCMAN D-121 Ⓢ	120	▬▬▬	○	⊖	⊖

RATINGS DETAILS   Models listed alphabetically

Denon DCM-340	Carousel turns both ways (speeds disc location).
Fisher DAC-503	Auto-edit. No headphone jack. Can't change discs while one is playing.
Goldstar FH-R20R	No headphone jack.
JVC XL-F211TN Ⓢ XL-F215TN, $320	Keypad on remote. Doesn't display time remaining on disc. Can start same-brand deck with remote. Can be controlled with same-brand receiver's remote. Can't change discs while one is playing.
JVC XL-V261TN	Console keypad. Auto-edit. Can start same-brand deck with remote. Can be controlled with same-brand receiver's remote.

JVC XL-M409TN Ⓓ	Auto-edit. Keypad on remote. Doesn't display time remaining on disc. Can be controlled with same-brand receiver's remote.
JVC XL-P80 Ⓢ XL-P60, $220	Doesn't display time remaining on disc. Can start tape deck.
Kenwood DP-2050 Ⓓ	Console keypad. Can start same-brand deck with remote. Can be controlled with same-brand receiver's remote.
Kenwood DP-M6650 Ⓢ DP-M5570, $229	Console keypad. Favorite track. Auto-edit. Keypad on remote. Also has single-play drawer. No Repeat-track switch. Can start same-brand deck with remote. Can be controlled with same-brand receiver's remote.
Kenwood DP-R5750 Ⓢ DP-R5070, $239	Keypad on remote. Can start same-brand deck with remote. Can be controlled with same-brand receiver's remote.
Magnavox CDC794 Ⓢ CDC745, $200	Console keypad. No Repeat-track switch. No headphone jack.
Onkyo DX-C110 Ⓢ DX-C211, $330	No Repeat-track switch. No headphone jack. Can be controlled with same-brand receiver's remote. Remote controls Onkyo decks. Carousel holds 6 discs.
Onkyo DX-710	Auto-edit. Can be controlled with same-brand receiver's remote. Remote also controls Onkyo tape decks.
Optimus CD-7500	Auto-edit. Can be controlled with same-brand receiver's remote.
Panasonic SL-S550 Ⓢ SL-S570, $250	Volume control on remote. Doesn't display time remaining on disc.
Philips CDC935 Ⓢ CDC936, $259	Console keypad. Favorite track. Auto-edit. No Repeat-track switch. Can start same-brand deck with remote. Can be controlled with same-brand receiver's remote.
Pioneer PD-202 Ⓢ PD-203, $220	Console keypad. Auto-edit. Volume control on remote. Can start same-brand deck with remote. Can be controlled with same-brand receiver's remote.
Pioneer PD-M702 Ⓢ PD-703, $315	Console keypad. Auto-edit. Volume control on remote. Keypad on remote. Can start same-brand deck with remote. Can be controlled with same-brand receiver's remote.
Sherwood CDC-5030R	Auto-edit. Volume control on remote. Can be controlled with same-brand receiver's remote.
Sony CDP-311 Ⓢ CDP-315, $200	Console keypad. Auto-edit.
Sony CDP-C435 Ⓢ C445, $330	Console keypad. Favorite track. Auto-edit. Volume control on remote. Keypad on remote.
Sony DISCMAN D-113CR Ⓢ D-137CR, $170	Doesn't display time remaining on disc.
Sony DISCMAN D-121 Ⓢ D-131, $140	No remote control. Doesn't display time remaining on disc.
Teac PD-555 Ⓓ	No Repeat-track switch. No headphone jack. Can start same-brand deck with remote. Can be controlled with same-brand receiver's remote.
Teac PD-D880 Ⓢ PD-D900, $269	Keypad on remote.

Ratings continued ▶

Ratings continued

Technics SL-PD947 Ⓢ SL-PD967, $250	Console keypad. Auto-edit. No Repeat-track switch. Can start same-brand deck with remote.
Technics SL-PG440	Console keypad. Auto-edit. Volume control on remote. Can start same-brand deck with remote.
Yamaha CDC-635 Ⓢ CDC-645, $299	Volume control on remote.

RATINGS   RECEIVERS

▶ **See report, page 39.** Last time rated in Consumer Reports: March 1994.

Brand-name recommendations: Choose any of the basic receivers in the first group if you use your system only to listen to music, or are content with stereo-only sound from your TV or VCR. A full-fledged home theater requires a receiver with Dolby Surround Pro Logic capability. Any of the low-priced Pro Logic models will meet the needs of most home theaters. Consider a mid-priced Pro Logic receiver only if your viewing habits and speakers warrant spending $100 or more for extra power in the main channels.

For a typical receiver, expect: ■ Excellent amplifier performance. ◨ Good or very good FM sensitivity. ■ At least very good FM selectivity. ■ Sufficient power to provide loud sound through typical speakers in a large room. ◨ Good to excellent FM tuner performance. ◨ Digital FM and AM tuning, with an ample 16 to 40 station presets. ◨ A remote control that operates all basic functions. ◨ A Loudness-compensation switch that can be turned off. ■ At least 1 switched AC outlet to allow other components to be plugged into it. ■ Direct tuning. ◨ 2 channels for stereo-only models; 4 channels for Dolby Pro Logic models. ◨ Minimum of 2 inputs and 2 outputs for video components or Dolby Pro Logic models.

Notes on the table: Price is the mfr.'s suggested retail. **Measured power** reflects our measurements of output in watts for the main channels in non-Dolby mode at three typical impedances. Ⓢ indicates tested model has been replaced by successor model; according to the mfr., the performance of new model should be similar to the tested model but features may vary. Not tested. Ⓓ indicates model is discontinued or replacement not similar.

RATINGS OVERVIEW
Within type, listed in order of performance and convenience

E ⊖ VG ⊖ G ○ F ◓ P ●

Brand and model	Price	Overall score				FM tuner	Ease of use	Measured power 8/6/4 OHM
STEREO-ONLY MODELS								
Sony STR-D311 Ⓢ	$165	███				⊖	⊖	77/87/①
Yamaha RX-460 Ⓓ	225	███				⊖	⊖	67/72/①
Onkyo TX930 Ⓓ	260	████				⊖	⊖	66/78/92

Brand and model	Price	Overall score	FM tuner	Ease of use	Measured power
					8/6/4 OHM
Fisher RS-717	$250		⊖	⊖	92/103/①
Sherwood RX-4030R	225		⊖	⊖	71/80/44
Kenwood KR-A5050 Ⓢ	225		⊖	⊖	113/126/95
Teac AG-620 Ⓢ	175		⊖	⊖	58/65/53
JVC RX-309TN Ⓓ	200		⊖	◯	113/103/①
Pioneer SX-312R Ⓓ	180		◯	⊖	76/83/①

LOW-PRICED PRO-LOGIC MODELS

Brand and model	Price	Overall score	FM tuner	Ease of use	Measured power
Onkyo TX-SV313PRO Ⓓ	360		⊖	⊖	77/88/①
Sherwood RV-5030R	370		⊖	⊖	87/98/①
Sony STR-D611 Ⓢ	280		⊖	⊖	79/89/①
JVC RX-509VTN Ⓓ	300		⊖	⊖	89/101/①
Technics SA-GX350 Ⓢ	280		◯	⊖	113/130/①
Kenwood KR-V6050 Ⓢ	325		◯	⊖	119/134/106
Optimus STAV-3270 Ⓓ	380		◯	⊖	85/96/①
Pioneer VSX-452 Ⓓ	280		◯	⊖	85/97/①

MID-PRICED PRO LOGIC MODELS

Brand and model	Price	Overall score	FM tuner	Ease of use	Measured power
Sony STR-D911 Ⓢ	390		⊖	⊖	113/129/①
Onkyo TX-SV515PRO	540		⊖	⊖	95/111/137
Yamaha RX-V470 Ⓓ	500		⊖	⊖	61/70/①
JVC RX-709VTN Ⓓ	400		⊖	⊖	110/127/①
Kenwood KR-V7050 Ⓓ	400		⊖	⊖	119/135/107
Denon AVR-800	400		⊖	⊖	73/84/①
Pioneer VSX-502 Ⓓ	380		⊖	⊖	113/126/①
Technics SA-GX650 Ⓢ	460		◯	⊖	143/166/198

① Mfr. does not recommend use with 4-ohm speakers.

RATINGS DETAILS Models listed alphabetically

Denon AVR-800	4 audio inputs, 2 outputs. Has Dolby 3 stereo. Has "ambience" sound effects.
Fisher RS-717	3 audio inputs, 2 outputs. Frequency response may degrade when main and extension ("B") pairs of speakers used.
JVC RX-309TN Ⓓ	3 audio inputs, 2 outputs. Remote works with some same-brand components. Frequency response may degrade when main and extension ("B") pairs of speakers used. Better than average at resisting interference from weak FM stations on the same frequency.

Ratings continued ▶

Ratings continued

JVC RX-509VTN Ⓓ	5 audio inputs, 3 outputs. Has Dolby 3 stereo. Has "ambience" sound effects for music. Remote works with some same-brand components. Frequency response may degrade when main and extension ("B") pairs of speakers used.
JVC RX-709VTN Ⓓ	5 audio inputs, 4 outputs. Has Dolby 3 stereo. Has "ambience" sound effects for music. Remote works with some same-brand components. Frequency response may degrade when main and extension ("B") pairs of speakers used.
Kenwood KR-A5050 Ⓢ KR-A5070, $199	5 audio inputs, 2 outputs. Better than average at resisting interference from weak FM stations on the same frequency.
Kenwood KR-V6050 Ⓢ KR-A6060, $299	5 audio inputs, 3 outputs. Has Dolby 3 stereo. Better than average at resisting interference from weak FM stations on the same frequency.
Kenwood KR-V7050 Ⓓ	5 audio inputs, 3 outputs. Has Dolby 3 stereo. Has "ambience" sound effects for music and at resisting overload from nearby FM transmitters and at resisting interference from weak FM stations on the same frequency.
Onkyo TX-SV313PRO Ⓓ	5 audio inputs, 3 outputs. Phono reproduction may be slightly inaccurate.
Onkyo TX930 Ⓓ	3 audio inputs, 2 outputs. Phono reproduction may be slightly inaccurate.
Onkyo TX-SV515PRO	4 audio inputs, 4 outputs. Phono reproduction may be slightly inaccurate. Has "ambience" sound effects for music. Remote operates in rooms other than where receiver is located. Better than average at resisting overload from nearby FM transmitters.
Optimus STAV-3270 Ⓓ	4 audio inputs, 2 outputs. Has Dolby 3 stereo. Remote works with some same-brand components. Remote operates in rooms other than where receiver is located.
Pioneer SX-312R Ⓓ	4 audio inputs, 2 outputs. Frequency response may degrade when main and extension ("B") pairs of speakers used. Better than average at resisting interference from weak FM stations on the same frequency.
Pioneer VSX-452 Ⓓ	4 audio inputs, 2 outputs. Has Dolby 3 stereo. Has "ambience" sound effects for music. Remote works with some same-brand components. Frequency response may degrade when main and extension ("B") pairs of speakers used. No 300-ohm FM input for some roof antennas and at resisting overload from nearby FM transmitters and at resisting interference from weak FM stations on the same frequency.
Pioneer VSX-502 Ⓓ	6 audio inputs, 4 outputs. Has Dolby 3 stereo. Has "ambience" sound effects for music. Remote works with some same-brand components. Remote operates in rooms other than where receiver is located. Frequency response may degrade when main and extension ("B") pairs of speakers used.
Sherwood RX-4030R	3 audio inputs, 1 output. Phono reproduction may be slightly inaccurate. Frequency response may degrade when main and extension ("B") pairs of speakers used.
Sherwood RV-5030	6 audio inputs, 3 outputs. Has Dolby 3 stereo. Has "ambience" sound effects for music. Remote operates in rooms other than where receiver is located. Frequency response may degrade when main and extension ("B") pairs of speakers used. Better than average at resisting interference from aircraft.

Sony STR-D311 Ⓢ STR-D315, $250	4 audio inputs, 3 outputs. Phono reproduction may be slightly inaccurate. Remote works with some same-brand components. Better than average at resisting overload from nearby FM transmitters.
Sony STR-D611 Ⓢ STR-D615, $350	4 audio inputs, 2 outputs. Has Dolby 3 stereo. Remote works with some same-brand components. Frequency response may degrade when main and extension ("B") pairs of speakers used. Better than average at resisting overload from nearby FM transmitters. Better than average at resisting interference from aircraft. Better than average at resisting interference from weak FM stations on the same frequency.
Sony STR-D911 Ⓢ STR-D915, $500	6 audio inputs, 4 outputs. Has Dolby 3 stereo. Has "ambience" sound effects for music. Remote works with some same-brand components. Frequency response may degrade when main and extension ("B") pairs of speakers used. Better than average at resisting overload from nearby FM transmitters. Better than average at resisting interference from aircraft. Better than average at resisting interference from weak FM stations on the same frequency.
Teac AG-620 Ⓢ AG-750, $259	3 audio inputs, 2 outputs.
Technics SA-GX35 Ⓢ SA-GX470, $300	4 audio inputs, 2 outputs. Has Dolby 3 stereo. Remote works with some same-brand components. Better than average at resisting interference from weak FM stations on the same frequency.
Technics SA-GX650 Ⓢ SA-GX670, $400	3 audio inputs, 2 outputs. Has Dolby 3 stereo. Remote works with some same-brand components. Remote is learning type.
Yamaha RX-460 Ⓓ	4 audio inputs, 2 outputs. No 300-ohm FM input for some roof antennas. Better than average at resisting interference from weak FM stations on the same frequency.
Yamaha RX-V470 Ⓓ	4 audio inputs, 2 outputs. Has Dolby 3 stereo. Has graphic equalizer. No 300-ohm FM input for some roof antennas. Better than average at resisting interference from weak FM stations on the same frequency.

RATINGS | CASSETTE DECKS

▶ **See report, page 47.** Last time rated in Consumer Reports: March 1994.

Brand-name recommendations: For those who don't need to copy tapes, any of the first six single-deck units will perform well. The *Sony TC-RX311* deserves consideration if you can find it for less than $200. For those who like long-playing background music, or who make tape-to-tape copies, the first four dual-deck units are worth considering.

For decks in this class, expect: ■ At least good dynamic range for mid and high frequencies. ■ Dolby B and C noise-reduction circuitry. ■ Compatibility with all types of tape. ■ Recording level and balance controls. ■ Light-touch keys. ■ Record-Mute. ■ Music search. ■ FM multiplex noise filter. ■ Adjustable bias. ■ AC timer control. ■ Headphone jack. ■ Relay mode (plays 2 or more tapes in sequence). ■ Next. ■ Normal Auto-reverse. ■ A cable to link to a same-brand receiver whose remote can control the deck. ■ CD Sync. ■ A digital and/or time counter. **A choice you'll have to make:** ■ Single or dual deck.

Notes on the table: Price is the mfr.'s suggested retail. **Flutter** indicates how free these decks are, in recording and playback, from a wavery sound caused by tape-speed irregularities. **Accuracy** shows how accurately a deck reproduced the level of a signal when recording and playing. Scores in parentheses are accuracy judgments for dubbing. ⑤ indicates tested model has been replaced by successor model; according to the mfr., the performance of new model should be similar to the tested model but features may vary. Not tested. ⓓ indicates model discontinued or replacement not similar.

RATINGS OVERVIEW — Within type, listed in order of overall performance

				E	VG	G	F	P
				⊖	⊖	○	⊖	●

Brand and model	Price	Overall score	Flutter	Accuracy	Ease of use CONVENIENCE	CONTROLS
SINGLE DECKS						
Sony TC-RX311	$250	▬▬▬▬	⊖	⊖	⊖	⊖
Technics RS-BX606 ⓓ	260	▬▬▬▬	⊖	⊖	○	⊖
Kenwood KX-5550 ⓓ	260	▬▬▬	⊖	⊖	⊖	⊖
Onkyo TA-203 ⓓ	290	▬▬▬	⊖	⊖	◐	⊖
Sony TC-C5 ⓓ	200	▬▬▬	○	⊖	⊖	⊖
Yamaha KX-360 ⓓ	250	▬▬▬	⊖	⊖	●	◐
Denon DRR-730	300	▬▬	⊖	⊖	○	○
JVC TD-R441TN ⓓ	280	▬▬	⊖	⊖	○	⊖
DUAL DECKS						
Technics RS-TR777 ⓓ	255	▬▬▬▬	⊖	⊖ (⊖)	⊖	○
Sony TC-WR635S ⑤	255	▬▬▬▬	⊖	⊖ (◐)	⊖	⊖
Onkyo TA-RW414	355	▬▬▬	⊖	⊖ (⊖)	○	◐

Brand and model	Price	Overall score					Flutter	Accuracy	Ease of use	
									CONVENIENCE	CONTROLS
Kenwood KX-W8050 Ⓢ	$285	▰▰▰					○	○ (◒)	◒	◒
JVC TD-W709TN Ⓓ	295	▰▰▰					◒	◒ (◒)	◒	◑
Yamaha KX-W262 Ⓢ	280	▰▰▮					◒	◒ (◒)	◑	●
Teac W-700R Ⓓ	150	▰▰▮					○	◒ (○)	◑	◑
Denon DRW-660	300	▰▰▮					○	◒ (◒)	○	○
Pioneer CT-W602R Ⓓ	250	▰▰					○	◒ (◒)	◒	◑
Pioneer CT-WM62R	525	▰▰					○	◒ (○)	○	◒
Optimus SCT-52 Ⓢ	230	▰▮					○	◒ (◒)	○	○
Philips FC930P Ⓢ	225	▰▮					◒	○ (◒)	●	○

RATINGS DETAILS Models listed alphabetically

Denon DRW-660	Noisier than most when changing functions.
Denon DRR-730	—
JVC TD-R441TN Ⓓ	—
JVC TD-W709TN Ⓓ	—
Kenwood KX-5550 Ⓓ	—
Kenwood KX-W8050 Ⓢ KX-W8070S, $299	Very difficult to see cassette tape. Noisier than most when changing functions.
Onkyo TA-203 Ⓓ	—
Onkyo TA-RW414	Very difficult to see cassette tape.
Optimus SCT-52 Ⓢ SCT-55, $250	Noisier than most when changing functions.
Philips FC930P Ⓢ FC931, $279	Recording-level meter coarsely graduated. Cannot properly record Type IV cassettes.
Pioneer CT-W602R Ⓓ	Has function to boost weak treble tones; may alter tape quality if used. Very difficult to see cassette tape. Noisier than most when changing functions.
Pioneer CT-WM62R	Changer model. Recording-level meter coarsely graduated. Has function to boost weak treble tones; may alter tape quality if used. Lacks headphone jack.
Sony TC-C5 Ⓓ	Changer model. Motor runs even when tape is stopped, accelerating wear.
Sony TC-RX311 **A BEST BUY**	Noisier than most when changing functions.
Sony TC-WR635S Ⓢ TC-WR6455, $350	Has Dolby S noise-reduction circuitry. Noisier than most when changing functions. Motor runs even when tape is stopped, accelerating wear.
TEAC W-700R Ⓓ	Noisier than most when changing functions.
Technics RS-BX606 Ⓓ	Motor runs even when tape is stopped, accelerating wear.

Ratings continued ▶

Ratings continued

Technics RS-TR777 Ⓓ	Noisier than most when changing functions.
Yamaha KX-W262 Ⓢ KX-W282, $249	Recording-level meter coarsely graduated.
Yamaha KX-360 Ⓓ	—

RATINGS VCRs

▶ **See report, page 32.** Last time rated in Consumer Reports: March 1994.

Brand-name recommendations: The top monophonic units, the *RCA VR526A,* $270, and the *GE VG4029,* $245, come with VCR Plus. The *RCA's* remote will work other manufacturers' TV sets; the *GE's* will work only *GE* sets. The top-rated hi-fi stereo VCRs—the *Sony SLV-700HF,* $410, and the *GE VG4210,* $295—offer a unified remote control, which works their own brand of TV set.

For the typical VCR in this class, expect: ■ Digital-quartz tuner that receives 125 cable channels. ■ Ability to record and play tapes recorded at SP, LP, and EP speeds. ■ On-screen programming of 8 events up to 1 year in advance, with options for daily and weekly recording. ■ Power on when tape is inserted and auto-rewind at end of tape. **A choice you'll have to make:** ■ Hi-fi or mono sound.

Notes on the table: Price is the mfr.'s suggested retail. **Overall score.** Differences of less than 20 points aren't significant. **Picture** indicates how clear the recorded and played-back pictures looked to our trained viewing panel at SP and EP speeds. **Remote control** indicates how user-friendly each remote was. **Channel rejection** gauges how well the VCR filters unwanted signals from channels next to the one being watched—important only for cable channels not received through a set-top box. Ⓢ indicates tested model has been replaced by successor model; according to the mfr., the performance of new model should be similar to the tested model but features may vary. Not tested. Ⓓ indicates model discontinued or replacement not similar.

RATINGS OVERVIEW — Within type, listed mainly in order of picture quality

Better ⊖ ⊖ ○ ◑ ● Worse

Brand and model	Price	Overall score	Picture SP/EP	Remote control	Channel rejection
HI-FI VHS (STEREO)					
Sony SLV-700HF Ⓢ	$410		⊖/○	⊖	◑
GE VG4210 Ⓓ	295		⊖/○	⊖	◑
Samsung VR8702 Ⓢ	270		⊖/○	⊖	◑
Toshiba M-649 Ⓢ	325		⊖/○	⊖	●
Mitsubishi HS-U48 Ⓓ	415		⊖/○	○	◑
Magnavox VR9260 Ⓢ	295		⊖/○	○	⊖

Brand and model	Price	Overall score					Picture	Remote control	Channel rejection
		P	F	G	VG	E	SP/EP		
Panasonic PV-4351 Ⓢ	$325						⊖/○	○	●
RCA VR601HF Ⓢ	295						⊖/○	⊖	⊖
Quasar VH434 Ⓓ	320						⊖/○	○	○
Zenith VRL4210HF Ⓢ	320						○/○	○	○
Fisher FVH-4909 Ⓢ	275						⊖/○	◒	◒
Hitachi VT-F370A Ⓢ	365						⊖/○	◒	◒
JVC HR-J600 Ⓢ	345						⊖/○	◒	○
Sharp VC-H904 Ⓓ	285						○/○	◒	○

MONOPHONIC VHS

Brand and model	Price	Overall score					Picture	Remote control	Channel rejection
RCA VR526A Ⓢ	270						⊖/○	⊖	○
GE VG4029 Ⓢ	245						⊖/○	⊖	○
Sanyo VHR-5418 Ⓢ	280						⊖/○	○	○
Panasonic PV-4314 Ⓢ	295						⊖/○	○	◒
Magnavox VR9242 Ⓢ	270						⊖/○	○	◒
Zenith VRL4170 Ⓢ	290						○/○	○	◒
Goldstar GVR-C435	300						○/○	○	○
Optimus Model 98 Ⓓ (Radio Shack)	300						⊖/○	◒	◒
JVC HR-VP404 Ⓢ	275						○/○	◒	○
Emerson VCR968 Ⓓ	190						○/○	◒	◒
Sharp VC-A504 Ⓓ	225						○/◒	◒	○
Signature 2000 (Ward's 20137) Ⓓ	200						○/◒	◒	○

RATINGS DETAILS Models listed alphabetically

Emerson VCR968 Ⓓ	Programs 4 events 28 days in advance. Console displays program settings. Poor instruction manual.
Fisher FVH-4909 Ⓢ FVH-49095, $350	Programs 6 events. Code-entry remote also controls cable boxes.
GE VG4029 Ⓢ VG4039, $300	VCR Plus. Fast rewind. Unified remote controls GE TV sets.
GE VG4210 Ⓓ	Fast rewind. Unified remote controls GE TV sets.
Goldstar GVR-C435	—

Ratings continued ▶

Ratings continued

JVC HR-VP404 Ⓢ HR-VP412, $330	VCR Plus. Can program from console or remote. Can't record at LP speed. Slow rewind. Front A/V jacks for camcorder.
JVC HR-J600 Ⓢ HR-J 610, $430	Can program from console or remote. Can't record at LP speed. HR-VP604, $380, is hi-fi, and has VCR Plus. Slow rewind. Front A/V jacks for camcorder.
Magnavox VR9260 Ⓢ VR9360AT, $300	Can't record at LP speed. Slow rewind. Unified remote controls Magnavox TV sets.
Magnavox VR9242 Ⓢ VR-9342, $280	Can't record at LP speed. Slow rewind. Front A/V jacks for camcorder.
Mitsubishi HS-U48 Ⓓ	Programs 4 events 30 days in advance. Can program from console or remote. Shows recording time left on tape. Can't record at LP. HS-U58, $470 is hi-fi, and has VCR Plus that controls cable box. Fast rewind. Childproof lock, power backup, front A/V jacks for camcorder.
Optimus 98 Ⓓ	Programs 6 events. Poor instruction manual. Power backup.
Panasonic PV-4314 Ⓢ PV-4414, $329	VCR Plus. Programs 30 days in advance. Code-entry remote also controls cable boxes. Power backup.
Panasonic PV-4351 Ⓢ PV-4451, $324	Programs 30 days in advance. Code-entry remote also controls cable boxes. Good instruction manual.
Quasar VH434 Ⓓ	Programs 4 events 30 days in advance.
RCA VR526A Ⓢ VR528, $350	VCR Plus. Fast rewind.
RCA VR601HF Ⓢ VR-610HF, $399	—
Samsung VR8702 Ⓢ VR8703, $579	Shows recording time left on tape. Slow rewind.
Sanyo VHR-5418 Ⓢ VHR-5420, $300	VCR Plus (also works cable box). Programs 6 events. Code-entry remote also controls cable boxes. Power backup.
Sharp VC-A504 Ⓓ	Programs 14 days in advance. Arbitrary counter (not in hr., min.). Childproof lock.
Sharp VC-H904 Ⓓ	Programs 14 days in advance. Arbitrary counter (not in hr., min.). Childproof lock.
Signature 2000 Ward's 20137 Ⓓ	Programs 14 days in advance. Arbitrary counter (not in hr., min.).
Sony SLV-700HF Ⓢ SLV-720HF, $549	Programs 30 days in advance. Shows recording time left on tape. Can't record at LP speed. United remote controls Sony TV sets. Power backup.
Toshiba M-649 Ⓢ M-650, $380	Shows recording time left on tape. Can't record at LP speed. Fast rewind. Front A/V jacks for camcorder.
Zenith VRL4170 Ⓢ VRM4170, $329	VCR Plus (also works cable box). Code-entry remote also controls cable boxes. Front A/V jacks for camcorder.
Zenith VRL4210HF Ⓢ VRM4220HF, $369	Unified remote controls Zenith TV sets. Power backup.

PHOTOGRAPHY

Technology keeps improving the camera. Blunder-proof, highly automated compact 35mm cameras have quickly become the amateur's best friend. With a built-in zoom lens, such cameras are almost as versatile as more professional single-lens reflex cameras—and they sell for hundreds less. At the same time, new, chip-driven features on single-lens reflex cameras (SLRs) can make that kind of camera more automatic and therefore less complex to use in the basic mode.

In a technology-driven marketplace, models quickly become obsolete, a reminder that you may not need all the benefits of technology to take prize-winning photos. You can still find basic models such as the *Pentax K-1000*, which has a built-in light meter but makes you set film speed, focus, and select shutter speed and aperture.

Technology has also touched film design. Kodak has reshaped the microscopic silver grains in some of its films to improve quality, for example. In Fuji Reala film, an extra color layer tries to reproduce hues more nearly as the human eye sees them.

Film processing is the final link between what you saw in the viewfinder and what you get. Developing and printing can be expensive, and the prints' quality can vary among labs, as our tests revealed.

A sturdy tripod lets photographers carefully frame a picture and use exposure settings that might cause blur in a hand-held shot. For camcorder work, a decent tripod designed for video use is a must.

Sales practices

Buying cameras and photographic gear is unique in some ways. List prices are pretty much fiction. The discount you get depends a lot on local competition and the customer service and convenience a store provides. For rock-bottom prices, check the mail-order ads in newspapers and photography magazines. Mail-order houses in New York and other big cities sell cameras and other gear, sometimes for half of list.

Watch out for high sales pressure and other questionable selling tactics. The classic is the bait-and-switch—"We're all out of that, but have something better." An unusually low advertised price for a brand-name SLR camera should arouse your suspicion—it may include a cheap off-brand lens. Another ploy: the tie-in, in which you're told you cannot buy an item at its advertised price without purchasing something else—a camera case, say. Try to find out beforehand which removable pieces—case, lens cap, strap—are standard on the item. Then you won't fall victim to the practice of "stripping": a store's removing standard equipment, then selling it back to you.

When photo equipment is imported by someone other than the manufacturer's au-

thorized U.S. subsidiary, it is known as "gray market" goods. There may be nothing wrong with the merchandise—but it may come with an "international" warranty or a camera-store warranty. With those warranties, you might have to send the camera abroad or deal with the retailer for repairs. If a store tells you that your sales slip is your warranty, the store, not the manufacturer, assumes responsibility for the warranty period. Some stores may give you a choice of goods with or without a U.S. warranty. Unless an advertisement specifically says "U.S. warranty," assume that the goods are gray-market.

For gear with few moving parts and little likelihood of breakage—tripods and many lenses—forgoing the premium-priced U.S. warranty poses little risk. For cameras, whose repair can be expensive, we'd think carefully about the risk.

Discounters may also try to sell you an extended warranty. We don't recommend it. See "Extended Warranties" on page 14.

Cameras & lenses

▶ **Ratings start on page 82.**

The 35mm format has become standard. The format's relatively large negative—about 1x1½ inches—yields sharper enlargements than the smaller negative from disc and 110 cameras. And a variety of film is available in black-and-white and in color.

Most 35mm cameras on the market are of two types—compacts, which have a built-in lens, and SLRs, which have inter-

changeable lenses. (A third type is the so-called bridge camera, a hybrid design that combines aspects of both.) Compacts far outsell SLRs. Kodak and Vivitar sell the most of that type—mainly cheaper models with little or no automation. Manufacturers such as Canon, Minolta, Olympus, Nikon, and Pentax account for most of the high-end compacts and SLRs sold.

Compact 35s

Some are pocket-sized; others, weighing more than a pound and bristling with ergonomic bulges and bulky zoom lenses,

would strain a coat pocket. Either way, compacts are designed for convenience—for easy use rather than for manual photographic control. Prices range from less than $10 to more than $300.

The choices

Single-use compacts—simple cameras preloaded with print film—appeared in the late 1980s and are the fastest-growing part of the market. Variations offer panoramic, telephoto, and even underwater capability. Models without a flash are limited to use in bright daylight. Single-use cameras sell for about $6 to $15.

Regular compact 35s come in two basic types. The simplest—and cheapest—euphemistically called "focus free," have a **fixed-focus** lens like that of most 110 and older box cameras.

More complex compact cameras are likely to offer **auto-focus**—automatic focus. And that's just the beginning of their automatic capabilities.

The type of lens also divides compacts along price lines. Cheapest are those with a **fixed-focal length lens**. At the other end, many compacts come with a **zoom lens** that covers the range from wide-angle (say, 35 mm) to modest telephoto (say, 105 mm), so that you can bring in more distant subjects and frame a scene even more tightly. Cheaper models offer a more limited range, perhaps 35 mm to 70 mm. A compromise often cheaper still: **dual-lens** models, which have a wide-angle setting, perhaps 28 mm or 35 mm, and a "second" setting, 45 mm or 70 mm. Prices of compacts run from $40 or less to more than $300, depending on the features. Fixed-focus models are typically priced at less than $100; auto-focus models, at more than $100.

Features and conveniences

Exposure. Most compacts have automatic exposure-control to help ensure proper exposure: A built-in light meter gauges the lighting and adjusts the aperture and shutter speed accordingly. Automatic exposure-control systems strike a balance between fast shutter speed (to prevent blurring of moving objects) and a small aperture (to enhance overall sharpness). Some compacts have a backlight switch to compensate for a bright background behind your subject.

Flash. All but the most rudimentary models sport a built-in electronic flash, which is generally on the weak side as flashes go. Most compacts fire the flash automatically when the exposure system senses insufficient light; a few let you turn off the flash for more natural-looking photos with available light.

Designs that reduce "red eye," typically by firing an extra flash burst before the main flash exposures, are common. (Light reflecting off people's retinas can make their eyes look red in photos; the preflash constricts the subject's pupils, reducing the chances of red eye.)

Film handling. Most compact 35s have automatic film handling: You insert the film, pull out enough film to reach a mark inside the camera, shut the back of the camera and the motor automatically threads the film. The motor also advances the film after each shot and rewinds the film at the end of the roll.

All but the cheapest models read the film's speed from the checkerboard DX-coding on the cartridge and set the camera's exposure meter for you. Some can read only the most popular speeds for color-print film, ISO 100 and 400; others read a range of speeds from as slow as 25, up to 5000, the full DX range. If you plan to use a variety of film speeds, make sure your camera covers a wide ISO range.

Focusing. With a fixed-focus model, a small lens aperture keeps all objects more than a few feet away reasonably sharp. But the small aperture rules out shooting in dim light unless you use flash. Auto-focus models set the lens for one of several distance zones. One zone might cover subjects 8 to 10 feet away; another, 10 to 14 feet, and so on. Some models use only two, very crude distance zones (near and far), others, dozens of zones. As a rule, the more zones, the better. Models with an infinity control—to set the focus to the farthest zone—are useful for shooting through glass or past an object in the foreground that might otherwise confuse the auto-focus.

Viewfinder. Some compacts have a bright-frame viewfinder; others have a sharp edge that frames the entire image. Both kinds are easy to use, even with eyeglasses. Our tests have shown that most such viewfinders are fairly accurate—what's visible in the finder is pretty much what's captured on the film. On the other hand, viewfinders with indistinct framing, which has indistinct edges that shift if you move your eye, make it really hard to know what part of a scene you're shooting.

Format. An increasing number of compacts offer the option of panoramic format. The first generation of these dual-format cameras required using an adapter, which was inserted into the back of the camera prior to loading the film. Newer designs allow the format to be changed midroll on a frame-by-frame basis, although automatic printing equipment may not cope with a mixture of normal and panoramic pictures.

Buying advice

Compact cameras have made it a snap to take crisp, properly exposed pictures. How you'll be using your camera will determine how much you spend and the features you'll need.

You may want the flexibility in composition that a zoom lens offers, for instance. Or you may be content with the slightly wide-angle view that most single-focal-length models give. Or, if you don't want to shoot night life, you won't need the best flash setup or a camera whose DX-reader can handle the fastest film speeds.

Consider, too, the camera's size. Models with zoom lenses are often the bulkiest, though most compacts weigh a fraction of a fully outfitted SLR camera.

Compact cameras don't allow much creative control. They don't allow you to use a variety of lenses and usually won't let you override the camera's automatic settings. But many a snapshooter is happy to trade that control for convenience and simplicity in a small package.

SLRs and 'bridge' cameras

These cameras can cost hundreds more than compacts 35s. For that you get flexibility and control. SLRs let you see through the picture-taking lens, not through a separate viewfinder. Because you see what the camera sees, you can use different lenses to change viewpoints. Highly automated models let you turn off their automatic features when you want to break the rules.

The choices

SLRs. The distinctive trapezoidal hump atop an SLR camera houses a prism mounted over a mirror, an arrangement that lets you see what the lens sees when you look through the eyepiece behind the hump. Sometimes you can choose from various "screens"—grids—to help you compose your shot. A built-in light meter also "sees" and evaluates what the lens takes in.

Single-lens reflex cameras were once strictly for serious hobbyists and professionals—photographers who knew the many ways of manipulating lenses, exposure controls, focus, and film types to create artistic effects. Recent innovations have automated so much of this that some SLRs can be as easy to work as a compact 35mm camera. (You can still find stripped-down manual-focus SLRs, though you may end up buying non-camera-brand lenses and accessories since camera makers have thrown more effort into their auto-focus rather than manual lines.)

Auto-focus SLR camera bodies range in price from $300 to more than $850, with $150 to $450 extra for a lens. Manual-focus models range from $150 to $500 for the body; $100 or more for a zoom lens to cover a range of focal lengths.

That's just the start, if you plan on collecting the extra lenses and paraphernalia that turn an SLR into a "camera system." Lenses, ranging from 180-degree-view fisheyes to telephotos so hefty a separate tripod is necessary to steady them, can add hundreds, even thousands, to the price.

'Bridge' models. Most bridge cameras offer less creative control than does the typical SLR but more versatility than a typical compact. These cameras, currently offered only by Canon and Olympus, fill the gap between interchangeable-lens SLRs and compacts. They may have an SLR viewfinder, but they don't accept interchangeable lenses. The built-in lens has a zoom range that covers 35 mm to 135 mm or more. The focusing and many other aspects of bridge cameras are automated, making the camera very easy to use. (But so are most auto-focus SLRs.) Prices range from about $400 to $600.

Features and conveniences

Lenses. The reflected image—the "reflex" in SLR—makes it practical to use a variety of lenses in addition to the "normal" 50mm lens. Attach a super-wide-angle lens and you gain appreciable peripheral vision, excellent for panoramas or photographing groups in tight spaces. Switch to a telephoto lens and you're looking through a

telescope, excellent for candid shots and bringing in distant objects without having to move in closer. Or you can use a zoom lens for a range of views.

The zoom has become the lens of choice: About 85 percent of SLR buyers fit their new camera body with a zoom, rather than the old standard 50 mm lens. A moderate-range zoom—35 mm to 105 mm or so—should cover most situations. Our tests show that the quality of SLR zoom lenses has improved markedly in recent years. Any lapses in sharpness are usually imperceptible except under high magnification.

The non-interchangeable zoom on a bridge camera often covers a wider range than do zoom lenses on compact cameras. Sometimes the viewfinder is also the SLR type, though it's generally less accurate than those on interchangeable-lens SLRs: Our tests have shown that framing errors of 10 or 15 percent of the picture area are common. Tests of the lenses themselves reveal quality typically about as good as that of a middling SLR zoom—very good, but not exceptional.

Exposure controls. Most auto-exposure models have a "program" mode, which selects both the aperture (the size of the lens opening) and shutter speed (how long the film is exposed) automatically. An aperture-priority exposure mode lets you set the lens opening (f-stop) while the camera automatically selects the right shutter speed. A shutter-priority exposure mode does just the opposite. Most can also be operated by hand, too: Typically, an indicator in the viewfinder confirms when you've manually set a combination of f-stop and shutter speed that works for a shot's lighting and film type. You may want to silhouette a model, say, or enhance blur in a moving object, which automated exposure would otherwise stymie.

All exposure systems rely on readings from a built-in light meter. Some systems (center-weighted) monitor the entire frame but give greater emphasis to the center; others (spot meters) check lighting only at the very center of the frame, where the subject is likely to be; yet others (multi-pattern metering) average the frame's light readings in a more complex manner. The photographer can select the metering mode if more than one mode is available.

Automatic film handling. As in compact cameras, motors help load, advance, and rewind the film. Most cameras with an auto-winder also let you fire off a quick series of shots, as fashion and sports photographers do. The feature, though, can devour a roll of film in no time. Automatic DX-code readers set the film speed.

Focusing. Some people find focusing by hand and eye to be tedious and slow. Typically, the center of a manual-focus SLR's viewfinder shows a split image whose halves you must align by turning the lens.

A GUIDE TO CAMERA AUTOMATION

Auto-focus. On most automated compact 35s and SLRs. Focuses automatically when shutter-release is partially pressed. (Indicator tells when subject is focused.) Variants on SLRs include: predictive focus, which tracks moving subjects; depth-of-field focus, which focuses on a point between the near and far subjects that you want to keep sharp; multispot focusing, which chooses one of four or five small focusing frames and focuses on whatever is in that frame; eye-control focus, which focuses with the focusing frame nearest to the area that your eye is looking at; and trap-focus, which lets the camera be focused manually, after which it automatically snaps any subject that moves into the frame's center at the preset distance (for wildlife photography). Autofocusing speeds up picture taking but may not work well in dim light or in scenes with repetitive graphic patterns or little contrast.

Auto-focus illuminator. On some SLRs. A red beam shines on the subject to help the auto-focus work in dim light conditions.

Auto-winder. On most automated cameras. This feature typically threads, advances, and rewinds the film. Some can fire off a series of shots to capture quick-moving sequences, as fashion and sports photographers sometimes do.

Auto-zoom. Found on some compact 35s and SLRs. Zooms to a focal length the camera "thinks" you are likely to want, or returns to a previous zoom setting. Can be more of a nuisance than a help; feature should have On/off switch. Some models can track a moving subject to keep its image size constant.

Built-in flash. On many automated models. Many turn on automatically when needed; otherwise an indicator signals the need to turn the flash on. Flash may be underpowered, however. Variations include: interlock, to prevent shooting until the flash is charged; red-eye reduction system, to reduce "red eye" in portraits, often by preflashing, to narrow the subject's pupils; hot shoe, to mount an external flash unit; and zoom flash, in which the flash widens

Or you must try to sharpen a shimmering ring around the split-image circle in the viewfinder's center.

Technology has solved the focusing problem. At the press of a button, computer chips and a miniature motor can now focus the lens in a split second, generally with pinpoint accuracy. Auto-focus models rarely provide a microprism ring or split-image circle in the viewfinder anymore.

Flash. Most highly automated cameras come with a built-in electronic flash, though it's apt to be low powered. Its fixed placement on the camera can throw harsh shadows against the backdrop when the subject is directly in front of the photographer.

Add-on flash units impart more power and versatility. They range from compact, low-powered models with limited features, selling for about $50, to high-powered, multifeatured units selling for more than $400.

The choice is limited by problems of or narrows its light beam depending on the angle the camera's zoom lens is covering.

Diopter adjustment. On some SLRs and compacts. Adjusts viewfinder for moderate near- or farsightedness, so many eyeglass wearers can focus and shoot without their spectacles.

DX sensing. On most automated cameras. Reads and sets film ISO speed from markings on the film cartridge—the photographer needn't worry about forgetting to set the speed and thus ruining a roll. Some models allow for only a limited set of speeds; others cover a wide range. Some allow you to turn off the sensing, to shoot film at the "wrong" speed (for creative effects, say).

Exposure control. On most compacts and SLRs. Program mode automatically sets shutter and aperture to give proper exposure for the lighting and film used. Variants: extra program modes, which can be set to favor a faster shutter (for action shots) or smaller aperture (for more depth of field); shutter priority, in which the photographer sets the shutter speed (often to stop action) and the camera calculates the necessary aperture, or f-stop, for proper exposure; and aperture priority, in which the photographer sets the f-stop and the camera finds the necessary shutter speed. Cameras with manual modification let a photographer set both shutter and aperture to "push" a film beyond its rated ISO speed, for creative control, or to "bracket" a shot (purposely over- and underexpose the picture, to see which works best).

Multisegment metering. On many automated SLRs. Bases exposure settings on readings from several areas in the picture. Can help camera choose correct exposure in tricky lighting, such as a bright window in the background. Some models, including compacts, have a Backlight switch, to compensate for strong light behind your subject.

Programmed image control. On highly automated SLRs. You match an icon to the type of shot—sports, portrait, landscape scene—and the camera adjusts its focus, shutter speed, and aperture settings for the best results; some also can be set to shoot continuously to capture an action sequence.

compatibility. Most camera manufacturers' flash units are dedicated, that is, each is designed for one or more models of the same camera brand and won't work satisfactorily with other brands, if at all. Consumers have to rely on salespeople or product literature to tell which flash does what on which cameras, particularly for flash units of non-camera-brand companies.

The expensive units put out more light and have special capabilities. They calculate exposure automatically with your camera's metering system, or let you override the setting manually. They can tilt toward the ceiling for "bounce" flash, a more pleasing effect than flatly lit head-on flash. Other features let you diffuse light to soften shadows about faces. Because they're offset further from the camera lens, flash units that mount atop a camera are much less prone to red eye than built-in flashes.

Other features. Automation has made cameras smart in many other ways, as noted in the box on page 76. Like many other complex products, however, highly automated cameras can also be complex to learn.

The tests

Key tests are for sharpness and for lens shortcomings such as flare, distortion, and chromatic aberration.

Tests of exposure accuracy tell how well a camera adjusts its shutter and aperture for a given scene and film; good accuracy is crucial when shooting slides. Other tests assess framing accuracy and the range and

uniformity of a camera's built-in flash. A camera's weight is also critical: The lighter, the better.

Buying advice

If you are or are willing to become knowledgeable about photography, consider an SLR without auto-focus. A manual-focus model is the cheapest kind of SLR and because you alone have to supply the brains, you'll have ample opportunity to learn the ropes—and to learn from mistakes.

On any SLR, consider carefully the weight of the camera and lens—lugging extra ounces around your neck or in your camera bag quickly takes a toll. The heavier the camera, the more likely it'll be left home on the shelf. If you buy a zoom lens, find out how close to an object you can focus it. Some zooms let you come to within a foot of your subject; others make you stand back a foot or more.

Bridge cameras offer different tradeoffs. We think most people with money and time to invest in learning photography will probably be happier with an interchangeable-lens SLR than with a bridge. And people with only a casual interest would probably be satisfied with a cheaper compact.

Whatever type of camera you settle on, select several models that pack the features you want. In the store, hold each camera to your eye and check its view, controls, grip, and balance. That's the only way to tell whether you'll be comfortable taking pictures with it.

Color print film

Kodak dominates the photographic-film market. Its familiar yellow boxes enclose three of every four rolls of film sold in the U.S. After *Kodak,* the most widely available film brand is *Fuji.* Then there's a handful of national brands—*Agfa, Polaroid, ScotchColor, Konica*—store brands such as *Kroger, Target,* K Mart's *Focal,* and private-label brands sold by mail-order processing firms such as Mystic Color Lab. Some cost only half as much as *Kodak* film.

Only a few companies manufacture film for consumers—Kodak and 3M Corp. in the U.S., Agfa in Germany, Fuji and Konica in Japan. The small number of film manufacturers makes it easy to identify a brand's origin. Kodak doesn't sell its film under other names, so any private-label brand made in the U.S. comes from 3M. In addition, 3M makes its own *ScotchColor* brand and Polaroid's ISO 200 35mm film, *Polaroid OneFilm*.

The choices

Film comes in various "speeds," a measure of sensitivity to light. The least sensitive, or "slowest," film demands more light and thus requires wider apertures or slower shutter speeds than does a "faster" film to capture the same photograph. Current color print films range in speed from ISO 25 (slowest) to ISO 3200 (fastest).

Traditionally, fast films reduce color accuracy and increase the graininess of the printed image, but technical innovations have improved the performance of fast films. In addition, color print film is more forgiving than it used to be. You can make all but the worst overexposures and the pictures will still turn out fine.

In general, the higher the film speed, the higher the price. While fast films contain more silver in their emulsion, the price difference appears mainly due to marketing factors.

Buying advice

Our tests show no compelling reason to prefer *Kodak* to film made by other major makers. However, film made by 3M was slightly grainier than the others. Since differences were subtle at best, we recommend buying by price.

Film is frequently a sale item, especially at peak shooting times like the holidays. We've seen advertised prices as low as $1.50 for a 24-exposure roll. Buying film in multiple-roll packs is usually less expensive than buying single rolls.

For the best-quality pictures, use the slowest film your shooting allows—your photographs will have slightly sharper images and slightly more accurate colors on average. Differences will be more noticeable in enlargements.

Most color print film is balanced for daylight or electronic flash. The processing lab can correct color balance when printing shots taken under incandescent or fluorescent light. However, for best results, film manufacturers recommend shooting with the appropriate color-correction filter.

Film processing

All photofinishing companies—from local one-hour outlets to giant mail-order operations—use highly automated equipment. The machines are geared to deliver good prints of average subjects captured under normal lighting so they're easily foiled by out-of-the-ordinary conditions. And those who run the machines don't always check the prints that come out. It's cheaper for the photofinisher to redo botched jobs only when customers complain. But many customers never complain.

Common lab mistakes include poor color balance, as evidenced by odd skin tones; overexposed prints, which look too dark; and underexposed prints, which look pale and washed out. Human errors at the lab include negatives marred by fingerprints, dirt, or scratches; film inadvertently exposed to light during processing; and negatives chopped in half. Muddy-looking prints from underexposed negatives are possibly caused by the camera user or the camera's metering system.

The choices

Mail-order labs. These businesses operate nationwide, with mailing envelopes that usually double as order forms. They're fairly low-priced—typically $3.50 to $7 for a set of 3½x5-inch prints from a 24-exposure roll. Turnaround is about one to two weeks.

Minilabs. These outfits, often in malls, can deliver prints within a few hours. Many promise one-hour service. You pay a premium for quick turnaround, generally $10 to $15 for a 24-exposure roll.

Wholesale companies. These processors operate through supermarkets, discount centers, and drugstores. Qualex is the dominant wholesaler. One of its branches is Kodalux, descended from Kodak's photofinishing operation and offered primarily through camera stores and prepaid mailers. Prices for wholesalers are comparable with those of the mail-order companies. Turnaround is about two days.

Buying advice

Several mail-order labs—Mystic Color Lab, Skrudland Photo, Seattle FilmWorks, Kodalux, and Custom Quality Studio—have consistently served us well over the past few years.

In our experience, wholesale labs and minilabs are, on average, pretty good overall but a notch or so poorer than the mail-order labs. One-hour minilabs charge considerably more than mail-order and wholesale labs for prints of comparable or lower quality.

Video & photo tripods

With today's fast films and quick shutter speeds you can create sharp pictures without "camera shake" even if your hands aren't steady. As a result, photo tripods have been relegated only to the most dedicated of photographers, those making "art." Tripods allow sharp pictures at long exposure times and enable you to compose a picture carefully.

For camcorder owners, however, a good tripod is a necessity if you want home videos to have a professional look. To achieve smooth panning (turning from side to side) or tilting (pointing the lens up or down), and to avoid incessant jiggling, a video tripod is indispensable.

The choices

A full-sized tripod is the most effective way to steady a camera, but there are other options: minipods, diminutive versions that fit into a camera bag or backpack; monopods, with one leg to rest on the ground or hoist above a crowd; car pods, which clamp onto rolled-down car windows; and shoulder pods, which brace a camera against the body. Some pros carry a bean bag, a cheap alternative that provides a steady resting place for the camera.

There are two types of full-sized tripods:

Video tripods. Camcorders, as a rule, work better with these. Video tripods have a fluid pan head—viscous friction on the pan and tilt movements to ensure smooth motion. Further, you can adjust the amount of friction so that the camera sits still when you release the pan handle and yet moves smoothly when you push on it. On a typical photo tripod, you must loosen and retighten tilt and pan locks frequently; it's very hard to follow the action without jerky motions.

Mid-priced video models generally sell for $100 to $150 and weigh around five pounds; some are a pound or so lighter. More expensive models tend to be taller and heavier; the less expensive ones, shorter and lighter.

Photo tripods. Because these tripods are less complex mechanically, they're a bit cheaper than video tripods. Photo tripods sell for about $75 to $120. They're also lighter, generally weighing three to four pounds.

Features and conveniences

A tripod has three principal parts: a pan head, which anchors the camera and controls its motion; a center column, which supports the pan head and periscopes up and down; and the legs.

Pan head. Video and still cameras need to pan from side to side and tilt up and down. A still camera should also be able to be tilted on its side, for vertical shots. Some pan heads can perform all three operations, but some lack the side-tilting axis. To use those tripods for taking vertical shots, you must tip the pan head 90 degrees, loosen the camera-mounting screw, and then rotate the camera.

Center column. A geared column lets you raise or lower the camera with a crank. The alternative, a simple sliding tube that you adjust with one hand and lock with the other, works fine if the camera or camcorder isn't too heavy.

Legs. A tripod's telescoping legs can make it slower or faster to set up. We think legs in three sections work best. Units with more leg sections take longer to set up; those with only two sections may be a little steadier but aren't as compact when folded for carrying and storage.

Look for legs that lock with levers or knobs instead of collets, small threaded rings that tend to jam when dirty. Lever locks are the fastest to operate.

Camera attachment. Most video tripods and some photo models have a quick-release insert—a small plastic piece with a protruding screw—that's supposed to expedite the union of camera or camcorder and tripod. Instead of making the connection in the traditional way (holding the camera over the tripod platform and tightening a screw from below), you screw the insert directly to the camera, then latch that combination onto a matching socket atop the pan head. But most such designs, we've found, make a camera less steady.

The surface on which the camera rests is often cork or rubber, which helps keep a camcorder from twisting as you pan. One feature that works even better is a tiny pin, called a video pin, found on the mounting platform of most video tripods and on some photo models. The pin fits into a matching hole on the bottom of a camcorder. Few, if any, still cameras have a hole for the pin, however. Some pins retract, but some must be removed before you attach a still camera, a task that may require a screwdriver.

Buying advice

Home videos greatly improve when a tripod is used. Hand-held camcorder shots, particularly telephoto shots, are never really steady and rapidly become tiring to watch. (For more information on camcorders, see the report on page 36.)

A tripod is also a must for still photography in dim light or with long telephoto lenses, which magnify even the smallest vibration. With less demanding photography, a tripod lets you frame and compose your pictures precisely and permits sharp pictures at long exposure times.

In general, look for a tripod that is stable and sturdy and that allows for fluid pans and tilts. Try it out in the store, and note how easy it is to set up and collapse.

RATINGS SLR CAMERAS

▶ **See report, page 72.** Last time rated in Consumer Reports: December 1993.

Brand-name recommendations: The four top-rated models are *Canons.* Each provides a wide range of automatic features and allows you to switch to full manual control. The lenses are especially quiet while their motor is focusing. But you needn't restrict your choices to a few top-rated models. The optical quality of all the brands is high. Your best guide, then, may be features and price.

For the typical auto-focus SLR, expect: ■ Automatic film handling—loading, advancing, and rewinding. ■ Automated DX film-speed range of ISO 25 to 5000. ■ Shutter-speed range of at least 30 sec. to 1/2000 sec. ■ Viewfinder that includes a ground-glass focusing screen plus displays that: show camera settings, when the subject is in focus or too close, when the flash is ready, and when film isn't advancing or battery is low. ■ Programmed exposure with multisegment metering; both aperture- and shutter-priority exposure modes plus other, specialized modes; exposure- and focus-lock to hold setting until shutter is released; spot metering; Match-indicator mode for setting both aperture and shutter speed manually; and Bulb Setting for time exposures. ■ Auto-focus that tracks moving subjects and sets focus to predicted point at exposure, and a manual-focusing option. ■ Built-in electronic flash and standard-shape hot shoe for add-on flash. ■ Features such as continuous-shot option, easy return to fully automatic operation, tripod socket, self-timer, provision for cable or remote release, and shutter lock.

Notes on the table: Prices are from a national survey. **Overall score** is based on image quality with the best of the tested lenses for that brand, and on weight, accuracy of viewfinder image, and versatility. In our tests, differences of less than 12 points on a 100-point scale weren't considered significant. **Weight** includes the body, film, and batteries, but not lens (except for bridge camera). **Zoom lens** score reflects quality of the best tested lens of that brand. **Flash guide number** is for ISO 100 film; to calculate maximum flash distance in ft., divide the guide number by the lens's widest f-number. **Viewfinder error** is the percentage of the actual picture area that doesn't show in the viewfinder. **Battery life** is an estimate of the number of rolls you can shoot with lithium or alkaline batteries. ▣ indicates model discontinued or replacement not similar.

RATINGS OVERVIEW	Within types, listed in order of overall quality			E ⊜	VG ⊖	G ○	F ◖	P ●	

Brand and model	Price	Overall score				Weight	Zoom lens	Flash GN	Viewfinder error	Battery life	
		F	G	VG	E					LITH.	ALKA.

INTERCHANGEABLE-LENS CAMERAS

Brand and model	Price	Overall score	Weight	Zoom lens	Flash GN	Viewfinder error	Battery life (LITH.)	Battery life (ALKA.)
Canon EOS A2E	$800	▬▬▬	25 oz.	⊜	50	-11%	22	—
Canon EOS A2	650	▬▬▬	25	⊜	50	-12	22	—
Canon EOS Rebel S II ▣	300	▬▬▬	17	⊜	40	-14	24	—
Canon EOS Elan	430	▬▬▬	21	⊜	44	-15	24	—

Brand and model	Price	Overall score				Weight	Zoom lens	Flash GN	Viewfinder error	Battery life	
		F	G	VG	E					LITH.	ALKA.
Minolta Maxxum 7xi	$560					24 oz.	⊖	41	-7%	17	—
Nikon N6006	470					24	⊖	—	-7	19	—
Nikon N8008S	640					28	⊖	—	-5	34	25
Nikon N90	830					30	⊖	64	-5	34	25
Minolta Maxxum 5xi	400					20	⊖	50	-5	17	—
Minolta Maxxum 3xi	280					16	⊖	35	-10	24	—
Minolta Maxxum 9xi	800					28	⊖	—	-7	35	25
Pentax PZ-20	410					19	⊖	43	-8	19	—
Nikon N5005	360					26	⊖	36	-9	54	36
Pentax PZ-1	600					24	⊖	34	-9	19	—
Pentax PZ-10	310					19	⊖	38	-13	19	—
Yashica 300 Auto Focus	370					16	⊖	37	-14	18	—

BRIDGE CAMERA (WITH BUILT-IN ZOOM LENS)

Brand and model	Price	Overall score				Weight	Zoom lens	Flash GN	Viewfinder error	Battery life	
Olympus IS-3 DLX	600					35	⊖	74	-21	14	—

RATINGS DETAILS   Models listed alphabetically

Canon EOS A2 — Very quiet rewind and auto-focus. Viewfinder has eyesight adjustment. One or more unmarked buttons or dials. Predictive auto-focus mode must be selected manually. Depth-of-field auto-focus mode. Depth-of-field preview or indicator. User-interchangeable focusing/framing screens. Metering mode adjusts weighting of parts of frame. User can change some default settings.

Canon EOS A2E — Very quiet rewind and auto-focus. One or more unmarked buttons or dials. Predictive auto-focus mode must be selected manually. Depth-of-field auto-focus mode. Depth-of-field preview or indicator. User-interchangeable focusing/framing screens. Metering mode adjusts weighting of parts of frame. User can change some default settings.

Canon EOS Elan — Very quiet auto-focus. One or more unmarked buttons or dials. Depth-of-field auto-focus mode. Depth-of-field preview or indicator. Metering mode adjusts weighting of parts of frame. User can change some default settings.

Canon EOS Rebel S II Ⓓ — Very quiet auto-focus. No provision for cable release or remote control. One or more unmarked buttons or dials. Depth-of-field auto-focus mode. Metering mode adjusts weighting of parts of frame.

Ratings continued ▶

Ratings continued

Minolta Maxxum 3xi	No provision for cable release or remote control. One or more unmarked buttons or dials. Metering mode adjusts weighting of parts of frame. No spot-metering mode. Flash is automatically activated as needed in Program mode.
Minolta Maxxum 5xi	One or more unmarked buttons or dials. Metering mode adjusts weighting of parts of frame. Flash is automatically activated as needed in Program mode.
Minolta Maxxum 7xi	One or more unmarked buttons or dials. Depth-of-field preview or indicator. Metering mode adjusts weighting of parts of frame. Flash is automatically activated as needed in Program mode.
Minolta Maxxum 9xi	Viewfinder has eyesight adjustment. One or more unmarked buttons or dials. Depth-of-field preview or indicator. Metering mode adjusts weighting of parts of frame. User can change some default settings. No built-in flash.
Nikon N5005	No easy reset to standard automatic mode. No provision for cable release or remote control. One or more unmarked buttons or dials. Metering mode adjusts weighting of parts of frame. Only one programmed auto-exposure mode. No spot-metering mode.
Nikon N6006	Predictive auto-focus mode must be selected manually. Metering mode adjusts weighting of parts of frame.
Nikon N8008S	Predictive auto-focus mode must be selected manually. Depth-of-field preview or indicator. User-interchangeable focusing/framing screens. Metering mode adjusts weighting of parts of frame. No built-in flash.
Nikon N90	Tracking auto-focus provided in Sports mode only. Predictive auto-focus mode must be selected manually. Depth-of-field preview or indicator. User-interchangeable focusing/framing screens. Metering mode adjusts weighting of parts of frame. No built-in flash.
Olympus IS-3 DLX	Tracking auto-focus provided in Sports mode only. Metering mode adjusts weighting of parts of frame. Slowest shutter speed, 15 sec.
Pentax PZ-1	Viewfinder has eyesight adjustment. Predictive auto-focus mode must be selected manually. Depth-of-field preview or indicator. Metering mode adjusts weighting of parts of frame. User can change some default settings.
Pentax PZ-10	Exposure program does not change with focal length. No exposure lock. Metering mode adjusts weighting of parts of frame. Only one programmed auto-exposure mode. No shutter priority metering mode.
Pentax PZ-20	No exposure lock. Metering mode adjusts weighting of various parts of frame. User can change some default settings.
Yashica 300 Auto Focus	Tested samples leaked light. No provision for cable release or remote control. One or more unmarked buttons or dials. Predictive auto-focus mode must be selected manually. No spot-metering mode. Slowest shutter speed, 8 sec.

RATINGS ZOOM LENSES

▶ **See report, page 72.** Last time rated in Consumer Reports: December 1993.

Brand-name recommendations: None of the zoom lenses disappointed us.

For the typical zoom lens, expect: ■ Above average color fringe toward the corners (chromatic aberration). ■ Below average or poor distortion.

Notes on the table: Prices are from a national survey. **Overall score** is based mainly on lens quality. In our tests, differences of less than 10 points on a 100-point scale weren't considered significant. **Maximum apertures** are the shortest and longest focal lengths. **Color fringe** around objects toward the corners is caused by chromatic aberration. **Flare** is one or more hot spots caused by reflections from elements in the lens. **Distortion** makes straight lines appear curved. Ⓢ indicates tested model has been replaced by successor model; according to the mfr., the performance of new model should be similar to the tested model but features may vary. Not tested.

| RATINGS OVERVIEW | | Within types, listed in order of overall quality | | | | E ⊖ | VG ⊖ | G ○ | F ◓ | P ● |

Brand and model	Price	Overall score	Maximum apertures	Sharpness	Color fringe	Flare	Distort.
		P F G VG E					

INTERCHANGEABLE LENSES FOR SLRs

Brand and model	Price	Overall score	Maximum apertures	Sharpness	Color fringe	Flare	Distort.
Nikon AF Nikkor D28-70mm	$415		f/3.5-4.5	○	⊖	⊖	○
Canon EF USM 28-80mm Ⓢ	320		f/3.5-5.6	⊖	○	⊖	◓
Canon EF USM 28-105mm	400		f/3.5-4.5	⊖	○	⊖	●
Nikon AF Nikkor 35-105mm	415		f/3.5-4.5	⊖	⊖	⊖	○
Nikon AF Nikkor 35-135mm	460		f/3.5-4.5	⊖	⊖	⊖	◓
Pentax SMC FA 28-105mm	390		f/4.0-5.6	○	⊖	⊖	○
Minolta Maxxum AF xi 28-80mm	210		f/4.0-5.6	○	⊖	⊖	○
Pentax SMC FA 28-80mm	265		f/3.5-4.7	○	⊖	⊖	◓
Minolta Maxxum AF xi 28-105mm	380		f/3.5-4.5	⊖	⊖	○	●

Ratings continued ▶

Ratings continued

Brand and model	Price	Overall score					Maximum apertures	Sharpness	Color fringe	Flare	Distort.
		P	F	G	VG	E					
Yashica AF Power 28-70mm	$170						f/3.5-4.5	○	⊖	⊖	●
Canon EF USM 35-80mm	150						f/4.0-5.6	○	⊖	○	◒

LENS SUPPLIED WITH BRIDGE CAMERA

Olympus IS-3 35-180mm	—						f/4.5-5.6	○	○	⊖	●

RATINGS DETAILS   Models listed alphabetically

Canon EF USM 28-80mm ⑤ EF USM 28-80 IImm, $320	Weight: 12 oz. Smallest field: 7 in.
Canon EF USM 28-105mm	Weight: 12 oz. Smallest field: 7 in.
Canon EF USM 35-80mm	Weight: 6 oz. Smallest field: 5 in.
Minolta Maxxum AF xi 28-80mm	Motorized manual focus and zoom only, judged inconvenient. Weight: 10 oz. Smallest field: 12 in.
Minolta Maxxum AF xi 28-105mm	Motorized manual focus and zoom only, judged inconvenient. Weight: 16 oz. Smallest field: 12 in.
Nikon AF Nikkor 35-105mm	Judged average in distortion. Weight: 13 oz. Smallest field: 6 in.
Nikon AF Nikkor 35-135mm	Weight: 24 oz. Smallest field: 11 in. (6 in. on separate macro setting).
Nikon AF Nikkor D 28-70mm	Weight: 24 oz. Smallest field: 11 in. (6 in. on separate macro setting).
Olympus IS 3 35-180mm	Motorized manual focus and zoom only, judged inconvenient. Can't zoom while in manual focus. Weight: Not separable from weight of bridge camera. Smallest field: 8 in. (6 in. on separate macro setting).
Pentax SMC FA 28-105mm	Manual and power zoom. Weight: 18 oz. Smallest field: 3 in.
Pentax SMC FA 28-80mm	Manual and power zoom. Weight: 14 oz. Smallest field: 5 in.
Yashica AF Power 28-70mm	Manual and power zoom. Weight: 12 oz. Smallest field: 7 in.

MAJOR APPLIANCES

A ds for major appliances often show them as nicely matched sets of *Maytag* kitchen or *Sears* laundry appliances. You won't go terribly wrong if you buy major appliances as pieces of a set—these machines are pretty old technology, dressed up in electronics though they may be, and appliance manufacturers know how to design a range or refrigerator or washer that works. Almost every major appliance we've tested in years can do its basic job. Differences often lie in niceties, like convenient controls, or nuance, like being able to heat the pasta water in 9 minutes instead of 12.

Every now and then, however, we find a product that misses—as we did with ranges recently—or a design that sets a new standard of quality—as with our last test of dishwashers. If you want to pick each appliance regardless of how it matches its mates, you can avoid some annoyances and profit from such progress. For years our tests have shown that no one company is best at making all these machines.

The brand names are familiar—the same, perhaps, that your parents owned years ago. But the manufacturers behind the logos may well have shifted. Most of the top 25 appliance brands are built by just five companies: General Electric, Whirlpool, Maytag, Raytheon, and Frigidaire. The General Electric brands include *Hotpoint* and *RCA* as well as *GE*. Whirlpool owns *KitchenAid*. Besides *Maytag*, Maytag sells *Jenn-Aire*, *Magic Chef*, and *Admiral* products. Raytheon sells *Amanas* and *Speed Queens*. Frigidaire uses its name and that of *White-Westinghouse*, *Gibson*, *Kelvinator*, and *Tappan*. And most microwave ovens, no matter what name they carry, are built by Japanese or Korean companies. Except for microwave ovens, which retailers treat more like TV sets, most of these products are sold in appliance and department stores. Many stores purport to be discounters, and some are, so it pays to shop around.

The price depends to some extent on where you live. In cities and suburban areas, where competition among merchandisers is keen, prices tend to be lower than elsewhere. Appliances are not discounted as sharply as audio and video equipment, but special sales are common. Discontinued models, which may be only slightly different from their newer replacements, may be a source of greater savings.

Kitchens and laundry appliances are not unlike most products—the more you pay, the more features you get. But don't be dazzled by features. Many represent a manufacturer's attempt to differentiate its product from the competition's or structure a line to represent a range of "price points" attractive to any buyer. Keep in mind that style and color, such as the white-on-white look, have long been used to create demand.

Electronic controls on major appliances add precision and versatility not possible with old-fashioned dials and switches. However, repair headaches sometimes accompany electronic sophistication. Features like ice-makers and water dispensers in refrigerators and electronic controls in ranges can actually make an appliance less reliable, as our brand Repair Histories show.

On the whole, new appliances are far stingier with energy than their predecessors. Federal standards for power-hungry refrigerators mandate that models built since 1993 be 25 percent more efficient than the 1990 standard required. New standards also require that dishwashers cut energy use. To check energy costs, use the bright yellow energy-guide label found on some appliances. It provides an estimate of yearly energy costs based on national average utility rates and other rates. It also compares the efficiency of the labeled model with others like it.

Microwave ovens

▶ **Ratings on page 103.** ▶ **Repair records on page 23.**

Consumers and manufacturers alike have concluded that the microwave oven isn't the do-all appliance they once thought. The microwave oven doesn't brown meat easily or well, despite a host of browning inventions. Nor does it bake well: A microwaved potato just isn't the same as a potato baked the traditional way. Still, the microwave oven provides the fastest, most convenient way to cook vegetables, reheat leftovers or coffee, defrost frozen foods and pop popcorn.

Sharp dominates the microwave-oven market. Other prominent brands include *General Electric, Panasonic, Sears Kenmore, and Tappan.* Most people shop for a microwave oven at discount stores Wal-Mart sells more than 15% of all microwave ovens. Appliance/TV stores and Sears are the next favorite places to shop for an oven.

The choices

Size and power. Microwave ovens come in small, medium, and large sizes. When appliance makers speak of "compact" or "large" ovens, they mean the size of the cooking cavity, which ranges from less than half a cubic foot to more than three times that. The Association of Home Appliance Manufacturers defines the sizes as follows: compact as .60 to .79 cubic feet, mid-sized as .8 to 1.09 cubic feet, and full-sized as 1.1 cubic feet and over.

Inside dimensions, while roughly comparable to those outside, depend on the cabinet design. Some models are low and long; others boxy. Big ovens typically sit on a countertop; small or medium-sized models may mount under cabinets or over a range.

Size aside, the main difference between big and small ovens is the amount of power produced by the magnetron, which generates the high-energy microwaves that do the cooking. The power output of full-sized models is usually 750 to 1000 watts; of mid-sized models, 600 to 800 watts; of small ovens, 500 to 700 watts.

More powerful ovens heat food faster, a difference especially noticeable when cooking large quantities. Many cookbooks and convenience-food package instructions are written for high-wattage ovens, so owners of less powerful models may have to adjust the time or power levels specified.

Full-sized ovens are the preferred size among today's consumers. They can accommodate lots of food—several containers of leftovers, two TV dinners, or a large casserole. But full-sized ovens take up lots of space—they're typically 22 to 24 inches wide and 15 to 19 inches deep. Price: $200 to $360.

The smallest ovens, just a bit larger than a toaster oven, may be too small for some frozen dinners. But for basic chores, like popping corn or warming beverages or leftovers, that may be big enough. Small ovens sell for $100 to $160.

Mid-sized ovens are much less bulky than big ovens, though they save just a few inches of counter space (they're typically 20 to 24 inches wide and 13 to 18 inches deep). In return, they sacrifice little in capacity, power, or versatility. Mid-sized models sell for about $130 to $250.

Combination ovens. Manufacturers have come up with various hybrid appliances to remedy the microwave oven's cooking deficiencies but none of them have taken off. One hybrid combines microwaving with convection cooking. The microwave/convection oven works fast, like an ordinary microwave. And like a traditional range oven, it browns food nicely. In convection cooking, a concealed electric element heats the air while a fan circulates it, crisping the outside as the heat works its way in. Most of those ovens can be set for a range of temperatures from 200° to 450°. Microwave/convection ovens typically sell for $470 to $600.

Features and conveniences

Features once found solely on high-end products now grace small, cheap models. Some features gradually disappear, like the temperature probe, once a premium feature. Here's a rundown of what you'll encounter when shopping:

Electronic controls. Nearly all models have dropped the mechanical timer for electronic controls, an important feature since seconds count in microwave cooking. (A mechanical timer could miss the mark by 20 or 30 seconds.) Most touchpads are easy to read and use. Ideally, numbers and letters should be printed clearly, and the control pad well labeled and laid out so that the buttons used in conjunction are near one another.

Programming automated features can be vexing. We like models with prompts that take you through each command step by step. By far the easiest automatic controls to use are those that scroll instructions across the display: When you press a touchpad, the display asks a question or tells you what to do next. Foods usually have number codes. Microwave ovens that have the codes printed right on the face of the oven are particularly convenient.

Quick-cook keys minimize button-pushing. One-button cooking—you press one key to start cooking—is almost a standard feature on mid-sized ovens and full-sized ovens. (Some models make you also hit a Cook or Time button.)

Power levels. Most ovens have at least six, some have as many as 10. We find that five well-spaced settings are plenty. In a few inexpensive ovens, power remains constant. Models with a high-power default automatically cook at that power unless programmed otherwise.

Turntable. Most models have a turntable. It improves heat distribution, but reduces an oven's usable space. A recessed or removable turntable doesn't cut down on space, but may create hard-to-clean nooks.

Multistage cooking programs. These programs instruct the oven to cook at one power level for a while, then switch to another—helpful for going directly from Defrost to Cook or for recipes that call for 10 minutes at high power and 5 at a reduced setting. Basic models typically allow two programs; fancy models offer several.

Automatic defrosting. Any microwave can adequately thaw out food if you break it apart as it defrosts and turn the pieces occasionally. Automatic-defrost reduces the labor. With some ovens, the feature works by lowering the power level during thawing; with others, it works for a programmed time period, based on the foods' weight. Some ovens signal when to turn the food or remove defrosted sections. They may also go into a "standing" mode periodically to let the temperature equalize. Models that thaw best—without cooking parts of the food while leaving icy spots—may not be the fastest, since uniform thawing takes more rather than less time.

Programmed cooking. Electronic controls give a microwave oven various programming capabilities. Many models have shortcut buttons that adjust the cooking time and power level for specific tasks, such as Pizza, Popcorn, and Beverage. Often you must estimate quantity or weight

for these shortcuts to work. Some models allow you to enter cooking instructions for your own recipes into computer memory or call up programmed instructions for a variety of foods at the touch of a button.

Delay start. This allows you to start the oven automatically at a specified time, a procedure suitable only for foods that don't require refrigeration.

Conveniences. Inspect any oven, plain or fancy, for basic conveniences. Can you see through the window to check on the progress of a dish? A door with a white screen tends to be harder to see through than one with a black-mesh screen. Look for an interior light bright enough to illuminate the food during cooking. A light that turns on when the oven door is opened and a bulb you can change yourself, without a service call, are worthwhile.

Does the oven have a shelf? It comes in handy for cooking more than one dish at a time, but it can compromise cooking uniformity: Food on the shelf can block the microwaves from reaching food on the oven floor.

Other useful touches include a lip or tray to contain spills and a clearly written, logically organized instruction book.

The tests

Our evaluation includes a judgment of heating speed based on heating measured amounts of water over fixed time periods and a battery of cooking tests mostly designed to gauge evenness of heating, a major concern in microwave cooking. We defrost ground beef, warm leftover mashed potatoes, melt cheese-topped slices of bread, pop popcorn, reheat dinners, and bake potatoes. We also measure usable capacity and review conveniences.

Reliability

Mid-sized microwave ovens have been slightly more reliable than full-sized models, our surveys show. Among full-sized models, *Panasonic* and *Sharp* have the best repair records for ovens bought between 1988 and 1993. Those brands, plus *Goldstar* and *Sanyo*, were the most reliable mid-sized ovens. See the brand Repair Histories on page 23.

Buying advice

Consider how much space you have available and how you plan to use the oven. Given their limited capacity and power, small ovens are worthwhile only if your kitchen space is truly at a premium. In our opinion, mid-sized models give the best value for the money. Many are priced just a little higher than small ovens but cook faster and offer more features. And they're small enough to fit under a cabinet or sit on a kitchen counter without hogging it.

Look for one-touch start and Quick cook keys to minimize button-pushing. A display that scrolls instructions beats referring to the instruction book.

Ranges, cooktops & ovens

▶ **Ratings start on page 106.** ▶ **Repair records on page 20.**

Today's "cooking center" may consist of a single basic range or a series of modular cooking appliances. Your choice depends largely on budget, personal preference, and cooking style. The kitchen layout, fuel source, and desired conveniences may also influence what you buy.

Whirlpool, *Sears*, and *General Electric* account for more than half of the electric ranges sold; other brands trail well behind. *GE* is number one in gas ranges, with *Magic Chef*, *Sears*, and *Tappan* on its heels. The big names in cooktops and wall ovens include *GE*, *Jenn-Air*, *Maytag*, *Magic Chef*, *Sears*, and *Whirlpool*.

Gas or electric?

This decision often depends on the utility hookup available. If you can choose, here are the major differences:

Gas burners respond quickly and let you see heat levels. Gas cooktops also stay usable in power outages. A gas cooktop isn't fussy about the flatness of the bottoms of pots. Sealed-burner units are fairly easy to clean. A gas range or cooktop is more expensive than a comparable electric model (there's more inside plumbing), but typically costs less to operate, especially now that automatic spark igniters have largely replaced pilot lights. Gas ovens are bigger than they used to be, but still smaller than the typical electric oven.

Electric cooktops, especially smoothtops, are easier to clean than conventional gas cooktops. Electric elements, particularly smoothtops and solid disks, require flat-bottomed pans. The oven is typically bigger than in comparable gas models; electrics broiled more evenly over a wider area in our tests. Electric ranges are also less likely to need repair.

Configurations

The kitchen cabinetry and floor plan probably dictate the range's width, whether the range fits between counters, is built into the cabinets or stands alone.

Freestanding models are the typical replacement ranges. They can be used in the middle or at the end of a counter. You'll find more models available than with other types. Width varies from 20 inches to 40 inches, but most are 30 inches wide. Price: $200 to $1600.

Built-in models can be of two types:

slide-ins, which fit into a space between cabinets, and drop-ins, which lack a storage drawer and fit into cabinets connected below the oven. Both types look "built-in." Price: $450 to $1400.

Dual ovens put two ovens together. The second oven—sometimes a microwave—may be up top or alongside the first. Price: $1300 to $1400.

Combination ovens combine two or even three methods of cooking in one cavity—microwaving or convection cooking along with regular thermal cooking. Most often, the second cooking method is convection, which uses a fan to circulate hot air. That's supposed to cook faster and seal in the juices. (Our tests in the past have shown that a convection oven was faster at roasting meat, but at the price of reduced oven capacity.)

A **cooktop** paired with a **wall oven** allows you to combine the instant on/off of a gas cooktop with the spaciousness of an electric oven. Most cooktops are glass and 30 inches wide, with four burners; some are 36 inches wide, with space for an extra burner. The burners can be gas or electric (with all the element types available on ranges), sealed or open. Wall ovens come in 24-, 27-, and 30-inch widths; they can be installed with the oven at eye level, or two can be stacked. Some cooktops are modular, with pop-in grills, rotisseries, and other options. Together, a cooktop and wall oven typically cost more than an all-in-one range. Price: $200 to $2000 for cooktop, $500 to $2000 for wall oven.

Element and burner types

Gas cooktops can be made of glass or steel finished with enamel. The burners are topped with the familiar grates, but some models have sealed burners, with no space between them and the cooktop to stop spills from seeping below. Gas burners tend to be slower than electric elements—even so-called high-speed burners.

Electric cooktops offer more choices:

Coil. Still the most common and least expensive type, coil cooktops usually have a porcelain surface. They offer the advantages of electric cooking: Fast heating and excellent low-temperature response. Coils are fairly forgiving of warped and dented pots and when broken are easy and cheap to replace. Cleanup isn't the easiest, although spills usually burn off elements and require no special care.

Solid element. Unlike electric coils, solid-disk elements remain gray even when very hot, so you may forget they're turned on. The disks are sealed to the cooktops, simplifying cleanup. Solid elements require perfectly flat pans and take a long time to heat and cool. Disks haven't performed as well or cleaned as easily as manufacturers hoped; they're on the way out.

Smoothtops. Elements on a smoothtop lie beneath a black or grayish white ceramic glass, often called Ceran. Patterned smoothtops, particularly the whitish gray ones, show smudges and fingerprints less than shiny black ones. Spills are easy to clean, but sugary foods, which could pit the glass, must be wiped up immediately. Manufacturers recommend a special cleaner. The elements under the glass may be radiant, halogen, or induction elements.

Radiant/halogen smoothtops. Radiant burners are essentially very thin coils; halogen burners are tungsten halogen bulbs. Indicator lights signal when the surface is hot, even if elements are off. A temperature limiter guards against overheating. For efficient heating, radiant/halogen burners require flat-bottomed pots with about the same diameter as the heating element. Halogen burners cook faster than radiant burners with the same wattage, but radiant burners come in higher wattages.

Induction smoothtops. This is the most expensive type, limited in availability. A high-frequency electrical coil beneath the smoothtop surface uses "magnetic friction" to heat the pot without heating the glass, using magnetic induction. Removing the pot from the surface turns off the heat. Heat is instant On and Off, much like gas cooking. Pots must be iron or steel (magnetic metal) but needn't be flat-bottomed.

Features and conveniences

Self-cleaning oven. A high-heat cycle (usually two to four hours at temperatures as high as 1000°) turns any accumulated goop into ash. When the cycle is complete, you wipe away the residue with a damp sponge. This worthwhile option adds $50 to $100 to an oven's price.

Alternatives: A "continuous clean" oven uses a special textured surface to camouflage dirt and is claimed to dissipate grime. Plain porcelain enamel ovens must be cleaned with oven cleaner.

Cleanup. Sealed elements or burners make cleaning easier. They add about $50 to $100 to the price of a range. Smoothtops are easiest to clean but require special cleaners and care.

Features that facilitate cleaning: seamless corners and edges (especially where the cooktop joins the backguard); a glass backguard instead of a painted one (glass won't scratch as easily); a raised edge around the cooktop to contain spills; no chrome edges. On a conventional range with coil elements or regular gas burners, deep wells and minimum clutter under the cooktop make cleanup easy. Make sure you can prop up or remove the cooktop for cleaning. Porcelain drip bowls are easier to clean than the chrome variety.

Oven capacity. Ovens in models with similar exterior dimensions often differ in capacity because of shelf supports and other protrusions. Some ovens won't let you cook casseroles on two racks at the same time. Ovens that double as convection

ovens typically lose some space to the fan.

Oven controls. Dials are generally less expensive than electronic controls. Dials have the advantage of being simpler and more straightforward to operate than some electronic controls. A nonelectronic control panel usually has an analog clock that controls the timer for starting and stopping the oven.

But digital timers with touchpads and light-emitting diode (LED) displays are more precise. The least complicated designs have prompts and a telephone-style keypad for entering time directly. A design with a smooth surface is easiest to clean.

Cooktop controls. Dials are still the norm. Freestanding ranges have controls laid out on the backguard (electric) or in front of the cooktop (gas). On electric ranges, controls can be split left and right, with the oven controls between, giving you some intuitive sense of which control works which element. Controls that are separated into right and left pairs and staggered front to back (rather than lined up) are easier to track with front and back elements. Controls clustered in the center of the backguard typically allow a tall pot to sit on a back element without blocking the controls. On gas ranges, only the oven controls are on the backguard, where they usually don't interfere with the use of large pots.

Downdraft vents. These vents eliminate the need for a range hood. They're useful for island or peninsula installations.

The tests

We judge speed of heating—the time it takes to heat measured quantities of water. To test simmering prowess, we melt baking chocolate in a saucepan, keep heat low for 10 minutes, and check for scorching. We judge evenness of oven and broiler heating by baking cakes and broiling burgers. We evaluate self-cleaning ovens by baking on and then removing a special blend of gunk. We assess cooktop space (clearance for a wide skillet, for example), cleanability, and features. We also evaluate oven and storage drawer capacity and safety, such as hot spots during self-cleaning.

Reliability

Electric ranges have proven more reliable than gas ranges, according to our reader surveys over the years. And, models with conventional dial controls have been more reliable than models that have electronic controls.

Our most recent survey showed *Whirlpool* and *Hotpoint* to be among the more reliable brands of electric ranges purchased from 1988 to 1993. Among gas ranges purchased between 1987 and 1993, *Whirlpool* had the best record of the six brands included in our survey, *Caloric* the worst.

For details, see the brand Repair Histories on page 20.

Buying advice

The least expensive and most common range is a freestanding electric model. A typical 30-inch model with four coil elements and a self-cleaning oven sells for around $450 to $600; a comparable gas range sells for $500 to $700. Sealed burners add to the price. On both types, electronic controls raise the price, too.

Gas has advantages: It's cheaper to cook with than electricity; the heat is easily and directly controlled; and gas cooktops remain usable during a power outage.

For the more stylish specialized and modular units—built-ins, cooktop and wall ovens, cooktop and dual or combination ovens—you pay a premium.

Refrigerators

▶ Repair records on page 21.

Refrigerators, one of the biggest energy-consuming appliances in the home, have chalked up impressive gains in efficiency. Today's models use half or less electricity than refrigerators did a decade ago. Responding to consumer demand and Government prodding, manufacturers keep devising new ways to reduce energy use. To meet new standards, refrigerators now have high-efficiency compressors, thicker insulation, and better door seals. Refrigerators of the future will be even better insulated, and run on refrigerants friendlier to the environment than chlorofluorocarbons, which are being phased out.

Efficiencies notwithstanding, a refrigerator's use of electricity adds up over its expected 15-year life span. By the end of its life, a refrigerator bought today is likely to have cost as much to operate as to buy.

Energy costs depend largely on the capacity and type you buy. But design matters, too. Our tests regularly show differences in the amount of electricity similarly configured refrigerators consume.

Sears, General Electric, and *Whirlpool* account for more than half of the refrigerators sold; other brands are small by comparison.

The choices

The main types you'll find are:

Top-freezer models. The most common type, top-freezer models are generally the least expensive to buy and the cheapest to run; they also give you the widest choice of capacities, styles, and features. The eye-level freezer offers easy access to its contents. The fairly wide shelves in the refrigerator compartment make it easy to reach things at the back, but you have to bend or crouch to reach items stored on bottom shelves. Nominal capacity ranges from about 10 to almost 26 cubic feet; width ranges from 24 to 35 inches. Typical 20- to 22-cubic-foot units sell for $400 to $1500.

Side-by-sides. These models are larger (about 19 to 27 cubic feet of capacity, 30 to 36 inches in width) and cost more to buy and run than other types. Advantages that may justify the expenditure: You can store food at eye level in both compartments. The tall, thin shape of the compartments makes it easy to find stray items (but hard to get at items in the back). Doors are narrower than those of a top-freezer model, requiring less clearance in front to swing open. The freezer is larger than in comparable top- or bottom-freezer models. Side-by-side models come in a fairly wide selection of capacities, styles, and features. Selling price: $800 to $2200, depending on size and features.

Bottom-freezer models. These refrigerators, a tiny part of the market, may be hard to find. They give you fairly wide, eye-level shelves in the refrigerator and easy access to its contents. The freezer is low, but often has a pull-out basket. Bottom-freezer models are more expensive ($800 to $1100) than top-freezer units. And features such as an in-door water dispenser are unavailable. Nominal capacity: 20 to 22 cubic feet; width, about 32 inches.

Built-in refrigerators. Built-ins are expensive appliances (usually $2000 and more), sized from 10 to 33 cubic feet. Designed to be installed flush with surrounding kitchen cabinets, they can be faced with custom door panels to match the cabinetry. To achieve that look, built-ins are only 24 inches deep, a half-foot shallower than conventional models; they're also taller and wider than typical refrigerators. Installation can be a major expense.

Compact models. No more than six cubic feet, they're handy for a college dorm,

office, or small apartment. None has much of a freezer. In this segment of the market, you'll find familiar appliance names, such as *General Electric* and *Whirlpool,* and also names known better in electronics, such as *Sanyo* and *Goldstar.* Prices range from about $100 to $350.

Mechanically, compacts are old-fashioned. Freezers, typically within the refrigerator compartment, get no colder than 15° or 20° and can keep ice cream for only a few hours before it goes soupy. If you adjust the control to make the freezer colder, items in the refrigerator compartment freeze, too. Nor do these models automatically defrost.

Small refrigerators such as compact models generally use energy less efficiently than larger models.

Features and conveniences

When evaluating a regular refrigerator, we use an 89-item checklist to rate how easy the unit would be to live with (the checklist for compacts has only 23 items). Minor items—poorly placed shelves, bins that don't glide smoothly—can mount up to major dissatisfactions in daily use.

Temperature controls. These are typically dials in the refrigerator compartment. With some designs, you may have to move food to adjust the controls. Some models have additional controls—a louver or valve for crispers or meat-keepers, say. The effectiveness of these controls has varied greatly in our tests.

Electronic touchpad controls, available on high-end models, are usually easy to use. They indicate when a door is ajar, when the unit is excessively warm, and when to clean the coils. In addition, such controls can flag problems needing repairs.

Shelves and bins. Shelves in the refrigerator compartment can usually be rearranged; so can some freezer shelves and door shelves. Tempered-glass shelves, increasingly common especially on high-end models, are preferable to wire shelves because they confine spills to one level and are easier to clean. Sliding shelves help you find stray items. Removable bins are handy for ice cubes.

On top-of-the-line refrigerators, you may find such niceties as a utility shelf fitted with storage and serving containers you can pop right into a microwave oven; adjustable, extra-deep door shelves for gallon-sized food or beverage containers; movable retainers on door shelves to keep tall bottles from toppling; and a built-in beverage container with its own spigot.

No-frost operation. This is practically a given these days, except on compact models. Most self-defrosting models defrost about once a day, after their compressor has run for a fixed number of hours.

Ice and water. An ice-maker is a mixed blessing. It can take up a cubic foot of freezer space and nearly double the chance that the unit will need repairs. Although it's built-in, the refrigerator must be connected to the home's cold-water line, a job do-it-yourselfers should be able to handle if there is a cold-water line nearby.

But ice-makers do keep you in ice cubes, about a pound of ice—four to six ice-trays' worth—a day. Most ice-makers shut off when their bin is full or when you raise and lock a wire arm.

Through-the-door ice dispensers can drop just a few cubes into a glass or fill an ice bucket. We like the push-in cradle dispenser, modeled after those in soda fountains. Dispensers using overhead push buttons often send ice to the floor instead of into the glass. Don't expect to get lots of cold water from a dispenser—reservoirs typically hold about 1½ quarts. Ice-makers, ice dispensers, and water dispensers jack up a refrigerator's price by $100 to $250. The plumbing connections for ice-makers and dispensers also come in kit form for as

little as $55 to $100. Such devices need to be used routinely to keep in working order and to keep their contents tasting fresh.

Door opening. Reversible doors are the most flexible; others have doors that are hinged on the right or left.

Reliability

Refrigerators with ice-makers were much more likely to need repairs than those without, according to data supplied by CONSUMER REPORTS readers. Among top-freezer models without ice-makers or water dispensers bought new between 1986 and 1993, *Magic Chef, Sears,* and *Whirlpool* were among the more reliable brands. Among side-by-side refrigerators purchased in that time, *GE* models' relatively poor record was probably due to faulty compressors used in the mid-1980s. See the brand Repair Histories on page 21.

Buying advice

Decide on type; then decide on capacity. Too large a model may be needlessly expensive, besides wasting space and energy. If your old model was big enough, then a similar-sized unit should be suitable.

Kitchen space is another consideration. Check how much clearance the door or doors need in front and at the side. Some doors demand an extra foot on the side so you can slide out bins and shelves.

A full refrigerator operates more efficiently than an empty one. To conserve energy further, make sure the door gasket seals tightly. You should also clean a refrigerator's condenser coil a few times a year with a special brush or a vacuum. When it collects dust, the coil becomes less effective at dissipating heat and may reduce efficiency. Some models locate the coil at the rear of the refrigerator; the coil gathers less dust there, but is hard to get at. Others models have the coil in front, located behind the grill at the bottom.

Dishwashers

▶ **Ratings on page 117.** ▶ **Repair records on page 23.**

Modern dishwashers use relatively little hot water—less than you'd likely use if you washed dishes under a faucet spewing hot water. Models built since mid-1994 are especially frugal, made to meet tough U.S. Department of Energy standards.

Top-selling brands are *Sears, General Electric, Whirlpool,* and *Maytag;* together they account for nearly three-fourths of the dishwashers sold.

The choices

Dishwashers range in price from about $200 to $600, but most people buy those selling in the $400-to-$500 price range. In that range, you get the kinds of features most buyers want: electronic controls, specialized cycles, and a self-cleaning filter. Spending more buys more sophisticated engineering and convenience features. State-of-the-art machines, priced at $750 and up, boast "fuzzy logic," a technology that enables the machine to adjust cycle times to the dirtiness of each load of dishes. European-made models—*Bosch, Miele, Asko*—and two models of GE's upscale *Monogram* line are exceptionally energy-efficient and quiet, and typically come with stainless-steel tub liners.

Nearly all dishwashers these days are built-in, under-counter models. Portable models with faucet hook up have been declining steadily in sales. Mechanically, the two types are similar.

Built-in models. This type is permanently attached to a hot-water pipe, a drain, and electrical lines. It generally fits into a 24-inch-wide space under the countertop between two kitchen cabinets. Compact models are designed to fit an 18-inch space.

Portable models. A portable has a finished exterior, wheels, a plug-in cord, and a hose assembly you attach to the sink faucet each time you use the machine. Most portables can be converted to an under-cabinet installation.

Features and conveniences

Controls. The choice is between manual or electronic. Neither is superior, in our view. Simple models that let you set everything with push buttons or buttons and a dial let you reset cycles quickly. Top-of-the-line models couple electronic touchpads with "systems monitor" displays. The circuitry displays the time for various dishwasher operations. Some displays flash warnings about clogged drains, blocked wash-arms, and so on. On some models a hidden touchpad locks the controls to keep kids from playing with them—a worthwhile feature for families with small children.

Cycles. A cycle is a combination of washes and rinses. Normal or Regular generally comprises two washes and two or three rinses. A Heavy cycle can entail longer wash cycles, second wash, hotter water, or all of those. A Light cycle usually includes one wash. Those three basic cycles are really all you need.

Dishwashers clean best on their heaviest cycles. But subjecting an ordinary load of dishes to extra washes and rinses wastes time and energy. And a heavy cycle may not clean a soiled load any better than a light cycle—dishes can get only so clean.

Extra cycles. Many models have a Rinse and Hold cycle that rinses dishes until you have enough for a full load. Additional cycles—Pot Scrubber, Soak and Scrub, and China and Crystal—exist mainly to justify a higher price tag. Regardless of what the names imply, a machine cannot scrub the way muscle and old-fashioned abrasive cleaners do. Nor can a dishwasher baby your heirloom crystal or good china. The machine jostles dishes, and harsh detergents can etch them. Gold trim may be especially vulnerable.

Noise. Quiet operation is a major selling point. Dishwashers as a class have become less raucous over the years. Insulating material and water pumps that run more quietly have helped. So has switching from porcelain to plastic tubs and redesigning the washer arms. In our most recent tests, the European-made models, even with their stainless steel tubs, were quietest. Only a few conventional models came close to being as quiet.

Saving water and energy. European-made models are typically more frugal with water than conventional models. In our tests, the Euromodels used 5½ to 8½ gallons per wash compared with 7½ to 13 gallons used by conventional models.

Most of the energy a dishwasher uses is in the form of hot water from your water heater. Electricity to run the pump, motor, and heating element can be less than a dime's worth at average rates calculated for efficient models. A booster heater system that checks the water temperature, heating it if necessary, lets you keep the water heater at a low, economical setting. A Delay-start setting lets you program the dishwasher to work when off-peak energy rates are in effect. All dishwashers let you choose between a heated dry cycle and the more energy-efficient air drying. A few also use a blower to aid drying, though some do just fine without one.

Filter. Look for a self-cleaning filter. Manual-cleaning filters require varying amounts of attention. One tested model required cleaning after each cycle; some required only occasional cleaning.

Soft-food disposer. Models with this feature grind and dispose of soft food. A few models accommodate hard food particles. In our tests, models with filters or soil separators did the best washing.

Rinse-aid dispenser. This releases a conditioning agent in the final rinse, which helps prevent water spots and speeds up drying. Some models indicate when the dispenser is empty.

Racks. Most racks hold cups and glasses on top and plates on the bottom. Some models have racks with folding shelves to let you add extra cups and glasses or small pressure-loaded arms to secure lightweight items. Others let you adjust the upper rack for tall glasses. Flatware baskets are typically in the main dish rack, occasionally on the door. Some have covered compartments to secure small items.

The tests

We judge performance by how well a dishwasher cleans place settings soiled with some of the most challenging foods we can find: chili, spaghetti, mashed potatoes, fried egg yolk, peanut butter, raspberry jam, cheese spread, cornflakes and milk, oatmeal, stewed tomatoes, and coffee. We let soiled dishes stand in the machines overnight. We run many loads in each machine, half with 140° water and half with 120° water. Most machines clean about the same at either temperature.

Reliability

Some of the more reliable brands, based on our readers' experience with dishwashers bought new since 1987, have been *Magic Chef, Whirlpool, Hotpoint, Amana, General Electric Monogram,* and *General Electric.* See the brand Repair Histories on page 23.

Buying advice

We usually find substantial performance differences among various brands of dishwashers—more than what we usually see with other major appliances. In our last test, price corresponded fairly closely to performance. So did quiet operation. Still, solid performers with dials and push buttons or electronic controls can be had for less than $500. Avoid budget models.

When shopping, look at the racks with your dishes in mind. The unit's construction is important, too. A porcelain-coated steel tub resists abrasion better than a plastic tub but is vulnerable to chipping. Stainless steel can be dented but is the most durable tub finish.

Washing machines

▶ **Repair records on page 22.**

Over the years, washer design has improved to the point where, virtually any machine can be expected to wash clothes satisfactorily, though some differences are still worth noting.

And substantive changes are not expected. Manufacturers met Federal energy standards that took effect in mid-1994 by simply eliminating warm-water rinses—a step worth taking on your own if your machine allows cold-water rinses. Future Federal standards are expected to require a level of energy efficiency that is likely to renew interest in front-loaders, which use less water, electricity, and detergent.

New washers are distinguished cosmetically with control-panel styling, and such attractions as quiet operation, electronic touchpad controls, extra cycles, and larger capacity. European models incorporate such features as a Delay-start cycle that lets you take advantage of off-peak electricity rates, or a built-in water heater, which saves money by reducing the burden on the household hot-water heater but lengthens overall wash time.

Just four brands—*Sears, Whirlpool, Maytag,* and *General Electric*—account for most of the washers sold in the U.S.

The choices

Washers range in price from about $250 to more than $800. Many models within a brand line are remarkably similar. They're often of the same design and boast the same basic components—wash tub, agitator, transmission, pump. Spending more typically buys more cycle-and-speed combinations, capacity, and a wider selection of water temperature and fill levels.

Top-load or front-load. Top-loaders are the biggest sellers in this country but aren't the most efficient type. Front-loaders use water much more efficiently than their cousins (typically 28 gallons versus 45 gallons in a regular wash cycle), but are more expensive and don't hold as big a load. In addition, their availability and selection is limited to *White-Westinghouse* models and a few imported brands. And, according to our readers' experiences, the *White-Westinghouse* front-loaders tended to break down more than top-loading machines. (See brand Repair Histories on page 22.)

Size. Most washers are 27 inches wide. Tub capacities usually vary between "large" and "extra large," but there's no standard definition of capacity: Our tests show washers deemed "extra large" can vary in capacity by as much as 50 percent. Models are also made for special installations—models "piggybacked" with a dryer permanently on top, or offering the option of stacking, and "portable" rolling models you hook up to a sink.

Multiple speeds. Most washers have

more than one wash/spin speed. A second, slower speed allows gentle handling for delicate items. Although some machines offer additional speeds, two speeds—a normal-speed agitation with normal spin and slow agitation/slow spin—suffice for most clothes.

Features and conveniences

Frills add to a model's price, not its performance. Here're some of those frills:

Extra cycles. Regular, Permanent Press, and Delicate are all you usually need. The cycle you choose may also determine the speed and water temperature, though on many models the choice is up to you. More expensive machines offer a Soak/Prewash for badly soiled laundry or an extra rinse cycle at the end. You can get the same result by manually resetting the dial.

Temperature settings. You generally need only three wash temperatures: hot, warm, and cold, followed by a cold rinse. Warm water doesn't rinse any better than cold water, and it wastes energy.

Water levels. The most economical way to wash is with a full load. When that's not practical, you lower the fill level to save water, detergent, and energy. On most large-tub models, the minimum fill requires roughly half as much water as the maximum. A selection of three fill levels is usually enough.

Controls. Washing-machine controls, whether knobs and buttons or electronic touchpads, are usually pretty straightforward. Large, clearly marked, easy-to-turn knobs are preferable. Electronic controls add to the price of a new machine and are likely to cost more to repair.

Finish. More and more machines have plastic-based finishes for the washer's top and lid. The new coatings, with trademarked names like Dura-Finish or Enduraguard, are tougher than enamels, but softer than porcelain.

Tubs. More plastic is used inside the machines, too. Some washers have a plastic tub, which should work as well as the porcelain-coated steel type. The polypropylene tub included with some models comes with a 25-year warranty.

Lid/door opening. Top-loaders have lids that open up, toward the back, or to the right or left. The direction isn't reversible so make sure it's suitable for a given installation. Front-loader washers open to the side or down, which makes a handy shelf but makes you stretch to reach into the tub.

Special features. Some machines have dispensers that release bleach and fabric softener at the appropriate time. Some models include an alternate agitator that's supposedly kinder to delicate fabrics. Others come with a little basket that fits inside the main tub for very small loads. A "Suds Saver" feature saves water by pumping the used wash water into an external tub for use with the next load.

Reliability

According to our reader survey, top-loaders with the *Hotpoint*, *Whirlpool*, *Maytag*, *General Electric*, and *Sears* nameplate purchased new between 1986 and 1993 have been among the more reliable brands of washing machines. Front-loaders from *White-Westinghouse*, the only front-loading washers on which we had reliability data, have been the most trouble-prone among the washers in our analysis. See the brand Repair Histories on page 22.

Buying advice

Look for a brand with a solid repair history. Top-of-the-line washers with fancy electronics and specialized settings don't provide good value. You'll get the best value by not buying more machine than you need. Don't be tempted by feature-ladened machines—a three-cycle, two-speed model should be ample for most chores.

Clothes dryers
▶ Repair records on page 22.

Just about any modern dryer will dry clothes adequately—particularly mixed loads of clothes. Performance differences are subtle and show up mainly in extreme conditions—when drying a tiny load of delicate fabrics, say.

Like washing machines, new clothes dryers must use energy efficiently. Because of standards that took effect in mid-1994, all dryers must now have at least one automatic-drying cycle.

Differences among dryers are a matter of convenience and capacity, much like washers. Some machines do all the figuring for you; others make you learn the setting that works best for your laundry. The highly automated models may sell for hundreds of dollars more than the simple ones. The biggest brands: *Sears, Whirlpool, General Electric,* and *Maytag.*

The choices

Dryer prices vary from under $200 to more than $650. Spend more, and you'll likely get electronic touchpad controls, greater drum capacity, more automatic settings, and a moisture sensor to control the drying time instead of a thermostat, which is not as precise.

The basic choices are:

Gas or electric. If you have the choice, you're better off with a gas model. Gas dryers tend to cost around $40 to $70 more than comparable electric models, but you'll recoup that in lower operating costs. (As a rule, if utility rates for a therm of gas are less than 25 times those for a kilowatt-hour of electricity—as they almost always are—running a gas dryer is cheaper.) But the extra plumbing in a gas dryer, often makes it slightly more trouble-prone.

Size. Full-sized models are 27 to 29 inches wide and have a drum capacity of 5 to 7 cubic feet. Some brands offer only one size of drum for all dryers in their line; others brands offer a larger drum in their top-of-the-line machines. The bigger the drum, of course, the more easily a dryer handles bulky items, such as a comforter. And with a larger drum, the less likely big loads are to come out wrinkled.

Manufacturers also make compact models (usually electrics only) with capacities of about 3½ cubic feet—about half that of full-sized models. Compacts can often be stacked on a companion washer. And they can be plugged into a regular outlet instead of a heavy-duty 240-volt line. But drying takes much longer with a compact. Compacts generally sell for about $300.

Features and conveniences

Here are the differences that separate models at the top of a brand line from their bare-bones brandmates:

Cycles. Bottom-of-the-line dryers offer just one automatic-drying cycle. More expensive models typically offer two or three auto-drying cycles—Regular, Permanent Press, and Knit/delicate, for instance—plus unheated settings. A "More Dry to Less Dry" range on the automatic settings lets you fine-tune the setting to suit the size and composition of each load.

Thermostat or moisture sensor. A thermostat checks the load's dampness indirectly. As clothes dry, air leaving the drum gets progressively hotter. When the temperature rises enough, the thermostat cycles off and the timer advances until the heat goes on again. The process is repeated until the heating part of the cycle has ended. New designs use moisture sensors that touch the clothes to gauge dryness. They are usually more accurate than thermostats, but not infallible. Moisture sensors are used in most top-of-the-line and some mid-priced models.

Two-way tumbling. Models with this feature tumble in one direction for about five minutes, then reverse direction for about half a minute. Frigidaire claims this feature cuts drying time by a third and reduces wrinkling.

Controls. Top-of-the-line dryers come with electronic controls. Such controls may prove slightly more convenient, but only after you've spent some time and effort to master them. Our tests show that electronic controls tend to work better than dial controls. Some electronic controls allow custom programming that you can create and save in "memory." Regular dial controls generally work well, as long as the designers don't try to squeeze too many choices onto too few controls.

Antiwrinkling. Most dryers let you extend the period of cool tumbling after the end of the automatic drying cycle—from 15 minutes to a couple of hours. This useful feature, sometimes called "Wrinkle Guard" or "Press Guard," helps prevent wrinkling if the cycle is completed but the dryer can't be emptied right away.

Less useful is what's called "Wrinkle Remove" (or similarly named feature) that promises to save you some ironing. It takes clean, wrinkled clothes and puts them through a short spell of tumbling at low or no heat followed by a cool-down. You can duplicate that on any dryer that has a temperature selector just by setting the selector to low or no heat and the tumble time to, say, 20 minutes.

Finish. The cabinet top and drum on most of today's dryers is finished with a coat of baked enamel.

End-of-cycle signal. Most models have a buzzer or other warning that sounds the end of the drying cycle; you may be able to disarm the signal or adjust loudness in some models. Some dryers also warn you when it's time to clean the lint filter.

Door opening. A large opening makes loading and unloading easier. Some doors open down, some open to the right, a few to the left, and a few are reversible. Those openings let you position the laundry basket under the opening. A door that opens down creates a useful shelf but requires you to stretch to reach into the drum.

Other features. A drum light can be useful for hunting down errant socks, even in a laundry room with good lighting. Some dryers come with a special rack for drying items like sneakers without tumbling.

Reliability

Our surveys show *Frigidaire* models purchased between 1987 and 1993 have been significantly more trouble-prone than other brands of electric dryers. Among gas dryers, *White-Westinghouse* models have been most troublesome. See the brand Repair Histories on page 22.

Buying advice

If you have a choice between an electric or gas clothes dryer, opt for the gas. Although gas dryers are higher priced, they are lesss expensive to run than electric models. The energy saved during the first year of ownership should offset the price difference of $40 to $70.

Even basic models now offer an automatic-drying cycle. Models with a moisture sensor can further help reduce wasteful overdrying. But you'll have to spend an extra $30 to $40 to get that feature.

Whichever clothes dryer you choose, make sure to clean the lint filter regularly. Ideally, that's after every load. Lint that's allowed to build up in the exhaust duct could cause a fire.

RATINGS | LARGE MICROWAVE OVENS

▶ **See report, page 88.** Last time rated in Consumer Reports: June 1994.

Brand-name recommendations: Most performed quite well indeed, but we recommend you focus on the top five. The *Quasar MQS1236H*, $249, offers auto-cook buttons that you can program and a display that scrolls instructions as you go. The *Tappan 56-5472*, $229, was the most powerful model we tested and a fast cooker. It also takes in sizable serving dishes. The *Panasonic NN-7603* is a fairly large oven, roomy inside. The more powerful *NN-6813A* is faster. Both feature displays that scroll programming instructions. But they sell for more than $200. If capacity isn't your overriding concern, consider the *Goldstar MA-1160M*, $259.

For the typical large microwave oven, expect: ■ A turntable. ■ Electronic controls with telephone-style keypad and lighted display that shows time of day when oven's not in use. ■ Maximum of 99 min., 99 sec. of cooking time. ■ 6 to 10 power levels, but cooking at full power as a default. ■ 2 to 4 cooking stages, such as defrost and then cook. ■ Interior light (which usually can't be changed by user). ■ Door that opens to the left with a push-button release. ■ Power draw of 1400 to 1600 watts.

Notes on the table: Price is the mfr.'s suggested or approx. retail. **Power** reflects our measurements in watts at the oven's highest setting. **Overall score** is based on our tests for heating speed, cooking uniformity, and defrosting, as well as various convenience features. ⑤ indicates tested model has been replaced by successor model; according to the mfr., the performance of new model should be similar to the tested model but features may vary. Not tested. Ⓓ indicates discontinued model or replacement not similar.

RATINGS OVERVIEW | Listed in order of performance and convenience

E ⊜ VG ⊜ G ○ F ◓ P ●

Brand and model	Price	Power	Overall score					Performance			
			P	F	G	VG	E	SPEED	UNIFORM-ITY	DEFROSTING	CONVEN-IENCE
Quasar MQS1236H	$249	910						⊜	⊜	⊜	⊜
Tappan 56-5472	229	1120						⊜	○	⊜	⊜
Panasonic NN-7603	270	950						⊜	⊜	⊜	○
Goldstar MA-1160M	259	870						○	⊜	⊜	⊜
Panasonic NN-6813A	299	1010						⊜	○	◓	○
Tappan 56-3872	199	1070						⊜	○	○	○
Sears 89345	200	850						⊜	○	⊜	⊜
Sharp R-5H85	299	890						⊜	○	⊜	⊜
Panasonic NN-6653A	250	920						⊜	○	⊜	○
General Electric JE1240L	260	920						⊜	◓	⊜	○

Ratings continued ▶

Ratings continued

Brand and model	Price	Power	Overall score						Performance			
			P	F	G	VG	E		SPEED	UNIFORM-ITY	DEFROSTING	CONVEN-IENCE
Whirlpool MT9160XYQ	$240	870							⊖	◖	⊖	○
Sharp R-4A95	219	890							⊖	○	○	○
Sharp R-4A54	200	900							⊖	○	◐	○
Samsung MW5510T	210	750							○	⊖	⊖	○
General Electric JE1237T Ⓓ	210	890							⊖	⊖	◐	○
Amana RSBG659P Ⓓ	275	1020							⊖	○	○	◐
Whirlpool MT6120XYB Ⓢ	170	790							○	○	○	⊖
General Electric JE1456LWH	270	890							⊖	○	◐	○
Emerson MT3122	200	750							○	○	○	○
Amana RWG322T1	225	790							○	◐	⊖	◐

RATINGS DETAILS — Models listed alphabetically

Amana RSBG659P Ⓓ	Generous usable space. Programmable settings. Temperature probe. Signal can be turned off. Beverage-reheat and Automatic potato-cooking performed well. User can change light bulb. Child lock-out feature. Confusing keypad layout. Inconvenient door handle; no cooking tray. No turntable. Draws more power than most.
Amana RWG322T1	Generous usable space. Programmable settings. Signal can be turned off. Beverage-reheat and Automatic potato-cooking performed well. User can change light bulb. Confusing keypad layout. Inconvenient door handle; no cooking tray. No turntable.
Emerson MT3122	Programmable settings. Dinner-plate reheat and Automatic potato-cooking performed well. Larger baking dishes wouldn't fit. Draws less power than most.
General Electric JE1237T Ⓓ	Dinner-plate reheat option performed well. Beverage-reheat performed well. Confusing keypad layout.
General Electric JE1240L	Generous usable space. Moisture sensor. Dinner-plate reheat performed well. Confusing keypad layout. No turntable.
General Electric JE1456LWH	Generous usable space. Temperature probe. Dinner-plate reheat and Beverage-reheat performed well. User can change light bulb. Confusing keypad layout. No turntable.
Goldstar MA-1160M	Limited usable space. Dinner-plate reheat and Automatic potato-cooking performed well. Child lock-out feature. Larger baking dishes wouldn't fit. Draws less power than most.
Panasonic NN-6653A	Display guides you through programming steps. Beverage-reheat and Automatic potato-cooking performed well. Child lock-out feature.

Panasonic NN-6813A	Moisture sensor. Display guides you through programming steps. Dinner-plate reheat option performed well. Automatic potato-cooking performed well. Has Child lock-out feature. Draws more power than most.
Panasonic NN-7603	Generous usable space. Display guides you through programming steps. Beverage-reheat option performed well. Automatic potato-cooking performed well. Child lock-out feature.
Quasar MQS1236H	Programmable settings. Moisture sensor. Display guides you through programming steps. Dinner-plate reheat option performed well. Child lock-out feature.
Samsung MW5510T	Limited usable space. Larger baking dishes wouldn't fit. Draws less power than most.
Sears 89345	Generous usable space. Child lock-out feature. Lacks Auto-cook and Auto-reheat controls but has Popcorn button.
Sharp R-4A54	Signal can be turned off. Dinner-plate reheat option performed well. Beverage-reheat option performed well. Automatic potato-cooking performed well. Child lock-out feature. Popcorn-cooking button performed worse than others.
Sharp R-4A95	Signal can be turned off. Dinner-plate reheat option performed well. Automatic potato-cooking performed well. Child lock-out feature. Popcorn-cooking button performed worse than others.
Sharp R-5H85	Generous usable space. Moisture sensor. Signal can be turned off. Dinner-plate reheat option performed well. Automatic potato-cooking performed well. Child lock-out feature.
Tappan 56-3872	Limited usable space. Programmable settings. Signal can be turned off. User can change light bulb. Lacks Auto-cook and Auto-reheat controls. Door has handle instead of push button. Draws more power than most.
Tappan 56-5472	Generous usable space. Programmable settings. Fits large casseroles and baking dishes. Signal can be turned off. User can change light bulb. Lacks Auto-cook and Auto-reheat controls. Door has handle instead of push button. Draws more power than most.
Whirlpool MT9160XYQ Ⓢ MT9160XB, $199	Generous usable space. Programmable settings. Signal can be turned off. Dinner-plate reheat option performed well. Beverage-reheat option performed well. Automatic potato-cooking performed well. Child lock-out feature.
Whirlpool MT6120XYB Ⓢ MT6120XXB, $169	Dinner-plate reheat option performed well. Beverage-reheat option performed well. Automatic potato-cooking performed well.

RATINGS GAS RANGES

▶ **See report, page 91.** Last time rated in Consumer Reports: January 1994.

Brand-name recommendations: All the ranges are competent, but the best are the *General Electric/Sears* siblings, largely because of their spacious oven in both gas and electric models. Their cooktop burners are particularly easy to regulate and are less likely than most to blow out when the oven door is slammed.

For the typical gas range in this class, expect: ■ Cooktop burners rated at about 9000 Btu/hr. ■ Self-cleaning oven. ■ Storage drawer. ■ Excellent baking performance. ■ 1 year parts and labor warranty, sometimes with shorter or longer periods for glass, finishes, and sealed burners. **Choices you'll have to make:** ■ Standard or sealed burners ■ Dial or electronic oven controls. ■ Window or no window. ■ Porcelain or chrome drip pans.

Notes on the table: Price is the mfr.'s suggested or approx. retail. ⑤ indicates tested model has been replaced by successor model; according to the mfr., the performance of new model should be similar to the tested model but features may vary. Not tested. ⑩ indicates model discontinued or replacement not similar.

RATINGS OVERVIEW

Listed in order of performance, oven capacity, and convenience

Better ← → Worse ⊖ ⊖ ○ ◒ ●

Brand and model	Price	Overall score P F G VG E	Oven SIZE	BROILING	OVEN	Cleaning WINDOW	COOKTOP
SEALED-BURNER MODELS							
General Electric JGBP34GEP3 ⑤	$749	▬▬▬▬	⊖	○	○	◒	○
Sears 73611 ⑤	699	▬▬▬▬	⊖	○	○	○	○
General Electric JGBP30GE02 ⑤	699	▬▬▬	⊖	○	○	○	○
Caloric RSK3700U	799	▬▬▬	⊖	⊖	⊖	○	⊖
Magic Chef 3488XRW ⑤	769	▬▬▬	⊖	○	⊖	○	○
Sears 73521 ⑤	599	▬▬▬	⊖	○	○	—	○
Tappan 30-3982	665	▬▬▬	○	○	⊖	○	○
Tappan 30-4942	740	▬▬	○	○	⊖	○	○
Whirlpool SF387PEY	749	▬▬	○	○	○	○	○
Wards KTM-2983-80A ⑤	630	▬▬	○	○	⊖	◒	○
Caloric RSS358U ⑤	599	▬▬	⊖	⊖	○	◒	◒

Brand and model	Price	Overall score					Oven		Cleaning		
		P	F	G	VG	E	SIZE	BROILING	OVEN	WINDOW	COOKTOP

TRADITIONAL-BURNER MODELS

Brand and model	Price	Overall score	SIZE	BROILING	OVEN	WINDOW	COOKTOP
General Electric JGBP26GEN4 Ⓢ	$699	▬▬▬	⊖	○	○	○	○
General Electric JGBP25GEN5 Ⓢ	699	▬▬▬	⊖	○	○	○	○
Sears 73321 Ⓢ	549	▬▬▬	⊖	○	○	—	○
Tappan 30-3981 Ⓓ	650	▬▬▬	○	○	⊖	○	⊖
Whirlpool SF365BEY	599	▬▬▬	○	○	⊖	—	○

RATINGS DETAILS   Models listed alphabetically

Caloric RSK3700U	Electronic oven controls. Fast, convenient controls. Small storage drawer; difficult to remove. Hot spots in front in self-cleaning.
Caloric RSS358U Ⓢ RSF 3300, $599	Dial oven controls. Controls are horizontally mounted: less accessible to children but reduce cooktop space. Small storage drawer. Hot spots in front in self-cleaning.
General Electric JGBP25GEN5 Ⓢ JGBP26GEV, $699	Dial oven controls. Smooth cooktop flame adjustment.
General Electric JGBP26GEN4 Ⓢ JGB26GEV, $699	Electronic oven controls. Smooth cooktop flame adjustment.
General Electric JGBP30GE02 Ⓢ JGBP34GEV, $699	Dial oven controls. Smooth cooktop flame adjustment.
General Electric JGBP34GEP3 Ⓢ JGBP34GEV, $749	Electronic oven controls. Smooth cooktop flame adjustment. Large window.
Magic Chef 3488XRW Ⓢ 3488XVW, $769	Electronic oven controls. Fast, convenient oven controls. Cooktop controls not conveniently arranged. Hot spots in front in self-cleaning.
Sears 73321 Ⓢ 73251, $549	Dial oven controls. Smooth cooktop flame adjustment. No window. No storage drawer.
Sears 73521 Ⓢ 75351, $599	Dial oven controls. Smooth cooktop flame adjustment. No window. No storage drawer.
Sears 73611 Ⓢ 75551, $699	Electronic oven controls. Smooth cooktop flame adjustment.
Tappan 30-3981 Ⓓ	Dial oven controls. Hot spots in front in self-cleaning oven.
Tappan 30-3982	Dial oven controls. Hot spots in front in self-cleaning.
Tappan 30-4942	Electronic oven controls. Buttons hard to push. Hot spots in front in self-cleaning.
Wards KTM-2983-80A Ⓢ 28584, $630	Dial oven controls. Hot spots in front in self-cleaning.
Whirlpool SF365BEY	Dial oven controls. No window. Hot spots in front in self-cleaning oven.
Whirlpool SF387PEY	Electronic oven controls. Display prompts, not helpful. Hot spots in front in self-cleaning.

RATINGS ELECTRIC RANGES

▶ **See report, page 91.** Last time rated in Consumer Reports: September 1993.

Brand-name recommendations: All but one would make a fine choice. The exception: The *General Electric JBP45GR,* the only model that couldn't bake cakes well on two shelves.

For the typical electric range in this class, expect: ■ Self-cleaning oven. ■ Storage drawer. ■ Automatic oven light. ■ Clock. ■ For conventional models: removable coil elements; prop-up cooktop; porcelain drip bowls; two 1500-watt elements; two 2600-watt elements; almond or white color. ■ For smoothtop models: radiant elements under glass; easy-to-clean cooktop but special cleaner required; black patterned or plain black surface; almond, black, or white color. **Choices you'll have to make:** ■ Dial or electronic controls. ■ Window or no window.

Notes on the table: All are 30-in. free-standing, self-cleaning models. **Price** is the mfr.'s suggested or approx. retail. **Overall score** is based on performance, cleanability, and capacity. **Speed** is how fast the burners brought a pot of water to boil. ⓢ indicates tested model has been replaced by successor model; according to the mfr., the performance of new model should be similar to the tested model but features may vary. Not tested. ⑩ indicates model discontinued or replacement not similar.

RATINGS OVERVIEW Within type, listed in order of performance

Better ◀———▶ Worse
⊖ ⊖ ○ ⊖ ●

Brand and model	Price	Speed	Oven			Cleaning	
			BAKE	BROIL	SIZE	OVEN	WINDOW
SMOOTHTOP MODELS							
DIAL CONTROLS							
Whirlpool RF366PXY ⓢ	$649	◒	⊖	⊖	⊖	⊖	⊖
General Electric JB575GS ⓢ	699	◒	⊖	⊖	○	⊖	○
Sears Kenmore 95629 ⓢ	649	◒	⊖	⊖	○	⊖	—
ELECTRONIC CONTROLS							
Whirlpool RF396PXY ⓢ	799	◒	⊖	⊖	⊖	⊖	⊖
Frigidaire Elite REGC39BN ⓢ	805	◒	⊖	⊖	⊖	⊖	◒
Tappan 31-5592-23	799	◒	⊖	⊖	⊖	⊖	●
General Electric JB578GS ⓢ	949	◒	⊖	⊖	○	⊖	○
Sears Kenmore 95929 ⓢ	879	◒	⊖	⊖	○	⊖	○
RADIANT/HALOGEN ELEMENTS AND CONVECTION							
KitchenAid Superba Selectra KERH507Y	1349	◒	⊖	○	◒	⊖	●

Brand and model	Price	Speed	Oven			Cleaning	
			BAKE	BROIL	SIZE	OVEN	WINDOW

CONVENTIONAL MODELS

DIAL CONTROLS

Brand and model	Price	Speed	BAKE	BROIL	SIZE	OVEN	WINDOW
Montgomery Ward KTM-4893 Ⓢ	$499	⊖	⊖	⊖	⊖	⊖	◑
White-Westinghouse KF480N Ⓢ	469	⊖	⊖	⊖	○	⊖	○
Sears Kenmore 93421 Ⓢ	499	⊖	⊖	⊖	○	⊖	○
General Electric JBP26GR Ⓢ	546	○	⊖	⊖	○	⊖	○
Whirlpool RF365PXY Ⓢ	479	◑	⊖	⊖	⊖	⊖	⊖

ELECTRONIC CONTROLS

Brand and model	Price	Speed	BAKE	BROIL	SIZE	OVEN	WINDOW
Tappan 31-3962-23	549	⊖	⊖	⊖	⊖	⊖	◑
Caloric Prestige Series ESK3700	675	○	⊖	○	⊖	⊖	◑
Sears Kenmore 93521 Ⓢ	529	⊖	⊖	⊖	○	○	○
Frigidaire Elite REG38BN Ⓓ	525	⊖	⊖	⊖	○	⊖	○
Whirlpool RF385PXY Ⓢ	549	◑	⊖	⊖	⊖	⊖	⊖
Hotpoint RB767GN Ⓢ	499	○	⊖	●	○	⊖	○
KitchenAid Selectra KER1500Y	699	○	⊖	○	○	⊖	◑
General Electric JBP45GR Ⓢ	579	○	◑	⊖	○	⊖	○

RATINGS DETAILS — Models listed alphabetically

Caloric Prestige Series ESK3700	Small storage drawer. Manual oven light. Oven controls fast, convenient.
Frigidaire Elite REGC39BN Ⓢ FEF367CAS, $804	Oven controls fast, convenient. Hard-to-clean back seam.
Frigidaire Elite REG38BN Ⓓ	Wide storage drawer. Oven controls fast, convenient. Shallow wells.
General Electric JB575GS Ⓢ JBP65GS, $699	Cooktop controls hard to remove. Hard-to-clean back seam.
General Electric JB578GS Ⓢ JBP79GS, $949	Cooktop controls hard to remove. Hard-to-clean back seam.
General Electric JBP26GR Ⓢ JBP65GS, $475	Cooktop controls hard to remove.
General Electric JBP45GR Ⓢ JBP45GS, $546	Cooktop controls hard to remove.
Hotpoint RB767GN Ⓢ RB757GT, $499	—
KitchenAid Selectra KERI500Y	Oven controls fast, convenient. Easy-to-use cooktop controls.
KitchenAid Superba Selectra KERH507Y	Warning light for hot cooktop. Easy-to-use cooktop controls. Oven controls fast, convenient. Helpful guide to center pots and pans.

Ratings continued ▶

Ratings continued

Montgomery Ward KTM-4893 Ⓢ 48464, $499	Cooktop controls hard to remove. Hard-to-clean back seam.
Sears Kenmore 93421 Ⓢ 93441, $499	Manual oven light. Contoured and comfortable knobs but hard to remove.
Sears Kenmore 93521 Ⓢ 93541, $529	Manual oven light. Contoured and comfortable knobs but hard to remove.
Sears Kenmore 95629 Ⓢ 95341, $649	Manual oven light. Bake/broil combined so can broil only at max. temperature. Hard-to-clean back seam.
Sears Kenmore 95929 Ⓢ 95849, $879	Manual oven light. Contoured and comfortable knobs. Has hard-to-clean back seam.
Tappan 31-3962-23	Cooktop controls hard to remove. Oven irksome to set.
Tappan 31-5592-23	Cooktop light's housing can fall off when changing bulb. Cooktop controls hard to remove. Oven irksome to set.
Whirlpool RF365PXY Ⓢ RF366PXD, $479	Manual oven light.
Whirlpool RF366PXY Ⓢ RF366BXD, $649	Warning light for hot cooktop. Large pot cannot be centered on rear element.
Whirlpool RF385PXY Ⓢ RF385PXD, $549	Prompts not helpful.
Whirlpool RF396PXY Ⓢ RF396PXD, $799	Warning light for hot cooktop. Prompts not helpful.
White-Westinghouse KF480N Ⓢ WEF350BA, $469	Wide storage drawer. Shallow wells.

RATINGS | WALL OVENS

▶ **See report, page 91.** Last time rated in Consumer Reports: July 1994.

Brand-name recommendations: When it comes to cooking and convenience, the top few models in each size performed very well. You can safely choose among them by price, color, or a contractor's tip. That said, if your kitchen has room, consider a 30-inch oven. They did best overall, and some cost less than smaller ovens.

For the typical wall oven in this class, expect: ■ Glass door with clear window. ■ Self-cleaning, with choice of duration. ■ Fan noise. ■ LED displays. ■ Porcelain-coated broiling pan; insert of chrome or easier-to-clean porcelain. ■ Oven light. ■ 2 chromed-steel shelves. **Choices you'll have to make:** ■ Gas or electric. ■ Size, usually 24, 27, or 30 in. for electric, 24 in. for gas. ■ All-electronic controls or electronic timers/dials. ■ Convection cooking or not. ■ Single or double oven.

Notes on the table: Model numbers are for white-on-white ovens. All the tested ovens also come in black; some in other colors. **Price** is the approx. average. **Overall score** is based on performance, convenience, and capacity. **Capacity** reflects an oven's ability to hold a 20-lb. turkey, 2 covered casseroles, and a large baking sheet. **Bake** reflects how evenly each oven baked 4 layers of cake. **Broil** reflects how many burgers could cook evenly. Ⓢ indicates tested model has been replaced by successor model; according to the mfr., the performance of new model should be similar to the tested model but features may vary. Not tested. Ⓓ indicates model discontinued or replacement not similar.

RATINGS OVERVIEW

Within type, listed in order of performance

E ⊜ VG ⊖ G ○ F ◒ P ●

Brand and model	Price	Overall score (P F G VG E)	Capacity	Bake	Broil	Clean (OVEN/WINDOW)
ELECTRIC						
30-INCH						
Maytag CWE9000BCE	$625		⊜	⊜	⊖	⊜/◒
Magic Chef 9875VRV	600		⊜	⊜	⊖	⊜/◒
General Electric JTP11WS Ⓓ	630		⊜	⊜	⊖	⊜/●
Whirlpool RB260PXYQ Ⓢ	650		⊜	⊜	⊖	⊜/○
Sears Kenmore 40995 Ⓢ	750		⊜	⊖	⊖	⊜/○
27-INCH						
General Electric Monogram ZEK735WP2	900		○	⊜	⊖	⊜/○
Frigidaire REG75WL-5 Ⓓ	630		○	⊖	⊖	⊜/○
Amana A027SEW Ⓢ	690		○	⊖	⊖	⊜/○
General Electric JKP14WOP Ⓢ	450		○	⊜	⊖	⊜/○

Ratings continued ▶

Ratings continued

Brand and model	Price	Overall score (P F G VG E)	Capacity	Bake	Broil	Clean (OVEN/WINDOW)
Sears Kenmore 47425 [D]	$700	▬▬▬	○	⊖	⊖	⊖/○
KitchenAid KEBI171Y [S]	750	▬▬▬	○	○	⊖	⊖/○
Maytag CWE6200ACE [D]	725	▬▬▬	○	○	⊖	⊖/⊖
Tappan 11-4989-00	600	▬▬	○	○	⊖	⊖/●
Jenn-Air W2720W [D]	625	▬▬	○	○	⊖	⊖/○
Whirlpool RB760PXYQ [S]	615	▬▬	○	●	⊖	⊖/●
27-INCH CONVECTION						
Jenn-Air W2780W	900	▬▬▬▬	○	⊖	⊖	⊖/○
General Electric Profile JKP17WOP [S]	830	▬▬▬	⊖	⊖	⊖	⊖/○
KitchenAid KEBSI77Y [S]	1095	▬▬▬	○	○	○	⊖/●
Modern Maid FDC250 [S]	979	▬▬▬	○	○	⊖	⊖/⊖
Thermador CT127NW	1455	▬▬	○	⊖	⊖	○/⊖
27-INCH DOUBLE						
General Electric JKP45WOP [S] [1]	1320	▬▬▬	○	⊖	⊖	⊖/○
24-INCH						
General Electric JRPI5WOP	620	▬▬▬	○	⊖	⊖	⊖/○
Sears Kenmore 40425 [D]	700	▬▬▬	○	⊖	⊖	⊖/○
Maytag CWE4700BCE [D]	550	▬▬▬	○	○	⊖	⊖/⊖
Whirlpool RB160PXYQ [S]	600	▬▬▬	⊖	●	⊖	⊖/⊖
GAS						
24-INCH						
Sears Kenmore 30425 [D]	800	▬▬	○	⊖	⊖	○/○
General Electric JGRP17WEP [S]	815	▬▬	○	⊖	⊖	○/○
Tappan 12-4990-00	700	▬▬▬	●	⊖	⊖	⊖/●

[1] Capacity score reflects capacity of each oven. Performance scores are similar for both ovens.

RATINGS DETAILS   Models listed alphabetically

Amana A027SEW [S] A027SEW1, $690	Porcelain broiler insert. Exterior fairly cool while broiling. Fan noise during Delay-cook. One broil setting.
Frigidaire REG75WL-5 [D]	Convenient electronic controls. Good view. Porcelain broiler insert. No fan noise. Vents dirty during Self-clean.
General Electric JGRP17WEP [S] JGR17WET, $815	Fan noise during Delay-cook. Vents dirty during Self-clean. Storage drawer.

General Electric JKP14WOP ⑤ JKP14WT, $450	No fan noise during Bake. Vents dirty during Self-clean.
General Electric JKP15WOP	Porcelain broiler insert. No fan noise during Bake. Vents dirty during Self-clean.
General Electric JKP45WOP ⑤ JKP45WT, $1320	Porcelain broiler insert. No fan noise during Bake. Vents dirty during Self-clean.
General Electric JTP11WS ⑩	Porcelain broiler insert. Exterior fairly cool while broiling. Fan noise during Delay-cook. Manual self-clean lock. Needs 33-in. cabinet.
General Electric Monogram ZEK735WP2	No fan noise. Vents dirty during Self-clean.
General Electric Profile JKP17WOP ⑤ JKP17WT, $830	Porcelain broiler insert. Quiet convection fan. Door, oven frames, and vents dirty during Self-clean. Convection cookbook. Convection roast rack.
Jenn-Air W2720W	Porcelain broiler insert. Exterior fairly cool while broiling. Timed oven feature hard to set. Dials set function and temp. Oven-on and Door-locked lights. Manual oven light. Manual self-clean lock.
Jenn-Air W2780W ⑩	Convenient electronic controls. Porcelain broiler insert. Exterior fairly cool while broiling.
KitchenAid KEBI171Y ⑤ KEBI171B, $750	Convenient electronic controls. Good view. Exterior fairly cool while broiling. Quiet fan.
KitchenAid KEBSI77Y ⑤ KEBSI77B, $1095	Convenient electronic controls. Good view. Exterior fairly cool while broiling. Quiet fans. Door handle discolored.
Magic Chef 9875VRV	Convenient electronic controls. Good view. Porcelain broiler insert. Exterior fairly cool while broiling. Manual oven light. Manual self-clean lock. Needs 33-in. cabinet.
Maytag CWE4700BCE ⑩	Good view. Porcelain broiler insert. Exterior fairly cool while broiling. Manual oven light. Manual self-clean lock. Dials set function and temp. Oven-on and Door-locked lights.
Maytag CWE6200ACE ⑩	Good view. Porcelain broiler insert. Exterior fairly cool while broiling. Timed oven feature hard to set.
Maytag CWE9000BCE	Convenient electronic controls. Good view. Porcelain broiler insert. Needs 33-in. cabinet.
Modern Maid FDC250 ⑤ FDC3502, $979	Convenient electronic controls. Porcelain broiler insert. Exterior fairly cool while broiling and self cleaning.
Sears Kenmore 30425 ⑩	Vents dirty during Self-clean. Fan noise during Delay-cook. Storage drawer.
Sears Kenmore 40425 ⑩	No fan noise during Bake. Vents dirty during Self clean.
Sears Kenmore 40995 ⑩	No fan noise. Dials set function and temp. Oven-on and Door-locked lights. Self-clean door latch concealed when not in use.
Sears Kenmore 47425 ⑩	No fan noise during Bake. Vents dirty during Self-clean.
Tappan 11-4989-00	Dials light when in use. No fan noise. Vents dirty during Self-clean. Dials set oven function and lamp. Oven-on and Door-locked lights.

Ratings continued ▶

Ratings continued

Tappan 12-4990-00	Convenient electronic controls. Porcelain broiler insert. No fan noise during Bake. Doesn't fit 14x16 in. cookie sheet. Nonremovable canopy. Vents dirty during Self Clean. Small storage drawer.
Thermador CT127NW	Good view. Exterior fairly cool while broiling and self cleaning. No seal at front of oven. Controls harder to use than others. Dial-type electronic temp. and timing controls, each with electronic display.
Whirlpool RB160PXYQ Ⓢ RB160PXBQ, $600	No fan noise. Display prompts not helpful.
Whirlpool RB260PXYQ Ⓢ RB260PXBQ, $650	No fan noise. Display prompts not helpful.
Whirlpool RB760PXYQ Ⓢ RB760PXBQ, $615	No fan noise. Display prompts not helpful.

RATINGS COOKTOPS

▶ **See report, page 91.** Last time rated in Consumer Reports: July 1994.

Brand-name recommendations: Except for a couple of low-rated gas models, very good performance was the norm. The least expensive type is coil; the top four models in that group deserve first consideration. Smoothtops—radiant/halogen and induction—are the most expensive type. The *GE JP3452S1WG*, $510, costs much less than the top-rated *Thermador CH30W*, $850, and was nearly as good. (That *GE* has been discontinued but may be available in some stores.) The *GE JP3930R1WG*, $825, is our first choice among induction models. Among gas models, the *KitchenAid KGCT305A*, $540, and the *Dacor SGG304W-1*, $680, (discontinued) were only slightly better than the less expensive *Magic Chef 8241RV*, $290.

For the typical cooktop, expect: ■ 30 in. x 21 in. deep. ■ 4 burners. ■ Dial controls (except electronic for induction models) that are continuously variable. ■ Easy-to-use controls. ■ For gas cooktops: sealed burners, spark igniter, convertibility to liquid propane, glass or porcelain surface. ■ For coil cooktops: wide availability, removable elements with drip bowls, porcelain surface. ■ For radiant/halogen smoothtops: On light, light to show burner is too hot to touch. ■ For induction smoothtops: lock feature, auto shutoff when pot is removed, auto shutoff if unit overheats.

Notes on the table: Model numbers are for the color tested, usually white. **Price** is the approx. retail. **Overall score** is based on performance, convenience, and features. **Cleaning** reflects how easy it was to get baked-on grime off cooktop surfaces. **Spills** reflect how easy it was to clean up liquid sloshed around the burner. Ⓢ indicates tested model has been replaced by successor model; according to the mfr., the performance of new model should be similar to the tested model but features may vary. Price is suggested retail. Not tested. Ⓓ indicates model discontinued or replacement not similar.

RATINGS OVERVIEW

Within type, listed in order of performance

Legend: E ⊖ VG ⊖ G ○ F ◐ P ●

Brand and model	Price	Overall score (P F G VG E)	Heat HIGH	Heat LOW	Cleaning	Spills	Controls

ELECTRIC

COIL

Brand and model	Price	HIGH	LOW	Cleaning	Spills	Controls
KitchenAid KECS100S	$265	⊖	⊖	⊖	⊖	⊖
Frigidaire FEC3X5XA	220	⊖	⊖	○	⊖	⊖
Sears Kenmore 42425 D	220	⊖	⊖	○	⊖	○
General Electric JP325R	230	⊖	⊖	○	⊖	○
Whirlpool RC8400XA	220	⊖	⊖	○	○	○
Tappan 13-3028	185	⊖	⊖	○	○	○
Magic Chef 8610PV	195	⊖	⊖	○	○	○
Jenn-Air CCE407W D	220	○	⊖	○	○	○

RADIANT/HALOGEN SMOOTHTOP

Brand and model	Price	HIGH	LOW	Cleaning	Spills	Controls
Thermador CH30W	850	○	⊖	⊖	⊖	○
General Electric JP3452S1WG D	510	⊖	⊖	⊖	⊖	○
Maytag CSE9000ACE	440	⊖	⊖	⊖	⊖	○
Amana AK2H30W1 S	655	⊖	⊖	⊖	⊖	○
Amana AK2T30W S	480	⊖	⊖	⊖	⊖	○
KitchenAid KECC500W	520	○	⊖	⊖	⊖	○
Whirlpool RC8600XXQ-1	500	⊖	⊖	⊖	⊖	○

INDUCTION SMOOTHTOP

Brand and model	Price	HIGH	LOW	Cleaning	Spills	Controls
General Electric JP3930R1WG	825	○	⊖	⊖	⊖	⊖
Sears Kenmore 42925 D	900	○	⊖	⊖	⊖	○

GAS

Brand and model	Price	HIGH	LOW	Cleaning	Spills	Controls
KitchenAid KGCT305A	540	◐	○	◐	◐	⊖
Dacor SGG304W-1 D	680	○	●	○	◐	○
Magic Chef 8241RV	290	○	●	◐	○	○
Maytag CSG7000BAE	385	◐	⊖	○	⊖	⊖
Thermador GG30WC-02 S	680	○	⊖	●	○	○
General Electric JGP331EP2WG S	475	○	○	○	◐	○
Sears Kenmore 32125 D	$480	○	◐	○	◐	○
Modern Maid PGT130UWW S	485	●	⊖	◐	◐	○
Whirlpool SC8630EXQ-5	275	○	●	○	⊖	○

Ratings continued ▶

Ratings continued

RATINGS DETAILS Models listed alphabetically

Amana AK2T30W Ⓢ AK2T30W1, $480	—
Amana AK2H30W1 Ⓢ AK2H30W2, $655	—
Dacor SGG304W-1 Ⓓ	Burners reignite when blown out.
Frigidaire FEC3X5XA Ⓢ JGPEVP331EV, $475	Front surface cooler than most. Opening around control stem sealed. Control markings especially clear. Knobs comfortable. Hinged, for easy cleaning.
General Electric JGP331EP2WG Ⓢ JGPEVP331EV, $475	Comfortable knobs.
General Electric JP3250R1	Opening around control stem sealed. Hinged, for easy cleaning. Comfortable knobs. Burner assembly looser than others.
General Electric JP3452S1WG Ⓓ	One dual burner. Opening around control stem sealed. Comfortable knobs. Front surface hotter than most.
General Electric JP3930R1WG	Front surface cooler than most. Each burner has an On light. Spills can leak inside unit and cabinet.
Jenn-Air CCE407W Ⓓ	Opening around control stem sealed. Front surface hotter than most.
KitchenAid KECC500W	Hot light for each burner. Comfortable knobs. Burner design aids in centering pot. Paint on metal rim came off easily on first sample tested; second sample OK.
KitchenAid KECS100S	Opening around control stem sealed. Easy to match control with burner. Hinged, for easy cleaning.
KitchenAid KGCT305A	Front surface cooler than most. Burners reignite when blown out. Control markings especially clear. Burner selection especially easy. Comfortable knobs.
Magic Chef 8241RV	Porcelain surface. Control markings especially clear. High-power burners look the same as low-power. Front surface hotter than most.
Magic Chef 8610PV	Front surface cooler than most. Opening around control stem sealed. Control markings especially clear.
Maytag CSE9000ACE	Opening around control stem sealed. Control markings better than others. Front surface hotter than most.
Maytag CSG7000BAE	Control markings especially clear. No shielding around control stem. Burner grates pop out of position more easily than others.
Modern Maid PGT130UWW	Front surface cooler than most. Burners reignite when blown out. Control selection very easy. Burner grates pop out of position more easily than most.
Sears Kenmore 32125 Ⓓ	—
Sears Kenmore 42425 Ⓓ	Opening around control stem sealed. Hinged, for easy cleaning.
Sears Kenmore 42925 Ⓓ	Front surface cooler than most. On light for each burner. Controls easy to use. Spills can leak inside unit and cabinet. Electronic touchpad control not sealed, spill leaked inside first sample; second OK.
Tappan 13-3028	Opening around control stem sealed. Hinged, for easy cleaning.

Thermador CH30W	One dual burner. Front surfaces cooler than most. Opening around control stem sealed. On light and Hot light for each burner.
Thermador GG30WC-02 Ⓢ GGN30W, $669	—
Whirlpool RC8400XA	Opening around control stem sealed. Control markings especially clear.
Whirlpool RC8600XXQ-1	Spills can leak inside cabinet. Front surface hotter than most. Two samples in black were defective.

RATINGS DISHWASHERS

▶ **See report, page 97.** Last time rated in Consumer Reports: October 1993.

Brand-name recommendations: We judged the three Euromodels excellent, but we think you'll get much more for your money with one of the conventional models judged very good. Consider first the *Maytag*, the *KitchenAids,* and the *In-Sink-Erator*.

For the typical dishwasher in this class, expect: ■ Heavy, Normal, and Light wash cycles plus a Rinse-and-Hold cycle. ■ Self-cleaning filter or soil separator. ■ Flatware basket. ■ Fold-down section(s) in upper rack for loading in 2 tiers. ■ Rinse-conditioner dispenser. ■ Exposed elements to heat water, if needed. ■ Push-button and/or dial controls.

Notes on the table: Price is mfr.'s suggested or approx. retail. **Overall score** reflects all judged attributes, with washing the most important. For **washing, energy** consumption, and **water use** ratings are based on performance using the Normal cycle. **Water use** is in gallons. Ⓢ indicates tested model has been replaced by successor model; according to the mfr., the performance of new model should be similar to the tested model but features may vary. Not tested. Ⓓ indicates model discontinued or replacement not similar.

RATINGS OVERVIEW
Within type, listed in order of overall performance

Better ◀——▶ Worse
◕ ◑ ○ ◐ ●

Brand and model	Price	Overall score		Washing	Noise	Energy	Water use
		P F G VG E					

CONVENTIONAL MODELS

Brand and model	Price	Overall score		Washing	Noise	Energy	Water use
Maytag DWU9200AAX	$494	▬▬▬▬▬		◑	◑	◑	10.0
Kitchen Aid KUDS230Y	699	▬▬▬		◑	◑	◑	7.5
Kitchen Aid KUDJ230Y	519	▬▬▬		◑	○	◑	7.5
In-Sink-Erator WS400	410	▬▬▬		◑	◐	◑	7.5
Sears Kenmore 15815	550	▬▬▬		◑	○	○	11.0
Sears Kenmore 16755	500	▬▬▬		◑	○	○	11.0
General Electric GSD2800 Ⓓ	470	▬▬▬		◑	◑	◐	12.5
Caloric DUS600WW	429	▬▬▬		◑	○	○	12.5

Ratings continued ▶

Ratings continued

Brand and model	Price	Overall score					Washing	Noise	Energy	Water use
		P	F	G	VG	E				

CONVENTIONAL MODELS *continued*

Brand and model	Price	Overall score					Washing	Noise	Energy	Water use
Amana DU6000BR	$450						⊖	◑	○	12.5
Sears Kenmore 15745	420						○	○	◐	12.0
Roper WU5750Y2	319						●	◐	⊖	9.0

EUROMODELS

Brand and model	Price	Overall score					Washing	Noise	Energy	Water use
General Electric Monogram ZBD4300SWH Ⓢ	930						⊖	⊖	⊖	7.0
Asko Premier 1303	699						⊖	⊖	⊖	5.5
Miele G572u	1000						⊖	⊖	⊖	8.5

RATINGS DETAILS Models listed alphabetically

Amana DU6000BR	Detergent dumped when cycle reset.
Asko Premier 1303	Filter needed occasional cleaning. Cannot easily fit large plates and cutting
Caloric DUS600WW	Cycle start can be delayed. Detergent dumped when cycle reset. Plastic interior stained.
General Electric GSD2800S Ⓓ	Cycle start can be delayed. Detergent dumped when cycle reset. Malfunctions displayed.
General Electric Monogram ZBD4300SWH Ⓢ ZBD4300SW, $930	Filter needed occasional cleaning. Detergent dumped when cycle reset.
In-Sink-Erator WS400	Cannot easily fit large plates and cutting boards.
KitchenAid KUDJ230Y	—
KitchenAid KUDS230Y	—
Maytag DWU9200AAX	Cycle start can be delayed.
Miele G572u	Filter needed occasional cleaning.
Roper WU5750Y2	Filter needed cleaning every cycle. Cycle start can be delayed. Detergent
Sears Kenmore 15745	Cycle start can be delayed. Plastic interior stained.
Sears Kenmore 15815	Cycle start can be delayed. Cannot easily fit large plates and cutting boards.
Sears Kenmore 16755	Cycle start can be delayed. Cannot easily fit large plates and cutting boards. Detergent dumped when cycle reset. Plastic interior stained.

SMALL APPLIANCES

In the early 1970s, Krups, the German appliance maker, redesigned the automatic drip coffee-maker pioneered by Mr. Coffee. Krups, Braun, and other European makers have since redesigned blenders, food processors, toasters, mixers, and other small appliances. American companies like Black & Decker and, finally, Mr. Coffee have followed suit. Countertop kitchen tools now are apt to be rounded, white, and sleekly styled.

At the same time, a "retro" look has developed a following, notably with blenders and toasters styled in the chrome and colors of the 1950s. While such appliances evoke the sentiments of an earlier age, they don't always live up to practicality as our recent tests of toasters demonstrated.

Breadmakers

▶ Ratings on page 141.

A breadmaker mixes up dough and bakes it, acting as both mixer and oven. You measure in ingredients, or pour a packaged bread mix into the pan; then, shut the lid, press some buttons, and walk away. A small, propeller-shaped paddle rotates to knead the dough, stops to let it rise, and sometimes repeats the cycle before the oven heats up to bake the bread. All breadmakers offer a basic yeast-bread cycle that takes about 2½ to 4 hours to complete.

Wellbilt and *DAK* (made by Wellbilt) dominate the market. Other brands include *Trillium, Hitachi, Regal, Seiko, Panasonic, Sunbeam, Oster, Black & Decker, Mr. Coffee, West Bend,* and *Betty Crocker.*

The choices

Size. Prices vary from $85 to $350. Less-expensive machines made bread just as well as their pricey relatives in our tests. Spending more usually buys greater capacity and more features. Breadmakers are available in 1-, 1½-, and 2-pound sizes. The 1½-pound size , which takes about three cups of flour, yields 10 to 14 thick slices—compared with 20 slices in a standard package of store-bought white bread. A 1-pound machine typically takes about two cups of flour and makes a loaf that delivers 8 to 10 thick slices.

Loaf shape. Some machines turn out familiar-looking rectangular loaves. Others make tall, squarish, or round loaves.

Features and conveniences

Controls. All models have a digital display indicating the stage of preparation and time left. The controls may be on the top at the side. Setting controls is generally easy; you push a few touchpad buttons and a Start button. The worst control panel was cramped and cluttered with buttons.

Specialty cycles. Most breadmakers have a rapid cycle that cuts an hour or so off the kneading and rising time; bread made the faster way is generally not as tall or fluffy as the standard-cycle bread. The Dough cycle, a feature on many models, prepares the dough so you can remove it to make rolls and other shapes for baking in a conventional oven. A **cool-down** cycle cools the bread and keeps it from turning gummy. Fancy models have programmed cycles with longer rising times for light or whole-grain breads. A few let you create

custom cycles. The absence of a labeled button with a cycle may not mean the machine can't do a task—just that it may need some manual assistance.

Delay-start timer. Most breadmakers let you add the ingredients and select a time (up to 13 hours in advance) for the bread to be ready.

Yeast dispenser. This feature, used in conjunction with Delay-start, allows the yeast to be released at the right time.

Viewing window. While most breadmakers have a small window on top to view the action, a few have a glass dome to let you see everything. But the domed models tend to produce unevenly colored crusts. Placing aluminum foil under the dome solves the problem but blocks the view.

Loading and cleanup. A nonstick bread pan is standard. Most machines let you remove the pan to load ingredients, the best design. Cleanup involves washing the pan and the kneading paddle.

A few machines use the hole-in-the-pan approach to loading: You put the pan in the machine, attach the paddle to a drive shaft that pokes through the hole, and add ingredients. That's bothersome and messy, leaving crumbs in the cavity after baking. But it does allow the bread to slide out easily since the kneading paddle comes with it.

The tests

We test breadmakers using three bread recipes and a packaged mix. We observe how well they bake basic loaves and handle complicated ingredients like whole-wheat flour and raisins. We note how easy they are to use and clean. And we evaluate the noise models make while kneading.

Buying advice

All breadmakers make very good bread, but those with well-designed controls that make cleanup and loading simple are easier to live with. Choose a size based on how much bread you expect to eat each week.

Most of the regular-loaf machines list for $300 or more; small-loaf models list for about $200. But that price is discounted, sometimes substantially. You'll find the greatest saving at mass merchandisers like Sears and warehouse clubs, or through mail order. Don't expect to recoup the machine's price by saving on bread: Unless you buy in large quantities, the price for ingredients is about what you'd pay for store-bought bread.

Food processors

▶ Ratings on page 134. ▶ Guide to food-fixers on page 137.

When the Cuisinarts Company introduced food processors two decades ago, some buyers assumed the gadgets would turn them into instant culinary experts. Aspiring chefs now know that food processors are great at some tasks, so-so at others. Processors easily chop vegetables for a soup or stew. They also make quick work of salad fixings like onions, mushrooms, and cucumbers, and they're handy for such baking chores as crumbling graham crackers for a crust and mixing pastry dough.

But for mashing potatoes or whipping cream, an electric mixer does better. And for liquefying foods, puréeing baby food, and concocting exotic drinks, nothing tops a standard countertop blender (see the guide to food-fixers on page 137).

After a shakeout in the mid-1980s, *Black & Decker* became the leading brand of food processor. Other makers include Hamilton Beach, Oster, and Sunbeam. Although the Cuisinarts Company no longer exists, Conair, took over the name.

The choices

Compact vs. full-sized. Food processors come in compact and full-sized versions, which vary widely. One manufacturer's "compact" may have a larger processing bowl than another's "full size." Models we consider full-sized have a bowl that holds at least 5½ cups of food. They're priced from $45 to $300. Compacts, priced from $35 to $215, hold 2½ to 4¼ cups. Even by that measure of capacity, some compacts are taller than full-sized models.

Compact models demand a bit less kitchen space, and are easier to lift and clean than full-sized models. Full-sized processors are useful if you regularly prepare ambitious menus or large meals.

Mini food-choppers/food processors. This variation chops, grinds, and purées in small quantities—half a cup or so at a time. Unlike a food processor, it cannot slice or shred. Price: $25 to $35.

Salad gun. The salad gun is essentially a feed tube fitted with a motorized cone that holds a slicing or shredding blade. The models in our tests sliced and shredded well and were simple to clean and move around. We especially liked the convenience of a Continuous-on switch. Compared with a food processor, they're much less effective or versatile. Price: from $25 to $45.

Multipurpose fixer. These megamachines combine a food processor, blender, salad maker, stand mixer, juice extractor, food mill; the mix varies with maker and model. Depending on the task, you attach an accessory to a motorized base. In our tests, no one model performed all its tasks well. Price: $250 to $300.

Features and conveniences

Chute. With most food processors, sliced or shredded food simply drops into a bowl, which must be emptied when full. Other machines are designed to let you process more than will fill the bowl with a separate chute you attach to divert the overflow of food, for instance, or a device that can "sling" food out of the bowl, through an opening in the lid, into another container.

Bowl. All food processors have a transparent plastic work bowl, usually with a convenient handle. A bowl can hold more dry food than liquid. Filled to capacity with a thin liquid, a bowl will usually leak during processing.

Blades and disks. An S-shaped metal chopping blade and a slicing/shredding disk are standard. Some models have separate slicing and shredding disks. Additional attachments, either standard or optional, may include thin and thick slicing/shredding disks, a cheese-grating disk, and a disk for cutting french fries. Attachments such as a plastic whipping accessory for cream or a plastic dough-mixing blade are less worthwhile.

Feed tube and pusher. With most models, you slice or shred food by inserting it into a feed tube on the bowl's lid using a plastic pusher to help if need be. If the tube is narrow, you'll have to trim the food into sizes that'll fit. Some models have a tube big enough to swallow a medium-sized tomato. Some tubes incorporate a slender inner tube for holding thin foods like carrots upright.

Safety. For safety reasons, no food processor can be turned on unless lid and bowl are latched.

Controls. Most compacts and all full-sized food processors have an On/off switch and a Pulse provision, which keeps the machine running as long as you depress a switch. Some processors have touchpad controls instead of switches; other models start whenever you move the lid in and out of a latch on the housing.

On some models, the switching mechanism may be part of the handle, which makes it convenient to turn on the machine continuously when you want to pulse and vice versa.

One speed—found on all compacts and most full-sized models—is all you need for food processing. Multiple speeds or variable speed controls are overkill.

Cleaning and storage. Machines with clean lines and no food-trapping gaps are the easiest to clean. Tough to clean: large, convoluted feed tubes. Most components are dishwasher-washable. Be sure to place them on the top rack, away from the heating element. And don't let blades soak in water overnight—they may rust.

The tests

To judge food processors, we spend hundreds of hours chopping, slicing, shredding, and mixing more than 30 different foods. We follow manufacturers' suggestions but also experiment to get the best results. We also judge convenience and safety factors.

Buying advice

If you're not an enthusiastic cook and don't make food for a crowd, consider a compact model. Don't count on a compact to save you much counter space, however. While they take slightly less space than full-sized models, they may actually be taller than their larger cousins.

If you need to chop, purée, mix, or slice on a grand scale, you may be glad to have a full-sized processor. A busy cook or baker is best off with a full-sized model.

You needn't pay top dollar. Processors sold at a Cadillac price, such as the *Cuisinart* and *Waring Professional*, are indeed powerful, quiet, and well appointed, but we've also found less expensive models that work quite well and may be more convenient to use.

Blenders
▶ **Guide to food-fixers on page 137.**

The repeal of Prohibition helped popularize the blender. With alcohol legal again, bars began using the machines to mix daiquiris and other frothy drinks. Standard blenders today are much like their Depression-era prototypes, but innovative designs are reshaping the market. Hand-held models take the mixing blades straight to the glass. KitchenAid entered the market in 1993, with two models capable of crushing ice. Also new: touchpad controls that simplify cleanup considerably.

Blenders are only made by a handful of companies. You'll see *Hamilton Beach* and *Oster* in most stores.

The choices

The basic choice is between the hand-held variety and standard, full-sized models.

Hand-held models. Hand-held blenders consist of a motor housing—with an On/off switch or dial that controls the speed—and a shaft with a blade at its end. You simply plunge the blade into a container of ingredients and blend. A hand-held model weighs only a couple of pounds, so it's easy to maneuver. It's also handy to use, since blended food or drink may be eaten or sipped from the container. Hand-held models are easily cleaned by holding the blades under hot running water. Most models work at one or two speeds. They're ideally suited to mixing liquids and making soups. Some also come with attachments for tasks such as chopping nuts and grinding cheese. Prices range from about $20 to $45.

Standard models. The standard blender—a mixing container with a rotating blade driven by a motor in the machine's base—is more powerful than the hand-held variety. Standard models generally come with a wider choice of speeds than is needed. Prices range from about $20 to $85.

Features and conveniences

Controls. Most models still use buttons, while more expensive units boast touchpad controls. One or two speeds, typical of a hand-held model, are enough for mixing liquids. Especially handy: a continuously variable speed. On standard models, a half-dozen speeds are enough for most chores. Pulse keeps the blades whirring only as long as you depress the control.

Containers. Markings that aid measuring are an obvious convenience. Wide-mouth containers make cleaning and loading food easy. Hand-held blenders usually come with plastic containers; standard models use plastic or glass. While plastic has the advantage of being lighter and more durable, it may get scratched and cloudy over time. Blend-and-store containers make leftovers easy to store and minimize cleanup.

Cleanup. Fewer controls make cleaning the base easier. Well-spaced buttons are easy to clean between, as are flat touchpad controls. Containers are almost always dishwasher-safe, but plastic may not hold up as well in the dishwasher as glass. Blades shouldn't be hard to clean but may rust if left to soak overnight.

Buying advice

A hand-held model lets you mix and serve in the same container. If you make a lot of foamy drinks and diet preparations, it's your best choice. If your blending tasks go beyond merely mixing liquids, consider a standard blender. Performance differences among them tend to be slight, so let convenience, features, and price guide you.

Portable & stand mixers

▶ **Ratings on page 136.** ▶ **Guide to food-fixers on page 137.**

Stand mixers are the traditional workhorses of mixers—most handle heavy bread and cookie dough in addition to lightweight tasks such as whipping cream and mixing cake batter. Their portable cousins, though, have far outdistanced stand mixers in sales because of convenience, price, and size.

Portable mixers come in plug-in or cordless (battery-powered) versions. Stand mixers come in heavy-, medium- and light-duty versions; though some heavy-duty models are more capable than others. Beyond that, the models may differ in the power of the motor and the number of speeds.

Black & Decker dominates sales of portables; *Kitchenaid* and *Sunbeam* are the big names in stand mixers.

The choices

Portables. An unadorned plug-in mixer sells for as little as $15 at discount. It typically offers three to five speeds and interchangeable beaters. More elaborate portables are priced as high as $60.

Cordless mixers free you from the electrical outlet, but when not in use they must be kept on a charging base that's plugged into an outlet. Package claims suggest that cordless units pack lots of power. They don't. Prices range from $35 to $60.

Stand mixers. Heavy-duty versions boast powerful motors and sturdier construction than most portables. Light-duty models can be detached and used as portables. Price: $100 and up for heavy- and medium-duty models; $35 to $80 for light-duty models.

Features and conveniences

Weight. Most portables weigh between 1¾ and 2¼ pounds. With time-consuming tasks, the heavier models may begin to feel leaden. Too light a mixer, though, may lack muscle. A comfortable handle makes weight easier to bear.

Stand mixers are considerably heavier than portables: The light ones weigh in at six pounds or less, the heavy-duty ones at more than 15 pounds. Medium-duty mixers weigh six to 8½ pounds.

Motor. A strong motor can keep the beaters turning through the stickiest dough, a challenge that could burn out a lesser motor. A special Power-boost switch found on some portables often provides the extra power needed.

Speeds. Though many models offer a generous number of speeds or a continuously variable speed, we've found that three well-spaced settings—slow, intermediate, and fast—are all you need. The slower the slow speed, in fact, the better to reduce the inevitable spattering.

For portable mixers, thumbwheel speed controls are more difficult to set than the typical speed switch. Controls located toward the front of the handle allow you to hold the mixer and adjust the speed singlehandedly. Look for a switch that's clearly labeled, located on top of the handle, and that can move sequentially from Off to Slow, Medium, and High.

A Pulse control is available on some stand mixers and works the same way as the Pulse button on food processors—it turns on the machine for as long as you depress the button.

Beaters and bowls. For most chores, beater shape doesn't much matter; for whipping air into foods like whipped cream, however, a wire whisk or beaters with no center post usually work best.

More important to the success of the task for portable models is the number of beaters. Cordless models that have only one beater don't mix food nearly as well as models with two.

Besides the basic beaters, some portables and most stand mixers come with a dough hook or a balloon whisk.

Stand mixers come with bowls made of glass, stainless steel, or plastic.

Cleaning. For portables, beaters with no center post and stainless-steel whisks or wire beaters tend to be the easiest to clean. Stainless-steel beaters are also more corrosion-resistant than the conventional chrome-coated ones. Most beaters and mixing bowls can be washed safely in the dishwasher.

Storage. A portable mixer with its beaters in place should be balanced enough to stand solidly on a countertop. Avoid portable mixers that have a narrow heel rest—they're the least stable.

A plug-in mixer doesn't take much space in a drawer or cupboard. Many portables can be wall-mounted. Some models have clips on the housing to hold the beaters. A cordless model needs room near an outlet for the charging base.

Stand mixers, especially the heavy-duty ones, are bulkier and take up more counter and storage space than a portable model.

Buying advice

If you bake a lot, consider a stand mixer. Although some portable mixers can manage dough, it takes a firm grip to keep the dough hooks from recoiling.

Spending $50 on a mixer isn't necessary if you use it just to mash potatoes once in a while. For occasional use, a conventional plug-in portable will do nicely. Cordless mixers are relatively expensive and many routine tasks leave them wheezing.

Drip coffee-makers

▶ **Ratings on page 138.**

While some coffee devotees boil their brew in a pot or swear by a percolator, the appliance of choice is a drip-style coffee-maker. Since Mr. Coffee pioneered it 20 years ago, the shape of the automatic coffee-maker has changed to the smooth, rounded look initiated by Krups and Braun.

Mr. Coffee still sells more coffee-makers than anyone else. *Black & Decker* and *Hamilton Beach* are also big brands in this market. *Braun* and *Krups* are small upscale brands popular among CONSUMER REPORTS readers. Melitta dominates sales of manual drip coffee-makers.

The choices

Electric. You'll see two electric types in stores—basic machines, which brew only

when you turn them on, and programmable models, which can also be set to begin brewing at a specific time.

Most automatic-drip machines have four parts: a water reservoir, a basket to hold the filter and coffee, a carafe to hold and serve coffee, and a hot plate to keep the carafe's contents warm. Electric elements heat the water and hot plate. To brew a pot of coffee, you pour a measured amount of cold tap water into the reservoir and flip a switch.

Drip models come in various sizes, from single-cup, personal-sized varieties to full-sized units that brew 12 cups. Ten-cup machines are the biggest sellers. Prices range from $20 to $100.

Manual. The simplest manual-drip brewers consist of a plastic cone to hold the paper filter and coffee and a glass carafe. To brew, you pour boiling water over the coffee. Price: $10 to $60.

Features and conveniences

Carafe. The carafes that come with most drip coffee-makers are glass and can be washed in the dishwasher. That's important, because to make good-tasting coffee, the carafe must be squeaky clean. Some carafes have cup markings to help measure water. Some coffee-makers come with a glass-lined thermal carafe. An insulated carafe is more delicate and tougher to keep clean than a regular one.

Reservoir. Look for one with a large, unobstructed opening, to make it easier to fill.

Basket. The basket holds the filter and coffee grounds. One that swings out is handier than one that slides out or sits directly on top of the carafe. It should be easy to remove and insert

Filters. Many units use the basket-style paper filter; others, the cone-style. Filters are typically paper, but permanent filters of metal or plastic are also available.

Controls. On a programmable model, watch out for controls that are crowded together and not well labeled. Since it's easy to forget the coffee-maker is on, a prominent On light is important. Auto shut-off turns off the machine after a certain amount of time, generally two hours.

Most models have drip-stop provision that lets you pour a quick cup before the coffee is completely ready without having coffee dribble onto the warming plate.

Some models have a brew-strength control. Our expert taster noticed little or no difference between coffee brewed at different settings. A simpler, less wasteful way to make a mild brew is to use less grounds.

More useful is a "small cup" switch designed to alter the brewing process when you make only a few cups of coffee. It worked well on our test models, eliminating the need to add a little more coffee per cup when brewing just a few cups.

The tests

To judge drip coffee-makers, an expert taster sips coffee freshly brewed by the machines. We use the same brand of coffee and the same amount of grounds for each cup. Since all the tested machines can make very good coffee, convenience and features figured prominently in our ratings.

Buying advice

A coffee-maker should turn out consistently good-tasting brew. Most do. Good models are also a pleasure to use.

If kitchen counter space is tight, or if you usually want only a cup or two at a time, consider a manual coffee-maker or a four-cup electric machine. A junior electric is no better or cheaper than the full-sized models, just smaller. A manual setup is less convenient but worth considering if you'd like to minimize appliances.

TIPS FOR FRESH BREW

Grinding whole beans just before brewing should make a fresher-tasting pot of coffee. Even if you don't go to such trouble, give yourself a shot at the freshest cup by taking care to store coffee in a sealed, dry, airtight container. Never store opened coffee at room temperature.

If you'll finish the coffee within a week, it's okay to keep it in the refrigerator. If you'll have it around longer, put it in the freezer. (You can grind and use frozen coffee without first defrosting it.) And if you buy coffee beans, patronize a store with lots of turnover in the coffee bins.

Toasters

▶ **Ratings on page 143.**

The mechanics of the pop-up toaster haven't changed much since Toastmaster pioneered the product in 1926. The basic components—spring-loaded carriage, hot wires, and rotary knob or sliding switch to regulate toast color—have been in use for decades.

Eight of 10 toasters sold are made by three companies: Toastmaster, Proctor-Silex, and Black & Decker.

The choices

The biggest difference among models remains capacity: two or four slices. New models have a long, slim profile with a single, elongated slot for two slices. Most four-slice toasters still have four individual slots. In addition, the traditional chrome finish has given way to an all-plastic housing that stays cool to the touch. At least one model mounts under cabinets.

Prices range from around $25 to $50 for two-slice models and $50 to $120 for the four-slicer models.

Features and conveniences

Wide slots. Some models advertised as "wide slot" have an opening no wider than the standard three-quarters of an inch. We've found the opening has to be at least 1⅛ inches wide for English muffins and other thick items to fit.

Controls. Most models are mechanical. A push-down lever lowers the bread; raising the lever interrupts toasting. When the toast is done, it pops up automatically.

Other designs include an electronic touchpad or a sliding lever to raise and lower the bread.

A Keep-warm setting lets the toast bask in the toaster's residual heat. A more so-phisticated version of that feature is the Warm-up setting, which cycles the power on and off for up to four minutes.

A well-designed four-slicer should have separate controls for each pair of slots. That way you won't heat all four elements to toast one; you can vary doneness, too.

Self-centering. This mechanism keeps the slices equidistant from the heat as a way to ensure even toasting. We didn't find any correlation between this feature and toasting performance.

Crumb cleanup. A removable crumb tray makes cleanup a snap. Most toasters provide a hinged tray on the bottom of the toaster through which you can shake out crumbs. Avoid models that need shaking upside down to remove crumbs.

Plastic housing. An insulated plastic exterior doesn't get as hot as a chrome one.

The tests

We look for toasters that make predictably, uniformly browned toast. We make toast one slice at a time, in full batches, and in consecutive batches. We also note conveniences.

Buying advice

If you eat a lot of toast, buy a toaster, not a toaster oven—they don't work quite as well as toasters. In general, we've found two-slice models work better than four-slicers, especially with thick slices of bread. If your taste runs to toasted bagels or thick hand-cut slices from crusty loaves, look for a toaster with slots that are at least 1⅛ inches wide.

If you need the capacity of a four-slice model, look for one with separate controls for each pair of slots.

Toaster ovens & broilers

▶ Ratings on page 145.

The toaster oven and its more popular cousin, the toaster-oven broiler, don't make better toast than a toaster—many make it worse. The particular strength of these little ovens is their ability to perform a variety of small cooking tasks: heating rolls and leftovers, making grilled sandwiches, baking potatoes. Unlike a microwave oven, they brown foods readily.

As toasters, the devices are lethargic, tending to leave bread with faint striping on the bottom. Of course, a toaster oven has some advantages over a regular toaster. You can monitor the color of the toast through the glass window. And it's easy to fit bulky items like bagels and English muffins, though they often need to go through two cycles to brown adequately.

Toaster ovens and oven-broilers are not precision cookers. Delicate foods, like fish, can become overdone easily. But you can usually quickly overcome a toaster oven's quirks and figure out the best time and temperature settings for a given task.

Broiler models, the most popular type, range from $40 to $150; plain toaster ovens go for $30 to $50. Spending more usually gets you a larger oven and such conveniences as a slide-out crumb tray and removeable door.

Black & Decker, Proctor-Silex, and Toastmaster account for 90 percent of sales.

The choices

Type. Toaster ovens heat food from above and below. In addition, a toaster-oven broiler can usually switch on its top element alone. Both types offer a temperature range similar to that of a conventional range oven: 200° to about 500°.

Size. Most toaster ovens take up only a little more counter space than a standard four-slice toaster. But models about the size of a small microwave oven are also available. Regular-sized models are big enough to hold two to four slices of bread. Large models are big enough to hold six slices of bread.

Features and conveniences

Controls. All have selections for Bake or Toast and let you set the temperature and toast color. Broilers have a seperate Broil setting. Recommended temperature settings printed on the control panel are handy. All have an On light to signal the oven is on. Also worthwhile: automatic shutoff when the door opens. Most resume when you shut the door. Some make you restart the oven—a safeguard in case you remove the food and forget to shut off the power.

A toast-ready bell is a nicety. A Keep-warm setting and a Defrost setting are fairly common, although setting the oven at a low temperature does the same job.

Some models have a top-brown setting for melting cheese or other toppings—better than the Broil setting because it usually shuts off on cue, so food won't burn as easily.

Toasting rack. It should be removable and should advance partway out when the door opens. Its height should be adjustable so you can move it closer to the heating element for broiling, farther from it for baking.

Cleanup. A removable rack and detachable door make cleaning easier. A removable crumb tray is easier to clean than a hinged one.

Don't be overly impressed by models with a "continuous clean" interior. Such an interior supposedly absorbs and disperses food spatters. In reality, it mostly masks the buildup and can't withstand scouring.

Pan and grid. A baking pan made of plated or porcelain-coated steel is sturdier than an aluminum pan. Models that lack the grid have you put food on the toast rack and juice drops onto the pan. That's messy and inconvenient.

The tests

We test these machines as toasters, evaluating the consistency and evenness of toasting. We test the ovens and broilers by broiling burgers to see how close each could come to turning out burgers that were well done on the inside and brown but not charred on the outside. To test baking performance, we bake potatoes and a packaged cake mix, which some models scorched.

We also note conveniences, space effi-ciency (interior space versus the overall size on countertop), and capacity.

Buying advice

Toaster ovens and oven-broilers handle a range of simple chores with reasonable com-petence. They're handy for quick warm ups, especially when you want crispness rather than the steamed texture of microwave cooking. They brown bread almost as well as a pop-up toaster, and they can easily ac-commodate bagels and English muffins.

The broiler models are more versatile than the plain ovens, and some cost only a little more. Performance differences among models in our tests tended to be slight, so your choice comes down to price, size, and convenience.

Look for features that make operation safe and cleaning easy. Make sure the mod-el is roomy enough—some can't hold more than two slices of toast or three burgers.

Juicers & juice extractors

▶ **Ratings on page 140.**

If you like the taste of fresh juice or find it more palatable than a plate of produce, a juicer or juice-extractor can fill the bill.

Citrus juicers are mechanized versions of the citrus reamer—you halve the fruit and press it to a moving reamer. Most citrus juicers are made by companies well known in the world of small appliances—Braun, Oster, and Black & Decker among them.

Juice extractors get juice out of various fruits and vegetables by pulping them. You'll find familiar appliance names here, too, along with names like *The Juiceman*, made famous by infomercials.

The choices

An extractor for vegetables and fruits costs anywhere from $30 to $300; a citrus juicer, usualy ranges from $10 to $25.

Citrus juicers. They're designed for or-anges, grapefruit, lemons, and limes. The reamer is typically set in the center of a strainer atop a detachable pitcher and mo-torized reamer. Citrus juicers work straight-forwardly. The juice flows from the reamer to a pitcher, leaving the seeds and most of the pulp behind in the strainer.

Most models are priced at $30 or less.

Extractors. These devices get the juice out of tomatoes, grapes, celery, peaches, and other produce. To use them, you must peel citrus fruits, remove hard pits from peaches and plums, destem grapes, and cut everything into pieces small enough to fit into a feed tube, much like a food pro-cessor's, in the top of the extractor. Food travels from the tube to a whirling cutter disk. Then the tiny pieces are spun to separate juice from pulp. The juice flows through a strainer to a spout, where it's ready to drink.

Extractors with a separate cutter and strainer extract the most juice. Models that combine cutter and strainer collect the pulp in a separate bin. These "pulp ejector" models are easier to clean but tend to extract less juice.

Juice extractors range in price from $50 to almost $300.

Citrus-juicer features

Capacity. A citrus juicer's capacity is limited by the size of its juice container or how much pulp it can collect. Capacities of the models we tested range from one to three cups in our tests.

Convenience. Controls are typically limited to just an On/off switch. Some models have a reamer that reverses direction with changes in hand pressure. That makes a juicer harder to use. Some citrus juicers come with a container to collect the juice; others have a spout under which you place a glass. Both methods work just as well, we've found.

Cleanup. Citrus juicers are a breeze to clean. They have few parts and few corners and crevices to collect pulp.

Extractor features

Speeds. Most extractors have one speed. Top-of-the-line models may boast two: Low for soft fruits such as grapes and tomatoes and High for hard foods such as apples and carrots.

Housing. Most models have plastic containers. Containers on the most expensive models are stainless steel.

Feed tube. Look for a wide feed tube. The wider the tube, the less time you spend cutting the food into small chunks.

Controls. A simple On/off switch is best. Avoid designs that make you rotate the housing to turn on the unit.

Spout. Check the height to make sure it accommodates containers you use.

Citrus attachment. A few extractors come with an attachment to juice citrus. As an extra-cost option, it's $30 to $40.

Pulp collection. Look for an extractor that allows you to see how much pulp has accumulated.

Cleanup. A pulp ejector, found on most models, directs most of the pulp to an easily emptied receptacle. A pulp container lined with a plastic bag eases the chore. In our tests, a dishwasher wasn't always able to get parts clean. Models with a detachable, one-piece top were the easiest to wash by hand.

The tests

To test juice extractors, we make a lot of juice from apples, carrots, and grapes. We observe how much juice and pulp each model produces. We also make juice from tomatoes, oranges, pineapples, celery, broccoli, and spinach to see if it's possible. And we note how easy each appliance is to operate and clean.

Buying advice

To squeeze fresh orange juice for breakfast or fresh limes for margaritas, look to a citrus juicer. Citrus juicers are modestly priced, simple to use, and relatively easy to clean. Cheaper still: a manual juicer—the old-fashioned reamer or squeezer.

If you favor carrot juice or exotic fruit cocktails, you'll want a juice extractor. Look for a model with the fewest components, nooks, and crannies—they're potential traps for pulp. An attachment to make citrus juice is a nice option. In our tests, price had little to do with performance: Models priced at less than $100 performed better than the $300 models. For the best price, look for special sales.

Garbage disposers
▶ Ratings on page 147.

A garbage disposer offers a tidy way (if occasionally noisy) to keep food waste out of the garbage cans. It's also good for the environment, since ground-up scraps flow directly from the sink to a sewage-treatment plant or septic system, where they break down more rapidly than they would in a landfill. And, despite the myth, a disposer uses relatively little water.

Out of the 20-odd brands on store shelves, *In-Sink Erator* and *Sears* are by far the biggest sellers. Despite the wide selection of brands, only five companies actually manufacture disposers.

The choices

Disposers need a fast-flowing faucet to work. Water and waste flow into a grinding chamber where metal impellers mounted on a fast-moving turntable grind food against a stationary metal ring. The ground-up waste flows through holes in the turntable and down the drain. Disposers work best with cold water, which solidifies grease, making it easy to carry away.

Disposers come in two varieties: batch-feed and continuous feed. There is virtually no difference in how they grind and dispose of waste. But they differ in other ways, including availability: Batch-feed disposers may be difficult to find outside of the Northeast.

Batch-feed disposers. With this type, you load the chamber one batch at a time. To activate the unit you push down or twist a stopper. You may have to load the chamber and activate the stopper more than once to handle a meal's typical waste.

Batch-feed models are less prone to hazards than continuous-feed models, since you can't turn them on unless the stopper is

in. The stopper also acts as a muffler, making operation a little quieter. Some stoppers can be bumped out of place by bones and other hard food; to keep the disposer going, you may have to hold the stopper down manually.

A batch-feeder is generally more expensive but cheaper to install than its continuous-feed cousin. Price: $20 to $250.

Continuous-feed disposers. Most people buy this type. A continuous-feed model is activated before loading, using a switch that's usually mounted on the wall close to the sink. You feed waste continuously through the drain opening—a special convenience with large quantities of food waste. Continous-feed models are generally less expensive than the batch-feeders but require installation of a separate switch. Price: $40 to $350.

Features and conveniences

Power. Batch-feeder models come in three motor-sizes: $\frac{1}{2}$, $\frac{3}{4}$, and 1 horsepower. Continous-feeders offer more choices—$\frac{1}{3}$, $\frac{1}{2}$, $\frac{3}{4}$, and 1 hp. The $\frac{1}{2}$-hp size is the one most sold. More power is usually more expensive, but the expense may not be worthwhile—we found little correlation between power and performance in our tests.

Antijamming devices. Jams in disposers are infrequent; when they occur, it's usually because a hard object—a bone or raw potato—gets stuck. A typical disposer has an overload switch to shut off the electric motor when a jam occurs.

Some models boast auto-reverse features to undo a jam automatically; none proved effective in our tests. Other models provide a wrench to unjam the disposer's driveshaft. You can dislodge most impediments in a disposer by poking a broom handle down the sink.

Splash guards. In our tests, a number of disposers of both types frequently backed up and flooded the sink, creating a mess. But only continuous-feed disposers splash water and eject food into the sink during disposal. The fixed or removable rubber splash guards that fit into the sink opening don't always solve the problem effectively we found.

Batch-feed models don't eject food, since the drain is covered during disposal. If the stopper is bumped out of place by bones, you have to hold the stopper down manually to keep the machine going.

Corrosion resistance. Disposers are made of corrosion-resistant materials. Nickel and chrome are the most effective materials but also the most expensive.

BEST PICKS IN GARBAGE BAGS

Just about any bag will hold light-weight trash. If you need a bag for heavier stuff, we recommend bags that excelled in strength: *Hefty Steel-Sak* (kitchen); *Glad* drawstring, *Hefty Steel-Sak*, or *A&P* (trash); *Hefty Cinch Sak*, *Glad* drawstring, or *Safeway* (lawn and leaf). For puncture resistance, we recommend *Hefty Steel-Sak* or *Sears Best Extra Heavy Duty* (kitchen); *Lady Lee* or *Hefty Cinch Sak* (trash); *Lady Lee* or *Hefty* twist tie (lawn and leaf). For tear resistance, we recommend *Seventh Generation* (kitchen); *Glad* handle tie (trash); *Safeway* (lawn and leaf.)

Our tests demonstrated that you can't judge a bag by its price or name. Some bags that did well overall didn't do well in every test. The quality of particular brands wasn't always consistent from size to size. And some individual products performed inconsistently from bag to bag.

Some models have a corrosion shield, a lining of polymer plastic over the metal drain chamber.

Dishwasher compatibility. Most disposers are designed to hook up to a dishwasher—not just the sink. The dishwasher's discharge tube connects to an opening in the disposer. However, if the discharge tube clogs and the disposer is poorly designed, waste can be diverted the wrong way—from disposer into dishwasher. We found two machines—the *Thermador TH800* and the *Sinkmaster 450*—to be unsuitable for connection to a dishwasher. (Dishwasher owners with a double-bowl sink can avoid the problem by connecting the dishwasher's drain line to the drain on the sink without the disposer.)

The tests

To measure the fineness of a disposer's grind, we feed every model beef ribs, carrots, celery, and lettuce. To test noise, we grind bones, vegetables, fruits, napkins, wax paper, and tea bags. To see how well the machines deal with taboo objects—seafood shells, artichoke leaves, corn husks—that are inadvertently dumped in the sink, we feed the disposers corn husks and metal spoons.

Buying advice

The more powerful the disposer, the more it will weigh and the higher the price. But our tests show that there's no link between power and performance. You can pay as little as $40 for a low-power, continuous-feed disposer that works very well.

If you contend with large amounts of waste, consider a continuous-feed disposer. They're more convenient, and generally less expensive than a batch-feed model and they're more widely available. The design of a batch feed disposer has a small edge in safety, however, a plus for household as with small children.

A typical professional installation can cost between $100 and $200 (replacement installations cost less) and is probably best left to a professional.

Disposers are not recommended for homes with cesspools. They may also be trouble in a house with a septic system. To find out whether a septic system is large enough to accommodate a garbage disposer, call your local Public Health Office.

Trash compactors

A compactor may save you some money if your community bases its garbage-hauling fees on the number of bags you produce. A compactor can reduce a bag of trash to less than half of its original volume.

Per bag billing may serve to renew interest in the trash compactor, sales of which have been declining for some years. *Sears Kenmore* is the clear market leader, accounting for 40 percent of all sales. Other key brands are *Whirlpool, General Electric,* and *KitchenAid.* Trash compactors range in price from $325 to $575.

The choices

The operation of a trash compactor is straightforward: Typically, you pull out a door, load your garbage in a bin lined with a bag designed to fit the bin, close the door, and turn a key lock. An electric motor then drives a steel ram downward to crush the trash. The bag is usually secured by retainer buttons on the bin. To remove the bag, you release a latch and (on most) you lift the bag out of a caddy.

Compactors come in three widths: 12, 15, and 18 inches. Regardless of width, they all have about the same capacity: 1½ cubic feet. Motors may be ⅓ or ½ horsepower. The more powerful motors showed no advantage in our tests.

Features and convenience

Compaction. The compactors we tested took about 20 to 60 seconds to crush their loads to 20 percent of their original volume. Some models have a special cycle

that compacts even more volume when left on overnight. You can get the same result with any compactor by turning off the motor with the ram in its lowest position.

Safety. Safety problems with home trash compactors are a rarity. An interlock keeps the compactor door from opening during a cycle; a key lock keeps children from starting the unit.

Loading/unloading. Most compactors have a handled sling to easily remove bags and retainer buttons to easily hold up the bags during compaction.

Bags. Special bags from compactor manufacturers are thicker and more expensive than standard trash bags. Most compactors can use generic trash-compactor bags sold in the supermarket in addition to the manufacturer's.

Buying advice

All of the compactors in our tests did their job with little fuss except for the *General Electric Monogram ZCG3300TWW,* which was plagued with serious design flaws. Apart from that model, differences among the test models were small, amounting mostly to price, size, and features.

While compressed trash may reduce landfill needs slightly, the home trash compactor offers few or no environmental advantages. For many households, buying one offers little except the opportunity to carry fewer, if heavier, loads of trash to the curb or the dump. However, for those with pay-as-you-throw garbage billing, a compactor should pay for itself quickly.

RATINGS FOOD PROCESSORS

▶ **See report, page 121.** Last time rated in Consumer Reports: August 1992.

Brand-name recommendations: The top-rated model, the *Braun UK11*, $104, boasts generous capacity (11½ cups); except for being noisy, it got high marks in most tasks. The *Panasonic MK-5070*, $100, was nearly as good and much quieter.

For the typical food processor, expect: ■ Transparent plastic bowl with a handle. ■ S-shaped metal chopping blade. ■ Slicing/shredding disk. ■ Feed tube with pusher to insert food. ■ Safety interlock that prevents operation unless lid and bowl are latched. ■ On/off switch and Pulse. ■ Single speed. ■ Blades to rust if left soaking. ■ Good or better performance at whipping cream, puréeing carrots, grinding peanuts and beef cubes, chopping carrots and prosciutto, slicing mushrooms, shredding zucchini and cabbage. **A choice you'll have to make:** ■ Full-sized or compact.

Notes on the table: Closely ranked models generally differed little in quality. **Price** is the mfr.'s suggested retail. **Size** measures capacity in cups of dry food, with bowl filled to rim and S-shaped chopping blade in place. **Power** is how well they did with heavy-duty tasks. **Blending** is tested with soup; grinding with graham crackers; slicing with carrots. Ⓢ indicates tested model has been replaced by successor model; according to the mfr., the performance of new model should be similar to the tested model but features may vary. Not tested. Ⓓ indicates model discontinued or replacement not similar.

RATINGS OVERVIEW

Within types, listed in order of performance

Better ◀———▶ Worse
⊖ ⊖ ○ ◔ ●

Brand and model	Price	Size	Power	Ease of use	Blend	Grind	Slice
FULL-SIZED MODELS							
Braun Multipractic UK11	$104	11½	○	⊖	○	○	◔
Panasonic Kitchen Wizard MK-5070	100	8¼	○	⊖	○	⊖	⊖
Cuisinart DLC-7 FPC	350	12¼	⊖	◔	●	◔	⊖
Cuisinart Custom 11 DLC-8M	199	10	⊖	◔	◔	○	⊖
Regal La Machine II K588GY	79	9½	○	⊖	●	○	⊖
Waring Professional PFP15	350	7¾	⊖	◔	○	○	○
Moulinex 305 Ⓓ	80	6½	◔	⊖	○	○	⊖
Braun Multipractic MC100	103	6½	◔	⊖	◔	◔	○
Braun Multipractic MC200	116	6½	◔	○	◔	○	⊖
Regal La Machine I K813GY	69	6½	◔	○	●	◔	○
Sunbeam Oskar 3000 14201	90	5½	◔	◔	⊖	⊖	⊖

Brand and model	Price	Size	Power	Ease of use	Blend	Grind	Slice
COMPACT MODELS							
Cuisinart Little Pro Plus	$100	4¼	—	⊖	○	⊖	⊖
Black & Decker Shortcut CFP10 Ⓓ	38	4¼	—	⊖	⊖	⊖	⊖
Black & Decker Handy Shortcut HMP30	39	2¼	—	⊖	○	⊖	⊖
Sunbeam Oskar 14181 Ⓢ	35	2¾	—	●	⊖	⊖	⊖

RATINGS DETAILS Models listed alphabetically

Black & Decker Handy Shortcut HMP30	Controls well marked, easy to use. All blades can be stored in bowl. Very narrow feed tube.
Black & Decker Shortcut CFP10 Ⓓ	Controls well marked, easy to use. Slicing/shredding disk easy and safe to mount and remove. No leaks with 1½ cups of liquid. All blades can be stored in bowl.
Braun Multipractic MC100	Blade stops instantly when switched off. Cord storage. Blade inserts pose slightly greater danger of cutting fingers. Hole on blade hub can admit foods, which can create a mess.
Braun Multipractic MC200	Blade stops instantly when switched off. Cord storage. Blade inserts pose slightly greater danger of cutting fingers. Hole on blade hub can admit foods, which can create a mess.
Braun Multipractic UK11	Has reversible thin/thick disks for slicing or shredding, disk for grating cheese, and disk for french fries. No leaks with 4 cups of liquid. Blade stops instantly when switched off. Cord storage.
Cuisinart Custom 11 DLC-8M	Controls well marked, easy to use. Good-sized feed tube but hard to use and clean. All blades can be stored in bowl. Liquids leaked.
Cuisinart DLC-7 FPC	Controls well marked, easy to use. Good-sized feed tube but hard to use and clean. All blades can be stored in bowl.
Cuisinart Little Pro Plus	Controls well marked, easy to use. Slicing/shredding disk easy and safe to mount and remove. Comes with regular lid and chute for slicing or shredding. All blades can be stored in bowl.
Moulinex 305 Ⓓ	Controls well marked, easy to use. All blades can be stored in bowl. Place to store cord. Blade inserts pose slightly greater danger of cut fingers.
Panasonic Kitchen Wizard MK-5070	Controls well marked, easy to use. No leaks even with 3⅓ cups of liquid. Blade inserts pose slightly greater danger of cutting fingers.
Regal La Machine I K813GY	Blade stops instantly when switched off. All blades can be stored in bowl. Liquids leaked. Blade inserts pose slightly greater danger of cutting fingers.
Regal La Machine II K588GY	Slicing/shredding disk easy and safe to mount and remove. Blade stops instantly when switched off. All blades can be stored in bowl. Cord storage.
Sunbeam Oskar 14181 Ⓢ 4817, $30	Hard-to-use chute instead of feed tube. Liquids leaked.

Ratings continued ▶

Ratings continued

Sunbeam Oskar 3000 14201 Ⓢ 4818, $90	Coarse shredding disk worked well. Cord storage. Poorly located On/off/pulse switch. Liquids leaked.
Waring Professional PFP15	Liquids leaked.

RATINGS | STAND MIXERS

▶ **See report, page 124.** Last time rated in Consumer Reports: November 1994.

Brand-name recommendations: If you need a stand mixer, choose the heavy-duty *KitchenAid K45SS,* $195, or the *KitchenAid KSM90,* $215. If you don't make much bread or cookie dough, consider the *Sunbeam 01401/2355,* $95, or *Oster 5600-20A/2381,* $110.

For the typical stand mixer, expect: ■ Excellent performance at whipping cream. ■ At least 1 beater and dough hook ■ 3 or more speeds. ■ Tilting head that locks in Down position. ■ For heavy-duty mixers: stainless-steel bowl that holds at least 4 qts.; wire whisk; ability to knead enough bread dough for two loaves; stationary bowl, moves as bowl spins; power take-off for optional attachments. ■ For medium-duty mixers: a 4-qt. stainless-steel or glass bowl plus a smaller bowl; bowl that rotates as beaters spin; 2 beaters that aren't interchangeable; ability to knead enough bread dough for one loaf; continuously variable speeds, and large, easy-to-use speed dial with mixing guide. ■ For light-duty mixers: body detaches and can be used like a hand mixer.

Notes on the table: Price is the estimated average based on a national survey. For **mixing**, we used cookie dough; for **mashing**, potatoes; for **kneading**, bread dough.

Within type, listed in order of performance and convenience

E VG G F P
⊜ ⊖ ○ ◖ ●

Brand and model	Price	Overall score					Performance			Comments
		P	F	G	VG	E	MIX	MASH	KNEAD	
HEAVY-DUTY MIXERS										
KitchenAid K45SS	$195						◖	⊖	◖	Little clearance to add ingredients.
KitchenAid KSM90	215						◖	⊖	◖	Little clearance to add ingredients. Handle on bowl.
KitchenAid K5SS	260						◖	⊖	◖	Little clearance to add ingredients. Handle on bowl. 5-qt. bowl.
Kenwood KM-210 (Rival Select)	202						◖	⊖	◖	Noisy. Beater hard to replace. Little clearance to add ingredients. Pulse, cont. variable speeds. 5-qt. bowl.
Kenwood KM220 (Rival Select)	254						◖	⊖	◖	Noisy. Beater hard to replace. Little clearance to add ingredients. Cont. variable speeds. 5-qt. bowl.

Brand and model	Price	Overall score					Performance			Comments
		P	F	G	VG	E	MIX	MASH	KNEAD	

MEDIUM-DUTY MIXERS

Brand and model	Price	Overall score	MIX	MASH	KNEAD	Comments
Sunbeam 01401/2355	$95	▬▬▬ (G)	◐	●	○	Glass bowls.
Oster 5600-20A/2381	110	▬▬▬ (G)	○	●	○	Stainless-steel bowls.
Sunbeam 2358	125	▬▬ (F–G)	○	●	◐	Quiet. Beaters hard to remove. Detachable body. Stainless-steel bowls.
Sunbeam 2360	114	▬▬ (F–G)	○	●	◐	Beaters hard to remove. Detachable body. Glass-bowls.

LIGHT-DUTY MIXERS

Brand and model	Price	Overall score	MIX	MASH	KNEAD	Comments
Krups 747	100	▬▬ (F)	●	◐	○	Good at whipping cream. Hard to set up. Beater-socket area hard to clean. Pulse setting, plastic bowl.
Hamilton Beach 64500	30	▬ (P–F)	●	◐	—	Fair at whipping cream. Noisy. Power-burst. Glass bowl.
Waring HM201	25	▬ (P)	●	◐	—	Poor at whipping cream. Noisy. Inconvenient speed controls. Small glass bowl. Whisk.

Buying the right food-fixer

	Standard blender	Hand-held blender	Portable mixer	Stand mixer	Food processor	Food chopper
Puréeing vegetables	✔					✔
Mixing frozen drinks	✔					
Mixing frozen shakes	✔	✔				
Whipping cream			✔	✔		
Mashing potatoes			✔	✔		
Mixing cake batter			✔	✔		
Mixing pie crust				✔	✔	
Mixing cookie dough				✔	✔	
Crumbling crackers					✔	
Shredding and slicing vegetables					✔	
Chopping vegetables					✔	✔
Grating Parmesan	✔				✔	✔

RATINGS DRIP COFFEE-MAKERS

▶ **See report, page 125.** Last time rated in Consumer Reports: October 1994.

Brand-name recommendations: All the test machines make a very good pot of coffee. The difference lies in their convenience and features. *Mr. Coffee* models top the list of basic machines. The two highest-rated programmable machines—the *Krups Coffee Time Plus 136*, 100, and *Braun FlavorSelect KF187, $109*—offer an unequaled array of features.

For the typical coffee-maker, expect: ■ Very good brewing performance. ■ A full carafe to brew in 8½ to 15 min. ■ A glass carafe with a claimed capacity of 10 or 12 cups (actual capacity may be up to 2 cups less). ■ A drip-stop feature, which lets you pour before brewing has stopped and minimizes drips. ■ A plastic housing. ■ A swing-out holder for basket or cone-shaped filters—more convenient than the pull-out type. ■ A warming plate with a nonstick coating. ■ For programmable models, a digital clock, automatic shut-off, and brewing that can be set up in advance.

Notes on the table: Price is the estimated average, based on a national survey. An * indicates the price we paid.

Within types, listed in order of convenience and features

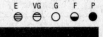

Brand and model	Price	Overall score					Ease of use	Comments
		P	F	G	VG	E		

BASIC MODELS

Brand and model	Price	Overall score	Ease of use	Comments
Mr. Coffee Accel PR12A	$27	▬▬▬▬	⊖	Filter basket has drip-stop on removable insert. Auto shut-off.
Mr. Coffee Accel PR16	25	▬▬▬▬	⊖	Filter basket has drip-stop on removable insert.
Braun FlavorSelect KF140	60	▬▬▬	⊖	Carafe has rim guard. Brew relatively hot.
Krups ProCafe Plus 201	50	▬▬▬▬	⊖	Carafe dribbled a lot when filling reservoir. Brew relatively hot.
Mr. Coffee BL110	22	▬▬▬	⊖	Pull-out filter basket. Brew relatively hot.
Proctor-Silex Morning Maker 42401	35	▬▬▬	⊖	Auto shut-off. Carafe dribbled a lot when filling reservoir. Warming plate uncoated.
Proctor-Silex Morning Maker 42301	20	▬▬	⊖	Warming plate uncoated.
Braun Aromaster KF400	35	▬▬▬	○	Carafe dribbled a lot when filling reservoir.
Krups Brewmaster Plus 140	40	▬▬▬	⊖	No drip-stop. Carafe has very comfortable handle, dribbled a lot when filling reservoir. Filter basket must be removed to pour coffee.

Brand and model	Price	Overall score (P F G VG E)	Ease of use	Comments
Black & Decker DCM901	$22	▬▬ (F–G)	○	Uncomfortable handle. Pull-out filter basket. Brew relatively hot.
Bunn NHB	40	▬▬▬ (G)	○	Porcelain-coated warming plate. Pull-out filter basket. Very comfortable handle. No drip-stop. Brew relatively hot.
Melitta Aroma Brew ACM-10S	*30	▬▬ (F)	○	Uncomfortable handle. No On light. Brew relatively cool.
Black & Decker DCM900WH	20	▬ (P–F)	◑	Pull-out filter basket. Uncomfortable handle. Reservoir hard to fill. No On light, drip-stop. Brew relatively hot.
West Bend Quik Drip 56660	35	▬ (P–F)	◑	Pull-out filter basket. Uncomfortable handle. Brew relatively hot.
Betty Crocker BC-1732	19	▬ (P)	◑	Reservoir inconvenient to fill. Carafe dribbled a lot when filling reservoir. Warming plate uncoated. Brew relatively cool.

PROGRAMMABLE MODELS

Brand and model	Price	Overall score (P F G VG E)	Ease of use	Comments
Krups Coffee Time Plus 136	100	▬▬▬▬ (VG)	◑	Carafe dribbled a lot. Filter basket has removable inserts with drip-stop. Brew relatively hot.
Braun FlavorSelect KF187	109	▬▬▬ (G)	◑	Metal filter. Carafe has rim guard. Beeps when coffee ready. Warming-plate temp. adjustable. Brew relatively hot.
Mr. Coffee Accel PRX20	50	▬▬▬ (G)	◑	Metal filter. Filter basket has removable insert. Brew relatively hot.
Betty Crocker BC-1740	35	▬▬▬ (G)	◑	Carafe dribbled a lot when filling reservoir. Has drip-stop on removable insert. Brew relatively hot.
Proctor-Silex A8737G or A8737T	40	▬▬▬▬ (VG)	◑	Metal filter. Easy to program. Dim On light. Brew relatively hot.
Black & Decker Spacemaker SDC3AG	50	▬▬▬ (G)	◑	Under-cabinet installation option. Reservoir can be filled at sink. Keep-warm coutdown timer. Uncomfortable handle. Carafe lacks markings on both sides. Pull-out filter basket. No drip-stop.
Black & Decker DCM903	32	▬▬ (F)	○	Easy to program. Uncomfortable carafe handle. Pull-out filter basket.
Panasonic Premiere Brew NC-F12MP	140	▬▬ (F–G)	○	Comes with water filter. Lid falls off during pouring. Beeps when coffee is ready. Brew relatively hot.
West Bend Quik Drip 56650	35	▬▬ (F)	◑	Keep-warm countdown timer. Pull-out filter basket. Uncomfortable carafe handle. Reservoir hard to fill.
Regal Kitchen Pro K7631BK	80	▬▬ (F)	◑	Plastic mesh filter. Keep-warm countdown timer. Reservoir difficult to see through. Uncomfortable carafe handle. Clock-timer hard to operate. Pull-out filter basket doesn't stand upright. Brew relatively hot.
Farberware L4260	50	▬▬ (F)	◑	Plastic mesh filter. Reservoir awkward to fill. Carafe dribbled a lot when filling reservoir.

RATINGS | JUICE EXTRACTORS

▶ **See report, page 129.** Last time rated in Consumer Reports: December 1992.

Brand-name recommendations: Two juice extractors stood out for quality and price: the *Panasonic MJ-65PR*, $80, and the *Sanyo SJ3020*, about $70.

For the typical juice extractor, expect: ■ 2- to 5½-cup capacity. ■ Centrifugal operation with combined cutter and strainer and separate bin to collect pulp. ■ Single speed. ■ Safety interlock that prevents operation without lid.

Notes on the table: Except where separated by a bold rule, closely ranked models differed little in quality. Bracketed models, judged about equal in quality, are listed alphabetically. **Price** is the mfr.'s suggested retail. Ⓢ indicates tested model has been replaced by successor model; according to the mfr., the performance of new model should be similar to the tested model but features may vary. Not tested. Ⓓ indicates model discontinued or replacement not similar.

RATINGS OVERVIEW — Within types, listed in order of performance

E ⊖ VG ⊖ G ○ F ◔ P ●

Brand and model	Price	Extraction (TOTAL)	Extraction (JUICE)	Capacity	Convenience	Cleaning
JUICE EXTRACTORS						
Panasonic MJ-65PR, **A BEST BUY**	$80	⊖	⊖	⊖	⊖	⊖
Sanyo SJ3020, **A BEST BUY**	70	⊖	⊖	○	⊖	○
Acme Supreme Juicerator 5001	206	⊖	⊖	⊖	◔	◔
Omega 1000	234	⊖	⊖	⊖	◔	◔
Waring JE504-1	77	○	⊖	⊖	◔	⊖
Braun MP80	75	○	◔	○	○	◔
Cuisinart JE-4	80	○	○	⊖	◔	○
Hamilton Beach 395W	53	○	◔	○	◔	⊖
Juiceman II by Trillium	150	●	◔	⊖	○	⊖
Krups VitaMight 294	40	○	◔	○	●	◔
Moulinex Deluxe 753 Ⓓ	69	○	○	○	○	○
Oster 323-08 Ⓢ	55	●	◔	⊖	○	○
Tefal Juice Master 8310 Ⓓ	60	○	◔	○	◔	◔

RATINGS DETAILS — Models listed alphabetically

Acme Supreme Juicerator 5001	Separate cutter and strainer that collects pulp. Quieter than most. No safety interlock. Disposable filters available. Many parts to clean.
Braun MP80	Separate pulp container.

Cuisinart JE-4	Citrus-juicer attachment. Small feed tube. Fragile clips hold upper housing.
Hamilton Beach 395W	Small feed tube. No safety interlock. Spout too low for 4¾-in.-high glass.
Kenwood JE-600	Spatters. 2 speeds.
Krups VitaMight 294	Small feed tube. Hard to clean lid switch.
Moulinex Deluxe 753 Ⓓ	Separate pulp container.
Omega 1000	Separate cutter and strainer that collects pulp. Quieter than most. Spatters. No safety interlock. Disposable filters available. Many parts to clean.
Oster 323-08 Ⓢ 3161, $110	Separate pulp container. Spatters. No safety interlock. 2 speeds.
Panasonic MJ-65PR, **A BEST BUY**	No safety interlock.
Sanyo SJ3020, **A BEST BUY**	No safety interlock. Spout too low for 4¾-in.-high glass.
Tefal 8310 Ⓓ	Citrus-juicer attachment.
Trillium Juiceman II	Separate pulp container. Hard-to-clean On/off switch. Glass juice container.
Waring JE504-1	Small feed tube. No safety interlock.

RATINGS | BREADMAKERS

▶ **See report, page 119.** Last time rated in Consumer Reports: December 1993.

See report, page 119.

Brand-name recommendations: All models made very good bread. Those in the top half of each size category would be a bit easier to live with.

For the typical breadmaker, expect: ■ Very good bread quality. ■ LED or LCD cycle-time display. ■ Delay-start timer. ■ Automatic dough cycle. ■ Adjustment to vary crust color. ■ At least 1 complete cycle that takes no more than 3¼ hr.

Notes on the table: Price is the mfr.'s suggested retail. Ⓢ indicates tested model has been replaced by successor model; according to the mfr. the performance of new model should be similar to the tested model but features may vary. Ⓓ indicates model discontinued or replacement not similar

Within types, listed in order of overall performance

Better ◀——▶ Worse
⊖ ⊖ ○ ◗ ●

Brand and model	Price	Overall score					Use	Clean-ing	Loaf shape	Comments
		P	F	G	VG	E				

REGULAR-LOAF MODELS

Brand and model	Price	Overall score					Use	Clean-ing	Loaf shape	Comments
Trillium Breadman TR-500	$199						⊖	⊖	☐	French-bread cycle. Mix-in signal. Keeps bread warm.
Zojirushi Home Bakery BBCC-S15	349						○	⊖	☐	French bread, cake, jam, custom cycles. Mix-in signal. Complicated Delay-start timer. Cools bread.

Ratings continued ▶

Ratings continued

Brand and model	Price	Overall score					Use	Cleaning	Loaf shape	Comments
		P	F	G	VG	E				

REGULAR-LOAF MODELS *continued*

Brand and model	Price	Overall score	Use	Cleaning	Loaf shape	Comments
Regal Kitchen Pro K6773	$159		⊖	⊖	☐	French- & sweet-bread cycles. Keeps bread warm.
Mister Loaf Home Bakery HB-215 Ⓓ	299		⊖	⊖	☐	French- & sweet-bread cycles. Bread sticks to paddle. Keeps bread warm.
Hitachi Home Bakery Breadmaster HB-B301 Ⓓ	399		⊖	⊖	☐	Cake, jam cycles. Mix-in signal. Loaves can be hard to release. Keeps bread warm.
Hitachi Home Bakery HB-B101 Ⓓ	229		⊖	⊖	☐	Mix-in signal. Loaves can be hard to release. Poor cool-down indicator. Cools bread.
National Bread Bakery SD-BT65N Ⓓ	399		○	○	☐	French- & whole-grain bread, cake, roll cycles. Cools bread.
Panasonic Bread Bakery SD-BT65P Ⓓ	399		○	○	☐	French- & whole-grain bread, cake, roll cycles. Cools bread.
Welbilt Homemade Bakery ABM-150R	249		○	◐	○	Whole-grain bread, cake, custom cycles. Crust has uneven color. Loading, cleaning difficult. Cluttered controls. Bread sticks to paddle. Cools bread.
Welbilt Bread Machine ABM-100-4	199		○	◐	○	French- & sweet-bread cycles. Mix-in signal. No short cycle. Crust has uneven color. Loading, cleaning difficult. Bread sticks to paddle. Cools bread.

SMALL-LOAF MODELS

Brand and model	Price	Overall score	Use	Cleaning	Loaf shape	Comments
Panasonic Bread Bakery SD-BT10P	199		⊖	⊖	☐	Whole-grain bread cycle. Keeps bread warm.
Toastmaster Bread Box 1150, Ⓢ 1153, $250	200		⊖	○	☐	Mix-in signal. Cools bread.
Maxim Accu-Bakery BB-1 Ⓓ	165		⊖	○	☐	French- & whole-grain bread cycles. Bread sticks to paddle. Keeps bread warm.
Mister Loaf Home Bakery HB-211 Ⓓ	179		⊖	○	☐	Bread sticks to paddle. No dough cycle. Delay-start timer, cycle-time display, crust-color choice. Keeps bread warm.
Welbilt Bread Baker ABM350-3	169		○	◐	○	Mix-in signal. Loading, cleaning difficult. Bread sticks to paddle. Keeps bread warm.
Welbilt Bread Oven ABM600-1	129		⊖	◐	○	Mix-in signal. Loading, cleaning difficult. Bread sticks to paddle. No Delay-start timer. Keeps bread warm.

RATINGS TOASTERS

▶ **See report, page 127.** Last time rated in Consumer Reports: August 1994.

Brand-name recommendations: For the most part, relatively small differences separate the better models. The best single-slot toasters were the *Oster 3826* and *Sunbeam 3824,* priced at $35. Nearly as good but cheaper were the single-slot *Maxim ET-9,* $25, and the *Betty Crocker BC-1613,* $19, a two-slot model. We judged each A Best Buy. The best of the four-slicers was the *Black & Decker T440,* $46.

For a typical toaster, expect: ■ White plastic housing. ■ Hinged tray that opens for crumb disposal. ■ Manual push-down/automatic pop-up carriage. ■ Rotary color control to set darkness. ■ 2-to 3-ft. power cord.

Notes on the table: Price is the estimated average, based on a national survey. * indicates price CU paid. **Cool touch.** A regular toaster's exterior can reach temperatures hot enough to scorch skin. Models insulated by a plastic shell stayed cool everywhere except near the slots. Ⓓ indicates model discontinued or replacement not similar.

Within type, listed in order of toasting performance and ease of use

E VG G F P
⊜ ⊜ ○ ◐ ●

Brand and model	Price	Overall score	Slot WIDTH/NO.	Cool touch	Ease of use	Comments
TWO-SLICE MODELS						
Oster 3826	$35		⊜/1	⊜	⊜	Centers bread. Hard to retrieve English muffins.
Sunbeam 3824	35		⊜/1	⊜	⊜	Centers bread. Hard to retrieve English muffins.
Krups 118	43		⊜/1	⊜	⊜	Centers bread. Warm-up setting. Removable tray. 4-ft. cord (with storage provision).
Maxim ET-9, **A BEST BUY**	25		⊜/1	⊜	⊜	Centers bread. Stores cord.
Cuisinart CPT-2	92		○/1	⊜	⊜	Electronic controls, programmable settings. Centers bread. Warm-up, Keep-warm settings. No tray. Hard to retrieve English muffins. Ready bell.
Betty Crocker BC-1613, **A BEST BUY**	19		⊜/2	⊜	⊜	Centers bread. Slide-lever color control. Thin bread slipped through carriage.
Rowenta TP-200	40		⊜/1	⊜	⊜	Centers bread. Removable tray. Keep-warm setting.

Ratings continued ▶

Ratings continued

Brand and model	Price	Overall score	Slot WIDTH/NO.	Cool touch	Ease of use	Comments
Toastmaster 740	$26		◑/1	⊜	○	Centers bread. Color control hard to adjust. Fuse shuts off power if carriage jams; technician must replace.
Salton TO-6	*26		◑/1	⊜	◐	Centers bread. Color control not clearly marked and hard to adjust. No tray.
Proctor-Silex T4300	26		○/2	⊜	◐	Centers bread. Hard to retrieve English muffins. Color control hard to adjust.
Black & Decker T215	23		◐/2	⊜	◐	Slide-lever color control (not clearly marked). Thin bread slipped through carriage.
Proctor-Silex T620B	13		◐/2	◐	◐	Slide-lever color control.
Sunbeam 3817	*20		◐/2	◐	○	Hard to retrieve English muffins.
Toastmaster B725 D	20		○/2	◐	◐	Slide-lever color control. Hard to retrieve English muffins.
Proctor-Silex T4400	20		○/2	◐	◐	Centers bread. Hard to retrieve English muffins.
Farberware T2920	21		◐/2	◐	◐	Color control not clearly marked. Hard to retrieve English muffins.
Sears Kenmore 084812 D	15		◐/2	◐	◐	Poorly balanced; pressing on lever to lower carriage toppled toaster. Slide-level color control. Keep-warm setting.
Sunbeam 3816	80		◐/2	○	○	Slide-lever color control. Self-lowering carriage (but didn't work on several samples). Hard to retrieve English muffins.

FOUR-SLICE MODELS

Brand and model	Price	Overall score	Slot WIDTH/NO.	Cool touch	Ease of use	Comments
Black & Decker T440	*46		◐/4	⊜	⊜	Slide-lever color control.
Proctor-Silex 24400	33		○/4	⊜	◐	Centers bread. Hard to retrieve English muffins.
Toastmaster D777	34		◐/4	⊜	⊜	Slide-lever color control.
Toastmaster 786	*76		◐/4	⊜	◐	Mounts under cabinet. Single color control for all 4 slots. Ready bell. Power-on light.

RATINGS TOASTER OVENS & BROILERS

▶ **See report, page 128.** Last time rated in Consumer Reports: October 1994.

Brand-name recommendations: The broilers are more versatile than the ovens, and some cost only a little more. Performance differences among models tended to be slight, so choose by price, size, and convenience. The top-rated *Black & Decker T660G,* $85, broiler performed well, but for a lot less money, you can choose the *Toastmaster 336V* broiler, $50. If you never broil, consider the *Toastmaster 319V,* $39.

For a typical model, expect: ■ Housing of plastic and metal. ■ Oven pan, hinged crumb tray, and broiling grid (on broiler models). ■ Clear glass door. ◘ 1200- to 1600-watt draw. ■ 2- to 3-foot power cord. ■ Exterior surfaces that become hot.

Notes on the table: Price is the estimated average, based on a national price survey. **Toasting performance. Color ranges** from imperceptibly toasted to very dark (but not burnt). We also made toast a **slice** at a time, and in three consecutive **loads. Ease of use** considers features and controls, and crumb disposal. **Capacity.** The max. number of standard-sized slices of bread each oven could take. Most oven-broilers could fit the same number of 3¼-in.-wide burgers as slices of bread. Ⓢ indicates tested model has been replaced by successor model; according to the mfr., the performance of new model should be similar to the tested model but features may vary. Not tested. Ⓓ indicates discontinued or replacement not similar.

RATINGS OVERVIEW

Within types, listed in order of performance and ease of use

E VG G F P
⊖ ⊖ ○ ⊜ ●

Brand and model	Price	Overall score					Toasting performance			Ease of use	Capacity slices
		P	F	G	VG	E	COLOR RANGE	SLICE	LOADS		
TOASTER OVEN/BROILERS											
Black & Decker T660G Ⓢ	$85	▬▬▬▬▬					⊖	⊖	⊖	⊖	6
Toastmaster 336V Ⓓ	50	▬▬▬▬▬					⊖	⊖	⊖	⊖	4 ①
DeLonghi XU-20L	130	▬▬▬▬					⊖	⊖	○	⊖	6
Proctor-Silex 03030	48	▬▬▬▬					⊖	⊖	⊖	⊖	4
Black & Decker SO-2500G	92	▬▬▬					○	⊖	⊖	⊖	6
Toastmaster 342 Ⓓ	60	▬▬▬					○	⊖	⊖	⊖	6
Munsey M-88	56	▬▬▬					⊖	⊖	○	○	6
Sears Kenmore 48216	70	▬▬▬					⊖	⊖	⊖	⊖	4
Proctor-Silex 03010	41	▬▬▬					○	⊖	○	⊖	4
Panasonic NT-855U Ⓢ	70	▬▬▬					⊖	⊖	⊖	⊖	2 ①
DeLonghi XU-14	69	▬▬▬					⊖	⊖	○	○	6
Black & Decker TRO-510	55	▬▬▬					○	⊖	⊖	⊖	4 ②

① But could fit 6 burgers.   ② But could fit only 3 burgers.

Ratings continued ▶

Ratings continued

Brand and model	Price	Overall score					Toasting performance			Ease of use	Capacity slices
		P	F	G	VG	E	COLOR RANGE	SLICE	LOADS		

TOASTER OVEN/BROILERS *continued*

Brand and model	Price	Overall score	Color range	Slice	Loads	Ease of use	Capacity slices
Black & Decker TRO-400	$50	▄▄▄	⊖	⊖	⊖	⊖	4 [2]
Hamilton Beach 336 [D]	40	▄▄	⊖ (half)	⊖	⊖	⊖	4 [2]

TOASTER OVENS

Brand and model	Price	Overall score	Color range	Slice	Loads	Ease of use	Capacity slices
Toastmaster 319V [D]	39	▄▄▄▄	⊖	⊖	⊖	⊖	4
Black & Decker TRO-200	40	▄▄	○	⊖	⊖	⊖	4
Proctor-Silex 03008	35	▄▄▄	○	⊖	◐	○	4

[1] But could fit 6 burgers. [2] But could fit only 3 burgers.

RATINGS DETAILS   Models listed alphabetically

Black & Decker SO-2500G — Removable door. Oven must be restarted once door is opened. Under-cabinet mounting. Toasting in batches better than average.

Black & Decker T660G [S] T670, $85 — Toast-ready bell. Oven must be restarted once door is opened.

Black & Decker TRO-200 — Top-brown setting. Under-cabinet mounting option.

Black & Decker TRO-400 — Scorched cake. Top-brown setting. Under-cabinet mounting option.

Black & Decker TRO-510 — Scorched cake. Toast-ready bell. Top-brown setting. Under-cabinet mounting option.

DeLonghi XU-14 — Toast color difficult to alter once timer is set. Toast-ready bell. Toast rack height adjustable. No broil grid. 18-in. power cord.

DeLonghi XU-20L — Toast color difficult to alter once timer is set. Toast-ready bell. Interior light. Toast rack height adjustable.

Hamilton Beach 336 [D] — Controls inconvenient. Scorched cake. Toast-ready bell. Oven must be restarted once door is opened.

Munsey M-88 — Toast color difficult to alter once timer is set. Toast rack height adjustable.

Panasonic NT-855U [S] NT-856P, $70 — Scorched cake. Toast-ready bell. Timer starts/stops oven and broiler. Sturdy oven pan. Toast rack not removable.

Proctor-Silex 03008 — Toast color difficult to alter once timer is set. Toast rack height adjustable. Top-brown setting. No oven pan.

Proctor-Silex 03010 — Toast rack height adjustable.

Proctor-Silex 03030 — Toast-ready bell. Toast rack height adjustable.

Sears Kenmore 48216 — Toast-ready bell. Toast rack height adjustable.

Toastmaster 319V [D] — Sturdy oven pan. Top-brown setting.

Toastmaster 336V [D] — Slower at broiling. Sturdy oven pan. Top-brown setting. No broil grid.

Toastmaster 342 [D] — Controls inconvenient to set. Scorched cake. Toast-ready bell. Toast rack height adjustable. Sturdy oven pan. Top-brown setting. No provisions for crumb disposal.

RATINGS   GARBAGE DISPOSERS

▶ **See report, page 131.** Last time rated in Consumer Reports: February 1994.

Brand-name recommendations: Of the continuous-feed models, the *Thermador THD800*, $179, grinds food faster and finer than any other model. But it is also expensive and unsuitable for connection to a dishwasher. Worthy alternatives include the *Sinkmaster 950*, $130; the *General Electric Disposall GFC1000G*, $170; and the *Sears Kenmore 6010*, A Best Buy at $40. Of the batch-feed models, the *Thermador THD800TC*, $219, performed best. However, the *General Electric Disposall GFB1050G*, $195, and *Sinkmaster BF891S*, $180, are the better buys, despite their slightly coarser grinding and the need to keep depressing their stoppers during bone-grinding.

For a typical disposer, expect: ■ Ability to handle most kitchen waste without jamming or clogging. ■ Overload switch that protects the motor by shutting off if a jam occurs. ■ Ability to accept waste from the sink and the dishwasher. ■ Professional installation to cost about $100 to $200 (replacement installations are less expensive). **A choice you'll have to make:** ■ Continuous-feed or batch-feed.

Notes on the table: Price is the mfr.'s suggested or approx. retail. **Overall score** is based primarily on fineness, with speed also considered. **Fineness** reflects the consistency to which the disposer was able to grind bones, celery, carrots, and lettuce.

Better ◀————▶ Worse
⊜ ⊖ ○ ◒ ●

Within type, listed in order of overall performance

Brand and model	Price	Overall score P F G VG E	Fine-ness	Comments

CONTINUOUS-FEED MODELS

Brand and model	Price	Overall score	Fine-ness	Comments
Sinkmaster 950	$130	▬▬▬	○	¾ hp. Processed corn husks faster than others. Removable splash guard. Narrow feed tube.
General Electric Disposall GFC1000G	170	▬▬▬	○	¾ hp. Processed corn husks faster than others. Removable splash guard. Narrow feed tube. Smaller chamber capacity.
Sears Kenmore 6010, A Best Buy	40	▬▬	○	⅓ hp. Speedier with soft than hard foods. Frequent splashing, ejection of food. Bones lodged under impellers. Fixed splash guard. Wrench for remedying jams.
In-Sink-Erator Classic	328	▬▬▬▬	◒	1 hp. Sink flooded frequently. Processed corn husks faster than others. Double splash guards: fixed and removable. Auto-reverse feature. Wrench for remedying jams.
In-Sink-Erator 333	125	▬▬	◒	½ hp. Clumpy discharge with corn husks. Fixed splash guard. Wrench for remedying jams.
Emerson E30	79	▬▬▬	◒	½ hp. Frequent splashing. Bones lodged under impellers. Fixed splash guard. Has wrench for remedying jams.

Ratings continued ▶

Ratings continued

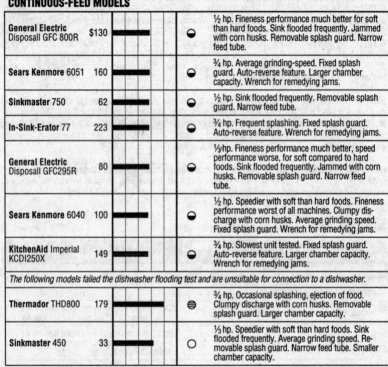

Brand and model	Price	Overall score P F G VG E	Fineness	Comments
CONTINUOUS-FEED MODELS				
General Electric Disposall GFC 800R	$130		⊖	½ hp. Fineness performance much better for soft than hard foods. Sink flooded frequently. Jammed with corn husks. Removable splash guard. Narrow feed tube.
Sears Kenmore 6051	160		⊖	¾ hp. Average grinding-speed. Fixed splash guard. Auto-reverse feature. Larger chamber capacity. Wrench for remedying jams.
Sinkmaster 750	62		⊖	½ hp. Sink flooded frequently. Removable splash guard. Narrow feed tube.
In-Sink-Erator 77	223		⊖	¾ hp. Frequent splashing. Fixed splash guard. Auto-reverse feature. Wrench for remedying jams.
General Electric Disposall GFC295R	80		⊖	⅓ hp. Fineness performance much better, speed performance worse, for soft compared to hard foods. Sink flooded frequently. Jammed with corn husks. Removable splash guard. Narrow feed tube.
Sears Kenmore 6040	100		⊖	½ hp. Speedier with soft than hard foods. Fineness performance worst of all machines. Clumpy discharge with corn husks. Average grinding speed. Fixed splash guard. Wrench for remedying jams.
KitchenAid Imperial KCDI250X	149		⊖	¾ hp. Slowest unit tested. Fixed splash guard. Auto-reverse feature. Larger chamber capacity. Wrench for remedying jams.
The following models failed the dishwasher flooding test and are unsuitable for connection to a dishwasher.				
Thermador THD800	179		⊜	¾ hp. Occasional splashing, ejection of food. Clumpy discharge with corn husks. Removable splash guard. Larger chamber capacity.
Sinkmaster 450	33		○	⅓ hp. Speedier with soft than hard foods. Sink flooded frequently. Average grinding speed. Removable splash guard. Narrow feed tube. Smaller chamber capacity.
BATCH-FEED MODELS				
Thermador THD800TC	219		⊜	½ hp. Center nut holding turntable in place became loose. Larger chamber capacity.
General Electric Disposall GFB1050G	195		○	¾ hp. Stopper pushed up during bone grinding. Processed corn husks faster than others.
Sinkmaster BF891S	180		○	¾ hp. Stopper pushed up during bone grinding.
In-Sink-Erator 17	269		⊖	¾ hp. Sink flooded frequently. Auto-reverse feature. Larger chamber capacity. Wrench for remedying jams.

HOME

Vacuum cleaners

Until manufacturers devise the perfect vacuum, deciding which type to buy depends mainly on what you clean most often. If most of your floors are carpeted, you'll need an upright vacuum or a canister model equipped with a power nozzle, which does the job of the upright's motorized brush. If you have only bare floors or if you expect to vacuum upholstered furniture, you need the kind of attachments and suction available in a canister model or an upright model with a power nozzle.

For small jobs, hand-held models fill the gap. Cordless models are best suited for quick pickups. Plug-in models deliver more power and better performance on carpet, especially those with a revolving brush.

Most vacuums are bought in discount or department stores. Relatively few are sold door-to-door these days. Four brands account for two-thirds of all vacuums sold: *Hoover, Eureka, Royal,* and *Sears Kenmore*. The *Electrolux* dominates sales of brand canister vacuums.

The choices

Uprights. As uprights grew more convenient, sales of canisters dropped. Uprights, which have a vertical bag, come in two basic designs: those with a soft bag and those with a bag enclosed in stiff plastic housing. The two types differ mainly in how dirt travels from floor to bag.

Uprights are generally good at carpet cleaning because their rotating brushes loosen and sweep up dirt lodged in the carpet's pile. They're not as good on hard surfaces because they generally have limited suction. Another drawback: Their business end tends to be large, often making them awkward in close quarters—too bulky to slip under a wing chair, too gangly for stairs. Uprights also tend to be noisier than canisters. Price: about $70 to $1000.

Canisters. Suction is the canisters' hallmark. They excel where uprights don't, on bare surfaces and upholstery.

With a canister, you push only the nozzle assembly. The stubby tank follows on wheels—a setup that usually makes the unit more agile than an upright, especially on stairs. But the canister's hose and numerous detachable wands are cumbersome to store, the bag is usually smaller than an upright's, and you have to give the hose a determined yank from time to time to keep the tank trailing behind you. Tug and twist the hose too much, however, and it's likely to become tangled. As a group, canisters weigh more: 20 to 25 pounds versus 10 to 25 for uprights. Price: about $75 to $1100.

Compact canisters. Predictably, compact canisters have smaller tanks than their full-sized cousins. Their compact size and light weight—only 10 to 15 pounds—make them easier to carry and store than full-sized canisters. The tradeoff for that convenience is limited performance. In our tests, compacts tended to be disappointing on all surfaces. Price: about $60 to $90.

Hand vacuums. Cordless, rechargeable models offer maximum portability. Cordless models rely mostly on suction for pickup, and thus they work best on hard, smooth surfaces. Some models can even handle wet debris and liquids. At about two pounds, they're a pound or so lighter than plug-ins. Typically, a fully

charged model runs for about 10 minutes.

Plug-in hand vacuums repress the free-roaming spirit of the cordless unit, although models with a long power cord—some extend 25 feet—are almost as convenient as their untethered siblings. Plug-ins have more power than the cordless variety and no battery to deplete. Most come with revolving brushes like those of full-sized uprights; brushes usually improve performance. Prices of cordless and plug-in vacuums overlap: about $30 to $90.

Car vacs. These look like cordless models but sport a 15- or 20-foot cord that plugs into the cigarette lighter. They can be used for extended periods without draining the car battery much. Price: about $30 to $90.

Other cleaning options exist, including central vacuum systems (found in some new homes), wet/dry shop vacs, and inexpensive electric brooms, or stick vacs, which are enjoying a renaissance of sorts.

Features and conveniences

Power nozzle. This extra-cost feature is found on most canisters, both full-sized and compact. It's basically a motorized brush to help remove dirt embedded in carpeting. Look for an automatic shutoff mechanism that prevents the power-nozzle motor from overheating and burning out when a scatter rug or object gets jammed in the rotating cylinder.

Assembly. An upright model requires little assembly, if any, to clean floors. A hose permanently attached to one end of the cleaner is the most convenient design for attaching tools. Some models make you snap on an adapter over the carpet brush or, worse, unhook the drive belt to connect the hose.

Putting together a canister is slightly harder. The basic drill involves inserting the hose, then attaching a metal or plastic wand that may consist of several pieces. Latches or clicking buttons hold metal wands together; friction holds plastic wands in place. Either type works well. With plastic wands, though, you must take care not to apply too little force, lest the fittings fall apart, while too much force could make them difficult to separate. The power nozzle and its wiring must be detached and set aside to attach other tools.

Controls. An On/off switch high on an upright's handle is easy to reach. On most canisters and a few uprights, the switch is on the base, where it's easy to work by foot. Most canisters have a separate foot switch to turn off the power nozzle—helpful when you're cleaning flat-weave rugs.

Suction adjustment. When vacuuming loose or billowy objects, excessive suction can cause the cleaner to inhale the fabric. Most canisters and some uprights let you reduce suction by uncovering a hole or valve near the handle. Models with more than one speed let you vary suction.

A revolving brush on a hand vac improves carpet cleaning, but it also competes with suction, flinging coarser soils about instead of ingesting them. A few battery-powered models come with a power-brush attachment, which improves pickup but can quickly drain batteries.

Adjustable brush height. Look for a model that allows raising or lowering the brush with dial, sliding lever, or foot pedal. Some models adjust height automatically.

Hoses. The most convenient swivel. Nonswiveling hoses can form annoying curlicues as you vacuum.

Pushing and carrying. The lighter the model, the easier to carry. That's a big selling point with compact canisters and *Eureka* uprights weighing less than 10 pounds. Power-assisted wheels are available on top-of-the-line uprights. This feature, found on about one-fourth of all sold, lets wheels glide easily over the plush carpet. On models that require pushing, large wheels or rollers make the job easier.

Uprights can usually be carried with one hand. Hoisting the tank and hose assembly of canisters requires two hands. Compact canisters sometimes come with a shoulder strap that makes them easy to carry and run, especially on stairs.

Vacuum bags. Most full-sized cleaners collect dirt in a disposable paper bag; some have a signal to show when the bag is full or airflow is blocked. Soft-body uprights have the largest bags (about a four-quart capacity). Hand vacuums have the smallest.

Installing a bag is easiest when you can drop the bag's cardboard collar into a slot. It's not as easy on models that make you slide the bag's sleeve over a tube and secure it with a spring band.

Most cordless vacuums come with an internal dust cup, which holds only a cup or two of debris. Plug-ins with an external dust bag can hold 6 to 11 cups.

Noise. No machine can be called quiet. The most offensive are uprights, especially the soft-bag models, according to our tests. Manufacturers recognize the problem and keep trying to design quieter models.

Dust control. We've found that paper dust bags in uprights or canisters are better at trapping fine dust than water-filtration or bagless dust collectors. The best solution for people who are severely allergic to dust may be to minimize carpeting.

Of late, companies have been offering special premium-priced, double-layered or microfiltration dust bags that supposedly minimize dirt dispersion. When we compared those bags to the cheaper ones, we found little difference.

Hand vacs sometimes shoot dirt and dust out of vent holes. It's more of a problem with cordless vacs than plug-ins because of the rear-mounted fan.

Cord storage. It's simplest on machines that have a spring-driven button or pedal that rewinds the long power cord for you. Otherwise, the usual arrangement is two hooks around which you wind the cord. If one hook swivels or retracts, you can loosen the cord quickly. Some canisters make you wrap the cord around the tank.

The tests

We judge a vacuum's deep-cleaning prowess as follows: We embed silica and talcum into sections of medium-pile carpet, pass each vacuum back and forth over the carpet eight times, and then weigh carpet and vacuum to see how much dirt is picked up. To judge suction, we measure airflow with a new bag, and then gradually feed each machine fine sawdust to measure how fast airflow falls off.

To test hand-held models, we spread various soils—sugar, sand, gravel, dog hair, and potting soil—on wood flooring and on low-pile carpeting, then count the number of passes each machine takes to remove the debris.

We also check edge-cleaning—how close to a wall each machine can vacuum. We measure noise levels, and for full-sized cleaners, gauge how well the various models keep dust from kicking up.

Buying advice

Of the two basic types, canisters offer greater versatility. They typically provide plenty of suction and, if equipped with a power nozzle, do a decent job on carpet. And their tools usually travel on board. But uprights, known primarily for carpet-cleaning, are becoming more versatile. More and more upright models accommodate the hose and gadgets on board now, sparing you the bother of rummaging through the closet for them. Upright models with on-board attachments now outsell all other vacuums.

You needn't pay top dollar. Although you can spend more than $1000 for a heavily chromed *Kirby*, sold exlusively through at-home demonstrations, plenty of models selling for $200 or so also work quite well.

For small spaces and undemanding tasks, you might be satisfied with a compact canister model.

Most hand vacs should work well on spills and small messes. A plug-in model with a revolving brush can gobble up dirt on carpet better than a battery-powered model, but a plug-in can also scatter bits of heavier debris. And, of course, a plug-in model lacks the mobility that originally made hand-held vacs popular.

The car vacs we've tested were mediocre. If there's an electric outlet close enough to your auto, you're better off using a plug-in hand vac or a regular full-sized vacuum.

Water treatment

Public concern over the quality of drinking water often centers on the obvious: how water looks, smells, or tastes. Ironically, water that is hazardous to your health usually looks, tastes, and smells just fine. Public supplies are either comparatively clean to start with or are purified to bring them up to par, but you wouldn't know that from the frightening picture painted by some unscrupulous vendors of water filters and other water-treatment equipment.

What gives those vendors some credibility is that real drinking water problems do exist. More than 70,000 water contaminants—including industrial and agricultural wastes, heavy metals, radon, and microbes—have been identified. Of those, more than 100 contaminants are subject to water-safety regulations. The level of risk each pollutant poses, and the number of people affected, varies widely.

Before buying any equipment, find out what's in your water. See "Getting Your Water Tested," on page 156.

Pollutants to worry about

Some substances in water such as calcium or iron, are harmless—they just make the water taste bad, refuse to lather, or mar fixtures or appliances. Other substances, like organic pollutants, typically present only localized problems. Three of the most widespread and serious water pollutants are lead, radon, and nitrate.

Lead. Significant levels of this toxic metal are more commonplace in drinking water than once assumed, and levels once considered safe are now seen as health concerns, particularly for pregnant women, infants, and children. Chronic lead exposure even at low levels may cause permanent learning disabilities and hyperactivity. In adults, such exposure is linked to high blood pressure and anemia.

Lead gets in water primarily from corrosion of household plumbing and service lines (the pipe connecting the home plumbing with the water main). There are three main sources: lead service lines (banned for nearly a decade, but widely used in many older homes), leaded solder (also banned since 1986) on copper pipes; and the brass in faucets and pumps. Very soft water and slightly acidic water leach lead from solder, pipes, and brass fixtures. To help minimize your exposure, use only cold water for cooking and drinking (hot water dissolves more lead). Running water for a minute or so to flush the pipes may help, but it's not a sure cure.

If you have more than five parts per billion of lead in your water even after letting it run, you should do something about it.

Radon. This probably poses a greater health risk than all other environmental pollutants combined. According to the U.S. Environmental Protection Agency, radon, a naturally ocurring radioactive gas, may cause between 10,000 and 20,000 lung-cancer deaths each year. Most of the radon seeps into homes from the ground. But some well water contains dissolved radon, which escapes into the air from sources like showers and washing machines.

Waterborne radon is usually confined to private wells or small community water systems. Large systems generally remove any radon before it reaches the tap. Before you test your water for radon, test the air inside your house. If the level is high and you rely on well water, have the water tested. If the air level is low, don't worry about the water.

Experts disagree as to the radon level in indoor air that should spur action. However, one EPA official we spoke with says you should take action if your water's radon level is 10,000 picocuries per liter or higher (about one picocurie per cubic meter of airborne radon). Radon is easily dispersed in outdoor air, so aerating the water before it enters the house is usually the simplest solution. Ventilating the bathroom, laundry room, or kitchen may also help. Other solutions include carbon filters.

Nitrate. Nitrate in water comes primarily from agricultural activities, especially chemical fertilizers and animal wastes.

High nitrate levels in water pose a risk mainly to infants. Bacteria in immature digestive tracts convert nitrate into nitrite, which in turn combines with hemoglobin in the blood to form methemoglobin, which cannot transport oxygen. The resulting ailment, methemoglobinemia, is rare but can result in brain damage or death. Some adults, including pregnant women, may also be susceptible to methemoglobinemia.

Rural families with private wells—especially those with infants or pregnant women—should have their water tested regularly. Some state health departments test wells for free. High nitrate levels may signal that other contaminants are also present.

Treatment devices

If your water is contaminated, consider a water-treatment device before taking the expensive route of buying bottled water or, if you have a well, digging deeper to an uncontaminated aquifer. The chart opposite shows which devices work best for which substances.

Some products on the market use just one of the techniques explained below; others combine two or more. However, none of these devices are suitable for treating bacteriologically contaminated water, which requires sterilization methods using ultraviolet rays, ozone, or chlorine.

Carbon filters. They're the most popular because they can overcome a variety of problems. They remove residual chlorine, which improves the water's taste, and can also remove organic compounds—such chemicals as pesticides, solvents, or chloroform. They're basically ineffective with hardness minerals, heavy metals like lead, or microbes; under certain conditions, they actually promote microbe growth

Carbon filters come in many forms. In-line filters, which serve a single cold-water faucet, are suitable for a household that uses lots of water. They range in price from $100 to $500. Tiny, faucet-mounted filters with a couple of ounces of carbon cost $10 to $20. Pour-through or pitcher devices are priced from $10 to $25. Whole-house carbon filters, with five-foot-high tanks that can be backwashed, are especially useful for removing radon from the household water. Prices start at $1500.

The most practical method of carbon filtration is an in-line filter that treats water at a single source, such as the kitchen sink. Some models are plumbed into the water line under the sink; others sit on the countertop and attach with flexible tubes.

Filters and cartridges need periodic replacement, at costs ranging from $5 to $40. Manufacturers typically recommend replacing a filter after a certain period of time or after a given quantity of water has passed through. Some filters have a water meter built in. Expect to change cartridges for a high-volume in-line filter every six months or 1000 gallons.

Lead-removing filters. Filters designed to remove lead come in different configurations: in-line filters (under-sink or countertop), faucet, or carafe. Price: $6 to $750. If lead is your only problem, activated alumina cartridges are an effective treatment; cartridges cost $100, the housing, $50. Reverse-osmosis devices and some carbon filters can remove lead.

Reverse-osmosis devices. These excel at removing inorganic contaminants, such as dissolved salts, ferrous iron, chloride, fluoride, nitrate, and heavy metals such as lead. A carbon filter is incorporated in most reverse-osmosis systems to remove organic chemicals. At the heart of these devices lies a fine sieve of cellophanelike material that screens out all but the smallest molecules. Under pressure, only water and other small molecules pass through.

High levels of hardness minerals can gum up these filtering devices. And reverse osmosis works slowly, producing only a few gallons of fresh water per day. Such devices are inefficient, wasting several gallons of water for every gallon they purify.

Some versions attach to the cold-water line under the sink; others sit on the counter. Under-sink models cost more than countertop models. Price range: $400 to $750.

Reverse-osmosis membranes need replacement every few years; filters, more often. Replacement membranes and filters cost $5 to $40.

Distillers. A distiller boils water, then cools and condenses the steam; the resulting distillate drips into a jug. Some models

Water problems and solutions

The maximum contaminant level is set by the Environmental Protection Agency. MCLs can be used as a general guide to safe and unsafe levels.

	Maximum contaminant level [1]	Carbon filter	Reverse osmosis [2]	Distiller	Water softener	Activated alumina cartridge	Aerator
AESTHETIC PROBLEMS							
Dissolved iron	—				✔		
Rust stains	—			✔			
Calcium	—				✔		
Magnesium	—				✔		
Chlorine	—	✔					✔
Salty taste	—		✔	✔			
'Skunky' taste	—	✔					
Total dissolved solids (TDS)	500 ppm		✔	✔			
HEALTH HAZARDS—Organic							
Benzene	5 ppb	✔					✔
Carbon tetrachloride	5 ppb	✔					✔
Lindane	0.2 ppb	✔		✔			
Methoxychlor	40 ppb	✔		✔			
Trichloroethylene	5 ppb	✔					✔
Trihalomethanes (THM)	100 ppb	✔					
HEALTH HAZARDS—Inorganic							
Arsenic	50 ppb		✔	✔			
Barium	2 ppm		✔	✔	✔		
Cadmium	5 ppb		✔	✔	✔		
Chromium	100 ppb		✔	✔			
Fluoride	4 ppm		✔	✔		✔	
Lead	15 ppb [3]	[4]	✔	✔		✔	
Mercury	2 ppb	✔	✔	✔			
Nitrate	10 ppm		✔	✔			
Selenium	50 ppb		✔	✔		✔	
HEALTH HAZARDS—Radiological							
Dissolved radon	10,000 pc/l	✔					✔

[1] ppm = parts per million; ppb = parts per billion; pc/l = picocuries per liter.
[2] Most will also remove organic substances.
[3] Action level.
[4] Some remove lead and accept lead-removing cartridges.

include a tiny carbon filter. Countertop units hold from one-half to 2½ gallons. Prices range from $150 to $425.

Distillers work best on brackish water or water polluted with heavy metals; they demineralize it. Anything that won't boil or evaporate remains in the boiling pot. Boiling water can also kill microorganisms, but don't rely on distillers for that purpose.

Distillers aren't effective against volatile organics like chloroform and benzene, which vaporize in the distiller and may wind up in the condensed water. A carbon filter might help remove such chemicals, but the filters incorporated into distillers are too small to do the job reliably.

Distillers are slow, taking a couple of hours to produce the first quart of water. Since they collect and concentrate minerals, scale can build up quickly and must be cleaned out. And, they use a lot of electricity—about three kilowatt-hours per gallon of purified water.

Water softeners. Water softeners, the

GETTING YOUR WATER TESTED

Despite possible contaminants, most people have water that's safe to drink. That's particularly true for people served by a large municipal water system. But if you have doubts about the water's quality, here's how you can find out if the water is fit to drink.

Consider the source. If you have municipal water, ask the utility for a copy of its latest water analysis. Federal law requires most public water companies to have the water tested regularly and to make the results available.

The test results will tell you the condition of the water when it left the reservoir or treatment plant. It won't tell you the condition at the tap—a shortcoming if you're concerned about lead, which generally leaches into the water from the plumbing.

Test for lead if your house is more than 30 years old or if the plumbing pipes are joined with lead solder. If you draw your water from a private well, call the local public health department to find out if any groundwater problems exist. If you drink well water, you should have it tested for radon, and periodically for bacteria, inorganic compounds, organic chemicals if the well is within a mile or two of a gasoline station or refinery, a chemical plant, a landfill, or a military base. If you live in an agricultural area, have the water tested for nitrate and pesticides.

Where to go for tests. Companies that sell water-treatment equipment often offer a free or low-cost water analysis as part of the sales effort. Don't depend on that kind of test: It's like asking a barber if you need a hair cut. Consult a state-certified, independent laboratory instead. You can often find one in the Yellow Pages under "Laboratories—Testing."

Or use a mail-order lab. Our past tests turned up three reliable labs: Clean Water Fund, 704 251-0518, $17 (lead only); Suburban Water Testing Labs, 800 433-6595; National Testing Laboratories, 800 458-3330.

Over the years, we've found that all labs tend to overstate or understate results occasionally. If a test report says the water has an especially high level of contaminant like lead, nitrate, or radon, have the water retested before taking costly remedial action.

granddaddy of water-treatment alternatives, remove calcium and magnesium, the hardness minerals, along with iron and lead. These devices don't remove radon, nitrate, or pesticides.

A water softener consists of a large tank of tiny resin beads loosely coated with sodium ions. When hard water flows in, minerals take sodium's place on the resin. The softener periodically reverses its flow, taking salt out of a tank to regenerate the resin beads. The minerals are flushed down the drain. Some models regenerate at preset intervals, using a timer. More sophisticated models ("demand control" models) regenerate according to water use.

Softeners differ in size. "Cabinet" units are the most compact. The average price for a softener is about $1000, but prices vary with installation, local water conditions, and competition among local dealers.

A water softener needs little maintenance, except for the salt you add periodically. You can adjust the level of salt consumption. A high setting ensures softer water but means more frequent refills. A lower setting saves salt and money, but the resin may regenerate less completely.

Iron removers. Iron dissolved in water can leave brown stains in the bathtub and sink, which are actually rust from the dissolved iron oxidizing with the air. You can use a water softener to remove the iron. Special devices are available for water where hardness is not a problem. An iron remover uses an oxidizing agent to precipitate the iron and is the best device for removing dissolved "ferrous" iron. One common design is a canister similar to a water softener. Iron removers are priced from $400 to $650.

Buying advice

The chart on page 155 summarizes the best way to treat the most common water problems. Before doing business with a water-treatment company, especially one with an unfamiliar name, it's a good idea to call the Better Business Bureau or a local consumer-protection agency to find out if there are unresolved complaints against the company.

In evaluating the various treatment systems, some key points to consider are:

■ **Carbon filter:** The more carbon the better. Based on our tests, small pour-through filters and fist-sized units that thread onto the faucet can improve the taste of water, but are simply too small to remove hazardous chemicals. High-volume under-sink or countertop filters do a much better job. Look for those with a replaceable filter cartridge. Cartridges made either with a "carbon block" or granulated carbon are better than those made with powdered carbon.

Carbon filters with a built-in sediment filter may clog before the carbon is used up if your water contains a lot of undissolved solids. To extend its life, install a separate sediment prefilter upstream of the carbon filter. A 5- to 10-micron mesh is fine enough. A clear plastic sump on the filter housing indicates when the cartridge needs changing.

■ **Distiller.** Check how easy the unit is to fill or clean. In our tests we found little variation in how well distillers removed inorganic compounds.

■ **Water softener.** Any model will do an acceptable job of removing minerals, according to our tests. For peak efficiency and minimum salt consumption where household water use varies from week to week, choose a demand-control model, which regenerates automatically according to water use.

■ **Iron removal.** Expensive models have the advantage of removing more iron and regenerating automatically rather than manually. They're designed for high iron levels. Aeration devices can precipitate and remove iron and also radon.

Paints, stains & finishes

▶ **Ratings of interior latex paints on page 185.**

Painting is the most common way to finish a surface. Paint provides a fairly tough film of resins and pigments that covers small blemishes and shields the surface from wear and weathering. It can be applied over primer or old paint and comes in almost every conceivable color.

Stain, which seeps into wood instead of covering it, is more subtle than paint, allowing the natural grain to show through. But stain allows fewer color choices, the most popular being browns, reds, grays, and whites for exterior, and wood colors for interior. Exterior stains tend to peel less than paint because of their greater penetration.

Interior transparent stains and clear finishes reveal wood in all its glory. Surface finishes (like varnish) form a hard, durable coat; they also may be waterborne or solventborne.

For help in choosing a finish for a surface, see the charts on pages 159 and 160.

Water-based, solvent-based

The make-up of paints and exterior stains is similar. Both contain binder, solvent, and pigment. The binder forms the film, holds the pigment, and gives adhesion. The solvent—water and alcohols in latexes and petroleum spirits in alkyds (oil-based paints)—helps determine how easily the paint goes on and its adhesion and coverage. Pigment provides hiding and color. Paint contains more pigment than most stains; as the transparency of stain increases, the amount of pigment decreases.

Paints and stains come in water-based (latex) and oil-based (alkyd) versions, with *Glidden, Sears, Sherwin-Williams, Dutch Boy,* and *Benjamin Moore* the leading brands of paint; *Olympic, Thompson's,* and

Behr, the leading brands of stain. Our advice: Use the same type of paint or stain that you paint over—oil over oil, latex over latex. (You can safely use latex over oil-based primer, however.) Consistently using the same type of paint minimizes stresses in the coating that can lead to blistering and peeling.

Latexes. The resin in latex paint consists of tiny plastic particles suspended in a solvent that's mostly water. As the water evaporates, the paint dries, allowing the resin particles to touch and coalesce into a film that remains somewhat permeable to air and water.

One of the appeals of water-based paints and stains is convenience. They're easier to apply than oil-based formulas. They can be applied to a damp surface. They dry quickly and without much odor. And, if you clean up promptly, you need only soap and water for the job. In addition, latex paints contain less air pollutants than are found in alkyd paints. Latexes also tend to remain more flexible than alkyds, making them less prone to crack.

But there's a tradeoff for those conveniences. Latex paint is somewhat more prone to damage from water and marring than alkyds. Latex, especially glossier latexes, may remain tacky long after drying, causing books to stick to shelving and windows to sills—a problem known as "blocking." And you have to be careful about storage—freezing can spoil latex, rendering it unusable.

Alkyds. Alkyd paints and stains—typically polymers of alcohol, organic acid, and vegetable oil dissolved in petroleum solvents—usually dry by oxidation rather than by evaporation. As alkyds combine with oxygen from the air, it forms a water-resistant skin of hardened resin. The initial hardening takes several days, but the polymerization may go on for years.

Consequently, oil-based paints and stains are very tough, the right choice when you want toughness, and extra resistance to water. Alkyds make sense for kitchens and bathrooms and for working surfaces such as bookshelves. They're especially adept at adhering to old painted surfaces, although some acrylic latexes are almost as good.

The petroleum-based chemistry of oil-based stains and paints, however, makes them messy to use. The brush may drag and leave drips and sags. Cleanup requires mineral spirits. For proper adhesion, oil-based finishes must be applied to a dry surface. They smell like solvent while drying and each coat needs about a day to dry.

The choices in paints

Interior paints. Latex paints are the typical choice for interior painting. They outsell the oil-based variety five to one.

Both latexes and alkyds come in various gloss levels. Unfortunately, there are no standard definitions for glossiness. One maker's "satin," for example may shine like another's "eggshell." The general rule is to use a flat paint for ceilings, eggshell and satin for walls, and a semigloss paint for most woodwork—moldings, baseboards, doors, and windows.

Exterior paints. Like interior paints, exterior paints come in a variety of sheens.

Matching interior surface to finish

	Latex, acrylic	Latex	Alkyd	Urethane, varnish	Stain	Floor paint	Aluminum paint
WOOD							
Floors				✔	✔	✔	
Paneling	✔	✔	✔	✔	✔		
Stair risers	✔	✔	✔	✔	✔		
Stair treads				✔	✔	✔	
Trim, furniture	✔	✔	✔	✔	✔		
MASONRY							
Concrete walls	✔					✔	
Kitchen/bath walls	✔		✔				
New masonry	✔						
Old masonry	✔						✔
Plaster		✔	✔				
Wall board	✔	✔	✔				
METAL							
Aluminum windows	✔	✔	✔				✔
Steel windows	✔	✔	✔				✔
Radiators, pipes	✔	✔	✔				✔

Note: Unless surface has been previously finished, primer or sealer may be required. Consult manufacturer's instructions.

House paint tends to be white or subdued colors, while trim hues are rich and bold.

Exterior latex and alkyd paints are formulated to withstand strong sunlight and the weather; most also combat mildew, latexes usually better than alkyds. A white paint that "chalks" continually sloughs off dirt along with the chalky powder, so the finish appears fresh and white longer.

Formulations may vary by region. "Southern" formulations of paint, for instance, usually contain more antimildew ingredients and are more apt to purposely chalk.

Specialty paints. *Rust-protecting paints* contain rust-inhibiting compounds. But if the surface is prepped correctly—you grind or sand off all rust to bright metal and prime the surface with a metal primer—you can

Matching exterior surface to finish

	Latex, acrylic	Alkyd	Wood stain	Trim paint	Porch paint	Urethane	Aluminum paint	Water repellent, preservative
WOOD								
Clapboard	✔	✔						
Natural siding/ trim			✔	✔		✔		
Shutters, trim	✔	✔	✔	✔				✔
Window frames	✔	✔	✔	✔				✔
Porch floor, deck					✔			✔
Shingle roof			✔					✔
MASONRY								
Brick	✔							✔
Cement, cinder block	✔							✔
Porches, floors	✔				✔			
Stucco	✔	✔						
METAL								
Aluminum windows	✔	✔		✔			✔	
Steel windows	✔	✔		✔			✔	
Metal siding	✔	✔		✔			✔	
Copper surfaces						✔		
Galvanized surfaces	✔			✔			✔	
Iron surfaces	✔	✔		✔			✔	

Source: Adapted from U.S. General Services Administration

use almost any paint for the top coat. Brushed-on coats are thicker, sturdier, and cover better than an aerosol enamel. Many thin coats are better than a few thick ones.

Don't count on a *basement-waterproofing paint* to halt outright seepage. Even the best we've tested allow a small amount of water to seep through. The most water-resistant are two-component epoxies—expensive, strong-smelling coatings that harden in a chemical reaction between a resin and catalyst. The epoxy must be mixed in precise amounts and applied to a sound surface. Next best: oil-based paint formulated for masonry. Cement-based powder and water-based paint are less effective.

The choices in stains

Interior stains. Unlike exterior stain, which resembles thinned paint, interior stain is more of a varnish with a dye. Colors are typically names of wood—walnut, cherry, mahogany. Many cabinet-quality stains are water-based. You brush them on, wipe off the excess, then seal the wood with varnish or polyurethane. Wiping off the stain takes a bit of finesse. Wipe too soon, and you may remove most of the color; wait too long, and the wood may be too dark.

Oil stains are better suited for the inexperienced. They're relatively simple to use, and their colors are easier to control.

Exterior stains. Like paint, stains come in latex or alkyd versions. Sales of solvent-based stains are double those of water-based stains. Leading brands include *Olympic, Thompson's, Behr,* and *Cabot.*

Stains come in transparent, semitransparent, and opaque (solid-color) varieties. Stains provide less surface film than paint and so peel less.

The choices in clear finishes

Varnish is a combination of resins and sometimes oils that coats the surface of the wood. It's much the same as paint, minus the pigment. The polyurethane widely used on floors is a urethane-oil-based varnish. Water-based varnishes, which clean up with soap and water, are also available. Either type comes in several gloss levels. Penetrating oils like tung oil or Danish oil soak into the wood's pores. They provide a natural-looking, low-luster finish.

Lacquers are resins dissolved in strong solvents. As the solvents evaporate, the lacquer dries to form a thin, tough film.

It's best to apply any clear finish in several thin coats and sand between coats. Trying to do the job with only one or two heavy coats may result in sagging, wrinkling, missed spots, or uneven gloss.

Environmental considerations

The solvents used in paints and other finishes include hydrocarbons and other volatile organic compounds (VOCs). Those solvents evaporate as the finish dries. They can react with other pollutants in the air to produce ozone, a major ingredient of smog.

Until recently, both oil- and water-based finishes contained VOCs. Oil-based products contained 40 to 50 percent VOCs; latex, 2 to 7 percent. VOC-free paints or low-odor paints, as they're advertised, have been used in Europe for several years, but only a few are available in the U.S.

Because of VOC regulations, the sale of solvent-based paint has been restricted in some states. In response to those restrictions, manufacturers have reformulated or discontinued making oil-based paints.

Until recently, most latex paints contained mercury compounds as bacteria- and fungus-fighting agents. In poorly ventilated rooms, mercury vapor escaping from drying paint could occasionally build up to high levels, posing a health hazard. The Government banned mercury in interior latex paint in 1990; outdoor paint containing mercury must be labeled as exclusively for exterior use.

Lead, once widely used in paint pigments and drying agents, was banned from house paints in the 1970s. But it continues to pose dangers. Old paint on walls and woodwork may contain lead, so great care must be taken when removing it.

The tests

We judge paint and stain after exposing them to typical conditions. For instance, we apply samples of outdoor paint to test panels left outside for months at our Yonkers, N.Y., headquarters and in Florida, where conditions favor mildew growth.

We evaluate each product for its workability—factors such as brushing ease, leveling (smoothness of the dried coating), and resistance to sagging (dripping) and blocking (residual tackiness).

We check how well interior products resist staining, scrubbing, blocking, spattering, and water. We measure gloss levels with an instrument called a gloss meter. We also test stain and paint to see how well they hide.

Buying advice

Choose a finish that's compatible with the surface you want to cover and make sure that it is clean and smooth.

Prices for indoor and outdoor paints range from less than $10 to more than $30 a gallon. Latexes tend to be cheaper than alkyds, and flat-finish paints cheaper than glossy ones. Stains are priced similarly.

We've recently found some standouts at the lower end of the price spectrum but over the years, bargain paints have fallen down in quantities such as hiding power, washability, and adhesion. As a result, we think you'd be better off selecting products from the high end of the brand lines.

The color you choose affects how much paint you'll need. Muted blacks, browns, blues, dark reds, and greens generally hide best. Most pale colors, especially golds and yellows, will probably need more than one coat. However, hiding is secondary to protection for exterior paint, where a sufficient film is required to resist the elements over a long period of time. Claims of one-coat hiding assume that you spread the paint thickly, covering only 450 square feet per gallon. On interior surfaces, that's easier to do with a brush than a roller. We've found that with normal rolling, a gallon covers up to 650 square feet, although at this spreading rate, the hiding suffers.

Some finishes exposed to bright sunlight are apt to fade. Among exterior paints, alkyds tend to whiten, while indoors, white alkyds yellow when shaded from the light. Reds and yellows typically fade the most.

STEPS TO A PERFECT PAINT JOB

- Prime new wood or metal.
- Clean all surfaces.
- Remove loose paint. If you scrape down to wood, apply a primer.
- Patch holes in plaster or wallboard with plaster or spackling compound. Sand lightly until smooth.
- Block rust and water. Remove rust down to bare shiny metal. Cover nail heads that could rust with wood filler and primer. Apply sealer over knots so they don't bleed. Caulk cracks and other sources of moisture penetration.
- Use the right tools. Brushes are best for exterior painting, especially on textured surfaces or shingles. Use a natural bristle brush with alkyd paints, synthetic bristles with latexes. Rollers make fast work of interior walls and ceilings.

Home security & safety

▶ Ratings start on page 180.

Too many people learn the hard way how well their home resists fire or theft. The following reports can help you assess your needs, take appropriate precautions, and choose the necessary equipment—locks, alarms, smoke detectors, carbon-monoxide detectors, and fire extinguishers—to avoid such calamities.

Door locks

You can reduce your risk of becoming a burglary victim by simply adding secure locks to your doors and by consistently using those locks. But our tests have shown a good lock is not enough. It needs to be installed with hardware of equal quality.

Even the most burglar-proof lock is only as secure as the door, frame, and hardware used to install it. The best doors are metal-clad or solid hardwood hung in metal or hardwood framing. The ¾-inch-long screws supplied with most lock strike plates barely penetrate the jamb; better are three-inch screws that sink well into the framing studs. A "high-security" strike plate of heavy-gauge construction and three-inch screws offers much better protection against kicking than ordinary strike plates.

You can spend a lot or a little for a door lock. The garden variety sold at hardware stores and home centers range in price from $10 to $100. You'll see names like *Schlage, Kwikset,* and *Weiser.* Heavy-duty, high-security locks such as *Medeco* are distributed primarily through locksmiths and can cost $200 or more.

The choices

Door locks are classified as either primary locksets, which lock automatically when you close the door, or as auxiliary locks, which have deadbolts that lock in place with the turn of the key or a thumb-turn. Five lock designs predominate:

Entry locksets. The primary locks found on most exterior doors use a short, spring-loaded latch opened by a knob or handle on the lock, and closed by a key on the outside or a button or lever on the inside. Guarding the main latch is a secondary latch that keeps intruders from pushing back the main latch with, say, a credit card forced between door and jamb.

Entry locksets with their short latches are vulnerable to prying, which frees the latch from the strike. Because the locking mechanism (cylinder) is enclosed in a knob or lever, the lock is vulnerable to physical attack from a burglar wielding a wrench, pliers, or hammer. An auxiliary deadbolt lock is likely to offer more resistance.

Doors that don't fit snugly may leave space for a hacksaw blade to work away at the latch or bolt. That's a problem if the latch of an entry lockset is the sole security for your door. Most dead-bolt locks have hardened inserts or bolts that resist sawing.

Entry handlesets. This type typically has a nonlocking latch that's manipulated by a thumb lever and an auxiliary key-operated cylinder deadbolt lock. A long, decorative handle is mounted below the lever.

Cylinder deadbolt locks. These are auxiliary locks installed separately from the entry lockset. The key and thumbturn at each end of the cylinder control a deadbolt that extends an inch or so into the door. Double-cylinder deadbolt locks have a keyed cylinder inside the door as well as outside. But these are banned in some areas since they prevent rapid egress in the event of an emergency.

Deadbolt locks are more resistant to prying than an entry lockset. But an ice pick can often disable such locks. Look for a model that shields its internal parts with a metal collar or housing around the lock mechanism or the bolt. Unlike spring-loaded latches on primary locks, deadbolts don't automatically engage when the door is closed; they must be locked manually.

Surface-mounted deadbolt locks. Also installed separately from the entry lockset, from the outside, these are unobtrusive; they mount flush with the door outside but protrude on the inside. Models have either a vertical or horizontal bolt. Surface-mounted deadbolts are the easiest locks to install. You don't have to drill holes for the bolt into the edges of the door and jamb—just one hole through the door for the cylinder. Surface-mounted vertical deadbolts, which hook into their strike plates, are generally impervious to jimmying.

Interconnected locksets are a kind of hybrid. Also known as a two-in-one lock, they contain both a typical entry lockset and a typical cylinder deadbolt lock. The two locks accept the same key and work in concert. Using the key to open the deadbolt from the outside also opens the latch; turning the knob to unlatch the door from the inside also opens the deadbolt. That's a feature that might buy you extra seconds in an emergency exit from your house. But such locks have an inherent weakness: Disarm one and you disarm the other.

Convenience

When it's time to leave the house, you want a door lock to open easily and quickly, especially in an emergency. Many entry locksets can be opened from inside with a turn of the knob, even when the latch is locked, making for an effortless exit. But, because the locked knob turns so freely in your hand, however, you can easily mistake it for an unlocked knob, which increases chances of locking yourself out. With other entry locksets and single-cylinder dead bolts, you must work a thumbturn or push button to unlock the door from the inside.

To exit a door with a double-cylinder lock, you must turn the door key inside. Typically, the key can be removed after the door is locked from the inside. Double-cylinder locks are intended for doors that have glass in or around them. Removing the key prevents a burglar from breaking the glass and then easily unlocking the lock from the inside. The tradeoff is that an occupant trying to flee would be trapped without the key. Because of that, some communities ban or restict the use of double-cylinder locks.

The tests

We mount the locks individually on a specially constructed door and mercilessly attack them. We use a mechanical basher to simulate a hefty person's kicks. We try prying, pulling, and wrenching the lock from the door. We assault the locks with a hammer, the lock cylinders with a drill. We also hire a locksmith to pick each lock.

Buying advice

Start by beefing up lock and door hardware. Use a high-security strike with three-inch screws.

If the primary locks on your door are entry locksets, and working well, you probably won't gain much by replacing them with a new set. No entry locksets afford great protection. Entry handlesets are somewhat better, largely because they include a cylinder deadbolt lock.

A single-cylinder deadbolt with an easily operated thumbturn on the inside allows a fast, safe getaway in an emergency.

If you don't mind their looks, consider a surface-mounted deadbolt lock. It offers good protection against burglars who try to kick or pry their way in. And it's generally straightforward to install.

Smoke detectors

Having a smoke detector in your home cuts the risk of dying in a fire by half, according to some studies. Homes would be safer still if more people took care of their smoke detectors. Though most homes now have smoke detectors, an estimated one-third of them would not properly warn of a fire because of dead or missing batteries.

BRK Electronics makes most of the smoke detectors sold in discount and hardware stores and home centers. BRK's *First Alert* and *Family Guard* brands account for three out of every four units sold. Brands sold through electrical suppliers include *BRK, Firex, Fyrnetics, Dicon*, and *Visual Alert*.

The choices

Smoke detectors are battery- or AC-powered. Most use a 9-volt battery. Detectors have long been required to sound a low-power warning when the batteries are weak. To ensure that the battery is in place and working, the latest models refuse to close without batteries in place or must signal visually if batteries are missing.

AC-powered models are wired directly into the household current, usually by an electrician. Most AC-powered models have a back-up battery so they can work in case of power failure. Such dual-powered units are required by more and more state and local building codes for newly built or renovated homes. The fact that AC-powered detectors don't rely on batteries is a strong advantage. Hard-wired detectors have another advantage: If two or more are interconnected, all sound the alarm when one

senses smoke. However, that installation may be practical only during construction.

Detectors also vary in how they work:

Ionization. This is by far the most widely sold and easiest type to find. Ionization detectors use a small amount of radioactive material (so small it poses no significant health or environmental threat) to make the air in the detector chamber conduct electricity. Smoke interferes with that electric current and triggers the alarm. Ionization detectors are the most effective way to sense blazes that give off little smoke. Battery-powered ionization detectors generally sell for less than $25.

Photoelectric. This type works by shining a small beam of light past a sensor. Smoke disperses the light, tripping the alarm. Photoelectric models are best at sensing a smoldering, smoky fire—the kind that might start, in upholstery, say.

Photoelectric detectors, priced at $20 to $30, remain scarce in stores. We suggest calling the following manufacturers for stores that carry them: BRK at 800 323-9005 or Dicon at 708 850-7255.

Combination. Some models use both ionization and photoelectric sensors. These models may be AC-powered, run on a battery, or offer both options. Price: $30 to $35.

For the hearing-impared. The most common type is an AC-powered ionization unit that rouses a sleeper with a strobe light flashing. Prices start at around $100.

Features and conveniences

Alarm testing. All models have a button to test whether the unit's circuitry, battery, and horn are working properly. Most also have a small LED (light-emitting diode) light that flashes every minute or so to indicate a state of readiness.

Most models let you activate the test button by depressing it with a broomstick; rounded buttons are the hardest to depress. You can test a few models with a flashlight beam, which is more convenient. Units with automatic testing sound the alarm briefly every week at the same time.

Alarm loudness. An industry standard specifies 85 decibels as the minimum loudness for an alarm. Many alarms are far more raucous, a consideration if you're hard of hearing.

Hush button. Detectors will sound as long as there is smoke to detect. Most are hard to silence once they go off, even if the reason is a piece of burnt toast. Many people resort to detaching the battery (but fail to reconnect it later). A Hush button solves the problem. It deactivates the alarm for 10 or 15 minutes—long enough for innocuous smoke to dissipate.

Weak-battery warning. All models chirp or beep periodically to indicate a weak battery. The warning continues for at least 30 days or until the battery is replaced.

Auxiliary light. When some models sound the alarm, they also turn on built-in reflector lights to help guide you through the smoke. But the lights are usually too small and weak to be of much use in a smoky fire; a large halogen-bulb flashlight would be more helpful.

The tests

We mount the detectors on the ceiling of a room-sized test chamber and high on its walls (the recommended installation sites) and pit them against several types of fires: a smoky paper blaze (which goes rapidly from hot smoke to leaping flames); a smouldering fire (whose smoke begins slowly and builds gradually); and a flaming fire

CARBON-MONOXIDE DETECTORS

Most at risk are people in homes with a fuel-fired hot-air furnace or space heater, a wood stove, or a fireplace—common sources of high levels of carbon monoxide. If the home is tightly weather-sealed, the risk is even greater.

The best way to reduce the risk of carbon monoxide poisoning is to maintain your home's heating system on a regular basis. As a backup, you can also install a carbon-monoxide (CO) detector that continuously monitors the air.

CO detectors look like smoke detectors and shriek the same way when the alarm is tripped. There are three types: battery-powered, plug-in, and sensor-card.

All the battery-powered or plug-in models we tested provide adequate warning. Both battery- and AC-powered electronic units have a test button you push to verify the detector is working. A few models provide some visual indication that batteries are missing. Electronic detectors typically cost from $40 to $75.

The third type of detector, the CO-sensing card, has a sensor "spot" on the card face that supposedly changes color in the presence of CO. Some of the tested cards didn't respond to hazardous levels of CO. And, none has an alarm—crucial since many people die from CO poisoning while sleeping. We have judged the cards Not Acceptable as a sole means of CO detection.

(which is largely smoke-free). Then we measure each model's response time.

Buying advice

You should have at least one smoke detector on every level of your house, preferably using at least one of each type, ioniza-

tion and photoelectric. Our tests have demonstrated that both types are necessary to be assured of an early warning of any fire.

If you already own detectors, make sure they all work. Any detector older than 10 years should be replaced.

Fire extinguishers

Extinguishers are sold mostly at home centers, discount stores, and hardware stores. There are two major brands—*Walter Kidde* and *First Alert*. Prices range from $10 for small extinguishers to $100 or so for the large sizes.

The choices

Underwriters Laboratories, an independent safety-testing organization, groups extinguishers both by capability—the kinds of fires they're meant to fight—and capacity—the size of fire they can fight.

Capability. Fires are classified as "A," "B," or "C," based on the kind of material burning. "A" fires involve ordinary combustibles—paper, wood, cloth, upholstery—and is the only kind of fire you can safely and effectively extinguish with water. "B" fires involve flammable liquids—cooking grease, gasoline, paint solvents, fuel oils. Unlike most liquid fires, grease fires are often contained and can usually be put out by smothering; if not, a dry-chemical extinguisher should work. "C" fires involve electrical equipment—a TV set, receiver, fuse-box, wiring, and the like.

A:B:C extinguishers, filled with ammonium phosphate, for instance, are multipurpose extinguishers used on most home fires. B:C extinguishers, filled with sodium bicarbonate, fight only fires involving flammable liquids and electrical equipment. The sodium bicarbonate in B:C types is particularly good at fighting a grease fire

because it smothers the fire and reacts chemically with fat to form a soapy film that blankets grease. But such chemicals can cause breathing difficulties, particularly for people with respiratory problems. And both sodium bicarbonate and ammonium phosphate leave a mess you should clean up quickly—the latter is especially corrosive.

Capacity. UL designations for fire extinguishers also include numbers preceding the "A" and "B" to denote the size of the fire they can fight. The result is a UL rating such as 2-A:10-B:C or 5-B:C (no size is assigned to "C" fires, the electrical variety). Other things being equal, an extinguisher rated at 10-B, say, will put out twice as much flaming liquid as a 5-B unit.

The UL ratings also tell how long each extinguisher can spray. The higher the number, usually, the longer the spray time. Spray time in our tests ranges from 9 to 24 seconds. A longer spray time buys you critical extra seconds to fight a fire—time you may need if you're unused to working the extinguisher and misdirect some of the spray. But big models are clumsy to store and may be too heavy to use.

Other types. Size is a drawback to several other types of extinguisher on the market. Those that spray water or carbon dioxide are effective on some types of fire but quite heavy. Carbon dioxide (B:C-type) extinguishers are not only heavy but expensive; they're ideally suited for use around electronic or computer gear because no corrosive, powdery mess is left. Halon-gas extinguishers, once the preferred type for fighting fires that involve electrical equipment, have all but disappeared from the market because halon vapor damages the earth's protective ozone layer. (If you own such a device and want to dispose of it, find a local fire-equipment service company that can safely reclaim the halon. Check the Yellow Pages under "Fire Extinguishers."

Features and conveniences

Weight. Multipurpose units range in weight from 4 to 37 pounds, B:C models, 1 to 33 pounds. Check the weight in the store; a unit that's too heavy is useless.

Pressure indicators. Extinguishers with a dial-type gauge are easiest to check—a needle shows at a glance whether the unit has sufficient working pressure. Some models use a pressure-check pin instead of a dial. You push down on the pin; if it pops back, the pressure is fine.

Mountings. Extinguishers come with a simple hanging bracket (hook), a marine bracket (ring), or both. It's usually easier to lift the tank off a regular bracket than a marine bracket, which makes you first unsnap the band that holds the unit to the hanging bracket. A marine bracket's circular retainer is useful for helping prevent an extinguisher from being accidentally knocked off the wall.

Rechargeability. Most extinguishers can be recharged after a fire or a drop in their pressure (for that service, check the Yellow Pages under "Fire Extinguishers").

While recharging the extinguisher is less wasteful than disposal, a recharge may cost as much as a new one and provide less firefighting capacity than the original charge.

The tests

We judge an extinguisher mostly on ease of use. We evaluate the security of its bracket and the effort needed to remove the extinguisher. We pull the safety catch or pin, and squeeze the handle or press the push button. We measure the unit's spray time. Durability testing tells us how well the tank and valve mechanism are apt to survive a fall or prolonged exposure to high temperatures.

Buying advice

Your first choice should be a large- or medium-sized multipurpose extinguisher, called "full-floor" models because they are large enough and versatile enough to cover one entire floor of a home against fires of all common burning materials. Give first consideration to an extinguisher rated at 3-A:40-B:C. Choose a medium-sized one (rated at 2-A:10-B:C) only if you can't handle a bigger model.

Small, supplemental models provide additional coverage for individual rooms. For instance, a small B:C extinguisher is worth considering for a kitchen because of its superior performance on a grease fire.

Burglar alarms

A house protected by a burglar alarm (or home-security system) is at least three times less likely to be burglarized than a house without one. When burglars do break into a protected house, they tend to get away with much less loot than is taken from an unguarded house.

A burglar alarm might confer peace of mind, but at a price, both in what you pay and how you'll have to live. A professionally installed security system can cost $1000 to more than $3000, a comparable do-it-yourself system, from $500 to $600. And if your system connects to a private security firm, you'll also have to pay a monthly fee.

A home-security system can also be annoying. You must remember to arm and disarm the alarm every time you go and come, and you must think before opening doors or windows. False alarms can irritate neighbors and subject you to fines.

Alarm systems are typically sold through contractors; some do-it-yourself kits are available in superstores such as Home Depot or specialty chains such as *Radio Shack. ADT, AT&T,* and *Brinks* are the big brand names.

The choices

A typical security system consists of sensors to detect an intruder, a remote or keypad-console control to arm and disarm the system, a central control unit to receive signals from the sensors, and a siren. The most sophisticated also provide a telephone dialer to alert a monitoring agency or call a number of your choice.

Once you know you want an alarm system, your choice is between a wired and a wireless system. The choice largely depends on whether you handle the installation yourself or hire a professional.

Wireless system. This type is the easiest to install. It's a good idea to mount the control center out of sight. Sensors communicate with the center via radio waves. In the simplest systems, one box houses everything but the sensors. Good systems have a remote alarm. Some door and window sensors come with self-stick pads to make installation especially easy. Most wireless systems have relatively plain controls and only a few operating options. And these systems generally can be armed and disarmed with a remote control.

Wired system. A wired system has strategically placed sensors that are physically linked to the central control unit. Installation requires drilling holes in walls and woodwork, fishing wire through walls and floors, and making electrical connections.

If you opt for professional installation of either type of system, you'll have to negotiate what it includes. Be prepared to steer the salesperson away from the contractor's most profitable products. Read contracts and sales agreements closely, and ask to change things you don't like.

Features and conveniences

Zone setup. With all wired and some wireless ones, you can divide a home into zones—a door, a room, a row of windows, for example. Zone control can help you find a door or window left open; a signal on the control panel tells you which part of the house is vulnerable. Wireless, single-zone systems are generally best suited for apartments or small houses.

Perimeter sensors. These protect the area around whatever boundary line you've established—along doors and windows, the edge of your yard, or both. Available types include:

■ A magnetic reed switch, which consists of a spring-loaded switch and magnet mounted side by side on a door or window and its adjacent frame. When the window or door opens, it breaks the connection. ■ Wired screens, which sound the alarm if the screen is cut or removed, let you leave windows open. ■ A mechanical plunger switch, used on steel doors or metal window frames, pops up to sound the alarm when the door or window opens. ■ Glass-break detectors, which are mounted directly on glass, are sensitive to vibration.

Area sensors. These can spot an intruder who eludes the perimeter sensors. They respond to motion by sensing a change within their field of "view"—an entire room, driveway, or even the backyard. Available types include:

■ Ultrasonic detectors, which emit sound waves beyond the range of human hearing that are reflected off objects in the protected area. Any motion that changes the pattern of the waves trips the alarm. Such waves may not be sensitive enough in rooms with heavy drapes or carpet, and they may be too sensitive to air currents, making ultrasonics near open windows or vents a poor choice. Loud noises may also cause them to react. ■ Microwave detectors pick up motion through changes in the pattern of high-frequency radio waves they emit. Microwaves have more penetrating power than ultrasound, so they're effective at greater ranges—so sensitive that radio transmissions or static from fluorescent lights can set them off. ■ Passive infrared detectors detect sudden changes in surrounding temperatures—changes that a warm body can cause. A passive infrared detector can be aimed fairly precisely.

Control unit. All units have backup batteries to keep the alarm working if the power fails or is interrupted by a burglar. A professionally installed system uses big, rechargeable batteries that are continually charged to stay at full capacity.

Operating modes. All systems have several operating modes. An Away mode gives you about 30 seconds to exit after arming the alarm or to disarm it when you enter. Some wireless systems require you to disarm the system with the remote *before* entering. A Home setting temporarily disables all interior motion detectors, so you can walk freely around the house. A Panic or Emergency mode sounds the alarm instantly, even if the system isn't armed.

Siren. To attract attention, you need a siren that delivers at least 80 decibels of loudness at a distance of 10 feet. Most wired systems let you choose where to put the siren. Wireless models usually have the siren built into the central control unit. An outdoor siren, usually optional, is a necessity for a single-family house.

An outdoor strobe light—an option generally available for all wired systems and a few wireless ones—also attracts attention. The light's high-intensity flashes can help identify the house whose siren is howling.

Monitoring services. Professionally installed systems usually require you to subscribe to a telephone-monitoring service for a given time. When the alarm sounds, an automatic dialer alerts the service's operators. An operator then calls your home. If no one answers, or if the person who answers fails to provide the proper code word, the operator calls the police.

Some systems provide a distress provision. If an intruder forces you to disarm the system or cancel an alarm, you can seem to comply but enter a special code instead. It will tell the monitoring service to call the police directly.

The tests

Since the components in most home-security systems generally work quite well, we concentrate on differences in their capability and convenience. We analyze the amount and type of protection offered—the number of sensors and protection zones provided, how the system is armed and disarmed, and the extras available.

Buying advice

A wireless, do-it-yourself system costs less than a comparable, professionally installed system. It can also be easier to use because it often lets you arm and disarm the alarm from outside. But its capabilities are more limited and may not provide the peace of mind you'd like.

Wired systems are pricey but generally more sophisticated and less obtrusive than wireless systems. You'll probably need a contractor to do the work.

Based on our experiences with professional installations, your getting an effective system probably depends more on the skill and conscientiousness of the dealer than on any hardware.

Garage-door openers

▶ Ratings on page 183.

A garage-door opener lets you open and close the door at the touch of a button, so there's no need to exit the car to do the job by hand. And once the door's shut, it locked.

Major brands are *Sears, Genie, Stanley,* and *Chamberlain.* Openers cost from $120 to $350. Most openers are do-it-yourself units sold in hardware stores or home centers; others are sold by dealers or installers.

Safety systems

Since 1982, all openers must include a mechanism that automatically reverses the door within two seconds of contacting anything in its path. Even so, many children have died after being trapped or crushed by a moving door. To further reduce the risk of deaths or injuries, openers made after January 1, 1993, must have additional safeguards. Most openers rely on an electric eye, mounted on the garage door's jamb, to detect anything in its path and trigger the auto-reverse. Others have a tape switch or door-edge sensor to trigger the auto-reverse.

The choices

All the openers come with a power unit that drives a trolley linked by an arm to the door, a remote, a wall switch, and a manual release cord. The power unit, mounted near the ceiling, uses a chain or worm gear to drive the trolley along a rail between the power head and the front of the garage. As the trolley moves, so goes the door. A remote control lets you operate the opener from the house or the car; a wall switch inside the garage does the same. A manual-release cord lets you disengage the opener. Most models work with a single- or double-width one-piece or sectional door, with or without tracks.

Installation. First, decide if you will do the work. The job requires respectable mechanical skills and several hours' time. Hiring someone to handle installation will cost about $70 to $100. Dealer installers tend to install premium-priced models.

Horsepower. The motors that drive the openers come in three sizes: ¼, ⅓, and ½ horsepower. Most consumers buy the ½-hp size. Our tests indicate that ¼ hp for a single door is perfectly adequate. In general, the brawnier motors don't work faster or compensate better for an unbalanced door.

Features and conveniences

Remote control. One battery-powered digital remote that operates up to several hundred feet away is standard. A second one costs $20 to $35. Compact remotes fit in a pocket; others clip on the car's sun visor.

To set the code that operates the remote, you generally flip small on-off switches in the remote that match settings on the switches in the power head. Most remotes provide at least 10 switches for both remote and receiver—enough for more than 1000 different code settings, which should deter any intruder. More elaborate remotes can learn a setting electronically, and remember up to five different settings keyed into from different remotes. Another type dispenses with switch-setting; it has built-in factory settings you activate by pressing two buttons. Basic models worked just as well as the fancier models in our tests.

Manual release. A rope-and-latch disconnect to disengage the trolley from the door with a tug on the rope is a necessity in a power failure. Look for one that lets you let go of the rope to work the door by hand after disconnecting the trolley. Having to keep the rope under constant tension when pulling the door is a nuisance, especially if the trolley stops in midcourse.

Lights. Every opener's power head has a provision for a light bulb. The bulb goes on when the door opens or closes and stays on for at least four minutes after the door closes. On many models the light also flashes when the electric eye reverses the door.

The small auxiliary light built into most wall controls guides you in the dark. A "vacation" switch that renders the opener deaf to all radio signals until you reset it; unplugging the opener works just as well.

Outside operation. You may have to open a locked garage when you don't have access to the remote. Three options help:

A key switch or a key disconnect are typically a $20 option. Neither switch is very secure. The most sophisticated option is a battery-powered, wireless keypad you mount on an outside wall near the garage door. A touch pad provides the best security. It costs about $40.

Installation. Openers weigh about 30 pounds—light enough for one person to set up (though the job is easier with two).

With openers sold at stores, you must assemble sections of rail, connect the rail to the power head, mount the works on the ceiling, and connect the opener to the door. Finally, you must install the electric eye, making adjustments to the door's travel and force. The job takes six to eight hours.

Most openers sold by garage-door specialists require less time to put together, mainly because the rails come fully assembled. Many such models tended to have incomplete or hard-to-follow instructions, and lacked necessary hardware.

The tests

We put each opener's safety features to the test, using a 16-foot-wide sectional door fitted in a garage-sized frame in our lab. We also assess how easily the openers are to assemble, install, adjust, and operate on a balanced and unbalanced door. Speed of door opening is another factor we gauge.

Buying advice

Good performance and a competent safety system are the norm so let price and features be your guide.

Power drills

▶ Ratings on page 189.

The most common power tool in the home workshop is a drill. Besides drilling holes, it can be adapted to sand, grind, polish, drive screws, and stir paint.

Black & Decker, Skil, and *Sears* are the most familiar brands. Names such as *Bosch, Makita,* and *DeWalt* usually represent the pricey "professional" grade of drill.

The choices

Virtually all power drills are variable-speed and reversible. Most models also have a ⅜-inch chuck (that is, they can hold

bits with a shank diameter of up to ⅜ inch).

Corded drills. Among drills, plug-in models are the workhorses. They deliver the most power—maximum turning speed and torque. The strongest drills tend to be the expensive "professional" models. Price: $30 to $300.

Cordless drills. Cordless drills draw power from nickel-cadmium batteries that need one to six hours to recharge. That's enough power for about 10 minutes of medium-duty drilling time. The best cordless drills in our tests could barely match the power of the weakest plug-in.

Cordless drills excel at driving screws. Most are equipped with an adjustable slip clutch that stops driving once the screw head is seated. Price: $30 to $350.

Features and conveniences

Chuck choices. Drills come with a Jacobs chuck that uses a key to tighten the bit or with a keyless chuck you tighten by hand. Both types work fine.

Speed. Drills have fixed or variable speed. Fixed-speed models come in two variations: a single speed, which is usually 600 revolutions per minute (rpm) or two speeds, typically 300 and 550 rpm. Variable-speed drills are continuously variable—the usual range among corded models is 0 to 1200 rpm; high-speed models go as high as 2500 rpm. Some cordless drills also have two speed ranges—0 to 400 rpm and 0 to 1000 rpm, say. The lower range sacrifices speed for increased torque.

A model's rated speed on the drill's nameplate is its maximum speed under light loads. The rated speed is a clue to what a drill is best suited for. A corded model rated for 1200 rpm is fine for general use. Drills at the 2500 rpm end of the range are best for light-duty work using light bits. The most flexible speed selection for a cordless drill is variable, with two ranges, which suits screw-driving and using large bits.

Trigger lock. All corded drills have a trigger lock to keep them in the On position. Less convenient is a recessed slide switch in front of the handle.

Reversing control. This is an interlock that protects the drivetrain by making you release the trigger before shifting into reverse. Even with that feature, you can still jolt the drill into reverse from forward.

Handles. Cordless models are more balanced, thanks to the weight of batteries in their handles. Most corded models have the handle at the end of the motor housing, which tends to give a nose-heavy feel. For a lot of rough drilling, consider a model with an auxiliary side-handle.

Electrical safeguards. Most corded-models have an all-plastic motor housing, which makes remote any bad shock. The shock potential is greater on models with a metal gear case at the front of the drill.

Double-insulated models with a two-pronged plug guard against shock. Two-prongers are preferable to the old three-pronged plug whose safety depends on use with a properly grounded power receptacle.

A cordless drill can be damaged if there's an overload. Look for a model with a circuit breaker or circuitry to shut off power.

Battery charging. Most batteries take about one and a half hours to recharge (not the one hour many claim). Batteries that recharge in about an hour appear to use "fast recharge" cells, which have a much shorter life expectancy.

The tests

We test for maximum power output, an advantage in long, tough jobs; sustained power, a measure of performance under ever-increasing loads without overheating; and stall torque, which reflects a drill's ability to keep from burning out when the bit binds suddenly. We also judge screw-driving ability, construction quality and, for cordless models, the amount of work possible on a single battery charge.

Buying advice

A ⅜-inch corded drill with variable-speed control is the best choice for most users. We recommend a variable-speed model with a top speed between 1000 and 1300 rpm—not a high-speed unit. Expect to pay $60 for a decent model.

A competent cordless drill costs around $150 to $200. We recommend a variable speed model with two speed ranges.

RATINGS DO-IT-YOURSELF HOME-SECURITY SYSTEMS

▶ **See report, page 168.** Last time rated in Consumer Reports: May 1994.

Brand-name recommendations: We prefer the *Radio Shack's Safe House 49-2010* and the *X-10 DS7000*. Basic sets sell for about $250 or less. Add 10 sensors (including a motion detector) and a separate siren, and the price nearly doubles. If you want a wired system, consider the *Safe House 49-485*. A setup comparable with the smallest dealer installation would run about $375.

For a typical do-it-yourself system, expect: ■ System price below $600. ■ Easy installation of central unit and sensors. ■ For wireless system, controls for arming, disarming, and Panic button located on remote control or at the console; for wired system, the controls are at the console. ■ Moderate security. ■ Relatively few features. **A choice you'll have to make:** ■ Wireless or wired system.

Notes on the table: Price. Basic prices are suggested retail for starter sets. System prices are for basic systems, augmented to include 9 door and window sensors, a motion detector, and a separate siren. **Sensors** lists the number in a basic set and the suggested retail price for each additional one. **Zones.** The number of control-center circuits (excluding those for a Panic button or smoke detector) available for dividing a dwelling into security areas.

Listed in order of versatility and convenience

Brand and model	Price		Sensors	Zones	Comments
	BASIC	SYSTEM	NO./PRICE		
WIRELESS					
Safe House 49-2010 (Radio Shack)	$200	$520	1/$30	16	Panic signal triggered by pressing any 2 remote-control buttons simultaneously. Main siren in console is disadvantage. Listening device "hears" an existing smoke detector and sounds alarm.
X-10 DS7000 Powerhouse	266	463	2/21	16	Alerts you before you enter the house if alarm tripped. Main siren in console is disadvantage.
X-10 SS5400 Powerhouse	110	388	1/21	16	Alerts you before you enter the house if alarm tripped. Main siren in console is disadvantage.
Dimango RC-2100	250	424	6/25	1	Alerts you before you enter the house if alarm tripped. No monitoring of sensor/transmitters from console of single-zone systems; sensors can be checked by opening doors or windows.
Linear Defiant Security DE90	169	487	2/32	1	Alerts you before you enter the house if alarm tripped. Main siren in console is disadvantage. Siren not loud enough. User can adjust entrance delay. No monitoring of sensor/transmitters from console of single-zone systems, but sensors can be checked with test buttons.
WIRED					
Safe House 49-485 (Radio Shack)	200	369	0/5	7	Users can adjust entrance and exit delay.

RATINGS   FIRE EXTINGUISHERS

▶ **See report, page 167.** Last time rated in Consumer Reports: May 1994.

Brand-name recommendations: For a full-floor model, consider the *Buckeye 5HI SA-40 ABC*, $45, and the *Ansul Sentry SY-0516*, $40, both 3-A:40-B:C models that weigh less than 10 pounds and have a wide spray pattern. Additional coverage for individual rooms is available from supplemental models: A multipurpose extinguisher such as the *Kidde FA110G*, $14, a 1-A:10-B:C model would be a good choice for a den. Consider the *Kidde FA5G*, $11, a 5-B:C model, and the *Kidde KK2*, $12, a 2-B:C model, for the kitchen.

For the typical fire extinguisher, expect: ■ Easy activation by handle after removing a safety pin. ■ A marine-bracket mounting. ■ Fire-engine-red finish. ■ 9 to 24 sec.'s spray of dry chemical, depending mostly on the extinguisher's size. ■ For full-floor models: rating of at least 2-A:10-B:C, indicating sufficient capacity and versatility to be the sole extinguisher on 1 level of a home; a dial gauge to check pressure conveniently; the capability to be recharged; a hose to help direct the spray. ■ For supplemental models: spray nozzle that provides less control than a hose; small and medium models that spray more slowly and are more susceptible to impact and high-temperature damage, the inability to be recharged. **A choice you'll have to make:** ■ Size (full-floor extinguishers, large or medium supplemental extinguishers).

Notes on the table: Within groups (full-floor and supplemental), extinguishers are separated by Underwriters Laboratories designations of capability and capacity. **Price** is the national average. An * indicates the price we paid. **Abuse** is based on tests of resistance to physical damage on impact and to high temperature.

Within type, listed in order of ease of use and durability

Better ◀—————▶ Worse
⊖ ⊖ ○ ◒ ●

Brand and model	Price	Overall score	Ease of use	Abuse	Spray time	Comments
		P F G VG E				

FULL-FLOOR MULTIPURPOSE MODELS

UL SIZE 3-A:40-B:C

Brand and model	Price	Overall score	Ease of use	Abuse	Spray time	Comments
Buckeye 5HI SA-40 ABC	$45	▬▬▬▬	⊖	⊖	⊖	Spray wider than most.
Ansul Sentry SY-0516	40	▬▬▬▬	⊖	⊖	⊖	Optional marine bracket. Spray wider, faster than most.
General TCP-5LH	38	▬▬▬▬	⊖	⊖	⊖	Needs forceful squeeze to spray. Spray narrower, faster than most.
American LaFrance 5MB-6H	38	▬▬▬▬	⊖	⊖	○	Optional marine bracket. Spray faster than most.
Kidde FA340HD	30	▬▬▬▬	○	⊖	⊖	Needs forceful squeeze to spray. Spray wider than most.

Ratings continued ▶

Ratings continued

Brand and model	Price	Overall score (P F G VG E)	Ease of use	Abuse	Spray time	Comments
UL SIZE 2-A:10-B:C						
Ansul Sentry SY-0515 [1]	$39	████████	⊖	⊖	⊖	Optional marine bracket.
First Alert FE2A10 [1]	30	████████	⊖	⊖	⊖	Pressure gauge. Wall hook.
American LaFrance 5MB-7H	37	███████	⊖	⊖	⊖	Optional marine bracket.
Buckeye M-5 ABC-II-100	55	██████	⊖	⊖	○	Pressure gauge.

SUPPLEMENTAL MODELS

Brand and model	Price	Overall score (P F G VG E)	Ease of use	Abuse	Spray time	Comments
LARGE MULTIPURPOSE (UL SIZE 1-A:10-B:C)						
Ansul Sentry SY-0216	28	█████	⊖	⊖	●	Optional marine bracket.
Kidde FA110G	14	████	⊖	⊖	○	Needs forceful squeeze to spray. Spray narrower than most. More susceptible than others to impact damage.
Fyr Fyter D1A10	20	████	⊖	○	○	No pressure gauge. More susceptible than others to impact damage. Safety catch is not a pin, but bracket prevents accidental discharge.
American LaFrance P250 MA-1	23	████	⊖	⊖	●	Optional marine bracket. Needs forceful squeeze to spray.
First Alert FE1A10	15	███	⊖	○	●	No pressure gauge. Spray narrower, faster than most. More susceptible than others to impact damage.
LARGE, FOR FLAMMABLE LIQUID AND ELECTRICAL FIRES (UL SIZE 10-B:C)						
Ansul Sentry SY-0236	31	██████	⊖	⊖	○	Optional marine bracket. Rechargeable.
General CP-21/2J	23	█████	⊖	⊖	●	Rechargeable. Spray narrower than most.
General CP-5J	41	█████	⊖	⊖	●	Rechargeable. Spray narrower, faster, than most.
American LaFrance 275RA-1	27	█████	⊖	⊖	●	Rechargeable. Spray narrower than most.
Buckeye 2.5 STD-100	35	████	⊖	○	●	Rechargeable. High temperatures damaged some samples.
Kidde FA10G	12	███	⊖	○	○	Spray wider than most. High temperatures damaged some samples. More susceptible than others to impact damage.

[1] *These two models are similar.*

Brand and model	Price	Overall score					Ease of use	Abuse	Spray time	Comments
		P	F	G	VG	E				
First Alert FE10	$14						⊖	○	⊖	No pressure gauge. Spray narrower than most. More susceptible than others to impact damage.
Fyr Fyter D250	23*						○	○	○	No pressure gauge. Optional marine bracket. High temperatures damaged some samples. More susceptible than others to impact damage. Safety catch is not a pin.

MEDIUM, FOR FLAMMABLE LIQUID AND ELECTRICAL FIRES (UL SIZE 5-B:C)

Brand and model	Price	Overall score					Ease of use	Abuse	Spray time	Comments
Kidde FA5G	11						⊖	○	○	Needs forceful squeeze to spray. Spray wider than most.
Fyr Fyter 210D	14						○	○	⊖	No pressure gauge. Push-button operation. Safety catch is not a pin.

SMALL, FOR FLAMMABLE LIQUID AND ELECTRICAL FIRES (UL SIZE 2-B:C)

Brand and model	Price	Overall score					Ease of use	Abuse	Spray time	Comments
Kidde KK2	12						⊖	○	⊖	No pressure gauge. Push-button operation. Spray narrower than most. Safety catch is not a pin. Wall hook.
Kidde PKG 200	13						⊖	○	⊖	Not damaged by high temperatures. Safety catch is not a pin. No bracket.
Fyr Fyter PKP 100	23 ②						⊖	○	⊖	No pressure gauge. Push-button operation. Spray narrower than most. Safety catch is not a pin. No bracket.

② *Price is per extinguisher in package of two.*

RATINGS SMOKE DETECTORS

▶ **See report, page 165.** Last time rated in Consumer Reports: May 1994.

Brand-name recommendations: We recommend both an ionization-type and a photo-electric-type detector for an early warning of any fire. All photoelectric detectors we tested proved competent. The *Double System* actually houses both types of detector, but its ionizing detector is less sensitive than that of the best ionization-only models. The three top-rated ionization detectors merit first consideration. Of the three, the *Firex* is the smallest, and thus the least obtrusive. The *Safe House* has a Hush button that silences the detector during false alarms.

For the typical smoke detector, expect: ■ Unit to carry Underwriters Laboratory (UL) certification. ■ For battery-powered models: a 9-volt battery, replaceable by user. ■ For photoelectric models: Best response to smoldering, smoky fires; limited availability; fewer false alarms triggered by cooking. ■ For ionization models: Best response to flaming fires with little smoke, wide availability.

Notes on the table: Price is a national average, batteries not included. An * indicates price CU paid. **Power** source is either a 9-volt battery (Bat.), household current (AC), or household current with battery backup (AC/Bat.). **Response** to fires is indicated for smoky fires, which smolder, and for flaming fires, which create little smoke. Ⓢ indicates tested model has been replaced by successor model; according to the mfr., the performance of new model should be similar to the tested model but features may vary. Not tested.

Listed in order of overall quality

E ⊜ VG ⊖ G ○ F ◖ P ●

Brand and model	Price	Power	Overall score					Response		Comments
			P	F	G	VG	E	SMOKY	FLAMING	
PHOTOELECTRIC MODELS										
First Alertz Double System SA301	$25	Bat.						⊜	○	Hard to test if ceiling-mounted.
Dicon Photoelectric 440	24	Bat.						⊜	◖	—
First Alert Photoelectronic SA203	20	Bat.						⊜	◖	Hard to test if ceiling-mounted.
IONIZATION MODELS										
Firex 0465/C	12	Bat.						○	⊜	Smaller than most. Loud alarm.
First Alert Hall/Stairway SA150LT Ⓢ SA150LTD, $25	20	Bat.						○	⊜	Can test with flashlight. Sounded cooking false alarm.
Safe House 49-458 (Radio Shack)	13	Bat.						○	⊜	Hush button. Sounded cooking false alarm.
Dicon Micro 300	11	Bat.						○	⊜	—

Brand and model	Price	Power	Overall score					Response		Comments
			P	F	G	VG	E	SMOKY	FLAMING	
First Alert Kitchen SA88	$15	Bat.	██████					⊖	⊖	Hush button. Can test with flashlight.
Code One 2000 D	13	Bat.	██████					⊖	⊖	Self-tests weekly. Smaller than most. Loud alarm.
Family Gard FG1000C	14	Bat.	█████					⊖	⊖	—
BRK 83R	14①	Bat.	████					⊖	⊖	Loud alarm. Sounded cooking false alarm.
Safety's Sake Petey-the-Puppy	18②	Bat.	████					⊖	⊖	Loud alarm. No monitor light. Designed for children.
Family Gard FG888D	7	Bat.	████					⊖	⊖	—
Dicon 370LB	24	AC/Bat.	████					⊖	⊖	Hush button.
Lifesaver 0918	16*	Bat.	████					⊖	⊖	Hush button. Hard to test if ceiling-mounted. Sounded cooking false alarm.
Lifesaver 1275	21*	AC/Bat.	████					⊖	⊖	Hush button. Hard to test if ceiling-mounted.
BRK 1839N12R	28*①	AC	████					⊖	⊖	Loud alarm. Sounded cooking false alarm. No backup battery.
First Alert SA86RAC	20	AC/Bat.	████					⊖	⊖	—
Firex 0440/FX 1218	18	AC/Bat.	████					⊖	⊖	Hard to test if ceiling-mounted.
Code One 2000 0192/E	16	Bat.	████					⊖	○	Loud alarm.
Kidde KSA-700	18*	Bat.	███					⊖	○	Loud alarm.
Generation 2 1001	23*	AC	███					⊖	○	Sounded cooking false alarm, hard to shut off. Mounts in ceiling light fixture.

① Not available in stores; call 800 323-9005.

② May be ordered directly from mfr. (800 877-1250); price includes shipping.

RATINGS DOOR LOCKS

▶ **See report, page 163.** Last time rated in Consumer Reports: May 1994.

Brand-name recommendations: None of the entry locksets afforded great protection, not even top-rated ones. The entrance handlesets did better, largely because they include a cylinder deadbolt lock. Good auxiliary locks will protect your home from all but the most determined burglars when equipped with the right hardware. The *National H479,* $30, stands out among the single-cylinder deadbolt locks we tested. Surface-mounted deadbolt locks offer good protection against kicking or jimmying. The best: the *Lori 1200,* $33.

For a typical door lock, expect: ■ Little protection from kicking or hammering using standard hardware. ■ Adequate installation instructions. ■ A 5-pin tumbler assembly that locks and unlocks by key from the outside and by thumbturn from the inside. ■ Compatibility with 2⅜-in. and 2¾-in. backsets.

Notes on the table: Price is approximate retail. **Overall score** is based mainly on ability to resist various types of assault. A skilled burglar could defeat every lock within 5 min. **Kicking** represents resistance to several simulated kicks with locks secured with 3-in. long strike screws and a high-security strike plate.

Within type, listed in order of resistance to physical attack

E VG G F P
⊖ ⊖ ○ ◑ ●

Brand and model	Price	Overall score					Kicking		Jimmy-ing	Extract-ing	Comments
		P	F	G	VG	E	LONG SCREWS	HEAVY STRIKE			

PRIMARY LOCKS: ENTRY LOCKSETS

Brand and model	Price	Overall score					Kicking LONG SCREWS	Kicking HEAVY STRIKE	Jimmy-ing	Extract-ing	Comments
Schlage F51NV	$21	■					●	○	●	●	Locked latch releases with turn of the knob from inside; no need to use thumbturn.
EZ-Set CS 100	10	■					●	●	●	◑	—
NT Harloc 59-700	17	■					●	◑	●	◑	Drive-in latch/bolt eliminates need to mortise door edge.
Titan 740	22	▬					●	◑	●	●	Has a 6-pin tumbler. Key needed for copying.
Kwikset 400T	12	▬					●	◑	●	●	Key needed for copying.
Weslock SV640	30	■					●	◑	●	●	Key needed for copying. Releases with turn of inside knob. Drive-in latch/bolt eliminates need to mortise door edge.

Brand and model	Price	Overall score					Kicking		Jimmy-ing	Extract-ing	Comments
		P	F	G	VG	E	LONG SCREWS	HEAVY STRIKE			
MasterLock 13232	$22	▪					●	●	●	●	More resistant to hammering than most of its type. Drive-in latch/bolt eliminates need to mortise door edge.
National H446	21	▪					●	●	●	●	Releases with turn of inside knob.

PRIMARY LOCKS: ENTRANCE HANDLESETS

Brand and model	Price	Overall score					Kicking		Jimmy-ing	Extract-ing	Comments
		P	F	G	VG	E	LONG SCREWS	HEAVY STRIKE			
National H425	64	▬	▬	▬			◑	⊖	⊖	⊖	Highly resistant to hacksawing.
Schlage F160NV	80	▬	▬	▬			●	◑	⊖	○	More resistant to hammering. Highly resistant to hacksawing. Comes with at least 3-in. screws. Plastic strike box.
Weslock 00361	76	▬	▬	▬			○	⊖	⊖	○	Key needed for copying. Bolt cannot be manipulated with ice pick. Highly resistant to hacksawing.
NT Harloc 49-1020	47	▬	▬	▬			◑	⊖	⊖	⊖	Key needed for copying. Highly resistant to hacksawing.
Kwikset 681-B	69	▬	▬	▬			◑	○	⊖	○	Key needed for copying.
EZ-Set CS 400	59	▬	▬	▬			◑	◑	⊖	○	Highly resistant to hacksawing.

AUXILIARY LOCKS: CYLINDER DEADBOLT MODELS

Brand and model	Price	Overall score					Kicking		Jimmy-ing	Extract-ing	Comments
		P	F	G	VG	E	LONG SCREWS	HEAVY STRIKE			
National H479	30	▬	▬	▬			○	◑	◑	⊖	Bolt cannot be manipulated with ice pick. Highly resistant to hacksawing. Plastic strike box.
National H474	18	▬	▬	▬			◑	⊖	⊖	⊖	Highly resistant to hacksawing.
MasterLock 1400330	22	▬	▬	▬			○	○	⊖	⊖	Bolt cannot be manipulated with ice pick. Highly resistant to hacksawing. Plastic strike box.
Weslock 486	32	▬	▬				◑	⊖	⊖	○	More resistant to hammering than most. Key needed for copying. Bolt cannot be manipulated with ice pick.
Segal 520	24	▬	▬	▬			○	○	⊖	●	Most resistant to kicking using standard hardware. Highly resistant to hacksawing. Metal strike box. Comes with hardware for a 2⅜-in. backset.
Weslock 371	19	▬	▬				◑	⊖	⊖	◑	Key needed for copying. Bolt cannot be manipulated with an ice pick.

Ratings continued ▶

Ratings continued

Brand and model	Price	Overall score					Kicking		Jimmy-ing	Extract-ing	Comments
		P	F	G	VG	E	LONG SCREWS	HEAVY STRIKE			

AUXILIARY LOCKS: CYLINDER DEADBOLT MODELS

Brand and model	Price	Overall score	Kicking LONG SCREWS	Kicking HEAVY STRIKE	Jimmy-ing	Extract-ing	Comments
Schlage B460	$28	▬▬	●	◑	⊖	⊖	More resistant to hammering than most. Highly resistant to hacksawing. Comes with at least 3-in. screws. Plastic strike box. Comes with hardware for a 2⅜-in. backset.
Schlage B160NV	21	▬▬	◑	◑	⊖	◐	Highly resistant to hacksawing. Comes with at least 3-in. screws. Plastic strike box.
Kwikset 660	14	▬▬	●	○	⊖	○	Key needed for copying. Comes with hardware for a 2⅜-in. backset.
EZ-Set CS200U	10	▬▬	●	◑	⊖	◑	Highly resistant to hacksawing.
NT Harloc 49-820	14	▬▬	●	○	⊖	◑	Highly resistant to hacksawing.
NT Harloc 59-920	18	▬▬	●	◑	⊖	●	Highly resistant to hacksawing. Drive-in latch/bolt eliminates need to mortise door edge.

AUXILIARY LOCK: DOUBLE CYLINDER DEADBOLT MODEL

Brand and model	Price	Overall score	Kicking LONG SCREWS	Kicking HEAVY STRIKE	Jimmy-ing	Extract-ing	Comments
Kwikset 587	24	▬▬▬	○	⊖	⊖	⊖	Key needed for copying. Bolt cannot be manipulated with an ice pick. Highly resistant to hacksawing and hammering.

AUXILIARY LOCKS: SURFACE-MOUNTED DEADBOLT MODELS

Brand and model	Price	Overall score	Kicking LONG SCREWS	Kicking HEAVY STRIKE	Jimmy-ing	Extract-ing	Comments
Lori 1200	33	▬▬	○	—	⊖	○	Key needed for copying. Highly resistant to hacksawing. Comes with hardware for a 2⅜-in. backset.
Segal 666	45	▬▬	⊖	—	⊖	⊖	Highly resistant to hacksawing. Comes with hardware for a 2⅜-in. backset.
Segal Slamlock 466	55	▬▬	⊖	—	⊖	⊖	Highly resistant to hacksawing. Comes with hardware for a 2⅜-in. backset. Deadbolt automatically locks when door is closed.

RATINGS | GARAGE-DOOR OPENERS

▶ **See report, page 171.** Last time rated in Consumer Reports: January 1994.

Brand-name recommendations: Every opener worked competently and safely in our tests. Price, not performance, separates these garage-door openers. If you hire some-one to handle the installation, plan to spend another $70 to $100 or so. And if you buy an opener from a garage-door installer, you'll pay a premium. The openers sold by installers are at the bottom of the Ratings because of price, not quality.

For the typical garage-door opener, expect: ■ Chain-and-cable drive. ■ Main auto-matic-reversal safety system controlled by an electric eye, with a secondary safety system that will reverse the door's direction within 2 sec. after contact with a person or an object. ■ Design that will open a hinged, sectional door up to 16 ft. wide; most also work with 1-piece tracked and trackless doors. ■ At least 1 digital remote control with an ample range, and a wall-mounted push-button control. ■ Built-in light that stays on at least 4 min. after door closes. ■ Lock-off feature for manual operation of door. ■ Light flash-es when electric eye triggers auto-reversal. **A choice you'll have to make:** ■ Whether you want a way to open the garage door from the outside without the remote control with a key switch, touch pad, or key-disconnect feature.

Notes on the table: A * preceding the model name denotes an opener sold only by profes-sional garage-door installers. **Price** is the mfr.'s suggested or approx. retail. **Speed.** All models opened or closed a door in 10 to 14 sec. **Reverse force** reflects the average max-imum force exerted before the opener reversed direction. Heaviest force: about 70 lbs., the equivalent of a strong push. **Assembly** shows how easy we found the openers to as-semble. Ⓢ indicates tested model has been replaced by successor model; according to the mfr., the performance of new model should be similar to the tested model but features may vary. Not tested. Ⓓ indicates model discontinued or replacement not similar.

Models listed in order of increasing price

Brand and model	Price	Speed	Reverse force	Assembly	Comments
Sears Craftsman 53225 Ⓓ	$140	⊖	○	○	Very easy to set code. Limited code-changing options.
Stanley ST200 Standard	129	○	○	○	Trolley easy to disengage. Lock-off was very easy to disengage. Trolley very easy to re-engage with door closed.
Sears Craftsman 53325	160	⊖	◒	○	Very easy to set code. Limited code-changing options. Remote can operate products connected to in-house receivers.
Chamberlain 2100 Standard Duty	139	⊖	○	◒	Very easy to set code. Limited code-changing options.
Stanley ST400 Deluxe	149	○	⊖	○	Trolley easy to disengage and very easy to re-engage with door closed. Lock-off was very easy to disengage.

Ratings continued ▶

Ratings continued

Brand and model	Price	Speed	Reverse force	Assembly	Comments
Genie G8000	$280	◐	◐	◐	Trolley easy to disengage. Lock-off was very easy to disengage. Needs more than 2-in. clearance between door and ceiling. Worm-gear drive.
Sears Craftsman 53425	160	◐	○	○	Very easy to set code. Limited code-changing options. Remote can operate products connected to in-house receivers.
Chamberlain 5100 Premium Heavy Duty	189	◐	○	◐	Very easy to set code. Limited code-changing options. Remote can operate products connected to in-house receivers.
Stanley SL700 Light Maker	189	○	◐	○	Trolley easy to disengage. Lock-off was very easy to disengage. Trolley very easy to re-engage with door closed.
Master Mechanic Premium	190	◐	○	◐	Very easy to set code. Limited code-changing options. Includes 2 remotes. Remote can operate products connected to in-house receivers.
Genie GXL9500	320	◐	◐	◐	Trolley easy to disengage. Lock-off was very easy to disengage. Includes 2 remotes. Remote can operate products connected to in-house receivers. Needs more than 2-in. clearance between door and ceiling. Worm-gear drive.
Sears Craftsman 53525	200	◐	◐	○	Very easy to set code. Limited code-changing options. Includes 2 remotes. Remote can operate products connected to in-house receivers.
***Lift-Master** 1260 Premium	195	◐	◐	◐	Very easy to set code. Limited code-changing options. Lacks hanging hardware. Chain drive.
***Challenger** 9500	180	◐	○	◐	Easy to change codes. Trolley very easy to re-engage with door closed. No lock-off when disengaging trolley. Lacks hanging hardware. Chain drive.
***Genie** Pro 98-S Premium	300	◐	◐	◐	Easy to change codes. Trolley easy to disengage. Lock-off was very easy to disengage. Lacks hanging hardware. Needs more than 2-in. clearance between door and ceiling. Worm-gear drive.
***Stanley** GT400	220	○	◐	○	Trolley easy to disengage. Lock-off was very easy to disengage. Heaviest tested (51 lb.). Needs more than 2-in. clearance between door and ceiling. Chain drive.
***Overhead** 656 Heavy Duty	285	◐	◐	◐	Very easy to set code. Trolley easy to disengage. Lock-off was very easy to disengage. Trolley hard to re-engage with door closed. Lacks hanging hardware. Includes 2 remotes. Remote can operate products connected to in-house receivers.
***Raynor** R-260 Ⓢ R-270, $260	304	◐	◐	◐	Easy to change codes. Lacks hanging hardware. Chain drive.

RATINGS INTERIOR LATEX PAINTS

▶ **See report, page 158.** Last time rated in Consumer Reports: February 1994.

Brand-name recommendations: When ranked by overall performance—water resistance, cleaning, spatter, fading, and hiding—*Tru-Test E-Z Kare EZ* came out on top. It sells for $19 a gallon, on average. Just as good was *Behr Premium Plus Flat*, $16, which ranked number two. *Wal-Mart Flat*, $7, combines very good performance and a very good price: We've judged it A Best Buy. But you need not limit your choice to the first few paints in the Ratings. Any of the top 10 are worth considering. And if hiding power matters far more to you than other factors, you can even look beyond the top 10.

For the typical interior latex paint, expect: ■ Very good to excellent resistance to water and to sticking. ■ Very good resistance to spatter. ■ Good or very good resistance to fading. ■ More stain resistance from low-luster and eggshell paints than flat. ■ 1-coat coverage with blue; 2-coats or more with off-white, gold, red, orange, green, and yellow. ■ Better color-matching with computers than by eye.

Notes on the table: We tested off-white, gold, red, orange, green, blue, and yellow in custom-mixed colors. The tinting base used and the accuracy of the color-matching can affect a brand's overall performance. **Price** is the estimated average, based on a national survey. An * indicates price we paid. **Gloss** is based on our measurements. Flat paint has essentially no gloss; low-luster has a very slight sheen; eggshell has the highest sheen. E=eggshell, F=flat, LL=low-luster. **Cleaning** scores show how well each paint held up to scrubbing and resisted stains. **Hiding** shows how well each paint covered the pattern of light-to-dark gray stripes on our hiding chart, with 1 coat and 2. The scores apply to the colors we tested, not to others in a brand. Resistance to fading was excellent for all the off-white paints. **Ratings Details:** Comments about color are called out only if that paint was exceptionally better or worse than the other colors and brands tested.

RATINGS OVERVIEW — Listed in order of overall performance

E=⊜ VG=⊜ G=○ F=◔ P=●

Brand and model	Price	Overall score	Gloss	Cleaning: Scrub	Cleaning: Stain	2-Coat Hiding	Fading
Tru-Test E-Z Kare EZ — True Value Hardware	*$19		E	⊜	⊜	⊜	⊜
Behr Premium Plus Flat	16		F	⊜	⊜	⊜	⊜
Behr Premium Plus Satin-Flat	17		F	⊜	⊜	⊜	⊜
Ace Seven Star Flat (Ace Hardware)	15		F	⊜	⊜	⊜	⊜
Ace Seven Star Satin (Ace Hardware)	14		E	⊜	⊜	⊜	○

Ratings continued ▶

Ratings continued

Brand and model	Price	Overall score (P F G VG E)	Gloss	Cleaning		Color properties	
				SCRUB	STAIN	2-COAT HIDING	FADING
Pratt & Lambert Accolade Velvet	$23	▬▬▬▬	E	⊖	⊖	⊖	○
Pittsburgh Manor Hall	21	▬▬▬▬	F	⊖	⊖	⊖	○
Wal-Mart Flat, **A BEST BUY**	7	▬▬▬	F	⊖	○	⊖	⊖
Benjamin Moore Regal Aquavelvet	23	▬▬▬	E	⊖	⊖	⊖	⊖
Fuller O'Brien Liquid Lustre	22	▬▬▬	LL	⊖	⊖	⊖	○
Dutch Boy Renaissance Flat	*17	▬▬▬	F	⊖	○	⊖	○
Fuller O'Brien Liquid Velvet	18	▬▬▬	F	⊖	◓	⊖	○
Tru-Test E-Z Kare EZF	12	▬▬▬	F	⊖	○	⊖	○
Dutch Boy Renaissance Satin	*19	▬▬▬	LL	○	⊖	⊖	○
Sears Best Easy Living Satin	18	▬▬▬	E	⊖	⊖	⊖	○
Wal-Mart Satin	8	▬▬▬	E	⊖	⊖	○	○
Devoe Wonder Tones Eggshell	17	▬▬▬	E	○	⊖	○	⊖
Glidden Spred Satin	12	▬▬	F	⊖	○	○	○
Dutch Boy Dirt Fighter Flat	12	▬▬	F	○	○	⊖	○
Valspar Flat	18	▬▬	F	○	○	⊖	⊖
Benjamin Moore Regal Wall Satin	18	▬▬	F	○	○	⊖	⊖
Devoe Wonder Tones Flat	16	▬▬	F	○	○	○	⊖
Dutch Boy Dirt Fighter Satin	14	▬▬	F	○	⊖	⊖	○
Sherwin Williams Classic 99 Flat	13	▬▬	F	○	◓	⊖	○
America's Finest Flat	9	▬▬	F	○	◓	⊖	◓
Sherwin Williams Super Paint Flat	18	▬▬	F	○	●	⊖	○
Sherwin Williams Classic 99 Satin	15	▬▬	F	◓	○	⊖	○

Brand and model	Price	Overall score					Gloss	Cleaning		Color properties	
		P	F	G	VG	E		SCRUB	STAIN	2-COAT HIDING	FADING
Performance Tough Flat, 10 yr. (Home Base)	$15	▬▬					F	◔	◔	⊖	⊖
Dutch Boy (K Mart) Fresh Look Flat	10	▬▬					F	●	◔	⊖	○
Glidden Spred Wall Flat	10	▬▬					F	●	●	⊖	⊖
Sherwin Williams Style Perfect Flat	9	▬					F	●	●	⊖	◔

RATINGS DETAILS   Models listed alphabetically

Ace Seven Star Flat	2-coat hiding: orange much worse than others.
Ace Seven Star Satin	Worse than others in resistance to sticking. All colors remained unchanged when scrubbed.
America's Finest Flat	1-coat hiding: gold, red, green much better than others. 2-coat hiding: yellow much worse than others. Scrub-resistance of paints made from deep base was better. Resistance to fading judged fair.
Behr Premium Plus Flat	1-coat hiding: gold, red, green much better than others. At least 3 colors suffered significant color change when scrubbed.
Behr Premium Plus Satin-Flat	1-coat hiding: green much better than others. White spattered much less than other colors. Resistance to spatter judged fair.
Benjamin Moore Regal Aquavelvet	2-coat hiding: orange much worse than others. Scrub-resistance of paints made from deep base was worse. Resistance to spatter judged fair.
Benjamin Moore Regal Wall Satin	2-coat hiding: orange, yellow much worse than others.
Devoe Wonder Tones Eggshell	Scrub-resistance of paints made from deep base was better.
Devoe Wonder Tones Flat	Scrub-resistance of paints made from deep base was better. We measured more volatile organic compounds in this brand than in others.
Dutch Boy (K Mart) Fresh Look Flat	Scrub-resistance of paints made from deep base was better. Significant amounts of stain penetrated coating. Resistance to water judged fair.
Dutch Boy Dirt Fighter Flat	1-coat hiding: gold, red much better than others. 2-coat hiding: yellow much worse than others. Scrub-resistance of paints made from deep base was better.
Dutch Boy Dirt Fighter Satin	2-coat hiding: yellow much worse than others. Green faded much more than others. Resistance to water judged fair.
Dutch Boy Renaissance Flat	1-coat hiding: green much better than others. Scrub-resistance of paints made from deep base was better.
Dutch Boy Renaissance Satin	Scrub-resistance of paints made from deep base was worse.
Fuller O' Brien Liquid Velvet	2-coat hiding: yellow much worse than others. Scrub-resistance of paints made from pastel base was worse.

Ratings continued ▶

Ratings continued

Fuller O'Brien Liquid Lustre	—
Glidden Spred Satin	Scrub-resistance of paints made from deep base was worse.
Glidden Spred Wall Flat	Scrub-resistance of paints made from deep base was better. At least 3 colors suffered significant color change when scrubbed. Significant amounts of stain penetrated coating.
Performance Tough Flat, 10 yr.	Significant amounts of stain penetrated coating.
Pittsburgh Manor Hall	1-coat hiding: red much better than others. 2-coat hiding: orange much worse than others. Scrub-resistance of paints made from deep base was better. All colors remained unchanged when scrubbed. Resistance to spatter judged fair.
Pratt & Lambert Accolade Velvet	1-coat hiding: red much better than others. 2-coat hiding: gold, orange, yellow, much worse than others. Green faded much more than others.
Sears Best Easy Living Satin	1-coat hiding: red, green much better than others. 2-coat hiding: orange much worse than others.
Sherwin Williams Classic 99 Flat	1-coat hiding: red, green much better than others. Orange faded much more than others. Scrub-resistance of paints made from deep base was better.
Sherwin Williams Classic 99 Satin	1-coat hiding: green much better than others. We measured more volatile organic compounds in this brand than in others.
Sherwin Williams Style Perfect Flat	1-coat hiding: green much better than others. At least 3 colors suffered significant color change when scrubbed. Significant amounts of stain penetrated coating. Resistance to water judged poor. Resistance to fading judged fair.
Sherwin Williams Super Paint Flat	1-coat hiding: gold, red, green much better than others. Orange faded much more than others. Scrub-resistance of paints made from deep base was better. At least 3 colors suffered significant color change when scrubbed.
Tru-Test E-Z Kare EZ	Worse than others in resistance to sticking. Gloss varied by base.
Tru-Test E-Z Kare EZF	Green faded much more than others. Scrub-resistance of paints made from deep base was better.
Valspar Flat	Scrub-resistance of paints made from deep base was better.
Wal-Mart Flat, **A BEST BUY**	2-coat hiding: gold, orange much worse than others. Scrub-resistance of paints made from pastel base was worse.
Wal-Mart Satin	—

RATINGS POWER DRILLS

▶ **See report, page 172.** Last time rated in Consumer Reports: January 1994.

Brand-name recommendations: The top-rated *Bosch 1001VSR* offers excellent value if you can find it, as we did, for less than $100 at retail. The closest runners-up among the standard, variable speed models—the *Makita 6402* and *Dewalt DW103*—are likely to have actual retail prices of about $25 more. For small occasional jobs, consider any of the inexpensive models. The better cordless drills were the *Sears 27139* and *Porter Cable 9852*.

For the typical ³⁄₈-inch power drill, expect: ■ Reversible direction. ■ Variable speed control. ■ For cordless drills: Nickel cadmium batteries, which take from 1 to 6 hr. to recharge (about 20 min. of drilling time); an adjustable slip clutch. **Choices you'll have to make:** ■ Corded or cordless. ■ Jacobs or keyless chuck.

Notes on the table: All are reversible, ³⁄₈-inch drills. Unless noted, all are above average or better in construction quality. Model numbers and prices in parentheses are for keyless-chuck drills, which are usually priced slightly higher than the traditional Jacobs-type chuck. **Price** is the mfr.'s suggested retail. Actual retail is less. At least 1 battery pack supplied with cordless models. **Power** is a short-term measure in watts of the effort a drill can exert when forced to work to the limit. **Speed** is the max. speed specified on each drill's nameplate. Variable-speed models have 2 numbers (separated by a dash); some have 2 ranges (stacked numbers). Fixed-speed models have a choice of 2 fixed speeds (separated by "or"). **Battery** is a rough index of the work cordless models could do on a single charge when run intermittently under a moderate load. **Stalling** represents turning effort when a drill is about to stall. Cordless models with a 2-speed transmission were tested in low gear. **Screws** is how well each drill drove screws. Weight is to the nearest quarter lb. Ⓢ indicates tested model has been replaced by successor model; according to the mfr., the performance of new model should be similar to the tested model but features may vary. Not tested. Ⓓ indicates model discontinued or replacement not similar.

RATINGS OVERVIEW

Within types, listed in order of overall quality

Better ◀————▶ Worse
⊖ ⊖ ○ ◓ ●

Brand and model	Price	Overall score					Power	Speed	Battery	Stalling	Screws	Weight
		P	F	G	VG	E						

CORDED MODELS

Brand and model	Price	Overall score	Power	Speed	Battery	Stalling	Screws	Weight
Bosch 1001VSR (1003VSR)	$160		475	0-1100	—	⊖	⊖	3¼
Bosch 1000VSR (1002VSR)	148		465	0-2100	—	○	○	3¼
Makita 6402 (6402X)	199		499	0-1200	—	⊖	⊖	3½
Dewalt DW103	207		466	0-1200	—	⊖	○	3¼
Sears Craftsman 27141	90		416	0-1200	—	⊖	⊖	4¼
Ryobi D38VSR	65		427	0-2500	—	◓	○	3½

Ratings continued ▶

Ratings continued

Brand and model	Price	Overall score (P F G VG E)	Power	Speed	Battery	Stalling	Screws	Weight
Porter Cable 2620 (2621)	$129	▬▬▬	374	0-1200	—	○	⊖	3¼
Dewalt DW100	118	▬▬▬	381	0-2500	—	⊖	○	3¼
Skil 6533 (6540) Ⓓ	124	▬▬	327	0-1200	—	⊖	⊖	3
Sears Craftsman 10144	80	▬▬	268	0-1200	—	⊖	⊖	3½
Milwaukee 0228-1	136	▬▬	292	0-1000	—	○	⊖	3½
Black & Decker 7193 (7196)	59	▬▬	355	0-2500	—	⊖	○	3¼
Makita 6510LVR	168	▬▬	284	0-1200	—	⊖	⊖	3¼
Milwaukee 0230-1	152	▬▬	319	0-1700	—	⊖	○	3½
Skil (6340)	(64)	▬	229	0-1300	—	⊖	⊖	3
Sears Craftsman 10143 (10146)	40	▬	195	0-1200	—	●	⊖	2¾
Black & Decker 7190 (7191) Ⓓ	34	▬	247	0-1200	—	⊖	○	2¾
Sears Craftsman 10142	30	▬	152	0-1200	—	●	⊖	2¾

CORDLESS MODELS

Brand and model	Price	Overall score (P F G VG E)	Power	Speed	Battery	Stalling	Screws	Weight
Sears Craftsman (27139)	(160)	▬▬▬	129	0-350 0-1000	⊖	⊖	⊖	4¼
Porter Cable 9852 (9853S)	196	▬▬▬	150	0-350 0-1000	⊖	○	⊖	4½
Ryobi TFD170VRK Ⓢ	198	▬▬▬	113	0-400 0-1200	○	⊖	⊖	4
Bosch 3050VSRK (3051VSRK)	235	▬▬▬	85	0-400 0-900	○	⊖	⊖	3¾
Skil 2735-02 (2736-04)	230	▬▬▬	132	0-500 0-1650	⊖	⊖	⊖	4¼
Milwaukee 0394-1 (0396-1)	191	▬▬▬	119	0-350 0-1000	○	○	⊖	3½
Dewalt (DW944K) Ⓢ	(155)	▬▬▬	97	0-350 0-1200	○	○	⊖	4¼
Makita 6093DW (6095DW)	283	▬▬	113	0-400 0-1100	○	⊖	⊖	3¾
Milwaukee 0384-1 (0386-1)	129	▬▬	62	0-600	○	●	⊖	2½
Skil 2535-02	132	▬▬	61	0-600	○	●	⊖	3
Sears Craftsman 11188	80	▬▬	55	0-600	○	●	○	3
Black & Decker CD4000 Ⓓ	63	▬	60	0-600	○	●	○	2¼

Brand and model	Price	Overall score					Power	Speed	Battery	Stalling	Screws	Weight
		P	F	G	VG	E						
Sears Craftsman 11186	$40	▬					51	300 or 500	◒	●	◒	2¼
Skil 2236	65	▬					57	300 or 600	◒	●	◒	2½
Black & Decker CD2000	60	▬					60	225 or 550	◒	●	◒	2

RATINGS DETAILS   Models listed alphabetically

Black & Decker CD2000	No interlock to prevent changing direction of spin while drill is running. No charging indicator light. Recommended recharging time of 3 hr. Below average construction quality.
Black & Decker CD4000 Ⓓ	Rear end of housing judged suitable for in-line grip. Built-in spirit level. Recommended recharging time of 3 hr. Average construction quality.
Black & Decker 7190 (7191) Ⓓ	Trigger lock can be set at any speed. Relatively low power level can safely be sustained for continuous use. Average construction quality.
Black & Decker 7193 (7196) Ⓓ	Trigger lock can be set at any speed. Built-in spirit level. Average construction quality.
Bosch 1000VSR (1002VSR)	Has trigger Off lock. Rear end of housing judged suitable for in-line grip.
Bosch 1001VSR (1003VSR)	Has trigger Off lock. Rear end of housing judged suitable for in-line grip.
Bosch 3050VSRK (3051VSRK)	Rear end of housing judged suitable for in-line grip. Adjustable slip clutch. Charger switches to trickle rate when battery is fully charged.
Dewalt DW100	Built-in spirit level.
Dewalt DW103	Relatively nose-heavy. Front of housing is metal, a possible shock hazard if drill pierces live wire.
Dewalt (DW944K) Ⓢ DW944K2, $303	Adjustable slip clutch. Charger switches to trickle rate when battery fully charged.
Makita 6402 (6402X)	Trigger lock can be set at any speed. Relatively nose-heavy. No interlock to prevent changing direction of spin while drill is running. Trigger On lock not shielded against accidental engagement.
Makita 6510LVR	No interlock to prevent changing direction of spin while drill is running. Trigger On lock not shielded against accidental engagement.
Makita 6093DW (6095DW)	Adjustable slip clutch. No interlock to prevent changing direction of spin while drill is running. No clearly set position for Off lock. Automatic brake stops bit spin on release of trigger. Circuit breaker guards against current overload.
Milwaukee 0228-1	Relatively nose-heavy. Front of housing is metal, a possible shock hazard if drill pierces live wire. Not double-insulated; has 3-wire line cord and plug. Automatic brake stops bit spin on release of trigger. Circuit breaker guards against current overload.
Milwaukee 0230-1	Relatively nose-heavy. Front of housing is metal, a possible shock hazard if drill pierces live wire. Not double-insulated; has 3-wire line cord and plug.

Ratings continued ▶

Ratings continued

Milwaukee 0384-1 (0386-1)	Circuit breaker guards against current overload.
Milwaukee 0394-1 (0396-1)	Adjustable slip clutch. Nominal recharging time ½ hr.
Porter Cable 9852 (98535)	Adjustable slip clutch. Charger switches to trickle rate when battery is fully charged.
Porter Cable 2620 (2621)	Relatively nose-heavy. Front of housing is metal, a possible shock hazard if drill pierces live wire.
Ryobi D38VSR	Trigger lock can be set at any speed. Built-in spirit level.
Ryobi TFD17OVRK Ⓢ TFD172VRK, $160	Rear end of housing judged suitable for in-line grip. Adjustable slip clutch. Automatic brake stops bit spin on release of trigger.
Sears Craftsman 10142	Below average construction quality.
Sears Craftsman 10143 (10146)	Trigger lock can be set at any speed. Relatively low power level can safely be sustained for continuous use. Average construction quality.
Sears Craftsman 10144	Trigger lock can be set at any speed. Auxiliary handle may be attached. Relatively nose-heavy. Front of housing is metal, a possible hazard if drill pierces live wire.
Sears Craftsman 11186	Rear end of housing judged suitable for in-line grip. Recommended recharging time 3 hr.
Sears Craftsman 11188	Adjustable slip clutch. Built-in spirit level. Circuit breaker guards against current overload.
Sears Craftsman (27139)	Rear end of housing judged suitable for in-line grip. Adjustable slip clutch. Built-in spirit level. Circuit breaker guards against current overload.
Sears Craftsman 27141	Trigger lock can be set at any speed. Auxiliary handle may be attached. Relatively nose-heavy. Front of housing is metal, a possible shock hazard if drill pierces live wire. Circuit breaker guards against current overload.
Skil 6340	Below average construction quality.
Skil 6533 (6540) Ⓓ	Trigger Off lock. Auxiliary handle may be attached.
Skil 2535-02	Adjustable slip clutch. Charger switches to trickle rate when battery is fully charged.
Skil 2236	Has low constant charging rate. Recommended recharging time 6 hr. No interlock to prevent changing direction of spin while drill is running. Average construction quality.
Skil 2735-02 (2736-04)	Adjustable slip clutch. Charger switches to trickle rate when battery is fully charged.

HEATING & COOLING

Fans

▶ Ratings on page 206.

There's nothing complicated about an electric fan. It's just a motor, propeller, switch, and housing. Fan makers arrange the basic pieces to assemble window, attic, floor, and ceiling fans.

Portable-fan brands include *Galaxy, Patton, Windmere*, and *Lakewood*. Major brands of ceiling fans include *Hunter, Fasco,* and *Casablanca*. K Mart, Sears, and Home Depot have their own brands.

The choices

Portable fans. Some can be used in or near a window, circulating air within a room. Box fans are often suitable for window use, though not always—check the instructions. Other portable models definitely don't belong in a window, where they may get wet. Floor fans come with a pedestal or stand. Some window models can be converted to floor fans by rotating their legs or stands. The better air-movers tend to be noisy and create turbulence. Portables have 9- to 20-inch blades, and range in price from less than $20 for a basic blower to $100 for a "high velocity" model with a souped-up motor.

Ceiling fans. These nostalgic appliances

have evolved from a utilitarian object into a prominent element in interior design. They move voluminous quantities of air unobtrusively. A large ceiling fan can, on higher speeds, recirculate cool air the way a portable fan does. Ceiling fans deliver a downdraft that's a foot or two wider than the blade's path. Typically, the edge of this column of air moves briskly; the "eye" of the column moves more gently. If the fan is centered in the ceiling, the air column reaches the floor, spreads out toward the walls, and turns upward to be recirculated. In general, large fans distribute air more uniformly than small ones, because their blades rotate slower. And due to their size, large fans disperse the air over a wider area.

Ceiling fans require an eight-foot ceiling to keep the blades a safe seven feet from the floor. Models you can flush mount against the ceiling provide more head room than those that hang. Remember, adding a lighting kit further reduces head room.

Most fans come with four or five blades measuring from 29 inches to 62 inches across. A 52-inch blade sweep is the most common. Prices vary widely: from $25 to more than $1000, although most are priced at $80 to $180. Models priced at $200 and up generally offer better workmanship and durability than cheaper models. Their heavy-duty castings, sealed bearings, weighted and well-balanced blades contribute to smooth, quiet operation.

Whole-house fans. Under the right conditions, a whole-house fan can ventilate an entire house on the electricity an air-conditioner would use to cool a single room. Large attic-mounted fans, whose blades range from 24 to 36 inches, can quickly draw copious amounts of fresh air through the entire house. If the outside temperature drops from, say, 85° to 75° in two hours, unassisted, the inside temperature will take another four hours to drop that much. A whole-house fan can do the job in a bit more than half that time.

On the downside, a whole-house fan requires substantial space and effort to install. You need two openings: one from the living space into the attic and another from the attic to the outdoors. The most effective way to do the job is to cut and frame the needed openings and fit them with shutters. "Automatic" shutters are simple and cheap. They move with the fan's sucking or blowing action. Shutters that open mechanically or electrically are more effective because they restrict airflow less.

Attic fans sell for about $200 to $400. Professional installation, adding louvers, shutters, remote-controlled switches, and other accessories can double the cost.

Features and conveniences

Controls. Portable models sometimes come with a variable-speed control, which lets you set the speed precisely; some also have a thermostat that cycles the unit on and off when the temperature drops below a certain setting.

Typically, a ceiling fan has a pull-chain to cycle through two or three speeds and turn the fan on and off and a switch to reverse the blades (and the direction of the air flow). A wall-mounted control is a necessity for a fan in a cathedral ceiling.

Some fancy ceiling fans offer a hand-held remote. On some models, the remote is the only means you have to control the fan. If you lose or break the gadget, you may or may not be able to get a replacement from the manufacturer.

Whole-house fans typically have two or three speeds, controlled by a wall switch.

Lights. Ceiling fans typically come with a light fixture under the fan or allow you to add a light, using a light-fixture kit.

Child safeguards. Child-safety features are especially important with portable fans. Look for grilles and housings with small, rigid openings that keep out fingers. Some models have a child-resistant On/off switch that, you must depress and turn at the same time, like a pill-bottle top.

Sizing the fans

In general, the larger the blade sweep, the greater a fan's air-moving capacity. But not always: Design differences help some smaller fans move more air than some of the larger models.

Size is especially critical with a whole-house fan, and there's a precise way to calculate what size machine to buy. First, figure out the cubic feet of the space to be ventilated. Include halls and stairways but exclude closets, pantries, store rooms, and the attic. If your summers are sweltering, go for a fan that can change house air completely every two minutes when running at maximum speed. Thus, for a house with 12,000 cubic feet of living space, you need a fan that can move 6000 cubic feet of air per minute. Where the heat is less intense, a model with a lower capacity should suffice.

Manufacturers rate their fans working against resistance (usually as 0.1 inch of water) or for "free-air delivery," which indicates the breeze churned when nothing restricts air flow. Free-air delivery isn't very realistic, since windows, furnishings, and a house's layout affect the air-flow. If the fan's air delivery when working against resistance is unavailable, use 80 to 85 percent of the free-air delivery rating.

The tests

A fan's air-moving ability and air distribution are key. We measure noise output and efficiency—how much air is moved Depending on fan type, we test for electric-shock hazard ("rain" test), stability, and evaluate child-safety features.

Buying advice

With a portable fan, first decide whether you want one that sits in or near the window. Next, decide if you want the fan to ventilate the room or just circulate the air. A box fan or large table and pedestal model are suitable for a single room. For ventilating more than one room, look to large fans.

Most portable fans do a fine job of circulating air in a room. If you don't mind the turbulence, you can stir up quite a breeze with a high-velocity unit. If you want quiet, buy a large fan. On low speed, it's likely to move as much air as a small fan on

AIR CLEANERS

Opening windows and eliminating pollution sources are the most effective ways to control indoor pollution. If the trouble is pollen, an air-conditioner set to recirculate indoor air should work. An air cleaner should be tried if those measures fail. If the problem is cigarette smoke, odors, or gases, most air cleaners won't help.

The best room models in our tests were electrostatic precipitators and those using a high-efficiency-particulate-arresting (HEPA) filter. In general, tabletop units weren't nearly as good; the best were ionizers with electret filters.

We found the contractor-installed electrostatic precipitators nearly as effective as the best room models. Two do-it-yourself in-duct filters were about equally effective, on a par with a small tabletop unit, at best.

Stay away from ozone generators; the two models we tested can generate unhealthy levels of ozone.

Energy and maintenance costs vary widely among models and, in some cases, can exceed the purchase price within just a year or two. Energy costs will range from about $20 to $60. HEPA replacement filters cost $30 to $120 a year; for other types, $20 to $80.

high, and do the job more quietly.

A ceiling fan's slow-turning blades create a quiet, gentle breeze. Spending more money buys a model with better construction and more durable parts.

A whole-house fan can make the entire house feel cool in a hurry. And in many parts of the country, drawing in the cool night air may be all you need to survive summer's heat.

Air-conditioners

▶ **Ratings on page 202.** ▶ **Repair records on page 24.**

A room air-conditioner that runs much of the year can use several hundred dollars' worth of electricity. Choosing an efficient air-conditioner helps reduce those costs. A model's efficiency rating—the EER (Energy Efficiency Rating) for a room unit, or SEER (Seasonal Energy Efficiency Rating) for other types—is marked on its yellow Energy Guide label. The higher the rating, the lower the energy cost to produce a given amount of cooling. Among room models, a rating of 9 or more can be considered high-efficiency. Central systems are required to have at least 10 SEER.

Choosing the right-sized model also helps reduce costs. The worksheet opposite can help you figure the cooling you need.

Sears Kenmore is the leading brand of room air-conditioner. *Sears*, along with *Whirlpool, Fedders,* and *GE,* accounts for more than half of all room models sold. Split-ductless models are a relatively new type of air-conditioner available under more than a dozen brand names, including *Mitsubishi* and *Sanyo.* Big names in central air-conditioning are *Carrier, Rheem, Trane,* and *Lenox.*

The choices

Although designs and styles vary, all air-conditioners contain pretty much the same components: outdoor compressor and condenser, and indoor fan and evaporator. The way those components are arranged is what distinguishes one type of cooling system from another. Each has advantages and disadvantages:

Central units. Central air is quiet and convenient. But it's expensive. The most widely used on central units are those that cool only. Another approach: the heat pump, a central system that can switch from cooling to heating. It makes the most sense for homeowners who cool more than heat and want to replace electric heating. Both types of central air-conditioning distribute air throughout the house through ducts in the walls.

Such systems are sold and installed by contractors. A good contractor will calculate the needed capacity room by room, allowing for climate, house construction, and other variables. Avoid rules of thumb, such as 12,000 British thermal units (Btu) per hour for every 1000 square feet. While these methods are fine for an initial estimate, a detailed worksheet is the only way to calculate your exact cooling requirement. (See opposite.)

If your house already has a duct system, you'll save on installation troubles and costs only if it is appropriately sized and located. Otherwise, you'll need a contractor to install a system. When installing ducts, the contractor should pay careful attention to balancing airflow into and out of each room to be cooled. Ducts should be firmly connected (not with duct tape), adequately supported (no sharp bend), and insulated where they pass through uncooled spaces.

Price without ducts: at least $3000 and up for a standard air-conditioner package that includes installation; $3000 and up for a dual-purpose heat pump.

Room models. The trend is toward small, light, and more efficient units. Manufacturers also offer "low profile" models designed to let you see through more of the window. Such models stow the bulk of their machinery outside and below the window; they tend to be noisier indoors than out.

Most room air-conditioners are designed to fit in a double-hung window; others are designed for casement windows or through-the-wall installation. These models vary in size and capacity. The smallest, suitable for a small bedroom, are generally rated at 5000 Btu per hour. The largest that run on normal household voltage are rated at 11,000 to 14,000 Btu per hour, enough to cool several rooms. To determine the general size you need, see right.

Small units starting at 5000 Btu are priced from $200; very large units, rated 12,000 Btu can cost as much as $850.

Split-ductless models. Something of a cross between a room unit and central air-conditioning, this typeof air-conditioner is widely used in Europe and Japan, but fairly new to the U.S. As in a central system, the compressor and condenser are located outdoors, but connected by tubing directly to a wall-mounted fan and evaporator in the room or rooms to be cooled. No ductwork is required. This arrangement ensures quiet operation and makes it possible to place the room component where it will cool most effectively without taking up a window. This type makes the most sense for cooling more than one room, or for cooling an addition to a house that has central air-conditioning.

Most split-ductless models range in capacity from 8000 to 24,000 Btu per hour. Some can double as a heat pump in winter. They're installed by contractors; prices

HOW BIG?

Don't depend on a salesperson to give you the straight dope about how much cooling capacity you need from a room air-conditioner. He or she may steer you toward the unit the store wants to sell, not the one that best meets your needs. This table, developed by a manufacturer, gives a rough guide to the capacity you need.

Room area in square feet	Capacity in Btu per hour
100 to 150	5,000
150 to 250	6,000
250 to 300	7,000
300 to 350	8,000
350 to 400	9,000
400 to 450	10,000
450 to 550	12,000
550 to 700	14,000
700 to 1000	18,000

- If the room is heavily shaded, reduce the capacity by 10 percent.
- If the room is very sunny, increase the capacity by 10 percent.
- If more than two people normally occupy the room, add 600 Btu for each additional person.
- If you're using the air-conditioner in a kitchen, increase the capacity by 4000 Btu to compensate for heat from cooking and appliances.

Source: Carrier Corp.

For a more precise cooling-capacity estimate, CU can provide a detailed worksheet, adapted from one published by the Association of Home Appliance Manufacturers. The worksheet is free. To order, send a stamped, self-addressed envelope to Consumers Union, Dept. DY, 101 Truman Ave., Yonkers, N.Y. 10703.

range from $1500 to nearly $4000, plus installation for the smallest capacities.

Features and conveniences

Energy-saving options. A 24-hour timer turns an air-conditioner on before you get home—no need for it to run all day. An Energy-saver setting, included on many models, cycles the fan on and off with the compressor instead of letting the fan run continuously. But without the fan, temperature control tends to suffer, something that some models compensate for.

Ductless models with a moisture-removal cycle dehumidify by turning the fan off when the compressor is off. They control the compressor's operating time and the temperature setting.

Controls. On room air-conditioners, look for a thermostat with clear markings. A few models have an electronic thermostat with a light-emitting diode (LED) readout of the room temperature and a signal light showing that the power is on.

Because ductless units are typically mounted near the ceiling, they come with some type of remote control. Wired or wireless remotes typically provide you with a temperature scale on the thermostat.

Louvers. Many room models lack a good way to direct air. Directional control is especially important if the unit is mounted in a corner or if you want spot-cooling. Models that let you close some louvers can redirect air with more force through the open ones. A Vent setting blows air outdoors; use it only for when the unit isn't cooling. Some models also draw in fresh air.

Slide-out chassis. A worthwhile feature on a room air-conditioner, this lets you secure the empty cabinet in the window, then slide the machine's innards into position. That makes installation safer and simplifies repair. All room units are heavy and, due to their bulk, should be installed by at least two people; low-profile models that must be lifted over the sill can easily become unwieldy.

The tests

We test air-conditioners by mounting them in a chamber within another chamber to create an "outside" and an "inside." Each unit's task is to maintain a temperature of about 75° when the "outdoor" temperature is kept at 95°. For room models, we keep outdoor humidity at 70 percent and measure the ability to keep variations from exceeding 5 percent. Sensors mounted in front of the fan determine how uniformly each model distributes cool air. To simulate a brownout, we boost the outside temperature to at least 120° and drop line voltage to 100 volts. At the lower voltage, we run a unit for an hour, turn the power off for three minutes, then try to restart it .

Reliability

Room air-conditioners are very reliable. On average, only about 1 in 22 models (of room models with capacities less than 10,000 Btu) purchased by our readers since 1988 has needed repairs. *Emerson Quiet Kool, Panasonic,* and *Sears* were among the most reliable brands. See the brand Repair Histories on page 24.

Buying advice

Where summers are dry and nights cool, a window or whole-house fan may be a sufficient alternative to air-conditioning—and much cheaper. Otherwise, consider an air-conditioner that cools just part of the house—a room model for a room or two, a split-ductless model for two rooms or more. In consistently hotter climes, consider central air-conditioning.

Among room units, don't assume the biggest is the best. The box on page 197 can help determine the right size. The higher the EER (SEER, for central and ductless models), the lower the operating cost.

Humidifiers

▶ **Ratings on page 209.**

When dry winter air saps moisture from your home, a humidifier can help. It reduces static electricity and protects wood furniture. It can make you feel warmer at relatively cool temperatures. It helps protect the respiratory system, aiding the body's defenses against viruses and air pollutants and helps alleviate dry, itchy skin.

Kaz is the leading brand. *Kaz, Duracraft, Holmes Air,* and *Sunbeam* account for more than half of all humidifiers sold. Others familiar names are *Emerson* and *Toastmaster.*

The choices

Humidifiers use various methods to add moisture to the air. The most common, **evaporative,** consumes little energy and can run on tap water. Capillary action draws water into a wick filter. A fan pulls air through the filter, allowing water to evaporate and sending it into the room. To prevent bacterial growth, these models need regular cleaning and filter replacement.

Impeller models sling droplets of water into the air. They are inexpensive to buy, but may require soft or distilled water or a demineralization cartridge, so a year's running cost can exceed the purchase price. Impellers can splatter water and spew microorganisms along with the water.

Models that use **steam mist** boil water to release steam. Boiling kills microorganisms, so filters aren't needed. (Still, bits of dead microorganisms may be emitted, which can trigger allergic reactions.) Steam-mist units use more energy than other types, and the heating element may be hard to clean when hard-water mineral deposits build up. There's a risk of scalding from the steam or the boiling water of a tipped-over tank. **Warm-mist** humidifiers work similarly to steam-mist units, except a fan mixes cool air with the steam. There's no scalding risk from the steam, but there is still boiling water.

Ultrasonic humidifiers, also known as cool-mist humidifiers, have fallen out of favor because of white dust. Hard water can produce a fine white dust that coats floors, walls, and furnishings and leaves mineral deposits that make the unit hard to clean. So they're best used with soft or distilled water, or a demineralization cartridge. These use little energy. Sizes of humidifiers vary, too:

Tabletop models. These small models are the best-selling type. They sell for about $20 to $100. Tabletop humidifiers are designed to humidify a room, or two at most.

Consoles. Furniture-sized consoles are typically the evaporative type. The smallest such model can humidify several rooms or an entire house. Prices range from about $100 to $200.

Central units. An in-duct humidifier, installed in a forced-air heating system, may cost about $125 to $250, in addition to installation, which may involve plumbing to provide water, electrical work, and sheet-metal work.

Features and conveniences

Controls. Tabletop models often lack a humidistat, a serious omission since it's essential for regulating humidity. Humidistats aren't always precise, but some control is better than no control. Also sometimes missing is an On/off switch. A switch that's separate from the humidistat and fan control saves resetting each time you turn the unit on. Fans can usually run at low or high; on high speed, some models can be as noisy as a room air-conditioner.

Indicator lights are helpful to warn when the water tank is empty or when it's time to clean the filter. Models with auto-shutoff turn themselves off when the tank runs dry.

Tank design. A tank needs a wide opening so you can quickly refill it (usually daily) and get your hand inside to clean (generally weekly). A full tank can be heavy, so carrying handles are important. Wheeled units can be rolled to the sink. A hose that connects to a faucet speeds filling.

The tests

We evaluate ease of cleaning and access to the interior. To see how long the humidifiers can run on a tank of water, we run them at high speed until they run dry—which took nine hours for the smallest to 2½ days for the largest. To see how neglected humidifiers fare, we run them with hard tap water for 1000 hours. Warm- and steam-mist models were hardly affected; the output of evaporative models decreased by nearly 25 percent.

Buying advice

The greater a humdifier's output, the faster a unit can humidify a given space.

But the rate should match your needs. Most tabletop humidifers have ample capacity for one or two rooms; small console models are fine for a large apartment or a moderate-sized house. The largest console is suitable for most homes.

Don't overlook the cost of operation and maintenance in making your choice. Most tabletop models use about $5 a year in electricity, at the national average rate of 8.4 cents per kilowatt-hour, while consoles use $11 to $14 a year. Humidifiers that vaporize water by boiling use about twice that amount of electricity.

Warm-mist and steam-mist models have essentially no maintenance costs. Tabletop evaporative units cost an estimated $9 to $23 a year in maintenance. Impeller models cost an estimated $20 to $40 a year, assuming they require distilled water or demineralization cartridges. Consoles cost about $20 to $50 a year.

Whatever type you choose, note that humidifiers need daily attention. The easiest to clean, we found, are those that are easy to disassemble and have a tank with a large opening and few nooks and crannies. Tanks on console models should be easy to drain and wipe dry.

Energy-saving thermostats

▶ Ratings on page 208.

You can save energy and money in the winter or summer with any thermostat if you remember to set and reset it daily. An automatic setback thermostat does the job, well, automatically. For example, in the winter it saves you the hassle of lowering the temperature at night or before you go out and raising it when you return or get up in the morning. The savings generated by setting back the temperature can be substantial. For example, in the upper Midwest, reducing the nighttime temperature setting from 68° to 55° in the winter can reduce a fuel bill by as much as $10 to $20 a month.

The choices

There are two types. Both are designed for do-it-yourself installation.

Electromechanical. This type, with the traditional round clock-timer, is the simpler. You program the setback On and Off times by adjusting movable tabs around the dial, and the temperatures by moving a couple of levers. This type lets you set two setback periods, each with one minimum and one maximum temperature. The setback times can't vary from day to day. Price: $50 to $75.

Electronic. This type is more flexible but more complicated. You can program multiple temperatures for different days of the week. The display looks like a digital clock. Programming, though, is tedious and frustrating you'll need the instruction book close by. Price: $30 to $130.

Features and conveniences

Features are more prolific among electronic models than electromechanical ones.

Display. Look for a readable display that also shows the current set temperature.

Usage tracking. A light that shows when the unit is calling for heating or cooling is helpful. A display of cumulative "on" time helps you track fuel use.

Ease of programming. Models that are easiest to program use only a few buttons and follow a fairly straightforward sequence of steps. Some thermostats offer "armchair" programming—those models detach easily from the wall so you can do the programming while comfortably seated.

Programming capability. The most versatile units let you program up to four different temperatures per day, with a different set schedule for each day of the week. With any, you can temporarily override the settings at any time.

The tests

To test each thermostat's ability to maintain a temperature setting, we put it in a 10x20-foot chamber designed to mimic a living room. Electric heaters substitute for a furnace and air-conditioning cools the room. We also program each thermostat and judge the quality of its display and controls.

Buying advice

If you want a thermostat to turn down the temperature in winter and turn it up in summer, but don't want to deal with programming, consider an electromechanical model. But keep in mind its limitation—the same two temperature levels every day unless you reset it. For a variety of settings on weekdays and weekends, you'll need a digital electronic model, preferably with "armchair" programming.

EXTERIOR CAULKING COMPOUNDS

Carefully applied around windows, doors, and siding, caulk not only blocks drafts, but also keeps water from seeping into walls. A good caulk should be easy to apply, without running, sagging, drying out, or cracking, and it should stay flexible through heat and cold. A 10-ounce tube typically costs $1 to $6.

Caulks come in two main types:

Silicone. With its rubbery consistency, this type shrank less over time than the others in our tests, a key measure of performance. But silicone won't mix with water, so you'll need mineral spirits to clean up hands and tools. And some brands can't be painted.

Latex. This is the easiest type to smooth, and it cleans up with water. Latex caulk is paintable. It's opaque when dry and shrinks more than silicone does. Also available is acrylic latex, which is often superior to plain latex.

Any caulk will be a compromise between convenience and durability, but silicone caulks performed the best overall. Some latex and silicone/latex caulks also did well; and they are paintable. See Ratings on page 204.

RATINGS LARGE-ROOM AIR-CONDITIONERS

▶ **See report, page 196.** Last time rated in Consumer Reports: June: 1994.

Brand-name recommendations: The models in the Ratings are quite powerful—9000 to 12,000 Btu per hour, suitable for large, sunny rooms or rooms that flow together. The higher your local electricity rate and the more you'll use the unit, the higher the energy efficiency (EER) you'll want. The *General Electric, Panasonic,* and *Quasar* models at the top of each Ratings group were among the quietest. Essentially similar units, they combine fine performance and good efficiency. Their only real drawback: They're not good at directing air sharply left or right.

For the typical large air-conditioner, expect: ■ A better job of directing air left than right. ■ At least 2 cooling speeds. ■ Fairly low indoor noise on Low; on High, somewhat noisier. ■ Expandable plastic side panels. ■ Adjustable louvers. ■ Removable air filter. ■ Vent for exhausting room air. ■ Power cord at least 60 in. long. ■ R-22 HCFC refrigerant (less harmful to the earth's ozone layer than other types). ■ Exterior support bracket. ■ Moisture removal of 3 or more pints per hour. **Choices you'll have to make:** ■ Capacity (Btu). ■ Energy efficiency (EER).

Notes on the table: Price is the mfr.'s suggested or approx. retail. **EER** is the Energy Efficiency Rating, a standard measure of efficiency. **Comfort** scores show how each air-conditioner cooled a room in its Regular mode, and in the Energy-saver mode found on some models. ⊡ indicates model discontinued or replacement not similar.

Within groups, listed in order of performance and efficiency

	E	VG	G	F	P
	⊖	⊖	○	◖	●

Brand and model	Price	Overall score					EER	Comfort		Comments
		P	F	G	VG	E		REG.	ENERGY-SAVER	

12,000 BTU-PER-HOUR CAPACITY

Brand and model	Price	Overall score	EER	REG.	ENERGY-SAVER	Comments
General Electric AMH12AA	$540		9.5	⊖	⊖	No ext. support bracket. Built-in timer. Powered louvers sweep side to side.
Quasar HQ2122GH	649		9.5	⊖	⊖	No ext. support bracket. Built-in timer. Hose can be used to route water. Powered louvers sweep side to side.
Montgomery Ward Signature 2000 5813	500		9.1	⊖	○	No ext. support bracket. In moderate-humidity, ice formed on indoor coil. Powered louvers sweep side to side.
Sharp AF-1203M6	565		9.2	⊖	○	Among best at moisture removal. No ext. support bracket. In moderate-humidity, ice formed on indoor coil.

Brand and model	Price	Overall score					EER	Comfort		Comments
		P	F	G	VG	E		REG.	ENERGY-SAVER	
Friedrich SS12H10A Ⓓ	$859			▬			10.0	○	⊖	Hose can be used to route water.
Carrier XCA121D	530			▬			10.0	○	⊖	No ext. support bracket. Hose can be used to route water. In moderate-humidity, ice formed on indoor coil.
Sears Kenmore 79128	480			▬			9.0	⊖	◗	Among best at moisture removal. No ext. support bracket. Easy-to-use controls with highly visible markings. Chassis doesn't slide out. Louvers adjust to side.
Whirlpool ACQ122XA	479			▬			9.0	⊖	—	No ext. support bracket.
White Westinghouse WAL123S1A	460			▬			9.0	⊖	—	Filter harder to service than most. Louvers adjust to side.
Sears Kenmore 79129	560			▬			9.0	⊖	●	Louvers provide high-thrust option. Easy-to-use controls. Hose can be used to route water. In moderate-humidity, ice formed on indoor coil.
Goldstar GA-1213LC	589			▬			9.0	○	—	No ext. support bracket. Hose can be used to route water.
Fedders A2T12F2C Ⓓ	689			▬			9.0	⊖	—	Among poorest at moisture removal. Chassis doesn't slide out.
Emerson Quiet Kool 12GT13 Ⓓ	689			▬			9.0	⊖	—	Among poorest at moisture removal. Chassis doesn't slide out.

9,000 TO 10,600 BTU-PER-HOUR CAPACITY

Brand and model	Price	Overall score					EER	Comfort		Comments
		P	F	G	VG	E		REG.	ENERGY-SAVER	
General Electric AMD10AA	500				▬		9.5	⊖	⊖	No ext. support bracket. Built-in timer. Powered louvers sweep side to side.
Panasonic CW-1004FU Ⓓ	600				▬		9.5	⊖	⊖	No ext. support bracket. Built-in timer. Hose can be used to route water. Powered louvers sweep side to side.
Sears Kenmore 78099	600				▬		10.5	⊖	○	Among poorest at moisture removal. Louvers provide high-thrust option. Easy-to-use controls. Hose can be used to route water.
Friedrich SM10H10A Ⓓ	849			▬			12.0	○	⊖	Hose can be used to route water.
Montgomery Ward Signature 2000 5174	580			▬			10.0	⊖	○	Built-in timer. Louvers provide high-thrust option. Fragile louver design.
Friedrich SS09H10A Ⓓ	695			▬			11.0	○	⊖	Among poorest at moisture removal. Hose can be used to route water.

Ratings continued ▶

Ratings continued

Brand and model	Price	Overall score					EER	Comfort		Comments
		P	F	G	VG	E		REG.	ENERGY-SAVER	

9,000 TO 10,600 BTU-PER-HOUR CAPACITY *continued*

Brand and model	Price	Overall score	EER	Comfort REG.	Comfort ENERGY-SAVER	Comments
Frigidaire FAL106P1A	$475	▬▬▬	9.5	⊖	—	Built-in timer. Easy-to-use controls. Fragile louver design.
Sharp AF-1002M6	429	▬▬▬	9.7	⊖	—	No ext. support bracket. In moderate-humidity, ice formed on indoor coil.
Gibson GAL108T1A	430	▬▬▬	9.3	⊖	—	Built-in timer. Easy-to-use controls. Powered louvers sweep side to side.
Carrier TCA101D	485	▬▬▬	9.0	⊖	—	Easy-to-use controls with highly visible markings. Hose can be used to route water. Chassis doesn't slide out. Fragile louver design.
White Westinghouse WAL117P1A	450	▬▬▬	10.0	○	—	Louvers adjust only to side.
Goldstar GA-1013LC	380	▬▬▬	9.5	○	—	Hose can be used to route water.
Amana 10QZ22TA Ⓢ 10QZ22TB, $539	485	▬▬▬	9.6	⊖	—	Louvers adjust only to side.
Fedders A2Q10F2A Ⓓ	450	▬▬▬	9.0	○	—	Chassis doesn't slide out. In moderate-humidity, ice formed on indoor coil. Louvers adjust to side.
Emerson Quiet Kool 10FC13 Ⓓ	440	▬▬▬	9.0	⊖	—	Chassis doesn't slide out. In moderate-humidity, ice formed on indoor coil.

RATINGS EXTERIOR CAULKS

▶ **See report, page 201.** Last time rated in Consumer Reports: October 1993.

Brand-name recommendations: Best overall were the *Ace, GE*, and *Red Devil* silicone caulks. The *M-D Paintable Silicone* is the highest-rated silicone that can be painted.

For the typical caulk, expect: ■ Smooth flow from the gun. ■ Adhesion without sagging. ■ For latex: easy application and cleanup; paintable. ■ For silicone: cleanup with solvent; not paintable (except *M-D Silicone*).

Notes on the table: Price is suggested retail, rounded to the nearest dollar, for a cartridge of about 10 oz. **Type:** S=silicone; L=latex; S/L=silicone/latex; AL=acrylic latex; B=butyl. **Weather** scores tell how well the caulk adhered and how well it resisted splitting and cracking. **Flex** scores show how flexible it stayed in high and below-freezing temperatures. **Mildew** and **dirt** scores indicate how well it resisted mildew growth and dirt. Ⓓ indicates model discontinued or replacement not similar.

Listed in order of performance based on lab tests and exposure to weather

Better ◐ ◐ ○ ◐ ● Worse

Brand and model	Price	Type	Overall score	Weather	Flex	Mildew	Dirt
Ace 50 Year Silicone [5]	$5	S		◐	◐	◐	◒
GE Silicone II Window & Door [5]	5	S		◐	◐	◐	◒
Red Devil 100% Silicone [5]	8	S		◐	◐	◐	◒
DAP '230' Advanced Latex	3	L		◐	◐	◐	○
HWI Do-it Best	2	S/L		◐	○	◐	○
M-D Paintable Silicone [5]	7	S		◐	○	◐	○
Elmer's Siliconized [1] [6]	4	S/L		◐	◐	○	◒
DAP Alex Plus	2	S/L		◐	◒	○	◒
Macco Super LC-130	3	S/L		◐	○	○	◒
M-D All Purpose [6]	4	AL		◐	◐	◒	○
DAP Dow Corning Silicone Plus [4]	5	S		○	◐	◐	◒
M-D Painter's	2	L		◐	○	○	◐
HWI Do-it [2]	2	AL		◐	◐	●	◒
Red Devil Acrylic 15-Year	3	AL		○	◐	◐	◒
UGL Duracalk	2	L		◐	◒	●	○
Phenoseal Surpass [6]	5	AL		◐	○	◒	◒
Red Devil Siliconized 25-Year	4	S/L		○	○	◐	◒
Tru-Test WeatherAll [1] [6]	3	S/L		◐	○	○	●
Shur-Stik 1345 Siliconized [2]	2	S/L		◐	○	●	○
M-D 25 Year	2	S/L		○	○	○	◒
Ace 25 Year Siliconized	2	S/L		◒	○	◐	◒
Seamseal Plus [D]	3	S/L		◒	○	○	○
M-D Butyl Rubber [3]	3	B		◒	◐	◐	●
Elmer's Weather-Tite [1] [6]	2	L		◒	◒	◒	●
DAP Butyl-Flex [2] [3]	3	B		◒	○	●	●

[1] At room temp., sagged in vertical aluminum, but not wood channel.
[2] Mildewed when painted with latex paint.
[3] Sticky and messy to apply and level.
[4] Painted sections stayed sticky and yellowish after a year indoors.
[5] Very low shrinkage.
[6] Very high shrinkage.

RATINGS CEILING FANS

▶ **See report, page 193.** Last time rated in Consumer Reports: June 1993.

Brand-name recommendations: Among the large fans, the ultramodern and pricey *Beverly Hills Stratos* topped the Ratings, with high marks for air-moving ability and air distribution. We consider two models Best Buys: The *Harbor Breeze Wellington* and the *J.C. Penney 854-8968-03* (and its successor), both about $100. The *Casablanca Lady Delta*, $224, was the top-rated small fan. It moved as much air as the best large fans but was a bit raucous and ran fast at high speed. But see page 372 for information about the recall of *Casablanca* fans.

For the typical ceiling fan, expect: ■ 4 to 6 blades. ■ 3 speeds. ■ Very good air distribution. ■ Pull-chain speed control (a few have wall-mounted control or a remote). ■ Do-it-yourself assembly. ■ Blades operate in reverse direction. ■ To provide 7-ft. clearance between blades and floor.

Notes on the table: Bracketed models were judged about equal in quality and are listed in order of increasing price. **Price** is the mfr.'s suggested retail. **Air-moving** indicates the amount of air pushed toward the floor on High. **Airflow range** is the range of air movement between High and Low. **Noise** is judged at high speed. Ⓢ indicates tested model has been replaced by successor model; according to the mfr., the performance of new model should be similar to the tested model but features may vary. Not tested. Ⓓ indicates model discontinued or replacement not similar.

Within type, listed in order of performance

Better ◐ ◑ ○ ◔ ● Worse

Brand and model	Price	Air moving	Airflow range	Noise	Comments
LARGE MODELS, 52-INCH					
Beverly Hills Stratos 4605	$374	◐	◐	◐	Very efficient. Inconvenient to reverse fan direction.
Casablanca Panama Gallery Edition 12002R/12002T	1032 800	◐	◐	○	Not efficient. Comes with light fixture kit.
Harbor Breeze Wellington 37771, **A BEST BUY** ①	97	◐	◔	◐	Very efficient. Comes with light fixture kit.
J.C. Penney 854-8968-03, **A BEST BUY** Ⓢ 832-1424, $100	100	◐	○	◐	Comes with light fixture kit.
Hunter Studio Series Remote 25730	160	◐	○	◐	—
Emerson Northwind Designer CF755BK	204	◐	○	◐	—
Hunter Orion ORN-03 25827	274	◐	○	◐	Comes with light fixture kit.

① Sold at Lowe's, a home-center chain in the South and Midwest.

Brand and model	Price	Air moving	Airflow range	Noise	Comments
Homestead Wind 1 WN11000R-6 [D]	$330	⊖	⊖	⊖	—
Fasco American Spirit Collection RM995BR [S] RM995BR, $249	460	⊖	⊖	⊖	Not efficient.
Encon Spectrum 5S-52WPB [S] 5AR52PBC, $149	60	⊖	○	⊖	Motor made noise. Comes with light fixture kit.
K Mart Atlantic Air 61-86-35	60	⊖	○	⊖	Motor made noise. Comes with light fixture kit.
Hampton Bay [D] The Beacon Hill 623-067	94	○	◐	⊖	Comes with light fixture kit. Lights above blades created a flickering effect.
Hunter Low Profile 22426	100	○	◐	⊖	—
Crest 4500 Series 04-599	49	⊖	○	⊖	Motor made noise. Comes with light fixture kit.
Crest 04-775	69	⊖	○	⊖	Motor made noise. Comes with light fixture kit.
Encon Contempra 5CP52PBP [S] 5RC52WPC, $129	60	◐	●	⊖	Not efficient. Blades were warped on 2 samples. Motor vibrated or wobbled and made noise. Comes with light fixture kit.

SMALL MODELS, 42- TO 44-INCH

Brand and model	Price	Air moving	Airflow range	Noise	Comments
Casablanca Lady Delta 16222D [S] 2722T, $400	224	⊖	⊖	○	—
Homestead UV 460-1 [D]	200	⊖	○	○	Very efficient.
Emerson Legend CF3342PB	344	⊖	⊖	○	Motor made noise.
Hunter Coastal Breeze CTL-0123500	70	○	◐	⊖	Very efficient. Motor made noise.
K Mart Atlantic Air 61-93-50	50	◐	●	⊖	Comes with light fixture kit.
Crest 5000 Series 05-001	29	◐	●	⊖	Motor made noise.
Encon Premier Deluxe PF-42ABA [S] CP42PBD, $49	45	◐	●	⊖	Blades were warped on 2 samples. Motor vibrated or wobbled. Comes with light fixture kit.
Fasco Gulf Stream 975-42BR	69	◐	●	⊖	—
Beverly Hills Designer Colors 2003	113	○	◐	⊖	Motor made noise.

RATINGS ENERGY-SAVING THERMOSTATS

▶ **See report, page 200.** Last time rated in Consumer Reports: October 1993.

Brand-name recommendations: If your family will be content with two temperature levels a day, then any of the three electromechanical models should do nicely. The *Emerson 7901* and the *Honeywell CT1501* were the easiest to use. For more versatility, any of the top four electronic thermostats would be a good choice. The *Sears Weekender* and the *Honeywell MagicStat* offer the convenience of completely independent programs for heating and cooling so you don't have to reprogram them when the seasons change.

For the typical thermostat, expect: ■ Control of heating and cooling (but not switched automatically) systems with a 24-volt AC circuit. ■ Battery backup (alkaline AA). ■ Adjustable cycle time/temperature swing. ■ At least 1 "comfort" temperature plus a second temperature to use as a lower "setback" (in winter) or a higher "setup" (in summer). ■ Digital display with time and room temperature. **A choice you'll have to make:** ■ Digital electronic or electromechanical.

Notes on the table: Price is the mfr.'s suggested retail. **Temperature swing:** V=varies. **Programs:** 2 = weekday & weekend; 3 = weekday, Sat., Sun.; 7 = daily; 1 = same one every day. Ⓓ indicates model discontinued or replacement not similar.

Within types, listed in order of overall quality

E VG G F P
⊖ ⊖ ○ ⊖ ●

Brand and model	Price	Overall score	Temp. swing	Setup	Programs	Comments
DIGITAL ELECTRONIC MODELS						
Honeywell MagicStat 33	$90		⊖	⊖	2	Independent programs for heating, cooling.
Honeywell PerfecTemp CT3400	130		⊖	⊖	3	—
Sears Weekender 91112	70		⊖	⊖	2	Lets you remove from wall to program. Independent programs for heating, cooling.
Emerson 7907	110		⊖	○	7	Limited temp. choice. Lets you remove from wall to program.
Jameson Deluxe 0940	80		○	⊖	7	Hard-to-read display.
Emerson 7903	60		⊖	●	2	Limited temp. choice. Independent programs for heating, cooling. Battery change wipes out program. Hard-to-push buttons.

Brand and model	Price	Overall score	Temp. swing	Setup	Programs	Comments
Hunter Auto Temp 44402 D	$55	▬▬▬	●	○	3	Batteries hard to change. Temp. swing, cycle time not adjustable.
Robertshaw TX1000	50	▬▬	◑	○	3	Hard to display setpoint temp. Hard to override temp. setting.
Hunter Set'n Save I 42204	29	▬▬	◑	○	2	Battery change erases program. Must be reprogrammed to switch from heat to cool. Temp. swing, cycle time not adjustable.
Jameson Economy 0925	40	▬▬▬	◑	◑	2	Limited temp. choice. Hard-to-read display.

ELECTROMECHANICAL MODELS

Brand and model	Price	Overall score	Temp. swing	Setup	Programs	Comments
Emerson 7901	52	▬▬▬▬	V	◒	1	Limited temp. choice.
Honeywell CT1501	85	▬▬▬▬▬	V	◒	1	Limited temp. choice.
Robertshaw T33-1044 D	49	▬▬▬	V	○	1	Limited temp. choice.

RATINGS HUMIDIFIERS

▶ **See report, page 199.** Last time rated in Consumer Reports: October 1994.

Brand-name recommendations: Among tabletop units, the best in our tests was a warm-mist model, the *Duracraft DH-904*, about $64. You can also consider three evaporative models: the *Duracraft DH-831*, the *Toastmaster 3408*, or the *Emerson HD850*. All should cost much less to run than the *Duracraft DH-904*. Among the console models, the *Toastmaster 3435* and *Emerson HD14W1* (and successor *HD15W*) are nearly equal in overall performance.

For the typical tabletop model, expect: ■ A portable tank with handles or side grips for convenience. ■ Sufficient capacity to humidify a medium- to large-sized room. **For the typical console model, expect**: ■ A humidistat to control relative humidity. ■ Sufficient capacity to humidify an average-sized house. ■ Casters or wheels. ■ A switch that shuts the unit off when the water tank is empty.

Notes on the table: Models are evaporative type unless otherwise noted. **Price** is an estimate of the average retail from the mfrs. An * indicates price we paid. **Operating** figures are based on 1000 hrs of use per year, at the highest output setting and includes energy cost (based on the national average electricity rate of 8.4¢). **Humidistat** scores reflect how precisely this control kept relative humidity steady. S indicates tested model has been replaced by successor model; according to the mfr. the performance of new model should be similar to the tested model but features may vary.

Ratings continued ▶

Ratings continued

Within type, listed in order of performance and convenience

Better ⊖ ⊖ ○ ◐ ● Worse

Brand and model	Price	Overall score					Operating cost	Humidi-stat	Comments
		P	F	G	VG	E			

CONSOLE MODELS

Brand and model	Price	Overall score (P–E)	Operating cost	Humidistat	Comments
Toastmaster 3435	$135	▬▬▬	$33	⊖	—
Emerson HD14W1 ⑤ HD15W, $145	145	▬▬	40	○	Variable fan speed or mist setting. Hose to fill tank.
Bemis 4973	140	▬▬	60	⊖	Variable fan speed or mist setting. Hose to fill tank.
Sears Kenmore 32-14412	115	▬▬	43	◐	Variable fan speed or mist setting.
Bionaire W-6S	168	▬▬	31	◐	Indicates if filter needs cleaning. Tank cap hard to use.

TABLETOP MODELS

Brand and model	Price	Overall score (P–E)	Operating cost	Humidistat	Comments
Duracraft DH-904	64	▬▬▬	28	⊖	Warm mist type.
Duracraft DH-831	74	▬▬▬	17	◐	—
Toastmaster 3408	53	▬▬▬	14	—	Tank is hard to fill or clean.
Emerson MoistAir HD850	59	▬▬▬	11	◐	No handle.
Kaz 3300	29	▬▬▬	10	—	Only 1 fan speed or mist setting.
Duracraft DH-805	64	▬▬▬	18	◐	—
Holmes Air HM-2000	43	▬▬▬	13	—	—
Bionaire CM-3 ⑤ CMD0300, $105	105	▬▬	32	◐	Tank cap hard to use. Hard to clean. Warm mist type.
Holmes Air HM-5150	55	▬▬	27	—	Steam mist type.
Holmes Air HM-460 or 460B	60	▬▬	19	—	Variable fan speed or mist setting. Tank cap hard to use. Splatters mist or water when running. Ultrasonic type.
DeVilbiss/Hankscraft 5920D/1100	*37	▬▬	12	—	Filter hard to install or remove.
Holmes Air HM-5100A	38	▬▬	26	—	Tank is hard to fill or clean. Only 1 fan speed or mist setting. Steam mist type.
Bemis 7260	45	▬▬	26	—	Filter hard to install or remove.

The following were downrated due to the high cost of using distilled water or a demineralization cartridge.

Brand and model	Price	Overall score (P–E)	Operating cost	Humidistat	Comments
Kaz 2000	27	▬▬	35	—	Splatters mist or water. Only 1 fan speed or mist setting. Impeller type.
Holmes Air HV-8005	27	▬▬	42	—	Splatters mist or water. Impeller type.
Sunbeam 658-8	*23	▬	32	—	Splatters mist or water. Only 1 fan speed or mist setting. Impeller type.
DeVilbiss/Hankscraft 0240D/1250	*25	▬	25	—	Tank cap hard to use. Splatters mist or water. Impeller type.

WORKING AT HOME

Desktop computers
▶ Ratings on page 224.

The home computer has finally arrived. Rising power and falling prices have produced a computer that, for less than $2000, can do all the usual computer tasks as well as show moving pictures and produce high-fidelity sound. The medium these multimedia machines run is CD-ROMs, and computer stores are now brimming with encyclopedias, games, "edutainment," and other interactive CD-ROM titles.

Another recent trend is toward energy efficiency. You can identify computers that comply with the U.S. Environmental Protection Agency's Energy-star program by the Energy-star logo.

The computer industry moves so quickly that many buyers hesitate to buy for fear that equipment sold today will soon be replaced by cheaper, faster gear. Competition among manufacturers and retailers is expected to remain fierce for the foreseeable future, with the choices in continual flux. You may be able to find good deals on machines only slightly out-of-date.

The choices

The computer market is divided primarily into two camps—IBM-compatible and Apple Macintosh. Differences between the two continue to shrink. In fact, a hybrid of the two may be on the horizon. For the present, here is what each type offers:

IBM-compatible. This term is a vestige of when manufacturers strove for compatibility with market leader IBM. Today, IBM shares the market with AST, Compaq, Dell, Gateway, Packard Bell, and Tandy. Most personal computers sold are IBM-compatibles. Most software in stores is designed to run on this type of machine.

IBM-compatibles are far easier to use than they used to be since nearly all now come with Microsoft Windows, a user interface that lets you work visually and carry out commands with a button's click. But older DOS-based software can't take full advantage of the friendliness of Windows.

Apple Macintosh. For over a decade, only Apple manufactured computers with the Macintosh interface. Although that's about to change. Macs are still a bit easier to use than an IBM-compatible machine with Windows. Apple's Power Macintosh, a powerful new type, should keep Macintosh competitive for many years to come.

Features and conveniences

Processor. This is the computer's brain. It determines how fast the computer runs and how much it costs. Motorola processors control Macintoshes; Intel processors—chiefly the 80486 and the Pentium—dominate IBM-compatible machines. Each chip has various models (designated SX, DX, DX2, DX4, etc.) at price points corresponding to performance. The speed of the processor's internal clock is expressed in megahertz (MHz), usually between 25 and 100. Combine those elements and you get the "models" shown in ads, such as 486SX-33.

A faster processor speeds up such tasks as searching through a document or performing complex calculations, but it won't speed up your hard drive or modem. Intel's new Pentiums achieve the blazing speeds it advertises only with special software. Without it, a 60 MHz Pentium is no faster than some of the speedier 486 processors.

Memory. Random access memory (RAM) determines how much data the computer can process at once. It is measured in megabytes (MB), each equal to a million typewritten characters. A program will run slowly, if at all, if the computer has insufficient memory. To run Windows at its best, an IBM-compatible machine needs at least 8 MB of RAM.

Video. Monitors come in various sizes, 14, 15, and 17 inches being the most common. "Dot pitch" describes the spacing between the display's color phosphors. "Non-interlaced" monitors are preferred because they result in less eye strain.

A monitor connects to a plug-in video card, which limits the monitor's speed and maximum resolution (number of rows and columns of dots on the screen). A "bus" ties the monitor and video card to the rest of the machine. Newer computers use VESA Local Bus (VLB) or Peripheral Component Interconnect (PCI).

For most uses, the following setup would be fine: a non-interlaced, 14-inch monitor with a 0.28 inch or finer dot pitch and SuperVGA resolution. The video card should have at least 512 KB of memory; the bus should be VLB or PCI (whichever your PC can handle).

Hard drive. This is the computer's storage compartment. Storage space is measured in megabytes; common sizes range from 120 MB to about 1000 MB. Prices run about 70 cents to $1 per megabyte and are constantly dropping. The two most popular drive types, roughly equal in speed, are Small Computer System Interface (SCSI) drives and the slightly cheaper Integrated Drive Electronics (IDE) drives.

Conventional wisdom says to buy the largest hard drive you can afford. Plan on at least 200 MB for a Windows computer; at least 120 MB if you're upgrading an old DOS-only machine; and at least 250 MB for a Macintosh. To upgrade a computer's storage capacity, file compression software is a cheap alternative to a new hard drive.

Multimedia. This requires a CD-ROM drive (a compact-disc player adapted for computers), a plug-in sound card, and speakers—components available already built in or sold separately. Installing a CD-ROM can be tricky, so it's best to buy a computer with the multimedia items already pre-installed.

The CD-ROM drive should be at least a double-speed drive; the sound card, 16 bit (a measure of how it moves data); and the loudspeakers, self-powered and magnetically shielded (to prevent interference with the monitor).

Fax/modem. With the rapid growth of the Internet and on-line services such as America Online, CompuServe, and Prodigy, many computers come with a fax/modem, typically an internal card that combines fax capability with the device computers use to communicate over the telephone. A fax/modem is a cost effective replacement for most fax uses. But it is no fax machine; you can send only what is already inside the computer and you can only receive faxes when the computer is turned on. Some fax cards can send, but not receive. (You'll need a computer scanner to convert paper documents into computer faxes.)

A modem gives you access to on-line services and can exchange files with another computer. An internal plug-in modem saves space on the desk, but can be tricky to install. An external modem connects to a socket in the back of the computer. Speeds range from 2400 to 28,800 baud; higher speed modems also operate at the lower speeds. Look for a 14,400 baud modem, which should cost around $100—little more than slower ones.

Buying advice

Whether to buy an IBM-compatible or Macintosh is a matter of personal prefer-

WHERE TO BUY

Computer stores. These include local shops and superstores like CompUSA. Both are likely to have knowledgeable salespeople. A local shop specializes in personal service; a superstore has the widest selection. With either type, it's easy to have a computer repaired or customized.

Consumer electronics stores. These have less to choose from than a computer store, and salespeople are likely to be less knowledgeable. An on-site repair shop is a plus here.

Office supply and department stores. These have just a few brands. Salespeople can range from knowledgeable to clueless. Don't count on being able to customize the computer.

Warehouse clubs. Don't expect much selection or service at places like Sam's Club or the Price Club. Models aren't the most up-to-date.

Mail order. Whether you buy from a dealer or directly from the manufacturer, mail-order buying often costs less and makes it easier to customize a system. But if the manufacturer includes a poor-quality display monitor, you won't know until the carton arrives at your door. Another risk is that some mail-order manufacturers may not be in business a year from now.

Regardless of where you buy, use a credit card for the buyer protection it offers and note the dealer's return policy.

ence. As a hedge against changing technology, we recommend an IBM-compatible machine that's upgradeable and can accept a faster replacement Pentium processor. If you're considering a Macintosh, look for one that can be upgraded to the PowerPC processor.

Computer printers

Technical innovation and competition are making computer printers better and cheaper than ever. The venerable daisy-wheel printer, the early standard bearer of print quality, has become a relic. Dot-matrix printers, the dominant breed for years, are on the decline, crowded out by the newest, most technologically advanced printers—ink-jet and laser models. Laser printers have become so popular that a host of stationery products specially designed for them—labels, calendars, business cards—are now available.

Street prices for personal laser printers have dropped to $500 and for color printers, well under $300. Brands you'll see include *Hewlett-Packard, Canon, Apple, Panasonic, Epson, Okidata,* and *Tandy.*

The choices

Printers have to be compatible with your computer type: PC or Macintosh. Since more PCs are made than Macs, you'll find a greater variety of PC printers than those designed for Macs.

Dot-matrix. Now, the bottom of the line. These printers' tiny metal pins form characters by hitting the paper hundreds of times a second while emitting a whine. The more dots in a printhead's matrix, the smoother and crisper its print. Prices are typically well below $200.

Ink-jet. This type uses an ink cartridge that feeds an array of nearly microscopic tubes, each with a heating element; when the element is energized, a small ink droplet in the corresponding tube squirts onto the paper. In our tests, most ink-jets' output quality has been nearly as good as a laser printer's, with very little noise. The technology is good enough to print color photographs that are reasonable facsimiles of the original. One drawback: Ink-jet cartridges are expensive, making operating costs about double that of laser or dot-matrix printers. Ink-jet printers typically are priced from $275 to $500. Color ink-jets run about $600, but prices are falling fast.

Laser. Using xerographic technology like that in photocopiers, these can reproduce an almost limitless variety of type forms and sizes, as well as complex graphics. Images are electronically created on a light-sensitive drum, usually with a scanning laser. Powdered toner sticks to areas where light touches the drum and then transfers to a sheet of paper, which is briefly heated to fuse the toner. The output is clean and crisp. In our tests, laser printers quietly printed nearly perfect renditions of test pages. And they printed each page in half the time of an ink-jet printer. Laser printer prices keep dropping, from $1000 a couple of years ago to as low as $500 for basic models, with some offering twice the resolution—600 dots per inch—of traditional laser models. Expect to pay more for models capable of printing Postscript documents, such as those created by page-layout programs.

Portables. As laptop and notebook computers have flourished, so have printers designed for life on the road. Such printers are typically ink jets, whose technology requires little electrical energy.

Features and conveniences

Paper feed. All printers can handle single sheets of letter-sized paper. Laser printers use an automatic feeder tray stacked with blank paper, an extra-cost option with some ink-jet models. Paper-tray capacity ranges from 30 sheets up to a 20-pound ream of paper. Some models feature an envelope feeder or offer it as an option.

Size. Most have a footprint on the desktop at least as large as letter-size paper. The most space-efficient are upright ink jets and lasers that stock paper vertically.

Buying advice

If your needs are limited to routine tasks like correspondence or you want the lowest cost per printed page, a 24-pin dot-matrix printer can do the job. For a few dollars more, an ink-jet printer can provide near-laser quality without taking a toll on your ears. Ink jet refills are priced at about $20 to $35. Color cartridges are more expensive.

Consider a laser model only if print quality and speed are important. Prices and models change rapidly. Before buying, check prices in computer magazines and the business section of your newspaper.

Telephones

Few products have become as protean as the telephone, its shape shifting according to decorative whimsy (football-shaped phones, neon phones) or in the name of real operational change (do away with the cord or the home base). Phones have become part of other devices—answering machines, fax machines, fax modems for computers. And phones themselves have bloomed with features, from memories of large proportions to the ability to show you who is calling before you pick up.

Telephones fall into three broad categories: corded phones, cordless phones, and cellular phones. Phones are sold under a multitude of brand names, many only regional. AT&T dominates the market in both corded and cordless phones. *Motorola* is the biggest brand name in the cellular-phone business.

Corded telephones

A conventional, corded phone has basically two pieces: a handset and a base that plugs into a telephone jack.

The choices

Two main types predominate: console and trim-style models.

Console models. These are the modern version of the traditional Bell desk phone, although most no longer sound the traditional Bell ring. This type has a separate handset, an array of push buttons, and a handset cradle or base. Console models range in price anywhere from $30 to more than $100.

Trim-style models. These are space-savers; the push buttons are on the handset itself, and the base is about half as wide as a console phone. They range in price from about $10 to $50.

Features and conveniences

Ring sound. Few models actually ring. The most common sound is a chirp; some emit a low warble.

Memory. This, more than anything, is responsible for the major technological changes in conventional telephones. Memory-related capabilities vary from model to model. Most phones with memory can store at least a dozen numbers of up to 15 digits—enough for all but some international calls. *Redial* recalls the last number dialed. A few models can redial a busy number several times automatically. *One-touch speed dialing* stores a number that you can then call by touching a single key. *Scratch pads* let you record a phone number during a conversation and, after you've hung up, dial the number. Electronic banking and voice-mail systems require you to enter lots of numbers via the telephone dial. Phones with *chain-dialing memory* can dial a long sequence of stored numbers.

Speakerphone. This common step-up feature lets you talk without the handset.

Multiline capability. Another common step-up feature is the ability to handle a second phone line.

Easy-to-see keys. Keys that are lighted let you dial in the dark. Big keys make dialing easy for kids or for those with poor eyesight or poor coordination.

Volume controls. One control raises or lowers the volume at the handset, as needed; another does the same for the phone's ring. Speakerphones also have a volume control for the speaker in the base. Mute disconnects the mike so a caller can't hear sounds from your end of the line.

Pulse/tone dialing. Most phones have a switch that lets you go back and forth between pulse and tone dialing. That enables you to use computer or voice-mail systems even if you don't have tone service.

Flash. This button briefly disconnects a call, useful if you have call-waiting, a service that lets you take two calls at once on the same phone.

Capacitors. These battery alternatives keep a phone's memory intact for up to 24 hours if you unplug the phone or if the phone line fails. Batteries can last longer, but need periodic replacement.

LCD display. This shows information such as the number dialed, time of day, and the caller's telephone number.

Buying advice

Most of the quirks in telephone performance were ironed out long ago. Sound quality—especially listening—may vary from model to model. That's something you'll know only after you get it home. You should be okay if you buy by features and price at a store with return privileges. Expect to pay more for two-line models and speakerphones.

Cordless phones

A cordless phone is basically a walkie-talkie. A radio transmitter and receiver, in both base and handset, beam the conversation between the two. The base stays plugged into your phone line; the handset is detachable, so you can make and take calls from hundreds of feet away from the base.

The technology, though improving, isn't perfect. Cordless phones are often vulnerable to static. They may pick up signals from other cordless phones or other devices or simply quit when approaching the limit of their range. Your voice may not come through as clearly to people you call as theirs will to you, if they're using a regular phone. And if you're remiss about replacing the handset in its charger, the batteries are likely to give out unexpectedly. Despite all their drawbacks, cordless phones are gaining in popularity.

Models we've tested lately demonstrate better sound quality and less background noise than older models. All now use a digital "combination code" to prevent "call stealing."

Makers are responding in other ways to complaints. Compander circuitry is now built into most models to supress background noise. Voice scrambling, found on a few brands, also cuts eavesdropping.

The choices

Replaceable batteries are now required on all cordless phones, and many manufacturers offer batteries that hold a charge for as long as three weeks without recharging.

2-channel models. These usually cost about $50 to $60 but are becoming increasingly rare. Their main shortcoming: vulnerability to interference from nearby cordless phones operating on the same radio channel.

10-channel models. These typically cost between $70 and $150. Should interference occur, most let you change channels while continuing to talk. Some models automatically select a clear channel when you first pick up the phone.

Some models have a speakerphone in the base, which permits hands-free operation. On some, the base and handset can work as an intercom system; other models offer two phone lines. Some have two keypads, one on the handset and one on the base, which makes the base, in effect, a complete phone. Others offer additional charging cradles or multiple handsets.

900 Megahertz models. These use a different transmission frequency than other cordless models, providing a wider operating distance and better ability to transmit around obstructions. The digital versions are completely static-free and virtually impossible to eavesdrop on without exotic equipment. They cost from $300 to $500.

Features and conveniences

Features adding to convenience include:

Two-way paging. Pushing a button on the base or handset sounds a paging signal on the other component. The signal can

also lead you to a misplaced handset.

Ringer in base. When you're near the base, this alerts you to an incoming call no matter where the handset may be.

Out-of-range tone. It warns you the handset is too far from the base.

Speed-call memory. This stores frequently called numbers and lets you dial them using one or two buttons. Many phones can store more than 10 phone numbers of up to 16 digits each.

Volume control. This boosts the loudness of the handset's speaker.

Mute/hold. This lets you talk to someone near you without letting the person on the phone hear.

Voice scrambling. This feature reduces the possibility of eavesdropping by inverting audio frequencies.

Low-battery indicator. Lets you know when to recharge the battery.

Rubber antenna. Rubber is more forgiving than a rigid, metal antenna. Its flexibility eliminates accidental bending and breaking.

Buying advice

Look for a model with at least 10 channels. For added range, you may want to spend extra for a 900 MHz model. Prices are expected to keep falling for this type as it gains wider acceptance.

Don't rely on a cordless phone to replace the regular phone in your house. Cordless phones won't work during a power failure unless you have the rare model that features a battery back up.

Cellular phones

Over the past few years, cellular phones have graduated from techno-toys for executives and owners of fancy cars to a practical consumer appliance. A recent survey of CONSUMER REPORTS readers shows that business use was the second-most-popular reason for buying a cellular phone. More readers bought phones to use in emergencies and to keep in touch with family members.

The increasing acceptance of cellular

phones is partly due to the billions of dollars invested by cellular carriers—the companies that operate local cellular systems—to expand service areas.

The phones themselves also are changing. Permanently installed mobile phones and bulky, heavy "bag" phones have been joined by hand-held portable models petite enough to fit in pocket. The mobile and transportable models still have an edge on the portables—they have more power and can make somewhat better connections.

The way phones and phone service are sold also attracts more users. In most areas, the price of the phone is contingent on signing up for service, a marketing technique called "bundling."

Motorola is the leading seller, accounting for one-fifth of cellular phones sold. Other brands include *Audiovox, Mitsubishi, NEC, Nokia, NovAtel, Panasonic,* and *Uniden*. Prices for the phone can be quite low—less than $100—because you're buying a phone *plus* a service contract. The contract requires you to purchase service for a set period. In effect, by signing a contract, you get a discount on the price of the phone; ordering the phone à la carte adds hundreds of dollars to its price.

The choices

Mobile phones. This type, the original type of cellular phones, is permanently installed in a vehicle, usually professionally. A mobile, or car, phone transmits 3 watts and requires an external antenna. Price: about $115 to $275.

Transportable phones. This is basically a mobile phone you can remove from the car. It draws power from a rechargeable battery pack or a car's cigarette-lighter plug. Though technically portable, such a phone can weigh more than you might care to tote—five pounds or so. Price: from $75 to $200.

Portable and microportable phones.

Lightweight, hand-held models are the best-selling type. A battery-operated, portable model looks like the handset of a cordless phone. Its power is limited—usually a mere 0.6 watts—so coverage in areas where cellular service is poor may be worse than with mobile or portable units. A kit that boosts that power to 3 watts is available for some models. Price: $125 to $475.

Features and conveniences

Cellular phones offer a host of features; here are the common ones:

Memory and speed dialing. Most models store at least 30 numbers. You can usually speed-dial a number by pressing two or three buttons.

Call timer. Because cellular calls are expensive, keeping track of air-time is important. Besides displaying elapsed time, some models have a second timer to tally all your calls over a given period. You can also set most phones to beep at fixed intervals for time keeping.

Battery-low indicator. Cellular-phone batteries, typically nickel-cadmium, sustain conversation for at least an hour and standby status for a minimum of eight hours. (Battery life may improve as new nickel-hydride batteries become more widespread.) An indicator warns visually or audibly that the battery is running low. If you're home, recharge the battery; if on the road, insert a fresh battery.

Own-number display. Every cellular phone has its own phone number. Should you forget it, the phone's display can summon the number up.

Roaming features. In cellular parlance, "roaming" is the term for leaving the area covered by your carrier. Calls made outside your area are charged at a higher rate. Most models can be assigned more than one phone number—you can register with more than one carrier to reduce roaming charges. All models can be programmed to halt roaming temporarily so you don't inadvertently run up extra charges.

Built-in help. With many phones, hitting a key or two displays instructions for features you don't use often.

Extra features and conveniences inlcude:

Automatic number selection. If you have numbers for more than one carrier, this feature switches them automatically.

Fast recharge. This cuts recharging time from more than eight hours to one or two. If your phone doesn't come with this, you can probably buy a separate one.

Answering features. These ease use while driving. Any-key answer lets you pick up incoming calls by pressing any key—not a particular key, as with many models. Automatic-answer picks up for you after a couple of rings.

One-touch dial. The dial has keys with preset numbers to shorten dialing time.

Speakerphone. With a speakerphone, you can talk with both hands on the wheel.

Voice activation. Mostly on mobile phones, this feature lets you verbally send and receive calls and access memory.

Buying advice

In cities or in areas with flat terrain, most models should be adequate. Suburban and rural areas, where cellular coverage may be spotty, make tougher demands of a cellular phone and carrier.

If you make most calls from a vehicle, a permanently installed mobile phone makes sense; it has more power and is usually less expensive than a portable model. Or consider a portable model with a kit that lets you power the phone from the car battery, boost transmitting power or an external antenna.

Because of the way cellular phones are bundled with a service commitment, identical models may differ in price by hundreds of dollars. Shop for a carrier and a contract as if they were part of the cost of the phone.

SELECTING CELLULAR SERVICE

Most carriers have plans tailored to common calling patterns. They stipulate a fixed fee for a monthly time allotment. Despite the fee, the sales brochures tout that time as "free." If you exceed the allotment, you pay a stated amount for each extra minute used during "peak" hours (usually daytime, Monday through Friday) and a lower amount for "off-peak" use.

If you're not sure which plan is best for you, or if you plan to use the phone only for emergencies, take the one with the lowest monthly fee until you establish a usage pattern. If you need to switch to a higher-volume plan before the contract is up, you shouldn't have any trouble. If you mostly call at night, look for the lowest "off-peak" rates.

Major differences between carriers can sometimes be hidden in fine print. We found a carrier that had three more peak hours per day than its competitor. A carrier that charges a full minute for an extra second's airtime is more expensive than one that measures airtime in 30-second increments.

Some carriers make you dial extra numbers to reach a long-distance company other than the one with which they're affiliated; others let you select your own company when you sign up.

Finally, think twice about using features such as conferencing, perhaps, or sports or weather hotlines. They run up airtime.

See "Selecting Cellular Service," above. Typically, you'll spend more for a year's service than you did for the phone itself. Monthly bills run about $60, on average, according to an industry trade group.

Phone answerers

Today's answering machine is smaller, smarter, and sleeker than the machines that first appeared in the late 70's. Improved technology keeps shrinking the machine's size and has automated such functions as playing back your recorded messages. The keypad of any touch-tone phone has replaced the remote beeper. Voice actuated circuits with "time-outs" that hang up automatically if no one speaks have made answering machines adroit at handling messages, both long and short.

AT&T accounts for about a third of all answering machines sold in the U.S. Other major names include *General Electric, Panasonic,* and *Phonemate*.

The choices

Built-in or stand-alone. A phone answerer can be a machine you attach to a phone, or it can come integrated with a phone. Some answerers are now integrated with fax machines. An answerer with a built-in phone saves space and may be less expensive than a separate phone and answerer. Such integrated units have become quite popular. The trouble with them is that, if any part fails, the entire unit goes to the repair shop. Integrated phone/answering machines are typically priced between $85 and $250; answer-only units, at less than $50.

Answerers, with or without phones, use various recording designs:

Single microcassette. Declining in popularity, this type records both the outgoing and incoming messages on a single microcassette. With only one cassette, the machine can be compact, but individual messages are often limited to a minute or two and callers must wait for the tape to shuttle forward before they can leave a message. This is the cheapest type.

Dual cassette. This type, also declining in popularity, uses two microcassette tapes. Callers can leave a message without delay and the outgoing message can be longer than on a single-cassette machine. A machine that uses an endless-loop tape for outgoing messages delays answering new calls for about 15 seconds after receiving a call—time for the tape to return to the out-going message.

Digital/microcassette and all-digital. This type is currently the most popular. Memory chips like those found in computers are used to store the greeting; a cassette records the message. All-digital machines do away completely with the cassette, storing messages and greeting on memory chips. Digital models are supposedly less likely to break down than cassette models, since digitals replace moving parts with circuits. Compared with tape, memory chips limit recording time, and are expensive—but prices are falling. In our tests, voice quality on machines with chips was clear, but sounded less natural than taped messages. These answerers tend to be smaller but more expensive than the other types.

Features and conveniences

Certain features have become standard:

Call screening. This lets you listen to a message as it comes in, so you can avoid nuisance calls and not miss important ones. If you decide to take a call, a machine with Auto-disconnect automatically stops recording as soon as you pick up any phone in the house; a machine with Auto-reset stops recording and resets itself.

Number of rings. You can set the number of rings the machine will wait before it answers the call—no need to race to the phone to beat the machine's pickup.

Pause and Skip. These help control playback of recorded messages. Pause temporarily stops a message so you can jot down a name or number. Skip speeds things up by moving the tape back or forward one message.

One-touch. This rewinds, plays messages, and sets the machine for new calls.

Call counters. Some machines use a light to signal that at least one message is waiting. Better are units that blink the light to tell you how many messages there are. The best displays provide a digital readout of the number of calls. Most counters ignore hang-ups occurring before the beep.

Power backup. Most machines keep their memory at least for a short time in the event of power failure, but some reset the call counter to zero. The best designs use a battery-strength indicator and a battery backup that holds the settings for hours.

Remote access. Almost all machines let you use a touch-tone phone to hear messages when away from home. Some prompt you with vocal messages, similar to voice mail. Some have a programmed security code; others let you set it yourself. Two- or three-digit codes offer the most security.

Toll-saver. This lets you avoid a charge for calling your machine long-distance to check for possible messages. You set the machine to answer the first call after four or five rings and later calls after only one or two. You save money because if the machine hasn't picked up by ring number three, you know there are no messages.

Higher-priced machines offer additional features, including:

Audible message indicator. Machines with this feature beep when a message has been received so you know if there's a new message without looking at the machine.

Greeting bypass. Callers who don't want to hear your outgoing message by-

pass it by pressing a certain touch-tone key, usually the asterisk.

Time and date. The machine notes the time and date of each incoming message and announces them when you play the message back.

Announce-only. This lets you post a greeting without recording the incoming calls.

Multi-outgoing greetings. This feature lets you program two greetings and switch between them, something that's useful for a home-based business.

Selective save and delete. Some digital answering machines can store or delete messages in a random fashion without losing space for additional incoming messages.

Voice mailboxes. Some digital answerers provide "mailboxes" for people who share an answering machine. Callers are instructed as to how to leave messages for the specific party that they are trying to reach.

Voice prompt. This instructs you on how to program for time, date, remote operation, and other functions.

Message transfer. This automatically dials a preprogrammed telephone number when a message comes in.

Buying advice

If your needs are simple and you don't want a new telephone, look for a plain answerer with dual cassettes or for a digital/microcassette machine. A digital machine is priced a few dollars more but should be less likely to need repairs.

You'll find similar answerer choices among answering machines with a built-in telephone. Choices in phones on those machines range from plain-vanilla telephones to cordless models with lots of features.

Answering machines are discounted heavily. Shop around before you buy.

An alternative to a phone-answering machine is a service offered by many local phone companies. When you're out or if your line is busy, the phone company receives and stores messages; you retrieve messages with a touch-tone phone. The advantages are obvious—no machine to break down, an increased capability for receiving messages, and the ability to take messages while the phone is in use. The drawbacks are serious: There's no provision to screen incoming calls; no visible indicator to tell you if you have messages; and no absolute guarantee of privacy. Network failures can destroy messages. Charges can run $5 to $10 per month.

Home fax machines

With little fanfare, the facsimile machine has claimed considerable turf in the nation's offices and on the telephone network. Trend seers say that the fax's next conquest will be the American home. Although the fax machine has found its way into only 2 percent of U.S. households, more and more people are using home faxes to order printed matter—newsletters, travel maps, reprints—or take-out food and mail-order purchases. Still others use home faxes to telecommute.

Four brands dominate sales of home fax machines: *Sharp*, *Panasonic*, *Canon*, and *Muratec* (formerly *Murata*).

The choices

Manufacturers aim their small models at the home-office market, which entails compromise. Absent are features big businesses demand, like fast printing speeds and the ability to print on plain rather than "fax" paper. Such machines generally list for $800 or more. But light-duty fax machines can be had for $350 and up—and prices are falling.

Home machines typically print incoming documents on long rolls of chemically treated stock, using a thermal system (tiny heating elements form the letters). That system helps keep both size and cost down.

The cheapest home fax machines lack a document feeder and an automatic paper cutter. Not having a feeder means each page sent must be inserted manually by someone standing over the machine; no cutter means someone has to cut scrolls of output into page-sized sheets.

But home fax machines also include amenities omitted on some big models. The faxes can photocopy (though the copies come out on fax paper) and, at the same time, some can enlarge or reduce copy. Home models usually have a Fax/voice switch, to make it easier for the machine to share the line with a regular phone. The circuitry listens for the data tone of a fax transmission to route incoming calls appropriately, to you or the machine. Most home machines also offer an answering-machine interface, which allows an answerer to take voice calls and messages the same way it does when you're not at home.

Features and conveniences

Sending modes. This determines the resolution of a faxed document and the speed at which it can be sent. In Standard mode, faxes break an inch of the page into 100 scan lines, each some 1700 dots across. Sending in Standard mode takes about a minute a page. Faxes can also be sent in Fine mode (twice the scan lines, double the time) for small print that might otherwise come out unreadable. Some models offer Superfine with still higher resolution but they only work with the same-brand machines. And many offer a Halftone mode, for photos and artwork, rendering grays in 16 or more steps from black to white. (Sending such a document can take five minutes or more per page.)

One-touch dialing. A fax machine's built-in memory typically sports at least a few buttons to program frequently dialed numbers. More numbers are usually programmable for speed-dialing (you press a special key, then a one- or two-digit code).

Auto retry. Typically, fax machines will persistently redial busy numbers for a few minutes until it connects.

Delayed sending. This allows you to set up a document for transmission at a later time, to take advantage of cheaper phone rates.

Remote start. If you answer an extension phone that shares the fax's line and find the call is an incoming fax, this feature lets you start your fax receiving by pressing a short code. Without it, you'd have to press the Start button.

Paper. Most machines use a glossy, slippery thermal paper, which is notorious for curling and being hard to handle. Some models take a grade of thermal paper that feels more like standard paper. Thermal paper comes in rolls of 49, 64, 98, and 328 feet. Rolls 98 feet or longer are more convenient than the 49-foot roll, which runs out quickly. Plain-paper fax machines are the standard in commercial use but cost twice as much as machines that use thermal paper.

Anticurl system. This feature flattens thermal fax paper.

Paper cutter. The cheapest machines use paper on a roll you must cut apart by hand. Paper-cutter models are more expensive but usually worth it.

Document feeder. A feeder tray lets you feed 5, 10, or 20 pages at one time rather than stand over the machine and insert the pages you're sending one by one.

Memory, broadcasting. If a fax runs out of paper when receiving, some models can capture a few pages of text in memory for later printing. Typically, those models are also able to use their memory to "broadcast" a document you want distributed to a routing list of phone numbers.

Activity reports. Most faxes print a listing of documents recently sent or received, along with phone numbers, times and dates, and can tell you whether or not the transmission went through.

Buying advice

If you only need a fax on rare occasions, consider using one in a nearby drug store, copy shop, or post office. That's still a lot cheaper than buying your own.

Judging from our tests, sending and printing clear text is not a problem for modern light-duty fax machines. Features, however, can make or break a machine.

Don't cut corners on paper-handling features. Two musts: a document feeder, to send long faxes, and an automatic cutter, to receive multipage documents.

Look for a machine that makes it easy to share the phone line with a regular phone. Many consumers with home offices probably cannot afford to install a telephone line just for the fax. A built-in Fax/voice switch you can set to pick up after a few rings can route voice calls to you and fax calls to the machine. You'll also want the capability to start the fax from an extension, along with an answering-machine interface (or built-in answering machine) that works smoothly and capably with the fax.

Special needs require special features. For faxing photos or artwork, look for a machine with a Halftone mode. If you do a lot of overseas faxing, choose a machine that lets you select a slower transmission speed to cope with electronic noise. For routinely sending the same documents to the same people, look for one with a built-in memory and the ability to broadcast to a routing list.

RATINGS DESKTOP COMPUTERS

▶ **See report, page 211.** Last time rated in Consumer Reports: November 1994.

Brand-name recommendations: Because of the fast-changing nature of the computer market, most of the models below are likely to be discontinued sometime in 1995. Our test results, however, should apply to the current members of the whole family, not just the model we tested. In general, we recommend the following: for an IBM-compatible, a 486SX-or DX33 or DX2-66 with 8 MB of RAM, at least a 200 MB hard drive, local BUS video, and 128-KB cache; for a Macintosh, we recommend a Performa with least 8 MB RAM and 250 MB hard drive. For both, we suggest a 14-inch .28 mm dot pitch, non-interlaced monitor.

For the typical desktop computer, expect: ■ DOS and Windows software for IBM-compatibles; System 7.X with Macs. ■ To purchase computer and monitor separately. ■ Color monitor. ■ Some upgrade options and multi-media and modem/fax options. ■ Good instructions for setup. **A choice you'll have to make:** ■ IBM-compatible or Mac.

Notes on the table: Family name is given first, then the tested model. Most were tested with 8 MB of RAM. **Price** is approx., rounded to nearest $100. **Overall score** summarizes judgments of performance and features with emphasis on display quality, ease of setup, and speed. **Display** considers contrast and clarity of monitor. **Application** shows how quickly the machines handled word processing, calculations, and games. **Video** shows speed of updating graphics.

RATINGS OVERVIEW
Within types, listed in order of performance and features

E VG G F P
◓ ◓ ○ ◑ ●

Brand and model	Price	Overall score	Display	Setup	Application			Video
					WP	FINANCE	GAMES	

IBM-COMPATIBLE: PENTIUM 60-MHZ PROCESSOR

Brand and model	Price	Overall score	Display	Setup	WP	FINANCE	GAMES	Video
Dell Dimension XPS XPS P60	$2600	▬▬▬▬	◓	◓	◓	◓	◓	◓
Gateway 2000 P5-60	2500	▬▬▬▬	◓	◓	◓	◓	◓	◓
Packard Bell Force Force 101CD	2300	▬▬▬	◓	○	◓	◓	◓	◓

IBM-COMPATIBLE: 486DX/2-T66-MHZ PROCESSOR

Brand and model	Price	Overall score	Display	Setup	WP	FINANCE	GAMES	Video
AST Advantage! Advantage! Plus Model 429	2900	▬▬▬▬	◓	◓	◓	○	◓	◑
Dell Dimension 466V	2000	▬▬▬▬	◓	○	◓	◓	◓	◑
Compaq Presario 860 Presario CDS 860	2300	▬▬▬	◓	◓	◓	○	◓	○
Packard Bell Legend 38CD Supreme	2200	▬▬▬	◓	○	◓	○	◓	◑

Brand and model	Price	Overall score	Display	Setup	Application			Video
					WP	FINANCE	GAMES	
Gateway 2000 P4D-66	$2600	▰▰▰	⊖	○	⊖	⊖	⊖	⊖
Tandy (Radio Shack) 4100MT	3100	▰▰▰	⊖	⊖	⊖	○	⊖	⊖
IBM PS/1 PS/1 2168-57C	2600	▰▰▰	⊖	●	⊖	○	⊖	⊖
Compaq Presario 866 Presario 866	2700	▰▰▰	⊖	●	⊖	○	⊖	⊖
AT&T Model 2445 Model 2445	2100	▰▰	○	⊖	⊖	○	⊖	⊖
Gateway 2000 Family PC 4DX2-66 Family PC	2000	▰	●	○	⊖	○	⊖	⊖

IBM-COMPATIBLE: 486 33-MHZ PROCESSOR

Brand and model	Price	Overall score	Display	Setup	Application			Video
					WP	FINANCE	GAMES	
IBM PS/1 PS/1 2168-SR1	1700	▰▰	⊖	⊖	◐	◐	◐	●
AST Advantage! Advantage! Adventure Model 213	1300	▰	⊖	⊖	◐	◐	◐	●
Compaq Presario 633 Presario CDS 633	1900	▰	⊖	○	◐	◐	◐	●
Compaq Presario 433 Presario 433	1200	▰	⊖	○	◐	◐	◐	●
AT&T Model 1151 Model 1151	1500	▰	○	◐	◐	◐	◐	●

MACINTOSH MODELS

Brand and model	Price	Overall score	Display	Setup	Application			Video
					WP	FINANCE	GAMES	
Apple Macintosh Performa 635CD Performa 635CD	1900	▰▰	⊖	⊖	⊖	⊖	○	○
Apple Power Macintosh 7100/66 Power Macintosh 7100/66	3500	▰▰	⊖	⊖	○	⊖	⊖	⊖
Apple Power Macintosh 6100/60 Power Macintosh 6100/60	2200	▰	⊖	⊖	○	○	●	⊖

RATINGS DETAILS — Models listed alphabetically

Apple Macintosh Performa 635CD	Tested with 5 MB RAM. Supports Energy-star energy saving.
Apple Power Macintosh 6100/60	—
Apple Power Macintosh 7100/66	Supports Energy-star energy saving.
AST Advantage! Advantage! Adventure Model 213	Tested with 4 MB RAM. Supports Energy-star energy saving.

Ratings continued ▶

Ratings continued

AST Advantage! Advantage! Plus Model 429	—
AT&T Model 1151 Model 1151	Tested with 4 MB RAM.
AT&T Model 2445 Model 2445	—
Compaq Presario 433 Presario 433	Tested with 4 MB RAM. Cannot fit internal CD-Rom drive. Features user-friendly front-end for Windows. Graphics sluggish with DOS.
Compaq Presario 633 Presario CDS 633	Tested with 4 MB RAM. Features user-friendly front-end for Windows. Graphics speedy with DOS.
Compaq Presario 860 CDS 860	Features user-friendly front-end for Windows.
Compaq Presario 866 Presario 866	Features user-friendly front-end for Windows.
Dell Dimension 466V	Graphics speedier than most with DOS.
Dell Dimension XPS XPS P60	—
Gateway 2000 Family PC 4DX2-66 Family PC	Supports Energy-star energy saving.
Gateway 2000 P4D-66	Supports Energy-star energy saving.
Gateway 2000 P5-60	Supports Energy-star energy saving.
IBM PS/1 PS/1 2168-SR1	Tested with 4 MB RAM. Supports Energy-star energy saving. "Resume" feature restores workpoint easily after turning computer off.
IBM PS/1 PS/1 2168-57C	Supports Energy-star energy saving. "Resume" feature restores workpoint easily after turning computer off.
Packard Bell Force Force 101CD	Features user-friendly front-end for Windows.
Packard Bell Legend 38CD Supreme	Features user-friendly front-end for Windows.
Tandy (Radio Shack) 4100MT	Supports Energy-star energy saving.

YARD & GARDEN

For do-it-yourselfers, basic lawn-care tools start with a lawnmower and include hoses, sprinklers, and perhaps a watering timer. An assortment of hand tools and perhaps a trimmer may be needed.

The lawn mower and string trimmer might be considered essential power equipment for any lawn. Other power tools may see action no more than once or twice a year. In such cases, renting makes the most sense. Then there's no need to store or service a bulky tiller or cultivator.

Whether you rent or buy, follow the tool's safety rules. In general, don't operate a power tool with children or pets close by, and wear protective clothing. Electric tools shouldn't be used when conditions are wet.

Gasoline-powered tools deserve special caution. Fill the fuel tank carefully, after the engine has cooled. Don't handle the blade of a machine unless the engine is stopped and the ignition disabled.

Lawn mowers

▶ **Ratings on page 234.**   ▶ **Repair records on page 24.**

There are people with a postage-stamp lawn who use a lawn tractor to cut the grass. And a few hardy souls with vast expanses of green still doggedly perform the weekly mowing chore with a manual reel mower. But it makes more sense to buy a machine that matches the lawn.

Size, terrain, and landscape all affect the

decision. A very hilly half-acre may need a different machine than a lawn that's flat. Even the simplest, flattest lawn may need some trimming with a walk-behind mower or a string trimmer. A lawn dotted with trees and flower beds will need a lot of trimming.

Lawn-mowing machines range from $80 reel mowers to 20-horsepower garden tractors priced upward of $2000. One company—American Lawn Mower Company/Great States Corp.—accounts for almost all the reel-mowers sold. Black & Decker, Sears, and MTD sell most of the electric mowers. Sears and Murray sell about half the gasoline mowers, mostly low-priced models. Other big names—Toro, Lawn-Boy, Snapper, Ariens, Honda, John Deere—concentrate on the pricey end of the market.

More and more people are choosing a new lawn-mowing option—mulching. When mulching, a mower chops clippings into small pieces and blows them down into the turf, hastening the return of nutrients to the soil and reducing the likelihood that the clippings will smother the grass. With no bags of clippings to empty, the mowing job becomes easier, but you may have to mow more frequently to avoid leaving too much grass behind. Most models that mulch can convert to a mower that deposits clippings into a bag or out a chute.

If you live where rainfall is scarce, you may decide to plant something other than a standard lawn. Choosing less thirsty grasses and plants could cut your water needs in half. For information, contact your local Cooperative Extension service or a local nursery or garden center.

Backyard pollution

Lawn mowers are beginning to change in response to new regulations aimed at limiting their emissions. The California Air Resources Board has estimated that mowing a lawn for a half hour with a typical mower can contribute as much smog as driving a car 172 miles. New regulations take effect first in California in 1995, with stricter standards due in 1999. The U.S. Environmental Protection Agency proposed Federal limits in April 1994; they're scheduled to take effect in 1996, though the industry has asked for a one-year delay.

To meet the first wave of regulations, mower designs may require only small adjustments in fuel mixture and ignition and valve timing. To meet 1999 emission limits, manufacturers may have to adopt some of the pollution-control devices used in cars—catalytic converters and sophisticated carburetion. The effect on price won't be much, at least for now. In 1999, when the stricter standards take effect, mower prices are expected to jump significantly.

Current lawn-mower designs vary in how much they pollute. A mower with an overhead-valve engine burns fuel more efficiently than the traditional side-valve machine. Four-stroke engines burn more cleanly than two-stroke ones. You can minimize emissions from mowing by regularly tuning up your mower and by buying a spillproof nozzle for its fuel container (spills from lawn and garden equipment cause a significant amount of emissions).

Safety

The Consumer Product Safety Commission requires manufacturers to equip walk-behind mowers with a deadman control that stops the blade when you let go of the handle. Such requirements seem to have made mowing safer. Injuries due to walk-behind mowers have dropped to about half what they were just 10 years ago. Still, thousands of people head to hospital emergency rooms every year because of an injury caused by a lawn mower or tractor.

When you mow, follow these rules:

■ Mow only when and where it's safe.

Don't mow when the grass is wet; your foot can slip under the mower. Push a mower across a slope, not up and down. If you have a riding mower or tractor, travel up and down, not across. If the slope is more than about 15 degrees, don't mow at all—on slopes that steep, a push-mower can get away from you, and a ride-on mower can tip over. Consider replacing some grassy areas with a different groundcover.

■ Dress for the job. Wear sturdy shoes and close-fitting clothes.

■ Prepare the area. Pick up toys, hoses, rocks, and twigs. Banish anyone nearby, including pets—a mower can hurl objects.

■ Use gasoline carefully. Fill the mower's fuel tank before you start, while the engine is cold. Before you refill, wait for the engine to cool (unless the tank is located away from the engine).

■ Keep hands and feet away from moving parts.

■ Don't defeat safety devices.

■ Don't let young children use a mower or tractor or ride a tractor.

The choices

Manual reel mower. Concern about hydrocarbon emissions from lawn mowers has focused new attention on this old product. The original lawn mower has been brought up to date with lightweight alloys and plastic parts. A series of blades linked to the wheels slice the grass. Cutting widths: 14 to 18 inches. For lawns up to about 5000 square feet, this is a quiet, no-pollution solution. But it's impractical for all but a small, level lawn.

Price: $100 or less.

Electric mower. The electric versions of the power mower use an electric motor ranging from 6.5 to 12 amp. to spin the blade while you push. The relatively low engine power makes electrics slower and less effective in tall grass than gasoline-powered mowers. Cutting widths: 18 to 20 inches. For lawns up to about one-quarter acre, an electric is a quiet, fumeless, fairly low-cost choice. Most are also mulching.

The power cord gets in the way, and it limits the range. A device to guide the cord across the handle when you change mowing direction helps keep the cord from tangling. Battery-powered models are starting to show up, made chiefly by Black & Decker and Ryobi. A full charge can cut about a quarter acre or so.

Price: $110 to $300 for corded models; $350 to $500 for battery models.

Push-type gasoline mower. The basic gasoline-powered mower, this type is best suited for mowing flat lawns up to about one-half acre and for trimming larger lawns. It has a one-cylinder, four-stroke engine that spins a 20- to 22-inch blade. Engine power ranges from 3.5 to 5.5 hp. A few models use a two-stroke engine, which requires a gasoline/oil fuel mixture and emits more pollutants.

Look for a deadman control that stops the blade but not the engine when you release the handle (called a blade-brake/clutch), rather than a control that stops both. A blade-brake/clutch can be found on higher-priced models, but the extra measure of safety and convenience is worth the cost.

Most models can mulch; they usually have more powerful engines (the better to grind up grass) than nonmulching models. A model with a grass-catcher bag at the rear is easier to maneuver around trees than one with the bag on the side.

Some models come with oversized rear wheels for smoother rolling on rough terrain. A mower with a deck that extends outboard of its wheels has a better chance of trimming close to a wall or fence than a mower whose wheels stick out. A folding handle allows more compact storage. Electric start eliminates tugging on a rope starter. For more information about features, see the box on page 238.

Price: $100 to $600.

Self-propelled mower. These mowers use the same general design as push-type mowers, but the engine also powers the front or rear wheels. This type is much easier to use, especially on hilly lawns, than push-type power mowers. It's good for lawns around one-half acre in size.

Look for the same features mentioned for push-type mowers. Variable or multiple drive speeds let you adjust speed to terrain. A clutch that lets you "feather" the mower into gear rather than start it abruptly makes maneuvering easier.

Price: $180 to $800.

Riding mower. These junior tractors suit lawns about one-half to one acre. They typically use a 30-inch blade and an 8- to 10-horsepower, rear-mounted, electric-start engine to power the wheels and blade. They can hold a large grass-catcher and typically offer a mulching conversion kit.

Look for a ride-on with one deadman control to stop the engine, the blade, or both if you dismount, another to stop the engine, the blade, or both if you dismount with the mower in gear.

Price: $900 to $4000.

Tractor. For lawns one acre or larger, this is the homeowner's version of the farmer's workhorse. Many cost no more than riding mowers, yet are much more versatile. Small versions—called lawn tractors—typically use a 12- to 14-hp engine, mounted in the front, to power the wheels and a 38- to 45-inch cutting deck with two or three blades. Mulching kits are often available, as are other attachments, including such accessories as snow plow and thrower, leaf vacuum, and cart. Large versions—garden tractors—use a 16- to 20-hp engine and take a wider range of attachments, including cultivators.

Look for positive gear-shift detents or for a hydrostatic transmission, which permits continuously variable speed. Make sure there are deadman controls like those we recommend for riding mowers.

Price: $900 to $4000 for lawn tractors, $2000 to $5000 for garden tractors.

The tests

CU tests mowers early each year, as soon as the new models become available. The grass at our New York headquarters is brown and dormant in winter, so we test mowers at a college campus in Florida. We assess each model's adeptness at several tasks: cutting evenly, dispersing clippings without clumping, cutting tall grass, and collecting clippings. For mowers that mulch, we see how well they disperse the grass.

We also look for designs that ease or hinder the chore and for anything that increases the risk of injury.

Reliability

The more complex the mower, the higher the probability that it will need repair, according to our readers' experience. One exception: *Hondas*. Their repair rates for push-type and self-propelled models were equally low. Overall, readers report that about 14 percent of push-type mowers purchased since 1988 needed repairs. About 23 percent of self-propelled models needed repair during the same time period. See brand Repair Histories on page 24.

Buying advice

Choose the type of mower that fits the size and nature of your yard. Don't buy more mower than you need.

Lawn mowers are heavily promoted in the spring, but the best prices are found after the Fourth of July. No matter when you buy, expect to pay more at a hardware store or specialty mower shop than at a home center, discount store, or catalog retail outlet. But smaller stores may offer better service and a higher-quality line of mowers.

String trimmers

String trimmers take care of what's beyond a mower's reach, effortlessly cleaning up the tough weeds and tall grass you used to tackle with clippers and shears. A trimmer works by spinning a plastic line fast enough to slice through leaf and stem but with too little inertia to maim a wayward foot. Still, a lashing from a trimmer's whirling line can draw blood from bare skin, and the line can fling dirt and debris with considerable force. Gasoline trimmers typically generate around 100 decibels of noise, enough to warrant use of hearing protection. We recommend wearing long pants, sturdy shoes, and goggles when using a string trimmer.

The choices

One-handled electric. For light trimming. These models cut a swath 8 to 10 inches wide and weigh about three pounds. Price: $25 to $35.

Two-handled electric. Some electric trimmers cut as well as gasoline-powered models, although the need for an extension cord limits the electrics' reach and convenience. The typical model has a motor mounted over the cutting head. They cut a swath 10 to 17 inches wide and weigh less than 10 pounds. Price: $35 to $80.

Battery-powered. These electric models offer freedom from both an extension cord and gasoline. The ones we've tested have run for about 20 minutes on a charge, typically with less power than plug-in electric trimmers. They cut a swath 6 to 10 inches wide and weigh three to five pounds. Price: $35 to more than $110.

Gasoline-powered. The heaviest, most powerful type cuts a swath 15 to 18 inches wide. These models weigh 9 to 15 pounds, enough to require two-handed operation. Most have a two-stroke engine located at the top of the shaft, but Ryobi has several models with a cleaner-burning four-stroke engine. Price: $80 to more than $350.

Wheeled. These gasoline-powered machines tackle areas of wood or plantings that are too large or rough for a power mower or that would require the prolonged use of an ordinary trimmer. They cut a swath 17 to 18 inches wide. Price: $400 and up.

Features and conveniences

String advancement. Most models use the bump-feed system. You tap or bump the trimmer head on the ground, and the line advances. A metal cutter on the head shears off any excess line. Even more convenient is automatic line-advance: The machine feeds out string as needed.

Brush-cutter blade. A metal blade can be substituted for the string to cut woody stems up to an inch thick.

Engine/motor location. With large gasoline-powered trimmers weighing nine pounds or more, good balance is critical to easy use. One of the best indicators of good balance is an engine or motor mounted high on the shaft, above the handle.

Shoulder strap. For heavy models, this is a way to improve balance. It also takes some load off arms.

Pivoting trimmer head. For edging, you typically have to orient the trimmer's head so the line spins vertically. A pivoting head makes the chore easier by letting you keep both handles in their regular position on the handle.

Translucent fuel tank. On gasoline-powered models, this makes the fuel level easy to check.

Buying advice

If your property is large, or if you must tackle heavy or woody undergrowth, consider a gasoline-powered trimmer. If overgrown weeds or the tether of an extension cord doesn't present a problem, a two-handled electric model may make the most sense. If you only need to touch up a small, well-tended plot, either a one-handled electric or a battery-powered trimmer should do the job nicely.

Garden hoses

Whatever you use a hose for—washing the car, filling the swimming pool, or watering the lawn—you want one that is flexible and deploys without kinking, while allowing a copious stream of water to flow through. Grade designations such as "good," "better," and "best" have no universally accepted meaning. Labels tout impressive bursting strengths, although just about any hose can handle normal water pressure without harm. Some promise lifetime guarantees. But that doesn't necessarily mean they're superior to models with a-year warranty or none at all.

The choices

Garden hoses range in price from $5 to $25. Factors that affect price: hose length, hose diameter, and hose material.

QUICK-CONNECT HOSE COUPLINGS

These attach to the threaded fittings at both ends of the hose and to the faucet, and the hose accessories. They make it easier to connect a hose to a faucet, to a sprinkler or to another length of hose. That saves trips back to the faucet and simplifies changing nozzles and hooking up to a sprinkler. In our tests, metal couplings ($4 to $7 a pair) attached and detached more easily, withstood more abuse, and restricted water flow less than plastic ones ($2 to $4).

Length and diameter. Fifty feet is by far the most common length, and $5/8$-inch is the most common (inside) diameter. That diameter is a good all-round choice. Half-inch hoses, either in 50- or 100-foot lengths, are suitable for most sprinklers and nozzles. But, if hooked up in more than two 50-foot lengths, those lengths may constrict water flow. Three-quarter-inch hoses let you reach beyond 150 feet and supply lots of water fast. Most ribbed "anti kink" hoses have a lower flow rate than a hose that's smooth or grooved inside.

Material. Hoses are made of four basic materials, none inherently better than the rest. Vinyl is the most common; often low-priced, it can be harder to coil in cool weather than hoses made of other materials. Rubber hoses have a reputation for quality, but we found little reason in our tests to justify their generally higher price. Rubber/vinyl hoses, are likely to handle better than all-vinyl hoses and cost less than all-rubber ones. Nylon hoses are rare these days.

Features and conveniences

Reinforcement. All but the cheapest hoses are reinforced with one or more layers of nylon or rayon fabric sandwiched between the vinyl or rubber layers. The fabric may be knit, wrapped in a spiral or dual-spiral pattern, or a combination of knit and spiral. The type of reinforcement doesn't much matter, we found—any kind of reinforcement helps strengthen the hose and makes it easier to use.

Faucet fittings. An octagonal hose-end fitting or a fitting with a plastic collar, either winged or round, is easier to use than a plain round knurled fitting.

Buying advice

You'll find the widest selection of lengths among the ⅝-inch hoses.

Consider a ½-inch hose only for short faucet-to-sprinkler reaches, and a ¾-inch hose only if you require more than 150 feet. The best values are reinforced models made of vinyl. The least likely to kink are reinforced vinyl/rubber models.

As with much yard equipment, you'll find the best prices at the end of the season.

Lawn sprinklers

Sprinklers come in various forms suitable for different-shaped lawns and gardens. Prices typically range from $5 to $30.

The choices

There are five basic types:

Stationary. These are probably the best known and least expensive. Their simple designs produce a variety of spray patterns: spots, rings, salt shakers, and turrets. Best for watering small areas. Price: less than $5.

Impulse. An impulse model is the most versatile type. Impulse sprinklers can cover areas ranging from very wide to small. The largest area it can cover—typically, a 70-foot-diameter circle—might take 10 to 14 hours to get an inch of water.

A spring-loaded flapper deflects the stream of water and turns the sprinkler's nozzle a few degrees each time it flaps. A set of stops lets you water a whole circle or an arc as narrow as 30 degrees. Other controls let you reduce the upward angle of the stream or break the stream into a spray; both reduce the diameter of the coverage but speed up water delivery. Avoid impulse models whose deflectors have to be adjusted directly by hand (you get splashed). Price: $4 to $35.

Rotary. These sprinklers whirl like a pinwheel, with two or three nozzles spreading a circular spray over a smaller area than that of impulse models. They are rel-

atively fast but cover a fairly small area. Some rotary sprinklers let you adjust the angle of the nozzle arms or the type of spray to reduce the area covered; others have a fan like deflector that makes a square watering pattern. Models whose nozzles lack labels are hard to set at the same angle. Price: $5 to $25.

Traveling. A mobile variation of the rotary sprinkler, this type lets you tailor the coverage to a large, irregularly shaped area. Most have a spray arm linked by gears to tractor-type wheels; as the nozzles whirl, the tractor base is slowly driven along by the water pressure using the laid-out hose as a guide. Price: $65 to $125.

Oscillating. On this type of sprinkler, a curved tube with holes or tiny nozzles slowly moves back and forth, quickly watering a small rectangular area. Oscillators usually let you make the rectangle shorter; some models also let you make it narrower. Price: $10 to $40.

Buying advice

Choose a model that suits your lawn. An impulse model covers the largest area, but it might take 10 to 14 hours to deliver an inch of water.

For a smaller lawn, a rotary or oscillating model will do the job in two to five hours. If your lawn has an irregular shape, look for a model that has adjustable patterns.

RATINGS PUSH-TYPE LAWN MOWERS

▶ **See report, page 227.** Last time rated in Consumer Reports: June 1994.

Brand-name recommendations: If you require a machine that cuts well in bagging, discharging, and mulching modes, consider the top-rated *Snapper X21500*, which costs $500 (the chute and mulching kit are extra). The *John Deere 14PZ*, $459, was the only model that gave an excellent cut in both bagging and side-discharge modes. If you seldom mow with the bag attached, look first to the best side-bagging mower, the *Montgomery Ward 37088*, $200. It has been discontinued but may still be available.

For mowers in this class, expect: ■ Good or very good evenness of cut when bagging but a wide range of bag capacities. ■ Good evenness of cut in mulching mode. ■ The ability to mow with the standard blade in 3 modes: discharging, bagging, and mulching. ■ Good or better convenience. ■ A 4-stroke, side-valve, 3.75 to 5 hp engine that starts with a pull cord and has a primer bulb rather than a choke control. ■ A deadman safety system that turns off the engine when the handle is released—less convenient than a system that stops only the blade. ■ A handle whose height is adjustable. ■ A steel deck. ■ Cutting swath 20 to 21 in. **A choice you'll have to make if you bag clippings:** ■ Rear bagger or side bagger.

Notes on the table: Price is the mfr.'s suggested or approx. retail. **Overall score** is based on performance, handling, and convenience. **Evenness** is mower's ability to produce a smooth, carpetlike cut. **Vacuuming** reflects the ability, when bagging, to leave the mowed lawn free from clippings. **Dispersal** reflects how uniformly clippings were distributed during discharging or mulching. **Tall grass** indicates performance on a plot of 12-in.-high grass. Ⓓ indicates model discontinued or replacement not similar.

RATINGS OVERVIEW Listed in order of performance

E ⊖ VG ⊖ G ○ F ◐ P ●

Brand and model	Price	Overall score P F G VG E	Bagging EVEN.	VAC.	Discharging EVEN.	DISP.	Tall grass	Mulching DISP.
REAR-BAGGING MODELS								
Snapper X21500	$500		⊖	⊖	⊖	⊖	⊖	⊖
John Deere 14PZ	459		⊖	⊖	⊖	○	⊖	○
Kubota W5021PC	659		⊖	⊖	○	⊖	⊖	—
Honda Harmony HRM215PXA	545		⊖	◐	⊖	◐	◐	⊖
Toro Recycler 20435	399		⊖	⊖	○	○	◐	⊖
Honda Harmony HRM215PDA	480		⊖	◐	⊖	◐	◐	⊖
Husqvarna Royal 48 Ⓓ	400		○	○	○	●	◐	
Homelite HSB21	380		⊖	⊖	○	⊖	⊖	—

Brand and model	Price	Overall score					Bagging		Discharging		Tall grass	Mulching
		P	F	G	VG	E	EVEN.	VAC.	EVEN.	DISP.		DISP.
Snapper R21400 Recycler/Mulcher	$400				▇		⊖	○	⊖	○	⊖	⊖
Ariens LM215 911051	529				▇		○	○	○	⊖	○	◐
Yard-Man 114-808L401	299			▇			⊖	⊖	⊖	○	⊖	⊖
Montgomery Ward PowrKraft 37288 Ⓓ	240			▇			⊖	⊖	⊖	⊖	⊖	○
Lawn-Boy Gold Series 10421	410			▇			⊖	○	○	◐	◐	⊖
Murray Convertible Mulcher 21677	180			▇			○	◐	○	◐	○	◐
Rally 4E372	200			▇			○	○	○	◐	○	⊖
Murray 3nOne Convertible 22355	399			▇			○	⊖	○	◐	●	○
Rally 2E372	185			▇			○	○	○	●	○	⊖
Wheeler WRBD5Q21	250			▇			○	○	○	⊖	⊖	○
White LC-428 114-428C190	319			▇			⊖	○	⊖	◐	○	⊖
Murray Vectra Convertible 22355X80	399			▇			○	⊖	○	◐	●	○
Sears Craftsman 38324 Ⓓ	240			▇			○	⊖	○	◐	○	⊖
Lawn Chief 81	240		▇				○	○	○	○	○	○

SIDE-BAGGING MODELS

Brand and model	Price	Overall score					Bagging		Discharging		Tall grass	Mulching
		P	F	G	VG	E	EVEN.	VAC.	EVEN.	DISP.		DISP.
Montgomery Ward Signature 2000 37088 Ⓓ	200				▇		⊖	⊖	⊖	⊖	⊖	○
Cub Cadet 108R	299				▇		⊖	⊖	⊖	○	⊖	○
White LC-108 114-108C190	279				▇		⊖	○	⊖	⊖	⊖	○
Toro 16400	319				▇		⊖	◐	○	○	⊖	—
Homelite HCM20	350			▇			⊖	⊖	⊖	⊖	○	⊖
Atlas A22551	250			▇			⊖	◐	○	○	⊖	○
Lawn Chief 94M	260			▇			○	⊖	○	⊖	◐	⊖
Lawn-Boy Silver Series 10202	270			▇			⊖	○	○	◐	◐	⊖
Sears Craftsman 38054	180		▇				○	⊖	○	○	○	⊖

Ratings continued ▶

Ratings continued

Brand and model	Price	Overall score					Bagging		Discharging		Tall grass	Mulching
		P	F	G	VG	E	EVEN.	VAC.	EVEN.	DISP.		DISP.
Sears Craftsman 38437	$250			▬			◓	○	◓	◓	○	◒
Murray 22277	139		▬				○	◓	◒	○	◒	○
Rally 1P209	115			▬			○	●	○	◒	◒	◒
Wheeler WDR4 Ⓓ	199		▬				○	○	◓	●	●	—

RATINGS DETAILS   Models listed alphabetically

Ariens LM215 911051	Easy to: maneuver; make U-turns; jockey side to side; start engine; use bag. Hard to: change modes; adjust cutting height. Has swiveling front wheels.
Atlas A22551	Easy to: maneuver; push; jockey side-to-side; change modes. Hard to adjust cutting height. Handle height not adjustable. Very small bag capacity.
Cub Cadet 108R	Easy to: maneuver; push; make U-turns; jockey side to side; change modes; Comfortable handle. Hard to: pull; use throttle.
Homelite HCM20	Easy to: push; adjust cutting height; change modes. Hard to: make U-turns; install bag. Noisy.
Homelite HSB21	Easy to: use throttle; change modes. Hard to: make U-turns; operate deadman; use starter cord. Noisy. Very large bag capacity.
Honda Harmony HRM215PDA	Easy to: use bag; adjust cutting height. Quiet. Discharge chute clogged. Different blade for mulching. Very large bag capacity.
Honda Harmony HRM215PXA	Deadman switch stops blade only. Easy to: start engine; use throttle; use bag; adjust cutting height. Quiet. Hard to: operate deadman. Discharge chute clogged. Different blade for mulching. Very large bag capacity.
Husqvarna Royal 48 Ⓓ	19-in. cutting swath. Easy to: maneuver; jockey side to side; operate deadman; empty bag; change modes; adjust cutting height. Comfortable handle. Quiet. Handle not adjustable and too high for short user. Vague throttle.
John Deere 14PZ	Easy to: maneuver; make U-turns; jockey side to side; use throttle; use bag; adjust cutting height. Comfortable handle. Different blade for mulching.
Kubota W5021PC	Deadman switch stops blade only. Easy to: start engine; operate deadman; use throttle; remove and replace bag; change modes. Quiet. Hard to: maneuver; push; make U-turns. Bag lacks rear handle.
Lawn Chief 81	Hard to: install bag; add fuel and oil. Bag lacks rear handle.
Lawn Chief 94M	Easy to: maneuver; make U-turns; change modes.
Lawn-Boy Gold Series 10421	Easy to: make U-turns; operate deadman; use throttle. Hard to: push and pull; jockey side-to-side. Discharge chute clogged. Handle vibrates. Clippings can blow at user when bag off.
Lawn-Boy Silver Series 10202	Easy to make U-turns. Hard to: jockey side-to-side; operate deadman; adjust cutting height. Discharge chute clogged. Clippings can blow at user when bag off. Bag has inconvenient zipper.

Montgomery Ward PowrKraft 37288 ⊡	Easy to adjust cutting height. Comfortable handle. Hard to: pull; make U-turns; pull starter cord. Handle vibrates, cannot fold. Very large bag capacity. Bag lacks rear handle.
Montgomery Ward Signature 2000 37088 ⊡	Easy to: maneuver; push; change modes. Hard to: pull; use throttle control.
Murray 22277	Easy to push. Hard to: jockey side to side; maneuver; adjust cutting height. Bag sticks out to the side. Handle height not adjustable. Very small bag capacity.
Murray 3nOne Convertible 22355	Easy to: remove and replace bag; use throttle; adjust cutting height. Hard to: push; jockey side to side; make U-turns. Discharge chute clogged. Bag lacks rear handle. Very large bag capacity.
Murray Convertible Mulcher 21677	Easy to: maneuver; change modes; empty bag; change air filter. Accumulated few clippings in mulching. Quiet. Hard to adjust cutting height.
Murray Vectra Convertible 22355X80	Easy to: remove and replace bag; adjust cutting height. Hard to: push; jockey side to side; make U-turns. Discharge chute clogged. Bag lacks rear handle.
Rally 1P209	Easy to: push; make U-turns. Quiet. Hard to: jockey side-to-side; change modes; add fuel and oil; assemble. Discharge chute clogged with bag. Different blade for mulching. Handle height not adjustable. Very small bag capacity.
Rally 2E372	Easy to change modes. Quiet. Discharge chute clogged. Bag lacks rear handle. Hard to adjust cutting height.
Rally 4E372	Easy to change modes. Quiet. Hard to make U-turns. Discharge chute clogged. Bag lacks rear handle.
Sears Craftsman 38054	Easy to: push; make U-turns; change modes. Hard to: maneuver; jockey side to side; adjust cutting height. Inconvenient to start. Noisy. Exhaust aimed at user. Very small bag capacity.
Sears Craftsman 38324 ⊡	Easy to change modes. Hard to adjust cutting height. Inconvenient to start. Noisy. Exhaust aimed at user. Bag lacks rear handle.
Sears Craftsman 38437	Easy to: push; make U-turns; change modes. Hard to: jockey side-to-side; adjust cutting height. Inconvenient to start. Discharge chute clogged. Very small bag capacity.
Snapper R21400 Recycler/Mulcher	Easy to: push; use throttle. Interlock requires chute or mulching cover in place. Hard to operate deadman. Inconvenient to start. Clippings can blow at user when bag off. Handle not adjustable; too high for short user. Different blade for mulching. Very large bag capacity.
Snapper X21500	Easy to: maneuver; use throttle; remove and replace bag; adjust cutting height. Comfortable handle. Different blade for mulching. Very large bag capacity.
Toro 16400	Heavy. Easy to: push; use throttle; adjust cutting height; change modes. Quiet. Bag sticks out to the side, has inconvenient zipper. Handle cannot fold. Very small bag capacity.
Toro Recycler 20435	Easy to: use throttle; adjust cutting height. Hard to install and remove bag.
Wheeler WDR4 ⊡	Easy to: push; change modes. Hard to: install catcher; adjust cutting height. Discharge chute clogged. Vague throttle. Bag sticks out to the side. Handle rust-prone, height not adjustable. Very small bag capacity.

Ratings continued ▶

Ratings continued

Wheeler WRBD5Q21	Hard to: push; install catcher. Bag lacks rear handle. Handle rust-prone; height not adjustable. Very large bag capacity.
White LC-108 114-108C190	Easy to: maneuver; push; make U-turns; change modes; jockey side to side. Comfortable handle. Hard to pull; use throttle.
White LC-428 114-428C190	Easy to maneuver. Comfortable handle. Hard to: pull; install bag; use throttle. Bag lacks rear handle.
Yard-Man 114-808L401	Easy to adjust cutting height. Hard to: pull; make U-turns; pull starter cord; use throttle. Handle vibrates; cannot fold. Bag lacks rear handle. Very large bag capacity.

GASOLINE PUSH MOWERS: A GUIDE TO BASIC FEATURES

Ways to start the engine. On most mowers you prime the cold engine with fuel by depressing a primer bulb. Better is a throttle lever you set to the Choke position and keep it there until the engine starts. All start by tugging a starter cord.

Deadman controls. Mandated by law, these stop the blade when the operator's hands leave the handle. Preferred, but rare in push mowers, are mowers whose deadman system stops only the blade. Their starter cords are mounted at the engine, allowing you to brace a foot against the mower's deck for leverage. Another, more conventional deadman design stops the engine as well. Such models have the cord on the handle so the deadman control must be held while starting the engine.

Cutting-height adjustments. A single control that moves all four wheels when you want to change cutting height is the best design. Cutting-height adjustments are more of a hassle with mowers that make you adjust each wheel separately. Mowers also vary in how readily the handle height can be adjusted. Some models allow no adjustment at all.

Grass catchers. Easiest to handle are catchers that simply lift into place and hook into slots. Less convenient are catchers that require you to engage both a tab for the discharge-chute door and a spring-loaded catch. With another design, when the catcher is removed, the chute stays in place, positioned so it can discharge clippings into the face of a operator who starts to mow without replacing the catcher.

Converting modes. Most mowers convert from bagging mode to mulching mode, which grinds up grass finely and returns it to the lawn. They can also be made to discharge to the side without mulching. Conversion is easiest when you don't have to remove and attach a lot of parts, when you don't need to use tools, and when parts line up readily. Most of the side-bagging mowers we've seen are easy to convert, as are several rear-bagging models. The worst design we've seen: a model that makes you install a plate, baffle, and blade in order to mulch.

RECREATION & EXERCISE

Exercise can strengthen the heart, improve circulation, help control weight, reduce cholesterol, ease hypertension, reduce stress, increase muscle tone, and improve sleep. It can also be fun, but that may be hard to believe.

Almost any form of physical activity can provide some health benefits. Bowling, golf, fishing, and gardening may not get your pulse pounding, but they're a lot better than watching TV.

For cardiovascular benefit, there are many aerobic exercises from which to choose. Among the best: running, brisk walking, cycling, rowing, swimming, stair-climbing, cross-country skiing, and aerobic dance. If you want to build muscle tone, no one has improved on resistance training such as weight-lifting.

You need very little equipment to set up a basic program of walking or running—a good pair of sneakers, a T-shirt, athletic socks and shorts, and maybe a towel. Of course, the companies that make athletic shoes and exercise equipment would like to sell you more. So they spend millions on advertising and deploy an arsenal of marketing tactics. They lend high style to products that were once utilitarian, such as bicycle helmets. They make athletic shoes dedicated to every sport, including previously unknown activities, like "cross training." They divide the market into specialized niches or uses—touring and racing bikes for riding on the road, mountain bikes for riding off road, and hybrid bikes for doing both—and then design products for each niche. And they invent elaborate equipment, such as home gyms, to do the job of simpler, less expensive equipment, such as free weights.

Before you start an exercise regime, the

standard words of caution apply. If you're out of shape, have a medical problem that could affect your ability to exercise, or are over 40, consult a doctor first. Stretch—without bouncing or jerking—before and after each workout. Warm up slowly. Don't try to do too much the first few times. Start with a short workout at moderate effort level and gradually increase duration and intensity. If you feel pain at any point, stop and walk until the pain goes away; if it doesn't, call it a day.

Don't feel that all your recreation has to involve a significant physical effort. There's nothing wrong with doing something simply because it's relaxing.

Exercise equipment

▶ Ratings start on page 250.

You can achieve fitness without buying an expensive machine. All you really need is a good pair of sneakers and the will to use them regularly. The scenery and fresh air of an outdoor workout can do a lot to banish the boredom of exercising. But many Americans feel that they need exercise equipment to assure them health and long life. Hence, an industry supplying treadmills, exercise bikes, stair climbers, and other home-fitness equipment.

Workouts on an exercise machine have advantages. You can use it when bad weather might otherwise encourage sloth. You can exercise in the privacy of your own home, even in the dead of night. There's no risk of injury from potholes, dogs, muggers, or cars. Terrain doesn't determine the effort you must expend. You can stop anytime without being miles from home. And you may be able to get a better workout, since a good machine makes it easy to maintain your aerobic target heart rate (220 minus your age; then 60 to 85 percent of that number).

Exercise machines vary in the kind of workout they give. Some machines work just the lower body. Others can improve the tone of the whole body. But if your reason for exercising is to achieve cardiovascular fitness, the kind of exercise matters less than the effort you put into it. Choose a machine that suits your personal preference—and your pocketbook. In weighing price against benefits, remember: A machine you don't enjoy is likely to turn into an expensive coat rack.

Before settling on any machine, ask your doctor if you're making the right choice. Some back problems, for example, might be aggravated by a rowing machine; some knee problems by a stair climber. The obese should probably avoid running on a treadmill, although walking is okay.

Home gyms

Home gyms are essentially scaled-down versions of the multistation gyms in health clubs and corporate fitness centers. The price is scaled down too, typically between $200 and $1500, compared with as much as $8000 for health club models.

Generally, home gyms consist of a metal frame, one or more padded seats or benches, and various levers, handles, or straps attached to a device that resists your pushing and pulling. A typical home gym offers a variety of exercises, which may include butterfly, triceps extension, pull-down, shoulder press, leg extension, leg curl, chest press, and biceps curl.

A home gym is primarily designed to build muscles, but you can use it to get the heart-strengthening benefits of mild aerobic exercise by "circuit training"—performing different strengthening exercises in rapid succession continuously for 20 minutes or more. (On some gyms, though, you have to pause so long between exercises to reconfigure the equipment that the aerobic value is diminished.)

All the home gyms we've tested are capable of providing an effective workout. But then so are free weights—and they cost much less. Home gyms allow some exercises that you can't do with free weights, and you don't need a spotter to catch the weight should you lose the strength to support it.

Some of the major manufacturers of home gyms are big names in home exercise or sports equipment—DP, BMI, Nordic Track, ProForm, and Schwinn. Others concentrate mainly in bodybuilding gear—Marcy, Soloflex, Trimax, and Weider.

The choices

Muscles get stronger by working against resistance. Doing a few repetitions with high resistance makes muscles bigger. Many repetitions with moderate resistance are better for toning muscles. Gyms use one of several methods to apply resistance:

Weights. A "captive" stack of heavy metal plates is lifted by a cable-and-pulley system. The more plates you engage with a pin, the higher the resistance.

Rubber bands. Thick rubber bands are attached at one end to the lever you push or pull and at the other end to the frame of the gym. You vary resistance by using bands of different thickness or by using more or fewer bands.

Flexible rods. One or more springy

plastic rods, mounted to the gym's frame, are attached to a cable you pull. As with bands, you vary resistance by your choice of number and thickness of rods.

Shock absorbers. Hydraulic or pneumatic cylinders that look and work like a car's shock absorbers resist your pushing or pulling. Changing the point at which the shocks are attached to the lever you push and pull changes the resistance.

Centrifugal brake. Brake shoes mounted on a spring-loaded pulley in a case lined with friction pads generate friction when you move a lever connected to the pulley. You can increase resistance by pulling harder on the lever and by rerouting the cable that connects the lever to the pulley.

Features and conveniences

A gym with plenty of padding keeps hard plastic and metal parts from hurting you while you exercise. A minimum of setup and changing makes it easier to do circuit training. A wide range of resistance settings keeps you from outgrowing the gym before you've attained the body you want.

The tests

Our engineers assemble each gym (with some models taking five hours), then test all the features of each machine. They judge fit (too big or too small?); body position (right for each exercise?); and range of motion (cramped or ample?). A pneumatic robot puts the gyms through the equivalent of a year's worth of intensive workouts in less than two days.

Buying advice

Spending more buys a better gym: heavier-gauge metal, more durable moving parts, smaller-increment resistance changes, and a wider range of resistance settings. More expensive gyms are likely to offer more comfortable stations and more stations, so that more than one person can use the machine simultaneously.

If possible, try out a gym before you buy. Look for a design that lets you get in and out of the stations easily. Changing resistance is easiest on gyms with weight stacks and elastic bands. For circuit-training workouts, choose a model that lets you zip from one exercise to another with little fussing. Watch out for models with potential pinch points. Finally, take note of a machine's size. Make sure the machine fits into the space available—some are quite bulky.

Treadmills

In essence, a treadmill is a belt stretched over a bed between two rollers that's driven by a motor or, in the case of "walking" models, the user. In practice, a treadmill is a way to walk or jog indoors at any time and as far as you want. Most models let you adjust the incline to simulate hills and increase the strenuousness of the workout. A monitor tells you speed, distance covered, time elapsed, and sometimes such things as heart rate and calories burned.

Walking at a brisk pace, jogging, and running are excellent aerobic conditioners. Increasing the incline can boost the exertion level of even a 3-mph walk to an aerobic level for a fit athlete. Walking and running improve lower-body muscle tone, but do nothing for upper-body muscles.

Treadmills for home use range from about $300 to $2200. Inexpensive brands include *Proform*, *Vitamaster*, *Sears*, *Tunturi*, *Voit*, and *DP*. Precor, Trotter, and Quinton make expensive versions. The more you spend, the bigger the motor, the wider and longer the bed, and the higher the top speed. High-priced units have automatic incline adjustments and easy-to-use controls.

The choices

The type of motor—AC or DC—affects the way the machine works. An AC motor runs at full speed all the time, relying on a transmission-like pulley system to vary the speed of the walking belt. Most such models can start up at full speed—a rude surprise if you're standing on the belt at the time. A DC motor can regulate speed and thus avoid this problem.

Motor size varies from half a horsepower to one and a half hp more. The more power, the better the ability to handle heavy loads or high speeds. Walking or jogging can be done on any unit, but jogging requires a treadmill that goes at least 5 mph. For a manual treadmill, you supply the power to move the belt.

Features and conveniences

A slow minimum speed makes starting safer. Automatic incline adjustments are helpful; treadmills that use pins to change the slope are a bother. A long, wide bed and full-length handrails make for comfortable, safe use. Some treadmills have movable ski-pole-like handles so you can get a moderate upper body workout while you walk or jog.

Buying advice

Before buying a treadmill, try one out in a health club first, to make sure indoor running or walking won't bore you.

When you shop, avoid treadmills that cost less than about $300; they're likely to be flimsy or to have a weak motor that won't stand up to heavy use. When you try treadmills in the store, make sure the belt is large enough to accomodate your full stride. The controls should be easy to reach, and the monitor should have the functions you want. Make sure you can bring a model back if you don't like it.

Exercise bikes

Cycling is an excellent aerobic conditioner. It can actually be easier to maintain a steady activity level on an exercise bike than on a bicycle, on which you may alternately pedal hard and coast.

Exercise bikes are made by bicycle companies such as Schwinn and Ross, as well as companies that first made their name in the exercise-equipment field, like Tunturi and Vitamaster. Lifecycle and Precor make home and health-club models that include programmable "courses" of hills and flats.

Most models range from about $200 to $800. Health-club type bikes can cost $1000 or more. Bikes that cost less than $150 tend to be flimsy and jerky, we've found.

The choices

Single-action models. This type looks like a one-wheeled bike. When you pedal, you drive a resistance device, such as a flywheel with a brake affixed to it. This type works only the legs. The main advantage is that you can change resistance with the twist of a knob.

Dual-action models. This type of bike works the arms as well as the legs. As you pedal, you pump handlebars back and forth. Models vary according to how they apply resistance. Some bikes couple their handlebars to the pedals; as you move the handlebars, the pedals rotate. Others use hydraulic shock absorbers for arm resistance. Most use a fan for resistance, others, a flywheel. To increase resistance on a fan model, you move arms and legs faster.

While you pedal, the fan cools you—in theory. But some models, we've found, produce barely a zephyr.

Recumbent models. This type lets you sit back in a chairlike seat, rather than perch on a bike seat. That position works the hamstring muscles more than an upright bike and is helpful for people who have back problems or trouble with balance—or who simply find a bicycle seat too uncomfortable.

Features and conveniences

A monitor keeps track of your speed, how far you've "traveled," and the elapsed time. Calibrated resistance settings let you work out at a specific, repeatable level. Pedal straps let your legs work on the upstroke as well as the downstroke. On dual-action models, "coaster" pedals let your feet momentarily stop while your arms do the work.

The flywheel or fan should rotate smoothly and the resistance control should be easy to work. The seat should be well padded and comfortably shaped. Seat height and resistance level should be easy to adjust. Make sure the bike isn't too small or too large for you. The bike should feel solid and pedaling should be smooth. Bikes that cost less than $150 or so are likely to be flimsy.

If you already own a bike, you can convert it to a stationary exercise bike by mounting it on a training stand. Training stands are typically priced under $200.

Stair climbers

A stair climber gives you the aerobic workout of climbing an endless flight of stairs, but with reduced stress on the knees. Most stair climbers are basically levers attached to a resistance device. Your legs pump the levers as if you were climbing stairs. Since your feet stay on the levers, stress on the knees is less than it would be for going up and down a real flight of stairs. A monitor displays steps-per-minute, elapsed time, and calories burned.

Stairmaster and *Lifestep* are leading brands of health-club models; *DP*, *Tunturi*, *Precor*, and *Sears* are popular brands among the home models. Stair climbers range in price from less than $200 to more than $2000, but many models meant for home use sell for less than $500.

The choices

Models vary according to how they apply resistance—with a hydraulic piston, flywheel, drivetrain, or fan. On many models, the "steps" are linked—as one goes down, the other goes up. Other models have independently moving steps, which give a better workout.

Steppers. This is the more common type of stair climber. On a stepper, you mimic the action of climbing stairs. Dual-action steppers exercise the arms as well as the legs.

Ladders. This type includes steps for the feet and "rungs" for the hands. Using it mimics the action of ascending a ladder.

Features and conveniences

Some machines have automatic resistance programming that changes at predetermined intervals. Also helpful is an indexed resistance knob you can adjust while you're exercising.

Buying advice

Try out a machine before you buy it. Designs are still being tried out, and the worst of them could sour you forever on this exercise.

Look for pedals and handles positioned so you have a comfortable posture; smooth pedal motion; a stable machine; monitors that are clear and versatile, but not overly complicated; easy-to-adjust resistance; pedals that provide a comfortable and secure stance; and comfortable handles.

Ski machines

Even if the nearest snow is 1000 miles—or six months—away, a ski machine offers you the considerable aerobic and muscle-toning benefits of cross-country skiing. The machines, first marketed in the mid-70s by NordicTrack, have slippery rollers to take the place of snow, skilike boards or sliding foot pads instead of skis. In place of separate ski poles, the machines use a rope-and-pulley arrangement, poles mounted to a swivel, or telescoping poles. Since you move both arms and legs on a ski machine, it can give you something most other exercise machines can't—an upper- as well as lower-body workout.

Besides market leader NordicTrack, manufacturers of ski machines include Precor, Tunturi, DP, and Vitamaster—all companies that make other exercise equipment as well. Basic ski machines start at $300 but can go as high as $1300. Swanky health-club versions cost more than $2000.

The choices

Ski machines have either **independent** leg motion or **dependent** leg motion, depending on whether or not the leg-motion devices are linked. An independent model has the disadvantage of being harder than a dependent model to master; coordinating the scissoring leg motion is awkward until you get the hang of it. (Typically, independent models are also more expensive.) But once you learn the technique, an independent model can give you a more vigorous workout and will let you use a more natural leg motion than will the dependent type.

Features and conveniences

Leg resistance that comes from an electromagnetic flywheel or from friction provided by a belt wrapped around a flywheel gives a "gliding" feeling similar to snow. Friction pads or straps used by some dependent models provide plenty of resistance but don't mimic the feel of real snow. Other dependents gave no leg resistance. A machine with variable incline increases the workout for the front thigh muscles. A monitor with a liquid-crystal display (LCD) is standard. Most show one function at a time and can scan through the displays. A readout of your heart rate helps you maintain an effective level of exertion. Some machines have indexed resistance settings; that makes it easier to repeat the difficulty level from one workout to the next, especially helpful if others will be using the machine at a different level. Wheels let you move the machine to its storage place without lugging it. Most machines fold up compactly and can be stored in a closet.

The tests

Human testers of varying heights put the machines through miles of simulated skiing, judging each machine's range of exercise intensity, comfort for people of different sizes, rigidity and stability, and usefulness of the electronic monitor. A robot-testing device gives the machines the equivalent of a year's worth of regular workouts in less than 100 hours.

Buying advice

Try a machine at a health club before you buy one. If you decide to go ahead, you'll probably want to choose a model with independent "skis." They take a bit longer to master than the kind with linked skis but offer a smoother, more skilike gait and let even very fit people work out at heart-strengthening intensity. A dependent model is worth a look if your level of fitness is fairly low or if you find it tough to get the hang of independent leg motion.

Running & walking shoes

If you're an athlete or reasonably active, you probably buy special shoes suited to your activity. Good shoes can reduce the risk of injury, a risk that is likely to increase the more you weigh, the faster you go, and the more miles you cover.

Major athletic-shoe manufacturers like Nike and Reebok spend millions advertising their wares. Those two companies account for about half the athletic shoes sold in this country. Other brands you'll encounter on store shelves: *New Balance, Avia,* and *Saucony.* Walking shoes are made by many of the same companies that make athletic shoes, and also by "sensible shoe" companies such as *SAS, Rockport,* and *Dexter.*

Athletic shoes are sold by mail and in athletic-footwear, sporting-goods, and department stores; unless you're sure of your size and brand preference, buy at a store with knowledgeable salespeople—and one where you can take your time trying on the shoes.

The choices

Athletic shoes are priced from less than $20 to $130 or so. The anatomy of a shoe is the same whether it's running or walking: an upper that lets the foot breathe; a toe box (the front of the upper) big enough for you to wiggle your toes; a heel counter and heel stabilizer to cup the heel and control lateral motion; a thin foam insole (a.k.a. sockliner) for some cushioning; a midsole that provides most of the cushioning and support; and an outsole, the bottom of the shoe, made of a durable material with texture for traction.

Many walking shoes have a "rocker" profile, turned up slightly at the front and beveled at the heel and essentially smooth soles. Running shoes turn up sharply at the front and have lugs or grooves in the soles to enhance off-road traction. Both types feature a shock-absorbent design; while shoes for basketball, aerobics, and court sports stress lateral support as well.

Features and conveniences

Comfort. A comfortable shoe has good arch support and adequate, but not overly spacious, toe room. It doesn't pinch or cause pain during or after exercise and is free of protrusions that can chafe the opposite leg. Its heel pad cushions the achilles tendon without restricting it.

Cushioning. The cumulative toll from thousands of footstrikes during a run can cause painful and disabling bone and joint injuries. Cushioning in a running shoe, especially the midsole, absorbs some of the shock. Walking causes less impact, though a walking shoe still needs cushioning. Manufacturers use a variety of midsole materials, including compressed gas, plastic foam, air, silicone gel, and rubber balls.

Flexibility. Proper walking or running form calls for the foot to land on the heel and roll forward, bending at the base of the toes as it pushes off. A shoe should be flexible enough to allow easy bending.

Stability. Many people's feet roll to the inside when they walk or run (called pronation); some roll to the outside (supination). Some shoes are designed to help control either tendency without clamping your foot.

Inner sleeve. This replaces the conventional tongue with a stretch fabric that hugs and supports the foot.

Ventilation. Materials that breathe in the shoe's upper let sweat evaporate to increase comfort.

Other features. Reflective tabs make you more visible to motorists at night. Lacing systems vary in the amount they let you adjust shoe tightness. The weight of a shoe can vary by several ounces, which over a long run or walk can add up.

Buying advice

If you buy athletic shoes just to wear to the supermarket, almost any brand will do. But serious athletes should be more choosy. Find a store that has a knowledgeable staff and sells a variety of brands. (Friends who are runners or fitness walkers may be able to recommend a store.)

Use the following tips to narrow your selection:

■ Find out if you're a pronator or supinator by looking for wear on your present shoes—when looked at from the back, a pronator's shoes will tilt to the the inside, a supinator's shoes will tilt to the outside. If the shoe doesn't tilt at all, you have a neutral running or walking style and don't need shoes with special motion control. Ask the salesperson for a shoe that will be suitable for your style.

■ Shop at the end of the day when feet are their largest, and wear the socks you wear for workouts.

■ If your feet are different sizes, buy for the larger foot. Use an insert to fill any gaps in the other shoe.

■ Look for defects in construction such as a shoe that tilts to one side. Check the seams to make sure all layers are firmly attached.

■ Run or walk on a hard surface to judge cushioning. Take a few steps and stop short to see if your feet slide inside the shoes, a sign that the shoes are too big. Check for adequate toe room by pushing down at your longest toe—there should be a thumbnail-sized space. Make sure the heel counter is snug around the back of your foot. Test the flexibility of the shoes by going up and down on your toes; the shoes should bend easily.

Bicycles

Walk into a bicycle store and you'll see a profusion of models across a broad range of types. The types and variants of types reflect the specialization that has occurred in the past decade or so. More and more, manufacturers cater to several distinct classes of bike rider: recreational, fitness, commuter, racer, around-town, or off-road. Which bike is best for you depends on where and how you ride—and your budget.

Discount stores such as K Mart and Toys 'R' Us usually sell bikes for less than $200. Typically, you'll find only a few brands—*Huffy, Murray, Roadmaster,* and *Kent.* Independent bike stores and sporting goods stores sell many brands priced $200 to $1000 and up. The biggest names include: *Trek, Cannondale, Specialized,* and *Schwinn.*

The choices

The world of bicycles can be divided into three main types:

Mountain bike. This is still the most popular type sold in the U.S. With the help of fat, knobby tires, 26-inch-diameter wheels, flat handlebars, a sturdy frame and, perhaps, a shock-absorbing suspension, the mountain bike moves competently over rough terrain but can feel a bit ungainly on pavement.

Road bike. Designed for racing or touring, this type of bike is lightweight and comes with thin tires and "drop" handlebars. It's fast and efficient but not particularly comfortable or suited to riding on rough surfaces. Although road bikes are the best choice if you ride fast or ride far,

they continue to decline in popularity.

Hybrid bike. Introduced in the late '80s, this type typically uses a lightweight frame, flat handlebars, and moderately knobby tires to marry a mountain bike's strength and comfort with a road bike's efficiency. A hybrid is a good choice for commuters or for those who occasionally travel a rough dirt road.

Features and conveniences

Frame. The diamond-shaped chassis— a bicycle's foundation—determines whether the bike will fit you. It's a major factor in the bike's weight and handling.

Frames are made from a variety of materials: heavy steel on the cheapest bikes; lightweight aluminum or carbon fiber or exotic metals like titanium or super-high-strength steel on the most expensive bikes. Frames on $300-to-$600 models are typically chromium-molybdenum steel or lightweight aluminum. Lower-priced chromoly mountain and hybrid bikes weigh about 30 pounds; an aluminum, titanium, or carbon-fiber road bike can weigh as little as 18 pounds. A frame's stiffness and geometry also affect a bike's performance.

Handlebars. Their size and shape influence riding efficiency and comfort. The bent-over posture required by the drop handlebars on road bikes, and to a lesser extent by performance-oriented mountain bikes, reduces wind resistance and shocks from bumps and improves handling. That posture also lets muscles work efficiently. But such benefits are unimportant for casual rides on pavement, where an upright position is more comfortable.

Gears. These let you pedal comfortably despite changes in road slope. With three sprocket wheels in front and six to eight in the rear, most mountain bikes and hybrids have 18 to 24 speeds. Off-road, we consider 18 the minimum needed. On pavement, 12 or 14 speeds may be enough.

As important as the number of gears are a bike's highest and lowest gear numbers. These numbers sum up the interaction between the front and rear gears and the wheel size. For challenging off-road rides, the lowest should be 28 or less. A road bike for general use should have a low of 40 or less. High gears around 100 help speed you downhill.

Shifters. These cause the derailleurs to move the drive chain from one sprocket wheel to another. Long a deterrent to would-be riders, old-fashioned "friction" shifters could be difficult to master until you developed a feel for them. "Indexed" shifters make changing gears far easier.

The most convenient indexed shifters are the under-the-bar lever and twist types. One caveat for off-road riding: If the derailleurs are thrown out of alignment by a fall, these shifters cannot revert to friction shifting. Some above-the-bar levers offer indexing with a friction mode as backup. For rough riding, that type may be the best choice.

Brakes. Road bikes typically use caliper brakes, poised over the tire. Most mountain and hybrid bikes have cantilever brakes mounted directly on the front wheel fork and the seat stay. According to our tests, both types are able to stop a bike quickly and controllably. If you ride in wet weather, avoid steel-rimmed wheels. In our wet-brake tests, they required a greater distance to stop than did wheels with aluminum rims.

Tires. A major factor in handling ability, these are easily changed to suit the terrain. For rough trails, a mountain bike's tires should be at least 1.9 inches wide, with very aggressive treads. Such tires produce a "buzzy" ride on pavement, though; smoother tires are better on paved roads.

Saddle. This won't affect performance much, but may determine how often or how long you ride. Look for one that's comfortable. Saddles are easy to change—don't let a poor saddle stop you from buying an otherwise good bike. Some manufacturers claim that seats filled with "gel" reduce shock and vibration. But our testers—of both sexes—found them no more comfortable than other types of bike seats.

Buying advice

Bicycle models and components change every fall, but the basics of a good bike remain the same. In September, last year's model may prove a good buy with no compromise in performance or features.

You'll see bikes priced less than $200 at Sears or discount stores and more expensive bikes at specialty stores. In our tests, bikes priced $300 to $600 provided pleasurable, trouble-free riding.

Narrow the field by selecting among bikes with frames that fit the rider. To find the right size, the rider should straddle the top tube with both feet flat on the floor. Allow three inches clearance between top tube and crotch for mountain bikes, two inches for hybrids, and one inch for road bikes. We recommend that both men and women buy a bike with a straight top tube if they intend to ride more than just casually.

Before buying, ride the bike over varying terrain to check handling; that your posture, the saddle, and the pedals feel comfortable; and that the brakes respond evenly, without grabbing, as you increase pressure. Many bike parts can be easily changed by the dealer for no extra charge or for a small extra charge and for the difference in the price of the components.

Bicycle helmets

▶ Ratings on page 254.

Today's helmets are brightly colored, aerodynamic, lightweight, and well ventilated. They're also effective. All the helmets in our tests provided at least adequate protection. Their plastic foam liner cushions the wearer's head in a crash by crumpling upon impact. Most helmets are certified to meet standards set by the Snell Memorial Foundation; some carry stickers indicating compliance with ANSI or ASTM standards.

Prices range from about $15 at stores such as K Mart, Wal-Mart, and Toys 'R' Us to up to $150 at bike stores. Most people pay about $30. Although there are more than 50 brands available, you're most likely to see *Bell, BSI,* and *Giro.*

The choices

Size. Helmets come in Adult, Youth (age 5 to 14), and Child (5 years and under) sizes. Most adult helmets come in Small, Medium, and Large, but there's little consistency from brand to brand in what those sizes mean. A youth helmet is also suitable for an adult with a small head.

Correctly fitted, a helmet should be level, covering the forehead, and all straps should be tight when the chin strap is buckled. To check roll-off protection, push up firmly on the front edge of the helmet with the heel of your hand. Helmets typically come with additional foam pads to fine-tune the sizing.

Weight. The lightest helmets—as light as a half-pound—are typically those that have no hard outer shell. Most helmets have a thin plastic shell, which may add one or two ounces. That shell also protects the liner from wear and tear. Only a few helmets still use a heavy plastic shell.

Heavier and thicker helmets, we've found, give no more overall protection than do lighter, thinner models.

Features and conveniences

Straps. All straps are adjustable on most helmets, so you can get a snug fit at front, back, and sides. That reduces the chance the helmet will roll off in an accident.

Buckles. The side-squeeze buckle is most prevalent and easiest to use.

Pads. Velcro pads can be repeatedly removed and replaced to fine-tune fit. The adhesive-backed pads on some helmets can be placed only once.

Vents. The coolest helmets have large air vents, ample air space between liner and head, and pads that don't block air flow.

Liners. Plastic foam forms the shock-absorbing barrier. Some liners are reinforced with plastic cages, lips, or linings to keep the liners from breaking apart in an accident.

The tests

To see how well the helmets absorb impact, we mount each onto a weighted metal headform and then drop "head" and helmet about 6½ feet onto a flat anvil. We test the straps to make sure they won't break, stretch, or slip, and find out how much they loosen when they get wet with sweat. We test a helmet's ventilation in a wind tunnel using an aluminum head fitted with temperature sensors. Finally, we check to see if a helmet will roll off the head, using real heads.

Buying advice

Any helmet that bears a Snell, ANSI, or ASTM safety label should offer adequate protection, as they did in our tests.

RATINGS SKI MACHINES

▶ **See report, page 244.** Last time rated in Consumer Reports: September 1994.

Brand-name recommendations: The independent *NordicTrack Pro*, $600, is our top-rated model: It's sturdy, operates smoothly, has plenty of useful features, and should stand up to heavy use. The *NordicTrack Challenger,* nearly as good at $340, is A Best Buy. The *Challenger* lacks an incline adjustment. Among independent machines, consider the *Vitamaster Northern Trails 83*, $300. It's a hybrid, letting you switch between dependent and independent leg motion. Used as an independent, it was just so-so; but as a dependent it was best in the class.

For the typical ski machine, expect: ■ Electronic monitor with various readouts. ■ Skiing motion from skis or foot pads riding on rollers or wheels. ■ Friction or flywheel/friction system for resistance. ■ Cord and pulley or poles for arm movement. ■ Unit that folds up. **A choice you'll have to make:** ■ Dependent or independent leg motion.

Notes on the table: Price is approx. retail. For mail-order models, shipping is extra. **Maximum exercise** indicates the intensity of aerobic exercise each machine can provide. **Fit** assesses the ergonomics of each machine—how well it positions users of various sizes. **Life** scores reflect durability after a mechanical exerciser put each model through a year's worth of use. **Rigidity** is how sturdy each machine feels in use. Ⓓ indicates model discontinued or replacement not similar.

RATINGS OVERVIEW

Within type, listed in order of performance and durability

E ⊖ VG ⊖ G ○ F ◖ P ●

Brand and model	Price	Overall score P F G VG E	Max. exercise	Fit	Life	Rigidity
INDEPENDENT LEG MOTION						
NordicTrack Pro Ⓘ	$600		⊖	⊖	⊖	○
Precor 515E	649		⊖	⊖	⊖	⊖
NordicTrack Challenger, **A BEST BUY** Ⓘ	340		⊖	⊖	⊖	○
NordicSport World Class Ski Ⓘ	770		⊖	⊖	⊖	○
Tunturi XC560 SkiFit	649		⊖	⊖	○	⊖
Vitamaster Northern Trails 83 (convertible to dependent)	300		⊖	⊖	◖	○
DEPENDENT LEG MOTION						
Fitness Master FM340	400		○	○	⊖	⊖
DP Prime Fit 17-0685 Ⓓ	290		○	○	○	○
Fitness Quest Fit One Ⓓ	295		○	○	○	◖
Proform Nordic XC Skier PF Ⓓ	220		◖	◖	⊖	○

Brand and model	Price	Overall score					Max. exercise	Fit	Life	Rigidity
		P	F	G	VG	E				
CSA Alpine XC E382	$193	▬					◓	◓	◒	○
CSA Alpine XC E272	100	▬▬					◓	◓	○	◓
Stamina 885 Aerobic Ⓓ (Wal-Mart)	100	▬					◓	◓	◓	◓

Ⓘ *Sold mainly by mail order; phone no.: 800 328-5888*

RATINGS DETAILS   Models listed alphabetically

CSA Alpine XC E272	Independent arm motion with poles. Quiet. No leg resistance; very low arm resistance. Foot pads make user's feet unsteady. Difficult assembly.
CSA Alpine XC E382	Dependent arm motion with ropes. No leg resistance. Abdominal pad forces user into awkward position. Foot pads scrape track for heavy users. Difficult assembly. Doesn't fold up.
DP Prime Fit 17-0685 Ⓓ	Dependent arm motion with poles.
Fitness Master FM340	Independent arm motion with poles. Friction leg resistance. Wheels for moving.
Fitness Quest Fit One Ⓓ	Independent arm motion with poles. Inconvenient monitor.
NordicTrack Challenger, **A BEST BUY**	Dependent arm motion with ropes. Indexed leg resistance. Abdominal pad hard to adjust. Friction/flywheel leg resistance. Feet can bump resistance unit. Detachable skis can hit or trip passerby. Noisy.
NordicTrack Pro	Dependent arm motion with ropes. Indexed arm and leg resistance. Adjustable incline. Adjustable abdominal pad. Friction/flywheel leg resistance. Wheels for moving. Monitor shows heart rate. Feet can bump resistance unit. Detachable skis can hit or trip passerby. Noisy.
NordicSport World Class Ski	Dependent arm motion with ropes. Indexed arm and leg resistance. Adjustable incline. Adjustable abdominal pad. Electromagnetic flywheel leg resistance. Monitors show heart rate. Max. leg resistance too low for strong users (but varied among samples). Settings to simulate skiing on different snow. Feet can bump resistance unit. Detachable skis can hit or trip passerby. Noisy.
Precor 515E	Dependent arm motion with ropes. Indexed leg resistance. Adjustable incline. Adjustable abdominal pad. Friction/flywheel leg resistance. Base can fall off incline mount during intense workout. Movement rougher after durability tests. Doesn't fold up.
Proform Nordic XC Skier PF Ⓓ	Independent arm motion with poles. Adjustable incline. Quiet. Very low arm resistance; no leg resistance except for incline of base. Foot pads cause feet to shift. Movement rougher after durability tests.
Stamina 895 Aerobic Ⓓ (Wal-Mart)	Independent arm motion with poles. Indexed arm resistance; no leg resistance. Arm mechanism became rougher and squeaked after durability tests. Part of frame broke during durability tests (machine still usable). Inconvenient monitor. Hard to change arm resistance.

Ratings continued ▶

Ratings continued

Tunturi XC560 SkiFit	Independent arm motion with poles. Adjustable abdominal pad. Electro-magnetic flywheel resistance. Wheels for moving. Max. leg resistance too low for strong users. Movement rougher after durability tests.
Vitamaster Northern Trails 83 (convertible to dependent)	Independent arm motion with poles. Indexed arm and leg resistance. Adjustable incline. Adjustable abdominal pad (but doesn't stay put). Friction/flywheel leg resistance. Wheels for moving. Max. leg resistance too low for strong users. Movement rougher after durability tests. Noisy.

RATINGS HOME GYMS

▶ **See report, page 240.** Last time rated in Consumer Reports: November 1993.

Brand-name recommendations: None of the models match what you find in health clubs. The best overall, the *BMI 9700* and the *Marcy Apex Plus* ($499 and $699, respectively) were only good. The *BMI* has been discontinued but may still be available in some stores. The *Trimax*, the most expensive gym, was barely fair.

For the typical home gym, expect: ■ Metal frame. ■ 1 or more padded seats or benches. ■ Various levers, handles, or straps attached to a device that resists pushing or pulling. ■ Variable resistance. ■ Do-it-yourself assembly.

Notes on the table: Price is mfr.'s suggested retail for the basic gym. Dimensions are height x width x depth. We judged each of 8 exercises: leg extension, leg curl, chest press, butterfly, lat pull-down, shoulder press, triceps extension, and biceps curl. Resistance range is as specified by the mfr.; the full range may not be available for all exercises. D indicates model discontinued or replacement not similar.

RATINGS OVERVIEW   Listed in order of performance based mainly on ergonomics

Brand and model	Price	Overall score					Comments
		P	F	G	VG	E	
BMI Challenger 9700 D	$499						Very good for triceps extension, biceps curl; fair for leg curls; poor for shoulder press; good for other exercises.
Marcy Apex Plus	699						Same ergonomic scores as the BMI except only fair for biceps curl.
Schwinn Bowflex Pro D	900						Good for upper body exercises except for pull-down, which was poor. Fair for lower body.
Nordic Flex Gold	999						Very good ergonomics for pull-down; good for butterfly, shoulder press; poor for chest press; fair for others.
Soloflex	1195						Good ergonomics for pull-down, butterfly, shoulder press; poor for chest press; fair for others.
Trimax	1320						Good for leg extensions, chest press, pull-down; fair for others.

RATINGS DETAILS Models listed alphabetically

BMI 9700 Ⓓ	85x58x90 in. Weight stack, 10-330 lb. Excellent for circuit training. Easy to change resistance. Large resistance increments. Vertical knee-raise station for abdominal workout and dips. Grips for one-arm and one-leg exercises. During durability test, some pulleys broke. Hard to assemble and move.
Marcy Apex Plus	82x38x95 in. Weight stack, 10-200 lb. Excellent for circuit training. Grips for 1-arm and 1-leg exercises. Easy to change resistance. Large resistance increments. Hard to assemble and move.
Nordic Flex Gold	75x49x75 in. Centrifugal brake, 0-450 lb. Poor for circuit training. Accessory electronic power meter (not tested) is only indication of workout intensity. Resistance applied in one direction only. Station for dips, pull-ups, and Roman sit-ups. Rerouting cables through pulleys changes lever speed and resistance ranges. Wobbly bench. Butterfly arms can pinch fingers while being attached or removed.
Schwinn Bowflex Pro Ⓓ	74x70x63 in. Flexible rods, 5-210 lb. Good for circuit training. Easy to vary resistance. Small resistance increments. Grips for 1-arm and 1-leg exercises. A sliding seat creates a rowing machine. Cables let you move your arms or legs in any motion. Getting into and out of position may be difficult.
Soloflex	72x42x65 in. Rubber bands, 10-350 lb. Poor for circuit training. Easy to vary resistance. Small resistance increments. Difficult to position for chest press. Wobbly bench without the optional leg exercise arm in place. Butterfly arms can pinch fingers while being attached or removed. Gym can tip forward if you attach only the leg exercise arm and sit at the end of the bench. (Other accessories restore balance.) Station for dips, pull-ups, and Roman sit-ups. Very quiet.
Trimax	64x51x89 in. Hydraulic cylinders, 0-500 lb. Good for circuit training. Moving the cylinders' attachment point changes the resistance range and lever speed. Pulse monitor (not tested) is only indication of workout intensity. Applies resistance to muscle group in one direction only. Butterfly arms can pinch bystander. Wrench needed to change height on the butterfly arms. Durability test wore out the cylinders.

RATINGS BICYCLE HELMETS

▶ **See report, page 249.** Last time rated in Consumer Reports: August 1994.

Brand-name recommendations: Any helmet in the Ratings—or, for that matter, any helmet that meets Snell, ANSI, or ASTM safety standards—should offer adequate protection, provided it's fitted correctly. Older adults, whose skulls may be especially vulnerable to impact injuries, may want to look first to the helmets that scored highest for impact protection: the *Schwinn Aeroflight*, $53, the *Bell Image*, $78, and the *Trek Micro*, $35 (discontinued but possibly still available). Athletic riders may prefer the lightweight *Vetta Testarossa*, $37 plus shipping, the best-ventilated helmet. The top six youth helmets and top three child helmets merit first consideration for youngsters.

For the typical bicycle helmet, expect: ■ At least adequate protection from head impact in most crashes. ■ Above average or better ventilation. ■ A thin plastic shell covering a plastic foam liner. ■ Adjustable chin and front and rear side straps. ■ Weight ranging from 8 to 13 oz. ■ Pads in various thicknesses that can be repositioned and are easy to use. ■ A side-squeeze quick-release buckle. ■ Fitting instructions.

Notes on the table: Youth helmets are usually designed to fit 5- to 14-year-olds; child helmets fit children up to about 5 years. **Price** is approx. retail. An * indicates price CU paid. **Overall score** is based primarily on impact absorption, with roll-off resistance, ventilation, weight, and ease of use also considered. **Roll-off** scores how well the helmet, when fitted to a panel of staffers, resisted attempts to push it out of place. Youth and children's models were judged by their design. Ⓢ indicates tested model has been replaced by successor model; according to the mfr., the performance of new model should be similar to the tested model but features may vary. Not tested. Ⓓ indicates model discontinued or replacement not similar.

Within types, listed in order of overall performance   Better ◀━━▶ Worse ⊖ ⊖ ○ ◖ ●

Brand and model	Price	Overall score (P F G VG E)	Impact	Roll-off	Strap use	Comments
ADULT HELMETS						
Schwinn Aeroflight	$53	▬▬▬▬	⊖	⊖	◖	—
Bell Image	78	▬▬▬▬	⊖	⊖	◖	Hook-type buckle; harder to use.
Vetta Testarossa SL	*37	▬▬▬	⊖	○	◖	No shell. Liner reinforced. Front and rear straps adjustable, but restrict buckle position. Straps stretch less than most when wet.
Spalding 79783 Ⓓ	*30	▬▬	⊖	○	○	Damaged in "hot trunk" test.
Scott Cross-V Ⓓ	*35	▬▬▬	⊖	⊖	○	Damaged in "hot trunk" test.

Brand and model	Price	Overall score (P F G VG E)	Impact	Roll-off	Strap use	Comments
Trek Micro D	$35	▬▬▬	⊖	⊖	○	Ventilation judged good. Damaged in "hot trunk" test.
Bell Image Pro	80	▬▬▬	○	○	⊖	Clam-style strap slide; very easy to use. Straps stretch less than most when wet.
Bell Razor Pump	114	▬▬▬	⊖	○	⊖	Ventilation judged good. Air-bladder sizing pad and clam-style strap slide; very easy to use. Straps stretch less than most when wet.
Bell Triumph	50	▬▬	○	⊖	○	Liner reinforced.
Aria Sonics Tempest SI	90	▬▬	⊖	⊖	○	Air-bladder sizing pad: very easy to use. Ventilation judged good.
Rhode Gear Ultra Light D	40	▬▬	○	⊖	◐	Hook-type buckle; harder to use. Lycra cover.
Horizon All American	*30	▬▬	⊖	○	⊖	Inside front-to-back space may be too short for large users. Only rear side strap, chin strap adjustable. Straps stretch less than most when wet. Damaged in "hot trunk" test.
Louis Garneau LG 8	65	▬▬	○	○	○	Thin-shell cover on bottom edge of helmet. Liner reinforced.
Specialized Team Force	40	▬▬	○	⊖	○	Some sizing pads adhesive-backed; can be positioned only once.
Pro-Tec Xcellerator	47	▬▬	○	⊖	○	Damaged in "hot trunk" test.
Giro Prolight D	52	▬▬	○	⊖	○	Ventilation judged good. Liner reinforced. Some sizing pads adhesive-backed; can be positioned only once. No shell, lycra cover.
Specialized Sub 6 Pro D	100	▬▬	○	○	○	Liner reinforced. Some sizing pads adhesive-backed; can be positioned only once.
Giro Hammerhead SC D	85	▬▬	○	○	○	Thin-shell cover on bottom edge of helmet. Liner reinforced. Some sizing pads adhesive-backed; can be positioned only once.
Performance Microtec ST II D	23	▬	⊖	◐	○	Straps must be very tight to prevent roll-off. Damaged in "hot trunk" test.

YOUTH HELMETS

Brand and model	Price	Overall score (P F G VG E)	Impact	Roll-off	Strap use	Comments
Bell Rebel	33	▬▬▬	⊖	○	○	Liner reinforced. Damaged in "hot trunk" test.
BSI Malibu	29	▬▬▬	⊖	○	○	Liner reinforced. Damaged in "hot trunk" test.

Ratings continued ▶

Ratings continued

Brand and model	Price	Overall score					Impact	Roll-off	Strap use	Comments
		P	F	G	VG	E				
Spalding Bullet	$*30						○	⊖	○	Damaged in "hot trunk" test.
Specialized Mega Force Ⓓ	39						○	⊖	○	Some sizing pads adhesive-backed; can be positioned only once. Damaged in "hot trunk" test.
Headwinds Shocker	19						○	⊖	○	Ventilation judged good. Damaged in "hot trunk" test.
Troxel Spirit Ⓓ	35						○	○	⊖	Ventilation judged good. Thin-shell cover on bottom edge of helmet. Front and rear straps adjustable, but restrict buckle position. Damaged in "hot trunk" test.
Pro-Tec XCalibre	40						○	⊖	○	Ventilation judged good. Damaged in "hot trunk" test.

CHILD HELMETS

Brand and model	Price	Overall score					Impact	Roll-off	Strap use	Comments
Bell Lil' Bell	38						⊖	⊖	○	Ventilation judged good. Damaged in "hot trunk" test.
BSI Cool Cap	17						○	⊖	○	Ventilation judged good. Damaged in "hot trunk" test.
CPC Sesame Street Helmet	21						○	⊖	○	Ventilation judged good. Straps stretch less than most when wet. Damaged in "hot trunk" test.
Troxel Nino Ⓢ Pro-Action Windrider, $30	30						○	◓	⊖	Ventilation judged good. Hard shell. Front- and rear-side straps not adjustable. Damaged in "hot trunk" test.

FAMILY & HEALTH

Blood pressure monitors

▶ Ratings on page 264.

For people diagnosed with hypertension, a home blood-pressure monitor can show whether drugs or alternatives to drug therapy—diet and exercise—are working, and how well. For those on medication for that condition, home monitoring can help the doctor determine the lowest effective dose.

A home monitor also allows patients to chart their progress in lowering pressure, a strong incentive to stay with a treatment regimen. Home monitoring can be especially useful when an person's pressure rises with the stress of having an office visit.

For those reasons, the National High Blood Pressure Education Program, a Government-sponsored effort, endorses home blood-pressure monitoring for people with hypertension, provided monitoring is done in collaboration with a physician and not as a means of self-diagnosis.

Prices of monitors range from $15 for a simple mechanical gauge to $75 for an electronic model with digital readout. Major brands: Omron, Sunbeam, and Lumiscope.

Drugstores used to be where you went for medical needs such as monitors. Now you can get pressure monitors in mass-merchandisers like K Mart and Wal-Mart.

The choices

Blood pressure, the force exerted by blood against the arteries, is expressed as a measure of height: the number of millimeters ("mmHg") that arterial pressure can push mercury up a vertical tube.

Traditionally, a nurse or doctor wraps an inflatable cuff around the upper arm and inflates the cuff by pumping a rubber bulb. The cuff acts as a tourniquet, cutting off blood flow below the elbow. While gradually deflating the cuff, the nurse listens with a stethoscope to the arm's main artery. As blood returns to the lower arm, sounds audible in the artery mark "systolic" pressure (the heart's pumping pressure) and "diastolic" pressure (the lower pressure occuring between heartbeats). Blood pressure is given as the systolic figure over the diastolic—120/80 mmHg, for example, more or less "normal."

To take your own pressure at home with some monitors, you do all the things the doctor or nurse does. Other devices use electronic circuitry to simplify matters.

Mechanical aneroid models. These are simple mechanical monitors that use a round dial-and-needle pressure gauge. (Home devices no longer use a mercury-filled aneroid tube—"aneroid" means "without liquid.") Mechanical monitors are relatively cheap at $15 to $20 and can be quite accurate if properly used. Proper use is the big drawback—you must don the cuff, pump it, and listen carefully to the artery as you turn a valve to slowly deflate the cuff while keeping an eye on the gauge's needle. The procedure takes practice. It demands good eyesight and hearing and the dexterity to do things with one hand.

Electronic models. These are the easiest to use and the best selling. By sensing pressure changes in the cuff—no stethoscope is needed—and passing data to a microchip in their console, the systolic and diastolic pressures are automatically calculated and flashed on a digital display. No human judgment is required. The circuitry can sometimes err—if you move your arm,

say, but an error code or an outlandish reading clearly signals mistakes.

The cheapest electronic monitors, priced about $30 to $40, require you to pump up the cuff, though deflation is automatic. More expensive models, ranging from $45 to $55, inflate the cuff automatically.

Another type of electronic monitor takes readings from the index finger, so you needn't even roll up your sleeve. You slip the finger into a loop, and the machine does its thing. Electronic finger monitors range in price from $70 to $75.

Features and conveniences

All arm models have a D-ring to make it easy to don the cuff with one hand—you form a loop and pull the cuff snugly around your arm, then fasten it with the plastic-loop closure. The ends of some cuffs, however, can easily slip out of the metal bar unless they have a retaining device sewn in. Cuffs of limp material are hard to handle.

A mechanical gauge is easier to use if the stethoscope's sensor is already sewn in place on the cuff (so you needn't hold the sensor down). Also, a sturdy metal deflation valve that works smoothly is easier to control than a plastic valve.

Electronic models vary in the clarity of their displays. Look for big, clear numbers at least three-quarters of an inch high.

The tests

Our main test uses a panel of staffers. We modify each model's tubing so that a nurse can take a simultaneous reading with a mercury gauge and stethoscope. By taking multiple readings at each sitting and comparing the nurse's figures with each monitor's, we're able to assess each model's variability from one reading to another.

Buying advice

Mechanical blood-pressure monitors offer the best value, if you're comfortable with them. They cost as little as $20 and, if correctly used, generally proved more accurate in our tests than electronic arm models. With practice, most people should have little trouble perfecting the technique.

The best electronic arm models approach the accuracy of the better mechanical units, or nearly so. Models that inflate automatically are easiest to use but also the most expensive. If you don't trust your ability to master a mechanical monitor, but don't want to pay top dollar, a good compromise is an electronic arm model whose cuff you inflate manually (but deflation is automatic). Such models are priced about half that of a fully automatic monitor.

With any arm model, you need the right-sized cuff to get accurate readings. People with large upper arms, those more than 13 inches around, may have difficulty with the cuffs supplied. Larger cuffs are available at extra cost from medical supply houses or from the manufacturer.

We do not recommend electronic finger models. Because the finger is smaller than the arm and farther from the heart, false readings are more likely. All of the finger models we tested in 1992 were rated Not Acceptable because of the great variability in the readings they gave.

Eyeglasses

There are more places selling glasses and more frames to choose from than ever before. There are also more lens choices beyond plastic or glass—special-purpose materials, lens coatings, and optical designs.

The industry's retailing extremes are the "superstore" and the warehouse store. Superstores are eyeglass emporiums where you can get eyes tested, choose from thousands of frames and, perhaps, have glasses made in an hour. Warehouse stores take the no-frills, mass-merchandising approach—a limited frame selection, possibly no optometrist on duty and no in-store lab. Of course, private practitioners—optometrists and ophthalmologists—still examine eyes and sell glasses.

In a recent survey of CONSUMER REPORTS subscribers who had bought spectacles in the previous two years, readers whose glasses came from a private practitioner tended to be the most satisfied. Some chains, though earned marks nearly as high.

Two further reasons favored the private practitioner: Readers had slightly fewer problems with glasses purchased from doctors than with those from the average chain. And more readers felt they got a more thorough exam from private eye-doctors than from those with the chains. While private doctors excel in service, the chains have the edge in frame selection and speed.

The choices

Besides selecting a frame, you'll need to make decisions about the lens material, special coatings, and optical design.

Lens materials. Glass resists scratching better than some plastic lenses, but it's heavy and more likely to shatter. *Regular plastic* (a resin called CR-39) is the most widely used material; it is half the weight of glass and more impact-resistant. *High-index plastic* is at least 30 percent thinner than CR-39, a boon for the very nearsighted, whose lenses can be thick at the edges; it can cost at least twice the price of regular plastic. *Polycarbonate lenses* are about as thin as high-index lenses but very impact-resistant, a plus for people who play sports. The price of polycarbonate lenses is about one-third more than regular plastic lenses.

Lens treatments. *Scratch protection* is for anyone who handles glasses roughly. Polycarbonate lenses are soft and typically come with this coating—you shouldn't pay extra for it. *UV protection* comes from a gray dye that shields wearers from ultraviolet rays—those associated with the formation of cataracts. The protection is most important for those who spend lots of time in strong sunlight. It's built into high-index and polycarbonate lenses—don't pay extra. *Antireflection* coating cuts some glare, a plus for night drivers and computer users.

Lens designs. *Bifocals* come in two traditional styles: flat-top, which have a small field at the bottom for close-up work, or *Franklin style*, where the entire bottom half of the lens is for near vision, giving good wide-field vision for work up close. *Progressive lenses* ("no-line bifocals") gradually change lens power to give a continuous range of clear vision as eyes move from the lens's top (distance vision) to bottom (close); the middle of the lens covers an arm's-length range, good for computer users. Progressive lenses take some getting used to and the lenses cost about twice as much as regular bifocals.

Aspheric lenses, typically for farsighted people, replace bulging convex lenses with a flatter lens so eyes look more natural.

Buying advice

Doctors not connected with a store have little incentive to prescribe new glasses and are more likely to be objective about problems with glasses bought elsewhere.

The readers surveyed were generally happiest with the places that charged the least. Some chains offer prices for complete eyeglasses; others charge á la carte for frames, lenses, and various lens options.

Bathroom scales
▶ **Ratings on page 266.**

Some bathroom scales talk. Others give you the news via a digital display or a dial and a pointer to display weight. Prices range from about $10 to $80.

The choices

Bathroom scales differ primarily in how they measure weight. Most use a calibrated spring to measure weight. Levers under the platform transmit the force of your weight to the spring, which stretches in proportion to the load. The spring moves a dial or pointer or activates a digital display.

The only truly electronic bathroom scale is the strain-gauge type. When you step on it, your weight bends a small steel beam. As the beam deflects, it stretches a wire, changing the electrical resistance in proportion to your weight. A microchip trans-

lates it for the digital display.

On a hydraulic scale, the weight on the platform forces fluid from one compartment to another. Changes in pressure provide the weight reading.

The balance-beam method resembles scales used in doctors' offices. This upright design has movable weights you slide across two bars until its beam is level.

The tests

To test accuracy, we compare the scales' readings with a series of known weights. To check consistency, we repeat the test five times with each scale at each given weight.

Buying advice

Spending more doesn't buy greater accuracy or consistency. We found accurate dependable scales for less than $20. We also found that with some bathroom scales, one sample of the same model would perform quite differently from another.

Cold, heat, and humidity can compromise the accuracy and consistency of any scale. Consider keeping your scale in a room other than the bathroom.

Cribs

Because babies spend so much time sleeping, cribs should be safe and secure as well as comfortable. Previous generations of crib design contributed to tens of thousands of accidents and upward of 150 deaths each year, often when an infant's head, or neck got caught between slats set too wide apart or when active babies tumbled over crib sides too low to safely contain them.

Government-mandated safety standards, in place since 1973, have fixed those problems by specifying acceptable measurements for slat separation, height from the mattress-support to the top of the sides, and mattress fit, among other factors. Most leading crib-makers supplement those standards with additional voluntary safeguards. The largest manufacturer of cribs is Child Craft. Besides that name, you'll also see brands such as *Simmons, Bassett, Welsh, Cosco,* and *Evenflo.*

The choices

Prices for cribs range from $70 to $600. The key choice involves the number of dropsides. Cribs with two dropsides give you easy access to a baby from the left or right. Models with one dropside are often $100 or cheaper and work just as well with the crib set up against a wall if head and foot board are finished the same.

Features and conveniences

Safety. With new cribs you generally needn't worry about safety, though occasionally a new model may not meet Federal standards. In our tests, we found one such model, an import, and judged it Not Acceptable. (That model has since been redesigned to meet Federal standards.) For extra assurance, look for cribs that bear the seal of the Juvenile Products Manufacturers Association. Such cribs meet mandatory Federal and voluntary safety standards. A crib without the seal, however, is not necessarily unsafe.

Assembly. Some models are easier to put together. The simplest take only 10 minutes to assemble and don't require tools; most take a half-hour.

CRIB MATTRESSES

Buying a mattress for a baby is much like buying one for an adult—you want the firmest you can find. In addition, a baby's mattress must keep out wetness and resist punctures and tearing.

The basic choice is between foam and innerspring models. Prices range from about $25 to more than $100. Foam is usually less expensive and easier to lift. Innerspring models usually keep their shape better, though high-density foam can be just as good.

Check firmness by squeezing the center and edges. Good mattresses offer quilted vinyl ticking or multiple layers of vinyl laminated together and reinforced with nylon. Look for fabric binding along the seams and plenty of vent holes, which help keep a mattress fresh by letting odors escape.

Casters. Look for spherical or hooded casters, to help roll the crib smoothly. Avoid narrow disk-shaped casters.

Dropside operation. We like the dropsides that operate with only one hand; that allows you to hold on to a baby with your free arm as you raise or lower the dropside. Many models use a foot treadle or rod or a combination of both to lower and raise the sides.

Mattress-height adjustment. You should also be able to adjust the mattress's height easily. As infants grow into toddlers, it's important that a crib's sides remain high enough to protect them, which is done by lowering the mattress support.

Buying advice

Models with one dropside are usually cheaper than those with two. If you put the crib against a wall, you can save money by buying a model with a single dropside.

Choose a double-dropside model if you want access from either side. A double dropside also gives you a backup, should one side's mechanism break.

Parents using older cribs or uncertain about a new model they're considering should be wary of these items:

■ Protruding corner posts.

■ Ornamentation that can break into small parts.

■ Decorative cutouts on end panels.

■ Slats more than 2⅜ inches apart.

■ A mattress that doesn't fit snugly.

■ End panels that do not extend below the mattress support in its lowest position.

■ Mattress support hooks that do not firmly stay in their brackets.

■ A lowered dropside that is less than nine inches above the mattress support at its highest setting or a raised side that is less than 26 inches above the mattress support at its lowest setting.

Strollers

Sales pitches for strollers have veered from selling basic transport to pushing prestige. High-status nameplates of imports like *Maclaren, Aprica,* and *Emmaljunga* sport price tags of more than $200; top-of-the-line *Aprica* or *Maclaren* strollers go for as much as $400. The typical stroller retails for about $100, but you can spend as little as $20.

We turned up more than 33 brands. Most familar are *Century, Graco,* and *Kolcraft.*

The choices

Carriage/stroller. This makes the most sense for a newborn. The seatback reclines enough to let the baby sleep. And, by raising the seatback and flipping the handle, you can convert the lie-down carriage into a sitting-position stroller. **Lightweight strollers,** usually the cheapest choice, fold

into a neat package you can carry.

Two-seater. This type is made for families with two stroller-age children. A **tandem,** which seats one child behind the other, offers easy maneuverability in tight quarters. A **side-by-side** model is wider and harder to maneuver.

Jogger. Instead of four sets of small wheels, these models sport three bicycle-type wheels. The design lets the runner or jogger in the family take the baby along, easily moving over rough terrain.

Car-seat combination. The newest type, it lets you move between sidewalk and car without lifting baby from the seat.

Features and conveniences

Strollers should be comfortable for child and grown-up. For the baby, that means good support from the back rest and adequate shock absorption. For the adult, it means a stroller that's easy to push and steer. The larger the wheels, usually, the more easily a stroller will handle curbs and uneven terrain. Models with swivel wheels and locks to stop the front wheels from veering on soft ground are easiest to maneuver. Strollers should be easy to open and fold up, preferably with one hand. They should have padding that's easily cleaned—preferably, removable and machine-washable. The handle should be at the right height—just below an adult's waist. (Few strollers, however, let you adjust the handles' height.)

Safety. Considering the 14,000 children injured annually in strollers (usually from falls), safety is paramount. Federal regulations bar sharp edges and points, and small parts, which a child can swallow or inhale. (A voluntary industry standard that most manufacturers follow supplements the Government regulations. Strollers that meet the supplementary standards carry a sticker or tag stating "compliance with ASTM F-833.")

Safety features to assess include:

Stability. A wide stroller with a long wheelbase and low-mounted seat set deep within the stroller frame is least likely to tip over. With the baby seated, the stroller should resist tipping as you press down lightly on the handles.

Frame. Sharp edges and protrusions, gaps between metal parts, uncovered coil springs, small holes, X-joints (where the frame tubes come together, scissors-style), loose plastic caps on frame ends—all have the potential to injure a child.

Restraints. The safety belt should wrap snugly and completely around the baby's waist, and there should be a crotch strap. We favor a T-shaped buckle attached to the strap, and waist belts that snap easily into the buckle. (Belts that thread through a buckle can slip, if improperly connected.)

Brakes. Most models have a foot-operated lock or bar to lock the rear wheels. A sprocket lock was more effective than a bar pressing against the tire, in our tests. Carriage/strollers should have two sets of brakes, so you can conveniently engage the brake regardless of handle's position.

Safety latches. Metal slip rings that slide over the frame's tubing are designed to lock the stroller open and hold its handles in place. But the rings can deform or change position, causing the stroller to collapse and possibly injure the child. Spring-loaded latches have largely replaced slip rings. Some latches have a lock plus a safety catch, which require two distinct actions to fold the unit.

Leg openings. Babies aged seven months or younger may creep backward while sleeping, slipping through the leg openings of a convertible carriage/stroller and trapping their heads. (Since the mid-1980s, the Government has documented just such a scenario as causing the asphyxiation or strangulation of 11 infants.) Some carriage/strollers let you close off the leg openings between the handrest bar and the front edge of the seat, blocking that danger zone.

Buying advice

Look for sturdy models that meet the voluntary safety standards (those with the ASTM F-833 sticker or tag). Carriage/strollers typically offer more comforts than do basic, umbrella models. Convertible carriage/strollers make the most sense for newborns for their comfort and the lie-down position. Once the baby has grown enough to sit up alone, you can flip the handle so the model can be used as a conventional stroller.

If you have two stroller-age children, opt for a tandem. It's easier to maneuver than a side-by-side model.

RATINGS | BLOOD-PRESSURE MONITORS

▶ **See report, page 257.** Last time rated in Consumer Reports: May 1992.

Brand-name recommendations: Look first to the mechanical monitors for the best value. They are the least expensive type and, if used correctly, are generally more accurate than electronic models. Anyone with poor eyesight, hearing, or dexterity, however, should consider the easier-to-use electronic models.

For the typical blood-pressure monitor, expect: ■ A cuff you inflate with a bulb or one that's self-inflating. ■ Metal D-ring on cuff for 1-handed use. ■ Stethoscope for mechanical models. ■ Storage case or pouch. ■ Rapid cuff deflation in emergency. **A choice you'll have to make:** ■ Mechanical model with dial-type gauge or electronic arm model, either manual- or auto-inflating type, with digital display.

Notes on the table: Except where separated by a bold rule, closely ranked models differed little in quality. **Price** is the mfr.'s suggested or approx. retail. **Consistency** is for systolic and diastolic pressure readings. Ⓓ indicates model discontinued or replacement not similar.

Within type, listed in order of performance, mainly consistency in use

Better ← → Worse
⊖ ⊖ ○ ◔ ●

Brand and model	Price	Consistency S / D	Ease of use	Instructions	Comments
MECHANICAL MODELS					
Marshall 104	$25	⊖/⊖	◔	⊖	Stethoscope sounds are easy to hear. Deflation valve must be closed manually. Cuff hard to apply.
Omron HEM-18	25	⊖/⊖	◔	○	Stethoscope sounds are easy to hear. Deflation valve must be closed manually. Cuff hard to apply.
Walgreens 2001	20	⊖/⊖	◔	⊖	Deflation valve must be closed manually. Cuff hard to apply because of tubing.
Lumiscope 100-021	20	⊖/⊖	●	◔	Deflation valve flimsy and hard to adjust; must be closed manually. Uncomfortable stethoscope yoke. Cuff hard to apply.
Sunmark 10	22	⊖/⊖	◔	○	Deflation valve flimsy and hard to adjust; must be closed manually. Uncomfortable stethoscope yoke. Cuff hard to apply.
Sunbeam 7627-10	20	○/⊖	●	○	Deflation valve flimsy and hard to adjust; must be closed manually. 1-person operation inconvenient. Uncomfortable stethoscope yoke.

Brand and model	Price	Consistency S / D	Ease of use	Instructions	Comments
ELECTRONIC ARM MODELS					
Omron HEM-704C	$80	⊖/⊖	⊖	⊖	Self-inflating. Cuff easy to don. Very large, clear digital readout.
Sunbeam 7621	40	⊖/⊖	○	◖	Cuff may be hard to inflate.
Sunbeam 7650	80	⊖/⊖	⊖	◖	Self-inflating. Very large, clear digital readout. End of cuff may slip out of D-ring.
Lumiscope 1081	80	⊖/⊖	⊖	◖	Self-inflating. Very large, clear digital readout. End of cuff may slip out of D-ring.
Marshall 91	80	⊖/⊖	⊖	⊖	Self-inflating.
AND UA-701	52	⊖/⊖	○	◖	End of cuff may slip out of D-ring. Cuff may be hard to inflate.
Omron HEM-713C	90	⊖/○	⊖	⊖	Self-inflating.
Sunmark 144	48	⊖/○	○	⊖	—
Omron HEM-413C	55	⊖/○	○	⊖	—
Walgreens 80WA	40	⊖/○	○	⊖	—
Marshall 80	55	⊖/○	○	⊖	—
Lumiscope 1065 Ⓓ	60	⊖/○	○	●	Deflation valve must be closed manually.
AND UA-731	90	◖/⊖	⊖	◖	Self-inflating. Very large, clear digital readout. End of cuff may slip out of D-ring.
Radio Shack Micronta 63-663 Ⓓ	50	◖/◖	○	⊖	—
Lumiscope 1060 Ⓓ	60	◖/◖	○	●	Deflation valve must be closed manually.

ELECTRONIC FINGER MODELS

The following models were judged Not Acceptable because of the great variability in the readings they gave. Listed alphabetically.

Brand and model	Price	Consistency S / D	Ease of use	Instructions	Comments
Lumiscope 1083	99	●/●	⊖	⊖	Self-inflating. Finger cuff difficult to adjust. Systolic and diastolic readings not separated.
Marshall F-89	138	●/●	⊖	⊖	Self-inflating. Inaccurate.
Omron HEM-815F	160	●/●	⊖	◖	Self-inflating. Inaccurate.
Sunbeam 7655-10	60	●/●	⊖	⊖	Self-inflating. Finger cuff difficult to adjust. Systolic and diastolic readings not separated.

RATINGS BATHROOM SCALES

▶ **See report, page 260.** Last time rated in Consumer Reports: January 1993.

Brand-name recommendations: The *Health O Meter 840,* $50, was top-rated because of its sample-to-sample consistency and high overall performance. But any of the next seven models gave consistently accurate and repeatable readings as well. Two models stood out for low price and high quality: the *Counselor Digital 850,* $22 (and its successor *34850,* $28), and the *Borg Digital 9855,* $23, which has been discontinued but may still be available in some stores.

For the typical bathroom scale, expect: ■ A spring mechanism to measure weight. (Other type, strain-gauge, is noted in Comments.) ■ Rectangular or square steel platform. ■ Readout interval of 1 lb. ■ Digital displays to use red LCD digits, 9-volt battery, tare-measurement capability. ■ Claimed maximum capacity of 300 lb. or more.

Notes on the table: Except where separated by a bold rule, closely ranked models differed little in quality. **Price** is the mfr.'s suggested retail. **Repeatable** is the ability to give consistent readings for the same weight. **Accuracy** is the ability to correctly display the weight of object being weighed. **Display** is a measure of reading ease. Ⓢ indicates tested model has been replaced by successor model; according to the mfr., the performance of a new model should be similar to the tested model but features may vary. Not tested. Ⓓ indicates model discontinued or replacement not similar.

Listed in order of performance, based primarily on repeatability

Better ◀——————▶ Worse
⊜ ⊖ ○ ◐ ●

Brand and model	Price	Repeat-able	Accuracy	Display	Comments
Health O Meter 840	$50	⊖	○	⊖	Strain-gauge. Accommodates large feet. Uncomfortable to bare feet. Can measure weights 5 lb. or less. Plastic base.
Thinner MS-7	50	⊖	○	○	Strain-gauge. Can measure weights 5 lb. or less. LCD display. Uses "lifetime" lithium battery.
Metro Thin Scale 9800	60	⊖	⊖	⊖	Strain-gauge. Accommodates large feet. Slides on dry floor easily. Not stable. Plastic base.
Borg Hot Dots 9144 Ⓢ 34-344-00-010, $34	28	⊖	○	⊖	Uncomfortable to bare feet.
Sunbeam Digital 12657	50	⊖	⊖	⊖	Strain-gauge. Slides on dry floor easily.
Counselor Digiscale 2121	40	⊖	○	⊖	Strain-gauge. Not stable.
Salter Electronic 971	50	⊖	⊖	○	Strain-gauge. Easy to clean. Slides easily. Can measure weights 5 lb. or less. Plastic base.
Counselor Digital 850, **A BEST BUY** Ⓢ 34850, $28	22	⊖	○	○	Slides on wet floor easily.

Brand and model	Price	Repeat-able	Accuracy	Display	Comments
Counselor Accucycle 1100 Ⓢ 3400, $41	$32	⊖	●	⊖	Accommodates large feet. Not stable. Can measure weights 5 lb. or less.
Health O Meter 811	38	⊖	○	⊖	Strain-gauge. Easy to clean. Accommodates large feet. Uncomfortable to bare feet. Can measure weights 5 lb. or less. Plastic base.
Health O Meter 190 Ⓓ	79	⊖	●	⊖	Strain-gauge. Accommodates large feet.
Metro Big Dial 1000	60	⊖	⊖	○	Speedometer. Accommodates large feet. Zero settings often shift. Display area not cleanable. Plastic base.
Borg Digital 9855, **A BEST BUY** Ⓓ	23	⊖	⊖	○	Slides on wet floor easily.
Health O Meter 1706	25	⊖	●	○	—
Sunbeam Thin Maxi 12573 Ⓢ 12557, $54	29	⊖	●	⊖	Max. claimed capacity less than 300 lb.
Sunbeam Eclipse II 12756 Ⓢ 12470, $30	22	⊖	○	○	—
Metro Digital 1600	30	⊖	○	○	Slides on wet floor easily. Not stable.
Seca Doctor's Scale 760	120	⊖	○	◒	Speedometer. Accommodates large feet. Zero settings often shifted.
Polder Swing Marble 6130	18	⊖	○	●	Rotating dial. Uncomfortable to bare feet.
Health O Meter 1715 Ⓓ	35	⊖	○	⊖	Accommodates large feet.
Metro Fashion 9500	23	⊖	⊖	◒	Rotating dial. Display area not cleanable. Slides easily. Not stable. Large feet block display. Uncomfortable to bare feet.
Counselor Monterey Wicker 410 Ⓢ 34410, $17	14	⊖	○	◒	Rotating dial. Zero settings often shift. Very hard to clean mat.
Sunbeam Thin Speedometer 12280	33	⊖	⊖	◒	Speedometer. Zero settings often shift. Display area not cleanable. Large feet block display. Mat peels off.
Polder Tic Tac Toe 6200	20	○	⊖	◒	Rotating dial. Slides easily. Not stable.
Medixact Proshape 6500 Ⓢ 33901, $49	35	⊖	●	○	Accommodates large feet. Zero settings often shift. Display area not cleanable. Not stable.
Sunbeam Granite Square 12509 Ⓢ 12484, $18	15	○	●	◒	Rotating dial. Max. claimed capacity less than 300 lb.
Counselor Leatherette 97 Ⓢ 34100, $16	10	○	○	◒	Rotating dial.

Ratings continued ▶

Ratings continued

Brand and model	Price	Repeat-able	Accuracy	Display	Comments
Salter Hampshire White 424	$19	○	◒	●	Rotating dial. Zero settings often shift. Slides easily. Max. claimed capacity less than 300 lb.
Health O Meter Professional 150	60	○	○	○	Speedometer. Accommodates large feet. Zero settings often shift.
Sunbeam The Classic 12200	30	○	◒	◒	Rotating dial. Accommodates large feet. Zero settings often shift. Max. claimed capacity less than 300 lb.
Counselor 550 Ⓢ 34560, $24	22	○	◒	○	Rotating dial. Zero settings often shift. Not stable.
Borg 3300 Ⓓ	12	◒	◒	○	Rotating dial. Zero settings often shift. Max. claimed capacity less than 300 lb.
Terraillon Eyedrop T1180	28	◒	○	◒	Rotating dial. Zero settings often shift. Slides easily. Max. claimed capacity less than 300 lb.
Health O Meter 50 Ⓓ	10	○	●	◒	Rotating dial. Zero settings often shift. Display area not cleanable. Slides on dry floor easily.
Metro Fashion 2000	13	○	●	◒	Rotating dial. Slides easily. Not stable. Max. claimed capacity less than 300 lb.
Health O Meter 180	30	◒	◒	◒	Speedometer. Zero settings often shift. Display area not cleanable. Slides easily. Large feet block display. Max. claimed capacity less than 300 lb.

AUTOS

Each year car manufacturers introduce about 175 "new" models of cars, minivans, and sport-utility vehicles. CONSUMER REPORTS tests and rates some 40 of those models during the year. And we are able to provide test information on many more models, for a couple of reasons:

■ Automakers often sell the same car under different nameplates. Many Dodges, Chryslers, and Plymouths, for instance, are essentially identical, many General Motors cars are fairly similar.

■ Many new models are essentially the same as previous years' models. Automakers typically redesign a particular model every three to five years. They may make cosmetic changes in years in between that don't affect the car's performance, such as a new grille or colors.

The key to car shopping is doing your homework. To help in your research, CONSUMER REPORTS provides information in three key areas: performance, reliability, and price. In addition, we report on auto-related products such as batteries.

Performance. In the Buying Guide, we present performance information in two forms:

■ Profiles of the 1994 cars, minivans, and sport-utility vehicles, which include judgments of a model's capabilities, comfort, and convenience, start on page 271. The profiles note the issue of CONSUMER REPORTS that contains the last full report. For the full test report, you can consult the monthly issues or you can order a report by fax (codes are noted in the profiles; for ordering information, see page 398).

■ Ratings of recently tested models,

which start on page 308.

Reliability. You can better the odds of getting sound transportation by choosing a car that our reader surveys show have been reliable in the past. In the Buying Guide, we sum up our readers' car experiences in two ways:

■ The trouble indexes summarize each model's reliability for the 1988 through 1993 model years. The indexes begin on page 324.

■ The Frequency-of-Repair records for 292 different models detail the trouble spots in each model's reliability history. They start on page 330.

Price. A new car's sticker price usually represents an asking, not a selling, price. A car typically costs the dealer 85 to 95 percent of the sticker price. If you know how to negotiate, you may be able to buy the car for close to cost or to get a better deal on a lease. The report on page 312 takes you through the negotiating process; the report on page 315 discusses the leasing process for a new car.

Although a used car presents more of a risk than a new one, it can also be a much better value, since someone else has suffered the sharp depreciation that occurs the instant a new car leaves the lot. The report on page 316 tells you how to shop for a used car.

Car prices, particularly for used cars, are too volatile to be listed in the Buying Guide. Each spring, we list general price ranges for the years' models in the April issue of CONSUMER REPORTS. Each fall, we update those prices and preview the new models in the New Car Yearbook, available on newsstands starting in mid-November. In addition, we offer up-to-date, customized price information by telephone for cars equipped as you want and sold in your region. See below for more information.

AUTO PRICE INFORMATION FROM CONSUMER REPORTS

New Car Price Service

Available by phone or mail, this service provides the latest price information for cars, minivans, sport-utility vehicles, or light trucks. Each Price Report covers:

■ Sticker price and dealer invoice for the model and all major options.

■ An itemized total of the sticker price and dealer cost for the model equipped as you want it.

■ The latest on rebates.

■ Options recommended by CONSUMER REPORTS auto experts.

■ Advice on dealing with the dealer. To order, see page 400.

Used Car Price Service

Available by phone, this service quotes purchase and trade-in prices for cars, minivans, sport-utility vehicles, and light trucks from 1986 to 1994. (Prices for used '94 models are available in January 1995.) The service covers:

■ Purchase and trade-in price information that takes into account the caller's region, the vehicle's age, mileage, major options, and condition.

■ For many models, the car's Trouble Index, based on CONSUMER REPORTS' Frequency-of-Repair data. To order, see page 399.

Profiles of the 1994 cars

Here, listed alphabetically by make and model, you'll find descriptions of nearly all the 1994 models of cars, minivans, and sport-utility vehicles. For most of these models, comments are based on a recent test, if not of the '94 model itself, then of its very similar '93 or '92 predecessor. If a vehicle has been recently redesigned, only data for models relevant to the 1994 models are included. In general, recommended models are those that performed competently in our tests and have been reasonably reliable in our surveys. For reference, we list the date of the **last full report**, which are also available by **fax,** using the fax code given (see page 398). **Predicted reliability** is a judgment based on our Frequency-of-Repair data for past models (see page 324). The **owner satisfaction** judgment reflects readers' responses to a question on our 1993 Annual Questionnaire. Judgments, based on the 1992 models, are compared with the average for each type of car. Best scores had 95 to 99 percent satisfied; worst, 79 to 85 percent. Throughout, **NA** means "not available." **New** means there's no data because the car is new or has been redesigned.

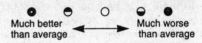

Much better than average ← → Much worse than average

ACURA INTEGRA *Small car* RECOMMENDED

▓ **Trim lines:** RS, LS, GS-R ▓ **Body style:** 4-door ▓ **Predicted reliability:** ◕ **Owner satisfaction:** New ▓ This small but expensive sedan is the entry-level model in Honda's luxury Acura line. Most drivers should be satisfied with the standard, 142-hp Four—it delivers more than enough pep—and the five-speed manual transmission. A 170-hp "VTEC" Four is also available. Interior space is decent in front; the seats are quite firm, perhaps too firm for some people. The rear seat is cramped for tall people. Most controls are nicely laid out and easy to use, but the climate-control slides are hard to adjust. **Last full report: Nov. '94 Fax: 9923**

ACURA INTEGRA COUPE *Sporty car under $25,000* RECOMMENDED

▓ **Trim lines:** RS, LS, GS-R ▓ **Body style:** 2-door hatchback ▓ **Predicted reliability:** ◕ **Owner satisfaction:** New ▓ This small, sporty two-door version of the Integra sedan competes with the likes of the Ford Probe, Mazda MX-6, and Toyota Celica. Although the standard, 142-hp Four delivers plenty of pep, the 170-hp "VTEC" Four is more in keeping with the engines of the Integra's competitors. The VTEC simultaneously delivers high performance and high fuel economy. Handling is steady and predictable. The front seats are nicely shaped but quite firm, perhaps too firm for some people. As in other small coupes, the back seat is tiny. **Last full report: June '94 Fax: 9742**

ACURA LEGEND *Mid-sized car over $25,000* RECOMMENDED

▓ **Trim lines:** L, LS, GS ▓ **Body styles:** 2-door, 4-door ▓ **Predicted reliability:** ◕ **Owner satisfaction:** ○ The Legend accelerates impressively, but expect only about 20 mpg overall—on premium fuel. The four-speed automatic transmission sometimes thumps. The car handles predictably but not nimbly. Mediocre tire grip limits cornering ability. Stops are straight, though

rather long. The ride is quiet and fairly taut. Most people should feel comfortable in front. The rear seat holds three in a pinch. The climate-control system works powerfully, but manually controlled dash vents are a nuisance. The gauges are clear, but the tiny horn buttons are hard to find. The front safety belts take up slack instantly in a frontal collision.
Last full report: Aug. '92 Fax: 7746

ACURA VIGOR *Mid-sized car over $25,000*

▓ **Trim lines:** LS, GS ▓ **Body style:** 4-door **Predicted reliability:** ◕ **Owner satisfaction:** ◓
This model might compete more successfully among sporty coupes than family sedans. Its sporty image seems to require a stiff ride. Quick, nimble handling is the car's greatest asset. Acceleration is vigorous, and braking is short and straight. Front seating is low, but the driver can see out well, and room is plentiful. Three are a crowd in back. Access is awkward. The climate-control system heats and cools quickly, most of the major controls are logical, and the gauges are easy to read. About the only major option you might consider is the automatic transmission—but we found that it shifts abruptly. **Last full report: Feb. '92 Fax: 7345**

AUDI 90 *Compact car over $20,000*

▓ **Trim lines:** S, CS, CS Quattro Sport, Cabriolet ▓ **Body styles:** 4-door, convertible ▓ **Predicted reliability:** NA **Owner satisfaction:** NA ▓ The Quattro's all-wheel drive provides superior traction on slippery roads. The brakes work powerfully, and handling feels safe but numb. Considerable noise reaches the interior. Acceleration is ample, but maximum performance requires a heavy throttle foot and lots of shifting. The five-speed manual transmission shifts fairly smoothly. An automatic transmission is unavailable in the Quattro. The rear seat is tight for three. The automatic climate-control system works powerfully. The odd controls and minor gauges need improvement. **Last full report: May '93 Fax: 7914**

AUDI 100 *Mid-sized car over $25,000*

▓ **Trim lines:** S, CS, CS Quattro ▓ **Body styles:** 4-door, 4-door wagon ▓ **Predicted reliability:** ◓ **Owner satisfaction:** ○ The optional automatic transmission is especially irritating: It shifts slowly and its shifter is awkward. The V6 feels sluggish. The two-wheel-drive version handles fairly smoothly but lacks agility. The ride ranges from jiggly to almost snappy. The front seats are quite comfortable and roomy. Two tall riders will find enough room in the rear, but the center position is no joy. Some of the controls are confusing, but most displays are legible. The manual climate-control system is fussy and weak; the automatic system is much better.
Last full report: Aug. '92 Fax: 7746

BMW 3-SERIES *Compact car over $20,000*   RECOMMENDED

▓ **Trim lines:** 318iS, 325iS, M3, 318i, 325i, 318iC, 325iC ▓ **Body styles:** 2-door, 4-door, convertible ▓ **Predicted reliability:** ○ **Owner satisfaction:** ○ The focus here is more on performance than luxury. The 325i's Six accelerates powerfully, and the optional four-speed automatic shifts smoothly. (The 318i version has a Four.) The car brakes superbly and carves through winding roads with the best of sports cars. Traction control in the 325 is a worthwhile option. The ride is firm and well controlled. Besides the sporty exhaust sound, we noted some road noise. The front seats provide good support; the rear seat is tight for tall people. The displays are clear, and the separate left and right climate-control systems are powerful.
Last full report: Aug. '94 Fax: 9792

BMW 5-SERIES *Luxury car* RECOMMENDED

▓ **Trim lines:** 525i, 530i, 540i, 525i Touring, 530i Touring ▓ **Body styles:** 4-door, 4-door wagon ▓ **Predicted reliability:** ◒ **Owner satisfaction:** ○ The BMW 530i and 540i came out in the middle of last year as 1994 models. These luxurious rear-wheel-drive sports sedans share their basic body with the 525i and they come with sophisticated, all-aluminum V8s instead of a Six. In either version, expect fine handling and a fairly firm ride. We recommend traction control. A smooth five-speed automatic transmission is standard in the 540i, optional in the 530i.
Last full report: May '94   Fax: 7732

BMW 740i *Luxury car*

▓ **Trim lines:** 740i, 740iL ▓ **Body style:** 4-door ▓ **Predicted reliability:** NA **Owner satisfaction:** NA ▓ These V8-powered models compete with the world's finest and costliest luxury sports sedans. The 740iL is four inches longer than the 740i. Both offer exceptional acceleration, superior handling, and all the fancy interior appointments one expects of cars in this price class. These models are substantially roomier than the 5-series BMWs. A five-speed automatic transmission is standard. Displays are quite clear, and nearly all controls are sensibly laid out and easy to reach. Redesigned for 1995.
Last full report: —   Fax: —

BUICK CENTURY *Mid-sized car under $25,000*

▓ **Trim lines:** Special, Custom ▓ **Body styles:** 4-door, 4-door wagon ▓ **Predicted reliability:** ◒ **Owner satisfaction:** ○ This aging and uninteresting model, made in the U.S. and Mexico, has one major advantage: Its repair record has been quite good. The Century and its corporate cousin, the Oldsmobile Cutlass Ciera, are no longer competitive with models such as the Ford Taurus. The optional 3.1-liter V6 and four-speed automatic make a much better choice than the standard 2.2-liter Four with its three-speed automatic.
Last full report: —   Fax: —

BUICK LE SABRE *Large car under $25,000* RECOMMENDED

▓ **Trim lines:** Custom, Limited ▓ **Body style:** 4-door ▓ **Predicted reliability:** ○ **Owner satisfaction:** ○ In standard form, this is a quiet, softly sprung car with sloppy handling. The Touring suspension improves handling somewhat. The V6 provides responsive acceleration, and the four-speed automatic shifts extremely smoothly. Seating is comfortable for five, less so for six. Controls are overstyled, but displays are clear, and the automatic climate-control system is powerful. The Le Sabre, Oldsmobile Eighty-Eight Royale, and Pontiac Bonneville are similar; the Bonneville is sportiest. The Buick Park Avenue and Oldsmobile Ninety-Eight Regency are longer but no roomier inside.
Last full report: Jan '92   Fax: 7965

BUICK PARK AVENUE *Large car over $25,000*

▓ **Trim lines:** Base, Ultra ▓ **Body style:** 4-door ▓ **Predicted reliability:** ○ **Owner satisfaction:** ○ This high-line freeway cruiser is a longer and more luxurious relative of the Buick Le Sabre. It competes among big, quiet luxury sedans such as the Oldsmobile Ninety-Eight Regency and Lincoln Town Car, with emphasis on a soft ride and every imaginable power convenience. The standard, 3.8-liter V6 is quite capable of powering this large car; the Ultra version comes with a snappier supercharged V6. Opt for the trailer-towing package; it includes a firmer suspension, which should improve handling.
Last full report: —   Fax: —

BUICK REGAL *Mid-sized car under $25,000* RECOMMENDED

▨ **Trim lines:** Custom, Limited, Gran Sport ▨ **Body styles:** 2-door, 4-door ▨ **Predicted reliability:** ○ **Owner satisfaction:** ○ This aging model shares major components with the Oldsmobile Cutlass Supreme and Pontiac Grand Prix, but it lacks the Pontiac's dual air bags and convenient front safety belts. The 3.8-liter V6 is peppier than the 3.1-liter V6 and only a bit thirstier. The four-speed automatic shifts very smoothly. Handling feels fairly sloppy in tight turns. Expect a comfortable ride on smooth roads, a slightly worse ride on broken pavement. The front and rear seats are roomy enough for tall people but lack support. The gauges are easy to read, but many minor controls are scattered haphazardly.

Last full report: Feb. '94 Fax: 7771

BUICK RIVIERA *Mid-sized car over $25,000*

▨ **Trim lines:** None ▨ **Body style:** 2-door ▨ **Predicted reliability:** New **Owner satisfaction:** New ▨ After a year's hiatus, the venerable Riviera nameplate was resurrected this year as a 1995 model for Buick's new "personal luxury coupe." The standard engine is Buick's tried-and-true (but "enhanced") 3.8-liter V6. A supercharged version is also available. The interior layout is thoroughly up-to-date. The split-bench front seat is unusual in a coupe. Bucket seats and a center console will be popular options.

Last full report: — Fax: —

BUICK ROADMASTER *Large car over $25,000*

▨ **Trim lines:** Base, Limited, Estate Wagon ▨ **Body styles:** 4-door, 4-door wagon ▨ **Predicted reliability:** ◒ **Owner satisfaction:** ○ This massive rear-wheel-drive model is the embodiment of automotive excess. A close cousin of the Chevrolet Caprice, it rides exceptionally smoothly and quietly—and that's pretty much where its virtues end. It guzzles fuel at the rate of 17 mpg on average. Handling is ponderous. Three people have lots of room in the rear, but three in front are tight. The driver can't see where the car ends in front, and wide rear roof pillars create a nasty blind spot. The climate-control system works well.

Last full report: Jan. '92 Fax: 7307

BUICK SKYLARK *Compact car under $20,000*

▨ **Trim lines:** Custom, Limited, Gran Sport ▨ **Body styles:** 2-door, 4-door ▨ **Predicted reliability:** ○ **Owner satisfaction:** ○ Though introduced in 1992, this design is based on the Chevrolet Corsica, little changed since 1987. The Skylark, Oldsmobile Achieva, and Pontiac Grand Am share many components, but each has a different image. The Skylark targets those who want some luxury with their sportiness. Even with the Gran Sport package, handling is just adequate. The 3.1-liter V6 is quieter and peppier than the 2.3-liter Four. The front seats are satisfactory; the rear is unfriendly even for two. Heating and cooling are effective but slow. The controls and displays need improvement. **Last full report: June '92 Fax: 7704**

CADILLAC CONCOURS/DE VILLE *Large car over $25,000*

▨ **Trim lines:** None ▨ **Body style:** 4-door ▨ **Predicted reliability:** New **Owner satisfaction:** New ▨ Cadillac's best-selling model line for years, the De Ville saw its first major redesign in a decade in 1994. Now built on a stretched version of the Cadillac Seville platform, it's a big, plush, four-door land yacht. The De Ville comes with a 4.9-liter V8. The upscale Concours gets

Cadillac's sophisticated Northstar all-aluminum 4.6-liter V8 and electronically controlled transmission and suspension. This car rides and handles relatively well.

Last full report: — Fax: —

CADILLAC ELDORADO *Mid-sized car over $25,000*

▨ **Trim lines:** Base, Touring Coupe ▨ **Body style:** 2-door ▨ **Predicted reliability:** ◗ **Owner satisfaction:** ◗ This showy luxury coupe offers a full array of safety and luxury features and two versions of the sophisticated Northstar all-aluminum V8. The Touring Coupe provides blazing acceleration, the electronic four-speed automatic transmission shifts very smoothly, and the traction control is exemplary on slippery roads. Handling is cumbersome. The car rides well on good roads, but bumps tend to trip it up. Though the front seat is roomy, support could be better. Two adults fit fairly nicely in the rear; access is awkward. The automatic climate-control system works quite well. The instruments are clear; some displays are poorly placed.

Last full report: July '93 Fax: 9325

CADILLAC FLEETWOOD *Large car over $25,000*

▨ **Trim lines:** Base, Brougham ▨ **Body style:** 4-door ▨ **Predicted reliability:** ● **Owner satisfaction:** NA ▨ In last year's redesign, the rear-wheel-drive Fleetwood became a replacement for the Cadillac Brougham. Built on the same chassis as the Buick Roadmaster and Chevrolet Caprice, it maintains the traditional characteristics of large domestic sedans, with a soft ride, quiet and plush interior, and enough muscle to haul a heavy trailer with ease. You'll find plenty of interior room front and rear, plus a large trunk. You'll also find the cumbersome handling and mediocre fuel economy inherent in this breed. **Last full report: — Fax: —**

CADILLAC SEVILLE *Luxury car*

▨ **Trim lines:** SLS, STS ▨ **Body style:** 4-door ▨ **Predicted reliability:** ◗ **Owner satisfaction:** ○ The Seville was designed to compete with sedans from Mercedes, BMW, Lexus, and Infiniti. Its Northstar system combines a modern all-aluminum V8, an electronic four-speed automatic transmission, traction control, and an active suspension that reacts to the road. The Seville accelerates faster than many performance cars. The STS version corners fairly crisply. The ride deteriorates considerably on poor roads. Some road and wind noise penetrates the cabin. Leg room is ample, but the sun-roof option robs head room. The front seats offer good support. The rear is several notches worse. **Last full report: Nov. '93 Fax: 7351**

CHEVROLET ASTRO/GMC SAFARI *Minivan*

▨ **Trim lines:** CS, CL, LT ▨ **Body styles:** regular, extended ▨ **Predicted reliability:** ◗ **Owner satisfaction:** ● (2WD) This old design hasn't aged well. The Astro and similar Safari suffer from clumsy handling, a trucklike ride, and poor reliability. The V6 and four-speed automatic transmission work smoothly. Optional all-wheel drive is useful on slippery roads. Lack of front foot room is a major discomfort. With the eight-passenger package, the second and third seats are comfortable for two but not for three. The digital displays are clear, the controls awkward. A huge cargo area—especially in the extended models—and impressive towing capability are pluses. **Last full report: Oct. '93 Fax: 7766**

CHEVROLET BERETTA *Compact car under $20,000*

■ **Trim lines:** Base, Z26 ■ **Body style:** 2-door ■ **Predicted reliability:** ◖ **Owner satisfaction:** ○ This model offers no surprises, good or bad. It represents the thrifty end of GM's compact models. The V6 is a better choice than the weak and noisy Four. The steering feels vague, and the car leans sharply in turns. The ride is busy but never harsh. The low front seats make it hard to see over the hood, and the seatbacks force occupants to slouch. Three adults feel crowded in back. Although the displays are clear, the controls are awkward and the climate-control system is weak. A split folding rear seatback is optional.

Last full report: June '92   Fax: 7704

CHEVROLET BLAZER/GMC YUKON *Sport-utility vehicle*

■ **Trim lines:** Cheyenne, Silverado, Sport ■ **Body style:** 2-door wagon ■ **Predicted reliability:** ● **Owner satisfaction:** ○ Built on a full-sized pickup-truck chassis, these vehicles lend themselves to hauling cargo or towing a heavy trailer. Don't confuse them with the compact-sized Chevrolet S-Blazer. The big versions feature four-wheel drive, a big V8, and antilock brakes. They ride surprisingly well and handle reasonably well. The best way to outfit the Blazer is with an automatic transmission, trailer-towing option, and Silverado Preferred Equipment Group 3, which includes many convenience items.

Last full report: —   Fax: —

CHEVROLET CAMARO *Sporty car under $25,000*

■ **Trim lines:** Base, Z28 ■ **Body styles:** 2-door, convertible ■ **Predicted reliability:** NA **Owner satisfaction:** NA ■ The Camaro and its corporate cousin, the Pontiac Firebird, are rear-wheel-drive muscle cars. The Z28 version uses a slightly detuned version of the potent V8 that powers the Chevrolet Corvette. A six-speed manual transmission is standard; a four-speed automatic is optional, as is traction control. The V8's effortless thrust makes the V6 seem sluggish. The ride is decent; the handling, precise but not nimble. The V8's wider tires grip better. Braking is competent. The front bucket seats cradle their occupants nicely and firmly. The rear seat is mostly for show.

Last full report: Oct. '93   Fax: 7341

CHEVROLET CAPRICE *Large car under $25,000*

■ **Trim lines:** Classic, Classic LS, Impala SS ■ **Body styles:** 4-door, 4-door wagon ■ **Predicted reliability:** ◖ **Owner satisfaction:** ◖ A quiet, pillowy ride is the main claim to fame of this rear-wheel-drive model. The optional 5.7-liter V8 produces gobs of power—but delivers only about 17 mpg overall. The four-speed automatic shifts very smoothly. The optional Sport Suspension improves handling. Seating is quite comfortable for two in front, not bad for three in the rear. Though slow to warm, the heater is strong and quiet. Instruments and controls are much friendlier than in earlier Caprices. Properly equipped, the Caprice can tow 5000 pounds.

Last full report: March '94   Fax: 9714

CHEVROLET CAVALIER *Compact car under $20,000*

■ **Trim lines:** Base, VL, RS, Z24 ■ **Body styles:** 2-door, 4-door, 4-door wagon, convertible ■ **Predicted reliability:** ● **Owner satisfaction:** ○ Why this humdrum little sedan and its cousin, the Pontiac Sunbird, remain among GM's top sellers is a mystery. The Four accelerates slowly and noisily; the V6 is a better choice. The automatic transmission occasionally hesitates and then bumps into gear. Stops are reasonably short, but the brakes fade more than we like in repeated stops. Expect good handling, but not a comfortable ride. The front seats are hard and low, and the rear seat is tight. A complete redesign is due for 1995.

Last full report: May '91   Fax: 7969

CHEVROLET CORSICA *Compact car under $20,000*

▓ **Trim lines:** None ▓ **Body style:** 4-door ▓ **Predicted reliability:** ◗ **Owner satisfaction:** ○ This model offers no surprises, good or bad. It represents the thrifty end of GM's compact models. The V6 is a better choice than the weak and noisy Four. The steering feels vague, and the car leans sharply in turns. The ride is busy but never harsh. The low front seats make it hard to see over the hood, and the seatbacks force occupants to slouch. Three adults feel crowded in back. Although the displays are clear, the controls are awkward and the climate-control system is weak. A split folding rear seatback is optional.

Last full report: June '92   Fax: 7704

CHEVROLET CORVETTE *Sports car over $25,000*

▓ **Trim lines:** Base, ZR-1 ▓ **Body styles:** 2-door, convertible ▓ **Predicted reliability:** ● **Owner satisfaction:** ○ This legendary model is an odd mix of old and new. The body flexes and twists. A huge V8 delivers blazing acceleration, while a sophisticated traction-control system minimizes wheel spin. The six-speed manual transmission shifts stiffly but precisely. Short drivers may have to stretch to depress the clutch pedal. Steering is quick and precise, but the Corvette feels too bulky to be nimble. It bounces badly on rough roads. It's hard to see over the hood. The climate-control system is effective but noisy at times. The gauges are legible, and the controls work quite well.

Last full report: Sept. '92   Fax: 7758

CHEVROLET LUMINA *Mid-sized car under $25,000*

▓ **Trim lines:** Base, LS ▓ **Body style:** 4-door ▓ **Predicted reliability:** New **Owner satisfaction:** New ▓ A redesigned version, due in late Spring as a 1995 model, offers a competitive ride, handling, and comfort. The new model remains fairly large and roomy, with more convenient instruments and controls and updated safety equipment.

Last full report: —   Fax: —

CHEVROLET LUMINA *Minivan*

▓ **Trim lines:** Base, LS ▓ **Body style:** minivan ▓ **Predicted reliability:** ◗ **Owner satisfaction:** ○ The plastic-clad Lumina is as competent as the similar Oldsmobile Silhouette and Pontiac Trans Sport, but not as reliable. The optional seven-seat package is versatile; its five modular seats are easy to fold, shift, or remove. A power side door is nice. The 3.1-liter V6 and three-speed automatic accelerate adequately; the 3.8-liter V6 and four-speed automatic do much better. Emergency handling is reasonably controllable. Seating is comfortable in the first two rows; access to the third row is awkward. The ride is comfortable for a van, and the climate-control system is powerful.

Last full report: July '94   Fax: 7789

CHEVROLET MONTE CARLO *Mid-sized car under $25,000*

▓ **Trim lines:** LS, Z34 ▓ **Body style:** 2-door ▓ **Predicted reliability:** New **Owner satisfaction:** New ▓ The Monte Carlo nameplate has resurfaced this year, attached to a coupe version of the redesigned '95 Chevrolet Lumina sedan. Where the Lumina aims squarely at the heart of the family-car market, the Monte Carlo courts those with a more youthful disposition. All versions come loaded with power accessories. The Z34 version has a 3.4-liter twin-camshaft V6 that is noisier and thirstier and not much stronger than the 3.1. **Last full report: — Fax: —**

CHEVROLET S-BLAZER/GMC JIMMY *Sport-utility vehicle*

▓ **Trim lines:** Standard, Tahoe, Tahoe LT ▓ **Body styles:** 2-door wagon, 4-door wagon ▓ **Predicted reliability:** ◓ **Owner satisfaction:** ◓ These models have changed little over the years. Don't confuse the S with the larger, plain Chevrolet Blazer. The S comes in two- and four-wheel-drive versions; we see little point in tolerating the discomforts of a sport-utility vehicle without the utility of four-wheel drive. The ride and handling are quite crude. To make this vehicle more competitive in its class, choose the 200-hp, 4.3-liter V6, along with the Tahoe LT package for its many convenience features. New versions will be introduced this summer as 1995 models. **Last full report: — Fax: —**

CHEVROLET SUBURBAN/GMC SUBURBAN *Sport-utility vehicle*

▓ **Trim lines:** Cheyenne, Silverado ▓ **Body style:** 4-door wagon ▓ **Predicted reliability:** ● **Owner satisfaction:** ○ Resembling an overgrown station wagon, the Suburban is built on a full-sized GM pickup chassis and comes in two- and four-wheel-drive versions. This sport-utility vehicle emphasizes utility over sport; it can haul lots of cargo or tow a heavy trailer. A redesign two years ago improved the handling and ride somewhat, but expect both to remain more trucklike than carlike. Instead of the thirsty 5.7-liter gasoline-powered V8, the powerful new 6.5-liter turbodiesel V8 may make sense for Suburban buyers who don't own a filling station. **Last full report: — Fax: —**

CHRYSLER CONCORDE *Large car under $25,000*   **RECOMMENDED**

▓ **Trim lines:** None ▓ **Body style:** 4-door ▓ **Predicted reliability:** ◓ **Owner satisfaction:** NA ▓ The Concorde and its siblings, the Dodge Intrepid and Eagle Vision, are top-rated among large cars. The 3.3-liter V6 accelerates responsively; the optional 3.5-liter V6 packs even more punch, but it's noisier. Both engines averaged about 21 mpg overall—the larger V6, on mid-grade fuel. The automatic shifts quite smoothly. The Concorde handles surprisingly nimbly for so large a car. The ride is firm and well controlled. The horn buttons are hard to find quickly, but the displays are clear. Seating is roomy and comfortable for five. **Last full report: March '93 Fax: 7948**

CHRYSLER LE BARON *Compact car under $20,000*

▓ **Trim lines:** LE, Landau ▓ **Body style:** 4-door ▓ **Predicted reliability:** ○ **Owner satisfaction:** ◓ This is the last year for this sedan. The V6, with four-speed automatic, accelerates well. These models handle well in routine driving. The steering responds predictably in abrupt avoidance maneuvers. Front seating is fairly comfortable for most people; short drivers need the power seat. Two tall people can fit easily in the rear seat; with three sitting abreast, the middle position has inadequate leg room. The heater is slow to warm the cabin. The split rear seatback can be folded. **Last full report: March '92 Fax: 7363**

CHRYSLER LE BARON CONVERTIBLE *Compact car under $20,000*

▓ **Trim lines:** GTC ▓ **Body style:** convertible ▓ **Predicted reliability:** ◓ **Owner satisfaction:** ○ This is one of the last models to be built on Chrysler's hoary K-car chassis, soon to enter retirement. Among the latest tweaks is the addition of dual air bags. Sales have been reasonably strong for such a dated and uninspired design, perhaps because it's one of few convertibles in its market niche. The last time we tested a Le Baron coupe (similar to the convertible), we were unimpressed with the handling and ride, particularly on poor roads. As in many other two-door models, the back seat is cramped and hard to reach. **Last full report: — Fax: —**

CHRYSLER LHS/NEW YORKER *Large car over $25,000* RECOMMENDED

▓ **Trim lines:** None ▓ **Body style:** 4-door ▓ **Predicted reliability:** ◑ **Owner satisfaction:** New ▓ These models are like the Chrysler Concorde/Dodge Intrepid/Eagle Vision triplets, which we consider the best large sedans on the market—but they're five inches longer. The LHS, with individual front seats, can seat five; the New Yorker, with a front bench seat, can seat six. The V6 gives spirited acceleration, and the four-speed automatic shifts fairly smoothly. These models handle relatively nimbly and ride comfortably. But unless you crave an expansive rear seat and trunk, get one of the smaller triplets and save several thousand dollars.
Last full report: March '94 Fax: 9714

CHRYSLER TOWN & COUNTRY *Minivan*

▓ **Trim lines:** None ▓ **Body style:** minivan ▓ **Predicted reliability:** ◖ **Owner satisfaction:** ○ Chrysler Corp.'s minivans continue to hold their own against tough new competition. This model is a loaded version of the Dodge Grand Caravan and Plymouth Grand Voyager. Handling is sluggish, but stops are short. The van rides pleasantly on smooth roads but shudders over bumps. The front seats are very comfortable. The rearmost seat is tight for three. The climate-control system is strong. Although the displays are clear, some controls could be better. The plain, shorter-bodied Dodge Caravan and Plymouth Voyager have been more reliable. A four-wheel-drive version is available. **Last full report: Oct. '92 Fax: 7766**

DODGE CARAVAN *Minivan* RECOMMENDED

▓ **Trim lines:** Base, SE, LE, ES ▓ **Body style:** minivan ▓ **Predicted reliability:** ○ **Owner satisfaction:** ○ The Caravan/Plymouth Voyager twins were our benchmark minivans for years, and they're still competitive. The V6 is strong. The automatic transmission sometimes shifts too often; a five-speed manual is available with the Four. The van handles sluggishly; an optional, stiffer suspension helps somewhat. The front seats are comfortable, and the climate-control system is powerful. The displays are clear, but minor controls could be better. The longer Chrysler Town & Country, Dodge Grand Caravan, and Plymouth Grand Voyager have been less reliable. **Last full report: July '94 Fax: 7789**

DODGE COLT *Small car*

▓ **Trim lines:** Base, ES ▓ **Body styles:** 2-door, 4-door ▓ **Predicted reliability:** NA **Owner satisfaction:** ◑ This model is also known as the Eagle Summit, Plymouth Colt, and Mitsubishi Mirage. The Colt is a price leader, destined for oblivion next year. Most cars on dealers' lots will be short on equipment such as antilock brakes—too bad, since the conventional brakes are poor. The ride is uncomfortable. The front seats provide satisfactory support. The rear seat can barely hold two six-footers. Major controls are easy to see and grasp, and the climate-control system works quickly. The split rear seatback can be folded.
Last full report: Aug. '93 Fax: 7302

DODGE GRAND CARAVAN *Minivan*

▓ **Trim lines:** Base, SE, LE, ES ▓ **Body style:** minivan ▓ **Predicted reliability:** ◒ **Owner satisfaction:** ○ Chrysler Corp.'s minivans continue to hold their own against tough new competition. This model and similar Chrysler Town & Country and Plymouth Grand Voyager are extended versions of the plain Caravan and Voyager. Handling is sluggish, but stops are short. The van rides pleasantly on smooth roads but shudders over bumps. Front seats are very comfortable. The rearmost seat is tight for three. The climate-control system is strong. Displays are clear. A four-wheel-drive version is available. The plain, shorter-bodied Dodge Caravan and Plymouth Voyager have been more reliable.   **Last full report: Oct. '92 Fax: 7766**

DODGE INTREPID *Large car under $25,000*   **RECOMMENDED**

▓ **Trim lines:** Base, ES ▓ **Body style:** 4-door ▓ **Predicted reliability:** ◒ **Owner satisfaction:** NA ▓ The Intrepid and its siblings, the Chrysler Concorde and Eagle Vision, are top-rated among large cars. The 3.3-liter V6 accelerates responsively; the 3.5-liter V6 packs even more punch. Both averaged about 21 mpg overall—the larger V6, on mid-grade fuel. The automatic transmission shifts quite smoothly. The Intrepid handles surprisingly nimbly for so large a car. The ride is firm but pleasant. The horn buttons are hard to find quickly, but the displays are clear. Seating is roomy and comfortable for five.   **Last full report: Feb. '94 Fax: 7771**

DODGE NEON *Small car*

▓ **Trim lines:** Base, Highline, Sport ▓ **Body style:** 4-door ▓ **Predicted reliability:** New **Owner satisfaction:** New ▓ The new Dodge/Plymouth Neon twins are among the very few small models to be designed and made entirely in the U.S. since Detroit all but abandoned the economy-car market to the imports years ago. Tagged as a 1995 model, the Neon is a smidgen larger than such competitors as the Honda Civic, Toyota Corolla, and Ford Escort, and the 2.0-liter Four accelerates aggressively. The Neon features standard-equipment dual air bags. The rear seatbacks fold down to expand the cargo space.   **Last full report: Oct. '94 Fax: 9923**

DODGE SPIRIT *Compact car under $20,000*

▓ **Trim lines:** None ▓ **Body style:** 4-door ▓ **Predicted reliability:** ○ **Owner satisfaction:** ○ This model (and its twin Plymouth Acclaim) will remain into 1995 for a few months until it's replaced by the new Dodge Stratus and the Chrysler Cirrus. The Four vibrates and growls; get the V6. Handling is predictable but not crisp in abrupt maneuvers. Front seating is fairly comfortable, though short drivers need the power-seat option. Toe space is tight for the front passenger. Two tall people fit easily in the rear, but a center passenger has too little leg room. A motorized right front safety belt is new this year. The heater works slowly, and the controls and displays could be better. The split rear seatback can be folded.
Last full report: March '92 Fax: 7363

DODGE STEALTH *Sports car over $25,000*

▓ **Trim lines:** Base, R/T, R/T Turbo ▓ **Body style:** 2-door hatchback ▓ **Predicted reliability:** ◒ **Owner satisfaction:** ○ In their sportiest form, the Stealth and its twin, the Mitsubishi 3000 GT, are technological tours de force. Price lines range from the base model, with front-wheel drive, on up to the R/T Turbo, with twin turbos, four-wheel steering, electronically adjustable suspension, and all-wheel drive. The R/T Turbo offers excellent steering response and traction, nimble cornering, exceptionally short stops, and blazing acceleration. The front seats are comfortable for most people. The tight rear seat is mostly for show. The automatic climate-control system works well. The controls could be a bit easier to use.   **Last full report: April '92 Fax: 9377**

EAGLE SUMMIT *Small car*

▩ **Trim lines:** DL, LX, ES, ESi ▩ **Body styles:** 2-door, 4-door ▩ **Predicted reliability:** NA **Owner satisfaction:** NA ▩ This model is also known as the Dodge Colt, Plymouth Colt, and Mitsubishi Mirage. By any name, it's a price leader. Most cars on dealers' lots will be short on equipment such as antilock brakes—too bad, since the conventional brakes are poor. The car rides uncomfortably. The front seats provide satisfactory support. The rear seat can barely hold two six-footers. Major controls are easy to see and grasp, and the climate-control system works quickly. The split rear seatback can be folded.   **Last full report: Aug. '93 Fax: 7302**

EAGLE SUMMIT WAGON *Small car*   RECOMMENDED

▩ **Trim lines:** DL, LX, AWD ▩ **Body style:** 3-door wagon ▩ **Predicted reliability:** ○ **Owner satisfaction:** NA ▩ This cross between a small wagon and a very small van also sells as the Mitsubishi Expo LRV and Plymouth Colt Vista. Tall and boxy, it has a high seating position and a sliding side door. The engine of choice, a 2.4-liter Four, feels lively. The tires squeal, the body leans, and the car plows ahead in tight turns. The ride is comfortable and quiet, and the Summit offers much more cargo space than do competing small wagons. Tall drivers need more leg room. The rear seat is roomy for two, tight for three. The climate-control system works well. The gauges are legible, but the controls could be handier.

Last full report: Sept. '93 Fax: 7331

EAGLE TALON *Sporty car under $25,000*

▩ **Trim lines:** DL, ES, TSi, TSi AWD ▩ **Body style:** 2-door hatchback ▩ **Predicted reliability:** ○ **Owner satisfaction:** ○ The Talon and similar Mitsubishi Eclipse are due for replacement in 1995. The optional turbocharger adds lots of power but hurts fuel economy somewhat. Handling feels responsive and stable. All-wheel drive in the top-line version improves handling. The ride isn't bad for a sporty car, but the seating is too low. The rear seat is just about useless. Luggage space is skimpy. The Talon is a competent car overall, but the Ford Probe, Honda Prelude, and Mazda MX-6 have better comfort and convenience features.

Last full report: Jan. '93 Fax: 7936

EAGLE VISION *Large car under $25,000*   RECOMMENDED

▩ **Trim lines:** ESi, TSi ▩ **Body style:** 4-door ▩ **Predicted reliability:** ◕ **Owner satisfaction:** NA ▩ The Vision and its siblings, the Dodge Intrepid and Chrysler Concorde, are top rated among large cars. The 3.3-liter V6 accelerates responsively; the optional 3.5-liter V6 packs even more punch, but it's noisier. Both engines averaged about 21 mpg overall—the larger V6, on mid-grade fuel. The automatic transmission shifts quite smoothly. The Vision handles surprisingly nimbly for so large a car. The ride is firm and well controlled. The horn buttons are hard to find quickly, but the displays are clear. Seating is roomy and comfortable for five.

Last full report: March '93 Fax: 7948

FORD AEROSTAR *Minivan*   RECOMMENDED

■ **Trim lines:** XL, XL Plus, XLT ■ **Body styles:** regular, extended ■ **Predicted reliability:** ○ **Owner satisfaction:** ○ This is a sound choice for carrying six or seven people or towing a trailer. Credit its strong optional 4.0-liter V6 and roomy cargo area. The four-speed automatic transmission can shift abruptly. The all-wheel-drive version handles more sure-footedly than the ponderous rear-wheel-drive version. The ride is good, the seating very comfortable. The dual climate-control systems work well. The front-wheel-drive Ford Windstar will replace the Aerostar in 1995.   **Last full report: Oct. '92 Fax: 7766**

FORD ASPIRE *Small car*

■ **Trim lines:** Base, SE ■ **Body styles:** 2-door hatchback, 4-door hatchback ■ **Predicted reliability:** New **Owner satisfaction:** New ■ This new model replaces the Ford Festiva, which anchored the small-car end of Ford's lineup. Like the Festiva, the Aspire is made in Korea by Kia. Think of it as a basic urban rúnabout, long on fuel economy but very short on performance. Its handling is very clumsy. The Aspire comes in an SE version, which aspires to be sportier than the normal two- or four-door hatchback.   **Last full report: Oct. '94 Fax: 9921**

FORD BRONCO *Sport-utility vehicle*

■ **Trim lines:** XL, XLT, Eddie Bauer ■ **Body style:** 2-door wagon ■ **Predicted reliability:** ● **Owner satisfaction:** ○ The elephantine Bronco weighs in solidly on the utility end of the sport-utility continuum, where it competes with the Chevrolet Blazer and GMC Yukon. This four-wheel-drive vehicle is a truck from the core outwards, but a truck that offers various levels of interior luxury appointments. It is designed for people who need to haul a lot of gear or tow a heavy trailer. Now available only with a V8 engine, the Bronco will sniff out every gas pump on its itinerary.   **Last full report: — Fax: —**

FORD CROWN VICTORIA *Large car under $25,000*   RECOMMENDED

■ **Trim lines:** Base, LX ■ **Body style:** 4-door ■ **Predicted reliability:** ○ **Owner satisfaction:** ○ The big Ford and similar Mercury Grand Marquis are among the last big freeway cruisers with a V8, full frame, and rear-wheel drive. A serene ride, huge trunk, and substantial trailer-towing capability are major advantages. The car accelerates well, and the four-speed automatic transmission shifts very smoothly. Steering response is fairly good. The Preferred Equipment Package 114A and the Handling and Performance Package materially improve braking and handling. The front seats lack sufficient padding. The rear offers room for three. The controls are mostly logical.   **Last full report: March '94 Fax: 9714**

FORD ESCORT *Small car*

■ **Trim lines:** Base, LX, GT ■ **Body styles:** 2-door hatchback, 4-door hatchback, 4-door, 4-door wagon ■ **Predicted reliability:** ○ **Owner satisfaction:** ○ Only the GT version offers antilock brakes—and without antilock, the Escort (and similar Mercury Tracer) stops poorly. The standard 1.9-liter Four gives lethargic and noisy acceleration. A sophisticated 1.8-liter Four in the GT is more powerful. The basic Escort handles sluggishly, but the GT's taut suspension makes the car feel nimble. Front seating is comfortable; the driver can see out well. The rear seat is roomy for six-footers, but isn't comfortable.   **Last full report: Sept. '93 Fax: 7331**

FORD EXPLORER *Sport-utility vehicle* RECOMMENDED

▓ **Trim lines:** XL, Sport, XLT, Eddie Bauer, Limited ▓ **Body styles:** 2-door wagon, 4-door wagon ▓ **Predicted reliability:** ○ **Owner satisfaction:** ○ Big and roomy, the four-door version easily seats five. (The Mazda Navajo is a two-door Explorer.) The V6 is adequate, and the four-speed automatic shifts smoothly. The optional four-wheel drive, without a center differential, is unsuited for dry roads. Handling is ponderous; we recommend the optional limited-slip rear axle and trailer-towing package. Resilient front seats partly make up for a bouncy ride. The rear seat can hold three six-footers. The climate-control system is strong. Most controls are convenient, and the displays are clear. **Last full report: Nov. '92 Fax: 7789**

FORD MUSTANG *Sporty car under $25,000*

▓ **Trim lines:** Base, GT ▓ **Body styles:** 2-door, convertible ▓ **Predicted reliability:** New **Owner satisfaction:** New ▓ The new-for-'94 Mustang continues as a rear-wheel-drive muscle car. The 1994 improvements are evolutionary rather than revolutionary. The Mustang offers a choice of 3.8-liter V6 or 5.0-liter V8. (A more modern, more powerful, and more refined 4.6-liter V8, similar to the one in the Lincoln Mark VIII, is due for next year.) Ride and handling are mediocre. The cabin is cramped; the rear seats are vestigial. Controls are easy to use, and displays are clear. **Last full report: June '94 Fax: 9742**

FORD PROBE *Sporty car under $25,000* RECOMMENDED

▓ **Trim lines:** Base, GT ▓ **Body style:** 2-door hatchback ▓ **Predicted reliability:** ○ **Owner satisfaction:** ○ This model and the Mazda MX-6 share many mechanical parts. The higher price line of each make is a step up in performance from the base four-cylinder version. The V6 accelerates with authority. We prefer the easy-shifting five-speed manual transmission. Handling is very smooth and predictable; the Probe GT's taut suspension and wide tires provide crisper handling, but the MX-6 rides a bit better. The front seats are comfortable, but reserve the rear seat for packages. There's lots of luggage room under the Probe's hatchback. **Last full report: Jan. '93 Fax: 7936**

FORD TAURUS *Mid-sized car under $25,000* RECOMMENDED

▓ **Trim lines:** GL, LX ▓ **Body styles:** 4-door, 4-door wagon ▓ **Predicted reliability:** ○ **Owner satisfaction:** ○ The Taurus and similar Mercury Sable deliver fine all-round performance. The four-speed automatic shifts smoothly. The Taurus handles well in normal driving but sluggishly in hard turns. The optional power seat comfortably accommodates drivers of nearly any size. The rear seat is roomy for two six-footers, adequate for three adults. The interior is quiet except for wind noise. Most of the controls are well designed. The optional automatic climate-control system works well. **Last full report: March '93 Fax: 7948**

FORD TAURUS SHO *Mid-sized car over $25,000* RECOMMENDED

▓ **Trim lines:** None ▓ **Body style:** 4-door ▓ **Predicted reliability:** NA **Owner satisfaction:** NA ▓ This high-performance version has a personality that is totally different from that of the sedate plain Taurus sedan. A very powerful V6 made by Yamaha accelerates impressively. The firm suspension provides responsive handling—though not quite as crisp and responsive as that of most BMW models and the Chrysler Concorde/Dodge Intrepid/Eagle Vision triplets. **Last full report: May '93 Fax: 7914**

FORD TEMPO *Compact car under $20,000*

■ **Trim lines:** GL, LX ■ **Body style:** 2-door, 4-door ■ **Predicted reliability:** ● **Owner satisfaction:** ◔ The Tempo and similar Mercury Topaz do everything adequately and nothing very well. This pair will be replaced in 1995 by the new Ford Contour and Mercury Mystique. Acceleration is leisurely; the automatic transmission shifts smoothly. The steering is slow and the body leans considerably in tight turns, although handling remains predictable. The driving position is fine for most physiques. The front seats offer good support, but the front passenger's toe space is skimpy. The rear-seat cushion is low and short. **Last full report: May '91 Fax: 7969**

FORD THUNDERBIRD *Mid-sized car under $25,000*

■ **Trim lines:** LX, SC ■ **Body style:** 2-door ■ **Predicted reliability:** ○ **Owner satisfaction:** ○ The Thunderbird and similar Mercury Cougar have received their first significant changes since 1989—exterior freshening and a new interior. Expect a decent ride, particularly for front-seat occupants, but fairly clumsy handling. The optional new 4.6-liter V8 develops about the same power as the old 5.0-liter V8 but is more refined and fuel-efficient. Standard equipment includes a wealth of power accessories such as air-conditioning, power windows, and power door locks. The old, awkward motorized safety belts are gone. **Last full report: — Fax: —**

FORD WINDSTAR *Minivan*

■ **Trim lines:** GL, LX ■ **Body style:** minivan ■ **Predicted reliability:** New **Owner satisfaction:** New ■ This front-wheel-drive minivan is lower slung and more carlike than the Ford Aerostar that it replaces. Unlike the Aerostar, the Windstar doesn't offer four-wheel drive. Its engine is the Ford Taurus's basic 3.8-liter V6. The Windstar is considerably roomier than the Mercury Villager/Nissan Quest twins, and even a bit roomier than the Plymouth Grand Voyager/Dodge Grand Caravan twins. The nicely designed interior has easy-to-reach controls and versatile rear seating. The third seat folds to increase cargo room. **Last full report: — Fax: —**

GEO METRO *Small car*

■ **Trim lines:** XFi, Standard ■ **Body styles:** 2-door hatchback, 4-door hatchback ■ **Predicted reliability:** ○ **Owner satisfaction:** ◔ This is not a car for freeway cruising. It feels zippy around town, but its small three-cylinder engine and cramped interior bode ill for long trips. The Metro is similar to, but cruder than, the Suzuki Swift, another inexpensive little runabout. Its pinchpenny practicality makes it popular with rental fleets. The four-door hatchback is the more practical version. The Metro will be redesigned for 1995. **Last full report: — Fax: —**

GEO PRIZM *Small car*   RECOMMENDED

■ **Trim lines:** Base, LSi ■ **Body style:** 4-door ■ **Predicted reliability:** ◑ **Owner satisfaction:** ◔ This high-rated model and the Toyota Corolla share powertrains, platform, and many body parts, but the Prizm has a firmer ride and sportier handling. Choose the 1.8-liter Four over the 1.6-liter Four, and the five-speed manual transmission over the automatic. The steering responds crisply, but backing off the accelerator in a hard turn can make the tail wag. Stops are quite short. The driving position is a bit cramped, and the optional sun roof robs lots of head room. The climate-control system works well. Most controls are easy to use, and the gauges are clear. The split rear seatback can be folded. **Last full report: Aug. '93 Fax: 7302**

GEO TRACKER *Sport-utility vehicle*

▓ **Trim lines:** Base, LSi ▓ **Body styles:** 2-door wagon, convertible ▓ **Predicted reliability:** ◒ **Owner satisfaction:** ○ This small, two-door, Jeep-like runabout is Geo's version of the Suzuki Sidekick. (If you want four doors, you have to buy the Sidekick.) The Tracker comes with two- or four-wheel drive. You can add optional fold-and-stow rear seats in the small cargo area behind the front seats. The hardtop version offers better weather protection than the convertible, at the expense of losing the open-air experience. The Tracker may be okay for running errands, but not for long trips. **Last full report: — Fax: —**

HONDA ACCORD *Mid-sized car under $25,000*   RECOMMENDED

▓ **Trim lines:** DX, LX, EX ▓ **Body styles:** 2-door, 4-door, 4-door wagon ▓ **Predicted reliability:** ● **Owner satisfaction:** New ▓ A complete redesign this year has made this fine model even better. The new Accord is a bit larger inside. We recommend the high-line EX version, which comes with a potent 2.2-liter "VTEC" Four that varies its valve timing to improve both power and fuel economy. The four-speed automatic transmission shifts smoothly; uphill, a "grade logic" feature prevents hunting between gears. Nimble handling and quick steering add to driver confidence. The suspension controls the ride nicely, and the seats offer good support. Noise is minimal. **Last full report: Jan. '94 Fax: 9392**

HONDA CIVIC *Small car*   RECOMMENDED

▓ **Trim lines:** CX, DX, VX, LX, Si, EX ▓ **Body styles:** 2-door, 2-door hatchback, 4-door ▓ **Predicted reliability:** ● **Owner satisfaction:** ○ Perennially one of our favorite small cars, the Civic feels peppy with the basic Four, even peppier with the "VTEC" Four. The optional four-speed automatic transmission sometimes shifts annoyingly back and forth uphill. The ride is firm on smooth roads, active on rough roads, and fairly noisy. Handling is a bit twitchy in abrupt maneuvers. Stops are short and straight. Front seating is low but comfortable. Two tall or three average-sized adults can fit in the rear. The displays are clear; the controls are nice except for tiny horn buttons. The climate-control system works well. **Last full report: May '92 Fax: 7397**

HONDA CIVIC DEL SOL *Sporty car under $25,000*

▓ **Trim lines:** S, Si, VTEC ▓ **Body style:** 2-door ▓ **Predicted reliability:** ◒ **Owner satisfaction:** NA ▓ Despite its detachable roof panel, the del Sol is no sports car. Think of it as a two-seat economy car. The base S version is peppy; the Si, faster; the VTEC, faster still. The Si's front end plowed a bit and the tail tended to slide out somewhat at our track. The ride is busy, and the body flexes and creaks on most roads. Braking is mediocre; too bad antilock brakes aren't available. Low seats and wide rear roof pillars create serious blind spots for the driver. Tall drivers will find plenty of room. The trunk is impressive, even with the roof panel stowed inside. **Last full report: Oct. '93 Fax: 7341**

HONDA PASSPORT *Sport-utility vehicle*

▓ **Trim lines:** DX, LX, EX ▓ **Body style:** 4-door wagon ▓ **Predicted reliability:** New **Owner satisfaction:** New ▓ Honda took a shortcut into the sport-utility market by simply rebadging an existing SUV, the Isuzu Rodeo. Both the Passport and Rodeo are made in Indiana. They feel more like station wagons than high, boxy trucks. Expect generous room for passengers, modest room for cargo, and a stiff ride. Skip the base Four in favor of the smooth 3.2-liter V6. You might as well choose the optional four-wheel drive as well; we see no point in enduring the discomforts of an SUV without that useful feature. **Last full report: July '94 Fax: 7789**

HONDA PRELUDE *Sporty car under $25,000*　　　　　**RECOMMENDED**

■ **Trim lines:** S, Si, Si 4WS, VTEC ■ **Body style:** 2-door ■ **Predicted reliability:** ◕ **Owner satisfaction:** ○ The VTEC engine is potent, but even the Si version feels punchy. The five-speed manual transmission shifts precisely, but depressing the clutch pedal requires a stretch. The steering feels nicely weighted and responsive, and the car handles well. Braking is respectable but not outstanding. The ride is jiggly, though well controlled on rough pavement, and quiet for a sporty car. The front seats are firm and comfortable, and large side bolsters cradle occupants during hard cornering. The rear seat is more decorative than functional. The layout of the controls and displays is haphazard. **Last full report: Jan. '93 Fax: 7936**

HYUNDAI ELANTRA *Small car*

■ **Trim lines:** Base, GLS ■ **Body style:** 4-door ■ **Predicted reliability:** ● **Owner satisfaction:** NA ■ This Korean-made model represents a small step up from the uninspired Hyundai Excel. It needs several more steps. The 1.6-liter Four is noisy and feels flat. The optional 1.8-liter Four is more powerful. The car handles well enough on smooth roads, but the suspension crashes and bangs on bumps that other cars take in stride. The front seats offer good all-round support, and the driver can see out well. The rear holds two tall passengers easily and accepts three average-sized adults in a pinch. Some switches are hard to operate, and the heater works well only on its highest and noisiest setting. **Last full report: May '92 Fax: 7397**

HYUNDAI EXCEL *Small car*

■ **Trim lines:** Base, GS ■ **Body styles:** 2-door hatchback, 4-door ■ **Predicted reliability:** ⊖ **Owner satisfaction:** NA ■ This model has changed little in the past few years; it's still one of the cheapest cars available, in the worst sense. Its good fuel economy and low price don't make up for its weak acceleration, crude handling, and subpar ride. Hyundai's unusual warranty pays for virtually all maintenance for the first two years, but the Excel has a poor reliability record. Replaced by the Accent in 1995. **Last full report: — Fax: —**

HYUNDAI SCOUPE *Sporty car under $25,000*

■ **Trim lines:** Base, LS, Turbo ■ **Body style:** 2-door ■ **Predicted reliability:** NA **Owner satisfaction:** NA ■ The Scoupe represents the low-budget act in the sporty-car arena, a basic car with trendy styling but a crude chassis. The high-trim-line Turbo version should at least provide peppy acceleration. Otherwise, the Scoupe is a modest all-round performer. The LS version comes with a reasonable level of standard equipment, and all versions offer adequate roominess in the front seats. The problem is, a sporty car should be fun to drive, and the Scoupe isn't. **Last full report: — Fax: —**

HYUNDAI SONATA *Mid-sized car under $25,000*

■ **Trim lines:** Base, GL, GL V6, GLS ■ **Body style:** 4-door ■ **Predicted reliability:** New **Owner satisfaction:** New ■ Hyundai models have competed well in price, but not much else. The previous Sonata has had a very poor reliability record. The latest one, introduced as a 1995 model, is larger in nearly every dimension. It's one inch longer than the Honda Accord, but still smaller than such competitors as the Toyota Camry. The standard engine, a 2.0-liter Four, is a smidgen more powerful than last year's. A 3.0-liter V6 is optional.   **Last full report: —   Fax: —**

INFINITI G20 *Compact car over $20,000*   RECOMMENDED

▓ **Trim lines:** G20, G20t ▓ **Body style:** 4-door ▓ **Predicted reliability:** ◕ **Owner satisfaction:** ◓ This "Japanese BMW" emphasizes performance without giving up much in luxury. The Four is powerful and economical. The optional four-speed automatic shifts smoothly except during hard acceleration. The car feels nimble and handles well. The front seats give good support, and accommodates all but the tallest drivers. The rear seat can hold two six-footers or three average-sized adults. The ride is firm but never punishing. Controls and displays are excellent, the climate-control system powerful. The trunk is roomy. **Last full report: Nov. '94 Fax: 9923**

INFINITI J30 *Mid-sized car over $25,000*   RECOMMENDED

▓ **Trim lines:** J30, J30t ▓ **Body style:** 4-door ▓ **Predicted reliability:** ◕ **Owner satisfaction:** NA ▓ This model is for people who want near-absolute isolation from the road. It's also for people who won't use the tight rear seat often and who don't need much trunk space. Acceleration is responsive, and the four-speed automatic shifts smoothly. The rear tires break loose fairly easily on slippery roads. Controlling tail wag is tricky in abrupt maneuvers. Stops are short and straight. The front seats provide exceptional comfort, and power adjustments can accommodate all but the tallest driver. The automatic climate-control system works very well. The major controls and displays are nicely designed.   **Last full report: May '93 Fax: 7914**

INFINITI Q45 *Luxury car*   RECOMMENDED

▓ **Trim lines:** Base, Q45t, Q45a ▓ **Body style:** 4-door ▓ **Predicted reliability:** ◓ **Owner satisfaction:** ○ The original Q45 scored points for its potent acceleration and superb handling. The later Q45 feels more like the Lexus LS400; performance is blunted in favor of a refined ride. Though too big to be agile, this rear-wheel-drive model grips the road well. The active-suspension version soaks up bumps, but the ride is fine even with the conventional suspension. Little noise penetrates the cabin. The front seats offer excellent though firm support. Adjustments accommodate just about any driver. The rear is comfortable for two but not three. Controls and displays are generally well designed; the trunk is large.   **Last full report: Nov. '93 Fax: 7351**

ISUZU AMIGO *Sport-utility vehicle*

▓ **Trim lines:** S, XS ▓ **Body style:** convertible ▓ **Predicted reliability:** NA **Owner satisfaction:** NA ▓ Think of it as a beach buggy with rear seats, a flashy runabout for the singles who inhabit beer commercials. Part pickup truck and part sport-utility vehicle, it lacks the utility of most pickups and the large enclosed cargo area of most SUVs. A removable canvas partial top lets two rear passengers (or cargo) face the elements. At least, with its wide stance, the Amigo should handle more stably than many other small SUVs. It comes with two- or four-wheel drive.   **Last full report: —   Fax: —**

ISUZU RODEO *Sport-utility vehicle*

▓ **Trim lines:** S, LS ▓ **Body style:** 4-door wagon ▓ **Predicted reliability:** ● **Owner satisfaction:** ◔ The smaller of Isuzu's two conventional sport-utility vehicles, the Rodeo is more like a station wagon than is the high, boxy Isuzu Trooper. It offers generous passenger room and modest cargo room—unless you fold down the split rear seatback. The 3.2-liter V6 is a big improvement over the fuel-guzzling 3.1-liter V6. The optional part-time four-wheel-drive can't be used on dry pavement. The front seats are well padded and high, but leg room is skimpy. The rear seat can hold three with ease. The controls are confusing and awkward. Heating is strong but uneven. **Last full report: July '94 Fax: 7789**

ISUZU TROOPER *Sport-utility vehicle* RECOMMENDED

■ **Trim lines:** S, RS, LS ■ **Body styles:** 2-door wagon, 4-door wagon ■ **Predicted reliability:** ○ **Owner satisfaction:** ○ The Trooper is more civilized than its boxy Trooper II predecessor. The 3.2-liter V6 in the LS version can't push the heavy vehicle along very quickly. The part-time four-wheel drive (standard equipment) isn't suitable for use on dry pavement. Handling is sloppy, and stops are long, with severe nosedive. Comfortable seats partly compensate for a bouncy ride. Tall and short drivers can get comfortable behind the wheel. The rear seat is designed for three but comfortably holds only two. The climate-control system is powerful. Most controls are convenient, and the displays are clear. **Last full report: Nov. '92 Fax: 7789**

JAGUAR XJ6 *Luxury car*

■ **Trim lines:** Base, Vanden Plas ■ **Body style:** 4-door ■ **Predicted reliability:** NA **Owner satisfaction:** NA ■ Jaguar keeps perfecting antiquated designs. The rear-wheel-drive XJ6's Six is smooth and powerful. Handling is crisp, the ride well mannered. Except for the wind, little noise intrudes. The chaotic control layout requires a strong tolerance for eccentricity. The front seats are nicely shaped but cramped, and the power adjustment is confusing and awkward. Tall drivers need more leg room. The rear seat comfortably holds three. Jaguars have a history of not holding up well. **Last full report: Nov. '93 Fax: 7351**

JEEP CHEROKEE *Sport-utility vehicle*

■ **Trim lines:** SE, Sport, Country ■ **Body styles:** 2-door wagon, 4-door wagon ■ **Predicted reliability:** ◕ **Owner satisfaction:** ○ The basic Cherokee has changed little in the last decade. It remains a harsh-riding vehicle with lots of cargo room and narrow seats that comfortably accommodate only slender people. The four-cylinder engine is sluggish; you're better off with the strong Six. The four-speed automatic shifts smoothly. Four-wheel drive is available. The Cherokee handles well in normal driving, though it rides stiffly and noisily. The air-conditioner is powerful, but the heater could be better. So could the controls and displays **Last full report: Sept. '91 Fax: 7976**

JEEP GRAND CHEROKEE *Sport-utility vehicle*

■ **Trim lines:** SE, Laredo, Limited ■ **Body style:** 4-door wagon ■ **Predicted reliability:** ● **Owner satisfaction:** NA ■ The upscale Grand Cherokee is vastly different from the plain Cherokee. Though it scored highest of any sport-utility vehicle we've tested, its reliability in its first year has been dismal. It comes with rear- and four-wheel drive. The Six accelerates well, the V8 even better. The four-speed automatic shifts smoothly. Handling is carlike, but the Jeep rocks annoyingly on bumps. The driving position suits both tall and short people. Seating is comfortable; three fit easily in back. The gauges are clear, and most controls are logical. The climate-control system is powerful. **Last full report: Nov. '92 Fax: 7789**

JEEP WRANGLER *Sport-utility vehicle*

▨ **Trim lines:** S, SE, Sport, Sahara, Renegade ▨ **Body style:** convertible ▨ **Predicted reliability:** ● **Owner satisfaction:** NA ▨ This is the closest surviving descendant of the old World War II Jeep, the seed that sprouted the entire sport-utility craze. It's the smallest, least expensive, and crudest Jeep. Nevertheless, its popularity with the off-road set endures. A basic four-wheel-drive vehicle with a hard, noisy ride and primitive handling, the Wrangler lives on because of its reputation for rugged durability in the wilds. If you must buy one, opt for the Six and antilock brakes. **Last full report: — Fax: —**

LEXUS ES300 *Mid-sized car over $25,000* RECOMMENDED

▨ **Trim lines:** None ▨ **Body style:** 4-door ▨ **Predicted reliability:** ● **Owner satisfaction:** ◓ This sophisticated model feels much like the bigger Lexus LS400, though sportier. It shares its engine, driveline, and chassis with the Toyota Camry V6, which costs thousands less—and which scored virtually the same in our tests. The ES300 accelerates powerfully, rides smoothly and very quietly, and offers excellent controls and displays. The four-speed automatic shifts imperceptibly. Emergency handling inspires confidence, and stops are short and straight. The front seats offer good support, and a multitude of adjustments allows everyone to find a comfortable driving position. The rear seat is roomy for three, and the trunk is large. **Last full report: Feb. '92 Fax: 7345**

LEXUS GS300 *Luxury car* RECOMMENDED

▨ **Trim lines:** None ▨ **Body style:** 4-door ▨ **Predicted reliability:** ● **Owner satisfaction:** NA ▨ This newest member of Toyota's luxury Lexus line nestles in size and price between the entry-level Lexus ES300 and the top-of-the-line Lexus LS400 sedan. The GS300 targets the sporty-sedan market, where it competes with the likes of the BMW 5-Series, Mercedes-Benz E-Class, and Saab 9000. Accommodations are top-notch, but the trunk is relatively small. This rear-wheel-drive model is powered by a detuned version of the six-cylinder engine used in the Lexus SC300 coupe. **Last full report: May '94 Fax: 7732**

LEXUS LS400 *Luxury car* RECOMMENDED

▨ **Trim lines:** None ▨ **Body style:** 4-door ▨ **Predicted reliability:** ● **Owner satisfaction:** ○ The LS400 aims to be one of the world's best luxury sedans, and it succeeds. It combines a sophisticated, powerful V8 with a lush interior. Not a driver's car, this rear-wheel-drive cruiser stresses isolation from the world outside. Virtually everything is electronically controlled. The four-speed automatic shifts exceptionally smoothly. The steering feels light, almost numb; emergency handling is sure-footed but not quick. Expect a quiet, unruffled ride. The cabin offers excellent front seating, with multiple adjustments that fit nearly any driver. Three can fit comfortably in the rear. Controls and displays are exceptionally well designed. **Last full report: Nov. '93 Fax: 7351**

LEXUS SC400/SC300 *Luxury car* RECOMMENDED

▨ **Trim lines:** None ▨ **Body style:** 2-door ▨ **Predicted reliability:** ● **Owner satisfaction:** ◓ This luxury-coupe version of the LS400 sedan delivers plenty of power to its rear wheels, and it handles winding roads as nimbly as a fine sports car. Traction control minimizes wheel spin. The firm suspension soaks up bumps without fuss. The front seats offer fine accommodation, but leave the rear uninhabited. The luminescent displays are excellent, but some secondary controls are awkwardly placed. The automatic climate-control system is superb. The trunk is small. The SC300's spirited Six isn't as smooth as the V8, but the car costs thousands less.

Last full report: July '93   Fax: 9325

LINCOLN CONTINENTAL *Large car* RECOMMENDED

■ **Trim lines:** Executive, Signature ■ **Body style:** 4-door ■ **Predicted reliability:** ○ **Owner satisfaction:** ○   The Continental is built on the Ford Taurus/Mercury Sable platform; next year will see a complete redesign on a new platform. No one could mistake the V6 for a V8; acceleration is leisurely. Last time we tested a Continental, a few years ago, we found the handling and steering a little sluggish and sloppy. But this year's suspension modifications may improve matters some. The spacious interior holds six with ease, and the cabin is very quiet. The trunk is huge.   **Last full report: —   Fax: —**

LINCOLN MARK VIII *Mid-sized car over $25,000* RECOMMENDED

■ **Trim lines:** None ■ **Body style:** 2-door ■ **Predicted reliability:** ◕ **Owner satisfaction:** NA ■ This rear-wheel-drive luxury coupe's strong point is a ride as smooth as any you'll find. Sophisticated features include a powerful aluminum V8, electronically controlled powertrain, and fully independent suspension with air cushions instead of springs. The traction control works only at low speeds. The Mark VIII maneuvers with surprising agility for such a large car. The front seats, each with power adjustment, offer good, firm support. Rear seating is cramped. The powerful automatic climate-control system is quiet, though a bit slow to start. Most controls are easy to see and reach, but the radio is needlessly complicated.

Last full report: July '93   Fax: 9325

LINCOLN TOWN CAR *Large car over $25,000*

■ **Trim lines:** Executive, Signature, Cartier, ■ **Body style:** 4-door ■ **Predicted reliability:** ○ **Owner satisfaction:** ◕ Despite its sophisticated V8 and full complement of safety features, the Town Car maintains the hoary tradition of domestic luxury turnpike cruisers. It comes with a full frame, rear-wheel drive, and a panoply of electronic gadgets and convenience features. Expect a soft, quiet ride and seating for six. To tame the Town Car's tendency to wallow on bad roads, choose the Ride Control package. A dual-exhaust system, made standard for 1994, has added significant power.   **Last full report: —   Fax: —**

MAZDA 323 *Small car*

■ **Trim lines:** None ■ **Body style:** 2-door hatchback ■ **Predicted reliability:** ● **Owner satisfaction:** ○ This basic little two-door hatchback is nearing the end of its life as Mazda's entry-level model in the shrinking small-car market, overtaken by the slightly larger and more powerful four-door Mazda Protegé sedan. The 323 offers a roomy interior for a small car, plus a fold-down rear seat that further expands the trunk space. This model lacks antilock brakes and air bags.   **Last full report: —   Fax: —**

MAZDA 626 *Compact car under $20,000* RECOMMENDED

■ **Trim lines:** DX, LX, ES ■ **Body style:** 4-door ■ **Predicted reliability:** ○ **Owner satisfaction:** ○ The 626 has much to recommend it. It comes with either an adequate Four or a powerful

V6. The optional four-speed automatic, recently improved, works well with either engine. The mid-line LX offers more value than the top-line ES. The 626 handles well; despite lots of body lean, its nimble handling and quick steering give the driver confidence. Expect a comfortable ride on most roads, thanks in part to the nicely shaped front seats. The rear seat can hold three. The controls are nicely laid out except for small, hard-to-find horn buttons. The split rear seatback can be folded. **Last full report: Jan. '94 Fax: 9392**

MAZDA 929 *Mid-sized car over $25,000*   RECOMMENDED

■ **Trim lines:** None ■ **Body style:** 4-door ■ **Predicted reliability:** ○ **Owner satisfaction:** ◒
The luxurious 929 retains its traditional rear-wheel drive, but all else is state of the art. The V6 takes off aggressively from a standstill. The four-speed automatic shifts very smoothly. Handling is smooth and steady in normal driving, queasy during hard cornering. The brakes perform admirably. The car rides very quietly and comfortably, even with a full load. The front seats could use more side support. A height adjustment assures a good view even for short drivers; tall drivers may find the accelerator too close. The rear is comfortable for two, much less so for three. Most controls and displays work well, as does the climate-control system. **Last full report: Aug. '92 Fax: 7746**

MAZDA MILLENIA *Mid-sized car over $25,000*

■ **Trim lines:** Base, S ■ **Body style:** 4-door ■ **Predicted reliability:** New **Owner satisfaction:** New ■ In size and price, this near-luxury model fits between Mazda's 626 and 929 sedans. New this year, the 1995 Millenia was originally designed as an entry-level model in a luxury line called Amati, which Mazda has aborted. The Millenia offers all the upscale features one expects in a car of this class: leather upholstery, sun roof, and power everything. But this model breaks no new technological ground except in its high-line S version, whose "Miller cycle" engine cleverly varies the valve timing for high power and high fuel economy. **Last full report: — Fax: —**

MAZDA MPV *Minivan*

■ **Trim lines:** 2.6L, 3.0L, 4WD ■ **Body style:** minivan ■ **Predicted reliability:** ○ **Owner satisfaction:** ○ Braking and ride are below par, handling is tail-happy during abrupt maneuvers, and cargo space is limited. Optional four-wheel drive improves handling somewhat. The V6 accelerates decently; the four-speed automatic sometimes bumps into gear. An optional load-leveling system smooths the rough ride somewhat. The front seats are comfortable but need more side support. The middle seats are adequate for two; the rear bench is very tight for three. The instruments are clear, but some controls are annoying. The climate-control system works well—especially with the optional rear air-conditioner. **Last full report: Oct. '92 Fax: 7766**

MAZDA MX-3 *Sporty car under $25,000*

■ **Trim lines:** Base, GS ■ **Body style:** 2-door hatchback ■ **Predicted reliability:** NA **Owner satisfaction:** ○ This is a small, agile coupe. The V6 version is quicker than the Four (discontinued for '95), but no match for, say, the Saturn SC. Steering is quick and accurate, though not strong on feel, and the tires grip well. But that edge in handling comes at the expense of a stiff and noisy ride. The optional antilock brakes are especially needed in this model. The seats offer plenty of support. A low roof, low seat cushions, and high sills hamper access. The instruments are easy to read, but the controls could be better. The climate-control system is quick and powerful, but distribution is spotty. **Last full report: July '92 Fax: 7734**

MAZDA MX-5 MIATA *Sports car under $25,000* RECOMMENDED

▨ **Trim lines:** None ▨ **Body style:** convertible ▨ **Predicted reliability:** ◉ **Owner satisfaction:** ◕ This rear-wheel-drive two-seater harkens back to the British sports cars of the 1950s and 1960s, with their hard and noisy ride, but the Miata is weathertight and reliable. A peppy Four and a crisp five-speed manual transmission with a short shift pattern enhance the sporty appeal. Nimble handling, precise steering, and powerful brakes add to the fun. Tall people may feel cramped. The exhaust note is music to a car buff's ears, but wind noise is a problem. The trunk is tiny. Most controls are easy to work, the displays are clear, and the climate-control system is capable. **Last full report: Oct. '93 Fax: 7341**

MAZDA MX-6 *Sporty car under $25,000* RECOMMENDED

▨ **Trim lines:** Base, LS ▨ **Body style:** 2-door ▨ **Predicted reliability:** ○ **Owner satisfaction:** NA ▨ This model and the Ford Probe share many mechanical parts. The higher price line of each make is a step up in performance from the base four-cylinder version. The V6 accelerates with authority. Both models handle very smoothly and predictably; the MX-6 rides a bit more comfortably, and the Probe handles a bit more crisply. The front seats are comfortable, but reserve the rear seat for packages. Unlike the Probe, which is a hatchback, the MX-6 has a conventional trunk. **Last full report: Jan. '93 Fax: 7936**

MAZDA NAVAJO *Sport-utility vehicle* RECOMMENDED

▨ **Trim lines:** DX, LX ▨ **Body style:** 2-door ▨ **Predicted reliability:** ○ **Owner satisfaction:** NA ▨ The Navajo and Ford Explorer are similar, but the Navajo comes only with two doors. The V6 is adequate, and the four-speed automatic shifts smoothly. The four-wheel drive, without a center differential, is unsuited for dry roads. Handling of our Explorer was ponderous; we recommend the optional limited-slip rear axle and trailer-towing package. Resilient front seats partly make up for a bouncy ride. The rear seat can hold three six-footers. The climate-control system is strong. Most controls are convenient, and the displays are clear. **Last full report: Nov. '92 Fax: 7789**

MAZDA PROTEGE *Small car*

▨ **Trim lines:** DX, LX ▨ **Body style:** 4-door ▨ **Predicted reliability:** ◕ **Owner satisfaction:** ○ This aging model will be replaced in 1995. The 1.8-liter Four delivers responsive performance. The Protegé generally handles well. Comfortable seats somewhat make up for a stiff ride. The rear seat is roomy enough for three adults if they sit up straight. The split rear seatback folds to enlarge the trunk. The controls are uncomplicated, the instruments simple and clear. This model lacks antilock brakes and air bags. Replacement due for 1995. **Last full report: — Fax: —**

MAZDA RX-7 *Sports car over $25,000* RECOMMENDED

▨ **Trim lines:** Base, R2, Touring ▨ **Body style:** 2-door hatchback ▨ **Predicted reliability:** NA **Owner satisfaction:** NA ▨ Cast as a return to the pure, uncompromising sports car, the RX-7 looks and feels the part. Practicality isn't part of the script. The RX-7 is cramped for a pair of average-sized people, pure misery for tall people. A rotary engine, with twin turbochargers driving the rear wheels delivers ferocious acceleration. The five-speed manual transmission feels precise. The brakes are exceptional. The RX-7 is nimble and responsive, but its ride is unusually hard and relentlessly noisy. The cockpit is stark, with practically no storage for odds and ends. The trunk is tiny. **Last full report: Sept. '92 Fax: 7758**

MERCEDES-BENZ C-CLASS *Mid-sized car over $25,000* RECOMMENDED

▦ **Trim lines:** C220, C280 ▦ **Body style:** 4-door ▦ **Predicted reliability:** New **Owner satisfaction:** New ▦ The new Mercedes C-Class replaces the aging 190 series and represents the entry level for this luxury nameplate. As in all Mercedes-Benzes, the drive wheels are in the rear. The two engine choices determine the models' names: the C220 comes with a 2.2-liter Four, the C280 with a 2.8-liter inline Six. You can expect the usual luxuriously appointed interior and full complement of safety features, along with a bit more room than in the old 190. The automatic climate-control system needs constant fiddling. **Last full report: Aug. '94 Fax: 9792**

MERCEDES-BENZ E-CLASS *Luxury car* RECOMMENDED

▦ **Trim lines:** E300 diesel, E320, E420, E500 ▦ **Body styles:** 2-door, 4-door, 4-door wagon, convertible ▦ **Predicted reliability:** ◕ **Owner satisfaction:** ○ E-Class is the new name for the fine Mercedes-Benz 300 series. In price and size, these luxurious four-door sedans represent the middle range of the Mercedes stable. The E320 has a 3.2-liter inline Six, the E420 a 4.2-liter V8. The front styling resembles that of Mercedes' top-of-the-line S-Class cars. E-Class models deliver precise handling, effortless performance, and an excellent ride, and they're loaded with the latest in safety and convenience features. **Last full report: May '94 Fax: 7732**

MERCURY CAPRI *Sporty car under $25,000*

▦ **Trim lines:** Base, XR2 ▦ **Body style:** convertible ▦ **Predicted reliability:** ● **Owner satisfaction:** NA ▦ It's no Mazda Miata, just a Miata wannabe. With a convertible top and vestigial rear seats, the Australian-made Capri seems to be designed to lure young people into a Mercury showroom. It's a tinny little sports car with unimpressive riding and driving qualifications. Handling is mediocre for a sports car; the ride is tiring on expressways and brutal on back roads. The driving position is uncomfortable, especially for tall people, and the rear seats are a bad joke. 1994 is the last year for the Capri. **Last full report: March '91 Fax: 9968**

MERCURY COUGAR *Mid-sized car under $25,000*

▦ **Trim lines:** XR7 ▦ **Body style:** 2-door ▦ **Predicted reliability:** ○ **Owner satisfaction:** ○ This model aims at a slightly higher-scale market than its near twin, the Ford Thunderbird. Its basic design dates back five years, but the latest model brings some modern tweaks, including a revised interior. More important, Mercury has added one of Ford's sophisticated "modular" 4.6-liter V8s. It delivers about as much power as the 5.0-liter V8 it replaces, though it's lighter and more economical. Dual air bags supersede the annoying motorized front safety belts, and lots of power conveniences are standard equipment. **Last full report: — Fax: —**

MERCURY GRAND MARQUIS *Large car under $25,000* RECOMMENDED

▦ **Trim lines:** GS, LS ▦ **Body style:** 4-door ▦ **Predicted reliability:** ○ **Owner satisfaction:** ○ The big Mercury and similar Ford Crown Victoria are among the last big freeway cruisers with a

V8, full frame, and rear-wheel drive. A serene ride, huge trunk, and substantial trailer-towing capability are major advantages. The car accelerates well, and the four-speed automatic shifts very smoothly. Steering response is fairly good. The Preferred Equipment Package 172A and the Handling Package materially improve braking and handling. The front seats lack sufficient padding. The rear offers room for three. The controls are mostly logical.

Last full report: March '94 Fax: 9714

MERCURY SABLE *Mid-sized car under $25,000*   RECOMMENDED

▓ **Trim lines:** GS, LS ▓ **Body styles:** 4-door, 4-door wagon ▓ **Predicted reliability:** ○ **Owner satisfaction:** ○ The Sable and similar Ford Taurus deliver fine all-round performance. The four-speed automatic shifts smoothly. These models handle well in normal driving but run wide in hard turns. The optional heavy-duty suspension improves neither the handling nor the ride. The optional power seat comfortably accommodates drivers of nearly any size. The rear seat is roomy for two six-footers, adequate for three adults. The interior is quiet except for wind noise. Most controls are well designed. The optional automatic climate-control system works well.

Last full report: March '93 Fax: 7948

MERCURY TOPAZ *Compact car under $20,000*

▓ **Trim lines:** GS ▓ **Body styles:** 2-door, 4-door ▓ **Predicted reliability:** ● **Owner satisfaction:** ● The Topaz and similar Ford Tempo do everything adequately and nothing very well. This pair has been replaced by the new Mercury Mystique and Ford Contour. Acceleration is leisurely; the automatic transmission shifts smoothly. The steering is slow and the body leans considerably in tight turns, although handling remains predictable. The driving position is fine for most physiques. The front seats offer good support, but the front passenger's toe space is skimpy. The rear cushion is low and short.   **Last full report: May '91 Fax: 7969**

MERCURY TRACER *Small car*

▓ **Trim lines:** Base, LTS ▓ **Body styles:** 4-door, 4-door wagon ▓ **Predicted reliability:** ○ **Owner satisfaction:** ○ Only the LTS version offers antilock brakes—and without antilock, the Tracer (and similar Ford Escort) stops poorly. The standard 1.9-liter Four provides noisy and lethargic acceleration. A sophisticated 1.8-liter Four in the LTS, though slightly smaller, is more powerful. The basic model handles sluggishly, but the LTS's taut suspension makes the car feel nimble. Front seating is comfortable, and the driver can see out well. The rear seat provides room enough for six-footers, but it isn't very comfortable. **Last full report: Oct. '94 Fax: 9921**

MERCURY VILLAGER *Minivan*   RECOMMENDED

▓ **Trim lines:** GS, LS, Nautica ▓ **Body style:** minivan ▓ **Predicted reliability:** ○ **Owner satisfaction:** NA ▓ The Villager and similar Nissan Quest are our top-rated minivans, though they don't offer the most cargo room. The V6 performs well, and the four-speed automatic generally shifts smoothly. Get the optional trailer-towing package. The ride is quite smooth and quiet, and handling is carlike. An optional heavy-duty suspension helps handling slightly. The brakes work well. The optional power seat accommodates tall and short drivers. The center-row captain's chairs are easier to remove than the standard bench. A few controls are hidden, and the gauges need more contrast. The climate-control system works well.

Last full report: Feb. '93 Fax: 7943

MITSUBISHI 3000 GT *Sports car over $25,000*

▓ **Trim lines:** Base, SL, VR-4 ▓ **Body style:** 2-door hatchback ▓ **Predicted reliability:** ◗ **Owner satisfaction:** NA ▓ In their sportiest form, the 3000 GT and its twin, the Dodge Stealth, are technological tours de force. Price lines range from the base model with front-wheel drive on up to the VR-4, with twin turbos, four-wheel steering, electronically adjustable suspension, and all-wheel drive. Our Stealth R/T Turbo, equivalent to the 3000 GT VR-4, gave good cornering grip, exceptionally short stops, and blazing acceleration. (The 1994 VR-4 is even faster.) The front seats are comfortable. The rear seat is mostly for show. The automatic climate-control system works well. The controls could be a bit easier to use.

Last full report: April '92   Fax: 9377

MITSUBISHI DIAMANTE *Mid-sized car over $25,000*   RECOMMENDED

▓ **Trim lines:** ES, LS ▓ **Body styles:** 4-door, 4-door wagon ▓ **Predicted reliability:** ○ **Owner satisfaction:** ○ Computers control the Diamante's power steering, suspension, brakes, starting traction, cabin temperature, locks, and interior lighting. But other models do very nicely without all that gadgetry. Acceleration is strong only at illegal speeds. The four-speed automatic usually shifts smoothly. Stops are rather long. The Diamante handles smoothly but not nimbly; the tail wags as the tires lose their grip. The ride is well controlled and quiet. The front seats are comfortable; the rear is tight even for two. The semi-automatic climate-control system works well, and the gauges are easy to read.   **Last full report: Feb. '92   Fax: 7345**

MITSUBISHI ECLIPSE *Sporty car under $25,000*

▓ **Trim lines:** Base, GS, GS DOHC, GS Turbo, GSX ▓ **Body style:** 2-door hatchback ▓ **Predicted reliability:** ○ **Owner satisfaction:** ○ The Eclipse and similar Eagle Talon are due for replacement in 1995. The optional turbocharger adds lots of power but hurts fuel economy somewhat. Handling feels responsive and stable. All-wheel drive in the top-line version improves handling. The ride isn't bad for a sporty car, but seating is too low. The rear seat is just about useless. Luggage space is skimpy. The Eclipse is competent overall, but more up-to-date models such as the Ford Probe, Honda Prelude, and Mazda MX-6 have better comfort and convenience features.   **Last full report: Jan. '93   Fax: 7936**

MITSUBISHI EXPO *Small car*

▓ **Trim lines:** Base, AWD ▓ **Body style:** 4-door wagon ▓ **Predicted reliability:** NA **Owner satisfaction:** ◓ This tall wagon with a rear liftgate is in a niche all its own—a hybrid of a van and a sport-utility vehicle. The Expo, entirely different from the smaller Expo LRV, has a fairly long wheelbase and three rows of seats; overall, it's about as long as a mid-sized sedan. Four-wheel drive is an option. To us, the Expo LRV makes more sense; it's a peppy little cargo hauler that's comfortable and economical. Discontinued in 1994.   **Last full report: —   Fax: —**

MITSUBISHI EXPO LRV *Small car*   RECOMMENDED

▓ **Trim lines:** Base, Sport ▓ **Body style:** 3-door wagon ▓ **Predicted reliability:** ○ **Owner satisfaction:** NA ▓ This cross between a small wagon and a very small van. Tall and boxy, it has a high seating position and a single sliding side door. The engine of choice, a 2.4-liter Four, feels lively. The tires squeal, the body leans, and the car plows ahead in tight turns. The LRV rides comfortably and quietly, and it offers much more cargo space than do competing small wagons.

Tall drivers need more leg room. The rear seat is tight for three. The climate-control system works well. The gauges are legible, but the controls could be handier. Discontinued in 1994.

Last full report: Sept. '93 Fax: 7331

MITSUBISHI GALANT *Compact car under $20,000*　　　　RECOMMENDED

▓ **Trim lines:** S, ES, LS, GS ▓ **Body style:** 4-door ▓ **Predicted reliability:** ◖ **Owner satisfaction:** New ▓ This model tested out well, but not as well as the excellent Toyota Camry and Honda Accord. The 1994 redesign slightly enlarged the body and added safety features. Acceleration is lively. The optional four-speed automatic sometimes downshifts when it shouldn't. The Galant handles controllably in tight turns, and the steering provides good road feel. The ride is smooth on good roads, but minor pavement flaws deliver jolts. Some may find the front-seat padding too thin. The rear seat holds three if need be. The gauges and controls are nicely designed. The rear seatback can be folded.　　**Last full report: Jan. '94 Fax: 9392**

MITSUBISHI MIRAGE *Small car*

▓ **Trim lines:** S, ES, LS ▓ **Body styles:** 2-door, 4-door ▓ **Predicted reliability:** NA **Owner satisfaction:** NA ▓ This model is also known as the Dodge Colt, Eagle Summit, and Plymouth Colt. By any name, it's a price leader. The non-antilock brakes are poor so try to get antilock. The ride is uncomfortable. The front seats provide satisfactory support. The rear seat can barely hold two six-footers. Major controls are easy to see and grasp, and the climate-control system works quickly. The split rear seatback can be folded.　　**Last full report: Aug. '93 Fax: 7302**

MITSUBISHI MONTERO *Sport-utility vehicle*

▓ **Trim lines:** LS, SR ▓ **Body style:** 4-door wagon ▓ **Predicted reliability:** NA **Owner satisfaction:** NA ▓ This high and boxy vehicle accelerates sluggishly with the 3.0-liter V6; the 3.5-liter V6 is a better bet. The Montero feels tippy in routine driving. Leave the "Active Trac" system in four-wheel drive to reduce the Montero's tendency to abruptly swing out its tail during hard cornering. The brakes perform adequately. Short drivers can see well over the hood; tall drivers need more leg room. The rear seat provides ample space for two, but not three, six-footers. The climate-control system is quick and powerful. The major controls work well, but the gauges aren't very legible.　　**Last full report: Nov. '92 Fax: 7976**

NISSAN 240SX *Sporty car under $25,000*

▓ **Trim lines:** SE ▓ **Body style:** convertible ▓ **Predicted reliability:** ◖ **Owner satisfaction:** ○ The 240SX has been redesigned for '94. Last year's convertible version of this model has continued into the 1994 model year. Despite a firm and abrupt ride typical of a small car, the 240SX's capable rear-wheel-drive chassis provides fine handling. The 2.4-liter Four offers peppy if noisy acceleration. Full, clear instrumentation complements generally well-designed controls. The firm bucket front seats provide adequate support. As with most small sportsters, the rear seat is best left uninhabited.　　**Last full report: — Fax: —**

NISSAN 300ZX *Sports car over $25,000*　　　　RECOMMENDED

▓ **Trim lines:** Base, with T-Bar, 2+2, Turbo ▓ **Body styles:** 2-door, convertible ▓ **Predicted reliability:** ○ **Owner satisfaction:** NA ▓ This rear-wheel-drive two-seater is everything a sports car should be and it's smooth and easy to drive. The twin-turbo V6 delivers blazing acceleration. The five-speed manual transmission shifts crisply. Handling is near perfect; four-wheel steering makes cornering precise. Stops are short and straight. The electronic suspension offers two settings; both feel stiff. The seats provide good support. The automatic climate-control system works well. Controls are hard to see; the small horn buttons are hard to find quickly. The cargo bay is roomy for a sports car.   **Last full report: Sept. '92   Fax: 7758**

NISSAN ALTIMA *Compact car under $20,000*   RECOMMENDED

■ **Trim lines:** XE, GXE, SE, GLE ■ **Body style:** 4-door ■ **Predicted reliability:** ● **Owner satisfaction:** NA ■ The Altima is not a sporty car. It leans noticeably when cornering, and it plows ahead through hard turns. It accelerates quite quickly, but the engine buzzes and hums. Stops are short. The ride is jittery and busy. Tall drivers will find the cockpit cramped; short drivers should have no problem. The front seats are low and lack thigh support. Rear seating is roomy enough for two tall people; three are a squeeze. The gauges are clear enough; the controls could be better. The GLE's automatic climate-control system works well, and the trunk is quite roomy.   **Last full report: Nov. '94   Fax: 9923**

NISSAN MAXIMA *Mid-sized car under $25,000*   RECOMMENDED

■ **Trim lines:** GXE, SE ■ **Body style:** 4-door ■ **Predicted reliability:** ● **Owner satisfaction:** ◔ The Maxima is a competent and well-rounded sedan. It provides precise handling, sporty acceleration, and a large measure of comfort. Nissan has moved the Maxima upscale to separate it further from the compact Nissan Altima. A 1995 Maxima, due this spring, retains last year's fine powertrain, but its new body resembles Nissan's premium Infiniti Q45.   **Last full report: Aug. '91   Fax: 7975**

NISSAN PATHFINDER *Sport-utility vehicle*   RECOMMENDED

■ **Trim lines:** XE, SE, LE ■ **Body style:** 4-door wagon ■ **Predicted reliability:** ◔ **Owner satisfaction:** ○ This model competes with the Chevrolet S-Blazer, Ford Explorer, and Jeep Grand Cherokee in the crowded SUV market. The Pathfinder rides almost as well as a sedan, and its V6 and optional automatic transmission form a peppy combination. The optional part-time four-wheel-drive system isn't suitable for dry pavement. The Pathfinder handles surprisingly well in normal driving, but it becomes rather sloppy in tight turns. Firm seating provides adequate support front and rear, but you'll find less cargo area here than in many other similar vehicles.   **Last full report: —   Fax: —**

NISSAN QUEST *Minivan*   RECOMMENDED

■ **Trim lines:** XE, GXE ■ **Body style:** minivan ■ **Predicted reliability:** ○ **Owner satisfaction:** NA ■ The Quest and similar Mercury Villager are our top-rated minivans, though they don't offer the most cargo room. The V6 performs well, and the four-speed automatic transmission generally shifts smoothly. The ride is quite smooth and quiet, and handling is carlike. An optional heavy-duty suspension helps handling slightly. The brakes work well. The optional power seat accommodates tall and short drivers. The center-row captain's chairs are easier to remove than the standard bench. A few controls are hidden, and the gauges need more contrast. The climate-control system works well.   **Last full report: Feb. '93   Fax: 7943**

NISSAN SENTRA *Small car*   RECOMMENDED

■ **Trim lines:** E, XE, SE, SE-R, GXE ■ **Body styles:** 2-door, 4-door ■ **Predicted reliability:** ◐
Owner satisfaction: ○ The Sentra offers a smooth and quiet ride and a sensible interior layout.
But the handling is just adequate; during hard cornering, the body leans and the tail wants to
slide out. Antilock brakes are available only in the upscale GXE sedan and sporty SE-R coupe.
The front seats offer good, firm support, but the rear seat is cramped. The controls and displays are logically placed and easy to use. The trunk is generous for a small model, and the
GXE version's split rear seatback can be folded for added luggage space. Replaced by a new
model for 1995.   **Last full report:** — **Fax:** —

OLDSMOBILE ACHIEVA *Compact car under $20,000*

■ **Trim lines:** S, SC, SL ■ **Body styles:** 2-door, 4-door ■ **Predicted reliability:** ○ **Owner satisfaction:** ○ Though introduced in 1992, this design is based on the Chevrolet Corsica, little
changed since 1987. The Achieva, Buick Skylark, and Pontiac Grand Am share many components, but each has a different image. The Achieva seems to woo conservative buyers. The
troublesome and noisy "Quad" Four performs weakly; we prefer the V6. Cornering is slow and
vague. The front seats give good support, but the driving position is low. The rear seat is a bit
more comfortable than the Skylark's and Grand Am's. Displays are clear except for occasional
reflections.   **Last full report: June '92 Fax: 7704**

OLDSMOBILE AURORA *Mid-sized car over $25,000*

■ **Trim lines:** None ■ **Body style:** 4-door ■ **Predicted reliability:** New **Owner satisfaction:**
New ■ The long-awaited Aurora, a 1995 model, borrows a revised form of Cadillac's sophisticated all-aluminum "Northstar" V8 as well. Though the interior isn't particularly roomy, it's very
contemporary. To compete with prestigious models such as the BMW 5-series and the Lexus
ES and GS300, the Aurora has almost every imaginable technological innovation but is too
heavy and feels it.   **Last full report:** — **Fax:** —

OLDSMOBILE BRAVADA *Sport-utility vehicle*

■ **Trim lines:** None ■ **Body style:** 4-door wagon ■ **Predicted reliability:** ○ **Owner satisfaction:** ○ This upscale, four-door version of the Chevrolet S-Blazer is due for redesign for 1996.
It's a trucklike vehicle with a choppy ride. The V6 accelerates well and the four-speed automatic
transmission shifts smoothly. Full-time all-wheel drive is standard. Handling is sloppy but controllable. The driving position is low and too close to the wheel. The front seats offer satisfactory support; the rear has ample room even for tall passengers. The rear seat easily folds flat,
forming a long cargo floor. Unless you choose the optional external spare-tire carrier, cargo
space is limited.   **Last full report: Sept. '91 Fax: 7976**

OLDSMOBILE CUTLASS CIERA *Mid-sized car under $25,000*

■ **Trim lines:** Special Edition, S ■ **Body styles:** 4-door, 4-door wagon ■ **Predicted reliability:**
◐ **Owner satisfaction:** ○ This aging and uninteresting model has one major advantage over
other large and mid-sized cars: reliability. The optional 3.1-liter V6 and four-speed automatic
transmission make a peppier combination than the standard 2.2-liter Four and three-speed
automatic. Don't expect sporty handling or high performance.   **Last full report:** — **Fax:** —

OLDSMOBILE CUTLASS SUPREME *Mid-sized car under $25,000*

▓ **Trim lines:** S, SL ▓ **Body styles:** 2-door, 4-door, convertible ▓ **Predicted reliability:** ○ **Owner satisfaction:** ○ This unexceptional model is similar in spirit to the Buick Regal and Pontiac Grand Prix. The 3.1-liter V6 is satisfactory. The 3.4-liter V6 is stronger but thirstier. The four-speed automatic transmission shifts very smoothly. Handling feels sluggish and sloppy but predictable. The ride is smooth on good roads, but the suspension runs out of travel on bumps. Get the six-way power seat. The heater is a bit slow to warm up. The controls need improvement, and the displays are small. Roomy trunk. **Last full report: Feb. '94 Fax: 7771**

OLDSMOBILE 88 ROYALE *Large car under $25,000*   RECOMMENDED

▓ **Trim lines:** Base, LS, LSS ▓ **Body style:** 4-door ▓ **Predicted reliability:** ○ **Owner satisfaction:** ○ This is a quiet, softly sprung car with sloppy handling. The touring suspension improves handling a bit. The V6 accelerates responsively, and the four-speed automatic transmission shifts extremely smoothly. Seating is comfortable for five, less so for six. The controls are much improved over those of previous models, and the displays are clear. The automatic climate-control system is powerful. The Eighty-Eight, Buick Le Sabre, and Pontiac Bonneville are similar, the Bonneville being the sportiest. The Buick Park Avenue and Oldsmobile Ninety-Eight are longer but no roomier. **Last full report: Jan, '92 Fax: 7307**

OLDSMOBILE 98 REGENCY *Large car over $25,000*

▓ **Trim lines:** Base, Elite ▓ **Body style:** 4-door ▓ **Predicted reliability:** ○ **Owner satisfaction:** ○ This near-twin to the Buick Park Avenue is Oldsmobile's biggest turnpike cruiser. It looks and feels like a traditional old-style luxury sedan, though it has a modern unitized body and front-wheel drive. Cars like this one emphasize a soft ride and a galaxy of power conveniences and luxury appointments. Handling tends to fall toward the sloppy end of the spectrum. **Last full report: — Fax: —**

OLDSMOBILE SILHOUETTE *Minivan*   RECOMMENDED

▓ **Trim lines:** None ▓ **Body style:** minivan ▓ **Predicted reliability:** ○ **Owner satisfaction:** ◒ The plastic-clad Silhouette is competent, overall, as are the similar Chevrolet Lumina and Pontiac Trans Sport. The seven-seat package is versatile; its five modular seats are easy to fold, shift, or remove. A power side door is nice. The 3.1-liter V6 and three-speed automatic transmission accelerate adequately; the 3.8-liter V6 and four-speed automatic do much better. Emergency handling is reasonably controllable. Seating is comfortable in the first two rows; access to the third row is awkward. The ride is comfortable for a van, and the climate-control system is powerful. **Last full report: July '94 Fax: 7789**

PLYMOUTH ACCLAIM *Compact car under $20,000*

▓ **Trim lines:** None ▓ **Body style:** 4-door ▓ **Predicted reliability:** ○ **Owner satisfaction:** ○ This model (and its twin Dodge Spirit) will remain into 1995 for a few months until replaced by new models. The Four vibrates and growls; get the V6. Handling is predictable but not crisp in abrupt maneuvers. Front seating is fairly comfortable, though short drivers need the power-seat option. Toe space is tight for the front passenger. Two tall people fit in the rear, but a center passenger has too little leg room. The motorized right front safety belt is new. The heater works slowly; the controls and displays could be better. **Last full report: March '92 Fax: 7973**

PLYMOUTH COLT *Small car*

■ **Trim lines:** Base, GL ■ **Body styles:** 2-door, 4-door ■ **Predicted reliability:** NA **Owner satisfaction:** NA ■ This model is also known as the Dodge Colt, Eagle Summit, and Mitsubishi Mirage. By any name, it's a price leader, destined for oblivion in 1995. Most cars on dealers' lots will be short on equipment such as antilock brakes—too bad, since the non-antilock brakes are poor. The car rides uncomfortably. The front seats provide satisfactory support. The rear seat can barely hold two six-footers. Major controls are easy to see and grasp, and the climate-control system works quickly. The split rear seatback can be folded.

Last full report: Aug. '93 Fax: 7302

PLYMOUTH COLT VISTA WAGON *Small car*   RECOMMENDED

■ **Trim lines:** Base, SE, AWD ■ **Body style:** 3-door wagon ■ **Predicted reliability:** ○ **Owner satisfaction:** NA ■ This cross between a small wagon and a very small van also sells as the Eagle Summit Wagon and Mitsubishi Expo LRV. Tall and boxy, it has high seating and a sliding side door. The engine of choice, a 2.4-liter Four, feels lively. The tires squeal, the body leans, and the car plows ahead in tight turns. The ride is comfortable and quiet, and there's much more cargo space than in competing small wagons. Tall drivers need more leg room. The rear seat is roomy for two, tight for three. The climate-control system works well. The gauges are legible, but the controls could be handier. Due for replacement in 1995.

Last full report: Sept. '93   Fax: 7331

PLYMOUTH GRAND VOYAGER *Minivan*

■ **Trim lines:** Base, SE, LE ■ **Body style:** minivan ■ **Predicted reliability:** ◒ **Owner satisfaction:** ○ Chrysler Corp.'s minivans continue to hold their own against tough new competition. This model and similar Chrysler Town & Country and Dodge Grand Caravan are extended versions of the plain Caravan and Voyager. Handling is sluggish, but stops are short. Four-wheel drive is available. The van rides pleasantly on smooth roads but shudders over bumps. Front seats are very comfortable. The rearmost seat is tight for three. The climate-control system is strong. Displays are clear, and controls are improved over those in previous models. The plain, shorter-bodied Dodge Caravan and Plymouth Voyager have been more reliable.

Last full report: Oct. '92   Fax: 7766

PLYMOUTH NEON *Small car*

■ **Trim lines:** Base, Highline, Sport ■ **Body style:** 4-door ■ **Predicted reliability:** New **Owner satisfaction:** New ■ The new Dodge/Plymouth Neon twins are among the very few small models to be designed and made entirely in the U.S. since Detroit all but abandoned the economy-car market to the imports years ago. Tagged as a 1995 model, it's a smidgen larger than such competitors as the Honda Civic, Toyota Corolla, and Ford Escort, and the 2.0-liter Four accelerates aggressively but noisily. It features standard-equipment dual air bags. The rear seatbacks fold down to expand cargo space. **Last full report: Oct. '94 Fax: 9921**

PLYMOUTH VOYAGER *Minivan*   RECOMMENDED

■ **Trim lines:** Base, SE, LE, LX ■ **Body style:** minivan ■ **Predicted reliability:** ○ **Owner satisfaction:** ○ The Voyager/Dodge Caravan twins were our benchmark minivans for years, and they're still competitive. The V6 is strong. The automatic transmission sometimes shifts too often; a five-speed manual is available with the Four. The van handles sluggishly; an optional, stiffer suspension helps somewhat. The front seats are comfortable, and the climate-control system is powerful. The displays are clear, but minor controls could be better. The longer Chrysler Town & Country, Dodge Grand Caravan, and Plymouth Grand Voyager have been less reliable. **Last full report: July '94 Fax: 7789**

PONTIAC BONNEVILLE *Large car under $25,000* RECOMMENDED

■ **Trim lines:** SE, SSE, SSEi ■ **Body style:** 4-door ■ **Predicted reliability:** ○ **Owner satisfaction:** ○ The Bonneville offers a tight, almost European feel, much better than that of the somewhat similar Buick Le Sabre and Oldsmobile Eighty-Eight Royale. The firm suspension and touring tires markedly improve handling and ride. Leave the supercharged engine to the hotrodders. The four-speed automatic transmission shifts responsively and very smoothly. Front seating is very comfortable; the rear is fine for two, ok for three. The automatic climate-control system works effectively, and the gauges are clear. **Last full report: March '94 Fax: 9714**

PONTIAC FIREBIRD *Sporty car under $25,000*

■ **Trim lines:** Base, Formula, Trans Am, Trans Am GT ■ **Body styles:** 2-door hatchback, convertible ■ **Predicted reliability:** NA **Owner satisfaction:** NA ■ The Firebird and its cousin, the Chevrolet Camaro, are rear-wheel-drive muscle cars. The Formula and Trans Am versions use a slightly detuned version of the potent V8 that powers the Chevrolet Corvette. A six-speed manual transmission is standard; a four-speed automatic is optional, as is traction control. The V8's effortless thrust makes the V6 seem sluggish. The ride is decent, the handling precise but not nimble. The V8's wider tires grip better. Braking is competent. The front bucket seats cradle their occupants firmly. The rear seat is mostly for show. **Last full report: Oct. '93 Fax: 7341**

PONTIAC GRAND AM *Compact car under $20,000*

■ **Trim lines:** SE, GT ■ **Body styles:** 2-door, 4-door ■ **Predicted reliability:** ○ **Owner satisfaction:** ○ Though introduced in 1992, this design is based on the Chevrolet Corsica, little changed since 1987. The Grand Am, Buick Skylark, and Olds Achieva share many components, but each has a different image. The flashy Grand Am aims at young buyers. Handling feels a bit clumsy, and the front end bounces disconcertingly on rough roads. The front seats give good support despite thin padding. The rear feels cramped. Heating and cooling are a bit slow but competent. Displays are easy on the eyes, but minor controls are clunky or poorly arranged. **Last full report: June '93 Fax: 9317**

PONTIAC GRAND PRIX *Mid-sized car under $25,000* RECOMMENDED

■ **Trim lines:** SE, GTP, GT ■ **Body styles:** 2-door, 4-door ■ **Predicted reliability:** ○ **Owner satisfaction:** ○ This aging model shares major components with the Buick Regal and Oldsmobile Cutlass Supreme. Of the three, only the Pontiac has dual air bags. The sedan has conventional front safety belts rather than awkward door-mounted ones. The 3.4-liter V6 is peppier than the 3.1-liter V6, but thirstier. The four-speed automatic transmission shifts smoothly. The steering is quick. The ride is firm on smooth roads, jolting on poor roads. The front seats look more comfortable than they are; the rear is roomy enough to hold three fairly painlessly. The gauges are logically arranged and easy to read. **Last full report: Feb. '94 Fax: 7771**

PONTIAC SUNBIRD *Compact car under $20,000*

■ **Trim lines:** LE, SE ■ **Body styles:** 2-door, 4-door, convertible ■ **Predicted reliability:** ● **Owner satisfaction:** NA ■ Why this little sedan and its cousin, the Chevrolet Cavalier, remain among GM's top sellers is a mystery. The Four accelerates slowly and noisily; the V6 is a better choice. The automatic transmission occasionally hesitates and then bumps into gear. Stops are reasonably short, but the brakes fade more than we like in repeated stops. Expect good handling, though not a comfortable ride. The front seats are hard and low, the rear seat, tight. Its replacement, the Sunfire, is due for 1995. **Last full report: May '91 Fax: 7969**

PONTIAC TRANS SPORT *Minivan* RECOMMENDED

■ **Trim lines:** SE ■ **Body style:** minivan ■ **Predicted reliability:** ○ **Owner satisfaction:** ○ The plastic-clad Trans Sport is competent, overall, as are the similar Chevrolet Lumina and Oldsmobile Silhouette. The seven-seat package is versatile; its five modular seats are easy to fold, shift, or remove. A power side door is nice. The 3.1-liter V6 and three-speed automatic transmission accelerate adequately; the 3.8-liter V6 and four-speed automatic do much better. Emergency handling is reasonably controllable. Seating is comfortable in the first two rows; access to the third row is awkward. The ride is comfortable for a van, and the climate-control system is powerful. **Last full report: July '94 Fax: 7789**

SAAB 900 *Compact car over $20,000* RECOMMENDED

■ **Trim lines:** S, SE ■ **Body styles:** 2-door hatchback, 4-door hatchback, convertible ■ **Predicted reliability:** New **Owner satisfaction:** New ■ This model, redesigned for this year, is more refined and looks much like the old Saab 900. Saabs have always had a unique personality, not to mention quirky touches like an ignition lock located on the floor rather than on the steering column. You can expect good handling, good performance, a large and versatile cargo area, and a full complement of safety features from this sturdy, solid car. Besides the standard-equipment 2.3-liter Four and optional 2.0-liter turbocharged Four, Saab offers a 2.5-liter V6. **Last full report: Aug. '94 Fax: 9792**

SAAB 9000 *Mid-sized car over $25,000* RECOMMENDED

■ **Trim lines:** CS, CSE, CDE, Aero ■ **Body styles:** 4-door, 4-door hatchback ■ **Predicted reliability:** ● **Owner satisfaction:** ○ Saab's biggest sedan is known for its solid performance, good handling, comfortable accommodations, and large and versatile cargo area. Besides the standard 2.3-liter Four, a turbocharged version is available in every body style and trim line. (That option adds several thousand dollars to the price.) All 9000s come with a wealth of safety and convenience equipment as standard. **Last full report: May '94 Fax: 7732**

SATURN *Small car* RECOMMENDED

■ **Trim lines:** SL, SL1, SL2, SW1, SW2 ■ **Body styles:** 4-door, 4-door wagon ■ **Predicted reliability:** ● **Owner satisfaction:** ◕ Saturn's reliability is exceptional for a domestic make. Stick with the SL2 version. It's powerful, though noisy. The optional automatic transmission shifts smoothly. Handling is nimble, the ride stiff. The front seats are firm and comfortable. The rear is very uncomfortable. Most controls and displays are sensibly designed. Heating and cooling are ample. The plastic body panels, held by fasteners, rebound rather than dent after a minor impact so replacement should be easy. **Last full report: Sept. '93 Fax: 7397**

SATURN SC *Sporty car under $25,000*   RECOMMENDED

▓ **Trim lines:** SC1, SC2 ▓ **Body style:** 2-door ▓ **Predicted reliability:** ● **Owner satisfaction:** NA ▓ Saturn is one of the few domestic makes that compete successfully with the Japanese in both performance and reliability. This sporty coupe combines quick acceleration, impressive fuel economy, and nimble handling. The Saturn is fairly quiet except when the engine is revved. The ride is stiff, even jarring. Tall drivers may want more head room. The gauges are easy to read. The climate-control system is strong but slow. The plastic body panels flex after a minor impact—and they're attached with fasteners, so replacement should be easy.

Last full report: July '92 Fax: 7734

SUBARU IMPREZA *Small car*   RECOMMENDED

▓ **Trim lines:** Base, L, LS ▓ **Body styles:** 2-door, 4-door, 4-door wagon ▓ **Predicted reliability:** NA **Owner satisfaction:** NA ▓ The base Impreza isn't all that imprezive, but the LS version with automatic transmission and antilock brakes holds its own. The steering is nicely weighted and responsive. All-wheel drive is available. The LS model, with bigger tires than those on the base L, handles more nimbly and crisply. The ride is smooth and gentle on the highway, jittery on bad roads. The front seats provide good support, though leg room is just adequate for tall people. The rear is awfully cramped for three. The instruments are clear.

Last full report: Aug. '93 Fax: 7302

SUBARU LEGACY *Compact car under $20,000*   RECOMMENDED

▓ **Trim lines:** L, LS, LSi ▓ **Body styles:** 4-door, 4-door wagon ▓ **Predicted reliability:** ◑ **Owner satisfaction:** ◑ This competent model has been redesigned for '95 model. It's the only mid-priced compact to offer all-wheel drive in some versions. Acceleration is adequate; a turbocharger is available. The four-speed automatic shifts quite smoothly. The Legacy rides well on the highway, but its tail wags easily in abrupt maneuvers. The front seats give good support. The climate-control system works quickly and powerfully. The gauges are clear, but the controls could be better. The split rear seatback can be folded.

Last full report: June '93 Fax: 9317

SUBARU SVX *Sporty car over $25,000*   RECOMMENDED

▓ **Trim lines:** L, LS, LSi ▓ **Body style:** 2-door ▓ **Predicted reliability:** ◑ **Owner satisfaction:** ◑ The SVX lacks the razor-sharp performance of a true sports car, but it offers the comfort and quietness of a luxury sedan and, optionally, the traction of all-wheel drive. Acceleration is ample, and the four-speed automatic transmission shifts smoothly. Normal handling feels very stable, but emergency handling lacks precision. The front seats are comfortable; two adults can tolerate the rear seat for short periods. The divided side windows make it hard to reach through—to pay a toll, say. The gauges are easy to read. Aside from tiny horn buttons, the controls are well designed.

Last full report: Sept. '92 Fax: 7758

SUZUKI SIDEKICK *Sport-utility vehicle*

▓ **Trim lines:** JS, JX, JLX ▓ **Body styles:** 4-door wagon, convertible ▓ **Predicted reliability:** ◐ **Owner satisfaction:** NA ▓ This tiny, Jeep-like runabout (a sibling to the Geo Tracker) comes in a wide range of styles: two or four doors; two or four seats; two- or four-wheel drive; fully enclosed or as a "convertible" with a soft top covering just the area behind the front seats. The four-door is more than a foot longer than the two-door and offers more standard equipment as well as more seating or cargo room in the rear. The Sidekick is better suited to running errands around town than cruising the turnpikes. **Last full report: — Fax: —**

SUZUKI SWIFT *Small car*

▓ **Trim lines:** GA, GS, GT ▓ **Body styles:** 2-door hatchback, 4-door ▓ **Predicted reliability:** NA **Owner satisfaction:** NA ▓ The Swift is much like the Geo Metro, but less basic and slightly peppier. It's a small, cheap runabout, better suited to zipping around town than cruising the turnpikes. The Swift, with its 1.3-liter Four, accelerates better than the Metro, with its 1.0-liter three-cylinder, while still delivering good fuel economy. The GT's perky 100-hp Four, combined with a generous amount of standard equipment, adds up to a spicy little runabout for about $10,000. **Last full report: — Fax: —**

TOYOTA 4RUNNER *Sport-utility vehicle*

▓ **Trim lines:** SR5 ▓ **Body style:** 4-door wagon ▓ **Predicted reliability:** ● **Owner satisfaction:** ○ Toyota's pickup truck provides the foundation for this sport-utility vehicle. That's why the 4Runner drives more like a truck than a car. Its V6 provides weak acceleration, and the cargo area is small. The front seats are reasonably comfortable, but the floor is high off the ground and the rear seat is tight for tall people. The interior is fairly quiet, but you can expect to be tossed around somewhat on poor roads. About the best one can say for the 4Runner is that it has been exceptionally reliable for a sport-utility vehicle, and it holds its resale value well. Four-wheel drive is available. **Last full report: — Fax: —**

TOYOTA CAMRY *Mid-sized car under $25,000* RECOMMENDED

▓ **Trim lines:** DX, LE, SE, XLE ▓ **Body styles:** 2-door, 4-door, 4-door wagon ▓ **Predicted reliability:** ● **Owner satisfaction:** ◕ One of the best family sedans under $25,000, the Camry drives like a luxury car. The V6 version scored about as well as the similar Lexus ES300, which sells for thousands more. The V6 is quiet and strong, but the Four is no slouch. Stops are short. Safe handling and a smooth and quiet ride are bonuses. Room in front is ample; short drivers may wish they could sit higher. The optional sun roof reduces rear head room. The gauges are clear, the controls straightforward. The climate-control system works effectively. **Last full report: Jan. '94 Fax: 9392**

TOYOTA CELICA *Sporty car under $25,000* RECOMMENDED

▓ **Trim lines:** ST, GT ▓ **Body styles:** 2-door, 2-door hatchback ▓ **Predicted reliability:** New **Owner satisfaction:** New ▓ The Celica's new body gives it a passing resemblance to a Lexus coupe, but the car retains last year's underpinnings. The Celica is a well-built little sports coupe, with comfortable front seats and a nice control layout. The only engine is a Four, but it's well up to the task of moving this fairly light car around. **Last full report: June '94 Fax: 9742**

TOYOTA COROLLA *Small car* RECOMMENDED

▓ **Trim lines:** Base, DX, LE ▓ **Body styles:** 4-door, 4-door wagon ▓ **Predicted reliability:** ● **Owner satisfaction:** ○ This high-rated model and the Geo Prizm share many mechanical and body parts, but the Corolla rides a bit better. It also tends to come with more standard equipment and cost more. Choose the 1.8-liter Four over the 1.6-liter Four. The Corolla handles predictably, but not very nimbly for a small car. The front seats are fine; the cramped rear seat holds only two in anything resembling comfort. The gauges are clear, and most controls are easy to use. The climate-control system works well. The split rear seatback can be folded down. **Last full report: Aug. '93 Fax: 7302**

TOYOTA LAND CRUISER *Sport-utility vehicle* RECOMMENDED

▨ **Trim lines:** None ▨ **Body style:** 4-door wagon ▨ **Predicted reliability:** NA **Owner satisfaction:** NA ▨ This very expensive sport-utility vehicle comes with all the fancy extras of a high-end sedan. As in most SUVs, high seats give a commanding view of the landscape. This vehicle offers a bouncy and jittery but quiet ride. Its Six delivers strong performance. Rugged construction, high ground clearance, and sophisticated full-time all-wheel drive make the Land Cruiser well suited for on- and off-road use. **Last full report: July '94 Fax: 7789**

TOYOTA MR2 *Sports car under $25,000* RECOMMENDED

▨ **Trim lines:** Base, Turbo ▨ **Body style:** 2-door ▨ **Predicted reliability:** ● **Owner satisfaction:** NA ▨ This rear-wheel-drive two-seater holds the fort as the only available small, mid-engined sports car. The engine balances weight fore and aft for nimble, ultra-responsive handling. The MR2 serves up lively acceleration, especially in its Turbo version. Stowage space is severely limited, even for a sports car. The MR2's escalating price and high insurance cost have hurt its sales in the supersaturated sports-car market. **Last full report: — Fax: —**

TOYOTA PASEO *Sports car under $25,000*

▨ **Trim lines:** None ▨ **Body style:** 2-door ▨ **Predicted reliability:** ● **Owner satisfaction:** ○ Unexciting acceleration, a soft suspension, and numb steering betray this model's plebeian Toyota Tercel lineage. Fuel economy is impressive. The five-speed manual transmission shifts accurately, but the shifter and clutch pedal feel too light. Bumps and wind gusts push the car off course. The non-antilock brakes need lots of room on wet pavement. The driving position is cramped for tall people. Consider the rear seat a shelf for packages. The controls and displays are fine, but the climate-control system is woefully inadequate.
Last full report: July '92 Fax: 7734

TOYOTA PREVIA *Minivan* RECOMMENDED

▨ **Trim lines:** DX, LE, LE S/C, DX All-Trac, LE All-Trac, LE All-Trac S/C ▨ **Body style:** minivan ▨ **Predicted reliability:** ● **Owner satisfaction:** ◖ This van is good for hauling people, not cargo. The load area is small, and the standard Four strains with a full load. The new supercharged Four should help. Uphill, the four-speed automatic shifts annoyingly back and forth. Cornering is reasonably steady; optional four-wheel drive helps on slippery roads. Drivers of all sizes can get comfortable. The rearmost seat is flat and hard. For the middle row, get optional swiveling captain's chairs. The controls work well once you figure them out, and the displays are legible. The climate-control system works effectively. **Last full report: Oct. '92 Fax: 7766**

TOYOTA SUPRA *Sports car over $25,000* RECOMMENDED

▨ **Trim lines:** Base, Turbo ▨ **Body style:** 2-door hatchback ▨ **Predicted reliability:** New **Owner satisfaction:** New ▨ Although previous Supra models emphasized the luxury end of the sporty-car spectrum, the 94's lighter and leaner model lunges into the high-performance arena of the true sports car, with a jarring and noisy ride. It competes with Japanese-bred road-eaters like the Dodge Stealth/Mitsubishi 3000GT, Mazda RX-7, and Nissan 300ZX. The Supra Turbo has a smooth-shifting six-speed manual transmission and a very hot twin-turbo-charged engine. It comes fully loaded with accessories.   **Last full report: June '94 Fax: 9742**

TOYOTA TERCEL *Small car*

▓ **Trim lines:** Base, DX ▓ **Body styles:** 2-door, 4-door ▓ **Predicted reliability:** ● **Owner satisfaction:** ○ First and foremost, this is an economy car. Tall drivers should try before they buy. The engine accelerates adequately but lacks pep. The Tercel handles nimbly, but the tail tends to swing out during hard cornering. Although the seats are firm and nicely shaped, space is in short supply. The ride is coarse even on good roads, and the car transmits a lot of tire and road noise to the cabin. As is typical in Toyota models, the Tercel's instruments are easy to see and read. Redesigned for 1995.   **Last full report: March '91 Fax: 7967**

VOLKSWAGEN CORRADO SLC *Sporty car under $25,000*

▓ **Trim lines:** None ▓ **Body style:** 2-door hatchback ▓ **Predicted reliability:** NA **Owner satisfaction:** NA ▓ The Corrado's V6 delivers smooth and strong performance. Expect near-perfect routine handling and smooth, responsive handling through hard turns. Many controls are poorly labeled; their functions may remain a mystery unless you consult the owner's manual. Front-seat comfort is very good. Though the Corrado has a rear seat, consider the car a two-seater for all practical purposes. If you're tall, pass up the sunroof; it robs head room.

Last full report: — Fax: —

VOLKSWAGEN EUROVAN *Minivan*

▓ **Trim lines:** CL, GL, MV ▓ **Body style:** minivan ▓ **Predicted reliability:** NA **Owner satisfaction:** NA ▓ A huge interior offers comfort for seven, and large windows provide a panoramic view. A delivery-truck heritage makes this van unpleasant to drive. Acceleration is anemic, and the optional four-speed automatic transmission shifts abruptly and often. The van leans sharply in tight turns, and the brakes are mediocre. The ride is bouncy and noisy. The dual climate-control systems work well, but the steering wheel is buslike, and the controls and displays need improvement. The 1995 model has dual air bags.   **Last full report: Feb. '93 Fax: 7943**

VOLKSWAGEN GOLF III *Small car*

▓ **Trim lines:** GL, Limited Edition, Cabrio ▓ **Body styles:** 2-door hatchback, 4-door hatchback, convertible ▓ **Predicted reliability:** NA **Owner satisfaction:** NA ▓ A responsive Four provides the power for the new Golf. Though the current model resembles the previous one on the outside, it has a slightly wider stance, larger (14-inch) tires, and a redesigned interior. The control layout is much improved over that of previous VWs. With a slick-shifting, five-speed manual transmission, the new Golf should be fun to drive. Consider only the models with dual air bags.   **Last full report: Oct. '94 Fax: 9921**

VOLKSWAGEN JETTA III *Small car*

▓ **Trim lines:** GL, GLS, GLX ▓ **Body style:** 4-door ▓ **Predicted reliability:** NA **Owner satisfaction:** NA ▓ The current Jetta offers a trifle more interior space than last year's model, while retaining a roomy trunk. A 2.0-liter Four is the standard engine in all but the sporty GLX version, which gets a powerful V6. Only the true 1994 models have air bags. The Jetta is made in Mexico—except for the GLX version, which comes from Germany.

Last full report: Nov. '94 Fax: 9923

VOLKSWAGEN PASSAT *Compact car over $20,000*

▨ **Trim lines:** GLX ▨ **Body styles:** 4-door, 4-door wagon ▨ **Predicted reliability:** NA **Owner satisfaction:** NA ▨ Despite some high spots, this model is riddled with annoyances. The V6 is smooth and strong, but the four-speed automatic transmission often shifts when it shouldn't. Handling is crisp, but the ride is stiff. The front and rear seats are comfortable, and the driving position accommodates people of almost any size. The gauges are clear, and the heating and ventilation work very well. Some controls are poorly labeled or hard to see. The station wagon's cargo area is especially roomy. The Passat will be redesigned later this year.

Last full report: — Fax: —

VOLVO 850 *Mid-sized car over $25,000*   RECOMMENDED

▨ **Trim lines:** Level I, Level II, Turbo ▨ **Body styles:** 4-door, 4-door wagon ▨ **Predicted reliability:** ◉ **Owner satisfaction:** NA ▨ Volvo is trying to shed its stodgy image with this sporty yet practical model. The four-speed automatic transmission usually shifts smoothly; a Winter mode allows starts in second or third. The ride is choppy. The steering isn't particularly quick, but handling is predictable. On dry pavement, the 850 stopped as short as any car we've tested; wet-pavement stops were also short. The driving position can accommodate people of nearly any size, and five can fit in exceptional comfort. The automatic climate-control system is powerful, and most displays and controls are easy to see and use.

Last full report: Aug. '94 Fax: 9792

VOLVO 940/960 *Mid-sized car over $25,000*   RECOMMENDED

▨ **Trim lines:** 940 Level I, 940 Level II, Turbo, 960 Level I, 960 Level II ▨ **Body styles:** 4-door, 4-door wagon ▨ **Predicted reliability:** ◒ **Owner satisfaction:** ○ The 940 has a Four; the 960, which we tested, has a peppy Six. Both versions provide many safety features, exceptional comfort for five, and a huge trunk. The wagon is especially roomy. The four-speed automatic transmission lets you start in any gear, and a locking differential limits wheel spin. Handling is predictable, though not nimble, and stops are short and straight. The ride is smooth. The climate-control system works superbly. Gauges are clear, and most controls are sensible. "Pretensioners" on the front safety belts instantly take up slack in a crash.

Last full report: Sept. '94 Fax: 9915

RATINGS | 1994 CARS

Notes on the table: Rated cars include only those for which we have recent test data. In some cases, our tests apply to more than one model. These models, called "siblings," are essentially similar models that are sold under different nameplates. They're grouped and marked with bullets in the charts below. **Fuel usage** is overall mpg and is based on our own tests on and off the track. **Tested model** notes the trim line, engine, drivetrain, and braking system of the model tested—items that can affect specific test results.

Within types, listed in order of overall quality

Model	Overall score (P F G VG E)	Fuel usage	Tested model
SMALL CARS			
Volkswagen Jetta III		23 mpg	GLX 2.8/V6; man/5.
Acura Integra		30	LS 1.8/4; man/5.
Volkswagen Golf III		30	GL hatchback; 2.0/4; man/5.
Dodge/Plymouth Neon		31	Highline 2.0/4; auto/3.
Geo Prizm		33	LSi 1.8/4; man/5; ABS.
Plymouth Neon		31	Sport 2.0/4; man/5.
Saturn		27	SL2 1.9/4; auto/4; ABS.
Honda Civic		29	EX 1.6/4; auto/4; ABS.
• Eagle Summit Wagon		24	Mitsubishi Expo LRV Sport 2.4/4; auto/4; ABS.
• Mitsubishi Expo LRV		24	Sport 2.4/4; auto/4; ABS.
• Plymouth Colt Vista Wagon		24	Mitsubishi Expo LRV Sport 2.4/4; auto/4; ABS.
Toyota Corolla		30	LE and DX 1.8/4; auto/4; ABS.
Subaru Impreza		29	L 1.8/Flat 4; man/5.
Nissan Sentra		28	GXE 1.6/4; auto/4; ABS.
Ford Escort		27	LX 1.9/4; auto/4.
Mercury Tracer		27	Base 1.9/4; auto/4.
Toyota Tercel		35	1.5/4; man/4.
• Dodge Colt		34	Eagle Summit ES 1.8/4; man/5.
• Eagle Summit		34	ES 1.8/4; man/5.
• Mitsubishi Mirage		34	Eagle Summit ES 1.8/4; man/5.
• Plymouth Colt		34	Eagle Summit ES 1.8/4; man/5.
Hyundai Elantra		25	GLS 1.6/4; auto/4.
Ford Aspire		36	Hatchback; 1.3/4; man/5.
COMPACT CARS UNDER $20,000			
Mazda 626		24	ES 2.5/V6; auto/4; ABS.
Mitsubishi Galant		24	LS 2.4/4; auto/4; ABS.
Nissan Altima		23	GLE 2.4/4; auto/4; ABS.

Model	Overall score					Fuel usage	Tested model
	P	F	G	VG	E		
Subaru Legacy						22 mpg	LS 2.2/Flat 4; auto/4; ABS.
▪ Ford Tempo						24	GL 2.3/4; auto/3.
▪ Mercury Topaz						24	Ford Tempo GL 2.3/4; auto/3.
Chrysler Le Baron						23	LX 3.0/V6; auto/4; ABS.
Buick Skylark						21	Gran Sport 3.3/V6; auto/3; ABS.
▪ Dodge Spirit						24	Plymouth Acclaim LE 2.5/4; auto/3.
▪ Plymouth Acclaim						24	LE 2.5/4; auto/3.
Pontiac Grand Am						20	GT 3.3/V6; auto/3; ABS.
Chevrolet Corsica						25	LT 2.2/4; auto/3; ABS.
Oldsmobile Achieva						24	S 2.3/4; auto/ 3; ABS.
▪ Chevrolet Cavalier						24	Pontiac Sunbird LE 2.0/4; auto/ 3.
▪ Pontiac Sunbird						24	LE 2.0/4; auto/3.

COMPACT CARS OVER $20,000

Model	Overall score					Fuel usage	Tested model
BMW 3-Series						22	325i 2.5/6; auto/4; ABS.
Infiniti G20						24	2.0/4; auto/4; ABS.
Saab 900						22	SE hatchback; 2.5/V6; auto/4.
Audi 90						22	90 CS Quattro Sport 2.8/V6; man/5; ABS.

MID-SIZED CARS UNDER $25,000

Model	Overall score					Fuel usage	Tested model
Toyota Camry						24	LE 2.2/4; auto/4; ABS.
Honda Accord						26	EX 2.2/4; auto/4; ABS.
▪ Ford Taurus						20	LX 3.8/V6; auto/4; ABS.
▪ Mercury Sable						20	LS 3.8/V6; auto/4; ABS.
Nissan Maxima						21	SE 3.0/V6; auto/4.
Pontiac Grand Prix						19	GT 3.4/V6; auto/4; ABS.
Buick Regal						20	Gran Sport 3.8/V6; auto/4; ABS.
Oldsmobile Cutlass Supreme						20	SL 3.1/V6; auto/4; ABS.

MID-SIZED CARS OVER $25,000

Model	Overall score					Fuel usage	Tested model
Volvo 850						22	2.3/5 turbo; auto/4; ABS.
Lexus ES300						20	3.0/V6; auto/4; ABS.
Volvo 960						20	2.9/Six; auto/4; ABS.
Saab 9000						21	CSE hatchback; 2.3/turbo 4; auto/4.
Infiniti J30						20	3.0/V6; auto/4; ABS.
Mazda 929						20	3.0/V6; auto/4; ABS.
Mercedes-Benz C-class						20	C280 2.8/6; auto/4.
Acura Legend						21	L 3.2/V6; auto/4; ABS.
Mitsubishi Diamante						20	LS 3.0/V6; auto/4; ABS.
Ford Taurus SHO						21	3.2/V6; auto/4; ABS.

Ratings continued ▶

Ratings continued

Model	Overall score					Fuel usage	Tested model
	P	F	G	VG	E		

MID-SIZED CARS OVER $25,000

Model						Fuel usage	Tested model
Lincoln Mark VIII						19 mpg	4.6V8; auto/4; ABS.
Acura Vigor						23	GS 2.5/5; auto/4; ABS.
Cadillac Eldorado						15	Touring Coupe 4.6/V8; auto/4; ABS.
Audi 100						21	S 2.8/V6; auto/4; ABS.

LARGE CARS

Model						Fuel usage	Tested model
▪ Chrysler Concorde						21	3.5/V6; auto/4; ABS.
▪ Dodge Intrepid						21	ES 3.5/V6; auto/4; ABS.
▪ Eagle Vision						21	TSi 3.5/V6; auto/4; ABS.
Chrysler LHS/New Yorker						20	3.5/V6; auto/4; ABS.
Pontiac Bonneville						19	SSEi 3.8/V6; auto/4; ABS.
▪ Ford Crown Victoria						19	LX 4.6/V8; auto/4; ABS.
▪ Mercury Grand Marquis						19	Ford Crown Victoria LX 4.6/V8; auto/4; ABS.
Chevrolet Caprice						17	Classic LS 5.7/V8; auto/4; ABS.
Buick Le Sabre						19	Oldsmobile Eighty-Eight LS 3.8/V6; auto/ 4; ABS.
Oldsmobile 88 Royale						19	LS 3.8/V6; auto/4; ABS.
Buick Roadmaster						17	5.7/V8; auto/4; ABS.

LUXURY CARS

Model						Fuel usage	Tested model
Mercedes-Benz E-Class						21	E320 3.2/6; auto/4.
BMW 5-Series						19	530i; 3.0/V8; auto/5.
Lexus LS400						19	4.0/V8; auto/4; ABS.
Infiniti Q45						17	Q45a 4.5/V8; auto/4; ABS.
Lexus SC400/300						19	4.0/V8; auto/4; ABS.
Cadillac Seville						17	STS 4.6/V8; auto/4; ABS.
Jaguar XJ6						18	4.0/6; auto/4; ABS.

SPORTS/SPORTY CARS UNDER $25,000

Model						Fuel usage	Tested model
Acura Integra Coupe						30	GS-R 1.8/4; man/5.
Ford Probe						24	GT 2.5/V6; man/5; ABS.
Chevrolet Camaro						17	Trans Am 5.7/V8; auto/4; ABS.
Pontiac Firebird						17	Trans Am 5.7/V8; auto/4; ABS.
Toyota Celica						28	GT hatchback; 2.2/4; auto/5.
Mazda MX-5 Miata						29	1.6/4; man/5; ABS.
Mazda MX-6						24	LS 2.5/V6; man/5; ABS.
Saturn SC						29	SC2 1.9/4; man/5; ABS.
Honda Prelude						26	Si 2.3/4; man/5; ABS.
Mazda MX-3						28	GS1.8/V6; man/5.

Model	Overall score					Fuel usage	Tested model
	P	F	G	VG	E		
▪ Eagle Talon						21 mpg	TSi 2.0/4 Turbo; man/5; ABS.
▪ Mitsubishi Eclipse						21	Eagle Talon TSi 2.0/4 Turbo; man/5; ABS.
Toyota Paseo						34	1.5/4; man/5.
Honda Civic del Sol						32	Si 1.6/4; man/5.
Mercury Capri						28	Base 1.6/4; man/5.

SPORTS/SPORTY CARS OVER $25,000

Model	Overall score					Fuel usage	Tested model
Toyota Supra						22	Turbo 3.0/turbocharged 6; man/6.
Chevrolet Corvette						17	Base 5.7/V8; man/6; ABS.
Nissan 300ZX						21	3.0/V6 Turbo; man/5; ABS.
Mazda RX-7						19	Touring1.3/2 rotary; man/5; ABS.
▪ Dodge Stealth						20	RT Turbo 3.0/V6; man/5; ABS.
▪ Mitsubishi 3000 GT						20	Dodge Stealth RT Turbo 3.0/V6; man/5; ABS.
Subaru SVX						19	LSi 3.3/Flat 6; auto/4; ABS.

MINIVANS

Model	Overall score					Fuel usage	Tested model
▪ Mercury Villager						20	GS 3.0/V6; auto/4; ABS.
▪ Nissan Quest						19	GXE 3.0/V6; auto/4; ABS.
Toyota Previa						18	LE All-Trac 2.4/4; auto/4; ABS.
▪ Dodge Caravan						19	ES 3.3/V6; auto/4; ABS.
▪ Plymouth Voyager						19	Dodge Caravan ES 3.3/V6; auto/4; ABS.
▪ Chevrolet Lumina						17	Pontiac Trans Sport SE 3.1/V6; auto/3.
▪ Pontiac Trans Sport						17	SE 3.1/V6; auto/3.
▪ Oldsmobile Silhouette						17	Pontiac Trans Sport SE 3.1/V6; auto/3.
Ford Aerostar						16	Eddie Bauer extended 4.0/V6; auto/4; rear ABS; AWD.
▪ Chrysler Town & Country						17	Dodge Grand Caravan LE 3.3/V6; auto/4; ABS.
▪ Dodge Grand Caravan						17	LE 3.3/V6; auto/4; ABS.
▪ Plymouth Grand Voyager						17	Dodge Grand Caravan LE 3.3/V6; auto/4; ABS.
Mazda MPV						16	3.0/V6; auto/4; rear ABS; AWD.
Volkswagen EuroVan						17	GL 2.5/5; auto/4; ABS.
Chevrolet Astro/GMC Safari						15	4.3/V6; auto/4; ABS; AWD.

SPORT-UTILITY VEHICLES

Model	Overall score					Fuel usage	Tested model
Jeep Grand Cherokee						16	Laredo 4.0/6; auto/4; ABS.
▪ Ford Explorer						15	Eddie Bauer 4.0/V6; auto/4; rear ABS.

Ratings continued ▶

Ratings continued

SPORT-UTILITY VEHICLES

Model	Overall score					Fuel usage	Tested model
	P	F	G	VG	E		
▪ Mazda Navajo						15 mpg	Ford Explorer Eddie Bauer 4/V6; auto/4; rear ABS.
Isuzu Trooper						15	LS 3.2/V6; auto/4; ABS.
Mitsubishi Montero						15	LS 3.0/V6; auto/4; ABS.
Jeep Cherokee						17	4.0/6; auto/4.
Honda Passport						16	EX 3.2/V6; auto/4.
Isuzu Rodeo						16	Honda Passport EX; 3.2/V6; auto/4.
Oldsmobile Bravada						18	4.3/V6; auto/4; ABS.

How to buy a new car

Traditionally, a new car's selling price depends on bargaining between buyer and dealer. But enough people find the rug-bazaar atmosphere of that transaction so unpleasant that a new type of sales strategy has emerged—the one-price policy. Dealers with such a policy set a nonnegotiable, take-it-or-leave-it price, which is generally well below the normal sticker price but well above their own cost. Prices of General Motors' Saturn cars are the full-sticker price. Saturn's success has inspired more than 1000 new-car dealers to adopt one-price selling on their own, but their non-negotiable price is usually based on a discounted price, not the full-sticker price.

The discounted no-haggle price, we've found, isn't always the lowest. While the preset price is usually discounted from the manufacturer's sticker price, hard bargaining can drive the price of a similar model lower still, judging by our shopping experience. People who don't know how to negotiate or who hate the process, however, may consider that money well spent.

And a no-haggle price means you know the price is the same for everyone.

As car prices have risen, dealers and automakers have increasingly promoted leasing as an alternative to buying. See the report on page 315 for more information.

Decide on the model

Falling in love with a specific car is a poor bargaining strategy. Unless the salesperson believes you're willing to shop elsewhere, there is little incentive to offer you the lowest possible price.

Whether or not you plan to bargain, first decide on the type and style of car that best suits your needs—a mid-sized sedan, for example, or a minivan. Then narrow the field to the makes and models in your price range.

Savings are sometimes possible by considering siblings—models that are similar in design but come with different nameplates and trim. The car profiles (page 271) and ratings (page 308) indicate which models are related.

Next, decide what equipment you want in your new car. Most models are sold in two or more trim lines (Base, GL, SLX, etc.). Each trim line has a different base price and selection of standard equipment.

In some cases, an apparently more expensive trim line may cost less than dressing up a basic model with all the options you want. Sometimes, too, desirable options are unavailable with the base model.

Option packages often bundle some useful with some frivolous equipment. If you want all or most of the extras, it's usually cheaper to buy the package

Learn the dealer's costs

To find the dealer's cost, you can consult price manuals available at public libraries. For more up-to-date information on models equipped exactly as you want, the Consumer Reports New Car Price Service provides prices for any make, model, and trim line. (See page 400.) Each Price Report printout notes the standard equipment, list price, and dealer cost of the basic car. It itemizes, by invoice number, all available factory-installed options and options packages, giving list prices and dealer invoice cost.

The service also notes current rebate offers, including unadvertised rebates to dealers. Since the dealer can either pocket that rebate or pass all or part of it on to the consumer, knowledge of such offers is useful leverage when you bargain.

Using the Price Report or other source prepare a worksheet that describes the car you want, its price to the dealer, and its list price. In two columns, list the price to the dealer and list price for the car and each option. At the bottom of each column, write in the destination charge. Finally, total both columns. The difference between the two totals is the room for negotiation.

If there's a factory-to-dealer rebate on the car, subtract its value from what the dealer pays. (In effect, such a rebate reduces that

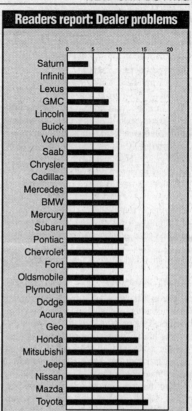

Readers report: Dealer problems

Makes are listed in order of overall rate of dissatisfaction as averaged across models. Makes were ranked based on reader complaints relating to the purchase of one or more individual models. Within makes, models often varied considerably. Data were adjusted for age of buyer; in general, younger buyers were less satisfied than older buyers. We included only those models receiving a minimum of 100 responses. Usually, however, we actually received many more than that. Honda Accord owners supplied the most responses: 7249.

figure.) If there's a factory-to-customer rebate, the check will come directly from the manufacturer. Or if you prefer, you can sign it over to the dealer as part of the down payment.

How much over dealer price should you expect to pay? On a mid-priced sedan in good supply, you may have to pay as little as $300 to $600 over the price to the car dealer. If the car is in tight supply and much in demand, however, you might find you can't get much of a discount. In that case, you may have to pay $1000 over cost.

Dealers sometimes sell cars below their apparent cost. An additional payment, called a holdback, that dealers often receive from the manufacturer at year's end lowers the dealer's cost. Holdbacks typically amount to 1 to 3 percent of the base sticker price on domestics and all but a few imports.

Resist add-ons

Dealers have come up with an amazing array of add-ons designed to improve their profits. The most common are "packs"— extras like a "protection package" that includes a fabric finish, a paint sealant, rustproofing, and undercoating. These are of little or no value. Pass them up.

Another costly extra is an extended warranty. Given the common three-to-seven-year warranty, an extended warranty is not worthwhile, especially for a model with a decent reliability record.

Some dealers charge a "conveyance" or "document" fee for the paperwork involved in selling and registering the car. You have to pay the state's registration fee, but the "conveyance" part may be negotiable.

Many dealers add an advertising surcharge—often more than $400 per car. Ask to see proof that the fee is legitimate.

Occasionally, a salesperson may point out that your figures don't include dealer preparation. In most cases, they shouldn't. Dealer preparation should be included in the base price of the car.

All too often, dealers will mention packs and fees only at the end of the bargaining, when it's time to sign the sales contract. Then, when the dealers cut the price of a pack or waive a fee, buyers feel they're getting a break. They're not.

Keep the deal simple

Trade-in. Salespeople usually ask early in the negotiations whether you have a trade-in. Your answer should be "no." You'll have plenty of time to reconsider later. If you talk trade-in too soon, the numbers become so confusing that you don't know how much you paid for the new car or got for the old one.

Selling your old car privately can be troublesome, but you'll probably get more for it than if you trade it in. You can learn what your car is worth by consulting price guides at the public library. Or, you can call the Consumer Reports Used Car Price Service, which provides up-to-date price information for your area (see page 400).

Financing. When sales are sluggish, automakers often offer below-market-rate loans. Compared with typical bank rates, promotional rates can save hundreds of dollars over the life of a loan. In many cases, however, low-rate financing applies to particular models or to short-term loans.

If low-interest financing isn't available on the car you want, don't accept the dealer's financing until you shop around. Credit unions, banks, and even auto-insurance companies may offer more favorable terms.

Shop around

With worksheet in hand, visit at least two or three dealers. Ask the dealership for its lowest figure, and say you're shopping around and are prepared to buy from the dealer who gives the lowest quote. Don't leave a deposit, even if it's refundable, until you're ready to sign the contract.

Before signing, take time to read the sales contract—including the fine print. If you see something you don't like—or if you don't see something that should be included—ask for changes.

If you turn in your old car on delivery of the new one several weeks later, the sales contract may allow the dealer to reappraise your car at that time. That's only fair. Much can happen to your car that may affect its value in the intervening weeks.

Make sure the sales contract states that you have the option to void the agreement and get your deposit back if, say, there's no delivery by a specified date. And make sure an officer of the dealership signs the agreement. The salesperson's signature alone may not be binding.

How to lease a new car

The least expensive way to buy a car is to pay cash for it. Financing is more costly, because of the interest you pay. Leasing is often costlier still, but in certain circumstances, it can make sense.

Many people cannot afford the cash outlay to buy a car outright. To them, leases are likely to look very tempting. There is often little or no down payment, and the monthly payments are lower than those for a typical auto loan.

The payments are lower because in essence you are borrowing money to cover only the depreciation of the car during the time you have it. But extra charges you may have to pay at lease end can turn a good deal into a poor one.

Sizing up a lease deal can be difficult. Key information you need to gauge a deal may be hard to come by.

Sizing up a lease

■ First, negotiate a price for the car exactly as if you were going to buy it. (See page 312.) Then ask for monthly lease payments based on that price.

■ Ask for the rate or "money factor" of the lease—similar to the annual percentage rate on a car loan. That number is usually a decimal like .0041. Convert it to a percentage rate by multiplying it by 2400 (.0041 works out to 9.84 percent). The lower the rate, the better.

■ Ask about the residual value of the car—the expected value of the car at the end of the lease. The higher the residual value, the better. Cars that hold their value well—such as *Hondas*, *Volvos*, and some *Toyotas*—often make the best lease deals. And cars that depreciate steeply, like *Hyundais*, may come with relatively high lease payments.

■ Read the entire leasing contract. Walk away if the lease company won't let you take home a copy of the contract to study.

■ Look for any setup fees, security deposit, or end-of-lease charges. Is the yearly mileage limit adequate for your needs? What is the charge for additional miles? Does the contract define "excess wear and tear"—damage you'll have to pay for at the end of lease? If not, you could face a big repair bill.

■ Find out what happens if you want to end the lease before it expires. You may have to make up the difference between the car's depreciation and what's paid.

■ Make sure "gap insurance" is included. It pays the difference between what you owe and what the car is worth if it's destroyed or stolen. Some lease companies toss it in free. It shouldn't cost more than $100 or $200.

■ Make sure the manufacturer's warranty will cover the car for the entire term of the lease. Otherwise, you may be liable for expensive repairs at lease end.

■ If there's an option to purchase the car at lease end, ask how the price will be determined.

It rarely makes economic sense to sign a lease for more than four years. Three years is the norm, and a few companies offer their best deals on two-year leases.

Consider only closed-ended leases, those that don't obligate you to buy the car at the end of the lease or require you to make up any shortfall in its residual value.

Be prepared for end-of-lease surprises. You may be asked to pay for excess wear and tear, for preparing the car for resale, and for wear on items like brakes, tires, and exhaust-system components. As a general rule, car dealers seem less likely to ambush consumers at lease end than private lease companies.

How to buy a used car

Used cars are often better values than new cars. The price of the average new car is up to nearly $19,000 and it depreciates by almost 15 to 20 percent in the first year. A used car costs an average of $8000 and depreciates more slowly.

The used-car marketplace, however, can be unsavory. Prices are highly elastic and subject to haggling. Paint and polish can be liberally applied to mask evidence of wear and tear, and odometers are often rolled back to hide the car's true mileage. Warranties are skimpy, if available. Finding out how much a car has suffered usually entails a good bit more than the proverbial kick in the tires.

Although you can't eliminate the risk when buying a used car, you can better the odds of getting sound transportation by learning how to shop.

What to consider

First, figure out what kind of car suits your life style and budget. Four-door sedans and station wagons usually provide the best used-car value. Chances are they've been driven and maintained more prudently than high-performance models. Convertibles, sporty coupes, and luxury models remain pricey even when used.

Next, consider cars that have held up well in the past. Our Frequency-of-Repair records, based on readers' experiences with more than 486,000 cars, trucks, sport-utility vehicles, and vans, describe the reliability history of 1988 through 1993 models. The better the car scored in the past, the less likely it is to have problems in the future. From those data, we have derived a list of reliable used cars (see page 319). We used the same data to identify models to avoid (see page 322). However, the older the car, the less important our records and the more important your inspection is.

To find out how much a model sells for in your area, you can use the Consumer Reports Used-Car Price Service, described on page 399. Price information also appears in various printed guides, available in public libraries.

Used-car leasing

Instead of buying a used car, you can lease one these days. General Motors and Ford lease models turned in at the end of new-car leases, generally ones that are two or three years old. Leasing sounds good on paper: A $50,000 car might lease for $600 a month when new, but for only $260 when three years old.

Many of the steps involved in leasing a used car are the same as those in leasing a new car, as described in "How to Lease a New Car," page 315. Take particular note that the mileage allowance covers the amount you expect to drive. Make sure the warranty covers the entire lease period, and that you know what parts are covered. And carefully document the condition of the car at the start of the lease.

Where to buy

Franchised new-car dealers are among the most trustworthy sources for late-model used cars. Such dealers often keep only the best trade-ins for resale, and often provide a warranty with service facilities to back it up. Of course, a car dealership's substantial overhead means you'll often pay more than you would elsewhere.

Independent used-car dealers offer lower prices, but their inventory is apt to be less desirable. Rejects from new-car dealers or weary specimens from police or taxi fleets are not uncommon. If you shop an independent dealer, choose one who's been in business for some time, and check with the Better Business Bureau.

Repossessed cars are periodically auctioned off. Check newspapers for advertisements. But be wary. Such cars may not have had the best care.

Auto-rental agencies such as Hertz, Avis, and National offer some cars to the public. While these cars may have been driven long and hard, most have been serviced regularly. And some companies provide a limited warranty. You can call the agencies' toll-free numbers to learn the location of their nearest used-car lot.

The Federal Trade Commission requires every used car sold by a dealer to display a "Buyer's Guide" label containing warranty information. Beyond that, only Massachusetts, New York, and Rhode Island have effective lemon laws to protect buyers from dealers who sell faulty merchandise. Protection extends to all but the oldest and cheapest used cars. Used-car warranty laws are on the books in Connecticut, Maine, Minnesota, Wisconsin, and the District of Columbia.

You can often get a good deal if you buy a car from a private party. That's because there is no dealer overhead and markup figured into the price. But in a private sale you normally get no guarantee, so it's best to buy from someone you trust. If you shop through a newspaper ad, ask about the car's condition and mileage, whether it's been in a wreck, and why it's being sold. Also ask whether the seller is a dealer. Some unethical operators pose as ordinary citizens to sell their cars.

Looking for trouble

Never buy on looks alone. After you've found a candidate, give it a thorough inspection—on the lot, on the road, and at the service station. Bring along a friend to help troubleshoot.

Here's what to look for:

Fluids. When the engine is cold, open the radiator cap and inspect the coolant; it shouldn't be rusty. Greenish stains on the radiator denote pinholes. To check an automatic transmission, warm up the engine and remove the dipstick. The fluid should be pinkish; it shouldn't smell burned or contain metal particles.

Leaks. Puddles or stains beneath the car are a bad sign. So is excessive residue of lubricants on the engine, transmission, hoses, and other underhood components.

Body integrity. Rust is ruinous. Check the wheel wells and rocker panels, the door bottoms, and the floor of the trunk, under the mat. Rust can also hide beneath blistered paint. Fresh welds in the car's underbody point to an accident. So does ripply body work, a part whose color or fit doesn't seem to match, and new paint on a late-model car. Fresh undercoating on older cars also is a giveaway.

Tires and suspension. A car with fewer than 25,000 miles should have its original tires. Uneven tread wear may merely indicate poor alignment, but it may also signal serious suspension damage. Grab the top of each tire and shake it. If there's play or a clunking sound, suspect loose or worn wheel bearings or suspension joints. Bounce the car a few times by pushing down each corner. When you let go, the car should rise and then settle. If it keeps bouncing, the struts or shock absorbers need replacing. Look at the car from the rear and the side. A lopsided stance could mean sagging springs.

Interior. A saggy driver's seat means heavy use or a heavy user. Excessively worn or brand new pedals might signal high mileage. Check under carpets for mildew or moisture. Musty odors suggest a water leak, often a costly fix because the source may be hard to find.

The road test

Plan to spend at least half an hour driving the car at various speeds on a variety of roads. But before you turn on the ignition, unlock the steering and turn the wheel. It shouldn't have much free play. Check the safety belts and all controls and accessories. Have your helper verify that all exterior lights, including brake and reverse lights, are working properly.

Engine. The car should start easily and pick up smoothly. Pings or knocks and blue or white smoke from the tailpipe could indicate oil guzzling. A bit of puffy white smoke on a cold day is OK; a lot could mean bad head gaskets. Black smoke may signal only a minor fuel adjustment. may be Ask a mechanic.

Transmission. A manual transmission shouldn't grab suddenly and make the car buck. An automatic shouldn't slam into gear or slip as you drive.

Brakes. Speed up to 45 mph on a flat stretch of traffic-free road. Try a series of stops from about 45 mph. Apply the brakes firmly. The car should stop quickly, evenly, and in a straight line. Repeat the exercise. To check for leaks in the brake system, press firmly on the pedal for 30 seconds. It shouldn't sink to the floor.

Alignment. Have someone stand behind the car while you drive straight ahead. The front and rear wheels should line up. Forget about the car if it scuttles sideways; the body is probably twisted. Pulling to one side may be less serious; the wheels may simply need alignment.

Exhaust. Blue smoke from the tailpipe means the car is burning oil—a costly fix. Billowy white smoke is serious as well. It means water is entering the combustion chamber. White vapor emerging briefly from the tailpipe on a cold morning is nothing to worry about.

Comfort and noise. Suspension work may be in order if the car bounces or rattles over rough roads at moderate speeds. Sputtering sounds from beneath the chassis indicate an exhaust-system leak.

Closing the deal

A car that's passed muster to this point is ready for checking by a reliable mechanic (that should cost $60 to $100). If you don't have a mechanic, consult the Yellow Pages for an auto diagnostic center. Make sure the mechanic performs a compression test on all cyclinders, mention any flaws you've found, and get a written estimate of repairs, to use in price negotiations.

The National Highway Traffic Safety Administration (800 424-9393) can tell you whether the model has ever been recalled. Also, check the Product Recalls chapter on page 375 for the auto recalls published in CONSUMER REPORTS from November 1993 through October 1994. If the car has been recalled, ask the seller for proof the problem was corrected.

Used cars—good & bad

The list of reliable used cars includes 1988 to 1992 models whose overall reliability has been better than average for their model year, according to our Frequency-of-Repair data (see page 324).

The list of used cars to avoid includes models whose overall records have been considerably worse than their model-year average for their model year.

Problems with the engine, engine cooling, transmission, driveline, clutch, and body rust—troubles likely to be serious and costly to repair—weighed more heavily than other problems in forming these lists.

For details on a model's reliability and systems that may have been troublesome, consult its Frequency-of-Repair chart. Charts start on page 330.

The reliable cars are grouped by price, as reported on pages 268 and 269 of the April issue of CONSUMER REPORTS. Prices are Midwestern averages for cars with average mileage, and with air-conditioning, AM/FM cassette stereo, and automatic transmission. (Prices for sporty cars, pickups, and sport-utility vehicles are with manual transmission.) Luxury cars are priced with leather seats, sunroof, and compact-disc player.

Abbreviations: RWD = rear-wheel drive; FWD = front-wheel drive; 2WD = two-wheel drive; 4WD = four-wheel drive.

Reliable used cars

$2000-$3500

CHEVROLET
Nova, '88
DODGE
Colt, '89
FORD
Festiva, '88, '89

$3500-$4000

FORD
Festiva, '90
MAZDA
323, '88
Pickup 2WD, '88
NISSAN
Sentra, '88 [1]
PLYMOUTH
Colt, '89
TOYOTA
Tercel, '88

$4000-$5000

DODGE/PLYMOUTH
Colt, '90; Colt Wagon, '89

HONDA
Civic, '88
ISUZU
Pickup 4 2WD, '89
MAZDA
323, '89
NISSAN
Pickup 4 2WD, '89
TOYOTA
Corolla 2WD, '88
Pickup 4 2WD, '88
Tercel, '89

$5000-$6000

DODGE/PLYMOUTH
Colt Wagon, '90
DODGE
Spirit 4, '90
FORD
Festiva, '91
GEO
Prizm, '90
HONDA
Civic, '89
CRX, '88

MAZDA
323, '90
626, '88 [1]
MX-6, '88 [1]
Pickup 2WD, '89
MITSUBISHI
Mirage, '90
NISSAN
Sentra, '89
Stanza Wagon 2WD, '88
TOYOTA
Corolla 2WD, '89; Corolla FX-16, '88 [2]
Pickup 4 2WD, '89
Tercel, '90

$6000-$7000

ACURA
Integra, '88
BUICK
Electra, '88
DODGE/PLYMOUTH
Colt, '91
EAGLE
Summit, '91

[1] Manual transmission only. [2] Automatic transmission only.

Continued ▶

Continued

FORD
LTD Crown Victoria, '88
GEO
Metro, 92
HONDA
Accord, '88
CRX, '89
ISUZU
Pickup 4 2WD, '91
MAZDA
626, '89 [1]
Pickup 2WD, '90
MERCURY
Grand Marquis, '88
NISSAN
Pickup 4 2WD, '90
Sentra, '90
Stanza, '89
PLYMOUTH
Acclaim 4, '90
TOYOTA
Celica, '88
Corolla 2WD, '90 & 4WD, '89
Pickup 4 2WD, '90; Pickup V6
  2WD, '89 & 4WD, '88

$7000-$8000

BUICK
Century V6, '90
DODGE/ PLYMOUTH
Colt, '92
FORD
LTD Crown Victoria, '89
GEO
Prizm, '91
HONDA
CRX, '90
MAZDA
323, '91
MX-6, '89 [1]
Pickup 2WD, '91
Protegé 2WD, '90
MERCURY
Grand Marquis, '89
MITSUBISHI
Galant, '89
Mirage, '91
NISSAN
240SX, '89
Maxima, '88 [2]

Pickup 4 2WD, '92 & 4WD,
  '90; Pickup V6 2WD, '89
OLDSMOBILE
Eighty-Eight, '89
TOYOTA
Camry 4 2WD, '88
Celica, '89
Corolla 2WD, '91 & 4WD, '90
Pickup 4 2WD, '91; V6 2WD, '90
Tercel, '91

$8000-$9000

ACURA
Integra, '89
BUICK
Electra, '89
Le Sabre, '89
DODGE
Spirit 4, '92
GEO
Prizm, '92
HONDA
Civic, '90
Civic Wagon 4WD, '91
LINCOLN
Town Car, '88
MAZDA
323, '92
626, '90
929, '88
Pickup 2WD, '92
Protegé 2WD, '91
NISSAN
240SX, '90
300ZX, '88
Pickup V6 2WD, '90
PLYMOUTH
Acclaim 4, '92
TOYOTA
Camry 4 2WD & 4WD, '89; V6,
  '89
Cressida, '88
Pickup 4 2WD, '92 & 4WD, '89
VOLVO
240 Sedan & Wagon, '88
740 Sedan, '88

$9000-$10,000

ACURA
Integra, '90

BUICK
Century V6, '91
Le Sabre, '90
Riviera, '89
CADILLAC
Sedan De Ville, '88
FORD
Probe V6, '91
HONDA
Accord, '89
Civic, '91
CRX, '91
Prelude, '89
MAZDA
MX-6, '90
Protegé, '92
MITSUBISHI
Galant, '90
NISSAN
300ZX Turbo, '88
Sentra, '91
Stanza, '90 [2]
SUBARU
Legacy 4WD, '90
TOYOTA
Camry 4 2WD, '90; V6, '90
Celica, '90
Corolla 2WD, '92 & 4WD, '91
Paseo, '92
Pickup 4 4WD, '90; V6 2WD,
  '91 & 4WD, '89, '90
Tercel, '92
VOLVO
740 Wagon, '88

$10,000-$12,000

ACURA
Integra, '91
Legend, '88 [2]
AUDI
100 Quattro Sedan, '89
100 Sedan & Wagon, '89
BUICK
Century V6, '92
Riviera, '90
CADILLAC
Fleetwood, '88
Sedan De Ville, '89
CHRYSLER
Le Baron Sedan 4, '92

HONDA
Accord, '90
Civic, '92
Prelude, '90
MAZDA
626, '91
929, '89
MX-5 Miata, '90
MITSUBISHI
Galant, '91
Montero V6, '89
NISSAN
Maxima, '89 ☑
Pathfinder V6, '88
Pickup V6 2WD, '92 & 4WD, '90
Sentra, '92
Stanza, '91 ☑
OLDSMOBILE
Cutlass Ciera V6, '92
SATURN
SC Coupe, '91
SL Sedan, '91, '92
SUBARU
Legacy 2WD, '91 & 4WD, '91 ☑
Loyale 4WD, '92
TOYOTA
4Runner V6 4WD, '88
Camry 4 2WD, '91
Cressida, '89
Pickup 4 4WD, '91, '92; V6 2WD, '92 & 4WD, '91
VOLVO
240 Sedan & Wagon, '90
760 Sedan V6 & Turbo Sedan, '88

$12,000-$15,000

ACURA
Integra, '92
Legend, '89 ☑
BMW
325i, '89
BUICK
Regal, '92
CADILLAC
Fleetwood, '89
Sedan De Ville, '90
Seville, '89
HONDA
Accord, '91, '92

Prelude, '91
INFINITI
G20, '91
JEEP
Cherokee 4 4WD, '92
LEXUS
ES250, '90
MAZDA
626, '92
MX-5 Miata, '91, '92
MITSUBISHI
Galant, '92
Montero, '90
NISSAN
240SX, '91, '92
Maxima, '90
Pathfinder V6, '89
Stanza, '92
SAAB
900 & 900 Turbo, '90
SATURN
SC Coupe, '92
SUBARU
Legacy 2WD & 4WD, '92
TOYOTA
4Runner V6 4WD, '89, '90
Camry 4, '92 & 4WD, '91; V6, '91
Celica, '91, '92
Cressida, '90
Land Cruiser Wagon, '89
MR2 & MR2 Turbo, '91
Pickup V6 4WD, '92
VOLVO
740 Sedan & Wagon, Turbo Sedan & Wagon, '89, '90
760 Sedan V6, '89; Turbo Wagon, '88

$15,000-$20,000

ACURA
Legend, '90
CADILLAC
Brougham, '91
Fleetwood, '90
HONDA
Prelude, '92
INFINITI
G20, '92
LEXUS
ES250, '91

MAZDA
MPV V6 2WD, '92
NISSAN
Maxima, '91, '92
Pathfinder V6, '90, '91 ☑
SUBARU
SVX, '92
TOYOTA
4Runner V6 4WD, '91 ☑
Camry V6, '92
Cressida, '91
Previa 2WD, '91, '92 & All-Trac 4WD, '91
VOLVO
740 Sedan & Wagon, '91 & Sedan, '92
760 Turbo Sedan & Wagon, '89
940 Sedan & Wagon, SE Sedan, Turbo Sedan & Wagon, '91

$20,000-$25,000

ACURA
Legend, '91 ☑
AUDI
100 S, '92
BMW
525i, '90, '91
INFINITI
Q45, '90
LEXUS
ES300, '92
NISSAN
Pathfinder V6, '92
TOYOTA
4Runner V6 4WD, '92
Land Cruiser Wagon, '91
Previa All-Trac 4WD, '92
VOLVO
740 Wagon, '92
940 SE Wagon, '91; 940 GLS Sedan, Turbo Sedan & Wagon, '92

$25,000-$30,000

ACURA
Legend, '92
AUDI
100 CS Sedan, '92

Continued

BMW
525i, '92
535i, '90, '91
LEXUS
LS400, '90
MERCEDES-BENZ
300E 2WD, '91

$30,000 AND UP

AUDI
100 CS Quattro Sedan &
 Wagon, '92
BMW
525i Touring, '92
535i, '92

INFINITI
Q45, '92
LEXUS
LS400, '91, '92
SC300, '92
SC400, '92
MERCEDES-BENZ
300CE, '91
300TE 2WD, '91

Used cars to avoid

ACURA

Legend, '88-89 ① , '91 ①

AUDI

100, '91

BUICK

Century V6, '88
Regal, '89
Roadmaster, Roadmaster
 Estate Wagon, '92

CADILLAC

Eldorado, '92
Seville, '91

CHEVROLET

Astro Van 2WD, '91, '92 &
 4WD, '92
Blazer, '88-92
Camaro, '88-92
Caprice V8, '91
Cavalier 4, '88-92; V6, '88 ② ,
 '89-92
Corsica, Beretta 4, '88, '90;
 V6, '88, '91
Corvette, '88-92
C1500-2500 Pickup V8, '88-
 89 ② , '91, '92
C/K 1500-2500 Pickup V6,
 '90 ② , '91
K1500-2500 Pickup V8, '88-92
Lumina APV Van, '90

S-10 Blazer V6 2WD & 4WD,
 '88 ② ; 2WD, '92; 4WD,
 '89-92
S-10 Pickup 4, '88 ① , '89-92;
 V6 2WD, '91, '92 & 4WD,
 '89, '92
Sportvan V8, '89-92
Sprint, '88 ①
Suburban 2WD & 4WD, '88-92

CHRYSLER

Le Baron Coupe/Convertible
 4; Turbo, '88, '89; V6, '90
Le Baron Sedan V6, '90
New Yorker, '89, '90, '92
Town & Country Van 2WD,
 '90-92 & 4WD, '92

DODGE

Caravan V6, '89, '90
Colt Vista Wagon, '88-89 ①
Dakota Pickup V6 2WD, '88-
 90 ② , '92; V8, '92
Daytona 4, '88, '89
Dynasty V6, '89-92
Grand Caravan 4, '88 ② , '89;
 V6 2WD, '88-92 & 4WD,
 '91, '92
Monaco, '90, '91
Omni, '89
Ram Van/Wagon B150-250
 V8, '88-90, '92
Shadow 4, '91
Spirit V6, '89, '90
Stealth 2WD, '91 ①

EAGLE

Premier V6, '88-91
Talon 2WD, '92; Turbo 4WD,
 '90-92

FORD

Aerostar Van 2WD, '88-91 &
 4WD, '90, '91
Bronco V8, '88-92
Bronco II 4WD, '88-90
Club Wagon, Van, '88-92
Escort, '88-90
Explorer 2WD & 4WD, '91;
 4WD, '92 ①
F150-250 Pickup 6 2WD &
 4WD, '88;
 4WD, '89, '90, '92; V8 2WD
 & 4WD, '88-92
Mustang 4, '88, '89; V8, '88-92
Probe 4, '89 ② , '91
Ranger Pickup 4 2WD, '92; V6
 2WD & 4WD, '88 ② ; V6
 4WD, '90-92
Taurus 4, '88; V6, '88 ② ;
 SHO, '89-91
Tempo 4, '88-90, '92
Thunderbird 4 Turbo, '88 ①

GEO

Metro, '91
Storm, '90

GMC

Jimmy, Yukon, '88-92
S-15 Jimmy V6 2WD & 4WD,
 '88 ② ; 2WD, '92; 4WD, '89-92

S-15 Sonoma Pickup 4, 88 ☐ ,
   89-92; **V6 2WD, '91, '92 &**
   4WD, '89, '92
Safari Van 2WD, '91, '92 &
   4WD, '92
Suburban 2WD & 4WD, '88-92

HONDA

Prelude, '88 ☐

HYUNDAI

Excel, '88-92
Sonata, '89-92

ISUZU

Rodeo V6, '91, '92
Trooper II 4, '89 ☐ ; **V6, '90,**
   '91; V6, '92 ☑

JEEP

Cherokee 4 4WD, '89, '90;
   Cherokee 6, '88-89 ☐ ;
   Cherokee/Wagoneer 6, '90,
   '91
Wrangler, '88-92

LINCOLN

Continental, '88-90
Town Car, '91

MAZDA

626 4, '88-89 ☑
929, '91
MPV V6 4WD, '90, '91
Navajo 4WD, '91; 4WD, '92 ☐
RX-7, RX-7 Turbo, '88 ☐

MERCURY

Capri 4, 4 Turbo, '91
Sable, '88
Topaz 4, '88-90, '92

MITSUBISHI

3000GT 2WD, '91 ☐
Eclipse 2WD, '92; Turbo 4WD,
   '90-92
Galant Sigma V6, '88 ☑

NISSAN

300ZX, 300ZX Turbo, '90 ☑ ,
   91 ☐
Maxima, '88 ☐
Sentra 2WD, '88 ☑

OLDSMOBILE

Cutlass Calais, '88-90
Cutlass Ciera V6, '88
Ninety-Eight, '88
Silhouette Van, '90

PLYMOUTH

Acclaim V6, '89, '90

Colt Vista Wagon, '88-89 ☐
Grand Voyager 4, '88 ☑ , **'89;**
   V6 2WD, '88-92 & 4WD,
   '91, '92
Horizon, '89
Laser 2WD & Turbo 4WD, '92
Sundance 4, '91
Voyager V6, '89, '90

PONTIAC

Firebird, '88-92
Grand Am 4, '88-91
Grand Prix V6, '88, '89
Le Mans, '88, '89
Sunbird, '88, '91, '92
Trans Sport Van, '92

SAAB

9000 Series, '89

SUBARU

Coupe, Sedan, Wagon 2WD,
   '88 ☐ **& 4WD, '88, '89 &**
   Turbo 4WD, '88
Justy, '88

VOLKSWAGEN

Fox, '89
Golf, GTI, '88-91
Jetta, '88-92
Passat, '90-92

BATTERY BASICS

There are three main types:

■ **Low-maintenance** batteries have caps or covers over their cells to permit periodic checking and refilling.

■ **Maintenance-free** batteries are the type in most new cars. They're designed to reduce water loss further; indeed, some have no refill caps. They may not endure a deep discharge as well as low-maintenance batteries.

■ **Dual** batteries typically combine a low-maintenance battery with separate back-up cells that for emergency power.

Size. Manufacturers categorize batteries by group size—24, 26, 34, and so forth—which denotes the size of the case (but has no direct bearing on the power output). You'll find the group-size on the old battery or in the battery dealer's book.

Cold-cranking amps. Manufacturers rate the cold-cranking amperage (CCA) of their models. The CCA is the amount of current a battery should be able to deliver at 0° without dropping below a certain cutoff voltage for 30 seconds. That translates into the battery's ability to supply power long enough to start your car in below-freezing weather.

Auto reliability

Small, compact, and mid-sized cars—the cars most people choose as the basic family car—are a fairly reliable lot. The reliability of vans, sport-utility vehicles, and pickup trucks—those vehicles whose sales are rising fastest—is less encouraging, according to our readers' experiences. The best of those vehicles are quite reliable but, overall, their reliability leaves a great deal to be desired.

Some domestic nameplates are becoming quite reliable—the *Saturn,* the *Chrysler Concorde,* the *Dodge Interepid,* and the *Eagle Vision.* (Some Chrysler Corp. models have recently been the subject of voluntary safety recalls, setbacks not yet reflected in our readers' reliability reports.)

We collect reliability data each year from CONSUMER REPORTS readers in order to assemble the most comprehensive picture available of auto reliability. We ask subscribers to tell us about problems they've had with their vehicles during the past year. The 1993 Annual Questionnaire, on which the Frequency-of-Repair records are based, brought in reports about 486,000 vehicles, reflecting subscribers' experiences between April 1992 and March 1993. Readers told us of problems they considered serious in the engine, ignition system, transmission, driveline, steering and suspension, air-conditioning, body, and exhaust system—17 trouble spots in all. (See page 329 for a detailed description.)

Our statisticians standardize the data for mileage. For some of the models identified as twins—that is, essentially identical models sold under different nameplates—data are pooled.

We use the statisticians' analysis to help car buyers in several important ways:

■ As the basis for our predicted-reliability judgments in the auto profiles (page 271).

■ To create the lists of reliable used cars and used cars to avoid (page 319).

■ To prepare the Frequency-of-Repair charts, which detail the reliability history of 292 models. See page 330.

■ To create the trouble indexes, starting below, which summarize reliability.

Trouble indexes, 1988 - 1993

The trouble indexes, beginning at right, summarize reliability, as reported by respondents to our Annual Questionnaire. The indexes show how each model compares with the average for that model year.

To come up with the score, our statisticians combine the problems reported for all 17 trouble spots to calculate an overall problem rate for each model in each model year. Because problems with the engine, engine cooling, driveline, transmission, clutch, and body rust tend to be the most serious and costly to repair, our statisticians weight those problems more heavily than other, less serious types of problems.

To score ◒ or ◓, a model had to differ from the average by at least 15 percent; to score ● or ◒, the difference had to be at least 35 percent.

Sometimes we don't have sufficient data to rate a car; such instances are marked with an *. A dash means that the model wasn't made in that year.

Other abbreviations: **RWD** = rear-wheel drive; **FWD** = front-wheel drive; **2WD** = two-wheel drive; **4WD** = four-wheel drive; **4** or **6** = four- or six-cyclinder engine; **V6** or **V8** = six- or eight-cyclinder engine.

Car name	'88	'89	'90	'91	'92	'93
Acura Integra	⊖	⊖	⊖	⊖	⊖	⊖
Acura Legend	⊖	⊖	⊖	⊖	⊖	⊖
Acura Vigor	—	—	—	—	○	*
Audi 5000, 100, Quattro	⊖	⊖	○	○	⊖	*
BMW 318i	—	—	—	○	*	*
BMW 325 Series (2WD)	⊖	⊖	○	*	◐	○
BMW 5 Series	⊖	⊖	⊖	⊖	⊖	*
BMW 7 Series	●	*	*	*	*	*
Buick Century 4	○	○	*	*	*	*
Buick Century V6	○	○	⊖	⊖	⊖	⊖
Buick Electra, Park Avenue	⊖	⊖	○	○	○	○
Buick Park Ave. Ultra Supercharged V6	—	—	—	—	⊖	*
Buick Le Sabre	⊖	⊖	⊖	⊖	○	○
Buick Regal	○	⊖	○	○	⊖	○
Buick Riviera	*	⊖	⊖	○	○	*
Buick Roadmaster	—	—	—	○	●	●
Buick Skylark	◐	○	○	○	⊖	*
Cadillac Brougham, Fleetwood (RWD)	○	⊖	○	⊖	*	●
Cadillac De Ville, Fleetwood (FWD)	⊖	⊖	⊖	○	○	○
Cadillac Eldorado	○	⊖	⊖	○	◐	*
Cadillac Seville	○	⊖	⊖	◐	○	●
Chevrolet Astro Van (2WD)	○	○	○	◐	●	●
Chevrolet Astro Van (4WD)	—	—	○	○	●	*
Chevrolet Blazer	◐	●	●	●	●	●
Chevrolet C/K1500-2500 Pickup V6	○	○	○	○	◐	○
Chevrolet C1500-2500 Pickup V8	○	○	○	◐	●	◐
Chevrolet K1500-2500 Pickup V8	●	●	●	●	●	◐
Chevrolet Camaro	●	●	*	●	●	*
Chevrolet Caprice V8	○	○	○	◐	○	◐
Chevrolet Cavalier 4	◐	◐	◐	●	◐	◐
Chevrolet Cavalier V6	○	◐	*	●	●	*
Chevrolet Celebrity 4	◐	⊖	*	—	—	—
Chevrolet Celebrity V6	○	○	○	—	—	—

Car name	'88	'89	'90	'91	'92	'93
Chevrolet Corsica, Beretta 4	◐	◐	◐	○	*	*
Chevrolet Corsica, Beretta V6	◐	○	○	◐	○	*
Chevrolet Corvette	*	●	*	*	◐	*
Chevrolet Lumina 4	—	—	◐	*	✳	*
Chevrolet Lumina V6	—	—	○	○	○	○
Chevrolet Lumina APV Van	—	—	◐	○	◐	●
Chevrolet Nova (FWD)	⊖	—	—	—	—	—
Chevrolet S-10 Blazer V6 (2WD)	◐	◐	*	◐	●	*
Chevrolet S-10 Blazer V6 (4WD)	◐	●	●	●	●	○
Chevrolet S-10 Pickup 4	◐	◐	◐	◐	◐	*
Chevrolet S-10 Pickup V6 (2WD)	○	○	◐	◐	◐	◐
Chevrolet S-10 Pickup V6 (4WD)	○	◐	*	◐	◐	*
Chevrolet Sportvan V8	○	●	●	●	●	*
Chevrolet Sprint	○	—	—	—	—	—
Chevrolet Suburban (2WD)	●	◐	◐	●	◐	◐
Chevrolet Suburban (4WD)	●	●	◐	●	●	●
Chrysler Concorde	—	—	—	—	—	⊖
Chrysler Le Baron Sedan 4	○	—	—	○	⊖	○
Chrysler Le Baron Sedan V6	—	—	○	○	○	○
Chrysler Le Baron Coupe & Conv. 4	○	○	*	*	*	*
Chrysler Le Baron Coupe & Conv. 4 Turbo	◐	◐	*	*	*	—
Chrysler Le Baron Coupe & Conv. V6	—	—	●	○	○	*
Chrysler New Yorker	○	◐	○	○	●	○
Chrysler Town & Country Van (2WD)	—	—	◐	●	◐	◐
Chrysler Town & Country Van (4WD)	—	—	—	—	●	○
Dodge Aries	○	○	—	—	—	—
Dodge Caravan 4	○	○	○	○	◐	○
Dodge Caravan 4 Turbo	—	○	*	—	—	—
Dodge Grand Caravan 4	◐	◐	—	—	—	—
Dodge Caravan V6 (2WD)	◐	◐	○	○	○	○

Continued ▶

Car name	'88	'89	'90	'91	'92	'93
Dodge Caravan V6 (4WD)	—	—	—	◐	*	*
Dodge Grand Caravan V6 (2WD)	◐	●	◐	●	◐	◐
Dodge Grand Caravan V6 (4WD)				●	●	○
Dodge Colt, Colt Wagon	⊖	⊖	⊖	⊖	⊖	*
Dodge Colt Vista Wagon	○	○	*	*	—	—
Dodge Dakota Pickup V6 (2WD)	○	○	○	○	●	◐
Dodge Dakota Pickup V6 (4WD)	○	◐	*	*	◐	*
Dodge Dakota Pickup V8		*	—	○	●	●
Dodge Daytona 4	◐	●	*	*	*	*
Dodge Dynasty V6	○	○	○	○	●	●
Dodge Intrepid	—	—	—	—	—	⊖
Dodge Monaco	—	—	●	●	*	—
Dodge Omni	○	◐	○	—	—	—
Dodge Ram 50 Pickup 4	⊖	*	*	*	*	*
Dodge Ram B150-250 Van, Wagon V8	○	●	●	○	●	*
Dodge Shadow 4	○	○	○	◐	○	○
Dodge Spirit 4	—	○	⊖	○	⊖	○
Dodge Spirit V6	—	○	○	○	○	○
Dodge Stealth (2WD)	—	—	—	○	○	●
Dodge Stealth Turbo (4WD)	—	—	—	*	●	*
Eagle Premier V6	●	●	●	●	*	—
Eagle Summit Coupe, Hatchback & Sedan	—	○	*	⊖	*	*
Eagle Summit Wagon	—	—	—	—	○	*
Eagle Talon (2WD)	—	—	○	○	●	○
Eagle Talon Turbo (2WD)	—	—	○	○	*	*
Eagle Talon Turbo (4WD)	—	—	●	◐	●	*
Eagle Vision	—	—	—	—	—	⊖
Ford Aerostar Van (2WD)	●	●	●	◐	○	⊖
Ford Aerostar Van (4WD)	—	—	●	●	○	●
Ford Bronco V8	●	●	◐	●	●	*
Ford Bronco II (4WD)	◐	◐	●	—	—	◐
Ford Club Wagon, Van	◐	◐	●	●	◐	◐
Ford Crown Victoria/ LTD Crown Victoria	⊖	⊖	⊖	○	○	○
Ford Escort	◐	◐	◐	○	⊖	○

Car name	'88	'89	'90	'91	'92	'93
Ford Explorer (2WD)	—	—	—	●	○	○
Ford Explorer (4WD)	—	—	—	◐	○	○
Ford F150-250 Pickup 6 (2WD)	◐	○	○	○	○	●
Ford F150-250 Pickup 6 (4WD)	◐	●	●	○	●	*
Ford F150-250 Pickup V8 (2WD)	◐	●	●	◐	●	◐
Ford F150-250 Pickup V8 (4WD)	●	●	●	●	●	○
Ford Festiva	⊖	⊖	⊖	⊖	●	*
Ford Mustang 4	◐	●	○	*	*	*
Ford Mustang V8	○	◐	◐	●	◐	*
Ford Probe 4	—	○	○	◐	○	○
Ford Probe 4 Turbo	—	○	◐	*	*	—
Ford Probe V6	—	—	○	⊖	○	○
Ford Ranger Pickup 4 (2WD)	○	○	⊖	○	◐	○
Ford Ranger Pickup V6 (2WD)	◐	○	○	⊖	○	⊖
Ford Ranger Pickup V6 (4WD)	◐	○	◐	●	●	○
Ford Taurus 4	●	◐	*	—	—	—
Ford Taurus V6	○	○	○	○	○	○
Ford Tempo 4	●	●	●	○	◐	◐
Ford Tempo V6	—	—	—	—	○	*
Ford Thunderbird 4 Turbo	○	—	—	—	—	—
Ford Thunderbird V6	○	○	○	○	○	⊖
Ford Thunderbird V8	⊖	—	—	○	○	*
Geo Metro	—	○	○	◐	⊖	◐
Geo Prizm	—	—	⊖	⊖	⊖	⊖
Geo Storm	—	—	◐	○	○	*
Geo Tracker (4WD)	—	○	○	○	○	*
GMC Jimmy, Yukon	◐	●	●	●	●	●
GMC S-15 Jimmy V6 (2WD)	◐	◐	*	◐	◐	*
GMC S-15 Jimmy V6 (4WD)	◐	●	●	●	●	○
GMC S-15 Sonoma Pickup 4	○	●	●	●	◐	*
GMC S-15 Sonoma Pickup V6 (2WD)	○	○	◐	◐	●	*

Car name	'88	'89	'90	'91	'92	'93
GMC S-15 Sonoma Pickup V6 (4WD)	O	⊖	*	⊖	⊖	*
GMC Safari Van (2WD)	O	O	O	⊖	●	●
GMC Safari Van (4WD)	—	—	O	O	●	*
GMC Suburban (2WD)	●	⊖	⊖	●	⊖	⊖
GMC Suburban (4WD)	●	●	⊖	⊖	●	⊖
Honda Accord	⊖	⊖	⊖	⊖	⊖	⊖
Honda Civic	⊖	⊖	⊖	⊖	⊖	⊖
Honda Civic Wagon (4WD)	⊖	*	*	⊖	—	—
Honda Civic del Sol	—	—	—	—	—	⊖
Honda CRX	⊖	⊖	⊖	⊖	—	—
Honda Prelude	O	⊖	⊖	⊖	⊖	*
Hyundai Excel	●	●	●	⊖	*	*
Hyundai Sonata	—	●	●	●	*	*
Infiniti G20	—	—	—	⊖	⊖	⊖
Infiniti J30	—	—	—	—	—	⊖
Infiniti Q45	—	—	⊖	O	⊖	*
Isuzu Pickup 4 (2WD)	*	⊖	O	⊖	O	*
Isuzu Rodeo V6	—	—	—	●	●	*
Isuzu Trooper II, Trooper 4	O	O	⊖	*	—	—
Isuzu Trooper II, Trooper V6	—	*	●	●	O	*
Jeep Cherokee 4 (4WD)	O	⊖	●	O	⊖	*
Jeep Cherokee, Wagoneer 6	O	O	⊖	●	O	●
Jeep Grand Cherokee 6	—	—	—	—	—	●
Jeep Grand Wagoneer, Grand Cherokee V8	*	*	*	*	—	●
Jeep Wrangler	●	●	●	●	●	●
Lexus ES 250	—	—	⊖	⊖	—	—
Lexus ES 300	—	—	—	—	⊖	⊖
Lexus LS 400	—	—	⊖	⊖	⊖	⊖
Lexus SC 300/400	—	—	—	—	⊖	⊖
Lincoln Continental	●	●	●	O	⊖	O
Lincoln Mark VII	O	O	O	*	*	—
Lincoln Mark VIII	—	—	—	—	—	⊖
Lincoln Town Car	⊖	O	O	●	O	⊖
Mazda 323	⊖	⊖	⊖	⊖	⊖	*
Mazda 626 4	⊖	⊖	⊖	⊖	⊖	⊖

Car name	'88	'89	'90	'91	'92	'93
Mazda 626 V6	—	—	—	—	—	⊖
Mazda 929	⊖	⊖	⊖	O	O	*
Mazda MPV 4	—	O	*	⊖	*	*
Mazda MPV V6 (2WD)	—	O	O	O	⊖	*
Mazda MPV V6 (4WD)	—	*	●	●	⊖	*
Mazda MX-3 4	—	—	—	—	O	*
Mazda MX-3 V6	—	—	—	—	●	*
Mazda MX-5 Miata	—	—	⊖	⊖	⊖	*
Mazda MX-6 4	⊖	⊖	⊖	⊖	⊖	⊖
Mazda MX-6 V6	—	—	—	—	—	⊖
Mazda Navajo (2WD)	—	—	—	—	O	O
Mazda Navajo (4WD)	—	—	—	⊖	O	O
Mazda Pickup (2WD)	⊖	⊖	⊖	⊖	⊖	⊖
Mazda Protege (2WD)	—	—	—	⊖	⊖	⊖
Mazda RX-7	O	*	O	*	—	*
Mercedes-Benz 300 Class 6, V8 (2WD)	⊖	O	⊖	⊖	⊖	*
Mercedes-Benz S Class	⊖	*	*	*	●	*
Mercury Capri 4	—	—	—	●	*	*
Mercury Cougar V6	O	O	O	O	O	⊖
Mercury Cougar V8	⊖	—	—	O	O	*
Mercury Grand Marquis	⊖	⊖	⊖	O	O	O
Mercury Sable V6	⊖	O	O	O	O	O
Mercury Topaz 4	●	●	●	O	⊖	●
Mercury Topaz V6	—	—	—	—	O	*
Mercury Tracer	O	⊖	—	O	⊖	⊖
Mercury Villager Van	—	—	—	—	—	O
Mitsubishi 3000GT (2WD)	—	—	—	O	O	●
Mitsubishi 3000GT Turbo (4WD)	—	—	—	*	●	*
Mitsubishi Diamante	—	—	—	—	⊖	*
Mitsubishi Eclipse (2WD)	—	—	O	O	●	O
Mitsubishi Eclipse Turbo (2WD)	—	—	O	O	*	*
Mitsubishi Eclipse Turbo (4WD)	—	—	—	●	⊖	*
Mitsubishi Expo LRV	—	—	—	—	O	*
Mitsubishi Galant 4	—	⊖	⊖	⊖	⊖	*
Mitsubishi Galant Sigma, Sigma V6	O	*	*	—	—	—

Continued ▶

Car name	'88	'89	'90	'91	'92	'93
Mitsubishi Mirage	✳	✳	⊖	⊖	✳	✳
Mitsubishi Montero V6	—	⊖	⊖	✳	✳	✳
Nissan 240SX	—	⊖	⊖	⊖	⊖	✳
Nissan 300ZX	⊖	✳	○	○	✳	✳
Nissan Altima	—	—	—	—	—	⊜
Nissan Maxima	⊜	⊜	⊜	⊜	⊜	⊜
Nissan Pathfinder V6	⊜	⊜	⊜	⊜	⊜	⊜
Nissan Pickup (2WD)	⊖	⊖	⊖	⊖	⊖	○
Nissan Pickup (4WD)	○	○	⊖	○	⊜	●
Nissan Pulsar NX, NX 1600/2000	⊖	✳	✳	✳	✳	✳
Nissan Quest Van	—	—	—	—	—	○
Nissan Sentra	⊖	⊖	⊖	⊖	⊖	⊖
Nissan Stanza	⊖	⊖	⊖	⊖	⊜	—
Oldsmobile 88	⊖	⊖	⊖	○	○	○
Oldsmobile 98	⊖	⊖	○	○	○	✳
Oldsmobile Achieva	—	—	—	—	○	✳
Oldsmobile Bravada	—	—	—	—	✳	✳
Oldsmobile Custom Cruiser Wagon	⊖	⊖	✳	⊜	✳	—
Oldsmobile Cutlass Calais	●	●	●	○	—	—
Oldsmobile Cutlass Ciera 4	○	○	⊖	✳	✳	✳
Oldsmobile Cutlass Ciera V6	○	○	○	○	⊜	⊜
Oldsmobile Cutlass Supreme V6	○	○	○	○	○	○
Oldsmobile Silhouette Van	—	—	⊜	○	⊜	✳
Oldsmobile Toronado	⊖	✳	⊜	✳	✳	—
Plymouth Acclaim 4	—	○	⊖	○	⊖	○
Plymouth Acclaim V6	—	○	○	○	○	○
Plymouth Colt, Colt Wagon	⊖	⊖	⊖	⊖	⊜	✳
Plymouth Colt Vista Wagon	○	○	✳	✳	○	✳
Plymouth Horizon	○	⊜	○	—	—	—
Plymouth Laser (2WD)	—	—	○	○	●	○
Plymouth Laser Turbo (2WD)	—	—	○	○	✳	✳
Plymouth Laser Turbo (4WD)	—	—	—	—	●	✳
Plymouth Reliant	○	○	—	—	—	—
Plymouth Sundance 4	○	○	○	⊜	○	⊜
Plymouth Voyager 4	○	○	○	○	⊜	○

Car name	'88	'89	'90	'91	'92	'93
Plymouth Voyager 4 Turbo	—	○	✳	—	—	—
Plymouth Grand Voyager 4	⊜	⊜	—	—	—	—
Plymouth Voyager V6 (2WD)	⊜	⊜	○	○	○	○
Plymouth Voyager V6 (4WD)	—	—	—	⊜	✳	✳
Plymouth Grand Voyager V6 (2WD)	⊜	●	⊜	●	⊜	⊜
Plymouth Grand Voyager V6 (4WD)	—	—	—	●	●	○
Pontiac 6000	○	○	○	✳	—	—
Pontiac Bonneville	○	○	⊖	○	○	⊜
Pontiac Firebird	✳	●	✳	●	✳	✳
Pontiac Grand Am 4	⊜	●	●	⊜	○	○
Pontiac Grand Am V6	—	—	—	—	○	○
Pontiac Grand Prix V6	○	⊜	○	○	○	○
Pontiac Le Mans	●	●	✳	✳	✳	✳
Pontiac Sunbird	⊜	○	⊜	●	⊜	✳
Pontiac Trans Sport Van	—	—	○	○	⊜	○
Saab 900	○	○	⊖	○	⊖	✳
Saab 9000	○	●	✳	○	○	⊖
Saturn	—	—	—	⊖	⊜	⊜
Subaru Coupe, Sedan & Wagon (2WD)	⊜	⊖	—	—	—	—
Subaru Coupe, Sedan & Wagon Turbo (4WD)	●	✳	—	—	—	—
Subaru Justy	○	✳	✳	✳	✳	✳
Subaru Legacy (2WD)	—	—	○	⊖	⊖	✳
Subaru Legacy (4WD)	—	—	⊖	⊖	⊖	○
Subaru Loyale Sedan, Wagon & Coupe (2WD)	—	—	○	○	○	✳
Subaru Loyale Sedan, Wagon & Coupe (4WD)	—	—	○	○	⊖	✳
Subaru SVX	—	—	—	—	⊖	✳
Suzuki Sidekick (4WD)	—	○	○	○	○	✳
Toyota 4Runner 4 (4WD)	⊖	✳	✳	✳	✳	✳
Toyota 4Runner V6	⊜	⊜	⊜	⊜	⊜	⊜
Toyota Camry 4 (2WD)	⊜	⊜	⊜	⊜	⊜	⊜
Toyota Camry 4 (4WD)	○	⊖	✳	⊖	—	—
Toyota Camry V6	⊜	⊜	⊜	⊜	⊜	⊜
Toyota Celica	⊖	⊜	⊖	⊖	⊖	⊖

Car name	'88	'89	'90	'91	'92	'93
Toyota Corolla (2WD)	⊖	⊖	⊖	⊖	⊖	⊖
Toyota Corolla (4WD)	✳	⊖	⊖	⊖	✳	—
Toyota Corolla FX, FX-16	⊖	—	—	—	—	—
Toyota Cressida	⊖	⊖	⊖	⊖	✳	—
Toyota Land Cruiser Wagon	⊖	⊖	✳	⊖	✳	✳
Toyota MR2	✳	✳	—	⊖	✳	✳
Toyota Paseo	—	—	—	—	⊖	✳
Toyota Pickup 4 (2WD)	⊖	⊖	⊖	⊖	⊖	⊖
Toyota Pickup 4 (4WD)	⊖	⊖	⊖	⊖	⊖	✳
Toyota Pickup V6 (2WD)	—	⊖	⊖	⊖	⊖	✳
Toyota Pickup V6 (4WD)	⊖	⊖	⊖	⊖	⊖	⊖
Toyota Previa Van (2WD)	—	—	—	⊖	⊖	⊖
Toyota Previa Van (4WD)	—	—	—	⊖	⊖	✳

Car name	'88	'89	'90	'91	'92	'93
Toyota Supra	⊖	○	✳	✳	✳	—
Toyota Tercel	⊖	⊖	⊖	⊖	⊖	⊖
Volkswagen Fox	○	◒	✳	✳	✳	✳
Volkswagen Golf, GTI	◒	●	●	●	✳	✳
Volkswagen Jetta	◒	○	●	●	●	✳
Volkswagen Passat	—	—	●	●	◒	✳
Volvo 240 Series	⊖	⊖	⊖	○	○	✳
Volvo 740 Series	⊖	⊖	⊖	⊖	⊖	—
Volvo 740 Series Turbo	⊖	⊖	⊖	✳	✳	—
Volvo 760	⊖	⊖	⊖	—	—	—
Volvo 850 GLT	—	—	—	—	—	⊖
Volvo 940	—	—	—	⊖	⊖	⊖
Volvo 960 Series	—	—	—	—	●	✳

Trouble spots explained

Trouble spot	Includes
Engine	Pistons, rings, valves, block, heads, bearings, camshafts, gaskets, turbo, belts & chains, oil pump, leaks, overhaul.
Engine cooling	Radiator, heater core, water pump, thermostat, hoses, intercooler & plumbing, overheating.
Fuel system	Choke, fuel injection, computer & sensors, fuel pump, tank, emissions controls, carburetion setting, leaks, stalling.
Ignition system	Spark or glow plugs, coil, distributor, electronic ignition, sensors, timing, too-frequent tune-ups, knock or ping.
Automatic transmission	Transaxle, gear selector, linkage, coolers & lines, leaks, malfunction or failure.
Manual transmission	Gearbox, transaxle, shifter, linkage, leaks, malfunction or failure.
Clutch	Lining, pressure plate, release bearing, linkage & fluids.
Driveline	Drive joints, drive axles, differential, wheel bearings, drive shaft, four-wheel-drive components.
Electrical system	Starter, alternator, battery, switches, controls, instruments, lights, radio, horn, accessory motors, electronics, wiring.
Steering/suspension	Linkage, power unit, pump, coolers, alignment, springs & torsion bars, ball joints, bushings, shocks/struts.
Brakes	Hydraulic system, linings, disks & drums; power boost, antilock system; parking brake & linkage, malfunction.
Exhaust system	Manifold, muffler, catalytic converter, pipes, leaks.
Body rust	Corrosion, pitting, perforation.
Paint & ext. trim	Fading, discoloring, chalking, peeling, cracking, loose trim, moldings, outside mirrors.
Body integrity	Air seals, weather stripping, air & water leaks, wind noise, rattles and squeaks.
Body hardware	Window, door, seat mechanisms, locks, safety belts, sunroof, glass, wipers.
Air-conditioning	Compressor, condenser, evaporator, expansion valves, hoses, dryer, fans, electronics, leakage.

Frequency-of-repair records, 1988 - 1993

The symbols in the charts reflect the percentage of cars with problems reported for each trouble spot, explained on page 329, in each model year.

At the time of the survey, the 1993 models were generally less than six months old, with an average of only 3000 miles. In our judgment, those cars should score ⊖ in all the trouble spots; a score of ○ or worse is a sure sign of trouble in a car that new. In older models, scores of ○ are not necessarily cause for alarm, but scores of ◒ or ● reflect too many problems for most trouble spots.

KEY TO PROBLEM RATES	
⊖	2.0% or less
◒	2.0% - 5.0%
○	5.0% - 9.3%
◑	9.3% - 14.8%
●	More than 14.8%
*	Insufficient data
□	Not applicable

ABBREVIATIONS USED	
—	model not made that year
RWD	rear-wheel drive
FWD	front-wheel drive
2WD	2-wheel drive
4WD	4-wheel drive
4 or 6	4- or 6-cylinder engine
V6 or V8	6 or 8-cylinder engine

TROUBLE SPOTS	Acura Integra '88	'89	'90	'91	'92	'93	Acura Legend '88	'89	'90	'91	'92	'93	Acura Vigor '88	'89	'90	'91	'92	'93	Audi 5000, 100, Quattro '88	'89	'90	'91	'92	'93
Engine	⊖	⊖	⊖	⊖	⊖	⊖	⊖	⊖	⊖	⊖	⊖	⊖					⊖		○	⊖	⊖	⊖	⊖	
Engine cooling	⊖	⊖	⊖	○	⊖	⊖	⊖	⊖	⊖	○	⊖	⊖					⊖		○	⊖	⊖	⊖	⊖	
Fuel system	⊖	⊖	⊖	⊖	⊖	⊖	⊖	⊖	⊖	⊖	⊖	⊖					⊖		○	◒	○	○	⊖	
Ignition system	●	●	⊖	⊖	⊖	⊖	⊖	⊖	⊖	⊖	⊖	⊖					◒		○	⊖	⊖	⊖	⊖	
Auto. transmission	⊖	⊖	⊖	⊖	⊖	*	○	⊖	⊖	⊖	⊖	⊖					⊖		*	*	○	◒	⊖	
Man. transmission	⊖	⊖	⊖	⊖	*	*	⊖	⊖	⊖	◒	*	*					*		*	*	*	*	*	
Clutch	○	⊖	⊖	⊖	⊖	⊖	●	●	○	●	*	*					*		*	*	*	*	*	
Driveline	⊖	⊖	⊖	⊖	⊖	⊖	⊖	⊖	⊖	⊖	⊖	⊖					⊖	Insufficient data	⊖	⊖	⊖	⊖	⊖	Insufficient data
Electrical system	◒	○	◒	○	◒	⊖	◒	◒	◒	◒	○	⊖					○		●	●	●	●	○	
Steering/suspension	⊖	◒	⊖	⊖	⊖	⊖	◒	◒	◒	⊖	⊖	⊖					⊖		◒	○	○	○	○	
Brakes	●	◒	⊖	⊖	⊖	⊖	◒	◒	○	⊖	⊖	⊖					⊖		◒	⊖	○	○	⊖	
Exhaust system	●	◒	⊖	⊖	⊖	⊖	⊖	⊖	⊖	⊖	⊖	⊖					⊖		○	⊖	⊖	○	⊖	
Body rust	○	⊖	⊖	⊖	⊖	⊖	⊖	⊖	⊖	⊖	⊖	⊖					⊖		⊖	⊖	⊖	⊖	⊖	
Paint	⊖	⊖	⊖	⊖	⊖	⊖	⊖	⊖	⊖	⊖	⊖	⊖					⊖		⊖	⊖	⊖	⊖	⊖	
Body integrity	○	⊖	○	○	⊖	⊖	○	○	○	⊖	⊖	⊖					◒		○	⊖	○	○	⊖	
Body hardware	○	◒	○	○	○	⊖	○	○	○	○	⊖	⊖					⊖		○	◒	○	○	⊖	
Air-conditioning	○	⊖	⊖	⊖	⊖	⊖	○	⊖	⊖	⊖	⊖	⊖					⊖		●	○	◒	○	⊖	

Top section

TROUBLE SPOTS	BMW 318i '89	'90	'91	'92	'93	BMW 325 Series (2WD) '88	'89	'90	'91	'92	'93	BMW 5 Series '88	'89	'90	'91	'92	'93	BMW 7 Series '88	'89	'90	'91	'92	'93
Engine		⊖				⊖	○	○		⊖	⊖	⊖	⊖	⊖	⊖	⊖		○					
Engine cooling		⊖				○	⊖	○		⊖	⊖	○	◑	⊖	⊖	⊖		●					
Fuel system		○				○	○	◑		○	⊖	⊖	⊖	⊖	⊖	○		⊖					
Ignition system		⊖				⊖	⊖	⊖		⊖	⊖	⊖	⊖	⊖	⊖	⊖		○					
Auto. transmission						*	*	*		◑	*	*	⊖	⊖	⊖	⊖		◑					
Man. transmission		⊖				*	⊖	*	Insufficient data	◑	*	*	*	*	*	*	Insufficient data		Insufficient data	Insufficient data	Insufficient data	Insufficient data	Insufficient data
Clutch		◑	Insufficient data	Insufficient data		*	⊖	*		◑	*	*	*	*	*	*							
Driveline		⊖				⊖	⊖	⊖		⊖	⊖	⊖	⊖	⊖	⊖	⊖		⊖					
Electrical system		◑				●	●	●		●	◑	●	●	●	●	○		●					
Steering/suspension		○				○	◑	◑		○	⊖	○	⊖	⊖	⊖	⊖							
Brakes		◑				●	◑	◑		○	⊖	●	◑	⊖	⊖	⊖							
Exhaust system		⊖				⊖	⊖	⊖		⊖	⊖	⊖	⊖	⊖	⊖	⊖		⊖					
Body rust						⊖	⊖	⊖		⊖	⊖	⊖						⊖					
Paint		○				⊖	⊖	○		⊖	⊖	○						○					
Body integrity		⊖				⊖	⊖	○		◑	⊖	⊖						○					
Body hardware		○				◑	○	○		○	⊖	○	○	○	⊖	⊖		●					
Air-conditioning		○				◑	○	○		○	⊖	○	○	○	⊖	⊖		●					

Bottom section

TROUBLE SPOTS	Buick Century 4 '89	'90	'91	'92	'93	Buick Century V6 '88	'89	'90	'91	'92	'93	Buick Electra, Park Avenue '88	'89	'90	'91	'92	'93	Buick Park Ave. Ultra Supercharged V6 '88	'89	'90	'91	'92	'93
Engine	○					○	⊖	⊖	⊖	⊖	⊖	⊖	⊖	⊖	⊖	⊖	⊖					⊖	
Engine cooling	○					○	⊖	⊖	⊖	⊖	⊖	○	⊖	⊖	⊖	⊖	⊖					⊖	
Fuel system	◑					●	○	⊖	⊖	⊖	⊖	⊖	○	⊖	⊖	⊖	⊖					⊖	
Ignition system	○					○	⊖	⊖	⊖	⊖	⊖	○	⊖	⊖	⊖	⊖	⊖					⊖	
Auto. transmission	⊖					⊖	○	⊖	⊖	⊖	⊖	○	○	⊖	⊖	⊖	⊖					⊖	
Man. transmission																							
Clutch																							
Driveline	⊖					⊖	⊖	⊖	⊖	⊖	⊖	⊖	⊖	⊖	⊖	⊖	⊖					⊖	
Electrical system	●					●	◑	◑	○	○	⊖	●	●	●	●	◑	○					◑	
Steering/suspension	●					◑	⊖	⊖	⊖	⊖	⊖	●	⊖	⊖	⊖	⊖	⊖					⊖	
Brakes	◑					●	●	●	○	◑	⊖	●	●	◑	○	○	⊖					⊖	
Exhaust system	⊖					○	⊖	○	⊖	⊖	⊖	⊖	⊖	⊖	⊖	⊖	⊖					⊖	
Body rust	⊖					⊖	⊖	⊖	⊖	⊖	⊖	⊖	⊖	⊖	⊖	⊖	⊖					⊖	
Paint	◑					●	○	⊖	○	○	⊖	◑	○	⊖	⊖	⊖	⊖					○	
Body integrity	○					○	○	○	○	○	○	○	⊖	○	●	◑	○					○	
Body hardware	○					◑	○	○	○	○	○	◑	⊖	○	◑	○	○					○	
Air-conditioning	⊖					○	○	○	⊖	⊖	⊖	⊖	○	⊖	○	⊖	⊖					⊖	

Buick Century 4 columns '90–'93: Insufficient data. Buick Park Ave. Ultra Supercharged V6 columns '88–'91, '93: Insufficient data.

Legend: ⊖ ⊖ ○ ◑ ● Few ← Problems → Many * Insufficient data

Buick Le Sabre

TROUBLE SPOTS	'88	'89	'90	'91	'92	'93
Engine	⊖	⊖	⊖	⊖	⊖	⊖
Engine cooling	⊖	○	○	⊖	⊖	⊖
Fuel system	⊖	◐	⊖	○	⊖	⊖
Ignition system	○	⊖	○	○	⊖	⊖
Auto. transmission	○	○	⊖	⊖	⊖	⊖
Man. transmission						
Clutch						
Driveline	⊖	⊖	⊖	⊖	⊖	⊖
Electrical system	●	◐	◐	◐	○	○
Steering/suspension	●	⊖	⊖	○	⊖	⊖
Brakes	●	◐	◐	○	⊖	⊖
Exhaust system	⊖	⊖	⊖	⊖	⊖	⊖
Body rust	○	○	○	○	⊖	○
Paint	○	○	○	○	◐	○
Body integrity	○	○	○	○	○	○
Body hardware	○	○	○	○	○	○
Air-conditioning	⊖	⊖	⊖	⊖	⊖	⊖

Buick Regal

TROUBLE SPOTS	'88	'89	'90	'91	'92	'93
Engine	○	○	⊖	⊖	⊖	⊖
Engine cooling	⊖	○	⊖	⊖	⊖	⊖
Fuel system	⊖	◐	○	⊖	⊖	⊖
Ignition system	⊖	◐	⊖	⊖	⊖	⊖
Auto. transmission	○	◐	⊖	⊖	⊖	⊖
Man. transmission						
Clutch						
Driveline	⊖	⊖	⊖	⊖	⊖	⊖
Electrical system	●	●	●	◐	○	○
Steering/suspension	○	○	⊖	○	○	⊖
Brakes	⊖	◐	⊖	○	⊖	⊖
Exhaust system	⊖	⊖	⊖	⊖	⊖	⊖
Body rust	⊖	⊖	⊖	○	⊖	⊖
Paint	○	○	○	○	○	○
Body integrity	○	○	○	○	○	○
Body hardware	○	●	◐	○	○	○
Air-conditioning	⊖	⊖	⊖	⊖	⊖	⊖

Buick Riviera

TROUBLE SPOTS	'88	'89	'90	'91	'92	'93
Engine		⊖	⊖	⊖	⊖	
Engine cooling		⊖	⊖	⊖	⊖	
Fuel system		⊖	⊖	⊖	⊖	
Ignition system		○	⊖	⊖	⊖	
Auto. transmission		○	⊖	⊖	⊖	
Man. transmission						
Clutch						
Driveline	Insufficient data	⊖	⊖	⊖	⊖	Insufficient data
Electrical system		●	●	●	◐	
Steering/suspension		●	⊖	⊖	⊖	
Brakes		●	◐	○	⊖	
Exhaust system		⊖	⊖	⊖	⊖	
Body rust		⊖	⊖	⊖	⊖	
Paint		○	○	○	⊖	
Body integrity		⊖	○	○	○	
Body hardware		○	●	⊖	⊖	
Air-conditioning		⊖	⊖	○	○	

Buick Roadmaster

TROUBLE SPOTS	'88	'89	'90	'91	'92	'93
Engine					⊖	⊖
Engine cooling					⊖	⊖
Fuel system					⊖	⊖
Ignition system					○	⊖
Auto. transmission					⊖	○
Man. transmission						
Clutch						
Driveline					⊖	⊖
Electrical system					○	◐
Steering/suspension					○	⊖
Brakes					⊖	⊖
Exhaust system					⊖	⊖
Body rust					⊖	⊖
Paint					⊖	⊖
Body integrity					◐	⊖
Body hardware					⊖	⊖
Air-conditioning					○	○

Buick Skylark

TROUBLE SPOTS	'88	'89	'90	'91	'92	'93
Engine	●	○	○	⊖	⊖	
Engine cooling	○	○	○	⊖	⊖	
Fuel system	○	○	○	⊖	⊖	
Ignition system	○	○	○	⊖	⊖	
Auto. transmission	⊖	⊖	⊖	⊖	⊖	
Man. transmission						
Clutch						
Driveline	⊖	⊖	⊖	⊖	⊖	Insufficient data
Electrical system	●	●	●	○	⊖	
Steering/suspension	⊖	⊖	⊖	○	⊖	
Brakes	⊖	◐	●	○	○	
Exhaust system	⊖	⊖	⊖	⊖	⊖	
Body rust	●	○	○	⊖	⊖	
Paint	●	●	○	○	○	
Body integrity	○	○	○	○	○	
Body hardware	○	○	○	○	○	
Air-conditioning	○	○	⊖	⊖	⊖	

Cadillac Brougham, Fleetwood (RWD)

TROUBLE SPOTS	'88	'89	'90	'91	'92	'93
Engine	○	○	○	⊖	⊖	⊖
Engine cooling	⊖	○	○	⊖	⊖	⊖
Fuel system	○	○	⊖	⊖	⊖	⊖
Ignition system	⊖	⊖	⊖	⊖	⊖	⊖
Auto. transmission	○	⊖	○	⊖		⊖
Man. transmission						
Clutch						
Driveline	⊖	⊖	⊖	⊖		○
Electrical system	●	●	◐	○	Insufficient data	○
Steering/suspension	○	○	○	⊖		⊖
Brakes	●	◐	○	⊖		⊖
Exhaust system	○	⊖	⊖	⊖		⊖
Body rust	○	⊖	⊖	⊖		⊖
Paint	●	○	⊖	⊖		⊖
Body integrity	⊖	○	○	○		○
Body hardware	⊖	○	○	○		○
Air-conditioning	⊖	○	○	○		⊖

Cadillac De Ville, Fleetwood (FWD)

TROUBLE SPOTS	'88	'89	'90	'91	'92	'93
Engine	○	⊖	⊖	○	⊖	⊖
Engine cooling	○	⊖	⊖	⊖	⊖	⊖
Fuel system	⊖	⊖	⊖	⊖	⊖	⊖
Ignition system	⊖	⊖	⊖	⊖	⊖	⊖
Auto. transmission	○	⊖	⊖	⊖	⊖	⊖
Man. transmission						
Clutch						
Driveline	⊖	⊖	⊖	⊖	⊖	⊖
Electrical system	●	◐	◐	○	⊖	⊖
Steering/suspension	◐	○	○	○	⊖	⊖
Brakes	●	●	◐	○	⊖	⊖
Exhaust system	⊖	⊖	⊖	⊖	⊖	⊖
Body rust	⊖	⊖	⊖	⊖	⊖	⊖
Paint	○	○	⊖	○	○	⊖
Body integrity	○	○	○	○	○	○
Body hardware	○	○	○	○	○	⊖
Air-conditioning	●	○	⊖	○	⊖	⊖

Cadillac Eldorado

TROUBLE SPOTS	'88	'89	'90	'91	'92	'93
Engine	⊖	⊖	⊖	⊖	⊖	
Engine cooling	●	⊖	⊖	⊖	⊖	
Fuel system	○	○	⊖	⊖	⊖	
Ignition system	⊖	◐	⊖	⊖	⊖	
Auto. transmission	○	○	⊖	⊖	⊖	
Man. transmission						
Clutch						
Driveline	⊖	⊖	⊖	⊖	⊖	Insufficient data
Electrical system	●	●	●	◐	⊖	
Steering/suspension	⊖	●	○	○	⊖	
Brakes	●	●	◐	○	⊖	
Exhaust system	⊖	⊖	⊖	⊖	⊖	
Body rust	⊖	⊖	⊖	⊖	⊖	
Paint	○	○	⊖	○	⊖	
Body integrity	○	○	○	○	●	
Body hardware	○	○	○	○	●	
Air-conditioning	●	○	⊖	○	⊖	

TROUBLE SPOTS	Cadillac Seville '89	'90	'91	'92	'93	Chevrolet Astro Van (2WD) '88	'89	'90	'91	'92	'93
Engine	⊖	⊖	⊖	⊜	⊖	◒	◒	⊖	⊜	⊖	⊖
Engine cooling	⊜	⊜	⊜	⊜	⊜	⊖	○	⊖	⊜	⊜	⊜
Fuel system	⊖	⊖	○	⊖	⊖	⊖	⊖	⊜	⊖	⊖	⊜
Ignition system	⊖	⊖	⊖	⊜	⊜	⊖	⊖	⊖	⊖	⊖	⊜
Auto. transmission	⊖	⊖	⊖	⊜	⊖	○	⊖	⊖	⊖	⊖	⊜
Man. transmission						*	*				
Clutch						*	*				
Driveline	⊜	⊜	⊜	⊜	⊜	⊜	⊜	⊜	⊜	⊜	⊜
Electrical system	●	●	●	◒	○	●	●	◒	◒	◒	⊖
Steering/suspension	⊖	⊖	○	○	⊖	●	◒	◒	○	⊖	⊖
Brakes	●	●	◒	⊜	⊖	●	●	●	●	◒	⊖
Exhaust system	⊜	⊜	⊖	⊜	⊜	○	⊖	⊖	⊜	⊜	⊜
Body rust	⊜	⊜	⊜	⊜	⊜	⊜	⊜	⊜	⊜	⊜	⊜
Paint	⊖	⊖	○	⊖	⊖	◒	○	◒	○	○	⊖
Body integrity	○	○	◒	●	◒	◒	◒	●	●	●	◒
Body hardware	◒	◒	○	◒	○	●	●	●	●	●	○
Air-conditioning	○	○	◒	⊜	⊖	○	○	○	⊜	⊖	⊖

TROUBLE SPOTS	Chevrolet Astro Van (4WD) '88	'89	'90	'91	'92	'93	Chevrolet Blazer '88	'89	'90	'91	'92	'93
Engine			⊖	⊖	⊖	Insufficient data	○	○	⊖	⊖	⊖	⊖
Engine cooling			⊜	⊖	⊖	Insufficient data	○	◒	○	○	⊜	⊜
Fuel system			⊖	⊜	⊖	Insufficient data	◒	○	○	⊖	⊖	⊜
Ignition system			⊜	⊜	⊜	Insufficient data	⊖	⊖	○	⊜	⊜	⊜
Auto. transmission			⊖	○	⊖	Insufficient data	◒	◒	*	⊖	○	⊖
Man. transmission						Insufficient data	*	*	*	*	*	*
Clutch						Insufficient data	*	*	*	*	*	*
Driveline			⊜	⊜	⊜	Insufficient data	⊜	⊜	⊜	⊜	⊜	⊜
Electrical system			◒	◒	○	Insufficient data	●	●	●	◒	◒	⊖
Steering/suspension			○	⊖	⊖	Insufficient data	◒	○	○	○	⊖	⊖
Brakes			●	◒	◒	Insufficient data	●	●	●	◒	○	⊜
Exhaust system			⊖	⊜	⊜	Insufficient data	◒	◒	◒	⊜	⊜	⊜
Body rust			⊜	⊜	⊜	Insufficient data	◒	◒	◒	○	⊖	⊜
Paint			◒	⊖	◒	Insufficient data	●	●	●	●	○	⊜
Body integrity			●	◒	●	Insufficient data	●	●	●	●	◒	◒
Body hardware			●	●	●	Insufficient data	●	●	●	●	◒	⊖
Air-conditioning			⊜	⊖	⊖	Insufficient data	○	⊖	⊜	⊖	○	⊜

TROUBLE SPOTS	Chevrolet C/K1500-2500 Pickup V6 '89	'90	'91	'92	'93	Chevrolet C1500-2500 Pickup V8 '88	'89	'90	'91	'92	'93
Engine	◒	⊖	⊖	⊖	⊜	◒	○	○	⊜	⊖	⊜
Engine cooling	○	○	⊜	⊜	⊜	●	○	⊖	⊖	⊜	⊜
Fuel system	⊖	⊖	⊖	⊜	⊜	○	○	⊖	○	⊖	⊜
Ignition system	○	○	⊖	⊖	⊜	○	⊖	○	⊖	⊜	⊜
Auto. transmission	⊖	◒	○	○	⊜	◒	◒	○	○	◒	⊖
Man. transmission	⊜	○	○	⊖	*	*	*	*	*	*	*
Clutch	○	○	◒	⊖	*	*	*	*	*	*	*
Driveline	⊖	⊜	⊜	⊜	⊜	⊜	⊜	⊜	⊜	⊜	⊜
Electrical system	●	◒	◒	◒	○	●	●	●	◒	◒	⊖
Steering/suspension	●	○	○	⊖	⊜	◒	◒	○	○	⊖	⊖
Brakes	◒	○	○	⊜	⊜	●	◒	◒	⊜	⊖	⊖
Exhaust system	○	⊖	⊖	⊜	⊜	◒	◒	○	⊖	⊜	⊜
Body rust	⊜	⊜	⊜	⊜	⊜	⊜	⊖	⊜	⊜	⊜	⊜
Paint	◒	○	○	○	⊖	◒	◒	◒	○	○	○
Body integrity	◒	◒	○	◒	○	◒	◒	○	◒	◒	○
Body hardware	◒	○	○	○	⊖	◒	◒	○	○	○	⊖
Air-conditioning	○	○	○	○	⊖	○	○	○	◒	⊖	⊜

TROUBLE SPOTS	Chevrolet K1500-2500 Pickup V8 '88	'89	'90	'91	'92	'93	Chevrolet Camaro '88	'89	'90	'91	'92	'93
Engine	◒	◒	○	⊖	⊖	⊜	◒	◒	Insufficient data	⊖	⊖	Insufficient data
Engine cooling	●	◒	⊖	⊜	⊜	⊜	●	◒	Insufficient data	⊖	⊜	Insufficient data
Fuel system	○	⊖	○	⊖	⊖	⊜	●	●	Insufficient data	◒	○	Insufficient data
Ignition system	○	○	○	⊖	⊖	⊜	◒	◒	Insufficient data	○	⊖	Insufficient data
Auto. transmission	◒	◒	◒	◒	◒	⊜	○	⊖	Insufficient data	⊖	○	Insufficient data
Man. transmission	*	*	*	*	○	*	*	*	Insufficient data	*	*	Insufficient data
Clutch	*	*	*	*	○	*	*	*	Insufficient data	*	*	Insufficient data
Driveline	⊖	⊖	⊖	⊜	⊜	⊜	⊜	⊜	Insufficient data	⊜	⊜	Insufficient data
Electrical system	●	●	●	◒	◒	⊖	●	●	Insufficient data	●	◒	Insufficient data
Steering/suspension	●	●	○	⊖	○	⊜	○	◒	Insufficient data	⊖	⊖	Insufficient data
Brakes	●	◒	◒	◒	⊖	⊜	○	◒	Insufficient data	◒	○	Insufficient data
Exhaust system	●	◒	⊜	⊖	⊜	⊜	●	○	Insufficient data	⊖	⊖	Insufficient data
Body rust	⊖	⊖	⊜	⊜	⊜	⊜	●	○	Insufficient data	⊖	⊜	Insufficient data
Paint	◒	◒	◒	◒	⊖	⊖	●	●	Insufficient data	●	◒	Insufficient data
Body integrity	◒	◒	◒	○	◒	○	●	●	Insufficient data	●	●	Insufficient data
Body hardware	●	◒	◒	○	○	○	●	●	Insufficient data	●	●	Insufficient data
Air-conditioning	○	○	○	○	⊖	⊜	○	⊖	Insufficient data	⊖	⊜	Insufficient data

⊜ ⊖ ○ ◒ ● *

Few ← Problems → Many Insufficient data

Chevrolet Caprice V8						Chevrolet Cavalier 4						TROUBLE SPOTS	Chevrolet Cavalier V6						Chevrolet Celebrity				
'88	'89	'90	'91	'92	'93	'88	'89	'90	'91	'92	'93		'88	'89	'90	'91	'92	'93	'88	'89	'90	'91	'92
○	○	⊖	⊖	⊖	⊖	○	◑	○	⊖	⊖	⊖	Engine	⊖	⊖		○	⊖	⊖	⊖	⊖			
○	○	⊖	⊖	⊖	⊖	○	○	○	⊖	⊖	⊖	Engine cooling	○	○		⊖	⊖	⊖	○	○			
⊖	○	⊖	⊖	⊖	⊖	⊖	⊖	⊖	⊖	⊖	⊖	Fuel system	●	●		⊖	⊖	⊖	⊖	○			
○	⊖	⊖	⊖	⊖	⊖	⊖	⊖	⊖	⊖	⊖	⊖	Ignition system	⊖	○		⊖	⊖	⊖	⊖	○			
○	⊖	⊖	⊖	⊖	⊖	⊖	⊖	⊖	⊖	⊖	⊖	Auto. transmission	⊖	⊖		*	*		⊖	⊖			
						*	*	*	*	*	*	Man. transmission	*	*		*	*						
						*	*	*	*	*	*	Clutch	*	*	Insufficient data	*	*	Insufficient data			Insufficient data		
⊖	⊖	⊖	⊖	⊖	⊖	⊖	⊖	⊖	⊖	⊖	⊖	Driveline	⊖	⊖		⊖	⊖		⊖	⊖			
⊖	○	⊖	○	○	⊖	●	●	●	●	⊖	⊖	Electrical system	●	●		●	●		●	⊖			
⊖	○	○	○	⊖	⊖	⊖	⊖	⊖	⊖	⊖	⊖	Steering/suspension	○	⊖		⊖	⊖		○	⊖			
⊖	○	○	○	⊖	⊖	●	●	●	●	⊖	⊖	Brakes	●	●		○	○		●	⊖			
●	○	⊖	⊖	⊖	⊖	⊖	●	⊖	⊖	⊖	⊖	Exhaust system	●	●		⊖	⊖		⊖	⊖			
○	○	⊖	⊖	⊖	⊖	●	●	⊖	○	⊖	⊖	Body rust	⊖	○		⊖	⊖		⊖	○			
○	○	⊖	⊖	⊖	⊖	●	●	●	⊖	⊖	⊖	Paint	●	⊖		⊖	⊖		⊖	○			
○	○	⊖	○	○	○	●	●	●	●	○	○	Body integrity	⊖	⊖		⊖	●		○	○			
⊖	⊖	●	●	○	⊖	●	●	●	⊖	○	○	Body hardware	⊖	⊖		●	●		○	○			
○	⊖	⊖	○	⊖	⊖	○	○	○	⊖	⊖	⊖	Air-conditioning	○	○		⊖	⊖		⊖	⊖			

Chevrolet Celebrity V6						Chevrolet Corsica, Beretta 4						TROUBLE SPOTS	Chevrolet Corsica, Beretta V6						Chevrolet Corvette				
'88	'89	'90	'91	'92	'93	'88	'89	'90	'91	'92	'93		'88	'89	'90	'91	'92	'93	'88	'89	'90	'91	'92
○	○	⊖				⊖	⊖	⊖	⊖			Engine	○	⊖	⊖	○	⊖			⊖			⊖
○	○	○				⊖	○	⊖	⊖			Engine cooling	⊖	○	⊖	⊖	⊖			●			⊖
⊖	●	⊖				⊖	⊖	⊖	⊖			Fuel system	●	●	⊖	⊖	⊖			⊖			⊖
⊖	⊖	⊖				○	⊖	○	⊖			Ignition system	⊖	⊖	⊖	⊖	⊖			○			⊖
○	⊖	⊖				○	⊖	⊖	⊖			Auto. transmission	○	⊖	⊖	⊖	⊖			*			*
*						*	*	*	*			Man. transmission	⊖	*	*	*	*			*			*
*						*	*	*	*	Insufficient data	Insufficient data	Clutch	●	*	*	*	*	Insufficient data	Insufficient data	*	Insufficient data	Insufficient data	*
⊖	⊖	⊖				⊖	⊖	⊖	○			Driveline	⊖	⊖	⊖	⊖	⊖			⊖			⊖
●	●	⊖				●	●	●	○			Electrical system	●	●	○	⊖	⊖			●			⊖
○	○	⊖				●	⊖	○	○			Steering/suspension	○	⊖	⊖	○	○			⊖			○
●	●	●				●	●	○	○			Brakes	●	●	⊖	○	○			⊖			⊖
●	●	⊖				●	●	○	⊖			Exhaust system	⊖	○	⊖	⊖	○			⊖			⊖
⊖	⊖	⊖				⊖	○	⊖	⊖			Body rust	⊖	⊖	⊖	⊖	⊖			⊖			⊖
●	⊖	○				●	●	●	⊖			Paint	●	●	●	○	⊖			○			○
○	○	○				●	⊖	○	⊖			Body integrity	●	⊖	⊖	○	⊖			●			●
●	○	⊖				●	●	○	○			Body hardware	●	●	●	○	○			●			○
○	○	⊖				○	⊖	⊖	⊖			Air-conditioning	○	○	⊖	⊖	⊖			●			⊖

Reliability chart. Symbol scale from "Few" problems to "Many" problems, with asterisk (*) indicating insufficient data.

Chevrolet Lumina 4

Trouble spot	'88	'89	'90	'91	'92	'93
Engine			⊖	*	*	*
Engine cooling		○		*(ins.)	*(ins.)	*(ins.)
Fuel system			◑			
Ignition system			◑			
Auto. transmission		⊖				
Man. transmission						
Clutch						
Driveline		⊖	●			
Electrical system		◑	●			
Steering/suspension		●	●			
Brakes		●	◑			
Exhaust system		⊖	◑			
Body rust		⊖	○			
Paint		◑	◑			
Body integrity		◑	●			
Body hardware		●	●			
Air-conditioning		○				

(Columns '91–'93: Insufficient data)

Chevrolet Lumina V6

Trouble spot	'88	'89	'90	'91	'92	'93
Engine		⊖	⊖	◑	⊖	⊖
Engine cooling		⊖	⊖	⊖	◑	⊖
Fuel system		○	⊖	◑	⊖	⊖
Ignition system		○	⊖	⊖	⊖	⊖
Auto. transmission		⊖	○	○	⊖	⊖
Man. transmission				*	*	*
Clutch				*	*	*
Driveline		⊖	⊖	⊖	⊖	⊖
Electrical system		◑	○	○	○	⊖
Steering/suspension		⊖	⊖	⊖	⊖	⊖
Brakes		●	●	○	⊖	⊖
Exhaust system		⊖	⊖	⊖	⊖	⊖
Body rust		⊖	⊖	⊖	⊖	⊖
Paint		◑	⊖	◑	⊖	⊖
Body integrity		●	●	◑	○	⊖
Body hardware		●	○	◑	◑	⊖
Air-conditioning		⊖	⊖	⊖	⊖	⊖

Chevrolet Lumina APV Van

Trouble spot	'88	'89	'90	'91	'92	'93
Engine			⊖	◑	⊖	
Engine cooling			●	◑	⊖	
Fuel system			⊖	◑	⊖	
Ignition system			⊖	◑	⊖	
Auto. transmission			⊖	⊖	⊖	
Man. transmission						
Clutch						
Driveline			⊖	⊖	⊖	
Electrical system			●	◑	○	
Steering/suspension			○	⊖	⊖	
Brakes			●	◑	○	
Exhaust system			⊖	⊖	⊖	
Body rust			⊖	⊖	⊖	
Paint			◑	⊖	⊖	
Body integrity			●	◑	○	
Body hardware			●	◑	●	
Air-conditioning			⊖	⊖	⊖	

(Column '93: Insufficient data)

Chevrolet Nova (FWD)

Trouble spot	'88	'89	'90	'91	'92	'93
Engine	⊖					
Engine cooling	⊖					
Fuel system	○					
Ignition system	⊖					
Auto. transmission	⊖					
Man. transmission	⊖					
Clutch	○					
Driveline	⊖					
Electrical system	⊖					
Steering/suspension	⊖					
Brakes	●					
Exhaust system	●					
Body rust	⊖					
Paint	⊖					
Body integrity	⊖					
Body hardware	⊖					
Air-conditioning	⊖					

Chevrolet S-10 Blazer V6 (2WD)

Trouble spot	'88	'89	'90	'91	'92	'93
Engine	◑	⊖		⊖	⊖	
Engine cooling	◑	○		⊖	⊖	
Fuel system	⊖	⊖		⊖	⊖	
Ignition system	◑	⊖		⊖	⊖	
Auto. transmission	⊖	⊖		⊖	⊖	
Man. transmission	*	*		*	*	
Clutch	*	*		*	*	
Driveline	●	●		◑	◑	
Electrical system	●	●		●	◑	
Steering/suspension	◑	●		○	◑	
Brakes	●	◑		◑	◑	
Exhaust system	◑	○		⊖	⊖	
Body rust	●	○		⊖	⊖	
Paint	●	●		●	◑	
Body integrity	●	●		●	●	
Body hardware	●	●		●	◑	
Air-conditioning	○			⊖	⊖	

(Columns '90, '93: Insufficient data)

Chevrolet S-10 Blazer V6 (4WD)

Trouble spot	'88	'89	'90	'91	'92	'93
Engine	⊖	⊖	⊖	⊖	⊖	⊖
Engine cooling	○	⊖	⊖	⊖	⊖	◑
Fuel system	⊖	○	⊖	⊖	⊖	⊖
Ignition system	⊖	⊖	◑	⊖	○	⊖
Auto. transmission	⊖	⊖	⊖	○	⊖	⊖
Man. transmission	*	*	*	*	*	*
Clutch	*	*	*	*	*	*
Driveline	●	●	◑	●	○	○
Electrical system	●	●	●	○	○	⊖
Steering/suspension	●	◑	○	◑	◑	⊖
Brakes	●	◑	◑	◑	○	⊖
Exhaust system	●	◑	○	○	⊖	⊖
Body rust	●	○	○	⊖	⊖	⊖
Paint	●	●	●	◑	○	⊖
Body integrity	●	●	●	●	●	○
Body hardware	●	●	●	◑	◑	○
Air-conditioning	⊖	⊖	⊖	⊖	⊖	⊖

Chevrolet S-10 Pickup 4

Trouble spot	'88	'89	'90	'91	'92	'93
Engine	○	○	○	○	◑	⊖
Engine cooling	○	○	⊖	○	◑	⊖
Fuel system	◑	◑	○	○	●	○
Ignition system	○	○	○	○	○	⊖
Auto. transmission	*	*	*	*	⊖	*
Man. transmission	⊖	⊖	*	○	○	
Clutch	◑	◑	*	●	◑	
Driveline	◑	◑	⊖	⊖	⊖	
Electrical system	●	●	●	◑	◑	
Steering/suspension	●	◑	◑	○	○	
Brakes	●	●	◑	◑	◑	
Exhaust system	●	◑	◑	○	○	
Body rust	●	○	⊖	⊖	⊖	
Paint	●	●	●	●	◑	
Body integrity	●	●	●	●	◑	
Body hardware	●	●	●	●	◑	
Air-conditioning	○	⊖	*	⊖	⊖	

(Column '93: Insufficient data)

Chevrolet S-10 Pickup V6 (2WD)

Trouble spot	'88	'89	'90	'91	'92	'93
Engine	◑	◑	⊖	⊖	⊖	⊖
Engine cooling	○	○	⊖	⊖	⊖	⊖
Fuel system	○	○	⊖	⊖	◑	⊖
Ignition system	○	○	⊖	⊖	⊖	⊖
Auto. transmission	⊖	⊖	⊖	⊖	⊖	⊖
Man. transmission	*	*	*	○	⊖	⊖
Clutch	*	*	*	○	◑	⊖
Driveline	●	◑	⊖	⊖	⊖	⊖
Electrical system	●	●	◑	○	○	⊖
Steering/suspension	◑	◑	○	⊖	⊖	⊖
Brakes	●	●	◑	◑	○	⊖
Exhaust system	●	◑	○	○	⊖	⊖
Body rust	●	○	⊖	⊖	⊖	⊖
Paint	●	●	●	◑	○	⊖
Body integrity	○	●	●	●	◑	⊖
Body hardware	○	●	●	●	◑	⊖
Air-conditioning	⊖	⊖	⊖	⊖	⊖	⊖

Legend: ⊖ Few ← Problems → ● Many · * Insufficient data

Top section

Trouble Spots	Chevrolet S-10 Pickup V6 (4WD) '88	'89	'90	'91	'92	'93	Chevrolet Sportvan V8 '88	'89	'90	'91	'92	'93	Chevrolet Sprint '88	'89	'90	'91	'92	'93	Chevrolet Suburban (2WD) '88	'89	'90	'91	'92	'93
Engine	○	○		⊖	○		○	○	⊖	⊖	⊖		○						○	○	○	⊖	⊖	⊖
Engine cooling	◐	○		⊖	⊖		○	○	⊖	○	⊖		◐						●	○	○	○	⊖	⊖
Fuel system	⊖	○		⊖	⊖		○	○	⊖	⊖	⊖		◐						○	○	⊖	⊖	⊖	⊖
Ignition system	⊖	○		⊖	○		⊖	⊖	⊖	⊖	⊖		○						○	○	○	⊖	⊖	⊖
Auto. transmission	○	○		⊖	○		○	○	○	⊖	⊖		✱						○	○	○	⊖	⊖	⊖
Man. transmission	✱	✱		✱	✱		✱	✱					⊖						✱	✱	✱			
Clutch	✱	✱		✱	✱		✱	✱					⊖						✱	✱	✱			
Driveline	⊖	⊖		⊖	⊖		⊖	⊖	⊖	⊖	⊖		⊖						⊖	⊖	⊖	⊖	⊖	⊖
Electrical system	●	●		◐	○		●	●	●	●	⊖		○						●	●	◐	◐	○	○
Steering/suspension	◐	◐		○	⊖		●	◐	◐	◐	⊖		⊖						○	○	○	⊖	⊖	⊖
Brakes	◐	○		⊖	⊖		●	●	●	○	○		●						●	◐	◐	⊖	⊖	⊖
Exhaust system	●	○		⊖	⊖		○	○	⊖	⊖	⊖		○						●	○	⊖	⊖	⊖	⊖
Body rust	◐	○		⊖	⊖		●	●	●	⊖	⊖		⊖						●	○	⊖	⊖	⊖	○
Paint	●	●		○	○		●	●	●	◐	⊖		○						●	◐	◐	◐	⊖	⊖
Body integrity	◐	○		⊖	⊖		●	●	●	⊖	⊖		⊖						●	●	●	◐	○	⊖
Body hardware	◐	◐		⊖	⊖		●	●	●	⊖	⊖		○						●	●	◐	◐	○	⊖
Air-conditioning	⊖	⊖		⊖	⊖		◐	◐	○	○	○		✱						●	○	⊖	⊖	○	⊖

Note: Columns '90, '92, '93 marked "Insufficient data" for Chevrolet S-10 Pickup V6 (4WD); columns '93 marked "Insufficient data" for Chevrolet Sportvan V8.

Bottom section

Trouble Spots	Chevrolet Suburban (4WD) '88	'89	'90	'91	'92	'93	Chrysler Concorde '88	'89	'90	'91	'92	'93	Chrysler Le Baron Sedan 4 '88	'89	'90	'91	'92	'93	Chrysler Le Baron Sedan V6 '88	'89	'90	'91	'92	'93
Engine	◐	○	⊖	⊖	⊖	⊖						⊖	○		○	⊖	⊖				⊖	⊖	⊖	⊖
Engine cooling	○	○	⊖	⊖	⊖	⊖						⊖	○		○	⊖	⊖				⊖	⊖	⊖	⊖
Fuel system	○	○	⊖	⊖	⊖	⊖						⊖	◐		⊖	⊖	⊖				⊖	⊖	⊖	⊖
Ignition system	⊖	⊖	⊖	⊖	⊖	⊖						⊖	○		⊖	⊖	⊖				⊖	⊖	⊖	⊖
Auto. transmission	◐	○	○	○	○	⊖						⊖	○		⊖	⊖	⊖				◐	○	○	⊖
Man. transmission	✱	✱	✱																					
Clutch	✱	✱	✱																					
Driveline	⊖	⊖	⊖	⊖	⊖	⊖						⊖	⊖		⊖	⊖	⊖				⊖	⊖	⊖	⊖
Electrical system	○	●	◐	●	○	○						⊖	●		○	○	⊖				◐	○	○	⊖
Steering/suspension	◐	○	◐	⊖	⊖	⊖						⊖	○		○	⊖	⊖				⊖	⊖	⊖	⊖
Brakes	●	●	●	◐	○	○						⊖	●		○	⊖	⊖				◐	⊖	⊖	⊖
Exhaust system	○	⊖	⊖	⊖	⊖	⊖						⊖	○		⊖	⊖	⊖				⊖	⊖	⊖	⊖
Body rust	●	◐	◐	⊖	⊖	⊖						⊖	⊖		⊖	⊖	⊖				⊖	⊖	⊖	⊖
Paint	●	●	◐	⊖	○	○						⊖	○		⊖	⊖	⊖				○	⊖	⊖	⊖
Body integrity	●	●	●	◐	○	○						⊖	◐		○	⊖	⊖				⊖	⊖	○	⊖
Body hardware	●	●	●	◐	○	○						⊖	○		⊖	⊖	⊖				⊖	⊖	⊖	⊖
Air-conditioning	○	◐	○	○	○	⊖						⊖	●		⊖	⊖	⊖				⊖	⊖	⊖	⊖

Trouble Spots — Chrysler

TROUBLE SPOTS	Chrysler Le Baron Coupe & Conv. 4 '88	'89	'90	'91	'92	'93	Chrysler Le Baron Coupe & Conv. 4 Turbo '88	'89	'90	'91	'92	'93	Chrysler Le Baron Coupe & Conv. V6 '88	'89	'90	'91	'92	'93	Chrysler New Yorker '88	'89	'90	'91	'92	'93
Engine	●	○					●	◐							○	⊖	⊖		⊖	⊖	⊖	⊖	○	⊖
Engine cooling	●	○					●	◐							⊖	⊖	⊖		○	⊖	⊖	⊖	⊖	⊖
Fuel system	◐	⊖					○	⊖							○	⊖	⊖		●	○	⊖	⊖	⊖	⊖
Ignition system	◐	⊖					⊖	⊖							⊖	⊖	⊖		⊖	⊖	⊖	⊖	⊖	⊖
Auto. transmission	◐	⊖	Insufficient data	Insufficient data	Insufficient data	Insufficient data	○	⊖	Insufficient data	Insufficient data	Insufficient data	Insufficient data			○	⊖	⊖	Insufficient data	○	●	○	○	○	⊖
Man. transmission	*	*					*	*							*	*	*							
Clutch	*	*					*	*							*	*	*							
Driveline	◐	⊖					⊖	⊖							⊖	⊖	⊖		⊖	⊖	⊖	⊖	⊖	⊖
Electrical system	●	○					●	●							●	●	●		●	●	○	○	○	⊖
Steering/suspension	●	○					●	●							⊖	⊖	⊖		●	○	○	○	⊖	○
Brakes	◐	⊖					⊖	●							●	●	○		●	●	○	○	⊖	⊖
Exhaust system	◐	⊖					⊖	⊖							⊖	⊖	⊖		⊖	⊖	⊖	⊖	⊖	⊖
Body rust	◐	○					◐	○							⊖	⊖	⊖		⊖	⊖	⊖	⊖	⊖	⊖
Paint	◐	○					◐	○							⊖	⊖	○		⊖	⊖	⊖	⊖	⊖	⊖
Body integrity	◐	○					●	●							●	○	◐		○	○	○	○	○	○
Body hardware							●	●							●	●	●		○	○	○	○	○	○
Air-conditioning		◐					●	●							⊖	⊖	⊖		●	○	○	○	○	○

Trouble Spots — Chrysler / Dodge

TROUBLE SPOTS	Chrysler Town & Country Van (2WD) '88	'89	'90	'91	'92	'93	Chrysler Town & Country Van (4WD) '88	'89	'90	'91	'92	'93	Dodge Aries '88	'89	'90	'91	'92	'93	Dodge Caravan 4 '88	'89	'90	'91	'92	'93
Engine		○	⊖	⊖	⊖						⊖	⊖	◐	◐					⊖	○	○	○	⊖	⊖
Engine cooling		○	⊖	⊖	⊖						⊖	⊖	○	⊖					⊖	○	⊖	⊖	⊖	⊖
Fuel system		⊖	⊖	⊖	⊖						⊖	⊖	◐	◐					⊖	○	○	⊖	⊖	⊖
Ignition system		⊖	⊖	⊖	⊖						⊖	⊖	○	○					⊖	○	⊖	⊖	⊖	⊖
Auto. transmission		●	○	○	⊖						○	⊖	⊖	⊖					⊖	⊖	⊖	⊖	⊖	⊖
Man. transmission													*	*					⊖	⊖	*		*	*
Clutch													*	*					○	○	*		*	*
Driveline		⊖	⊖	⊖	⊖						⊖	⊖	⊖	⊖					⊖	⊖	⊖	⊖	⊖	⊖
Electrical system		◐	⊖	◐	⊖						◐	⊖	◐	○					●	●	○	○	⊖	⊖
Steering/suspension		○	⊖	⊖	⊖						⊖	⊖	◐	○					⊖	⊖	○	⊖	⊖	⊖
Brakes		◐	⊖	◐	⊖						○	⊖	●	●					●	●	○	○	⊖	⊖
Exhaust system		⊖	⊖	⊖	⊖						⊖	⊖	⊖	⊖					⊖	⊖	⊖	⊖	⊖	⊖
Body rust		⊖	⊖	⊖	⊖						⊖	⊖	○	○					⊖	⊖	⊖	⊖	⊖	⊖
Paint		⊖	⊖	⊖	⊖						○	⊖	◐	⊖					⊖	⊖	⊖	⊖	⊖	⊖
Body integrity		◐	◐	◐	○						○	○	●	●					○	○	○	◐	○	○
Body hardware		◐	●	◐	⊖						◐	⊖	◐	●					●	◐	○	○	○	○
Air-conditioning		○	⊖	⊖	⊖						⊖	⊖	●	●					●	○	○	○	○	○

Legend: ⊜ ⊖ ○ ◐ ● — Few ← Problems → Many   * Insufficient data

Dodge Caravan 4 Turbo / Dodge Grand Caravan 4 / Dodge Caravan V6 (2WD) / Dodge Caravan V6 (4WD)

TROUBLE SPOTS	Caravan 4 Turbo '88	'89	'90	'91	'92	'93	Grand Caravan 4 '88	'89	'90	'91	'92	'93	Caravan V6 (2WD) '88	'89	'90	'91	'92	'93	Caravan V6 (4WD) '88	'89	'90	'91	'92	'93
Engine	○						●	◐					●	●	●	○	⊖	⊖				⊖		
Engine cooling	◐						◐	○					◐	◐	○	⊖	⊖	⊖				○		
Fuel system	⊖						◐	○					●	○	○	⊖	⊖	⊖				○		
Ignition system	⊖						⊖	◐					⊖	⊖	⊖	⊖	⊖	⊖				⊖		
Auto. transmission	⊖						◐	●					○	◐	◐	○	⊖	⊖				◐		
Man. transmission	*						*	*																
Clutch	*						*	*																
Driveline	⊖						⊖	⊖					⊖	⊖	⊖	⊖	⊖	⊖				⊖		
Electrical system	◐						●	◐					●	○	◐	◐	○	⊖				◐		
Steering/suspension	○						◐	○					◐	○	⊖	⊖	⊖	⊖				⊖		
Brakes	●						●	●					◐	◐	○	○	⊖	⊖				◐		
Exhaust system	⊖						⊖	⊖					⊖	⊖	⊖	⊖	⊖	⊖				⊖		
Body rust	⊖						⊖	⊖					⊖	⊖	⊖	⊖	⊖	⊖				⊖		
Paint	⊖						○	⊖					⊖	⊖	⊖	⊖	⊖	⊖				⊖		
Body integrity	○						○	◐					○	◐	◐	⊖	⊖	⊖				◐		
Body hardware	◐						●	●					●	●	●	◐	⊖	○				○		
Air-conditioning	◐						◐	◐					●	○	⊖	⊖	⊖	⊖				⊖		

Caravan 4 Turbo: Insufficient data '89–'93. Grand Caravan 4: Insufficient data '90–'93. Caravan V6 (4WD): Insufficient data except '91.

Dodge Grand Caravan V6 (2WD) / Dodge Grand Caravan V6 (4WD) / Dodge Colt, Colt Wagon / Dodge Colt Vista Wagon

TROUBLE SPOTS	Grand Caravan V6 (2WD) '88	'89	'90	'91	'92	'93	Grand Caravan V6 (4WD) '88	'89	'90	'91	'92	'93	Colt, Colt Wagon '88	'89	'90	'91	'92	'93	Colt Vista Wagon '88	'89	'90	'91	'92	'93
Engine	●	●	○	⊖	◐	⊖				⊖	⊖	⊖	●	○	○	⊖	⊖		●	◐				
Engine cooling	◐	◐	○	⊖	⊖	⊖				⊖	⊖	⊖	○	⊖	⊖	⊖	⊖		◐	○				
Fuel system	●	○	◐	⊖	⊖	⊖				⊖	⊖	⊖	○	⊖	⊖	⊖	⊖		◐	○				
Ignition system	⊖	⊖	⊖	⊖	⊖	⊖				⊖	⊖	⊖	⊖	⊖	⊖	⊖	⊖		⊖	⊖				
Auto. transmission	◐	●	●	◐	○	⊖				◐	○	⊖	⊖	⊖	*	*	*		*	*				
Man. transmission													⊖	⊖	⊖	⊖	⊖		●	◐				
Clutch													⊖	⊖	⊖	⊖	⊖		○	○				
Driveline	⊖	⊖	⊖	⊖	⊖	⊖				⊖	⊖	⊖	⊖	⊖	⊖	⊖	⊖		○	◐				
Electrical system	●	◐	○	◐	○	⊖				●	◐	⊖	◐	○	○	⊖	⊖		◐	○				
Steering/suspension	◐	○	○	⊖	⊖	⊖				◐	◐	⊖	○	⊖	⊖	⊖	⊖		◐	○				
Brakes	●	◐	◐	○	⊖	⊖				●	◐	⊖	●	◐	○	⊖	⊖		○	○				
Exhaust system	⊖	⊖	⊖	⊖	⊖	⊖				◐	⊖	⊖	⊖	⊖	⊖	⊖	⊖		⊖	⊖				
Body rust	⊖	⊖	⊖	⊖	⊖	⊖				⊖	⊖	⊖	⊖	⊖	⊖	⊖	⊖		⊖	⊖				
Paint	○	○	⊖	⊖	⊖	⊖				○	⊖	⊖	○	○	⊖	○	○		⊖	○				
Body integrity	○	○	◐	⊖	⊖	○				◐	○	○	○	○	◐	◐	○		⊖	○				
Body hardware	●	●	○	◐	⊖	○				●	◐	⊖	○	○	◐	⊖	⊖		⊖	○				
Air-conditioning	●	◐	○	⊖	⊖	⊖				⊖	⊖	⊖	○	○	⊖	⊖	⊖		◐	○				

Grand Caravan V6 (4WD): Insufficient data '88–'90. Colt, Colt Wagon: Insufficient data '93. Colt Vista Wagon: Insufficient data '90–'93.

Symbol key: ◓ = few problems · ⊖ · ○ · ◒ · ● = many problems · ✳ = insufficient data

Upper section

TROUBLE SPOTS	Dodge Dakota Pickup V6 (2WD) '88	'89	'90	'91	'92	'93	Dodge Dakota Pickup V6 (4WD) '88	'89	'90	'91	'92	'93	Dodge Dakota Pickup V8 '88	'89	'90	'91	'92	'93	Dodge Daytona 4 '88	'89	'90	'91	'92	'93
Engine	◓	⊖	○	◓	◓	⊖	○	○	*Insufficient data*		⊖	*Insufficient data*	*Insufficient data*			⊖	◓	⊖	◓	◓	*Insufficient data*			
Engine cooling	⊖	○	◓	⊖	⊖	⊖	○	○			○					⊖	⊖	⊖	◓	○				
Fuel system	●	⊖	○	◓	◓	⊖	●	○			○					⊖	◓	⊖	○	◓				
Ignition system	◓	◓	○	◓	◓	⊖	●	○								⊖	◓	⊖	○	○				
Auto. transmission	⊖	◓	◓	○	○	⊖	✳	✳			●					⊖	◓	○	○	○				
Man. transmission	✳	✳	✳	✳	✳	✳	✳	✳			✳					⊖	✳							
Clutch	✳	✳	✳	✳	✳	✳	✳	✳			✳					⊖	✳							
Driveline	⊖	○	⊖	⊖	⊖	⊖	○	⊖			⊖					⊖	⊖	⊖	⊖	⊖				
Electrical system	◓	○	○	⊖	⊖	⊖	⊖	⊖			⊖					⊖	⊖	○	○	⊖	●	●		
Steering/suspension	◓	○	○	◓	⊖	⊖	◓	⊖			⊖					⊖	⊖	⊖	◓	⊖	●	⊖		
Brakes	●	◓	◒	⊖	⊖	⊖	●	◓			⊖					⊖	⊖	○	◓	◓	●	◒		
Exhaust system	◓	○	⊖	⊖	⊖	⊖	⊖	○			⊖					⊖	⊖	⊖	◓	◓	○	⊖		
Body rust	⊖	⊖	⊖	⊖	⊖	⊖	⊖	⊖			⊖					⊖	⊖	⊖	⊖	⊖	○	⊖		
Paint	◓	○	○	⊖	⊖	⊖	◓	◓			○					○	⊖	⊖	●	◒				
Body integrity	◓	○	◓	⊖	⊖	⊖	⊖	⊖			○					○	⊖	⊖	●	◒				
Body hardware	◓	○	○	⊖	⊖	⊖	○	○			○					⊖	○	○	●	◒				
Air-conditioning	⊖	◓	○	⊖	⊖	⊖	✳	✳			⊖					⊖	⊖	⊖	●	◒				

Lower section

TROUBLE SPOTS	Dodge Dynasty V6 '88	'89	'90	'91	'92	'93	Dodge Intrepid '88	'89	'90	'91	'92	'93	Dodge Monaco '88	'89	'90	'91	'92	'93	Dodge Omni '88	'89	'90	'91	'92	'93
Engine	◓	○	○	◓	⊖	⊖						⊖			○	○			○	⊖	⊖			
Engine cooling	⊖	○	○	⊖	⊖	⊖						⊖			○	○			○	○	○			
Fuel system	●	◓	⊖	⊖	⊖	⊖						⊖			○	○			◓	○	○			
Ignition system	◓	○	◓	⊖	⊖	⊖						⊖			○	○			○	○	◓			
Auto. transmission	○	●	◓	◓	○	⊖						⊖			◓	◓	*Insufficient data*		⊖	⊖	✳			
Man. transmission																			○	✳	✳			
Clutch																			○	✳	✳			
Driveline	⊖	◓	⊖	◓	⊖	⊖						⊖			⊖	⊖			⊖	⊖	⊖			
Electrical system	●	◓	●	○	◓	○						⊖			●	●			◓	●	○			
Steering/suspension	◓	○	○	◓	○	○						⊖			○	○			○	○	◓			
Brakes	◓	●	◓	○	◓	○						⊖			●	●			●	◓	○			
Exhaust system	⊖	◓	○	◓	⊖	⊖						⊖			⊖	⊖			⊖	⊖	⊖			
Body rust	○	◓	⊖	◓	⊖	⊖						○			⊖	⊖			○	○	⊖			
Paint	●	○	○	○	○	○						⊖			●	○			●	○	○			
Body integrity	●	◓	○	○	◓	○						○			○	●			●	◓	○			
Body hardware	◓	○	○	○	◓	○						⊖			⊖	◓			○	⊖	○			
Air-conditioning	⊖	◓	⊖	⊖	◓	⊖						⊖			●	⊖			●	⊖	✳			

Legend: ◓ ⊖ ○ ◒ ● — Few ← Problems → Many · ✳ Insufficient data

Symbols: ● = filled, ⊖ = half, ○ = open, * = (insufficient/not applicable)

Dodge Ram 50 Pickup 4 & Dodge Ram B150-250 Van, Wagon V8 / Dodge Shadow 4 / Dodge Spirit 4

TROUBLE SPOTS	Ram 50 '88	Ram 50 '89	Ram 50 '90	Ram 50 '91	Ram 50 '92	Ram 50 '93	Van '88	Van '89	Van '90	Van '91	Van '92	Van '93	Shadow '88	Shadow '89	Shadow '90	Shadow '91	Shadow '92	Shadow '93	Spirit '88	Spirit '89	Spirit '90	Spirit '91	Spirit '92
Engine	⊖	*	*	*	*	*	○	⊖	⊖	⊖	⊖	*	⊖	⊖	○	○	○	⊖	○	○	○	⊖	⊖
Engine cooling	⊖						○	⊖	○	⊖	⊖		⊖	⊖	○	⊖	⊖	⊖	○	⊖	⊖	⊖	⊖
Fuel system	○						⊖	○	○	⊖	○		○	⊖	○	⊖	⊖	⊖	○	⊖	⊖	⊖	⊖
Ignition system	⊖						⊖	○	○	⊖	⊖		○	⊖	⊖	⊖	⊖	⊖	○	⊖	⊖	⊖	⊖
Auto. transmission	*						⊖	●	●	⊖	○		⊖	⊖	⊖	⊖	⊖	⊖	⊖	⊖	⊖	⊖	⊖
Man. transmission	⊖												*	*	*	⊖	⊖	*	*	*	*	*	*
Clutch	○												*	*	*	⊖	⊖	*	*	*	*	*	*
Driveline	⊖						⊖	⊖	⊖	⊖	⊖		⊖	⊖	⊖	⊖	⊖	⊖	⊖	⊖	⊖	⊖	⊖
Electrical system	○						⊖	●	●	●	●		⊖	⊖	○	○	○	⊖	⊖	○	○	○	⊖
Steering/suspension	○						⊖	●	⊖	●	⊖		⊖	⊖	○	⊖	⊖	⊖	○	⊖	⊖	○	⊖
Brakes	○						⊖	●	⊖	⊖	⊖		●	●	●	○	⊖	⊖	⊖	●	⊖	⊖	⊖
Exhaust system	⊖						⊖	○	⊖	⊖	⊖		⊖	⊖	⊖	⊖	⊖	⊖	⊖	⊖	⊖	⊖	⊖
Body rust	⊖						○	○	○	⊖	⊖		⊖	⊖	⊖	⊖	⊖	⊖	⊖	⊖	⊖	⊖	⊖
Paint	⊖						⊖	●	⊖	⊖	○		⊖	⊖	○	○	⊖	⊖	⊖	○	⊖	⊖	⊖
Body integrity	⊖						⊖	●	●	⊖	●		⊖	⊖	⊖	○	⊖	⊖	⊖	⊖	⊖	○	⊖
Body hardware	⊖						⊖	⊖	○	○	●		●	●	⊖	⊖	⊖	⊖	⊖	●	○	⊖	⊖
Air-conditioning	⊖						●	●	⊖	○	⊖		●	●	⊖	⊖	⊖	⊖	⊖	○	⊖	⊖	⊖

(Ram 50: '89–'93 Insufficient data. Van: '93 Insufficient data. Spirit 4: '93 column cut off at page edge.)

Dodge Spirit V6 / Dodge Stealth (2WD) / Dodge Stealth Turbo (4WD) / Eagle Premier V6

TROUBLE SPOTS	Spirit V6 '88	Spirit V6 '89	Spirit V6 '90	Spirit V6 '91	Spirit V6 '92	Spirit V6 '93	Stealth '88	Stealth '89	Stealth '90	Stealth '91	Stealth '92	Stealth '93	Turbo '91	Turbo '92	Turbo '93	Premier '88	Premier '89	Premier '90	Premier '91	Premier '92
Engine		○	⊖	⊖	⊖	⊖				⊖	⊖	⊖		⊖		⊖	⊖	○	○	
Engine cooling		⊖	⊖	⊖	⊖	⊖				⊖	⊖	⊖		⊖		●	●	○	○	
Fuel system		⊖	⊖	⊖	⊖	⊖				⊖	⊖	⊖		⊖		⊖	⊖	○	○	
Ignition system		⊖	⊖	⊖	⊖	⊖				⊖	⊖	⊖		⊖		⊖	⊖	○	○	
Auto. transmission		●	⊖	○	○	⊖				*	*	*				⊖	⊖	⊖	○	
Man. transmission										○	⊖	*		○						
Clutch										⊖	⊖	*		⊖						
Driveline		⊖	⊖	⊖	⊖	⊖				⊖	⊖	⊖		⊖		⊖	⊖	⊖	⊖	
Electrical system		●	⊖	○	○	⊖				⊖	○	○		●		●	●	●	●	
Steering/suspension		○	⊖	○	○	⊖				⊖	⊖	⊖		○		⊖	⊖	⊖	○	
Brakes		⊖	●	⊖	⊖	○				⊖	⊖	⊖		○		●	●	⊖	⊖	
Exhaust system		⊖	⊖	⊖	⊖	⊖				⊖	⊖	⊖		⊖		●	⊖	⊖	⊖	
Body rust		⊖	⊖	⊖	⊖	⊖				⊖	⊖	⊖		⊖		⊖	⊖	⊖	⊖	
Paint		⊖	○	⊖	⊖	⊖				○	⊖	⊖		⊖		⊖	⊖	⊖	⊖	
Body integrity		○	⊖	⊖	○	○				○	●	⊖		○		⊖	○	⊖	○	
Body hardware		⊖	●	○	○	⊖				○	●	⊖		○		●	●	●	⊖	
Air-conditioning		⊖	⊖	⊖	⊖	⊖				⊖	●	⊖		⊖		●	●	⊖	⊖	

(Spirit V6: '88 Insufficient data. Stealth 2WD: '88–'90 Insufficient data. Stealth Turbo 4WD: '91 and '93 Insufficient data. Eagle Premier V6: '92 Insufficient data; '93 column cut off at page edge.)

Top section

TROUBLE SPOTS	Eagle Summit Coupe, Hatchback & Sedan '89	'90	'91	'92	'93	Eagle Summit Wagon '88	'89	'90	'91	'92	'93	Eagle Talon (2WD) '88	'89	'90	'91	'92	'93	Eagle Talon Turbo (2WD) '88	'89	'90	'91	'92	'93
Engine	⊖	⊖								⊖			⊖	⊖	○	⊖	⊖			⊖	⊖			
Engine cooling	⊖	⊖								⊖			⊖	⊖	⊖	⊖	⊖			⊖	⊖			
Fuel system	○	⊖								⊖			⊖	⊖	⊖	⊖	⊖			⊖	○			
Ignition system	⊖	⊖								⊖			⊖	⊖	⊖	⊖	⊖			⊖	⊖			
Auto. transmission	⊖	✻								⊖			⊖	⊖	○	✻					✻			
Man. transmission	⊖	✻								✻			○	⊖	⊖	✻				○	✻			
Clutch	⊖	✻								✻			⊖	⊖	⊖	✻				○	✻			
Driveline	⊖	⊖								⊖			⊖	⊖	⊖	⊖	⊖			⊖	⊖			
Electrical system	○	○								○			⊖	●	○	○	⊖			⊖	⊖			
Steering/suspension	○	⊖								⊖			⊖	⊖	⊖	⊖	⊖			⊖	⊖			
Brakes	⊖	⊖								⊖			○	○	⊖	⊖	⊖			○	○			
Exhaust system	⊖	⊖								◑			⊖	⊖	●	●	⊖			⊖	⊖			
Body rust	⊖	⊖								⊖			⊖	⊖	⊖	⊖	⊖			⊖	⊖			
Paint	○	⊖								○			⊖	⊖	⊖	⊖	⊖			○	⊖			
Body integrity	●	●								○			○	○	○	⊖	⊖			⊖	⊖			
Body hardware	○	○								◑			○	⊖	⊖	⊖	⊖			⊖	⊖			
Air-conditioning	○	⊖								⊖			⊖	⊖	⊖	⊖	⊖			⊖	⊖			

Columns '91 '92 '93 for Eagle Summit Coupe, Hatchback & Sedan marked "Insufficient data."
Column '93 for Eagle Summit Wagon marked "Insufficient data."
Columns '92 '93 for Eagle Talon (2WD) marked "Insufficient data."
Columns '92 '93 for Eagle Talon Turbo (2WD) marked "Insufficient data."

Bottom section

TROUBLE SPOTS	Eagle Talon Turbo (4WD) '89	'90	'91	'92	'93	Eagle Vision '88	'89	'90	'91	'92	'93	Ford Aerostar Van (2WD) '88	'89	'90	'91	'92	'93	Ford Aerostar Van (4WD) '88	'89	'90	'91	'92	'93
Engine	⊖	⊖	○								⊖	⊖	⊖	○	○	⊖	⊖		●	⊖	⊖	⊖	
Engine cooling	⊖	⊖	⊖								⊖	●	●	○	○	⊖	⊖		○	⊖	⊖	⊖	
Fuel system	⊖	○	⊖								⊖	○	○	○	⊖	⊖	⊖		⊖	⊖	⊖	⊖	
Ignition system	⊖	⊖	⊖								⊖	○	●	○	○	⊖	⊖		○	○	⊖	⊖	
Auto. transmission		✻	✻								⊖	●	○	○	○	⊖	⊖		○	○	⊖	⊖	
Man. transmission	⊖	○	○									✻	✻	✻	✻	✻	✻						
Clutch	○	⊖	○								⊖	✻	✻	✻	✻	✻	✻						
Driveline	⊖	⊖	⊖								⊖	⊖	⊖	⊖	⊖	⊖	⊖		⊖	⊖	⊖	⊖	
Electrical system	⊖	◑	⊖								⊖	●	●	●	○	○	⊖		⊖	⊖	⊖	○	
Steering/suspension	⊖	⊖	⊖								⊖	●	●	○	○	⊖	⊖		○	○	○	⊖	
Brakes	◑	◑	⊖								⊖	●	●	●	○	⊖	⊖		●	●	○	⊖	
Exhaust system	⊖	⊖	⊖								⊖	○	○	⊖	⊖	⊖	⊖		⊖	⊖	⊖	⊖	
Body rust	⊖	⊖	⊖								⊖	○	○	⊖	⊖	⊖	⊖		⊖	⊖	⊖	⊖	
Paint	⊖	○	○								⊖	○	○	⊖	○	⊖	⊖		⊖	○	○	⊖	
Body integrity	○	○	○								○	●	○	○	⊖	○	⊖		○	⊖	⊖	⊖	
Body hardware	⊖	○	○								⊖	●	●	⊖	⊖	○	⊖		⊖	●	⊖	⊖	
Air-conditioning	⊖	⊖	⊖								⊖	●	●	●	⊖	○	⊖		●	●	⊖	⊖	

Columns '92 '93 for Eagle Talon Turbo (4WD) marked "Insufficient data."

Legend

⊖   ⊖   ○   ◑   ●   ✻

Few ←— **Problems** —→ Many   Insufficient data

Top section

Ford Bronco V8						Ford Bronco II (4WD)						TROUBLE SPOTS	Ford Club Wagon, Van						Ford Crown Victoria LTD Crown Victoria				
'88	'89	'90	'91	'92	'93	'88	'89	'90	'91	'92	'93		'88	'89	'90	'91	'92	'93	'88	'89	'90	'91	'92

Trouble spots (top section): Engine, Engine cooling, Fuel system, Ignition system, Auto. transmission, Man. transmission, Clutch, Driveline, Electrical system, Steering/suspension, Brakes, Exhaust system, Body rust, Paint, Body integrity, Body hardware, Air-conditioning

(Ford Bronco II column marked "Insufficient data" for '91–'93)

Bottom section

Ford Escort						Ford Explorer (2WD)						TROUBLE SPOTS	Ford Explorer (4WD)						Ford F150-250 Pickup 6 (2WD)				
'88	'89	'90	'91	'92	'93	'88	'89	'90	'91	'92	'93		'88	'89	'90	'91	'92	'93	'88	'89	'90	'91	'92

Trouble spots (bottom section): Engine, Engine cooling, Fuel system, Ignition system, Auto. transmission, Man. transmission, Clutch, Driveline, Electrical system, Steering/suspension, Brakes, Exhaust system, Body rust, Paint, Body integrity, Body hardware, Air-conditioning

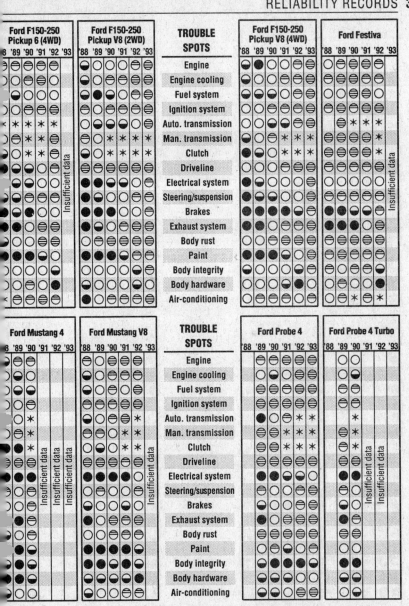

TROUBLE SPOTS

Top panel vehicles (years '88 '89 '90 '91 '92 '93):

- Ford F150-250 Pickup 6 (4WD)
- Ford F150-250 Pickup V8 (2WD)
- Ford F150-250 Pickup V8 (4WD)
- Ford Festiva

Bottom panel vehicles (years '88 '89 '90 '91 '92 '93):

- Ford Mustang 4
- Ford Mustang V8
- Ford Probe 4
- Ford Probe 4 Turbo

Trouble spots (rows, both panels):

Engine
Engine cooling
Fuel system
Ignition system
Auto. transmission
Man. transmission
Clutch
Driveline
Electrical system
Steering/suspension
Brakes
Exhaust system
Body rust
Paint
Body integrity
Body hardware
Air-conditioning

Legend:

Few ⟵ **Problems** ⟶ Many   ✱ Insufficient data

Trouble Spots — Ford Probe V6, Ford Ranger Pickup 4 (2WD), Ford Ranger Pickup V6 (2WD), Ford Ranger Pickup V6 (4WD)

TROUBLE SPOTS	Probe V6 '88	'89	'90	'91	'92	'93	Ranger 4 (2WD) '88	'89	'90	'91	'92	'93	Ranger V6 (2WD) '88	'89	'90	'91	'92	'93	Ranger V6 (4WD) '88	'89	'90	'91	'92	'93
Engine			⊖	⊖	⊖	⊖	●	○	○	⊖	⊖	⊖	⊖	⊖	○	⊖	⊖	⊖	⊖	⊖	○	⊖	⊖	⊖
Engine cooling			⊖	⊖	⊖	⊖	○	○	⊖	⊖	⊖	⊖	●	○	○	⊖	⊖	⊖	●	○	○	⊖	⊖	⊖
Fuel system			◐	⊖	⊖	⊖	○	○	○	⊖	⊖	⊖	○	⊖	⊖	⊖	⊖	⊖	○	○	⊖	⊖	⊖	⊖
Ignition system			⊖	⊖	⊖	⊖	○	○	○	⊖	⊖	⊖	⊖	⊖	⊖	⊖	⊖	⊖	○	⊖	⊖	⊖	⊖	⊖
Auto. transmission			○	⊖	*	*	*	*	*	*	*	*	●	○	○	○	⊖	⊖	⊖	*	○	○	⊖	*
Man. transmission			⊖	*	*	⊖	⊖	⊖	○	⊖	⊖	⊖	⊖	⊖	○	⊖	⊖	⊖	○	⊖	*	○	⊖	*
Clutch			⊖	*	*	⊖	○	○	○	⊖	⊖	⊖	○	⊖	⊖	⊖	⊖	⊖	○	⊖	*	⊖	⊖	*
Driveline			⊖	⊖	⊖	⊖	⊖	⊖	⊖	⊖	⊖	⊖	⊖	⊖	⊖	⊖	⊖	⊖	⊖	○	○	⊖	⊖	⊖
Electrical system			●	●	●	⊖	⊖	⊖	○	○	○	⊖	⊖	⊖	⊖	○	○	⊖	⊖	⊖	○	○	○	⊖
Steering/suspension			⊖	⊖	⊖	⊖	⊖	⊖	⊖	⊖	⊖	⊖	⊖	⊖	○	○	⊖	⊖	○	○	○	○	⊖	⊖
Brakes			○	⊖	⊖	⊖	○	●	○	○	⊖	⊖	⊖	●	○	○	⊖	⊖	○	○	○	⊖	⊖	⊖
Exhaust system			⊖	⊖	⊖	○	●	●	○	○	○	⊖	⊖	●	○	○	⊖	⊖	○	○	○	⊖	⊖	⊖
Body rust			⊖	⊖	⊖	○	⊖	⊖	⊖	⊖	⊖	⊖	⊖	⊖	⊖	⊖	⊖	⊖	○	⊖	⊖	⊖	⊖	⊖
Paint			⊖	⊖	⊖	⊖	○	⊖	⊖	⊖	○	○	○	⊖	○	○	○	○	○	○	○	○	○	○
Body integrity			●	⊖	⊖	⊖	○	○	○	⊖	⊖	○	○	○	○	○	○	○	○	○	○	○	○	○
Body hardware			○	○	⊖	⊖	○	○	○	⊖	⊖	○	○	○	○	○	○	○	○	○	○	○	○	○
Air-conditioning			○	○	⊖	⊖	⊖	●	○	○	⊖	*	●	●	●	○	⊖	⊖	⊖	○	○	⊖	⊖	⊖

Trouble Spots — Ford Taurus 4, Ford Taurus V6, Ford Tempo 4, Ford Tempo V6

TROUBLE SPOTS	Taurus 4 '88	'89	'90	'91	'92	'93	Taurus V6 '88	'89	'90	'91	'92	'93	Tempo 4 '88	'89	'90	'91	'92	'93	Tempo V6 '88	'89	'90	'91	'92	'93
Engine	●	○					○	○	⊖	⊖	⊖	⊖	●	●	○	○	⊖	⊖					⊖	
Engine cooling	●	◐					◐	○	⊖	⊖	⊖	⊖	●	●	○	○	⊖	⊖					⊖	
Fuel system	●	○					◐	○	⊖	⊖	⊖	⊖	●	●	◐	○	○	⊖					⊖	
Ignition system	⊖	⊖					⊖	○	○	⊖	⊖	⊖	○	○	⊖	⊖	⊖	⊖					⊖	
Auto. transmission	●	○					◐	○	⊖	○	⊖	⊖	◐	○	⊖	⊖	⊖	⊖					⊖	
Man. transmission	*							○	○	⊖	⊖	*	⊖	⊖	*	*	*	*					*	
Clutch	*							●	●	⊖	◐	*	◐	○	*	*	*	*					*	
Driveline	⊖	⊖					⊖	⊖	⊖	⊖	⊖	⊖	⊖	⊖	⊖	⊖	⊖	⊖					⊖	
Electrical system	●	●					●	●	◐	○	○	○	●	●	◐	○	○	⊖					◐	
Steering/suspension	●	◐					●	◐	○	⊖	⊖	⊖	●	●	◐	⊖	⊖	⊖					○	
Brakes	●	●					●	◐	○	○	⊖	⊖	●	●	◐	○	⊖	⊖					⊖	
Exhaust system	●	○					⊖	⊖	⊖	⊖	⊖	⊖	●	●	◐	○	⊖	⊖					⊖	
Body rust	⊖	⊖					○	⊖	⊖	⊖	⊖	⊖	○	⊖	⊖	⊖	⊖	⊖					○	
Paint	◐	○					⊖	○	⊖	⊖	⊖	⊖	●	⊖	○	○	⊖	⊖					○	
Body integrity	●	◐					○	○	○	○	◐	○	●	◐	○	○	●	○					◐	
Body hardware	●	●					◐	○	○	⊖	⊖	○	●	●	○	○	○	⊖					◐	
Air-conditioning	●	○					●	○	⊖	⊖	⊖	⊖	●	◐	◐	⊖	⊖	⊖					⊖	

Note: "Insufficient data" is indicated in the blank year columns for Ford Taurus 4 (1990–1993) and Ford Tempo V6 (1988–1991).

Reliability Records — Trouble Spots

Symbol key: ⊖ = few problems · ○ = average · ◒ = some · ● = many problems · * = insufficient data

Ford Thunderbird 4 Turbo / Ford Thunderbird V6 / Ford Thunderbird V8 / Geo Metro

Trouble Spots	T-Bird 4 Turbo '89	'90	'91	'92	'93	T-Bird V6 '88	'89	'90	'91	'92	'93	T-Bird V8 '88	'89	'90	'91	'92	'93	Geo Metro '88	'89	'90	'91	'92	'93
Engine						○	⊖	⊖	⊖	⊖	⊖	○			⊖	⊖		○	⊖	⊖	⊖	⊖	
Engine cooling						○	⊖	⊖	⊖	⊖	⊖	○			⊖	⊖		⊖	⊖	⊖	⊖	⊖	
Fuel system						◒	○	⊖	⊖	⊖	⊖	○			⊖	○		⊖	⊖	⊖	⊖	⊖	
Ignition system						○	⊖	⊖	⊖	⊖	⊖	⊖			⊖	○		○	⊖	⊖	⊖	⊖	
Auto. transmission						⊖	⊖	⊖	⊖	⊖	⊖	○			⊖	⊖		*	*	*	*	*	*
Man. transmission																		*	⊖	⊖	⊖	⊖	
Clutch																		*	⊖	⊖	⊖	⊖	
Driveline						⊖	⊖	⊖	⊖	⊖	⊖	⊖			⊖	⊖	⊖	⊖	⊖	⊖	⊖	⊖	
Electrical system						●	●	●	◒	○	⊖	●			◒	○		●	◒	◒	○	⊖	
Steering/suspension						○	○	○	⊖	⊖	⊖	◒			◒	○		○	○	⊖	⊖	⊖	
Brakes						●	●	●	◒	○	⊖	●			◒	○		○	○	⊖	⊖	⊖	
Exhaust system						●	⊖	⊖	⊖	⊖	⊖	●			⊖	⊖		●	⊖	⊖	⊖	⊖	
Body rust						○	⊖	⊖	⊖	⊖	⊖	⊖			⊖	⊖		⊖	⊖	⊖	⊖	⊖	
Paint						◒	◒	○	○	○	⊖	◒			◒	◒		◒	◒	○	○	⊖	
Body integrity						○	◒	○	○	○	○	○			○	○		●	◒	●	○	○	
Body hardware						◒	●	●	◒	○	⊖	○			◒	◒		●	◒	◒	○	⊖	
Air-conditioning						○	◒	◒	◒	○	⊖	⊖			○	○		*	⊖	○	◒	*	

Ford Thunderbird V8 '92–'93: Insufficient data

Geo Prizm / Geo Storm / Geo Tracker (4WD) / GMC Jimmy, Yukon

Trouble Spots	Prizm '89	'90	'91	'92	'93	Storm '88	'89	'90	'91	'92	'93	Tracker 4WD '88	'89	'90	'91	'92	'93	GMC Jimmy/Yukon '88	'89	'90	'91	'92	'93
Engine		⊖	⊖	⊖	⊖			⊖	⊖	⊖				⊖	⊖	○		○	○	⊖	⊖	⊖	⊖
Engine cooling		⊖	⊖	⊖	⊖			⊖	⊖	⊖				⊖	⊖	⊖		○	○	○	⊖	⊖	⊖
Fuel system		⊖	⊖	⊖	⊖			⊖	⊖	⊖				○	⊖	⊖		○	○	⊖	⊖	⊖	⊖
Ignition system		⊖	⊖	⊖	⊖			⊖	⊖	⊖				⊖	⊖	⊖		○	○	⊖	⊖	⊖	⊖
Auto. transmission		⊖	⊖	⊖	⊖			*	*	*				*	*	*	*	◒	◒	*	⊖	○	⊖
Man. transmission		⊖	⊖	⊖	*			⊖	⊖	*				*	*	*	⊖	*	*	*	*	*	*
Clutch		⊖	⊖	⊖	*			○	○	*				*	*	*	⊖	*	*	*	*	*	*
Driveline		⊖	⊖	⊖	⊖			⊖	⊖	⊖				⊖	⊖	⊖		⊖	⊖	⊖	⊖	⊖	⊖
Electrical system		○	○	◒	⊖			●	○	⊖				◒	○	○		●	●	◒	◒	○	⊖
Steering/suspension		⊖	○	⊖	⊖			○	○	⊖				◒	○	○		●	●	◒	○	⊖	⊖
Brakes		○	⊖	⊖	⊖			◒	○	⊖				●	●	○		●	●	●	◒	○	⊖
Exhaust system		◒	⊖	⊖	⊖			●	○	⊖				●	◒	○		⊖	⊖	◒	⊖	⊖	⊖
Body rust		⊖	⊖	⊖	⊖			⊖	⊖	⊖				○	⊖	⊖		●	⊖	⊖	⊖	⊖	⊖
Paint		○	○	⊖	⊖			○	○	○				○	○	◒		●	●	●	◒	⊖	⊖
Body integrity		◒	○	○	⊖			◒	○	◒				◒	○	◒		●	●	●	◒	◒	◒
Body hardware		●	◒	○	⊖			●	○	⊖				◒	○	◒		●	●	●	◒	◒	⊖
Air-conditioning		⊖	⊖	⊖	⊖			⊖	○	⊖				*	*	*	⊖	○	⊖	⊖	○	⊖	⊖

Geo Storm '92–'93, Geo Tracker '88 and '92–'93: Insufficient data

Legend: ⊖ ⊖ ○ ◒ ● * — Few ←— Problems —→ Many · Insufficient data

Legend of symbols used: ● = solid circle, ◐ = half-filled circle, ⊖ = circle with horizontal bar, ○ = open circle, ✱ = asterisk (not applicable). Shaded year columns marked "Insufficient data".

TROUBLE SPOTS	GMC S-15 Jimmy V6 (2WD) '88	'89	'90	'91	'92	'93	GMC S-15 Jimmy V6 (4WD) '88	'89	'90	'91	'92	'93
Engine	◐	◐		⊖	⊖		◐	⊖	⊖	⊖	⊖	⊖
Engine cooling	◐	○		⊖	⊖		○	⊖	⊖	⊖	⊖	⊖
Fuel system	⊖	⊖		⊖	⊖		○	⊖	⊖	⊖	⊖	⊖
Ignition system	○	⊖		⊖	⊖		⊖	○	⊖	⊖	⊖	⊖
Auto. transmission	◐	⊖	Insufficient data	⊖	⊖	Insufficient data	◐	⊖	○	⊖	○	⊖
Man. transmission	✱	✱		✱	✱		✱	✱	✱	✱	✱	✱
Clutch	✱	✱		✱	✱		✱	✱	✱	✱	✱	✱
Driveline	⊖	⊖		⊖	⊖		⊖	⊖	⊖	⊖	⊖	⊖
Electrical system	●	●		◐	○		●	●	●	◐	○	○
Steering/suspension	○	⊖		○	⊖		●	◐	○	⊖	⊖	⊖
Brakes	◐	⊖		○	⊖		●	●	◐	○	⊖	⊖
Exhaust system	◐	⊖		⊖	⊖		⊖	⊖	◐	⊖	⊖	⊖
Body rust	○	○		⊖	⊖		⊖	⊖	⊖	○	○	⊖
Paint	●	◐		●	○		●	●	◐	○	⊖	⊖
Body integrity	●	●		◐	◐		●	●	●	◐	◐	○
Body hardware	●	◐		◐	◐		●	●	◐	◐	◐	○
Air-conditioning	○	○		⊖	⊖		⊖	⊖	⊖	⊖	⊖	⊖

TROUBLE SPOTS	GMC S-15 Sonoma Pickup 4 '88	'89	'90	'91	'92	'93	GMC S-15 Sonoma Pickup V6 (2WD) '88	'89	'90	'91	'92	'93
Engine	○	○	○	◐	⊖		◐	⊖	⊖	⊖	⊖	⊖
Engine cooling	○	○	○	⊖	⊖		○	⊖	⊖	⊖	⊖	⊖
Fuel system	◐	○	○	○	⊖		○	⊖	⊖	⊖	⊖	⊖
Ignition system	○	○	○	○	⊖		○	○	⊖	⊖	⊖	⊖
Auto. transmission	✱	✱	✱	⊖	✱		⊖	⊖	⊖	⊖	⊖	⊖
Man. transmission	⊖	⊖	✱	○	⊖		✱	✱	✱	○	○	⊖
Clutch	◐	◐	✱	●	⊖		✱	✱	✱	○	○	⊖
Driveline	⊖	⊖	⊖	⊖	⊖	Insufficient data	⊖	⊖	⊖	⊖	⊖	⊖
Electrical system	◐	○	○	◐	○		●	●	◐	○	○	⊖
Steering/suspension	○	○	○	○	⊖		●	◐	○	⊖	⊖	⊖
Brakes	⊖	⊖	◐	○	⊖		●	●	◐	○	⊖	⊖
Exhaust system	●	⊖	○	○	⊖		●	◐	◐	○	⊖	⊖
Body rust	○	⊖	○	⊖	⊖		⊖	○	○	○	⊖	⊖
Paint	●	●	◐	◐	○		●	●	◐	○	○	⊖
Body integrity	●	◐	○	◐	◐		●	●	◐	◐	○	○
Body hardware	◐	◐	◐	○	○		●	●	◐	◐	○	○
Air-conditioning	○	⊖	✱	⊖	⊖		⊖	⊖	⊖	⊖	⊖	⊖

TROUBLE SPOTS	GMC S-15 Sonoma Pickup V6 (4WD) '88	'89	'90	'91	'92	'93	GMC Safari Van (2WD) '88	'89	'90	'91	'92	'93
Engine	○	○		⊖	○		◐	◐	⊖	⊖	⊖	⊖
Engine cooling	◐	○		⊖	○		⊖	○	⊖	⊖	⊖	⊖
Fuel system	⊖	○		⊖	○		⊖	⊖	⊖	⊖	⊖	⊖
Ignition system	⊖	○		⊖	○		⊖	⊖	⊖	⊖	⊖	⊖
Auto. transmission	○	○		⊖	○		○	⊖	⊖	⊖	⊖	⊖
Man. transmission	✱	✱		✱	✱		✱	✱				
Clutch	✱	✱	Insufficient data	✱	✱	Insufficient data	✱	✱				
Driveline	⊖	⊖		○	○		⊖	⊖	⊖	⊖	⊖	⊖
Electrical system	●	●		◐	○		●	●	○	○	◐	⊖
Steering/suspension	◐	○		○	⊖		●	●	⊖	○	⊖	⊖
Brakes	◐	⊖		○	⊖		●	●	◐	○	⊖	⊖
Exhaust system	●	◐		○	⊖		○	⊖	○	⊖	⊖	⊖
Body rust	◐	○		⊖	⊖		⊖	⊖	⊖	⊖	⊖	⊖
Paint	●	◐		○	○		●	○	○	●	◐	○
Body integrity	◐	◐		○	○		◐	⊖	●	●	●	◐
Body hardware	◐	◐		○	⊖		⊖	○	●	●	●	○
Air-conditioning	⊖	⊖		⊖	⊖		○	○	⊖	⊖	⊖	⊖

TROUBLE SPOTS	GMC Safari Van (4WD) '88	'89	'90	'91	'92	'93	GMC Suburban (2WD) '88	'89	'90	'91	'92	'93
Engine			⊖	⊖	⊖		○	○	○	⊖	⊖	⊖
Engine cooling			⊖	⊖	⊖		●	○	⊖	⊖	○	⊖
Fuel system			⊖	⊖	⊖		⊖	⊖	⊖	○	⊖	⊖
Ignition system			⊖	⊖	⊖		⊖	⊖	⊖	⊖	⊖	⊖
Auto. transmission			⊖	○	⊖		○	○	○	○	⊖	⊖
Man. transmission							✱	✱	✱			
Clutch							✱	✱	✱			
Driveline			⊖	⊖	⊖	Insufficient data	⊖	⊖	⊖	⊖	⊖	⊖
Electrical system			◐	○	○		●	●	◐	○	○	⊖
Steering/suspension			○	○	○		●	●	◐	○	⊖	⊖
Brakes			●	◐	○		●	●	●	◐	○	⊖
Exhaust system			⊖	⊖	⊖		●	◐	○	○	⊖	⊖
Body rust			⊖	⊖	⊖		●	○	○	⊖	⊖	⊖
Paint			⊖	⊖	○		●	●	◐	○	○	⊖
Body integrity			●	●	◐		●	●	●	◐	○	○
Body hardware			●	●	◐		●	●	●	◐	◐	○
Air-conditioning			⊖	⊖	⊖		⊖	⊖	○	⊖	⊖	○

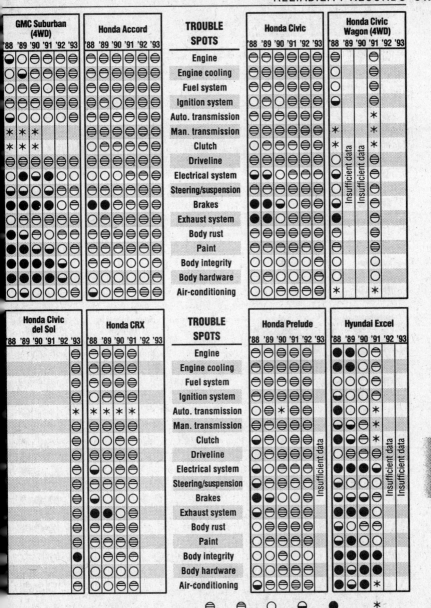

TROUBLE SPOTS

Engine · Engine cooling · Fuel system · Ignition system · Auto. transmission · Man. transmission · Clutch · Driveline · Electrical system · Steering/suspension · Brakes · Exhaust system · Body rust · Paint · Body integrity · Body hardware · Air-conditioning

Top row vehicles: GMC Suburban (4WD), Honda Accord, Honda Civic, Honda Civic Wagon (4WD) — years '88–'93

Bottom row vehicles: Honda Civic del Sol, Honda CRX, Honda Prelude, Hyundai Excel — years '88–'93

Legend: Few ← Problems → Many   * Insufficient data

Legend: ● = filled circle · ○ = open circle · ⊖ = half circle (average) · ✱ = not applicable/insufficient

Hyundai Sonata / Infiniti G20 / Infiniti J30 / Infiniti Q45

TROUBLE SPOTS	Hyundai Sonata '89	'90	'91	Infiniti G20 '91	'92	'93	Infiniti J30 '93	Infiniti Q45 '90	'91	'92
Engine	⊖	⊖	⊖	⊖	⊖	⊖	⊖	⊖	⊖	⊖
Engine cooling	⊖	⊖	⊖	⊖	⊖	⊖	⊖	⊖	⊖	⊖
Fuel system	○	⊖	⊖	⊖	⊖	⊖	⊖	⊖	⊖	⊖
Ignition system	○	⊖	○	⊖	⊖	⊖	⊖	⊖	⊖	⊖
Auto. transmission	●	✱	✱	⊖	⊖	✱	⊖	⊖	○	○
Man. transmission	✱	✱	✱	⊖	⊖	✱				
Clutch	✱	✱	✱	⊖	⊖	✱				
Driveline	⊖	⊖	⊖	⊖	⊖	⊖	⊖	⊖	⊖	⊖
Electrical system	●	●	●	○	⊖	⊖	⊖	○	○	⊖
Steering/suspension	○	○	⊖	⊖	⊖	⊖	⊖	⊖	⊖	⊖
Brakes	●	●	○	⊖	⊖	⊖	⊖	●	○	⊖
Exhaust system	●	●	○	⊖	⊖	⊖	⊖	⊖	⊖	⊖
Body rust	○	⊖	⊖	⊖	⊖	⊖	⊖	⊖	⊖	⊖
Paint	⊖	⊖	⊖	⊖	⊖	⊖	⊖	⊖	⊖	⊖
Body integrity	⊖	●	○	⊖	⊖	⊖	⊖	⊖	⊖	⊖
Body hardware	●	●	●	○	⊖	⊖	⊖	●	○	○
Air-conditioning	●	●	●	⊖	⊖	⊖	⊖	●	○	⊖

Hyundai Sonata: '88, '92, '93 — Insufficient data. Infiniti G20: '88–'90 — Insufficient data. Infiniti J30: '88–'92 — Insufficient data. Infiniti Q45: '88, '89, '93 — Insufficient data.

Isuzu Pickup 4 (2WD) / Isuzu Rodeo V6 / Isuzu Trooper II, Trooper 4 / Isuzu Trooper II, Trooper V6

TROUBLE SPOTS	Pickup 4 '89	'90	'91	'92	Rodeo V6 '91	'92	Trooper 4 '88	'89	'90	Trooper V6 '90	'91	'92
Engine	⊖	⊖	⊖	○	○	○	●	○	⊖	○	○	⊖
Engine cooling	⊖	○	⊖	⊖	○	⊖	●	○	⊖	○	○	⊖
Fuel system	⊖	⊖	⊖	⊖	⊖	⊖	○	⊖	⊖	⊖	○	⊖
Ignition system	⊖	⊖	⊖	⊖	⊖	⊖	⊖	⊖	⊖	⊖	⊖	⊖
Auto. transmission	✱	✱	✱	✱	✱	✱	○	✱	✱	✱	✱	⊖
Man. transmission	✱	⊖	⊖	✱	✱	⊖	⊖	⊖	⊖	✱	○	✱
Clutch	✱	⊖	⊖	✱	✱	⊖	○	⊖	⊖	✱	○	✱
Driveline	⊖	⊖	⊖	⊖	⊖	⊖	⊖	⊖	⊖	⊖	⊖	⊖
Electrical system	○	○	○	○	●	○	⊖	○	○	○	⊖	●
Steering/suspension	⊖	○	⊖	⊖	○	⊖	⊖	⊖	⊖	●	●	⊖
Brakes	○	●	●	⊖	⊖	○	●	●	⊖	●	●	⊖
Exhaust system	●	⊖	⊖	⊖	⊖	⊖	●	○	⊖	⊖	⊖	⊖
Body rust	○	⊖	⊖	⊖	○	⊖	○	⊖	⊖	⊖	○	○
Paint	○	○	○	⊖	●	⊖	○	⊖	⊖	⊖	○	○
Body integrity	⊖	⊖	⊖	⊖	●	○	○	⊖	○	⊖	○	○
Body hardware	○	○	○	⊖	●	○	○	○	○	○	○	⊖
Air-conditioning	✱	✱	✱	✱	○	⊖	○	⊖	⊖	○	⊖	⊖

Isuzu Pickup 4 (2WD): '88, '93 — Insufficient data. Isuzu Rodeo V6: '88–'90, '93 — Insufficient data. Isuzu Trooper II, Trooper 4: '91–'93 — Insufficient data. Isuzu Trooper II, Trooper V6: '88, '89, '93 — Insufficient data.

Legend: ⊖ = Few problems · ○ = · ◐ = · ● = Many problems · * = Insufficient data

Jeep Cherokee 4 (4WD)

Trouble Spots	'88	'89	'90	'91	'92	'93
Engine	○	○	⊖	⊖	⊖	*Insufficient data*
Engine cooling	○	○	○	⊖	⊖	
Fuel system	○	○	○	⊖	⊖	
Ignition system	⊖	○	⊖	⊖	⊖	
Auto. transmission	●	○	⊖			
Man. transmission	*	*	*	*	*	
Clutch	*	*	*	*	*	
Driveline	⊖	⊖	⊖	⊖	⊖	
Electrical system	●	●	●	○	○	
Steering/suspension	○	○	◐	○	⊖	
Brakes	●	●	⊖	⊖	⊖	
Exhaust system	●	⊖	⊖	⊖	⊖	
Body rust	○	⊖	⊖	⊖	⊖	
Paint	●	⊖	⊖	○	○	
Body integrity	●	●	●	◐	○	
Body hardware	●	◐	○	◐	○	
Air-conditioning	○	○	⊖	⊖	⊖	

Jeep Cherokee, Wagoneer 6

Trouble Spots	'88	'89	'90	'91	'92	'93
Engine	○	○	⊖	○	⊖	⊖
Engine cooling	◐	○	○	⊖	⊖	⊖
Fuel system	○	○	◐	⊖	⊖	⊖
Ignition system	⊖	⊖	⊖	⊖	⊖	⊖
Auto. transmission	⊖	○	*	*	*	*
Man. transmission	⊖	○	*	*	*	*
Clutch						
Driveline	⊖	⊖	⊖	⊖	⊖	⊖
Electrical system	●	●	●	●	○	○
Steering/suspension	○	◐	○	⊖	⊖	⊖
Brakes	●	●	●	⊖	⊖	⊖
Exhaust system	●	⊖	⊖	⊖	⊖	⊖
Body rust	⊖	⊖	⊖	⊖	⊖	⊖
Paint	⊖	⊖	⊖	○	○	○
Body integrity	●	●	●	◐	◐	◐
Body hardware	◐	●	●	◐	◐	◐
Air-conditioning	○	⊖	○	○	⊖	⊖

Jeep Grand Cherokee 6

Trouble Spots	'88	'89	'90	'91	'92	'93
Engine	*Insufficient data*					⊖
Engine cooling						⊖
Fuel system						⊖
Ignition system						⊖
Auto. transmission						⊖
Man. transmission						
Clutch						
Driveline						⊖
Electrical system						○
Steering/suspension						○
Brakes						⊖
Exhaust system						⊖
Body rust						⊖
Paint						⊖
Body integrity						○
Body hardware						◐
Air-conditioning						⊖

Jeep Grand Wagoneer, Grand Cherokee V8

Trouble Spots	'88	'89	'90	'91	'92	'93
Engine	*Insufficient data*					⊖
Engine cooling						⊖
Fuel system						⊖
Ignition system						⊖
Auto. transmission						⊖
Man. transmission						
Clutch						
Driveline						⊖
Electrical system						○
Steering/suspension						
Brakes						⊖
Exhaust system						
Body rust						⊖
Paint						⊖
Body integrity						◐
Body hardware						○
Air-conditioning						⊖

Jeep Wrangler

Trouble Spots	'88	'89	'90	'91	'92	'93
Engine	●	○	⊖	⊖	⊖	⊖
Engine cooling	●	○	○	⊖	⊖	⊖
Fuel system	●	●	●	○	⊖	⊖
Ignition system	●	○	⊖	⊖	⊖	⊖
Auto. transmission	*	*	*	*	*	*
Man. transmission	○	*	○	*	○	*
Clutch	*	○	*	⊖	○	*
Driveline	○	⊖	○	⊖	⊖	⊖
Electrical system	●	○	○	◐	○	⊖
Steering/suspension	○	○	◐	○	○	⊖
Brakes	●	●	◐	⊖	⊖	⊖
Exhaust system	●	●	●	⊖	⊖	⊖
Body rust	○	○	○	○	○	⊖
Paint	●	○	○	○	○	○
Body integrity	●	●	●	●	●	●
Body hardware	●	●	○	○	◐	○
Air-conditioning	*	*	*	*	*	*

Lexus ES 250

Trouble Spots	'88	'89	'90	'91	'92	'93
Engine			⊖	⊖		
Engine cooling			⊖	⊖		
Fuel system			⊖	⊖		
Ignition system			⊖	⊖		
Auto. transmission			⊖	⊖		
Man. transmission			*	*		
Clutch			*	*		
Driveline			⊖	⊖		
Electrical system			○	○		
Steering/suspension			⊖	⊖		
Brakes			⊖	⊖		
Exhaust system			⊖	⊖		
Body rust			⊖	⊖		
Paint			⊖	⊖		
Body integrity			○	⊖		
Body hardware			○	○		
Air-conditioning			⊖	⊖		

Lexus ES 300

Trouble Spots	'88	'89	'90	'91	'92	'93
Engine					⊖	⊖
Engine cooling					⊖	⊖
Fuel system					⊖	⊖
Ignition system					⊖	⊖
Auto. transmission					⊖	⊖
Man. transmission					*	*
Clutch					*	*
Driveline					⊖	⊖
Electrical system					⊖	⊖
Steering/suspension					○	⊖
Brakes					⊖	⊖
Exhaust system					⊖	⊖
Body rust					⊖	⊖
Paint					⊖	⊖
Body integrity					○	⊖
Body hardware					⊖	⊖
Air-conditioning					○	⊖

Lexus LS 400

Trouble Spots	'88	'89	'90	'91	'92	'93
Engine			⊖	⊖	⊖	⊖
Engine cooling			⊖	⊖	⊖	⊖
Fuel system			⊖	⊖	⊖	⊖
Ignition system			⊖	⊖	⊖	⊖
Auto. transmission			⊖	⊖	⊖	⊖
Man. transmission						
Clutch						
Driveline			⊖	⊖	⊖	⊖
Electrical system			⊖	⊖	⊖	⊖
Steering/suspension			○	⊖	⊖	⊖
Brakes			⊖	⊖	⊖	⊖
Exhaust system				⊖	⊖	⊖
Body rust			⊖	⊖	⊖	⊖
Paint			⊖	⊖	⊖	⊖
Body integrity						
Body hardware			⊖	⊖	⊖	⊖
Air-conditioning			⊖	⊖	⊖	⊖

⊖ ⊖ ○ ◐ ● *
Few ← **Problems** → Many   Insufficient data

Symbol key used below: ● = filled circle, ◐ = half-filled circle, ○ = open circle, ⊖ = circle with bar, * = insufficient data point.

Lexus SC 300/400 · Lincoln Continental · TROUBLE SPOTS · Lincoln Mark VII · Lincoln Mark VIII

Trouble spot	Lexus SC 300/400 '88	'89	'90	'91	'92	'93	Lincoln Continental '88	'89	'90	'91	'92	'93	Lincoln Mark VII '88	'89	'90	'91	'92	'93	Lincoln Mark VIII '88	'89	'90	'91	'92	'93
Engine					⊖	⊖	●	◐	○	⊖	⊖	⊖	⊖	⊖	⊖									⊖
Engine cooling					⊖	⊖	○	⊖	○	⊖	⊖	⊖	○	⊖	⊖									⊖
Fuel system					⊖	⊖	●	◐	○	⊖	⊖	⊖	○	○	○									⊖
Ignition system					⊖	⊖	○	◐	○	⊖	⊖	⊖	⊖	⊖	○									⊖
Auto. transmission					⊖	⊖	⊖	◐	○	⊖	⊖	⊖	⊖	○	⊖									⊖
Man. transmission					*	*																		
Clutch					*	*																		
Driveline					⊖	⊖	⊖	⊖	⊖	⊖	⊖	⊖	⊖	⊖	⊖									⊖
Electrical system				○	○	○	●	●	●	◐	○	○	●	●	●									⊖
Steering/suspension					⊖	⊖	⊖	●	◐	○	⊖	⊖	⊖	●	◐									⊖
Brakes					⊖	⊖	●	●	●	●	○	⊖	●	●	⊖									⊖
Exhaust system					⊖	⊖	●	●	◐	○	⊖	⊖	●	◐	○									⊖
Body rust							⊖	⊖	⊖				⊖	⊖	⊖									⊖
Paint					⊖	⊖	○	○	○				⊖	⊖	⊖									⊖
Body integrity					⊖	⊖	○	○	⊖				○	○	⊖									⊖
Body hardware					⊖	⊖	●	●	●				●	●	●									⊖
Air-conditioning					⊖	⊖	●	◐	○	○	⊖	⊖	●	◐	⊖									⊖

(Lincoln Mark VII '91–'93: Insufficient data)

Lincoln Town Car · Mazda 323 · TROUBLE SPOTS · Mazda 626 4 · Mazda 626 V6

Trouble spot	Lincoln Town Car '88	'89	'90	'91	'92	'93	Mazda 323 '88	'89	'90	'91	'92	'93	Mazda 626 4 '88	'89	'90	'91	'92	'93	Mazda 626 V6 '88	'89	'90	'91	'92	'93
Engine	○	⊖	⊖	⊖	⊖	⊖	○	⊖	⊖	⊖	⊖		○	⊖	⊖	⊖	⊖	⊖						⊖
Engine cooling	○	○	⊖	⊖	⊖	⊖	⊖	⊖	⊖	⊖	⊖		⊖	⊖	⊖	⊖	⊖	⊖						⊖
Fuel system	○	○	⊖	⊖	⊖	⊖	⊖	⊖	⊖	⊖	⊖		⊖	⊖	⊖	⊖	⊖	⊖						⊖
Ignition system	⊖	⊖	⊖	⊖	⊖	⊖	⊖	⊖	⊖	⊖	⊖		⊖	⊖	⊖	⊖	⊖	⊖						⊖
Auto. transmission	⊖	○	⊖	⊖	⊖	⊖	○	○	⊖	⊖	*		●	◐	⊖	⊖	⊖	⊖						⊖
Man. transmission							⊖	⊖	⊖	⊖	⊖		⊖	⊖	⊖	⊖	⊖	⊖						*
Clutch							○	⊖	⊖	⊖	⊖		⊖	⊖	⊖	⊖	⊖	⊖						*
Driveline	⊖	⊖	⊖	⊖	⊖	⊖	⊖	⊖	⊖	⊖	⊖		⊖	⊖	⊖	⊖	⊖	⊖						⊖
Electrical system	●	●	●	●	○	○	○	○	⊖	○	○		○	○	○	○	○	⊖						⊖
Steering/suspension	○	●	○	⊖	○	⊖	○	⊖	⊖	○	⊖		⊖	⊖	⊖	⊖	○	⊖						⊖
Brakes	○	●	●	○	⊖	⊖	●	●	○	○	⊖		●	●	○	○	⊖	⊖						⊖
Exhaust system	●	○	○	⊖	⊖	⊖	○	⊖	○	○	⊖		●	●	○	⊖	⊖	⊖						⊖
Body rust	⊖	⊖	⊖	⊖	⊖	⊖	⊖	⊖	⊖	⊖	⊖		⊖	⊖	⊖	⊖	⊖	⊖						⊖
Paint	○	○	○	○	⊖	⊖	○	○	○	○	⊖		⊖	⊖	⊖	⊖	⊖	⊖						⊖
Body integrity	○	○	○	⊖	○	⊖	○	○	○	○	⊖		◐	○	○	○	○	○						⊖
Body hardware	●	○	●	○	⊖	⊖	○	○	○	○	○		●	○	○	○	○	○						⊖
Air-conditioning	●	○	○	⊖	⊖	○	○	⊖	⊖	⊖	○		○	⊖	⊖	⊖	⊖	⊖						⊖

(Mazda 323 '93: Insufficient data)

Mazda 929

TROUBLE SPOTS	'88	'89	'90	'91	'92	'93
Engine	⊖	⊖	⊖	⊖	○	
Engine cooling	⊖	⊖	⊖	⊖	⊖	
Fuel system	⊖	⊖	⊖	⊖	⊖	
Ignition system	⊖	⊖	⊖	⊖	⊖	
Auto. transmission	⊖	⊖	○	○	⊖	
Man. transmission						
Clutch						
Driveline	⊖	⊖	⊖	⊖	⊖	
Electrical system	○	○	○	○	○	
Steering/suspension	○	○	⊖	○	○	
Brakes	●	●	◑	⊖	⊖	
Exhaust system	○	○	○	⊖	○	
Body rust	⊖	⊖	⊖	⊖	⊖	
Paint	⊖	○	○	○	○	
Body integrity	⊖	○	○	○	○	
Body hardware	○	○	○	○	⊖	
Air-conditioning	○	⊖	⊖	⊖	⊖	

Mazda MPV 4

TROUBLE SPOTS	'88	'89	'90	'91	'92	'93
Engine	○	Insufficient data	⊖	Insufficient data	Insufficient data	Insufficient data
Engine cooling	⊖		⊖			
Fuel system	⊖		⊖			
Ignition system	○		⊖			
Auto. transmission	○		*			
Man. transmission	*		*			
Clutch	*		*			
Driveline	⊖		⊖			
Electrical system	◑		○			
Steering/suspension	○		⊖			
Brakes	●		●			
Exhaust system	●		⊖			
Body rust	⊖					
Paint	⊖		○			
Body integrity	○		○			
Body hardware	◑		○			
Air-conditioning	○		*			

Mazda MPV V6 (2WD)

TROUBLE SPOTS	'88	'89	'90	'91	'92	'93
Engine	◑	○	○	⊖	Insufficient data	Insufficient data
Engine cooling	⊖	⊖	⊖	⊖		
Fuel system	⊖	⊖	⊖	⊖		
Ignition system	⊖	⊖	⊖	⊖		
Auto. transmission	○	⊖	⊖	⊖		
Man. transmission	*					
Clutch	*					
Driveline	⊖	⊖	⊖	⊖		
Electrical system	◑	◑	○	⊖		
Steering/suspension	⊖	⊖	⊖	⊖		
Brakes	●	●	●	◑		
Exhaust system	◑	○	⊖	⊖		
Body rust	⊖	⊖	⊖	⊖		
Paint	⊖	⊖	⊖	⊖		
Body integrity	⊖	⊖	⊖	⊖		
Body hardware	◑	○	◑	⊖		
Air-conditioning	○	○	⊖	⊖		

Mazda MPV V6 (4WD)

TROUBLE SPOTS	'88	'89	'90	'91	'92	'93
Engine	Insufficient data	Insufficient data	○	⊖	Insufficient data	Insufficient data
Engine cooling			⊖	⊖		
Fuel system			⊖	⊖		
Ignition system			⊖	⊖		
Auto. transmission			◑	○		
Man. transmission			*			
Clutch			*			
Driveline			⊖	⊖		
Electrical system			○	◑		
Steering/suspension			⊖	⊖		
Brakes			●	○		
Exhaust system			⊖	⊖		
Body rust			⊖	⊖		
Paint			⊖	⊖		
Body integrity			⊖	⊖		
Body hardware			◑	⊖		
Air-conditioning			○	⊖		

Mazda MX-3 4

TROUBLE SPOTS	'88	'89	'90	'91	'92	'93
Engine				Insufficient data	⊖	Insufficient data
Engine cooling					⊖	
Fuel system					○	
Ignition system					⊖	
Auto. transmission					*	
Man. transmission					*	
Clutch					*	
Driveline					⊖	
Electrical system					○	
Steering/suspension					⊖	
Brakes					⊖	
Exhaust system					⊖	
Body rust					⊖	
Paint					○	
Body integrity					●	
Body hardware					○	
Air-conditioning					*	

Mazda MX-3 V6

TROUBLE SPOTS	'88	'89	'90	'91	'92	'93
Engine					⊖	Insufficient data
Engine cooling					⊖	
Fuel system					⊖	
Ignition system					⊖	
Auto. transmission					*	
Man. transmission					*	
Clutch					*	
Driveline					⊖	
Electrical system					○	
Steering/suspension					⊖	
Brakes					⊖	
Exhaust system					⊖	
Body rust					⊖	
Paint					◑	
Body integrity					●	
Body hardware					●	
Air-conditioning					*	

Mazda MX-5 Miata

TROUBLE SPOTS	'88	'89	'90	'91	'92	'93
Engine	Insufficient data	Insufficient data	⊖	⊖	⊖	Insufficient data
Engine cooling			⊖	⊖	⊖	
Fuel system			⊖	⊖	⊖	
Ignition system			⊖	⊖	⊖	
Auto. transmission				*	*	
Man. transmission			⊖	⊖	⊖	
Clutch			⊖	⊖	⊖	
Driveline			⊖	⊖	⊖	
Electrical system			○	⊖	⊖	
Steering/suspension			⊖	⊖	⊖	
Brakes			⊖	⊖	⊖	
Exhaust system			○	⊖	⊖	
Body rust			⊖	⊖	⊖	
Paint			⊖	○	○	
Body integrity			○	○	○	
Body hardware			○	⊖	◑	
Air-conditioning			⊖	⊖	⊖	

Mazda MX-6 4

TROUBLE SPOTS	'88	'89	'90	'91	'92	'93
Engine	○	⊖	⊖	⊖	⊖	⊖
Engine cooling	⊖	⊖	○	⊖	⊖	⊖
Fuel system	⊖	⊖	⊖	⊖	⊖	⊖
Ignition system	⊖	⊖	⊖	⊖	⊖	⊖
Auto. transmission	○	◑	○	⊖	*	*
Man. transmission	⊖	⊖	⊖	⊖	*	*
Clutch	⊖	⊖	⊖	⊖	*	*
Driveline	⊖	⊖	⊖	⊖	⊖	⊖
Electrical system	◑	○	○	○	○	○
Steering/suspension	◑	○	○	⊖	⊖	⊖
Brakes	◑	○	○	⊖	○	⊖
Exhaust system	●	◑	○	⊖	⊖	⊖
Body rust	⊖	⊖	⊖	⊖	⊖	⊖
Paint	○	○	⊖	◑	○	○
Body integrity	○	○	●	◑	○	●
Body hardware	◑	○	●	○	○	◑
Air-conditioning	⊖	⊖	⊖	⊖	⊖	⊖

Legend: ⊖ Few ← Problems → Many ●   * Insufficient data

Top section

TROUBLE SPOTS	Mazda MX-6 V6 '88	'89	'90	'91	'92	'93	Mazda Navajo (2WD) '88	'89	'90	'91	'92	'93	Mazda Navajo (4WD) '88	'89	'90	'91	'92	'93	Mazda Pickup (2WD) '88	'89	'90	'91	'92	'93
Engine						⊖					⊖	⊖				⊖	⊖	⊖	○	⊖	⊖	⊖	⊖	⊖
Engine cooling						⊖					⊖	⊖				●	⊖	⊖	○	⊖	⊖	⊖	⊖	⊖
Fuel system						⊖					⊖	⊖				⊖	⊖	⊖	○	⊖	⊖	⊖	⊖	⊖
Ignition system						⊖					⊖	⊖				⊖	⊖	⊖	○	⊖	⊖	⊖	⊖	⊖
Auto. transmission						⊖					⊖	⊖				○	⊖	⊖	*	⊖	⊖	⊖	*	*
Man. transmission						⊖					○	*				⊖	⊖	⊖	⊖	⊖	⊖			*
Clutch						⊖					⊖	*				⊖	⊖	⊖	⊖	⊖	⊖	⊖		*
Driveline						⊖					○	⊖				⊖	⊖	⊖	⊖	⊖	⊖	⊖	⊖	⊖
Electrical system						○					○	⊖				⊖	⊖	⊖	○	⊖	⊖	⊖	⊖	⊖
Steering/suspension						⊖					○	○				○	○	⊖	○	⊖	⊖	⊖	⊖	⊖
Brakes						⊖					○	⊖				○	○	⊖	●	○	●	⊖	⊖	⊖
Exhaust system						⊖					⊖	⊖				⊖	⊖	⊖	●	⊖	⊖	⊖	⊖	⊖
Body rust						⊖					⊖	⊖				⊖	⊖	⊖	⊖	⊖	⊖	⊖	⊖	⊖
Paint						⊖					○	⊖				⊖	○	⊖	⊖	○	⊖	⊖	⊖	⊖
Body integrity						○					○	⊖				○	○	⊖	○	⊖	⊖	⊖	⊖	⊖
Body hardware						●					○	⊖				○	○	⊖	⊖	⊖	○	○	⊖	⊖
Air-conditioning						⊖					⊖	⊖				○	⊖	⊖	⊖	⊖	⊖	⊖	⊖	⊖

Bottom section

TROUBLE SPOTS	Mazda Protege (2WD) '88	'89	'90	'91	'92	'93	Mazda RX-7 '88	'89	'90	'91	'92	'93	Mercedes-Benz 300 Class 6, V8 (2WD) '88	'89	'90	'91	'92	'93	Mercedes-Benz S Class '88	'89	'90	'91	'92	'93
Engine			⊖	⊖	⊖	⊖	⊖		⊖				⊖	○	○	⊖	⊖	○	○				⊖	
Engine cooling			⊖	⊖	⊖	⊖	○		⊖				⊖	○	○	⊖	⊖	○	⊖				⊖	
Fuel system			⊖	⊖	⊖	⊖	⊖		⊖				○	○	○	⊖	⊖	○	⊖				⊖	
Ignition system			⊖	⊖	⊖	⊖	⊖		○				○	⊖	⊖	⊖	⊖	○	⊖				○	
Auto. transmission			⊖	⊖	⊖	*	*		*				⊖	⊖	⊖	⊖	○		⊖				⊖	
Man. transmission			⊖	⊖	⊖	*	⊖		*				*											
Clutch			⊖	⊖	⊖	*	●		*				*											
Driveline			⊖	⊖	⊖	⊖	⊖		⊖				⊖	⊖	⊖	⊖	⊖		⊖				⊖	
Electrical system			○	⊖	⊖	⊖	●		●				●	●	⊖	○	○		●				⊖	
Steering/suspension			○	○	⊖	⊖	⊖		⊖				⊖	⊖	○	○	○		⊖				●	
Brakes			○	○	⊖	⊖	⊖		○				●	●	○	○	○		⊖				○	
Exhaust system			⊖	⊖	⊖	⊖	⊖		⊖				⊖	⊖	⊖	⊖	⊖		⊖				⊖	
Body rust			⊖	○	○	⊖	⊖		⊖				⊖	⊖	⊖	⊖	⊖		⊖				⊖	
Paint			○	○	○	⊖	⊖		⊖				⊖	⊖	○	○	○		⊖				○	
Body integrity			⊖	○	○	⊖	⊖		●				⊖	⊖	○	○	○		○				○	
Body hardware			●	⊖	○	⊖	⊖		●				●	○	⊖	○	○		○				●	
Air-conditioning			⊖	⊖	⊖	⊖	○		*				●	⊖	⊖	⊖	⊖		○				○	

Note: columns marked "Insufficient data" (Mazda RX-7 '91, '92, '93; Mercedes-Benz 300 Class '93; Mercedes-Benz S Class '88, '89, '90, '91, '93).

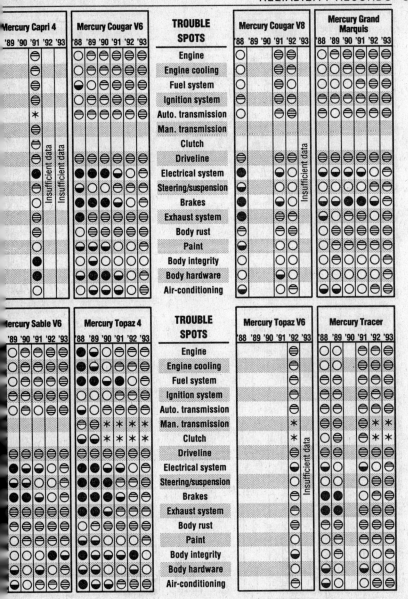

Mercury Capri 4 — '89 '90 '91 '92 '93
Mercury Cougar V6 — '88 '89 '90 '91 '92 '93
TROUBLE SPOTS
Mercury Cougar V8 — '88 '89 '90 '91 '92 '93
Mercury Grand Marquis — '88 '89 '90 '91 '92 '93

Mercury Sable V6 — '89 '90 '91 '92 '93
Mercury Topaz 4 — '88 '89 '90 '91 '92 '93
TROUBLE SPOTS
Mercury Topaz V6 — '88 '89 '90 '91 '92 '93
Mercury Tracer — '88 '89 '90 '91 '92 '93

Trouble spots: Engine · Engine cooling · Fuel system · Ignition system · Auto. transmission · Man. transmission · Clutch · Driveline · Electrical system · Steering/suspension · Brakes · Exhaust system · Body rust · Paint · Body integrity · Body hardware · Air-conditioning

Legend: Few ← Problems → Many · ✳ Insufficient data

Top Section

TROUBLE SPOTS	Mercury Villager Van '88 '89 '90 '91 '92 '93	Mitsubishi 3000GT (2WD) '88 '89 '90 '91 '92 '93	Mitsubishi 3000GT Turbo (4WD) '88 '89 '90 '91 '92 '93	Mitsubishi Diaman '88 '89 '90 '91 '92
Engine				
Engine cooling				
Fuel system				
Ignition system				
Auto. transmission				
Man. transmission				
Clutch				
Driveline				
Electrical system				
Steering/suspension				
Brakes				
Exhaust system				
Body rust				
Paint				
Body integrity				
Body hardware				
Air-conditioning				

(Mitsubishi 3000GT Turbo (4WD): columns '88–'91 and '93 marked "Insufficient data")

Bottom Section

TROUBLE SPOTS	Mitsubishi Eclipse (2WD) '88 '89 '90 '91 '92 '93	Mitsubishi Eclipse Turbo (2WD) '88 '89 '90 '91 '92 '93	Mitsubishi Eclipse Turbo (4WD) '88 '89 '90 '91 '92 '93	Mitsubishi Expo LR '88 '89 '90 '91 '92
Engine				
Engine cooling				
Fuel system				
Ignition system				
Auto. transmission				
Man. transmission				
Clutch				
Driveline				
Electrical system				
Steering/suspension				
Brakes				
Exhaust system				
Body rust				
Paint				
Body integrity				
Body hardware				
Air-conditioning				

(Mitsubishi Eclipse Turbo (2WD): columns '92 and '93 marked "Insufficient data"; Mitsubishi Eclipse Turbo (4WD): column '93 marked "Insufficient data")

Top group

TROUBLE SPOTS	Mitsubishi Galant 4 '88	'89	'90	'91	'92	'93	Mitsubishi Galant Sigma, Sigma V6 '88	'89	'90	'91	'92	'93	Mitsubishi Mirage '88	'89	'90	'91	'92	'93	Mitsubishi Montero V6 '88	'89	'90	'91	'92	'93
Engine	○	○	◐	⊖	⊖	ID	◐	ID		ID	ID	ID	ID	ID	○	⊖	ID	ID	ID		⊖	○	ID	ID	ID
Engine cooling	⊖	⊖	⊖	⊖	⊖		○								⊖	⊖					⊖	⊖			
Fuel system	⊖	⊖	⊖	⊖	⊖		⊖								⊖	⊖					⊖	⊖			
Ignition system	⊖	⊖	⊖	⊖	⊖		⊖								⊖	⊖					⊖	⊖			
Auto. transmission	○	○	⊖	⊖	⊖		●								⊖	⊖					⊖	⊖			
Man. transmission	⊖	⊖	⊖	⊖	*		*								*	*					*	*			
Clutch	○	○	○	⊖	*		*								*	*					*	*			
Driveline	⊖	⊖	⊖	⊖	⊖		⊖								⊖	⊖					⊖	⊖			
Electrical system	●	○	○	○	⊖		●								○	⊖					○	○			
Steering/suspension	⊖	⊖	⊖	⊖	⊖		●								○	⊖					○	○			
Brakes	●	○	○	⊖	⊖		●								○	○					○	○			
Exhaust system	⊖	⊖	⊖	⊖	⊖		⊖								⊖	⊖					⊖	⊖			
Body rust	⊖	⊖	⊖	⊖	⊖		⊖								⊖	⊖					⊖	⊖			
Paint	⊖	⊖	⊖	⊖	⊖		⊖								○	⊖									
Body integrity	⊖	⊖	⊖	⊖	○		⊖								●	◐					○	○			
Body hardware	○	○	○	○	○		○								○	○					○	○			
Air-conditioning	⊖	⊖	⊖	⊖	⊖		○								⊖	⊖					⊖	⊖			

(ID = "Insufficient data" printed vertically in the column)

Bottom group

TROUBLE SPOTS	Nissan 240SX '88	'89	'90	'91	'92	'93	Nissan 300ZX '88	'89	'90	'91	'92	'93	Nissan Altima '88	'89	'90	'91	'92	'93	Nissan Maxima '88	'89	'90	'91	'92	'93
Engine	⊖	⊖	⊖	⊖	ID	ID	⊖	ID	⊖	⊖	ID	ID						⊖	⊖	⊖	⊖	⊖	⊖	⊖
Engine cooling	⊖	⊖	⊖	⊖			⊖		⊖	⊖								⊖	⊖	⊖	⊖	⊖	⊖	⊖
Fuel system	⊖	⊖	⊖	⊖			○		⊖	○								⊖	⊖	⊖	⊖	⊖	⊖	⊖
Ignition system	⊖	⊖	⊖	⊖			⊖		⊖	⊖								⊖	⊖	⊖	⊖	⊖	⊖	⊖
Auto. transmission	⊖	○	⊖	*			*		◐	*								⊖	⊖	⊖	⊖	⊖	⊖	⊖
Man. transmission	⊖	⊖	⊖	⊖			*		⊖	⊖								⊖	○	⊖	⊖	⊖	⊖	*
Clutch	○	○	⊖	⊖			*		○	○								⊖	●	◐	○	⊖	⊖	*
Driveline	⊖	⊖	⊖	⊖			⊖		⊖	⊖								⊖	⊖	⊖	⊖	⊖	⊖	⊖
Electrical system	●	○	⊖	⊖			●		○	○								⊖	●	○	◐	○	⊖	⊖
Steering/suspension	⊖	⊖	⊖	⊖			⊖		⊖	⊖								⊖	○	⊖	⊖	⊖	⊖	⊖
Brakes	○	○	⊖	⊖			○		●	●								⊖	●	●	◐	⊖	⊖	⊖
Exhaust system	○	⊖	⊖	⊖			○		⊖	⊖								⊖	⊖	⊖	⊖	⊖	⊖	⊖
Body rust	⊖	⊖	⊖	⊖			⊖		⊖	⊖								⊖	⊖	⊖	⊖	⊖	⊖	⊖
Paint	⊖	⊖	⊖	⊖			⊖		⊖	⊖								⊖	○	⊖	⊖	⊖	⊖	⊖
Body integrity	○	○	⊖	⊖			○		○	○								⊖	○	○	⊖	⊖	⊖	⊖
Body hardware	●	⊖	○	○			○		○	○								⊖	○	◐	○	⊖	⊖	⊖
Air-conditioning	⊖	⊖	⊖	⊖			○		⊖	⊖								⊖	○	⊖	⊖	⊖	⊖	⊖

Legend: ⊖   ⊖   ○   ◐   ●   *
Few ← Problems → Many   Insufficient data

Nissan Pathfinder V6

TROUBLE SPOTS	'88	'89	'90	'91	'92	'93
Engine	⊖	⊖	⊖	⊖	⊖	⊖
Engine cooling	⊖	⊖	⊖	⊖	⊖	⊖
Fuel system	○	⊖	⊖	○	⊖	⊖
Ignition system	⊖	⊖	⊖	⊖	⊖	⊖
Auto. transmission	⊖	*	⊖	○	⊖	⊖
Man. transmission	⊖	⊖	⊖	⊖	⊖	*
Clutch	○	⊖	⊖	⊖	⊖	*
Driveline	⊖	⊖	⊖	⊖	⊖	⊖
Electrical system	◖	○	○	○	○	⊖
Steering/suspension	◖	○	⊖	⊖	⊖	⊖
Brakes	◖	○	⊖	⊖	⊖	⊖
Exhaust system	●	◖	○	⊖	⊖	⊖
Body rust	⊖	⊖	○	⊖	⊖	⊖
Paint	⊖	⊖	⊖	⊖	⊖	⊖
Body integrity	○	○	○	○	⊖	⊖
Body hardware	◖	○	○	⊖	⊖	⊖
Air-conditioning	⊖	⊖	⊖	⊖	⊖	⊖

Nissan Pickup (2WD)

TROUBLE SPOTS	'88	'89	'90	'91	'92	'93
Engine	⊖	⊖	⊖	⊖	⊖	⊖
Engine cooling	⊖	⊖	⊖	⊖	⊖	⊖
Fuel system	○	○	⊖	⊖	⊖	⊖
Ignition system	⊖	⊖	⊖	⊖	⊖	⊖
Auto. transmission	*	*	○	○	⊖	⊖
Man. transmission	⊖	⊖	⊖	⊖	⊖	⊖
Clutch	○	⊖	⊖	⊖	⊖	⊖
Driveline	⊖	⊖	⊖	⊖	⊖	⊖
Electrical system	◖	◖	○	⊖	⊖	⊖
Steering/suspension	○	⊖	⊖	⊖	⊖	⊖
Brakes	○	○	⊖	⊖	⊖	⊖
Exhaust system	◖	○	○	⊖	⊖	⊖
Body rust	⊖	○	⊖	⊖	⊖	⊖
Paint	○	○	⊖	⊖	⊖	⊖
Body integrity	○	○	⊖	⊖	⊖	⊖
Body hardware	◖	○	○	⊖	⊖	⊖
Air-conditioning	○	⊖	⊖	⊖	⊖	⊖

Nissan Pickup (4WD)

TROUBLE SPOTS	'88	'89	'90	'91	'92	'93
Engine	○	⊖	⊖	⊖	⊖	⊖
Engine cooling	⊖	⊖	⊖	⊖	⊖	⊖
Fuel system	●	⊖	⊖	⊖	⊖	⊖
Ignition system	⊖	⊖	⊖	⊖	⊖	⊖
Auto. transmission	*	*	*	*	*	*
Man. transmission	*	⊖	*	⊖	⊖	*
Clutch	*	⊖	*	⊖	⊖	*
Driveline	○	○	⊖	⊖	○	⊖
Electrical system	⊖	○	⊖	○	○	⊖
Steering/suspension	○	◖	⊖	⊖	⊖	○
Brakes	○	◖	⊖	⊖	⊖	⊖
Exhaust system	●	◖	○	○	⊖	⊖
Body rust	●	○	⊖	⊖	⊖	⊖
Paint	○	○	⊖	⊖	⊖	⊖
Body integrity	○	⊖	⊖	○	○	○
Body hardware	○	◖	○	○	⊖	⊖
Air-conditioning	*	*	*	*	*	*

Nissan Pulsar NX, NX 1600/2000

TROUBLE SPOTS	'88	'89	'90	'91	'92	'93
Engine	○					
Engine cooling	⊖					
Fuel system	○					
Ignition system	⊖					
Auto. transmission	*					
Man. transmission	*					
Clutch	*					
Driveline	⊖	Insufficient data	Insufficient data	Insufficient data	Insufficient data	Insufficient data
Electrical system	◖					
Steering/suspension	◖					
Brakes	●					
Exhaust system	●					
Body rust	⊖					
Paint	○					
Body integrity	◖					
Body hardware	⊖					
Air-conditioning	○					

Nissan Quest Van

TROUBLE SPOTS	'88	'89	'90	'91	'92	'93
Engine						⊖
Engine cooling						⊖
Fuel system						⊖
Ignition system						⊖
Auto. transmission						⊖
Man. transmission						
Clutch						
Driveline						⊖
Electrical system						○
Steering/suspension						⊖
Brakes						⊖
Exhaust system						⊖
Body rust						⊖
Paint						⊖
Body integrity						○
Body hardware						○
Air-conditioning						⊖

Nissan Sentra

TROUBLE SPOTS	'88	'89	'90	'91	'92	'93
Engine	○	⊖	⊖	⊖	⊖	⊖
Engine cooling	○	⊖	⊖	⊖	⊖	⊖
Fuel system	⊖	⊖	⊖	⊖	⊖	⊖
Ignition system	⊖	⊖	⊖	⊖	⊖	⊖
Auto. transmission	◖	○	○	⊖	⊖	⊖
Man. transmission	⊖	⊖	⊖	⊖	⊖	⊖
Clutch	⊖	⊖	⊖	○	⊖	⊖
Driveline	⊖	⊖	⊖	⊖	⊖	⊖
Electrical system	●	◖	○	○	○	⊖
Steering/suspension	○	○	⊖	⊖	⊖	⊖
Brakes	●	◖	○	○	⊖	⊖
Exhaust system	●	◖	⊖	⊖	⊖	⊖
Body rust	⊖	⊖	⊖	⊖	⊖	⊖
Paint	○	⊖	⊖	⊖	⊖	⊖
Body integrity	○	○	○	⊖	○	○
Body hardware	○	○	⊖	⊖	⊖	⊖
Air-conditioning	○	⊖	⊖	⊖	⊖	⊖

Nissan Stanza

TROUBLE SPOTS	'88	'89	'90	'91	'92	'93
Engine	⊖	⊖	⊖	⊖	⊖	
Engine cooling	⊖	⊖	⊖	⊖	⊖	
Fuel system	⊖	⊖	⊖	⊖	⊖	
Ignition system	⊖	⊖	⊖	⊖	⊖	
Auto. transmission	○	⊖	⊖	⊖	⊖	
Man. transmission	*	*	⊖	⊖	⊖	
Clutch	*	*	○	⊖	⊖	
Driveline	⊖	⊖	⊖	⊖	⊖	
Electrical system	●	◖	◖	○	⊖	
Steering/suspension	○	⊖	⊖	⊖	⊖	
Brakes	●	◖	○	⊖	⊖	
Exhaust system	●	●	⊖	⊖	⊖	
Body rust	⊖	⊖	⊖	⊖	⊖	
Paint	○	⊖	⊖	⊖	⊖	
Body integrity	◖	○	○	○	⊖	
Body hardware	●	◖	○	⊖	○	
Air-conditioning	○	⊖	⊖	⊖	⊖	

Oldsmobile 88

TROUBLE SPOTS	'88	'89	'90	'91	'92	'93
Engine	⊖	⊖	⊖	⊖	⊖	⊖
Engine cooling	○	○	⊖	⊖	⊖	⊖
Fuel system	◖	○	○	⊖	○	⊖
Ignition system	○	○	⊖	⊖	⊖	⊖
Auto. transmission	○	⊖	⊖	⊖	⊖	⊖
Man. transmission						
Clutch						
Driveline	⊖	⊖	⊖	⊖	⊖	⊖
Electrical system	◖	●	●	○	○	○
Steering/suspension	●	●	◖	○	⊖	⊖
Brakes	●	●	◖	○	○	⊖
Exhaust system	⊖	⊖	⊖	⊖	⊖	⊖
Body rust	○	⊖	⊖	⊖	⊖	⊖
Paint	◖	○	○	⊖	⊖	⊖
Body integrity	○	○	○	⊖	⊖	○
Body hardware	○	○	○	⊖	○	○
Air-conditioning	○	○	⊖	⊖	⊖	⊖

Oldsmobile 98

TROUBLE SPOTS	'89	'90	'91	'92	'93
Engine	⊖	⊖	⊖	⊖	*Insufficient data*
Engine cooling	○	○	⊖	⊖	
Fuel system	○	○	⊖	⊖	
Ignition system	○	⊖	⊖	⊖	
Auto. transmission	⊖	⊖	⊖	⊖	
Man. transmission					
Clutch					
Driveline	⊖	⊖	⊖	⊖	
Electrical system	●	●	●	◐	
Steering/suspension	⊖	⊖	⊖	⊖	
Brakes	●	◐	○	○	
Exhaust system	⊖	⊖	⊖	⊖	
Body rust	⊖	⊖	⊖	⊖	
Paint	○	○	○	○	
Body integrity	○	○	○	●	
Body hardware	⊖	⊖	⊖	⊖	
Air-conditioning	○	○	○	○	

Oldsmobile Achieva

TROUBLE SPOTS	'88	'89	'90	'91	'92	'93
Engine					⊖	*Insufficient data*
Engine cooling					⊖	
Fuel system					⊖	
Ignition system					⊖	
Auto. transmission					⊖	
Man. transmission					*	
Clutch					*	
Driveline					⊖	
Electrical system					○	
Steering/suspension					⊖	
Brakes					⊖	
Exhaust system					⊖	
Body rust					⊖	
Paint					○	
Body integrity					●	
Body hardware					◐	
Air-conditioning					⊖	

Oldsmobile Bravada

TROUBLE SPOTS	'88	'89	'90	'91	'92	'93
Engine				⊖		
Engine cooling				⊖		
Fuel system				⊖		
Ignition system				⊖		
Auto. transmission				⊖		
Man. transmission						
Clutch						
Driveline				⊖	*Insufficient data*	*Insufficient data*
Electrical system				◐		
Steering/suspension				⊖		
Brakes				◐		
Exhaust system				⊖		
Body rust				⊖		
Paint				○		
Body integrity				◐		
Body hardware				●		
Air-conditioning				⊖		

Oldsmobile Custom Cruiser Wagon

TROUBLE SPOTS	'88	'89	'90	'91	'92	'93
Engine	○	○		⊖		
Engine cooling	○	○		⊖		
Fuel system	◐	⊖		○		
Ignition system	○	⊖		⊖		
Auto. transmission	○	⊖		⊖		
Man. transmission						
Clutch						
Driveline	⊖	⊖	*Insufficient data*	○	*Insufficient data*	
Electrical system	◐	●		◐		
Steering/suspension	○	○		○		
Brakes	◐	○		○		
Exhaust system	⊖	⊖		⊖		
Body rust	○	○		⊖		
Paint	○	○		○		
Body integrity	○	○		○		
Body hardware	⊖	⊖		○		
Air-conditioning	○	○		○		

Oldsmobile Cutlass Calais

TROUBLE SPOTS	'89	'90	'91	'92	'93
Engine	◐	●	⊖	⊖	
Engine cooling	○	◐	○	⊖	
Fuel system	◐	⊖	○	⊖	
Ignition system	◐	⊖	○	⊖	
Auto. transmission	○	⊖	⊖	○	
Man. transmission	*	*	*		
Clutch	*	*	*		
Driveline	◐	⊖	⊖	⊖	
Electrical system	●	●	◐	○	
Steering/suspension	○	⊖	⊖	⊖	
Brakes	●	●	◐	⊖	
Exhaust system	◐	●	◐	⊖	
Body rust	○	○	⊖	⊖	
Paint	◐	●	○	⊖	
Body integrity	○	○	○	○	
Body hardware	◐	○	○	⊖	
Air-conditioning	○	⊖	⊖	⊖	

Oldsmobile Cutlass Ciera 4

TROUBLE SPOTS	'88	'89	'90	'91	'92	'93
Engine	⊖	⊖	⊖			
Engine cooling	○	○	○			
Fuel system	○	○	⊖			
Ignition system	○	○	⊖			
Auto. transmission	○	○	⊖			
Man. transmission						
Clutch						
Driveline	⊖	⊖	⊖	*Insufficient data*	*Insufficient data*	*Insufficient data*
Electrical system	●	●	○			
Steering/suspension	⊖	⊖	⊖			
Brakes	●	●	⊖			
Exhaust system	◐	⊖	⊖			
Body rust	○	○	⊖			
Paint	◐	○	⊖			
Body integrity	○	⊖	○			
Body hardware	○	○	○			
Air-conditioning	⊖	⊖	⊖			

Oldsmobile Cutlass Ciera V6

TROUBLE SPOTS	'88	'89	'90	'91	'92	'93
Engine	○	⊖	⊖	⊖	⊖	⊖
Engine cooling	●	○	○	⊖	⊖	⊖
Fuel system	◐	○	○	⊖	⊖	⊖
Ignition system	○	○	⊖	⊖	⊖	⊖
Auto. transmission	○	○	⊖	⊖	⊖	⊖
Man. transmission						
Clutch						
Driveline	⊖	⊖	⊖	⊖	⊖	⊖
Electrical system	●	●	○	○	⊖	○
Steering/suspension	⊖	⊖	⊖	⊖	⊖	⊖
Brakes	●	●	◐	○	⊖	○
Exhaust system	○	⊖	⊖	⊖	⊖	⊖
Body rust	○	○	○	⊖	⊖	⊖
Paint	○	○	○	⊖	⊖	⊖
Body integrity	○	⊖	○	○	⊖	○
Body hardware	○	○	○	○	⊖	⊖
Air-conditioning	⊖	⊖	⊖	⊖	⊖	⊖

Oldsmobile Cutlass Supreme V6

TROUBLE SPOTS	'88	'89	'90	'91	'92	'93
Engine	⊖	⊖	⊖	⊖	⊖	⊖
Engine cooling	○	○	○	⊖	⊖	⊖
Fuel system	○	○	○	⊖	⊖	⊖
Ignition system	○	○	○	⊖	⊖	⊖
Auto. transmission	○	○	○	⊖	⊖	⊖
Man. transmission		*	*		*	*
Clutch		*	*		*	*
Driveline	⊖	⊖	⊖	⊖	⊖	⊖
Electrical system	●	●	●	◐	○	○
Steering/suspension	●	◐	○	⊖	⊖	⊖
Brakes	●	●	●	◐	○	○
Exhaust system	○	○	⊖	⊖	⊖	⊖
Body rust	○	○	○	⊖	⊖	⊖
Paint	●	◐	○	○	⊖	○
Body integrity	●	◐	○	○	○	○
Body hardware	●	◐	○	○	⊖	⊖
Air-conditioning	○	○	⊖	⊖	⊖	⊖

⊖ ⊖ ○ ◐ ● ＊
Few ← Problems → Many   Insufficient data

Reliability symbols shown as: ● (worse), ◐ (partial), ⊖ (average), ○ (better), ✱ (asterisk / not applicable). Cells left blank where no data shown.

Oldsmobile Silhouette Van

TROUBLE SPOTS	'88	'89	'90	'91	'92	'93
Engine			⊖	⊖	⊖	*Insufficient data*
Engine cooling			●	⊖	⊖	
Fuel system			⊖	⊖	⊖	
Ignition system			⊖	⊖	⊖	
Auto. transmission			⊖	⊖	⊖	
Man. transmission						
Clutch						
Driveline			⊖	⊖	⊖	
Electrical system			●	◐	○	
Steering/suspension			○	⊖	⊖	
Brakes			○	◐	⊖	
Exhaust system			⊖	⊖	⊖	
Body rust			⊖	⊖	⊖	
Paint			●	◐	⊖	
Body integrity			◐	◐	○	
Body hardware			●	●	●	
Air-conditioning			○	⊖	⊖	

Oldsmobile Toronado

TROUBLE SPOTS	'88	'89	'90	'91	'92	'93
Engine	⊖	*Insufficient data*	⊖	*Insufficient data*	*Insufficient data*	*Insufficient data*
Engine cooling	○		○			
Fuel system	⊖		⊖			
Ignition system	○		◐			
Auto. transmission	○		⊖			
Man. transmission						
Clutch						
Driveline	⊖		⊖			
Electrical system	●		●			
Steering/suspension	○		◐			
Brakes	◐		●			
Exhaust system	⊖		⊖			
Body rust	⊖		⊖			
Paint	○		○			
Body integrity	○		●			
Body hardware	◐		●			
Air-conditioning	○		○			

Plymouth Acclaim 4

TROUBLE SPOTS	'88	'89	'90	'91	'92	'93
Engine		○	○	○	⊖	⊖
Engine cooling		○	⊖	⊖	⊖	⊖
Fuel system		○	⊖	⊖	⊖	⊖
Ignition system		⊖	⊖	⊖	⊖	⊖
Auto. transmission		⊖	⊖	⊖	⊖	⊖
Man. transmission		✱	✱	✱	✱	✱
Clutch		✱	✱	✱	✱	✱
Driveline		⊖	⊖	⊖	⊖	⊖
Electrical system		○	○	○	○	⊖
Steering/suspension		○	○	⊖	⊖	⊖
Brakes		●	◐	⊖	⊖	⊖
Exhaust system		⊖	⊖	⊖	⊖	⊖
Body rust		⊖	⊖	⊖	⊖	⊖
Paint		○	⊖	⊖	⊖	⊖
Body integrity		⊖	⊖	⊖	⊖	⊖
Body hardware		⊖	⊖	⊖	⊖	⊖
Air-conditioning		◐	○	⊖	⊖	⊖

Plymouth Acclaim V6 (partially cut off at page edge)

TROUBLE SPOTS	'88	'89	'90	'91	'92
Engine		○	⊖	⊖	⊖
Engine cooling		⊖	⊖	⊖	⊖
Fuel system		⊖	⊖	⊖	⊖
Ignition system		⊖	⊖	⊖	⊖
Auto. transmission		◐	○	○	⊖
Man. transmission					
Clutch					
Driveline		⊖	⊖	⊖	⊖
Electrical system		●	◐	○	⊖
Steering/suspension		○	◐	○	⊖
Brakes		●	◐	⊖	⊖
Exhaust system		⊖	⊖	⊖	⊖
Body rust		⊖	⊖	⊖	⊖
Paint		○	⊖	⊖	⊖
Body integrity		○	⊖	⊖	⊖
Body hardware		○	⊖	⊖	⊖
Air-conditioning		⊖	⊖	⊖	⊖

Plymouth Colt, Colt Wagon

TROUBLE SPOTS	'88	'89	'90	'91	'92	'93
Engine	●	○	○	⊖	⊖	*Insufficient data*
Engine cooling	○	⊖	⊖	⊖	⊖	
Fuel system	○	⊖	⊖	⊖	⊖	
Ignition system	⊖	⊖	⊖	⊖	⊖	
Auto. transmission	⊖	⊖	✱	✱	✱	
Man. transmission	⊖	⊖	⊖	⊖	⊖	
Clutch	⊖	⊖	⊖	⊖	⊖	
Driveline	⊖	⊖	⊖	⊖	⊖	
Electrical system	○	○	○	⊖	⊖	
Steering/suspension	○	⊖	⊖	⊖	⊖	
Brakes	●	◐	○	⊖	⊖	
Exhaust system	⊖	⊖	⊖	⊖	⊖	
Body rust	⊖	⊖	⊖	⊖	⊖	
Paint	○	○	⊖	○	○	
Body integrity	○	○	⊖	⊖	○	
Body hardware	○	○	⊖	⊖	⊖	
Air-conditioning	○	○	⊖	⊖	⊖	

Plymouth Colt Vista Wagon

TROUBLE SPOTS	'88	'89	'90	'91	'92	'93
Engine	●	◐	*Insufficient data*	*Insufficient data*	*Insufficient data*	⊖
Engine cooling	⊖	○				⊖
Fuel system	⊖	⊖				⊖
Ignition system	⊖	⊖				⊖
Auto. transmission	✱	✱				⊖
Man. transmission	●	◐				✱
Clutch	○	○				✱
Driveline	○	⊖				⊖
Electrical system	○	○				○
Steering/suspension	○	○				⊖
Brakes	○	○				○
Exhaust system	⊖	⊖				◐
Body rust	⊖	⊖				⊖
Paint	⊖	○				⊖
Body integrity	⊖	○				○
Body hardware	⊖	○				◐
Air-conditioning	⊖	○				⊖

Plymouth Horizon

TROUBLE SPOTS	'88	'89	'90	'91	'92	'93
Engine	○	⊖	⊖			
Engine cooling	○	◐	○			
Fuel system	⊖	⊖	⊖			
Ignition system	○	○	⊖			
Auto. transmission	⊖	⊖	✱			
Man. transmission	○	✱	✱			
Clutch	○	✱	✱			
Driveline	⊖	⊖	⊖			
Electrical system	⊖	●	⊖			
Steering/suspension	○	○	○			
Brakes	●	●	◐			
Exhaust system	⊖	⊖	⊖			
Body rust	○	○	⊖			
Paint	●	◐	○			
Body integrity	●	●	●			
Body hardware	○	◐	○			
Air-conditioning	●	●	✱			

Plymouth Laser (2WD)

TROUBLE SPOTS	'88	'89	'90	'91	'92	'93
Engine			⊖	⊖	⊖	
Engine cooling			⊖	⊖	⊖	
Fuel system			⊖	⊖	⊖	
Ignition system			⊖	⊖	○	
Auto. transmission			○	○	✱	
Man. transmission			○	⊖	✱	
Clutch			⊖	⊖	✱	
Driveline			◐	○	⊖	
Electrical system			⊖	⊖	⊖	
Steering/suspension			○	⊖	⊖	
Brakes			◐	●	⊖	
Exhaust system			⊖	⊖	⊖	
Body rust			⊖	○	⊖	
Paint			○	◐	⊖	
Body integrity			⊖	◐	⊖	
Body hardware			⊖	⊖	⊖	
Air-conditioning			⊖	⊖	⊖	

Plymouth Laser Turbo (2WD)

Trouble Spots	'88	'89	'90	'91	'92	'93
Engine		⊖	⊖			
Engine cooling		⊖	⊖			
Fuel system		⊖	○			
Ignition system		⊖	⊖			
Auto. transmission			*			
Man. transmission		○	*			
Clutch		○	*			
Driveline		⊖	⊖	Insufficient data	Insufficient data	
Electrical system		◐	◐			
Steering/suspension		⊖	⊖			
Brakes		○	○			
Exhaust system		⊖	⊖			
Body rust		⊖	⊖			
Paint		○	⊖			
Body integrity		○	⊖			
Body hardware		○	⊖			
Air-conditioning		⊖	⊖			

Plymouth Laser Turbo (4WD)

Trouble Spots	'88	'89	'90	'91	'92	'93
Engine			○			
Engine cooling			⊖			
Fuel system			⊖			
Ignition system			⊖			
Auto. transmission						
Man. transmission			○			
Clutch			○			
Driveline			⊖	Insufficient data		
Electrical system			○			
Steering/suspension			○			
Brakes			⊖			
Exhaust system			⊖			
Body rust			⊖			
Paint			○			
Body integrity			○			
Body hardware			◐			
Air-conditioning			⊖			

Plymouth Reliant

Trouble Spots	'88	'89	'90	'91	'92	'93
Engine	⊖	⊖				
Engine cooling	○	⊖				
Fuel system	⊖	○				
Ignition system	○	○				
Auto. transmission	⊖	⊖				
Man. transmission	*	*				
Clutch	*	*				
Driveline	⊖	⊖				
Electrical system	○	◐				
Steering/suspension	◐	○				
Brakes	●	●				
Exhaust system	⊖	⊖				
Body rust	○	○				
Paint	○	◐				
Body integrity	●	●				
Body hardware	●	●				
Air-conditioning	●	◐				

Plymouth Sundance 4

Trouble Spots	'88	'89	'90	'91	'92	'93
Engine	⊖	⊖	○	○	○	⊖
Engine cooling	⊖	⊖	○	⊖	⊖	⊖
Fuel system	⊖	○	○	○	⊖	⊖
Ignition system	○	⊖	⊖	⊖	⊖	⊖
Auto. transmission	⊖	⊖	⊖	⊖	⊖	⊖
Man. transmission	*	*	*	⊖	⊖	*
Clutch	*	*	*	⊖	⊖	*
Driveline	⊖	⊖	⊖	⊖	⊖	⊖
Electrical system	◐	○	◐	○	○	⊖
Steering/suspension	⊖	⊖	○	⊖	⊖	⊖
Brakes	●	●	◐	⊖	⊖	⊖
Exhaust system	⊖	⊖	⊖	⊖	⊖	⊖
Body rust	⊖	⊖	⊖	⊖	⊖	⊖
Paint	○	⊖	⊖	⊖	⊖	⊖
Body integrity	○	○	⊖	◐	⊖	⊖
Body hardware	●	◐	○	⊖	⊖	⊖
Air-conditioning	●	◐	⊖	⊖	⊖	⊖

Plymouth Voyager 4

Trouble Spots	'88	'89	'90	'91	'92	'93
Engine	◐	○	○	○	⊖	⊖
Engine cooling	◐	○	○	⊖	⊖	⊖
Fuel system	◐	○	○	⊖	⊖	⊖
Ignition system	◐	⊖	○	⊖	⊖	⊖
Auto. transmission	⊖	○	○	⊖	⊖	⊖
Man. transmission	⊖	⊖	*		*	*
Clutch	○	○	*		*	*
Driveline	⊖	⊖	⊖	⊖	⊖	⊖
Electrical system	●	○	◐	●	⊖	⊖
Steering/suspension	●	○	○	⊖	⊖	⊖
Brakes	●	◐	○	⊖	⊖	⊖
Exhaust system	⊖	⊖	⊖	⊖	⊖	⊖
Body rust	⊖	⊖	⊖	⊖	⊖	⊖
Paint	⊖	⊖	○	⊖	⊖	⊖
Body integrity	⊖	○	⊖	○	⊖	⊖
Body hardware	◐	○	◐	◐	⊖	○
Air-conditioning	⊖	○	○	⊖	⊖	⊖

Plymouth Voyager 4 Turbo

Trouble Spots	'88	'89	'90	'91	'92	'93
Engine	○					
Engine cooling	◐					
Fuel system	⊖					
Ignition system	⊖					
Auto. transmission	⊖					
Man. transmission	*					
Clutch	*					
Driveline	⊖	Insufficient data				
Electrical system	◐					
Steering/suspension	○					
Brakes	◐					
Exhaust system	⊖					
Body rust	⊖					
Paint	⊖					
Body integrity	○					
Body hardware	◐					
Air-conditioning	◐					

Plymouth Grand Voyager 4

Trouble Spots	'88	'89	'90	'91	'92	'93
Engine	●	◐				
Engine cooling	⊖	○				
Fuel system	⊖	○				
Ignition system	⊖	⊖				
Auto. transmission	○	●				
Man. transmission	*	*				
Clutch	*	*				
Driveline	⊖	⊖				
Electrical system	●	○				
Steering/suspension	◐	○				
Brakes	●	●				
Exhaust system	⊖	⊖				
Body rust	⊖	⊖				
Paint	○	⊖				
Body integrity	○	⊖				
Body hardware	●	●				
Air-conditioning	◐	○				

Plymouth Voyager V6 (2WD)

Trouble Spots	'88	'89	'90	'91	'92	'93
Engine	●	◐	○	⊖	⊖	⊖
Engine cooling	●	○	○	⊖	⊖	⊖
Fuel system	●	○	○	⊖	⊖	⊖
Ignition system	⊖	⊖	⊖	⊖	⊖	⊖
Auto. transmission	○	⊖	◐	○	⊖	⊖
Man. transmission						
Clutch						
Driveline	⊖	⊖	⊖	⊖	⊖	⊖
Electrical system	●	◐	◐	○	○	⊖
Steering/suspension	○	○	◐	○	⊖	⊖
Brakes	●	◐	○	○	⊖	⊖
Exhaust system	⊖	⊖	⊖	⊖	⊖	⊖
Body rust	⊖	⊖	⊖	⊖	⊖	⊖
Paint	○	⊖	⊖	⊖	⊖	⊖
Body integrity	○	○	◐	○	⊖	⊖
Body hardware	●	◐	○	○	○	○
Air-conditioning	●	○	⊖	⊖	⊖	⊖

Legend: ⊖ ⊖ ○ ◐ ● Few ← Problems → Many   * Insufficient data

Plymouth Voyager V6 (4WD)

Trouble Spots	'88	'89	'90	'91	'92	'93
Engine			⊖			
Engine cooling			⊖			
Fuel system			○			
Ignition system			⊖			
Auto. transmission			⊖			
Man. transmission						
Clutch				Insufficient data	Insufficient data	
Driveline			⊖			
Electrical system			◒			
Steering/suspension			⊖			
Brakes			⊖			
Exhaust system			⊖			
Body rust			⊖			
Paint			◒			
Body integrity			⊖			
Body hardware			○			
Air-conditioning			⊖			

Plymouth Grand Voyager V6 (2WD)

Trouble Spots	'88	'89	'90	'91	'92	'93
Engine	●	●	○	⊖	⊖	⊖
Engine cooling	⊖	○	○	⊖	⊖	⊖
Fuel system	●	○	⊖	⊖	⊖	⊖
Ignition system	⊖	⊖	⊖	⊖	⊖	⊖
Auto. transmission	●	●	●	○	⊖	⊖
Man. transmission						
Clutch						
Driveline	⊖	⊖	⊖	⊖	⊖	⊖
Electrical system	●	○	○	○	⊖	⊖
Steering/suspension	○	⊖	⊖	○	○	⊖
Brakes	●	●	◒	⊖	⊖	⊖
Exhaust system	⊖	⊖	⊖	⊖	⊖	⊖
Body rust	⊖	⊖	⊖	⊖	⊖	⊖
Paint	○	○	⊖	⊖	⊖	○
Body integrity	○	⊖	○	○	⊖	○
Body hardware	●	●	◒	⊖	⊖	○
Air-conditioning	●	◒	○	⊖	⊖	⊖

Plymouth Grand Voyager V6 (4WD)

Trouble Spots	'88	'89	'90	'91	'92	'93
Engine			⊖	⊖	⊖	
Engine cooling			⊖	⊖	⊖	
Fuel system			⊖	⊖	⊖	
Ignition system			⊖	⊖	⊖	
Auto. transmission			⊖	○	⊖	
Man. transmission						
Clutch						
Driveline			⊖	⊖	⊖	
Electrical system			●	◒	⊖	
Steering/suspension			⊖	⊖	○	
Brakes			⊖	○	⊖	
Exhaust system			⊖	⊖	⊖	
Body rust			⊖	⊖	⊖	
Paint			○	⊖	⊖	
Body integrity			⊖	⊖	⊖	
Body hardware			●	◒	⊖	
Air-conditioning			⊖	⊖	⊖	

Pontiac 6000

Trouble Spots	'88	'89	'90	'91	'92	'93
Engine	○	○	⊖			
Engine cooling	●	⊖	○			
Fuel system	●	●	○			
Ignition system	○	○	⊖			
Auto. transmission	○	○	⊖			
Man. transmission	*					
Clutch	*					
Driveline	⊖	⊖	⊖			
Electrical system	●	●	◒	Insufficient data		
Steering/suspension	●	●	○			
Brakes	●	●	●			
Exhaust system	◒	◒	⊖			
Body rust	○	○	⊖			
Paint	●	◒	⊖			
Body integrity	◒	◒	⊖			
Body hardware	●	○	⊖			
Air-conditioning	○	○	⊖			

Pontiac Bonneville

Trouble Spots	'88	'89	'90	'91	'92	'93
Engine	⊖	⊖	⊖	⊖	⊖	⊖
Engine cooling	◒	⊖	⊖	⊖	⊖	⊖
Fuel system	◒	○	○	○	⊖	⊖
Ignition system	○	○	○	⊖	⊖	⊖
Auto. transmission	○	⊖	⊖	⊖	⊖	⊖
Man. transmission						
Clutch						
Driveline	⊖	⊖	⊖	⊖	⊖	⊖
Electrical system	●	●	●	◒	○	⊖
Steering/suspension	○	◒	⊖	○	⊖	⊖
Brakes	●	●	○	○	⊖	⊖
Exhaust system	⊖	⊖	⊖	⊖	⊖	⊖
Body rust	⊖	⊖	⊖	⊖	⊖	⊖
Paint	○	○	⊖	⊖	⊖	⊖
Body integrity	○	◒	⊖	◒	⊖	⊖
Body hardware	○	○	◒	◒	⊖	⊖
Air-conditioning	⊖	⊖	⊖	⊖	⊖	⊖

Pontiac Firebird

Trouble Spots	'88	'89	'90	'91	'92	'93
Engine		⊖		○		
Engine cooling		⊖		○		
Fuel system		⊖		⊖		
Ignition system		⊖		⊖		
Auto. transmission		○		*		
Man. transmission		*		*		
Clutch		*		*		
Driveline		⊖	Insufficient data	⊖	Insufficient data	Insufficient data
Electrical system	Insufficient data	●		●		
Steering/suspension		⊖		⊖		
Brakes		○		⊖		
Exhaust system		⊖		⊖		
Body rust		⊖		⊖		
Paint		●		●		
Body integrity		●		●		
Body hardware		●		◒		
Air-conditioning		○		⊖		

Pontiac Grand Am 4

Trouble Spots	'88	'89	'90	'91	'92	'93
Engine	●	●	○	⊖	⊖	⊖
Engine cooling	◒	○	○	⊖	⊖	⊖
Fuel system	○	○	○	⊖	⊖	⊖
Ignition system	○	○	○	⊖	⊖	⊖
Auto. transmission	⊖	⊖	⊖	⊖	⊖	*
Man. transmission	*	*	*	*	*	*
Clutch	*	*	*	*	*	*
Driveline	⊖	⊖	⊖	⊖	⊖	⊖
Electrical system	●	●	◒	○	○	○
Steering/suspension	○	◒	○	⊖	⊖	⊖
Brakes	●	●	◒	◒	⊖	⊖
Exhaust system	●	●	◒	⊖	⊖	⊖
Body rust	○	◒	⊖	⊖	⊖	⊖
Paint	●	●	◒	◒	⊖	⊖
Body integrity	◒	◒	○	○	⊖	⊖
Body hardware	○	○	○	⊖	⊖	⊖
Air-conditioning	⊖	⊖	⊖	⊖	⊖	⊖

Pontiac Grand Am V6

Trouble Spots	'88	'89	'90	'91	'92	'93
Engine					⊖	⊖
Engine cooling					⊖	⊖
Fuel system					⊖	⊖
Ignition system					⊖	⊖
Auto. transmission					⊖	⊖
Man. transmission						
Clutch						
Driveline					⊖	⊖
Electrical system					○	⊖
Steering/suspension					⊖	⊖
Brakes					○	⊖
Exhaust system					⊖	⊖
Body rust					⊖	⊖
Paint					⊖	⊖
Body integrity					⊖	○
Body hardware					⊖	⊖
Air-conditioning					○	⊖

TROUBLE SPOTS	Pontiac Grand Prix V6						Pontiac Le Mans					
	'88	'89	'90	'91	'92	'93	'88	'89	'90	'91	'92	'93
Engine	○	⊖	⊖	⊖	⊖	⊖	●	●				
Engine cooling	○	○	⊖	⊖	⊖	⊖	●	●				
Fuel system	○	◐	⊖	⊖	⊖	⊖	●	●				
Ignition system	○	○	⊖	⊖	⊖	⊖	◐	●				
Auto. transmission	○	○	○	⊖	⊖	⊖	*	*				
Man. transmission	*	*	*	*	*	*	*	*				
Clutch	*	*	*	*	*	*	*	*				
Driveline	⊖	⊖	⊖	⊖	⊖	⊖	⊖	⊖	Insufficient data	Insufficient data	Insufficient data	Insufficient data
Electrical system	●	●	●	◐	◐	○	●	●				
Steering/suspension	●	●	◐	●	○	○	●	●				
Brakes	⊖	⊖	◐	○	○	⊖	●	●				
Exhaust system	⊖	⊖	⊖	⊖	⊖	⊖	●	●				
Body rust	○	⊖					○	⊖				
Paint	○	○	○	○	○	⊖	⊖	●				
Body integrity	○	○	○	○	○	○	⊖	●				
Body hardware	○	●	⊖	○	○	○	●	●				
Air-conditioning	○	⊖	⊖	⊖	⊖	⊖	●	*				

TROUBLE SPOTS	Pontiac Sunbird						Pontiac Trans Sport Van					
	'88	'89	'90	'91	'92	'93	'88	'89	'90	'91	'92	'93
Engine	●	●	○	◐	○				⊖	⊖	⊖	⊖
Engine cooling	●	○	○	○	○				○	⊖	⊖	⊖
Fuel system	○	⊖	○	○	○				⊖	⊖	⊖	⊖
Ignition system	○	⊖	⊖	⊖	⊖				⊖	⊖	⊖	⊖
Auto. transmission	⊖	⊖	⊖	⊖	⊖				⊖	○	⊖	⊖
Man. transmission	*	*	*	*	*	Insufficient data						
Clutch	*	*	*	*	*							
Driveline	⊖	⊖	⊖	⊖	⊖				⊖	⊖	⊖	⊖
Electrical system	●	●	●	●	○				●	◐	○	●
Steering/suspension	○	○	⊖	⊖	⊖				⊖	⊖	⊖	⊖
Brakes	●	●	●	●	●				●	●	●	◐
Exhaust system	●	○	○	⊖	◐				⊖	⊖	⊖	⊖
Body rust	●	○	⊖	⊖					⊖	⊖		
Paint	○	○	○	○	○				○	○	○	●
Body integrity	⊖	⊖	⊖	○	○				○	●	○	○
Body hardware	○	○	○	◐	●				●	●	●	○
Air-conditioning	⊖	⊖	⊖	⊖	⊖				○	⊖	○	⊖

TROUBLE SPOTS	Saab 900						Saab 9000					
	'88	'89	'90	'91	'92	'93	'88	'89	'90	'91	'92	'93
Engine	○	○	⊖	⊖	⊖			○	○		⊖	⊖
Engine cooling	○	●	⊖	⊖	⊖			○	●		⊖	⊖
Fuel system	○	○	⊖	⊖	⊖			○	○		⊖	⊖
Ignition system	○	⊖	⊖	⊖	⊖			⊖	⊖		⊖	⊖
Auto. transmission	*	*	*	*	*			*	*	○	*	*
Man. transmission	○	⊖	*	*	*			*	*	⊖	*	*
Clutch	○	⊖	*	*	*	Insufficient data		*	*	⊖	*	*
Driveline	⊖	⊖	⊖	⊖	⊖			⊖	⊖	⊖	⊖	⊖
Electrical system	●	●	●	●	◐			●	●	●	◐	○
Steering/suspension	○	◐	○	○	⊖			○	⊖	○	○	⊖
Brakes	⊖	○	○	○	⊖			●	●	○	○	⊖
Exhaust system	⊖	⊖	⊖	⊖	⊖			⊖	⊖	⊖	⊖	⊖
Body rust	○	○	⊖	⊖				⊖	⊖	⊖		
Paint	○	○	○	◐	○			○	○		○	○
Body integrity	○	●	○	○	○			●	●	○	○	○
Body hardware	⊖	○	○	○	○			○	○	○	⊖	⊖

TROUBLE SPOTS	Saturn						Subaru Coupe, Sedan & Wagon (2WD)					
	'88	'89	'90	'91	'92	'93	'88	'89	'90	'91	'92	'93
Engine				⊖	⊖	⊖	●	●				
Engine cooling				⊖	⊖	⊖	●	○				
Fuel system				⊖	⊖	⊖	⊖	⊖				
Ignition system				⊖	⊖	⊖	○	⊖				
Auto. transmission				⊖	⊖	⊖	⊖	⊖				
Man. transmission				⊖	⊖	⊖	⊖	*				
Clutch				⊖	⊖	⊖	●	*				
Driveline				⊖	⊖	⊖	⊖	⊖				
Electrical system				○	○	○	○	○				
Steering/suspension				○	○	○	○	○				
Brakes				○	○	○	○	○				
Exhaust system				⊖	⊖	⊖	⊖	○				
Body rust				⊖	⊖	⊖	⊖	⊖				
Paint				⊖	⊖	⊖	⊖	○				
Body integrity				○	○	○	○	○				
Body hardware				○	○	○	○	○				
Air-conditioning				⊖	⊖	⊖	○	○				

Legend: ⊖ ⊖ ○ ◐ ●   *
Few ← Problems → Many   Insufficient data

Symbol key (as read): ● = filled • ◐ = half-filled • ⊖ = circle with dash (average) • ○ = open • * = asterisk • (blank) = no symbol

Subaru Coupe, Sedan & Wagon (4WD) / Subaru Justy / Subaru Legacy (2WD) / Subaru Legacy (4WD)

Trouble Spots	Coupe/Sedan/Wagon (4WD) '88	'89	Justy '88	Legacy (2WD) '90	'91	'92	Legacy (4WD) '90	'91	'92	'93
Engine	●	●	○	⊖	⊖	⊖	⊖	⊖	⊖	⊖
Engine cooling	●	◐	○	⊖	⊖	⊖	⊖	⊖	⊖	⊖
Fuel system	⊖	⊖	◐	⊖	⊖	⊖	⊖	⊖	⊖	⊖
Ignition system	⊖	⊖	⊖	⊖	⊖	⊖	⊖	⊖	⊖	⊖
Auto. transmission	⊖	*		○	○	⊖	○	○	⊖	*
Man. transmission	⊖	⊖	◐	⊖	*	⊖	⊖	⊖	⊖	*
Clutch	◐	⊖	○	⊖	*	⊖	⊖	⊖	⊖	*
Driveline	⊖	⊖	⊖	⊖	⊖	⊖	⊖	⊖	⊖	⊖
Electrical system	○	○	◐	○	⊖	⊖	⊖	○	⊖	⊖
Steering/suspension	⊖	⊖	◐	⊖	⊖	⊖	⊖	○	⊖	⊖
Brakes	○	◐	○	●	○	⊖	◐	○	⊖	⊖
Exhaust system	◐	⊖	●	⊖	⊖	⊖	⊖	⊖	⊖	⊖
Body rust	○	○	⊖	⊖	○	○	⊖	○	○	⊖
Paint	○	○	○	○	○	○	○	○	○	⊖
Body integrity	○	○	◐	○	○	○	○	○	○	⊖
Body hardware	○	○	◐	●	○	○	◐	○	○	⊖
Air-conditioning	⊖	○	*	○	⊖	⊖	⊖	⊖	⊖	⊖

(Justy '89–'93: Insufficient data. Legacy 2WD '88, '89, '93: Insufficient data. Legacy 4WD '88, '89: Insufficient data.)

Subaru Loyale Sedan, Wgn & Coupe (2WD) / Subaru Loyale Sedan, Wgn & Coupe (4WD) / Subaru SVX / Suzuki Sidekick (4WD)

Trouble Spots	Loyale (2WD) '90	'91	'92	Loyale (4WD) '90	'91	'92	SVX '92	Sidekick (4WD) '89	'90	'91	'92
Engine	●	⊖	⊖	○	⊖	⊖	⊖	⊖	○	⊖	⊖
Engine cooling	○	⊖	⊖	○	⊖	⊖	⊖	⊖	⊖	⊖	⊖
Fuel system	⊖	⊖	⊖	⊖	⊖	⊖	⊖	○	○	⊖	⊖
Ignition system	⊖	⊖	⊖	⊖	⊖	⊖	⊖	⊖	⊖	⊖	⊖
Auto. transmission	*	*	*	*	*	*	⊖		*	*	*
Man. transmission	*	*	*	⊖	⊖	⊖		*	*	*	⊖
Clutch	*	*	*	○	⊖	⊖		*	*	*	⊖
Driveline	⊖	⊖	⊖	⊖	⊖	⊖	⊖	⊖	⊖	⊖	⊖
Electrical system	○	⊖	○	○	○	⊖	●	◐	○	○	○
Steering/suspension	⊖	⊖	⊖	⊖	⊖	⊖		⊖	⊖	○	○
Brakes	⊖	○	⊖	○	○	⊖	⊖	●	●	◐	○
Exhaust system	⊖	⊖	⊖	○	⊖	⊖	⊖	○	⊖	○	○
Body rust	⊖	○	○	⊖	⊖	⊖	⊖	○	○	○	○
Paint	○	○	○	○	○	○	⊖	○	○	○	○
Body integrity	○	○	○	◐	○	◐	○	◐	○	◐	◐
Body hardware	⊖	○	○	○	○	⊖	○	◐	○	◐	◐
Air-conditioning	*	⊖	⊖	○	⊖	⊖	⊖	*	*	*	⊖

(Loyale 2WD '88, '89, '93: Insufficient data. Loyale 4WD '88, '89, '93: Insufficient data. SVX '88–'91, '93: Insufficient data. Suzuki Sidekick '88, '93: Insufficient data.)

Toyota 4Runner / Camry

Trouble Spots	Toyota 4Runner 4 (4WD) '88	'89	'90	'91	'92	'93	Toyota 4Runner V6 '88	'89	'90	'91	'92	'93	Toyota Camry 4 (2WD) '88	'89	'90	'91	'92	'93	Toyota Camry 4 (4WD) '88	'89	'90	'91	'92	'93
Engine	⊖						○	⊖	⊖	⊖	⊖	⊖	○	⊖	⊖	⊖	⊖	⊖	◓	⊖		⊖		
Engine cooling	⊖						⊖	○	⊖	⊖	⊖	⊖	⊖	⊖	⊖	⊖	⊖	⊖	○	⊖		⊖		
Fuel system	⊖						⊖	○	⊖	⊖	⊖	⊖	⊖	⊖	⊖	⊖	⊖	⊖	○	○		⊖		
Ignition system	⊖	Insufficient data	Insufficient data	Insufficient data	Insufficient data	Insufficient data	⊖	⊖	⊖	⊖	⊖	⊖	⊖	⊖	⊖	⊖	⊖	⊖	○	⊖		⊖		
Auto. transmission	✱						✱	✱	⊖	⊖	⊖	⊖	⊖	⊖	⊖	⊖	⊖	⊖		⊖	Insufficient data	⊖		
Man. transmission	⊖						✱	✱	⊖	⊖	⊖	✱	⊖	⊖	⊖	⊖	⊖	✱	⊖	✱				
Clutch	⊖						✱	✱	⊖	○	○	✱	○	⊖	⊖	⊖	⊖	✱	○	✱				
Driveline	○						⊖	⊖	⊖	⊖	⊖	⊖	⊖	⊖	⊖	⊖	⊖	⊖	⊖	⊖		⊖		
Electrical system	○						○	⊖	⊖	⊖	⊖	⊖	◓	○	○	○	⊖	⊖	◓	◓		◓		
Steering/suspension	○						○	○	○	○	⊖	⊖	○	○	⊖	⊖	⊖	⊖	○	○		○		
Brakes	○						○	⊖	⊖	⊖	⊖	⊖	◓	◓	○	◓	⊖	⊖	◓	◓		○		
Exhaust system	○						⊖	○	⊖	⊖	⊖	⊖	●	●	○	⊖	⊖	⊖	●	◓		⊖		
Body rust	○						⊖	⊖	⊖	⊖	⊖	⊖	⊖	⊖	⊖	⊖	⊖	⊖	⊖	◓		⊖		
Paint	○						○	⊖	○	⊖	⊖	⊖	○	○	⊖	⊖	⊖	⊖	◓	◓		◓		
Body integrity	○						⊖	○	○	⊖	⊖	⊖	○	○	⊖	⊖	⊖	⊖	⊖	⊖		⊖		
Body hardware	○						○	○	○	○	⊖	⊖	◓	○	⊖	⊖	⊖	⊖	◓	◓		⊖		
Air-conditioning	○						⊖	⊖	○	○	⊖	⊖	⊖	⊖	⊖	⊖	⊖	⊖	⊖	⊖		⊖		

Toyota Camry V6 / Celica / Corolla

Trouble Spots	Toyota Camry V6 '88	'89	'90	'91	'92	'93	Toyota Celica '88	'89	'90	'91	'92	'93	Toyota Corolla (2WD) '88	'89	'90	'91	'92	'93	Toyota Corolla (4WD) '88	'89	'90	'91	'92	'93
Engine	○	⊖	⊖	⊖	⊖	⊖	○	⊖	⊖	⊖	⊖	⊖	⊖	⊖	⊖	⊖	⊖	⊖		⊖	⊖	⊖		
Engine cooling	⊖	⊖	⊖	⊖	⊖	⊖	⊖	⊖	⊖	⊖	⊖	⊖	⊖	⊖	⊖	⊖	⊖	⊖		⊖	⊖	⊖		
Fuel system	⊖	⊖	⊖	⊖	⊖	⊖	⊖	⊖	⊖	⊖	⊖	⊖	⊖	⊖	⊖	⊖	⊖	⊖		⊖	⊖	⊖		
Ignition system	○	⊖	⊖	⊖	⊖	⊖	⊖	⊖	⊖	⊖	⊖	✱	○	⊖	⊖	⊖	⊖	⊖		⊖	⊖	⊖		
Auto. transmission	○	⊖	⊖	⊖	⊖	⊖	⊖	⊖	⊖	⊖	⊖	✱	⊖	⊖	⊖	⊖	⊖	⊖		✱	✱	✱		
Man. transmission	✱	✱	✱	✱	✱	✱	⊖	⊖	⊖	⊖	⊖	✱	⊖	⊖	⊖	⊖	⊖	⊖	Insufficient data	⊖	✱	✱	Insufficient data	
Clutch	✱	✱	✱	✱	✱	✱	⊖	⊖	⊖	⊖	⊖	✱	○	⊖	⊖	⊖	⊖	⊖		⊖	✱	✱		
Driveline	⊖	⊖	⊖	⊖	⊖	⊖	⊖	⊖	⊖	⊖	⊖	⊖	⊖	⊖	⊖	⊖	⊖	⊖		⊖	⊖	⊖		
Electrical system	○	◓	○	○	⊖	⊖	⊖	◓	○	⊖	⊖	⊖	◓	○	○	○	⊖	⊖		○	○	○		
Steering/suspension	○	◓	○	○	⊖	⊖	⊖	○	⊖	⊖	⊖	⊖	○	○	○	⊖	⊖	⊖		⊖	⊖	⊖		
Brakes	◓	◓	○	◓	⊖	⊖	◓	○	⊖	⊖	⊖	⊖	●	◓	○	⊖	⊖	⊖		◓	⊖	⊖		
Exhaust system	●	◓	○	◓	⊖	⊖	●	●	○	⊖	⊖	⊖	●	●	○	⊖	⊖	⊖		●	⊖	⊖		
Body rust	⊖	◓	⊖	⊖	⊖	⊖	⊖	⊖	⊖	⊖	⊖	⊖	⊖	⊖	⊖	⊖	⊖	⊖		⊖	⊖	⊖		
Paint	○	◓	○	○	⊖	⊖	○	○	○	⊖	⊖	⊖	○	○	⊖	⊖	⊖	⊖		⊖	○	⊖		
Body integrity	○	◓	○	⊖	⊖	⊖	○	○	○	○	○	⊖	○	○	⊖	⊖	⊖	⊖		⊖	○	⊖		
Body hardware	◓	●	◓	○	⊖	⊖	○	○	○	○	○	○	◓	○	○	⊖	⊖	⊖		⊖	○	⊖		
Air-conditioning	⊖	◓	○	○	⊖	⊖	⊖	○	○	⊖	⊖	⊖	⊖	⊖	⊖	⊖	⊖	⊖		⊖	✱	✱		

Legend: ⊖ Few ← Problems → ◓ ● Many   ✱ Insufficient data

Symbol key used below: ● much worse · ◐ worse · ⊖ average · ○ better · * insufficient data

Top section

Trouble Spots	Corolla FX, FX-16 '88	Cressida '88	'89	'90	'91	Land Cruiser Wagon '88	'89	'90	'91	'92	'93	MR2 '88	'89	'90	'91	'92	'93
Engine	⊖	○	⊖	⊖	⊖	◐	○		⊖						⊖		
Engine cooling	⊖	○	⊖	⊖	⊖	◐	○		⊖						⊖		
Fuel system	⊖	⊖	⊖	⊖	⊖	○	◐		⊖						⊖		
Ignition system	⊖	⊖	⊖	⊖	⊖	⊖	⊖		⊖						⊖		
Auto. transmission	⊖	⊖	⊖	⊖	⊖	⊖	⊖		⊖						*		
Man. transmission	⊖														⊖		
Clutch	◐														⊖		
Driveline	⊖	⊖	⊖	⊖	⊖	⊖	⊖	*Insufficient data*	⊖	*Insufficient data*	*Insufficient data*	*Insufficient data*	*Insufficient data*	*Insufficient data*	⊖	*Insufficient data*	*Insufficient data*
Electrical system	○	●	○	○	○	○	○		○						○		
Steering/suspension	○	⊖	⊖	⊖	⊖	⊖	⊖		⊖						○		
Brakes	●	◐	◐	○	○	◐	○		◐						⊖		
Exhaust system	●	○	⊖	⊖	⊖	○	⊖		○						⊖		
Body rust	⊖	⊖	⊖	⊖	⊖	○	○		⊖						⊖		
Paint	○	⊖	⊖	⊖	⊖	⊖	○		⊖						⊖		
Body integrity	◐	⊖	⊖	○	○	⊖	⊖		○						○		
Body hardware	○	◐	⊖	⊖	⊖	○	○		○						⊖		
Air-conditioning	○	○	○	○	⊖	⊖	⊖		○						⊖		

Bottom section

Trouble Spots	Paseo '93	Pickup 4 (2WD) '88	'89	'90	'91	'92	'93	Pickup 4 (4WD) '88	'89	'90	'91	'92	'93	Pickup V6 (2WD) '90	'91	'92	'93
Engine	⊖	⊖	⊖	⊖	⊖	⊖	⊖	⊖	⊖	⊖	⊖	⊖		⊖	⊖	⊖	⊖
Engine cooling	⊖	○	○	⊖	⊖	⊖	⊖	◐	○	⊖	⊖	⊖		⊖	⊖	⊖	⊖
Fuel system	⊖	⊖	⊖	⊖	⊖	⊖	⊖	⊖	⊖	⊖	⊖	⊖		⊖	⊖	⊖	⊖
Ignition system	⊖	⊖	⊖	⊖	⊖	⊖	⊖	⊖	⊖	⊖	⊖	⊖		⊖	⊖	⊖	⊖
Auto. transmission	⊖	⊖	⊖	*	⊖	⊖	*	*	*	*	*	*		⊖	*	*	*
Man. transmission	⊖	⊖	⊖	⊖	⊖	⊖	⊖	⊖	⊖	⊖	⊖	⊖		⊖	*	*	*
Clutch	⊖	○	⊖	⊖	⊖	⊖	⊖	○	⊖	⊖	⊖	⊖		○	*	*	*
Driveline	⊖	⊖	⊖	⊖	⊖	⊖	⊖	⊖	⊖	⊖	⊖	⊖	*Insufficient data*	⊖	⊖	⊖	⊖
Electrical system	⊖	⊖	⊖	⊖	⊖	⊖	⊖	⊖	⊖	⊖	⊖	⊖		⊖	○	⊖	⊖
Steering/suspension	⊖	⊖	⊖	⊖	⊖	⊖	⊖	⊖	⊖	⊖	⊖	⊖		⊖	○	○	⊖
Brakes	⊖	◐	○	⊖	⊖	⊖	⊖	○	○	○	⊖	⊖		◐	○	○	⊖
Exhaust system	⊖	○	○	⊖	⊖	⊖	⊖	◐	●	⊖	⊖	⊖		○	⊖	⊖	⊖
Body rust	⊖	○	⊖	⊖	⊖	⊖	⊖	○	⊖	⊖	⊖	⊖		⊖	⊖	⊖	⊖
Paint	○	⊖	⊖	⊖	⊖	⊖	⊖	⊖	⊖	⊖	○	⊖		⊖	⊖	○	⊖
Body integrity	⊖	⊖	⊖	⊖	⊖	⊖	⊖	⊖	⊖	⊖	⊖	⊖		⊖	⊖	⊖	⊖
Body hardware	⊖	⊖	⊖	⊖	⊖	⊖	⊖	⊖	⊖	⊖	⊖	⊖		○	○	⊖	⊖
Air-conditioning	⊖	⊖	⊖	⊖	⊖	⊖	⊖	○	⊖	*	⊖	⊖		⊖	⊖	⊖	⊖

Paseo: Insufficient data for '88–'92.

Upper section

Trouble Spots	Toyota Pickup V6 (4WD) '88	'89	'90	'91	'92	'93	Toyota Previa Van (2WD) '88	'89	'90	'91	'92	'93	Toyota Previa Van (4WD) '88	'89	'90	'91	'92	'93	Toyota Supra '88	'89	'90	'91	'92	'93
Engine	⊖	⊖	⊖	⊖	⊖	⊖				⊖	⊖	⊖				⊖	⊖		○	○				
Engine cooling	⊖	⊖	⊖	⊖	⊖	⊖				⊖	⊖	⊖				⊖	⊖		○	○				
Fuel system	⊖	⊖	⊖	⊖	⊖	⊖				⊖	⊖	⊖				⊖	⊖		⊖	○				
Ignition system	⊖	⊖	⊖	⊖	⊖	⊖				⊖	⊖	⊖				⊖	⊖		⊖	⊖				
Auto. transmission	*	*	*	*	*	*				⊖	⊖	⊖				⊖	⊖		⊖	*				
Man. transmission	○	⊖	⊖	⊖	⊖	*				*	*	*				*	*		⊖					
Clutch	○	○	⊖	○	⊖	*				*	*	*				*	*		○	○				
Driveline	○	⊖	⊖	⊖	⊖	⊖				⊖	⊖	⊖				⊖	⊖	Insufficient data	⊖	⊖	Insufficient data	Insufficient data	Insufficient data	
Electrical system	○	⊖	⊖	⊖	⊖	⊖				○	⊖	⊖				○	⊖		◐	○				
Steering/suspension	⊖	⊖	⊖	⊖	⊖	⊖				⊖	⊖	⊖				⊖	⊖		○	⊖				
Brakes	◐	⊖	○	⊖	⊖	⊖				⊖	⊖	⊖				⊖	⊖		○	◐				
Exhaust system	⊖	○	○	⊖	⊖	⊖				⊖	⊖	⊖				⊖	⊖		○	○				
Body rust	⊖	⊖	⊖	○	⊖	⊖				⊖	⊖	⊖				⊖	⊖		○	○				
Paint	⊖	⊖	⊖	⊖	⊖	⊖				⊖	⊖	⊖				⊖	⊖		○	○				
Body integrity	⊖	⊖	⊖	○	⊖	⊖				○	⊖	⊖				⊖	⊖		○	⊖				
Body hardware	⊖	⊖	⊖	◐	⊖	⊖				◐	⊖	⊖				○	⊖		◐	○				
Air-conditioning	*	⊖	⊖	⊖	⊖	*				◐	⊖	⊖				⊖	⊖		◐	●				

Lower section

Trouble Spots	Toyota Tercel '88	'89	'90	'91	'92	'93	Volkswagen Fox '88	'89	'90	'91	'92	'93	Volkswagen Golf, GTI '88	'89	'90	'91	'92	'93	Volkswagen Jetta '88	'89	'90	'91	'92	'93
Engine	○	⊖	⊖	⊖	⊖	⊖	○	○					○	○	○	⊖			○	○	○	○		
Engine cooling	○	○	◐	⊖	⊖	⊖	◐	◐					●	●	●	⊖			●	●	●	⊖		
Fuel system	○	○	⊖	⊖	⊖	⊖	○	○					●	●	◐	⊖			⊖	⊖	◐	○		
Ignition system	○	○	⊖	⊖	⊖	⊖	◐	○					○	○	⊖	⊖			⊖	⊖	⊖	○		
Auto. transmission	⊖	⊖	⊖	⊖	⊖	*							*	*	*	*			⊖	○	*	*	*	
Man. transmission	○	⊖	⊖	⊖	⊖	⊖	⊖	○					○	⊖	*	*			○	⊖	⊖	⊖	*	
Clutch	○	⊖	⊖	⊖	⊖	⊖	○	○					⊖	⊖	*	*			⊖	○	⊖	⊖	*	
Driveline	○	○	⊖	⊖	⊖	⊖	⊖	○					○	⊖	⊖	⊖	Insufficient data	Insufficient data	⊖	⊖	⊖	⊖		Insufficient data
Electrical system	⊖	○	⊖	⊖	⊖	⊖	●	●	Insufficient data	Insufficient data	Insufficient data	Insufficient data	●	●	●	⊖			●	●	●	◐	⊖	
Steering/suspension	○	○	⊖	⊖	⊖	⊖	⊖	○					○	⊖	⊖	⊖			⊖	◐	◐	○	⊖	
Brakes	⊖	○	○	⊖	⊖	⊖	●	○					○	◐	⊖	⊖			⊖	◐	◐	○	⊖	
Exhaust system	⊖	○	○	⊖	⊖	⊖	●	○					●	◐	⊖	⊖			⊖	◐	◐	⊖	⊖	
Body rust	○	○	○	⊖	⊖	⊖	○	○					⊖	⊖	⊖	○			⊖	⊖	⊖	○	○	
Paint	⊖	○	○	⊖	⊖	⊖	○	○					⊖	⊖	◐	⊖			⊖	◐	◐	○	○	
Body integrity	○	○	⊖	⊖	⊖	⊖	○	○					◐	●	◐	⊖			●	●	●	●	⊖	
Body hardware	⊖	⊖	⊖	⊖	⊖	⊖	⊖	○					●	●	●	⊖			●	●	●	◐	⊖	
Air-conditioning	⊖	⊖	⊖	⊖	⊖	*	⊖	⊖					⊖	⊖	○	*			○	○	⊖	⊖	⊖	

Legend: ⊜ ⊖ ○ ◐ ● — Few ← Problems → Many • * Insufficient data

TROUBLE SPOTS	Volkswagen Passat '88	'89	'90	'91	'92	'93	Volvo 240 Series '88	'89	'90	'91	'92	'93	Volvo 740 Series '88	'89	'90	'91	'92	'93	Volvo 740 Series Turbo '88	'89	'90	'91	'92	'93
Engine			○	⊖	⊖		⊖	⊖	⊖	⊖	⊖		○	⊖	⊖	⊖	⊖		◐	○	⊖			
Engine cooling			◐	◐	⊖		○	○	⊖	⊖	⊖		○	⊖	⊖	⊖	⊖		○	○	○			
Fuel system			○	○	⊖		⊖	○	⊖	⊖	⊖		⊖	○	○	⊖	⊖		⊖	⊖	⊖			
Ignition system			○	○	⊖		⊖	○	⊖	⊖	⊖		⊖	⊖	⊖	⊖	⊖		⊖	⊖	⊖			
Auto. transmission			◐	*	*		⊖	⊖	⊖	⊖	⊖		⊖	⊖	⊖	⊖	⊖		⊖	*	⊖			
Man. transmission			*	*	*		⊖	*	*	*	*		*	*	*				*	*	*			
Clutch			*	*	*		⊖	*	*	*	*		*	*	*				*	*	*			
Driveline			⊖	⊖	⊖		⊖	⊖	⊖	⊖	⊖		⊖	⊖	⊖				⊖	⊖	⊖			
Electrical system			●	◐	○		⊖	⊖	●	◐	⊖		●	●	◐	○	◐		○	◐	●			
Steering/suspension			◐	○	⊖		⊖	⊖	⊖	⊖	○		⊖	⊖	⊖	⊖	⊖		○	⊖	⊖			
Brakes			●	●	●		⊖	●	●	●	○		●	●	●	○	⊖		●	●	●			
Exhaust system			⊖	⊖	⊖		○	⊖	⊖	⊖	⊖		⊖	○	⊖	⊖	⊖		⊖	⊖	⊖			
Body rust			⊖	⊖	⊖		⊖	⊖	⊖	⊖	⊖		⊖	⊖	⊖	⊖	⊖		⊖	⊖	⊖			
Paint			⊖	⊖	⊖		⊖	⊖	⊖	⊖	⊖		⊖	⊖	⊖	⊖	⊖		○	⊖	⊖			
Body integrity			◐	○	○		○	○	○	○	○		○	⊖	⊖	○			○	○	○			
Body hardware			●	◐	○		○	○	○	◐	○		●	◐	○	○			●	◐	○			
Air-conditioning			⊖	⊖	⊖		●	○	⊖	⊖	⊖		●	◐	⊖	⊖	⊖		◐	◐	○			

Note: Volkswagen Passat and Volvo 240 Series '93 columns, Volvo 740 Series '93 and Volvo 740 Series Turbo '92–'93 columns marked "Insufficient data."

TROUBLE SPOTS	Volvo 760 '88	'89	'90	'91	'92	'93	Volvo 850 GLT '88	'89	'90	'91	'92	'93	Volvo 940 '88	'89	'90	'91	'92	'93	Volvo 960 Series '88	'89	'90	'91	'92	'93
Engine	⊖	○	⊖									⊖				⊖	⊖	⊖						⊖
Engine cooling	○	○	⊖									⊖				⊖	⊖	⊖						⊖
Fuel system	⊖	⊖	○									⊖				⊖	⊖	⊖						⊖
Ignition system	⊖	⊖	○									⊖				⊖	⊖							○
Auto. transmission	⊖	⊖	⊖									⊖				⊖	⊖	⊖						○
Man. transmission												*												
Clutch												*												
Driveline	⊖	⊖	⊖									⊖				⊖	⊖	⊖						⊖
Electrical system	○	◐	○									⊖				○	⊖	○						●
Steering/suspension	○	○	○									⊖				○	⊖	⊖						⊖
Brakes	◐	●	●									⊖				⊖	⊖	⊖						⊖
Exhaust system	⊖	⊖	⊖									⊖				⊖	⊖	⊖						⊖
Body rust	⊖	⊖	⊖									⊖				⊖	⊖	⊖						⊖
Paint	⊖	⊖	⊖									⊖				○	⊖	⊖						⊖
Body integrity	◐	⊖	○									⊖				○	⊖	⊖						⊖
Body hardware	●	●	○									⊖				○	○	○						◐
Air-conditioning	●	○	○									⊖				⊖	⊖	⊖						⊖

Note: Volvo 850 GLT data shown in the '93 column only; Volvo 940 data shown in '91–'93 columns; Volvo 960 Series data shown in the '92 column only, '93 marked "Insufficient data."

PRODUCT RECALLS

Products ranging from cars to toys are recalled when there are safety defects. Various Federal agencies—the Consumer Product Safety Commission, the National Highway Traffic Safety Administration, the U.S. Coast Guard—monitor consumer complaints and injuries and, when there's a problem, issue a recall. A selection of those recalls are published monthly in CONSUMER REPORTS. This section covers recalls from November 1993 through October 1994. For the latest information, see the current issue of CONSUMER REPORTS.

Children's products

Animal Shape Wagon pull toys
Small parts could come off and choke child. Also, excessive lead in yellow and green paint could be toxic to children.

Products: 1000 toys sold 10/10-11/18/93 by mail order through Hanover House and 6-12/93 in stores for $8. Wooden wagon is 10½ inches long and 5 inches wide, with animal-shaped cutouts on top and sides. Ten colored animal figures fit through cutouts. Wagon also has 4 red wheels on wooden axles, 2 round red headlights, and pull cord. Label on box reads: "Animal Shape Wagon, ITEM NO. 9638. . . MADE IN CHINA."

What to do: Return toy to Hanover House or store for refund of purchase price plus shipping. For further information, call 800 841-1007.

Baby's Bucket-Sorting Toy
Small parts could come off and choke child.

Products: 5000 toys sold 3/93-2/94 for $2-$3. Toy consists of 17¼-inch round bucket with handle and

9 shaped pieces, which fit through corresponding cutouts in bucket's yellow lid. Square, hexagonal, triangular, and circular pieces have attached small animal figure, which could come off. Label on box says "MADISON LTD., HACKENSACK, NJ, . . . MADE IN CHINA."

What to do: Return toy to store for refund.

Baby Trend and Baby Express Home and Roam portable playpens
Could collapse and strangle child.

Products: 65,000 mesh-sided playpens sold '92-93 for $68-$130. Playpen measures 40x40 or 28x40 in. Words "Home and Roam" and either "Baby Trend" or "Baby Express" appear on two of four top rails. Playpen is secured by rotating pivot hinge in center of each rail. To lock rails, hinge must be turned 180 degrees from collapsed position. Because hinges are covered by fabric, consumers may rely on sense of touch to determine whether hinge has been rotated fully. Partially rotated hinge can give false impression that rail is locked.

What to do: Note model and lot number on foot of playpen, and call 800 234-1879 for label and small gift.

Buddy L My First Buddys Police Car and My First Buddys Dumper
Small parts could come off and choke child.

Products: 138,000 police cars and 201,000 dump trucks sold singly or in 4-piece gift packs that contain one or both of affected toys. Recalled toys were sold 1/90-12/92. Other toys included in gift packs—pumper, scooper, helicopter, wrecker ball—aren't subject to recall. Individual toys sold for $5; gift packs, for $17. Blue and white police car is 7 in. long, 3¾ in. wide, and 4 in. high, and has handle that extends from top of windshield to trunk. Toy clicks and plastic flasher with red rectangular block moves from side to side when rear wheels are moved. Interior, bumper guards, and hub caps are white; wheels are red. Gold sticker with "POLICE" in black print appears on windshield. "POLICE" also appears in white on both sides of car. "BUDDY L" is on both license plates. White police badge on hood reads "My First Buddys Police Patrol." Label under car reads, in part: "BUDDY L CORP, MADE IN CHINA." Dumper is yellow and is same size as police car. White handle extends from front bumper guard to cab. Dumper bed can be lifted and lowered, and "DUMPER" is printed in red on both sides of bed. Wheels are red with white hub caps. Toy clicks when front wheels are moved. "BUDDY L" is on both license plates. Label on floor of dumper bed reads, in part: "BUDDY L CORP, MADE IN CHINA."

What to do: Return toy to store for refund.

Cosco 2-rod guard rail for toddler beds
Child could be trapped and asphyxiated by metal rods.

Products: 75,000 guard rails made 8/1/91-6/10/92 and sold with Cosco toddler beds, models 10T23 and 10T33, or separately (model 10T71). Guard rails are red, white, or blue, have ¾-inch tubular metal frame, and 2 thin horizontal metal rods within frame. Guard rails with 3 thin metal rods are not affected; nor are guard rails for full-sized beds. Check label for 4-digit date-of-manufacture code. First 2 digits are week of year; last 2 digits are year.

What to do: Call 800 267-2614 for free modification kit.

Deary Baby Rattle Baby Soother Spain Style pacifier
Poses multiple choking hazards: Nipple can separate from base. Also, shield lacks ventilation holes, and it can penetrate too far into mouth.

Products: 194,000 pacifiers sold 8/92-11/93 in Ariz., Calif., Ill., Md., Mo., N.Y., and Tex. Pacifier has pink, yellow, or blue shield and ring with rubber nipple. Packaging consists of plastic bubble attached to perforated display panel that reads: "Deary Baby Rattle Baby Soother Spain Style." Package also shows blond baby with pacifier in mouth.

What to do: Destroy pacifier or mail it to Eugene Trading Co., 3841 Broadway Pl., Los Angeles, Calif. 90037, for refund.

Dubby pacifier-thermometers
Nipple could come off and choke child.

Products: 340 pacifier-thermometers sold at pharmacies and through mail-order catalogs 4/93-8/93 for up to $12.50. Device is pink or blue with clear silicon rubber nipple. Built-in electronic LCD thermometer displays temperature when baby sucks on nipple. Product was sold in blue box with "Dubby" on top panel; sticker reads, "Made in Taiwan."

What to do: Return product to store or mail-order house.

Gerry Splash Seat baby-bathing device
Suction cups may not stick adequately to bathtub or base of seat; seat could tip and injure child.

Products: 176,000 seats, model 455, with white suction cups, sold 3/93-3/94. Box in which seat was sold bears UPC nos. 0-37434-45508-3 or 0-37434-45500-7. Units with blue suction cups are not affected.

What to do: Call 800 278-8881 for replacement suction cups.

Graco Carrier and Convert-a-Cradle swings

In fully reclined position, infant could fall out.

Products: 208,000 swings sold 11/91-10/92 for $60 to $100. Product has detachable carrier seat with 3-position handle to adjust angle of recline. Carrier seats with only 2 recline positions are not subject to recall.

What to do: Do not use fully reclined position. Call 800 217-7822 for kit that eliminates that position.

Kenner Fastblast Spray Art Design craft set and ink-refill assortment

Ink contains high level of ethylene glycol, which could poison children.

Products: 45,000 Fastblast craft sets, model 60090, and 29,000 Fastblast ink refills, model 60091, sold 11/93-3/94 for about $10 and $4, respectively. Toy is intended to create various designs with stencils and airbrush that sprays washable colored inks. Craft set contains sprayer, 2 washable color inks, 3 stencils, and 10 sheets of paper. Refill assortment contains 3 colored inks.

What to do: Return products to store for refund.

Kouvalias musical toy

Small parts could come off and choke child.

Products: 18,400 toys sold '89-7/93 for $45. Toy consists of 5-inch-diameter wooden base that houses music box; 3½-inch-diameter wooden platform attached to base; and 2-inch wooden ball connected to platform. Nine colored wooden balls are attached to 2-inch ball via small metal coil springs. Music box plays when platform is turned. Label beneath base reads: "A Kouvalias S.A. . . . MADE IN GREECE."

What to do: Return toy to store for refund.

Levi Strauss & Co. Jeans, Shortalls, Rompers, and Koveralls for children 12-24 months old

Snap fasteners could come off and choke child.

Products: 40,000 boys' garments sold 7/93 to early '94 and girls' garments sold since 5/92. Recalled boys clothes include Rib Bottom Jeans (product code 29370-7011); Koverall, pants-length version of traditional adult overall (code 19379-7011); Shortall, short-pants version of adult overall (code 19375-7011); and Romper, loose-fitting denim play suit (code 19377-7011). Garments are in dark blue or indigo-blue stonewash with gray trim. Recalled girls' garment is Koverall with pink elastic suspenders; item is in indigo-blue stonewash (code 38966-0491), bleached blue (code 38966-0435), pink stonewash (code 38966-1088), or pink (code 38966-1287). Product code is on underside of care label.

What to do: Return garment to store for refund.

Little Tykes High Back Toddler Swing

Lacks safety belt. Child could fall out.

Products: All swings, model 4309, sold 1/93-9/93. (High back swings made beginning 10/93 have safety belt.) Affected model is made of blue or green plastic, with yellow ropes that attach to backyard swing set. Little Tykes label is on T-bar across front of chair.

What to do: Call 800 868-2276 to get safety belt.

Mini-Racer F-1 toy race-car sets

Small parts could come off and choke child.

Products: 28,800 car sets sold 11/1/92-5/31/93 for 99 cents, mostly at following chains: Britts, Elmore, G.C. Murphy, H.L. Green, J.J. Newberry, Kress, McClellan, McCrory, Silver, and T.G. & Y; also, at independent stores. Sets contain 6 brightly colored plastic racing cars in blister package. Each car measures 3½ in. long, has number on hood, 2 sets of wheels in front and 1 set in back, silver engine, driver, and airfoil with "Fire Bird" decal.

What to do: Return toy to store for refund.

Rosalco bunk beds

Could collapse. (This is not a recall. Rosalco has cooperated with the Consumer Product Safety Commission and is offering free reinforcement brackets to avoid further incidents.)

Products: 175,000 glossy tubular-framed red, white, blue, or black beds sold since 1/90 for $150-$300. Recalled units bear model nos. 3006, 3007, 3026, 3027, 3206, 3207, 3226, and 3227. Beds come with metal ladder that attaches to side and use twin-sized mattress on top bunk and either twin or full-size mattress on bottom. Rectangular metal side rails that support mattress measure 1 in. wide by 2 in. high. (Beds whose rails measure 1½ in. wide and ¾ in. high are not subject to recall.)

What to do: Contact store to determine whether you have Rosalco bed. If so, phone 800 833-1545 for kit containing reinforcement brackets and installation instructions.

See-Thru Bi-plane toy airplane

Small parts could come off and choke child.

Products: 2000 toys sold 12/92-3/94 in Northeast for $3. Plane is 5½ in. long and 3½ in. high. Clear plastic body has multicolored gears inside; wings and propeller are yellow, pilot's head is red. When plane is pushed, propeller spins and gears turn. Decal on top wing reads: "907 Skeletplane," "MADE IN CHINA . . . © U.S.A. 1992, U.K. 1992 MCT" is embossed under lower wing.

What to do: Return toy to store for refund.

Three-piece outfits for newborn boys sold at K Mart stores
Snap fasteners could come off and choke child.

Products: 6500 outfits sold 1/94-2/94 for $13. Outfit consists of cotton/polyester cardigan sweater, short-sleeved top, and checkered pants. Outfits came in two shades of blue and white and have airplane appliques on sweater and top.

What to do: Return outfit to K Mart for refund.

Thunderbat toy baseball bat with noisemaker
When bat is swung, end cap and noisemaker could fly off and injure bystanders.

Products: 172,000 yellow hard-plastic bats sold with white plastic ball 12/92-9/93 for $5. Noisemaker mimics cracking sound of bat hitting ball. Recall involves only bats with yellow end cap and words "Thunderbat" and "Tim Mee Toy" on plastic covering.

What to do: If end cap isn't stapled securely to bat, return bat to store for refund or replacement.

Tubular metal-framed bunk beds
Could collapse and injure occupants.

Products: 17,530 bunk beds, including: 8600 red, blue, black, or white twin-sized/full-sized (model 3013) and twin/twin (model 3012) beds, sold in Calif. 12/91-2/93 by MPC Trading Co. Also, 8000 red, blue, black, or white twin/full (model 504), twin/twin (model 508), and twin/full-futon (model 510) beds, sold by International Express Mfg. 6-12/92 for $140 to $200; gold sticker on headboard or footboard reads "IEM" and "International Express Mfg." Also, 930 twin/full beds sold in Dela., N.J., N.Y., and Pa. by World Imports Ltd. 8/92-10/93; beds have C-shaped headboard and footboard and came in red (model 02-2332), white (model 02-2343), blue (model 02-2354), and black (model 02-2365); gold "Warning" label appears on top of end frame at head or foot of upper bunk.

What to do: Ask store where bed was bought whether bed was from firm named above. With MPC bed, have store repair or replace bed or refund purchase price. With International Express bed, call 800 869-1688 (or, in California, 213 888-1688) for repair kit or replacement frame. World Imports will also provide repair kit; call 800 486-4710. With any other metal bunk bed, inspect all 8 mattress-support corners; if you see cracks in metal or paint around welds, call Consumer Product Safety Commission at 800 638-2772.

Tubular metal-framed bunk beds
Could collapse and injure occupants.

Products: 123,500 bunk beds, including: 50,000 twin-sized/full-sized and twin/twin beds distributed by Gold Key Enterprises and sold '88-9/93. Beds have protruding metal mattress-support tongues that extend from corner posts and slide into top and bottom mattress frames. Most models have distinctive scrollwork on headboard, footboard, and guardrails. 11,000 twin/full beds, models 354 (black), 364 (white), 464 (red), and 465 (blue), distributed by Bernards Inc., and sold since 5/92. Beds have mattress-support tongues similar to above. 2700 twin/full beds, models 6202B (black), 6202L (blue), 6202R (red), and 6202W (white), distributed by S&A Imports Inc., and sold '91-93. Beds have mattress-support tongues similar to those above. 4800 beds, designated "Slumberama" (twin/full) or "Double Decker" (twin/twin), distributed by Fashion Bed Group (previously known as Berkshire Furniture Co.) and sold 1-5/91. 23,000 twin/full beds, models 440 (red), 446 (white), 447 (blue), and 448 (black), distributed by L. Powell Co., and sold 6/92-3/31/93. Beds have C-shaped headboard and footboard frames, partial guardrails on both sides of upper bunk, and middle leg on side rail of bottom bunk. 13,000 twin/full beds, model 66-72995 (red or white), distributed by Montgomery Ward '90-91; models with fifth, center leg on lower full-sized portion are not affected. 6000 twin/full beds, nos. BB-104-2 (red), BB-105-2 (white), BB-106-2 (blue), and BB-107-2 (black), distributed by Southern Enterprises and sold since 1/90. Affected models have rectangular mattress support side rails that measure ¾x1½ in. 13,000 beds, models 2330, 2331, 2332, and 2335, distributed by Coaster Co. of America and sold 5-12/92. Beds have 13 cross bars on top and bottom mattress supports and center brace on bottom mattress support.

What to do: Inspect all 8 mattress-support corners for cracks, and ask at store where bed was bought whether bed was imported by firm named above. If it was, ask store for importer's toll-free phone number. If bed has no cracks, you'll get repair kit with reinforcement brackets and instructions. If bed has cracks, you'll get new bed. Call Consumer Product Safety Commission at 800 638-2772 if bed has cracks and was not imported by firm named above.

Wooden puzzle sets sold through "Learn & Play" mail-order catalog
Red plastic pegs could come off puzzle pieces and choke child.

Products: 8219 toys sold 1/92-12/93. "Basic Skills Puzzle Set" sold for $15 and consists of 4 3x11-in. wooden puzzles: "Hatch-A-Chick," "Pretty Posies," "Wacky Creatures," and "Animal Friends Train."

Puzzles have 4 or 5 pieces with red plastic peg attached to each piece. Labels on box and puzzles read, in part: "© 1993 Troll Associates...Made in Taiwan." "Wooden Pegged Puzzle Set" sold for $30 and consists of 4 11¾x8½-in. puzzles: "Learning World," "On-the-Go," "My Home," and "Animal Friends." Puzzles have 8 or 9 pieces with red plastic peg attached to each piece. Labels on box and puzzles read, in part: "© 1992 Troll Associates... Made in Taiwan."

What to do: Return puzzles to Troll Associates for refund of purchase price and shipping costs. Mail to company at: 4600 Pleasant Hill Road, Memphis, Tenn. 38118. For recall information, call Learn & Play catalog service department at 800 942-0781.

Zenital 16-in. sidewalk bicycles with training wheels

Lack foot brakes, a violation of Federal safety standard for sidewalk bikes. Also, lack insertion marks on stem of handlebar to ensure proper stem depth, another violation.

Products: 7900 bicycles, model B-1601, sold at swap meets in southern Calif., Ariz., and Tex. 9/92-4/93 for $30.

What to do: Call 800 888-3558 for modification.

Household products

American Camper NY90 rope hammock
Could break.

Products: 14,400 hammocks sold 2/92-10/93. Hammock is 90 in. long by 48 in. wide with knotted cotton ropes and 49-in. wooden spreader bars.

What to do: Return hammock to store for refund.

Armadillo figures made in Mexico
Excessive lead in green, red, and purple paint could be toxic to children.

Products: 5000 various-sized armadillos, imported by Colbert Collection and sold 1/90-12/93 for $7.50-$18. Armadillo body is gourd; legs, tail, and movable head are wood. Label underneath reads: "HECHO EN MEXICO." Product was not intended for use as child's toy.

What to do: Take armadillo away from children and return to store for refund. For further information, call 203 379-9289.

Beef-Iron and Wine liquid dietary supplement
Lacks child-resistant packaging; too much iron could cause serious illness or death.

Products: 2000 1-pint bottles sold at health-food and nutrition stores 1/1-12/1/93. Brown plastic bottle has conventional white screw-on plastic cap; label says: "Beef-Iron and Wine . . . Hematinic . . . Alcohol 10% by volume . . . 16 FL. OZ. (1 PINT) . . . DISTRIBUTED BY METRO INTERNATIONAL DISTRIBUTORS, INC., 217 Washington Avenue-A, Carlstadt, N.J. 07072."

What to do: Return bottle and remaining contents to store for refund or replacement.

Bissell Trio Vac vacuum cleaners
Plastic fan in motor housing could break, and flying pieces could injure bystanders.

Products: 13,000 vacuum cleaners, models 3005 (single speed) and 3005W (canister kit) sold '92-6/93 for $50-$60. Date of manufacture is stamped on inside of bottom of motor housing. To find date, remove dirt-collection tank. First 2 numbers of 6-digit code are year. If numbers are 92 or if no numbers are visible, vacuum is subject to recall. If nos. are 93, vacuum is not recalled.

What to do: Call 800 237-7691 for replacement.

Black & Decker and General Electric under-cabinet coffee-makers
Could catch fire.

Products: 750,000 coffee-makers, models SDC 1, SDC 2, and SDC 3, made 2/84-5/88 and sold for $45 to $72. Recalled units bear 3-digit date code, which runs sequentially from 406 to 822. Date code appears on outside of plug prong.

What to do: Have Black & Decker service center inspect unit for faulty thermostat and replace, if necessary. (If no repair is needed, coffee-maker will be returned to you.) Instead of free repair, company will let you buy new coffee-maker at discount. For information and location of nearest service center, call 800 826-1070.

Borg-Warner, Luxaire, Fraser-Johnson, and Montcrief Heatpipe furnaces
Deadly carbon monoxide gas could leak out.

Products: 4000 furnaces sold '84-88 by York International under several brand names. Recalled units bear following model nos.: PAUT-LD08N073, PAUT-LD12N073, PAUT-LD12N105, PAUT-LD16N105. (Luxaire, Fraser-Johnson, Montcrief); P1NUD08N06301, P1NUD12N06301, P1NUD12N08901, P1NUD16N08901 (Borg-Warner and York).

What to do: Call 800 310-3476 or contact any authorized York, Fraser-Johnson, or Luxaire dealer for free replacement furnace. York will also pay $200 toward installation.

Bumble Bee Solid White Tuna in Water

Can may be cut or punctured, which could contaminate food, causing serious illness or death, if eaten.

Products: 1.5 million 6⅛-oz. cans, sold in packs of 4 or 6 cans, distributed 8/1/93-3/17/94 in the following states: Alaska, Ariz., Calif., Colo., Hawaii, Idaho, Iowa, Kan., Mo., Mont., Neb., Nev., N.M., Ore., Tex., Utah, Wash., and Wyo. Recalled cans were primarily sold in warehouse clubs and similar discount-type stores. Nearly 600,000 of the potentially defective products have been recovered by the manufacturer.

What to do: If you suspect you may have any of the suspect cans, contact Bumble Bee Seafood consumer affairs department at 619 550-4000.

Candoliers electric candle decorations

Pose shock and fire hazard.

Products: 300,000 candles sold at K Mart and Builders Square stores during 1993 winter holiday season, and 364, 400 candles sold at K Mart during 1992 holiday season. Candles sold at K Mart in '93 are 10-in.-high cream-colored plastic with clear bulb. They cost 99 cents. Builders Square candles are identical, but sold in packages of two for $1.97. Candles sold in '92 have either one or three clear or orange bulbs and are made of off-white plastic. Single-bulb candles are 11 in. high and sold for 99 cents. Triple-bulb candles have 6-in. outer candles and 7-in. center candle and sold for $4.59.

What to do: Return candle to store for refund.

Casablanca ceiling fans (all models)

Could fall from ceiling mount.

Products: 3.3 million fans sold 1/81-9/93. Fans are identifiable by word "Casablanca" on metal nameplate on fan exterior. Recalled models also have serial no. on nameplate whose second letter is either A, B, C, O, P, R, S, T, U, V, W, X, or Y. Recall doesn't involve Pasadena brand fans, which are made by Casablanca.

What to do: Call 800 390-3131 for repair kit and instructions. Consumers can also arrange for free installation. (Because fans made before 3/91 were marketed by another company, free installation may not be available; phone to find out whether your model qualifies.)

Citronella-scented lawn torch

Could spatter hot wax and burn bystanders.

Products: 362,000 torches sold 1-8/93. Painted 33-in. bamboo stake supports cylindrical wax candle. "Loomis Sales Co." appears on packaging.

What to do: Return torch to store for refund.

Columbia Wire & Cable Corp. 12-foot ground-fault circuit interrupter extension cord

Will not protect against severe electric shock if short or ground fault occurs. Also, connecting cord to electrical device with 3-prong plug creates shock hazard.

Products: 53,600 white extension cords, model GF1812, sold in '92 for $4. Most were sold at Odd Lots and Big Lots stores in Midwest and Southeast; some may have been sold by unidentified retailers. Top side of white two-pronged plug has red button labeled "RESET," and embossed label that says "WARNING: To reduce the risk of shock, do not immerse, remove, or modify this plug." Label on bottom of plug reads: "Cat. No. 6575, E-96425." Three-hole receptacle at other end bears letters "JC." Cord may be labeled in part, "...E90165...18AWX3C Da Tung," or "E56274...18AWG/3C Cableton."

What to do: Return cord to store for refund. For information, call 800 877-1253. If cord was not bought at Odd Lots/Big Lots store, call Consumer Product Safety Commission at 800 638-2772.

Dell 14-inch SVGA color computer monitor

Could overheat and cause fire.

Products: 63,000 monitors, model DL-1460NI, sold by Dell, Sam's Club, Costco, Price Club, and CompUSA '92-93. Model no. appears on label on back of monitor.

What to do: Unplug monitor and call 800 913-3355 to arrange for free pickup and repair.

Electric potpourri pots sold at Walgreen stores

Poses electric-shock hazard.

Products: 14,400 ceramic potpourri pots sold until 6/92. White ceramic pots hold about 1½ cups of water. Blue design on side depicts wreath, flower basket, sea shells, or fruit. Ceramic lid is blue, power cord is white. "Model WA-00117" is on black plastic bottom.

What to do: Return pot to store for refund or replacement.

Fem-Plus with iron nutritional supplement for women

Lacks child-resistant packaging; too much iron could cause serious illness or death.

Products: 4435 bottles containing 60 capsules, with 25 mg of iron per capsule, sold at health-food and nutrition stores 6/1/91-8/2/93. Product comes in opaque white plastic bottle with blue screw-on plastic cap. Bottle is labeled: "HERBAL BIO-THERAPY . . . Fem-Plus . . . NO. 811 . . . . 60 CAPSULES." Label also reads: "MANUFACTURED EXCLUSIVELY FOR ENZYMATIC THERAPY, INC., GREEN BAY, WISCONSIN 54311." Recall does not apply to later samples with white child-resistant caps labeled "push down and turn."

What to do: Return product to store for replacement or refund.

Henrob 2000 welding torch

Gas valve may corrode and leak, and flame may not extinguish immediately when valve is shut off.

Products: 1704 welding torches, made 3/16/93-8/31/93, with serial nos. H or M followed by 04421-06125.

What to do: Call 800 443-6762 for modification kit and installation instructions.

Hunter ceiling fan wireless remote control

Touching exposed end of receiver's antenna, mounted in ceiling fixture, poses shock hazard.

Products: 6865 remotes, model 22788, sold 11/16/93-3/30/94 for $45. Device, sold as option, consists of receiver and 3-button hand-held transmitter that controls light and fan. Affected units bear serial nos. 029936 to 051679. Model and serial no. appear on nameplate on top of receiver in upper canopy of fan.

What to do: Call 901 745-9318 for instructions on how to disconnect fan and get free replacement remote control.

Imported two-layer skirt with sheer chiffon fabric over gauze lining

Skirt is dangerously flammable, and will burn faster than newsprint if it catches fire. That poses risk of serious burn injuries.

Products: 250,000 skirts made in India and sold for the past several years for $6 to $80. Long, full skirt, designed for summer and fall use, is all rayon or rayon-cotton blend, has elastic waist band, and may also have drawstring at waist. General information on label recommends user separately hand-wash item in cold water or have it dry cleaned. Brands that failed flammability test include 2 Kool Look; Ann Simone; Carla Freeman; Casual Designs by RAVIA; Exclusif; F b i; Founded 1976 D II K by K.V.M.; Giallo Napoli; Gold Star; LeGebi; Masone II; Minti Mode; Papillon; Phool; Renuka; Short Circuit; Steed Import Inc.; Vile Parle; Xessorium; and Zero Zero. Other brands may be involved in recall as well. Garments lacking brand information may bear the following nos. on label: RN 81177; RN 74867; RN 50971; or RN 57716. Skirts were sold in boutiques and large chains including Abraham & Straus Basement; Ames Ladies Wear; Annie Sez; Bealls Outlet Stores; Burlington Coat Factory; Cost Plus; Dayton's; Filenes Basement; Gantos; Hudson's; Jean Nicole; Loehmann's; Marianne; Marshalls; Marshall Field's; One Price; Ross; and T.J. Maxx.

What to do: Return skirt to store for refund. For more information, call U.S. Consumer Product Safety Commission's toll-free hotline at 800 638-2772.

Keebler Fudge Shoppe Fudge 'n Caramel Shortbread cookies

Label does not note that cookies contain peanuts, which could cause fatal reaction in allergic people.

Products: 32,232 11-oz. packages sold 10/93-2/94. Affected products bear lot number L261 on package label.

What to do: Return cookies to store for refund.

Mighty Lite halogen clamp light

If lamp head is allowed to rotate, wire insulation could chafe, creating shock hazard.

Products: 2000 clamp lights sold in California at Northern California Yardbirds stores and nationwide at Sears stores 7-8/93 for $20. Light is yellow with black hook and handle and spring-loaded clamp base with yellow vinyl grips. Handle is labeled "the Designers EDGE." At back of lamp head, molded into metal, is phrase: "SUITABLE FOR WET LOCATION MISC. FIXTURE QH-250N 1G96."

What to do: If light was bought at Sears, return it to Sears store for refund. If light was bought at Northern California Yarbirds store, check lamp cord; if cord lacks date code, return light to store for refund or replacement. (Lamps with 7/93 or later date code are not affected.)

NEC Technologies laptop computers
Battery could explode and catch fire.

Products: 13,000 computers, models PC-17-01 and PC-17-02, sold 12/88-4/90. Model no. appears on bottom of computer.

What to do: Turn on computer with AC adapter disconnected and allow battery to discharge fully. Call 800 237-2913 for replacement battery and $100 bonus.

Novelty cigarette lighters shaped like tractor trailer
Child could mistake lighter for toy and start fire or suffer burns.

Products: 200,000 lighters sold 12/93-3/94 at convenience stores for $1.50. One side has picture of truck along with eagle's head, U.S. flag, or full moon. Sticker on back says "Made in Philippines."

What to do: Keep lighter out of child's reach and return it to store for replacement gift.

Outdoor fluorescent deck lights
Pose electric-shock hazard.

Products: 9300 Builders Square fluorescent "wall bracket lights" and unknown number of Pay-N-Pak "Deck Lite Fixtures," models 302048 and 302049. Fixtures were sold 7/91-3/92 for $15. Builders Square unit is black diecast aluminum with clear plastic globe. Original U-shaped fluorescent lamp is labeled: "DLS 9W, LIGHT 21." Back of fixture has three labels: "UL Incandescent Fixture, Issue No. 696089, Suitable For Wet Locations," "E117402, Made In Korea," and "Wall Mount Only." Pay-N-Pak unit is probably similar, but description is unavailable.

What to do: Return Builders Square fixtures to any Builders Square store for refund. Pay-N-Pak models should be discarded, since company is out of business.

PRO1600 hair dryer sold at Wal-Mart stores
When dryer is plugged in and turned off, heater could go on without fan, creating fire hazard.

Products: 900 dryers sold 1/92-4/93 for $10. Beige dryer's black fan is visible from back. "MODEL PRO1600" is on handle. Later dryers with gray fan are not affected.

What to do: Send dryer to Hartman Prods., 4949 W. 147th St., Hawthorne, Calif. 90250, for replacement or refund plus shipping.

'Professional Styler' hairdryers
Pose electrocution hazard if dryer is submerged.

Products: 10,000 dryers sold mostly in Florida '90-8/93. "Professional Styler" or "Professional Styler by Pomair" is printed on nozzle. Model no. 600-53000 is on handle.

What to do: For refund plus postage, mail dryer to MBR Ind., Customer Service, P.O. Box 640364, N. Miami, Fla. 33164.

Scotsman home ice-cube machine
Could catch fire.

Products: 121,000 machines made before 9/91, including models DC33A-1A, DC33A-1B, DC33A-1W, DC33PA-1A, DC33PA-1B, DC33PA-1W, and DC33PA-1A-PB. Model number and date code appear on label attached to left side of base, behind front grill. On some machines, information also appears on second label attached to control-box cover at lower front of unit. Serial no. consists of 6 digits immediately preceded or followed by number-letter combination that represents machine's date code. Affected units bear letters D, E, F, G, H, J, S, T, U, V, W, or X in date code or have date code of 01K, 02K, 07K, 08K, 09K, 10K, 11K, or 12K.

What to do: Turn control knob to Off and call 800 733-5383 for free repair.

Solgar diet supplements containing iron
Tablets and capsules do not come in child-resistant packaging, as required by law. Products with iron could be fatal if swallowed by child.

Products: 17,500 brown glass bottles with yellow screw-on cap, containing 50 to 1000 tablets or capsules, sold 1/93-4/93. Products include Natural Amino Acid Chelated Iron, Gentle Iron Vegicaps, Hematinic Formula, Prenatal Nutrients, and Trace Elements.

What to do: For refund, return bottle with unused portion to store or mail to Solgar, 410 Ocean Ave., Lynbrook, N.Y. 11563, Att: Recall.

Sunbeam and Oster 1000-watt indoor electric grills
Accumulated grease can create fire hazard.

Products: 4500 variable-temperature grills, Sunbeam model 4757 and Oster model 4772, sold 9/92-6/93 for $30 and $45, respectively. Recalled models have "1000-watt" and "E992"stamped on heating element where it attaches to temperature control. Grill sits atop gray "Nu-Stone" plastic base and has Griffo porcelain cooking grid.

What to do: Send grill to company for replacement or refund. Call 800 986-0008 for prepaid mailing carton.

Sweda Juice Factory electric juicer

If juicer isn't reassembled properly after cleaning, upper plastic body could shatter and cause serious injury.

Products: 6000 juicers sold at Caldor and Jamesway stores since 4/2/92 for $30-$50.

What to do: Call 800 269-1572 for instructions on how to return juicer, with proof of purchase, for refund of purchase price and postage.

Synergy Plus Chewables Vitabots iron-containing supplement for children

Lacks child-resistant packaging. Too much iron could make child seriously ill.

Products: 2500 amber-glass bottles containing 90 light-brown tablets, sold at health-food and nutrition stores 7/1/92-7/31/93 for $9 or $10. Label says "Synergy Plus (For Children Over 4 Years) Chewables Vitabots Multiple Vitamins & Minerals with Digestive Enzymes and Oat Bran" and "Manufactured by SYNERGY PLUS, Union, N.J. 07083 USA." Label also says "Non-Toxic," which is erroneous, according to Consumer Product Safety Commission.

What to do: Return bottle and unused tablets to store or phone 201 371-7300 for instructions on mailing product to manufacturer for refund plus shipping costs.

Marine products

'93 Blue Water 17- and 19-foot aluminum boats

Fuel tank could break loose, creating fire hazard.

Models: 76 boats with inboard/outboard engine.
What to do: Have dealer install bottom support for fuel tank. For further information, call 503 741-1111.

'90-91 Nissan 5-hp outboard engine

Fuel tank could leak, creating fire hazard.

Models: 829 engines made 9/90-11/91.
What to do: Have dealer replace metal fuel tank with plastic one.

'94 Pontoon and Tracker boat trailers

Handrails for steps on winch stand could break in use and allow user to fall.

Products: 777 trailers made 8/93-10/93, including Pontoon Bass Buggy 18, Fishin' Barge 21, Party Barge 21, Party Barge 24, and Tracker Pontoon.
What to do: Have dealer remove handrail.

'94 Tracker boat trailers

Wheel could come off and cause accident.

Products: 321 boat trailers, including Magna 17', Magna 19', Magna 19' tandem axle, Nitro 160 (brake), Nitro 170 (brake), Nitro 180, Nitro 190, Nitro 190 tandem axle, Nitro 2000, Bass Buggy 18, Fishin' Barge 21, Party Barge 24, Party Hut 30, and Party Cruiser 32, made 3-4/94.
What to do: Have dealer install new threaded wheel studs and lug nuts.

Cars

'89-93 BMW models

Fuel feed hose could leak at engine fitting and create under-hood fire hazard.

Models: 116,300 cars made 6/88-2/93, including 318i, 318iC, 318iS, 325i, 325iC, 325iS, 325iX, 525i, 535i, 735i, 735iL.
What to do: Have dealer replace fuel hose and clamp.

'92-94 BMW 318i and 318iS

In very cold weather, engine could keep racing when accelerator is released.

Models: 23,500 cars made 2/92-1/94.
What to do: Have dealer install redesigned throttle-body heater.

'93 BMW 740

Throttle cable could break and cause engine to return to idle even if accelerator is depressed.

Models: 2306 cars made 10/92-1/93.
What to do: Have dealer replace throttle cable.

'94 BMW 540i, 840Ci, 850Ci, 850CSi

Antitheft remote control can operate power windows and sun roof when operator is not in car's immediate vicinity. That could allow windows or sun roof to be closed inadvertently on someone's arm or neck.

Models: 1400 cars with remote activation device made 6/93-10/93.
What to do: Have dealer install rear-view mirror with activation receiver that will control door locks and theft alarm, not windows and sun roof.

'90 Buick Regal, Chevrolet Lumina, Oldsmobile Cutlass, and Pontiac Grand Prix

Wheels could crack and come off.

Models: 160,000 cars, with steel wheels, including Regals made 4/88-1/90; Luminas, 2/89-1/90; Cutlasses and Grand Prix, 4/88-2/90.
What to do: Have dealer check and, if necessary, replace wheels.

'91 Buick Regal with 3.8-liter V-6

Fuel hose could leak, causing fire hazard.

Models: 11,432 cars made 11/90-12/90.
What to do: Have dealer replace hose.

'93 Buick Century, Chevrolet Cavalier, Oldsmobile Ciera, and Pontiac Sunbird

Defective brake hoses could hamper stopping.

Models: 2848 cars made 4/93.
What to do: Have dealer replace right front brake-hose assembly on Century and Ciera, and both rear hoses on Cavalier and Sunbird.

'93 Buick Regal, Chevrolet Lumina, Oldsmobile Cutlass, Pontiac Grand Prix

Front seatbacks could recline suddenly.

Models: 5574 cars made 2/93.
What to do: Have dealer replace manual seat-recliner mechanism.

'93 Buick Skylark, Oldsmobile Achieva, and Pontiac Grand Am

Engine could be started with automatic transmission in forward or reverse gear, resulting in unexpected movement. Also, engine may not start when ignition key is turned.

Models: 1103 cars with automatic transaxle made 5/93.
What to do: Have dealer replace neutral-start switch and, if necessary, manual switch of transaxle assembly.

'94 Buick Century

Water may have entered accelator-control cable conduit. In very cold weather, accelerator could require high effort, or engine could continue to race after accelerator has been released.

Models: 10,646 cars made 6/93-12/93.
What to do: Have dealer purge water from cable.

'94 Buick Century and Oldsmobile Ciera

Should main accelerator-return spring fail, backup spring may not return throttle to fully closed position, and racing engine could cause loss of control.

Models: 49,047 cars, with 3.1-liter V6, made 8/93-10/93.
What to do: Have dealer replace backup spring.

'94 Buick Century and Oldsmobile Cutlass with 3.1-liter V6 and cruise control

Throttle could stick open.

Models: 579 cars made 8/93.
What to do: Have dealer replace cruise-control cable.

'94 Buick Roadmaster, Cadillac Fleetwood, and Chevrolet Caprice

Engine oil-cooler hose could rub against steering gear and leak, creating fire hazard.

Models: 8475 cars, with engine-oil cooler, made 3-10/93.
What to do: Have dealer reroute and, if necessary, replace hose.

'94 Buick Roadmaster, Cadillac Fleetwood, and Chevrolet Caprice

Wheels could break off, causing loss of control.

Models: 139 cars made 3/93-3/94 and sold in U.S. territories and possessions (Puerto Rico, Guam, etc.).
What to do: Have dealer remove paint from all 4 wheel mounting surfaces. Also, inspect and, if necessary, replace wheel studs.

'93 Cadillac Eldorado and Seville

Fuel leak could cause fire hazard.

Models: 10,146 cars, with 4.6-liter "Northstar" V8, made 8/92-1/93.
What to do: Have dealer inspect and, if necessary, adjust or replace fuel lines.

'93 Cadillac Fleetwood

Passenger-side air bag may not provide proper crash protection.

Models: 37 cars made 10/92-11/92.
What to do: Have dealer replace passenger-side air bag.

'94 Cadillac Eldorado and Seville

Throttle could stick open or closed.

Models: 8545 cars made 6/93-8/93.
What to do: Have dealer secure throttle cable with tie strap.

'91-92 Chevrolet Camaro and Pontiac Firebird
Fuel and vapors could leak from filler neck, causing fire hazard.

Models: 232,988 cars made 10/89-8/92.
What to do: Have dealer inspect and, if necessary, replace fuel-tank assembly.

'92 Chevrolet Lumina with methanol/ethanol fuel system
Fuel leak could cause fire.

Models: 1058 cars made 4/92.
What to do: Have dealer replace fuel tank.

'94 Chevrolet Camaro and Pontiac Firebird
Fuel hose could contact hot-air check valve and melt, spilling fuel and causing fire hazard.

Models: 6807 cars with 5.7-liter V8, made 8/93.
What to do: Have dealer reroute and, if necessary, replace fuel hose.

'87-91 Chrysler Corp. cars (various models)
Emission-control system may discharge excessive pollutants.

Models: 726,873 vehicles including the following: '87 Renault Alliance GTA (with 2-liter engine); '87-90 Jeep Cherokee, Comanche, and Wagoneer (4-liter engine); '88-89 Eagle Premier (2.5-liter engine); '88-91 Eagle Premier (3-liter engine); '88-91 Dodge Monaco (3-liter engine).
What to do: Have dealer make necessary repairs.

'94 Chrysler Concord, LHS, and New Yorker, Dodge Intrepid, and Eagle Vision
Electrical wiring harness could rub against steering component and short-circuit, stalling engine or allowing it to start with shifter in position other than Park or Neutral.

Models: 110,000 cars made 7/93-12/93.
What to do: Have dealer install redesigned wiring harness and protective sleeve.

'94 Chrysler Lebaron, Dodge Spirit, and Plymouth Acclaim
Safety belts could fail.

Models: 200 cars made 9/93-11/93.
What to do: Have dealer modify belts.

'90-92 Dodge Monaco and '89-92 Eagle Premier
Hot engine coolant could spill into passenger compartment and burn driver's feet. Also, steam could fog windshield and impair driver's vision.

Models: 136,000 cars made 7/87-6/92.
What to do: Have dealer install temperature-controlled heater-bypass valve.

'92-93 Dodge Daytona
Body may suffer structural weakness with time; doors may not open properly, metal may crack, and protection could suffer in crash.

Models: 17,000 cars made 10/91-11/92.
What to do: Have dealer secure dash panel to front rails with additional nuts and bolts.

'95 Dodge and Plymouth Neon
Brakes could fail partially.

Models: 2700 cars with antilock brakes made 11/93-1/94.
What to do: Have dealer inspect and, if necessary, replace master cylinder.

'95 Dodge and Plymouth Neon
Engine could stall unexpectedly. Also, brakes could fail partially.

Models: 7100 cars made 11/93-2/94.
What to do: Have dealer replace powertrain control module and screws that retain rear brake-hose bracket.

'86-88 Ford Taurus and Mercury Sable and '88 Lincoln Continental
Road salt could corrode subframe components and cause loss of control.

Models: 500,000 Taurus and Sables built 10/14/85-8/19/88 and Continentals made 11/4/87-9/30/88. Recall affects only cars sold or registered in Conn., Ill., Ind., Me., Mass., Mich., N.H., N.J., N.Y., Ohio, Pa., Vt., and Wisc.
What to do: Have dealer install corrosion-resistant reinforcing plate and new bolt on each rear subframe mount.

'93 Ford Escort
Driver's seat could move in crash, increasing risk of injury.

Models: 3500 cars made 5-6/93.
What to do: Have dealer replace inboard seat track.

'93 Ford Mustang with V8 engine
Fuel-system component could break and spill fuel, causing fire hazard.

Models: 4100 cars made 4/93-5/93.
What to do: Have dealer replace component.

'89-93 Geo Metro
Hood may not latch fully when closed and could open suddenly while car is moving, blocking driver's view.

Models: 356,097 cars made 8/88-7/92.
What to do: Have dealer install nuts and bolts to secure striker-plate assembly and tighten fasteners on latch assembly.

'92-94 Honda Civic and '94 Acura Integra
Shifter may indicate wrong gear position, resulting in unexpected vehicle movement.

Models: 191,289 cars with automatic transmission made 3/92-9/93.
What to do: Have dealer replace clip that connects transmission shift cable to shift lever.

'89-94 Hyundai Sonata
Motorized shoulder belts might travel slowly, chatter in track, or stop working.

Models: 100,000 cars made 12/88-9/93.
What to do: Have dealer lubricate belt tracks and, if necessary, repair or replace belt components.

'86-89 Hyundai Excel with manual 4- or 5-speed transmission
Wheels could lock up and stop car abruptly.

Models: 515,000 cars made 1/86-4/89.
What to do: Have dealer change transmission oil.

'88-89 Hyundai Excel
Hot engine coolant could leak from stem assembly in heater core.

Models: 270,000 cars made 4/88-2/89.
What to do: Have dealer install heater-stem assembly that includes bonnet made from more heat-resistant material.

'90-94 Hyundai Excel
Excessive fuel could spill from tank in side impact, causing fire hazard.

Models: 257,001 cars made through 10/93.
What to do: Have dealer make necessary repairs.

'94 Hyundai Elantra and Excel
Defective component in ignition system could stall engine suddenly.

Models: 600 cars made 1-2/94.
What to do: Have dealer inspect and, if necessary, replace component.

'87-92 Jaguar (various models)
Motorized safety belts could jam and become unusable.

Models: 52,102 cars made 10/87-7/92, including '87-89 XJS, and '89-92 Majestic, Sovereign, Vanden Plas, and XJ6.
What to do: If belt jams at any time during life of car, have dealer repair it.

'92 Lexus ES300
If primary hood latch fails, secondary latch may not prevent hood from opening suddenly.

Models: 16,036 cars made 7/91-1/92.
What to do: Have dealer replace secondary hood latch.

'88-91 Mazda 626 and 929
Door could open suddenly when window is lowered.

Models: 372,796 cars. Mazda 626s were made 5/87-6/91; 929s, 3/87-6/91.
What to do: Have dealer replace door-handle latch assembly.

'91-92 Mercedes-Benz 400E
Fuel vapor from charcoal canister could ignite and cause under-hood fire.

Models: 5900 cars made 5/91-10/92.
What to do: Have dealer reposition canister's vent hose and install fused wiring harness and larger heat shield on preresistor of electric auxiliary radiator fan.

'93 Mercedes-Benz (all models)
Driver's-side air bag may not provide proper crash protection.

Models: 480 cars made 9/92-4/93.
What to do: Have dealer inspect and, if necessary, replace air bag.

'94 Mercedes-Benz C220
Engine may not slow down when cruise control is disengaged.

Models: 1822 cars made 1-12/93.
What to do: Have dealer replace cruise-control linkage.

'93 Mercury Capri with automatic transmission
Tube could come loose from transmission and spill fluid onto hot exhaust, causing fire hazard.

Models: 3750 cars made 5/92-5/93.
What to do: Have dealer install redesigned tube.

'90-94 Mitsubishi Precis
In crash, excessive fuel could leak from tank, creating fire hazard.

Models: 12,890 cars made 8/90-10/93.
What to do: Have dealer install protector on left rear suspension arm.

'93 Mitsubishi Diamante
Rear safety belts could fail.

Models: 300 cars made 9/92-2/93.
What to do: Have dealer tighten safety-belt components.

'92-93 Nissan Maxima with air bag
Air bag could inflate unexpectedly.

Models: 65,000 cars made 8/91-9/92.
What to do: Have dealer install redesigned air-bag sensor.

'93-94 Nissan Altima
Engine could keep racing when accelerator is released.

Models: 206,000 cars made 6/92-2/94.
What to do: Have dealer reposition and secure throttle-cable housing.

'87-91 Peugeot 405 sedan and station wagon
Fuel hose could leak and create fire hazard.

Models: 8341 vehicles made 11/87-7/91.
What to do: Have dealer replace 3 fuel hoses, clamps, and mounting clips and reroute hoses away from high-voltage ignition wire.

'88-91 Pontiac Le Mans
Front safety belts may not latch or relase.

Models: 182,045 cars made 12/86-8/91.
What to do: Have dealer repair or replace belt buckles.

'92-93 Pontiac Sunbird
In cold weather, throttle cable could freeze and jam throttle in open or closed position.

Models: 108,898 cars made 3/91-4/93.
What to do: Have dealer replace accelerator control assembly.

'89-92 Porsche 911 and Carrera
Resistor for rear heater blower in engine compartment could overheat and cause fire hazard.

Models: 11,346 cars made 4/88-1/92.
What to do: Have dealer install resistor that contains circuit breaker.

'91 Porsche 944 and 968
Windshield wipers could fail.

Models: 1178 cars made 7/90-11/91.
What to do: Have dealer replace cover over windshield-wiper motor to keep out water.

'91-93 Porsche 911 Turbo and 911 America roadster
Rear wheels could lock up, causing loss of control.

Models: 1149 cars made 7/90-10/92.
What to do: Have dealer install redesigned brake-pressure reduction valve.

'92-93 Saab 9000
Fuel-filler and tank-ventilation hoses could leak, creating fire hazard.

Models: 5824 cars made 5-10/92.
What to do: Have dealer replace hoses and install redesigned clamps.

'92-93 Saab 9000
Fuel could leak and create fire hazard.

Models: 5000 cars made 6/92-11/92.
What to do: Note vehicle identification number and ask dealer whether your car is affected. If it is, have dealer install redesigned fuel-filler and vent hoses and new clamps.

'93 Saab 900
Water, slush, and road salt could build up on front brakes and hamper stopping ability.

Models: 7443 4-door cars made 8/93-3/94.
What to do: Have dealer install redesigned front brake shields and make other modifications.

'93 Saab 9000
Brake-lights may not work properly.

Models: 9747 cars made 6/92-6/93.
What to do: Have dealer inspect brake lamp switches and, if necessary, replace.

'94 Saab 900
Seatback could fold backward in rear-end crash, increasing risk of injury to occupants.

Models: 3252 hatchbacks, with nonpower front driver's seat, made 8/93-1/94.
What to do: Have dealer replace front-seat frame rails.

'94 Saab 9000 CD and CDE
Brake lights may not go on properly when brake pedal is pressed.

Models: 59 cars made 12/93-3/94.
What to do: Have dealer rewire outboard brake-light assemblies.

'93 Saturn
Brakes could fail during hard braking.

Models: 3661 cars made 2/93, with 034 or 035 as last three digits of date-code tag on brake master cylinder.
What to do: Have dealer replace brake-booster assembly.

'90-93 Subaru Legacy, Loyale, and XT-6
In extremely cold and humid conditions, transmission could seize, stopping vehicle abruptly.

Models: 31,295 cars, including Legacy and XT-6, with manual transmission and all-wheel drive, and Loyale, with manual transmission and 4-wheel drive, made 9/89-9/92.
What to do: Have dealer modify dipstick pipe and modify or replace dipstick.

'93 Subaru Impreza with all-wheel drive
Fuel leak could cause fire hazard.

Models: 3351 cars made 11/92-3/93.
What to do: Have dealer install modified fuel vent pipe.

'89-93 Suzuki Swift
Hood may not latch fully when closed and could open suddenly while car is moving, blocking driver's view.

Models: 38,229 vehicles made 1/88-1/93.
What to do: Have dealer install nuts and bolts to secure striker-plate assembly and tighten fasteners on latch assembly.

'91 Toyota Camry and Previa
Radio could short-circuit, causing fire hazard.

Models: 155,809 cars, with Fujitsu Ten radio, made 8/90-8/91.
What to do: Have dealer make necessary repairs.

'91 Toyota Previa
Windshield wipers could fail.

Models: 75,863 minivans made 1/90-6/91.
What to do: Have dealer install new wiper motor and replace and tighten other components.

'87-89 Volkswagen Cabriolet
Fuel could leak from crack in tank and create fire hazard.

Models: 7500 cars made 8/86-8/89.
What to do: Have dealer inspect and, if necessary, replace fuel tank.

'92-93 Volkswagen Corrado
Electrical wiring in engine compartment could abrade, short out, and stall engine, or stop radiator fan and cause engine overheating.

Models: 4300 cars made 8/91-11/92.
What to do: Have dealer route wiring away from edge of sheet metal.

'93 Volkswagen Passat
Lock nuts that secure left and right front axles could break and cause loss of control.

Models: 1200 cars made 1/93-3/93.
What to do: Have dealer replace lock nuts.

'94 Volvo 850
May produce excessive exhaust emissions and make Check Engine warning light go on.

Models: 14,500 sedans and wagons with nonturbocharged engine and automatic transmission. In affected sedans, last 6 digits of vehicle-identification number are 100496 through 131601, in recalled wagons 012016 through 037597.
What to do: Have dealer replace oxygen sensor.

Sport-utility vehicles, trucks & vans

'85-91 Chevrolet and GMC vans and utility vehicles with bucket seats and knob-type recliner mechanisms

Seatback could recline suddenly and cause loss of vehicle control.

Models: 604,207 vehicles made 8/84-1/91, including '85-91 Chevrolet Astro and GMC Safari, and '89-90 Chevrolet and GMC Suburban.

What to do: Have dealer modify recliner mechanisms.

'88-92 Chevrolet and GMC light trucks and vans

Corrosion from road salt could make brake rotors come apart, reducing stopping ability and causing loss of control.

Products: 341,364 vehicles made 4/86-12/91, including '88-92 Chevrolet and GMC K100 and K200, '88-92 GMC L, and '90-92 Chevrolet L. Recall affects vehicles sold or registered only in Conn., Ill., Ind., Me., Mass., Mich., N.H., N.J., N.Y., Ohio, Pa., R.I., Vt., and Wisc.

What to do: Have dealer install redesigned front brake rotors. (Recall doesn't include free replacement of worn brake pads.)

'91-93 Chevrolet and GMC pickup trucks converted to run on compressed natural gas

Fuel tank could rupture, creating fire hazard.

Models: 2500 2-wheel-drive pickup trucks, converted by PAS, Inc., made 10/91-6/93, including: Chevrolet C10, C20, and C30, and GMC C15, C25, and C35.

What to do: Stop using truck and let engine run until fuel tank is less than one-quarter full. Then call Chevrolet at 800 334-5370 or GMC at 800 462-7000. Manufacturer will exchange truck for comparable '94 gasoline-powered ½- or ¾-ton pickup or will repurchase vehicle.

'92-93 Chevrolet, Oldsmobile, and Pontiac minivans

Safety-belt retractor could lock up, making it impossible to withdraw belt.

Models: 157,740 Chevrolet Lumina, Oldsmobile Silhouette, and Pontiac Trans Sport minivans made 6/91-6/93. Problem affects left third-row seat in 6-passenger vans and center second-row seat in vans.

What to do: If belt locks up, have dealer replace it.

'93 Chevrolet and GMC 4-wheel drive pickup trucks

Vehicle could be in gear and move unexpectedly though automatic-transmission shifter appears to be in Park.

Models: 72,664 pickup trucks, including Chevrolet Blazer and T10 and GMC Jimmy and Sonoma, made 8/92-1/93.

What to do: Have dealer inspect and, if necessary, replace transmission.

'93 Chevrolet and GMC pickup trucks

Rear bench seat could come loose in crash.

Models: 303 pickups, with folding rear bench seat, made 4/93-5/93. Models include Chevrolet C30 and K30 and GMC C35, K35, and Sierra.

What to do: Have dealer replace rivets that secure latch mechanism with bolts.

'93 Chevrolet and GMC G20 vans

Vehicle came with wrong spare wheel. In use, wheel could crack and come off, causing loss of control.

Models: 1793 vans made 8/93-4/94.

What to do: Have dealer replace spare wheel.

'93-94 Chevrolet Lumina APV, Oldsmobile Silhouette, and Pontiac Transport

Second row, passenger-side shoulder belt may not retract properly, resulting in inadequate protection in a crash.

Models: 5294 minivans, with optional power sliding door, made 11/92-3/94.

What to do: Have dealer replace door-frame pillar trim panel.

'94 Chevrolet Blazer and GMC Jimmy

Trailer hitch could separate from towing vehicle and cause accident.

Models: 740 4-door multipurpose vehicles, with weight distribution trailer-hitch (VR4) option, made 2-3/94.

What to do: Have dealer tighten trailer-hitch bolts to specified torque.

'94 Chevrolet and GMC C107 and K207 extended-cab pickup trucks

Trailer could come loose from towing vehicle.

Models: 4821 trucks, with weight-distribution trailer-hitch (VR4 option), made 8-11/93.

What to do: Have dealer install additional fasteners on trailer-hitch platform.

'94 Chevrolet and GMC C10703 and K10703 pickup trucks

Fuel tank could sag and touch road, spilling fuel and creating fire hazard.

Models: 976 half-ton short-box trucks made 10/93.
What to do: Have dealer tighten tank's front strap bracket.

'94 Chevrolet and GMC C and K series pickup trucks

Front-end components could come apart, causing loss of control.

Models: 30,148 pickup trucks made 11-12/93, including Chevrolet C 10, C20, C30, K10, K20, and K30; also, GMC C15, C25, C35, K15, K25, and K35.
What to do: Have dealer tighten rear nut that secures left lower-control arm to frame.

'94 Chevrolet and GMC light trucks and vans

Brakes could fail.

Models: 70,154 vehicles made 7/93-8/93, including Chevrolet C10, C20, C30, G Van, K10, K20, and K30, and GMC C15, C25, C35, G Van, K15, K25, and K35.
What to do: Have dealer make sure that brake-pedal push-rod retainer is in place.

'94 Chevrolet Lumina, Oldsmobile Silhouette, and Pontiac Trans Sport vans

Center rear safety belt may not lock in crash.

Models: 1238 minivans made 8/93-9/93.
What to do: Have dealer inspect and, if necessary, replace safety-belt retractor assembly.

'94 Chevrolet S10 and GMC S15 pickup trucks

In crash, fuel leakage could create fire hazard.

Models: 117,200 light trucks made 3/93-1/94.
What to do: Have dealer replace fuel-filler pipe.

'93 Chrysler Town & Country, Dodge Caravan, and Plymouth Voyager

Wheels could come off.

Models: 600 minivans with 15-in. stamped steel road wheels or spare wheel, made 4/93.
What to do: Have dealer replace wheels.

'94 Dodge BR1500, BR2500, and Ram pickup trucks

Vehicles have risk of fuel spill in rear-end collision, a violation of Federal safety regulation.

Models: 7000 trucks, without rear bumper, made 7/93-8/94.
What to do: Have dealer make necessary repairs.

'94 Dodge Dakota pickup truck with 4-wheel drive

Steering could fail.

Models: 1500 trucks made 11/93.
What to do: Have dealer replace upper control-arm bolts.

'94 Dodge Dakota pickup truck

Fuel tank could fall off.

Models: 9000 vehicles made 7/93-12/93.
What to do: Have dealer tighten tank's support straps.

'94 Dodge Ram light trucks

Seatback may not latch securely and could fly forward in crash or during hard braking, increasing risk of injury.

Models: 17,000 vehicles made 7-10/93.
What to do: Have dealer replace seatback latch assembly.

'94 Dodge Ram pickup truck with 4-wheel drive

Failure of front suspension could cause loss of control.

Models: 3900 light-duty trucks made 7/93-9/93.
What to do: Have dealer tighten track-bar attachment.

'94 Dodge Ram

Front suspension could fail, resulting in loss of steering control.

Models: 400 light trucks, 3500 series with 4-wheel drive, made 10/93.
What to do: Have dealer replace front-suspension track bar.

'93 Explorer and Tiara van conversions

Left front safety belt won't fit all drivers when seat is adjusted fully forward.

Models: 1089 Explorer conversions and 8283 Tiara conversions of '93 Chevrolet Astro and GMC Safari ¾-ton vans. Explorer vans were made 9/92-8/93; Tiara vans, 9/92-9/93 .
What to do: Have dealer install extendable buckle assembly.

'90-91 Ford F250, F350, and Super Duty pickup trucks and chassis

Fuel hoses could leak, creating fire hazard.

Models: 89,770 trucks, with 7.5-liter engine and gross vehicle-weight rating of more than 8500 pounds, made 8/89-8/91.
What to do: Have dealer replace steel fuel-return hoses with flexible hoses.

'90-93 Ford F150, F250, F350, and F Super Duty gasoline-powered light trucks and chassis cabs with dual fuel tanks
Fuel could flow from one tank to the other, overflow, and create fire hazard.

Products: 1,131,000 vehicles made 7/89-12/92.
What to do: Have dealer replace fuel-pressure regulator and install additional check valves.

'93 Ford Bronco and F150
In 4-wheel drive, transmission could slip out of gear and cause loss of control.

Products: 1389 vehicles, with "touch drive" electric-shift transfer case, made 11/92-12/92.
What to do: Have dealer replace transfer case.

'93-94 Ford light pickup trucks and sport-utility vehicles
Front bumper could fall off.

Models: 370,000 vehicles, made 4/93-12/93, including '93-94 Bronco, F150, F250, and F350, and '94 F Super Duty.
What to do: Have dealer replace bumper fasteners.

'94 Ford F-Super Duty CH, F250, and F350
Under heavy load with cruise control engaged, throttle might not respond immediately when load on engine decreases. That could cause sudden and unexpected acceleration burst.

Models: 900 pickup trucks and chassis-cabs, with direct injection turbodiesel engine, 5-speed manual transmission, and over 8500-pound gross vehicle rating, made 2-3/94.
What to do: Have dealer replace electronic engine-control module.

'94 Ford F150 and F250 light trucks
Air bag might not deploy in crash.

Models: 3322 trucks made 8/93-9/93.
What to do: Have dealer inspect vehicle and, if necessary, replace air-bag diagnostic module.

'94 Ford F150 and F250 light trucks with air bags
Driver's air bag could deploy if right door is slammed while ignition key is in Start position.

Models: 1500 trucks made 8/93.
What to do: Have dealer replace air-bag diagnostic module.

'94 Ford Ranger and Mazda B-series pickup trucks
Fuel may leak from crack in hose to cause fire.

Models: 11,400 Rangers and 1868 B-Series trucks, with 3.0- and 4.0-liter engines, made 4-5/94.
What to do: Have dealer inspect front fuel-hose assembly and, if necessary, replace.

'93-94 Geo Tracker and Suzuki Sidekick
Rear-axle could break, causing loss of control and partial brake failure.

Models: 39,419 vehicles made 8/92-9/93 including 34,172 Trackers and 5247 Sidekicks.
What to do: Have dealer inspect and, if necessary, replace axle assembly.

'94 Geo Tracker
Steering could fail.

Models: 2502 vehicles made 12/93.
What to do: Have dealer inspect and, if necessary, replace steering shaft.

'87-93 Jeep Wrangler
Fuel could leak from tank and cause fire.

Models: 230,000 sport-utility vehicles, with plastic fuel tank, made 2/86-8/93.
What to do: Have dealer replace gasket on fuel-tank sending unit.

'89 Jeep Wrangler
Windshield wipers could fail.

Models: 11,000 sport-utility vehicles made 8/88-10/88.
What to do: Have dealer reinforce windshield frame and replace wiper-linkage parts.

'93 Jeep Cherokee
Label specifying minimum tire and wheel size is wrong. Installation of wrong tires could result in failure of tire and loss of vehicle control.

Models: 3400 sport-utility vehicles with 4.0-liter Six, made 7/92-12/92.
What to do: Have dealer provide correct label.

'93 Jeep Grand Cherokee and Grand Wagoneer
Liftgate could open while vehicle is moving.

Products: 80,000 sport-utility vehicles made 1/92-10/92.
What to do: If liftgate seems difficult to latch, have dealer replace it.

'93 Jeep Grand Cherokee and Grand Wagoneer
Steering assembly could come apart, causing loss of control.

Models: 115,000 sport-utility vehicles made 12/92-7/93.

What to do: Have dealer install special sleeve on steering assembly.

'94 Jeep Cherokee
Rear safety belts could fail.

Models: 12,000 sport-utility vehicles made 7/93-8/93.
What to do: Have dealer install longer bolts on rear inboard safety-belt anchors.

'94 Oldsmobile Bravada
May have wrong owner's manual.

Models: 6315 multipurpose vehicles made 5/93-2/94.
What to do: Have dealer supply correct manual.

'93 Range Rover County and County LWB
Power windows and sun roof could keep closing after switch has been released, causing injury.

Products: 463 sport-utility vehicles made 8/92-9/92.
What to do: Have dealer replace necessary electrical parts.

'86-91 Volkswagen Vanagon
Center ventilation duct could break and fall on passenger.

Models: 29,500 vans, with factory-installed air-conditioner, made 8/85-6/91.
What to do: Have dealer install reinforcement plates at center and rear airflow ducts.

'93 Volkswagen Eurovan
Parking brake could release unexpectedly.

Models: 2400 vans made 7/92-11/92.
What to do: Have dealer replace bolt in steering assembly.

'93 Volkswagen Eurovan
Steering could fail.

Models: 8350 vans made 7/92-1/93.
What to do: Have dealer replace spring in parking-brake handle.

Child car seats

Kolkraft child safety seats
Tongue plate of buckle may corrode and discourage use, increasing risk of injury.

Products: 307,017 child safety seats, including Automate model made 1/24/91-3/22/93 and Playschool and Traveler 700 models made 1/24/91-6/30/93.
What to do: Call 800 453-7673 for replacement harness assembly and installation instructions.

Evenflo child safety seats (various models)
Plastic sleeve near buckle can become torn, split, or slip out of position, making buckle difficult to latch.

Products: 308,271 seats, made 2/8-8/4-93 including Champion, model 224; Ultara 1, model 231; and Ultara II, model 232. Model designation and date of manufacture appear on label on seat shell.
What to do: Call Evenflo at 800 837-4002 for instructions on how to remove plastic sleeve. Removal of sleeve won't reduce seat's safety, according to company.

Renolux GT7000 child-safety seat with electric recliner
Wiring connecting seat to cigarette lighter could overheat, creating fire hazard.

Products: 891 seats made 1/89-8/92. Date of manufacture and model information appear on label on seat shell.
What to do: Call 800 476-5273 for replacement seat.

Renolux child-safety seats
Fabric cover on pad burns too rapidly, in violation of Federal safety standard.

Products: 5000 seats, models GT2000, GT4000, GT5000, and GT7000, made 5/89-6/93. Affected models have blue tweed seat cover with red and yellow stripes. Model and date of manufacture appear on label on seat shell.
What to do: Call 800 476-5273 for replacement cover.

Motorcycles, bicycles & snowmobiles

'94 BMW R1100 motorcycle
Battery connector cable could short, creating fire hazard and reducing stopping ability or making engine run roughly.

Models: 772 motorcycles made 2/93-6/93.
What to do: Have dealer remove positive terminal extension and bolt battery cable connector directly to battery.

'94 BMW R1100 motorcycle
Ridden hard on off-roads terrain, suspension parts could come loose, resulting in loss of steering control.

Models: 716 motorcycles made 2-6/94.
What to do: Have dealer apply stronger adhesive to bearing pin in rear swinging arm and tighten to spec-

ification, and replace flange nut in front strut with self-tightening nut.

'93-94 Harley-Davidson FLHTC and FLTC motorcycles
Throttle could bind and cause loss of control.

Models: 4038 motorcycles made 8/92-10/93.
What to do: Have dealer repair throttle cable.

'94 Harley-Davidson XLH motorcycle
Front fender could loosen, rub against tire, and cause loss of control.

Models: 1077 motorcycles made 9/93-10/93.
What to do: Have dealer replace bolts that retain front fender.

'92-94 Suzuki Intruder VS800 GL motorcycle
Handlebar could loosen and cause loss of control.

Models: 9965 motorcycles made 9/91-10/93.
What to do: Have dealer replace handlebar and stay-cushion rubbers.

'90-92 Polaris LP snowmobiles
If left engaged in use, parking brake could overheat and cause fire hazard.

Products: All hydraulic-brake models sold 4/89-12/91.
What to do: If you don't need parking brake, have dealer remove parking-brake lever.

Motor homes

'89 Fleetwood Bounder and Flair motor homes
Windshield wipers may not work properly.

Models: 74 motor homes made 1/89-2/89.
What to do: Have dealer modify mounting of windshield-wiper hardware and replace passenger-side pivot arm.

'93 Fleetwood Bounder motor home
Hydraulic hose for leveling jack could contact hot exhaust manifold and leak, posing fire hazard.

Models: 72 motor homes made 7/92-11/92.
What to do: Have dealer replace and reroute hose.

'93 Fleetwood Flair motor home
Main door-entry step could break off.

Models: 128 motor homes made 12/92-3/93.
What to do: Have dealer make necessary repairs.

'93 Fleetwood Rio Grande folding camper trailer
Raising or lowering folding top could damage wiring to exterior lights, creating fire hazard.

Models: 1122 trailers made 7/92-3/93.
What to do: Have dealer install plastic wire protector around lifting cable.

'93-94 Fleetwood Bounder motor homes
Propane gas pipes at rear of vehicle could leak from contact with axle, causing explosion.

Models: 131 motor homes, with Mor/Ryde "AO" type rear tag-axle suspension, made 11/93-5/94.
What to do: Have dealer replace iron LP gas pipe in rear of vehicle with copper tubing rerouted to avoid axle swing area.

'94 Fleetwood motor homes
Insulation on battery cable could contact hot exhaust manifold and ignite.

Models: 458 motor homes made 9/93-12/93, including Arrow, Jamboree, Montara, Rallye, Searcher, and Tioga.
What to do: Have dealer relocate and, if necessary, replace battery.

'94 Fleetwood Flair motor home
Vibration could cause spare-tire-and-wheel assembly, suspended under front of vehicle, to descend and contact pavement.

Models: 121 motor homes made 1-2/94.
What to do: Have dealer install square chain connector in chain-and-pulley mechanism that holds tire-and-wheel assembly. Also, install additional chain, bracket, and chain connector to secure assembly to undercarriage.

'94 Fleetwood Prowler, Terry, and Wilderness travel trailers
Stove, made for natural gas, can generate high level of deadly carbon-monoxide gas when used with propane gas.

Models: 142 travel trailers, with Magic Chef stove, made 10/93-2/94.
What to do: Have dealer convert stove for propane use.

'89-93 Ford F Super Duty motor-home chassis
Brakes could fail.

Models: 17,400 chassis made 5/89-3/93.
What to do: Have dealer install heat shield and insulation on brake hoses.

'92-94 Gulf Stream Tourmaster motor home

Engine may not slow down when accelerator is released.

Models: 302 motor homes, with Spartan Motors Diesel Pusher chassis, made 11/91-4/94

What to do: Have dealer install bracket to keep throttle cable away from exhaust manifold.

'93-94 Holiday Rambler Alumalite and '94 Imperial motor homes

Steering could fail.

Models: 102 Class A motor homes, on Spartan diesel "pusher" chassis, made 2/93-1/94.

What to do: Have dealer tighten or replace slip-shaft fasteners on steering column.

'88-89 Itasca and Winnebago motor homes

Fuel tank could leak and create fire hazard.

Models: 11,353 motor homes made 7/87-8/89, including Itasca Flyer, Suncruiser, and Windcruiser, and Winnebago Chieftain, Elandan, and Super Chief.

What to do: Have dealer inspect and, if necessary, replace fuel tank.

'90-91 Itasca and Winnebago 321RG motor homes

Under certain conditions, generator exhaust system could contact pavement, resulting in damage to the system and under-floor storage area.

Models: 401 motor homes, with 110-volt Onan generator, made 5/89-8/91.

What to do: Have dealer replace generator exhaust system.

'91-93 Jayco Designer, Eagle, and Jay trailers with slide-out room

Slide-out room could open unexpectedly and cause accident.

Models: 3143 fifth-wheel trailers and travel trailers made 6/90-6/93.

What to do: Have dealer inspect and, if necessary, repair or replace slide-out switch and control module.

'89-90 Layton, Nomad, and Skyline travel trailers

Suds and water could reach washing-machine motor switch, causing overheating and fire hazard.

Products: 112 travel trailers, with 24-in. laundry center, made 8/89-1/90.

What to do: Have dealer secure shield over washing-machine with stronger adhesive and install redesigned motor switch.

'93 Monaco Crown Royale Signature motor home

Windshield wipers could fail.

Models: 85 motor homes made 6/92-4/93.

What to do: Have dealer install redesigned wiper motor.

'86-89 Winnebago Spectrum motor homes

Hot exhaust gases could ignite engine hoses.

Models: 88 motor homes, model WWR32RQ, made 6/86-2/89.

What to do: Ask dealer for information on replacing exhaust check valves.

'88 Winnebago Spectrum 32-ft. motor home

Engine compartment could catch on fire.

Models: 85 motor homes made 6/86-2/89. Vehicle was recalled earlier this year, but manufacturer was unable to correct problems.

What to do: Phone 800 537-1885 to find out how to exhange motor home for another.

'93 Winnebago Vectra motor home

Front-end components may wear prematurely.

Models: 227 motor homes on Spartan Motors chassis, model WSM35RQ9, made 9/92-3/93.

What to do: Have dealer replace front axle and springs.

Vehicle accessories

Chico LBL and Choice Lite LBL Winner motorcycle helmets

Might not provide adequate protection in accident.

Products: 4000 helmets made 8/91-1/93.

What to do: Send helmet to Helmet Recall, Box 21338, Fort Lauderdale, Fla. 33335. If you don't get refund within reasonable time, call manufacturer at 305 566-2426.

Cooper CMXT and CT240 steel-belted radial tires

Could fail.

Products: 574 tires, load range G, made 1-2/94, including the following: 230 tires, model CXMT 340, size 11R22.5 and bearing DOT nos. 3D3TCX2044 (Last three nos. are date of manufacture; "044" represents fourth week of '94.), 3D3TCX2054, and 3D TCX2064; 100 tires, model CXMT 340, size 295/75R22.5, DOT nos. 3D37CX2044, 3D37CX2054, and 3D37CX2064; 126 tires, model CT240 tires, size 11R22.5, DOT nos. 3D3TC1X044 and 3D3TC1X054; and 105 tires, model CT240, size 295/75R22.5, DOT nos. 3D37C1X054 and 3D37C1X064.

What to do: Have dealer replace tires.

Dick Cepek light-truck tires
Could fail.

Products: 569 tires, size 33/1450R16.5, made by Denman Tire Corp. 5/89-10/91. Sidewalls are branded "DICK CEPEK RADIAL F-C" and bear serial nos. DYV6 GSA239-411. (Last three nos. are date of manufacture; for example, "411" represents 41st week of '91.)

What to do: Have dealer replace tires.

Eldorado polyester/steel radial tires
Air leak from tiny hole in sidewall could cause tire failure.

Models: 1762 tires, size P205/75R15, load range B, with medallion no. "D06L," bearing DOT identification nos. U9ULEHA143, U9ULEHA153, U9ULEHA 163, U9ULEHA173, or U9ULEHA183. (Last three nos. are date of manufacture; for example, "143" represents 14th week of '93.)

What to do: Have dealer replace tires.

Kelly Springfield Douglas Xtra-Trac all-weather tires
Could fail.

Products: 990 tires, size P165/80R13, bearing D.O.T. no. PLJYDAJR402. (Last three nos. are date of manufacture; "402" represents 40th week of '92.)

What to do: Have dealer replace tires.

'85-87 Toyota MR2 exhaust pipe installed by Midas muffler shops
Exhaust heat shield could rub against oil pan, causing oil leak, engine damage, and fire.

Products: 1102 pipes, Midas part no. 3E9395, made 5/90-4/93.

What to do: If exhaust pipe was installed by Midas approximately 5/90-4/93, have Midas replace pipe.

Remington Rimfire and Centennial Canyon Climber light-truck tires
Could fail.

Models: 1230 tires, size P205/75R15, bearing DOT identification no. DBULH45033. (Last three nos. are date of manufacture; "033" represents 3rd week of '93.)

What to do: Have store replace tires.

Trailer hitch for Dodge, Isuzu, Mitsubishi, and Toyota sport-utility vehicles
Hitch could break, allowing trailer to come loose.

Products: 670 Class II trailer hitches, part no. 0607, made by Reese Prods. 3/92-6/93 for '87-91 Dodge Raider, '89-91 Isuzu Amigo, '86-91 Isuzu Trooper and Trooper II, '91-92 Mitsubishi Montero, and '91-93 Toyota Land Cruiser.

What to do: Have dealer replace trailer hitch.

WARCO Hi-Performance Brake Fluid
Could cause brakes to fail.

Products: All WARCO brake fluid. Manufacturer is out of business, so product can't be recalled.

What to do: If brake system contains substantial amount of WARCO fluid, drain and flush and use other fluid.

Buying Guide index

This index is for information in the 1995 Buying Guide. For an eight-year index to the last full report in CONSUMER REPORTS, see page 390.

Consumer Reports:
8-year index to last full report

This index indicates when the last full report on a given subject was published in issues of CONSUMER REPORTS from 1987 through October 1994. Bold type indicates Ratings reports or brand-name discussions; italic type indicates corrections or follow-ups. Numbers at the left of each entry are codes for ordering reports by fax or mail. (No code or * means a report is not available by fax.) To order, call 800 896-7788. You can use MasterCard or Visa. Each report is $7.75. When you call, have ready the report's code and your charge-card. Before ordering a report, check to see if it's in the Buying Guide.

STATEMENT OF OWNERSHIP, MANAGEMENT, AND CIRCULATION
(Required by 39 U.S.C. 3685)

1. Title of Publication: CONSUMER REPORTS. 1A. Publication No: 0010-7174. 2. Date of Filing: September 16, 1994. 3. Frequency of issue: Monthly, except semi-monthly in December. 3A. No. of Issues Published Annually: 13. 3B. Annual Subscription Price: $22.00. 4. Complete Mailing Address of Known Office of Publication: 101 Truman Avenue, Yonkers, New York 10703-1057. 5. Complete Mailing Address of the Headquarters of General Business offices of the Publisher: 101 Truman Avenue, Yonkers, New York 10703-1057. Full Names and Complete Mailing Address of Publisher, President, Editor, & Executive Editor. Publisher: Consumers Union of United States, Inc. 101 Truman Avenue, Yonkers, New York 10703-1057. President: Rhoda H. Karpatkin; Editor: Joel Gurin; Executive Editor: Eileen Denver. 7. Owner: (If the publication is published by a nonprofit organization, its name and address must be stated.) Name: Consumers Union of United States, Inc., a nonprofit organization. Address: 101 Truman Avenue, Yonkers, New York 10703-1057. 8. Known Bondholders, Mortgagees, and Other Securities (if there are none, so state): None. 9. For Completion by Nonprofit Organizations Authorized to Mail at Special Rates (Section 424.12 DMM only). The purpose, function, and nonprofit status of this organization and the exempt status for Federal Income tax purposes has not changed during preceding 12 months. 10. Extent and Nature of Circulation.

	Average no. copies each issue during past 12 mo.	Actual no. copies of single issue published nearest to filing date
A. Total no. of copies (net press run)	5,552,797	5,556,773
B. Paid and/or requested circulation		
1. Sales through dealers, carriers, street vendors, counter sales	136,736	123,178
2. Mail subscription (paid and/or requested)	5,134,447	5,201,468
C. Total paid and/or requested circulation (sum of 10B1 and 10B2)	5,271,183	5,324,646
D. Free distribution by mail, carrier or other means Samples, complimentary, and other free copies	13,942	13,840
E. Total distribution (sum of C and D)	5,285,125	5,338,486
F. Copies not distributed		
1. Office use, left over, unaccounted, spoiled after printing	77,773	44,597
2. Return from news agents	189,899	173,690
G. TOTAL (sum of E, F1 and 2 should equal net press run shown in A)	5,552,797	5,556,773

11. I certify that the statements made by me above are correct and complete.
Louis J. Milani, Director, Business Affairs

Give $1000.
Get a whole
lot more.

Giving away $1000 may not seem like a way to increase your assets. But consider all you get back when you give $1000 to Consumers Union:

1. You become a Lifetime Member of Consumers Union.

2. You receive Consumer Reports every month for the rest of your life.

3. Your name is inscribed on the permanent Honor Roll in the Consumer Reports National Testing and Research Center.

4. Your gift qualifies for a tax deduction (less subscription value) as allowed by law.

5. Your Lifetime Membership is acknowledged in a special listing published periodically in Consumer Reports—unless you'd prefer to remain anonymous.

6. Your contribution helps build a stronger Consumers Union. This means better values in the products and services you buy. Safer products for you and those you care about. More protection against fraud and deceit. A fairer world for the consumer—in so many ways.

As you may know, CU accepts no contributions from business. No outside advertising. No contributions larger than $5000 from anyone.

More than 6000 of our readers have increased their assets by contributing $1000 to Consumers Union. Join them by becoming a Lifetime Member today. Please use the coupon when you send your check.

Yes, I'd like to enjoy the benefits of Lifetime Membership in Consumers Union with a tax deductible contribution of:

☐ $1000   ☐ $1500   ☐ $2000
☐ Other $ _____ (Maximum: $5000)
☐ My check is enclosed.
☐ I wish to contribute in quarterly installments.
☐ My first installment is enclosed.
☐ I cannot be a Lifetime Member now, but here is my gift for $ _____

Name _____

Address _____

City _____ State _____ Zip _____
Name to be entered as Lifetime Member (if different):

_____

☐ Yes, you may list my name in Consumer Reports.   KLGGG
☐ Don't list my name.
Mail this coupon to:
CONSUMERS UNION
Dept. MEM, 101 Truman Ave., Yonkers, N.Y. 10703

CONSUMERS UNION OF U.S., INC., 101 Truman Ave., Yonkers, N.Y. 10703, is a not-for-profit, tax-exempt organization, contributions to which are tax-deductible in accordance with law. Contributions are not accepted from any commercial interest. A copy of our latest financial report filed with the New York Department of State may be obtained by writing: Office of Charities Registration, Department of State, Albany, NY 12231, or from CU at the address above. Residents of Virginia: State Division of Consumer Affairs, PO Box 1163, Richmond, VA 23209.